D0759573

Redefining Judaism in an
Age of Emancipation

Studies in European Judaism

VOLUME 13

Redefining Judaism in an Age of Emancipation

Comparative Perspectives on Samuel Holdheim (1806–1860)

Edited by
Christian Wiese

BRILL
LEIDEN • BOSTON
2007

Publication of the Salomon Ludwig Steinheim–Institute for German-Jewish History, Duisburg

This book is printed on acid-free paper.

Library of Congress Cataloging-in-Publication Data

Redefining Judaism in an age of emancipation : comparative perspectives on Samuel Holdheim (1806–1860) / edited by Christian Wiese.
    p. cm. — (Studies in European Judaism; v. 13)
    Includes bibliographical references and index.
    ISBN 90-04-15265-2 (hardback)
    1. Holdheim, Samuel, 1806–1860. 2. Reform Judaism – Germany – history – 19th century. I. Wiese, Christian, 1961–

BM755.H646R43 2006
296.8'341092–22   2006049685

ISSN 1568-5004
ISBN-10 90 04 15265 2
ISBN-13 978 90 04 15265 6

PRINTED IN THE NETHERLANDS

CONTENTS

ABBREVIATIONS

AJA = American Jewish Archives
AJS = Association for Jewish Studies
AZJ = *Allgemeine Zeitung des Judenthums*
CAHJP = Central Archives for the History of the Jewish People
CCAR = Central Conference of American Rabbis
CJA = Centrum Judaicum-Neue Synagoge Berlin, Archiv
DIGB = Deutsch-Israelitischer Gemeindebund
EJ = *Encyclopedia Judaica*
GstA PK = Geheimes Staatsarchiv, Preußischer Kulturbesitz
HUCA = *Hebrew Union College Annual*
JJGL = *Jahrbuch für jüdische Geschichte und Literatur*
JJS = *Journal of Jewish Studies*
JQR = *Jewish Quarterly Review*
JPS = Jewish Publication Society
JSS = Jewish Social Studies
LBI = Leo Baeck Institute
LBIYB = *Leo Baeck Institute Yearbook*
LHA Schwerin = Landeshauptarchiv Schwerin
MfBB = Ministerium für Volksbildung
MGWJ = *Monatsschrift für die Geschichte und Wissenschaft des Judentums*
SächsHSTA = Sächsisches Hauptstaatsarchiv
SUNY = State University of New York
ZRGG = *Zeitschrift für Religions- und Geistesgeschichte*

CONTRIBUTORS AND EDITORS

RALPH BISSCHOPS (Ph.D, 1992, Free University of Brussels) is research associate at the German Department of Ghent University and staff member of the Adult Education Centre of the Brussels Chamber of Commerce. He was visiting professor at the University of Duisburg where he lectured on German-Jewish history. He is the author of a book on metaphorical language and ethics (*Die Metapher als Wertsetzung*, 1994) and together with James Francis he edited the volume *Metaphor, Canon and Community – Jewish, Christian and Islamic Approaches* (1999). He has published articles, reviews and essays on theory of metaphor, literary criticism and exegesis of the Hebrew Bible. Dr. Bisschops is also editor of the periodical *Shofar – Revue de la Communauté Israélite Libérale de Belgique*.

ANDREAS BRÄMER (Ph.D, 1997, Free University of Berlin) is Associate Director of the Institut für die Geschichte der deutschen Juden, Hamburg, and reader (Privatdozent) at Hamburg University. He is the author of *Rabbiner und Vorstand. Zur Geschichte der jüdischen Gemeinde in Deutschland und Österreich 1809-1871* (1999), *Rabbiner Zacharias Frankel. Wissenschaft des Judentums und konservative Reform im 19. Jahrhundert* (2000), *Judentum und religiöse Reform. Der Hamburger Tempel 1817-1938* (2000), *Leistung und Gegenleistung. Jüdische Religions – und Elementarlehrer in Preußen 1823/24 bis 1872* (2006). He is also co-editor of *Das Jüdische Hamburg* (2006). Currently he is working on a biography of Rabbi Joseph Carlebach (1883-1942).

DAVID ELLENSON (Ph.D, 1981, Columbia University) is President of Hebrew Union College-Jewish Institute of Religion (HUC-JIR) and I.H. and Anna Grancell Professor of Jewish Religious Thought He is a distinguished rabbi, scholar, and leader of the Reform Movement who is internationally recognized for his publications and research in the areas of Jewish religious thought, ethics, and modern Jewish history. He is a Fellow at the Shalom Hartman Institute of Jerusalem and a Fellow and Lecturer at the Institute of Advanced

Studies at Hebrew University in Jerusalem. His extensive publications include *Tradition in Transition: Orthodoxy, Halakhah and the Boundaries of Modern Jewish History* (1989), *Rabbi Esriel Hildesheimer and the Creation of a Modern Jewish Orthodoxy* (1990), *Between Tradition and Culture: The Dialectics of Jewish Religion and Identity in the Modern World* (1994), and *After Emancipation: Jewish Religious Responses to Modernity* (2004).

JUDITH FRISHMAN (Ph.D, 1992, Leiden University) is Professor of the History and Culture of Rabbinic Judaism in the Faculty of Catholic Theology at University of Tilburg, the Netherlands. Between 1995 and 2005 she has also occupied the special chair for the history of Jewish-Christian Relations in Modernity in the Theological Faculty of Leiden University. She is author of *The Ways and Means of the Divine Economy. An Edition, Translation and Study of Six Biblical Homilies by Narsai* (1992) and has co-edited, amongst others, *Expectation and Confirmation. Two Hundred Years of Jewish Emancipation in the Netherlands* (1996), *The Book of Genesis in Jewish and Oriental Christian Interpretation* (1997), *Religious Identity and the Problem of Historical Foundation* (2004), and *Dutch Jewry in a Cultural Maelstrom, 1880-1940* (forthcoming). Her interests include modern religious reform and Jewish-Christian relations in antiquity and modernity.

ANDREAS GOTZMANN (Ph.D, 1995, Freie Universität Berlin), is Professor of Jewish Studies at Erfurt University, Chair for Jewish Religious and Cultural History. Among other writings he is the author of *Jüdisches Recht im kulturellen Prozeß: Die Wahrnehmung der Halacha im Deutschland des 19. Jahrhunderts* (1997) and *Eigenheit und Einheit: Modernisierungsdiskurse des deutschen Judentums der Emanzipationszeit* (2002); he is also co- editor of *Juden — Bürger — Deutsche: Zu Vielfalt und Grenzen in Deutschland* (2001), *Modern Judaism and Historical Consciousness: Identities — Encounters — Perspectives* (forthcoming 2007), and editor of *Kehilat Friedberg: Jüdisches Leben in Friedberg im 16.-18. Jahrhundert* (2 vols., 2002). His special fields of interest are German-Jewish History, Jewish Religious and Cultural History from Early Modern to Modern Time, theory and methods of Cultural History.

KATRIEN DE GRAEF (Ph.D, 2004, University of Ghent, Belgium) is Assistant Professor at the Department Languages and Cultures of the Near East, research-unit Assyriology, University of Ghent, Belgium.

She is the author of several articles on the socio-economic history of the Old Babylonian period and has published two MDP-volumes: *Les archives d'Igibuni. Les documents Ur III du chantier B à Suse* (2005) and *De la dynastie Simashki au sukkalmahat. Les documents fin PE II début PE III du chantier B à Suse* (2006); she is also editor of *Ba'al Milim. Liber Amicorum Julien Klener* (2004). Her research interests include the socio-economic history of the Old Babylonian period in Mesopotamia and Susa, the historical geography of Mesopotamia (based on cuneiform and rabbinical sources) and the history of nineteenth-century Reform Judaism in Europe.

KLAUS HERRMANN (Ph.D, 1990, Freie Universität Berlin) is lecturer at the Institute for Jewish Studies in Berlin. Previously he was research assistant in the project: "Early Jewish Mysticism (Hekhalot literature)" at the universities of Cologne and Berlin and, in 1993-1994, visiting fellow at the Hebrew University. He is the author of *Massekhet Hekhalot. Traktat von den himmlischen Palästen* (1994) and co-editor of *Übersetzung der Hekhalot-Literatur* (1995) as well as *Studies in Jewish Manuscripts* (1998). His areas of research include Jewish mysticism, Palaeography and the Jewish Reform Movement in Germany.

ROBIN JUDD (Ph.D, 2000, University of Michigan) is an Assistant Professor of History at the Ohio State University in Columbus, Ohio. She is the author of *Cutting Identities: Jewish Rituals and German Politics* (forthcoming 2007) and a number of articles concerning Jewish ritual behavior and the formation of German-Jewish politics. She is currently working on a new research project, "Love at the Zero Hour: European War Brides, GI Husbands, and Reconstruction Politics."

KEN KOLTUN-FROMM (Ph.D, 1997, Stanford University) is Associate Professor of Religion at Haverford College, where he has taught since 1997. He is the author of *Moses Hess and Modern Jewish Identity* (2001) and *Abraham Geiger's Liberal Judaism: Personal Meaning and Religious Authority* (2006). His interests include modern Jewish identity, cultural studies, and the interplay between American Jewish thought and material culture.

MICHAEL A. MEYER (Ph.D, 1964, HUC-JIR) is the Adolph S. Ochs Professor of Jewish History at Hebrew Union College-Jewish Institute of Religion in Cincinnati and the International President of the Leo Baeck Institute. Among other works, he is the author of *The Origins of the Modern Jew: Jewish Identity and European Culture in Germany, 1749-1824* (1967), *Response to Modernity: A History of the Reform Movement in Judaism* (1988), and *Judaism within Modernity* (2001). He is also the editor of *Ideas of Jewish History* (1974) and *German-Jewish History in Modern Times* (4 vols., 1996-1997).

MARGIT SCHAD (Ph.D, 2004, University of Duisburg) is a research associate at the University of Tübingen with a project about German-Jewish sermons during World War I. Previously she was associate of the edition of Moses Mendelssohn's *Gesammelte Schriften (Jubiläumsausgabe)*. She is the author of *Judentum als Lebensanschauung und Literatur. Michael Sachs (1808-1864) — Rabbiner, Prediger und Übersetzer* (2006).

CÉLINE TRAUTMANN-WALLER (Ph.D, 1995, Paris) is Professor of German Studies at the University of Paris III since 2005. She is the author of *Philologie allemande et tradition juive. Le parcours intellectuel de Leopold Zunz* (1998) and *Aux origines d'une science allemande de la culture. Linguistique et psychologie des peuples chez Heymann Steinthal* (2006). She has edited *Références juives et identités scientifiques en Allemagne* (Revue germanique internationale 17/2002) and *Quand Berlin pensait les peuples. Anthropologie, ethnologie et psychologie (1850-1890)* (2004). Her research interests include Cultural History of German Jews and History of Human Sciences in Germany (nineteenth century).

CHRISTIAN WIESE (Ph.D, 1997 University of Frankfurt am Main) is Director of the Centre for German-Jewish Studies and Reader at the History Department at Sussex University, Great Britain. Previously he held positions at Duisburg University and Erfurt University, and has been visiting faculty at McGill University (Montreal), Dartmouth College, and Trinity College (Dublin). He is the author of *Challenging Colonial Discourse: Jewish Studies and Protestant Theology in Wilhelmine Germany* (2005) and *The Life and Thought of Hans Jonas: Jewish Dimensions* (forthcoming 2007), and has co-edited *Weiterwohnlichkeit der Welt: Zur Aktualität von Hans Jonas* (2003); *Modern Judaism and Historical Consciousness: Identities — Encounters — Perspectives* (forthcoming 2007); *Judaism and the Phenomenon of Life: The Legay of Hans Jonas. Historical and Philosophical Studies* (forthcoming 2007). He is also the editor of *Hans Jonas, Erinnerungen* (2003). His research interests include Jewish-Christian relations, modern Jewish History and Thought, American-Jewish History, and Zionism.

CARSTEN WILKE (Ph.D, 1994, University of Cologne) is research fellow at the Salomon Ludwig Steinheim-Institut für deutsch-jüdische Geschichte in Duisburg and visiting professor at the Institute of Jewish Studies at Düsseldorf University He has previously been visiting professor at the Hochschule für Jüdische Studien in Heidelberg and held research positions in Paris and Mexico City. His publications on European Jewish history include *Jüdisch-christliches Doppelleben im Barock* (1994), *Den Talmud und den Kant: Rabbinerausbildung an der Schwelle zur Moderne* (2003), *Biographisches Handbuch der Rabbiner, part I: Die Rabbiner der Emanzipationszeit in den deutschen, böhmischen und großpolnischen Ländern, 1781-1871* (2 vols., 2004), *Histoire des juifs portugais* (forthcoming 2007). He is also the editor of the posthumous works of *I. S. Révah, Antonio Enríquez Gómez, un écrivain marrane* (2003) and *Uriel da Costa et les marranes de Porto* (2004). He is currently working on the research project "The Alliance Israélite Universelle in Germany, 1860-1914."

INTRODUCTION

Christian Wiese

On July 4, 1906, at the annual meeting of the Central Conference of American Rabbis in Indianapolis, David Philipson, one of the most prominent American Reform rabbis at the beginning of the twentieth century and author of the first comprehensive historical representation of Reform Judaism written in the United States,[1] honored the memory of Samuel Holdheim on the occasion of the centenary of the reformer's birth in 1806 in a lecture analyzing the latter's intellectual profile and work in the broader historical context of the German-Jewish Reform movement in the nineteenth century. In his lecture with its historical depictions and characteristic contemporary ideological overtones, he described Reform as the "religious counterpart" of the movements for German Jewry's political and educational emancipation. While political emancipation "transformed the Ghetto-Jew into a citizen of a fatherland" and educational emancipation turned the "heder-Jew" into a man of modern culture, religious emancipation "transmuted the shulhan-arukh Jew into the reformer for whom Judaism spelt universalism and not Orientalism, prophetism and not rabbinism, world-wide Messianism and not Palestinianism."[2] This movement, however, Philippson continued, needed "prophets" who would succeed in creating a spiritual, prophetic, universalistic reading of Judaism and in recognizing ethical monotheism as its essential teaching; it found such a prophet in Samuel Holdheim, "the keenest and most incisive thinker" among the early leaders of the Reform movement and "the man, who, with Abraham Geiger, will always occupy the foremost place among the rabbis of Reform Judaism's creative period."[3]

---

[1] David Philipson, *The Reform Movement in Judaism* (New York: Macmillan, 1907).
[2] Idem, "Samuel Holdheim, Jewish Reformer (1806-1860)," *Central Conference of American Rabbis Year Book* 16 (1906), 305-329 (quoted from the offprint, Indiana: s.n., 1906, 3).
[3] Ibid., 6.

The image of Holdheim drawn by Philipson, very much based on the description of the reformer's intellectual development presented by his disciple and biographer, Immanuel Heinrich Ritter,[4] is that of [the gradual radicalization of an originally traditional Jewish scholar and rabbi who, through inner struggles and conflicts with other contemporary scholars, eventually created an interpretation of Jewish religion in the age of emancipation characterized by both revolutionary redefinitions and a fundamental loyalty to Judaism.] Comparing Holdheim to Abraham Geiger, the second among the "twin stars in the firmament of Jewish religious liberalism," he depicted Holdheim as the "arch-radical reformer," the "iconoclast without mercy" who, in contrast to Geiger' reverence for the institutions and forms of Jewish life that had developed historically, had no scruples to have his radical theories realized in immediate practice.[5] As a leading participant of the stormy Reform controversies of the 1840s, Holdheim, the "radical of the radicals," was, as Philipson recalled, famously denounced by Heinrich Graetz as a reincarnated Paul of Tarsus who, by his resolute denial of the authority of rabbinic tradition and his rejection of the significance of Jewish ceremonial law had dangerously undermined Judaism;[6] the Cincinnati rabbi then went on to condemn Graetz's judgment, characterizing it as the expression of a bitter partisan antagonism against the Reform movement in general, and defended Holdheim against the charge of attempting to destroy Judaism:

> Whatever he may or may not have been, he was certainly a Jew with all his heart and soul; he had no intention or purpose to undermine Judaism and replace it by another religion as did Paul; his interpretation of Judaism and its ceremonies may have been individual and too radical, but he rooted in Judaism; he never wished to be anything else but a follower and teacher of Judaism and in the history of modern Judaism he must always be given, as he will always have, a foremost place.[7]

---

[4] Heinrich Immanuel Ritter, *Geschichte der jüdischen Reformation*, vol. 3: *Samuel Holdheim. Sein Leben und seine Werke, Ein Beitrag zu den neuesten Reformbestrebungen im Judenthum* (Berlin: W. J. Peiser, 1865).

[5] Philipson, "Samuel Holdheim, Jewish Reformer (1806-1860)", 10f.

[6] See Heinrich Graetz, *Geschichte der Juden von den ältesten Zeiten bis auf die Gegenwart*, 2nd edition, vol. 11 (Leipzig: O. Leiner, 1900), 515: "Since Paul of Tarsus Judaism had not experienced such an enemy from within, who tried to shake the entire structure down to its foundations."

[7] Philipson, "Samuel Holdheim, Jewish Reformer (1806-1860)", 12.

It is quite interesting and, as we will see, quite appropriate that Philipson, after having described the development of Holdheim's radical Reform theory on the basis of his most important publications, pointed to his sermons as a genre revealing a different side of his personality and religious identity and characterizing him as a preacher "imbued with true sentiments" and a sincere scholar "who had drunk very deeply at the sources of Jewish learning"[8]—thus countering the image, painted by his opponents, of a reformer alienated from tradition and willing to opportunistically sacrifice Jewish identity for the sake of civil equality and social integration. However, what Philipson most admired in Holdheim, was the clear and unmistakable elimination of the national or political aspect of Judaism in his writings as well as his vision of a universalistic Jewish mission in modern European society, and he used the occasion of the centenary of his birth as an opportunity to polemically assert the utter incompatibility of Reform Judaism and Zionism. Himself involved in fierce debates on the emerging Zionist movement in the United States at the turn of the twentieth century, Philipson viewed Holdheim as a founding father of Reform who, more than any other reformer, lent authority to his own anti-Zionist attitude and embodied an interpretation of Judaism that excluded any kind of Jewish national identity:

> Reform Judaism and nationalism, or let me use the synonym for Jewish nationalism now in vogue, Zionism, are absolutely incompatible and irreconcilable. Reform Judaism is spiritual, Zionism is political; Reform Judaism is universal, Zionism is oriental. Reform Judaism looks to the future, Zionism to the past; the outlook of Reform Judaism is the world, the outlook of Zionism is a corner of Western Asia [...] Zionism means a surrender of all the ideals for which Reform Judaism stands.[9]

This passage of the commemoration speech shows that Holdheim, for Philipson, was more than just an influential early reformer; rather, he served him as an authoritative voice supporting his own ideological assumptions with regard to contested contemporary political issues like the Reform Jewish stance on the emerging Zionist movement. While Philipson had only praising words for the theoretical implications of Holdheim's universalistic, non-nationalist reinterpretation of Jewish tradition, including the replacement of the doctrine

---

[8] Ibid., 25.
[9] Ibid., 14f. For Philipson's attitude toward Zionism, see idem, *The Jew in America* (Cincinnati, OH: CCAR, 1909).

of Israel's election by the idea of a universal covenant of love between
God and man, he also expressed a certain criticism with regard to
the radical practical consequences he had drawn from it. Echoing
thoughts voiced forty years earlier by Abraham Geiger[10] and apparently influenced by a certain distance of the younger generation of
American Reform rabbis to the radical ideas expressed e.g. by reformers like David Einhorn and Kaufmann Kohler,[11] he deplored
Holdheim's a-historical disregard of deeply rooted elements of Jewish
life and characterized him as a purely philosophical thinker who was
not aware of the need of a less iconoclastic approach:

> The serious mistake which he made was that he was guided altogether
> by intellectual forms and took no sufficient note of historical forces
> and social determinants. No religion, Judaism or any other, is simply
> a philosophical discipline; the forces that have been at work in shap-
> ing the expression a religion takes, must enter largely into the reformer's
> workshop. No reformer can begin *de novo*; he is not a creator, he is
> not God; he must work with the material in hand; true, he must
> remove abuses which have sprung up in the course of time, he must
> necessarily destroy, but much more, he must reinterpret, re-adapt, re-
> construct. [...] Holdheim who was all intellect had little patience with
> anything that conflicted with his intellectual conclusions; his system of
> theology gave not sufficient place to the historical element of Jewish
> development, in his broad conception of the principle of tradition he
> disregarded too much special traditions and ceremonies that still might
> have had and did have potency and power. He proceeded from an
> "absolute" instead of a "relative" point of view. In one way he saw
> too clearly, impatiently brushing away everything that obstructed his
> vision, in another he was short-sighted in that he failed to appreciate
> that religion, and notably the Jewish religion, is a life, the century-old
> experience of a community which developed along particular lines.
> Reform can not proceed according to a program as iconoclastic as
> Holdheim's; not only the intellect must be reckoned with, but also the

---

[10] See Abraham Geiger, "Die religiösen Thaten der Gegenwart," *Wissenschaftliche
Zeitschrift für jüdische Theologie* 6 (1847), 1-16, here 11ff. And see idem, "Review of
Samuel Holdheim, Sein Leben und seine Werke, by Immanuel Ritter," *Jüdische
Zeitschrift für Wissenschaft und Leben* 3 (1864/65), 216-218, especially 216f.: "In our
relation of love and high esteem during a quarter of a century, we most readily
agreed on the justification of our divergent opinions, conceding to each other honesty of purpose both spiritually and morally, yet we knew always very well how to
find the line where our views differed. Holdheim was of a dogmatic, dialectic nature;
mine was, and is, decidedly and preponderatingly historical."

[11] For the stage of "radical" Reform in the United States leading to the Pittsburgh
Platform 1885 and the subsequent redefinition of Reform Judaism under different
historical circumstances, see Michael A. Meyer, *Response to Modernity: A History of the
Reform Movement in Judaism* (New York: Oxford University Press, 1988), 264-334.

historical consciousness of the people; not only the spirit of the age must be considered but also the genius of Israel. This explains in chief part why the Berlin Congregation [the radical Berlin Reform Congregation for which Holdheim served as a rabbi betwen 1847 and 1860] which translated Holdheim's interpretation of Judaism into practice remained so isolated a phenomenon in the life of German Jewry.[12]

Given the dramatic historical changes since 1906, including the destruction of German and European Judaism during the Holocaust, the rise of Zionism as a forceful intellectual and political reality, the establishment of the State of Israel, as well as the profound changes Reform Judaism has undergone in the twentieth century, commemorating Samuel Holdheim another hundred years later, on the occasion of his two-hundredth anniversary, is a task that has to be fullfilled in an entirely different context. On the one hand, this implies a much more complicated process of historical reflection, since some of the apparently clear categories employed by Philipson—e.g. universalistic versus national interpretations of Judaism—have to be differentiated and reinterpreted; on the other hand, the growing historical distance to the beginnings of the Reform movement in nineteenth-century Germany allows contemporary historiography to look at the phenomenon of "radical Reform" in general and at Samuel Holdheim's life and Reform concept in particular from a fresh perspective, especially since such an endeavor can be undertaken in a much more academic manner, without being part of ideological or political conflicts between different currents within Judaism.

A thorough reinterpretation of Samuel Holdheim's biography, work, and ideology from a variety of perspectives is certainly still a desideratum. While some of the figures of the Reform movement, including the representatives of its more conservative variant, have already found their biographers,[13] especially those rabbis and philosophers associated with the radical Reform movement in Germany and the United States, like Holdheim, Samuel Hirsch, David Einhorn, Kaufmann Kohler, or Emil G. Hirsch, still await a detailed historical analysis. As far as Holdheim is concerned, the history of

---

[12] Philipson, "Samuel Holdheim, Jewish Reformer (1806-1860)," 28.

[13] See, e.g., Andeas Brämer, *Rabbiner Zacharias Frankel. Wissenschaft des Judentums und konservative Reform im 19. Jahrhundert* (Hildesheim: Olms, 2000); Margit Schad, *Judentum als Lebensanschauung und Literatur. Michael Sachs (1808-1864)—Rabbiner, Prediger und Übersetzer* (Hildesheim: Georg Olms Verlag, 2006); Susannah Heschel, *Abraham Geiger and the Jewish Jesus* (Chicago: Chicago University Press, 1998).

historiography on his role within the Reform movement can be told
rather quickly. The still detailed biography by Immanuel Heinrich
Ritter is a valuable tool for a reconstruction of his ideological development on the basis of an analysis of his writings and a description
of his rabbinical activities in Frankfurt an der Oder (1836-1840),
Schwerin (1840-1847), and the radical Reform congregation in Berlin
(1847-1860), and it certainly helps present scholarship to identify crucial breaks and lines of continuity within his intellectual path. Although
far from being a hagiographic work, this biography nonetheless clearly
reflects its author's strong identification with Holdheim's agenda and
generally lacks a critical, contextualizing, or comparative analysis of
the reformer's theory and practice. The same is true for Emanuel
Schreiber's characterization of Holdheim in his book, *Reformed Judaism
and Its Pioneers* (1892), which is admittedly largely dependant on
Ritter's representation, although he claims to be "less prepossessed
in favor of Holdheim."[14] The Moravian-born Reform rabbi, who
emigrated to the United States in 1881, eventually being offered the
pulpit of the congregation Emanu-el in Chicago, characterized
Holdheim as "a giant wrestling with the demons of prejudice and
superstition, and conquering them" by a remarkable inner evolution,[15] and he praisingly described his role during the Reform controversies of the 1840s. Emil G. Hirsch, the important representative
of classical American Reform at the turn of the twentieth century,
saw Holdheim's importance mainly in the solution he provided for
the problem of "how loyalty to Judaism could be combined with
unqualified allegiance to [...] German nationality."[16] An interesting
remark in his encyclopedia-article refering to Holdheim as one of
the "pioneers of modern Jewish homiletics"[17] points to a dimension
of his work that deserves much more attention in the future: while
his published reform writings were often prompted by the immediate needs of responding to intellectual challenges within the context
of the Reform controversies, thus reflecting his role as a polemical
theoreticist, the abundance of his sermons published in several volumes or separately throughout his career shed a slightly different

---

[14] Emanuel Schreiber, *Reformed Judaism and Its Pioneers: A Contribution to Its History*
(Spokane: Spokane Printing Company, 1892), 179-254, here 254.

[15] Ibid., 245.

[16] Emil G. Hirsch, "Samuel Holdheim," in The Jewish Encyclopedia, vol 6 (New
York: Funk and Wagnalls Company, 1904), 436-439, here 437.

[17] Ibid., 438.

light on his biography, and a future detailed analysis of his profile
as a reformer as reflected in his homiletic activity promises to discover facets that might easily be overlooked when focusing entirely
on the genre of reform treatises.

While scholars associated with the Reform movement generally
shared a rather positive view of Holdheim and tended to emphasize
similar aspects of his intellectual profile, and while conservative historians like Heinrich Graetz usually condemned him, thus reflecting
the ideological boundaries between radical Reform and Positive-
Historical Judaism, a different accent emerges in the writings of
authors affiliated with Zionism or other forms of Jewish nationalism.[18] The only more detailed reference to Holdheim among scholars who embraced Zionist views is that of Max Wiener in his 1933
book on *Jüdische Religion im Zeitalter der Emanzipation*, a critical analysis of nineteenth-century German-Jewish intellectual history from the
perspective of the experience of the Weimar Republic and the beginning threat by Nazism. Very much in contrast to David Philipson's
anti-Zionist-motivated appraisal of Holdheim's main intellectual
achievement, the separation between Judaism's religious and national
elements, Wiener, although himself belonging to Liberal Judaism,
expressed a strongly critical judgment on the reformer's interpretation of the religious essence of Jewish tradition. Holdheim's aim of
a thorough de-nationalization and confessionalization of Judaism
deprived the Jewish religion, according to Wiener, of its "specific
correlation with its history as well as with the fate of a special group
that stands out from its surroundings," thus making it a purely individual confessional matter. This kind of reform, however, displayed
"an unmistakable similarity with the Protestant-Lutheran one."[19]
Furthermore, Wiener deplored that Holdheim's universalism was much
too strongly connected with an ideology of political liberalism and
abstract humanism, to the extent that a serious attempt of fullfilling
the "Jewish mission" in modern society instead of just internalizing

---

[18] See, e.g., Simon Dubnow, *Weltgeschichte des jüdischen Volkes*, vol. 9 (Berlin: Jüdischer
Verlag, 1929), 100-102; Raphael Mahler, *Divre yeme yisrael: Dorot aharonim*, vol. 2
(Merhavjah: Sifriyat Po'alim, 1980), 153-155; and see Michael A. Meyers inter-
pretation in his contribution to this volume.

[19] Max Wiener, *Jüdische Religion im Zeitalter der Emanzipation* (Berlin: Philo Verlag,
1933), 87-113, here 97. For Wiener's intellectual development toward a Jewish
national interpretation of Liberal Judaism, see Robert S. Schine, *Jewish Thought
Adrift: Max Wiener (1882-1950)* (Atlanta, Ga: Scholar's Press, 1992).

the need of divesting Judaism of its national elements was never undertaken and Jewish Messianism was simply identified with the liberal political idea of progress.[20] Finally, he criticized Holdheim's underestimation of the power and relevance of the irrational elements of Judaism, including more traditional forms of Jewish life and national sentiments which, as he indicated, might be inseparably linked with Judaism "according to its very concept of religion."[21]

After 1933, only very few scholars referred to Holdheim, whose interpretation of Judaism seemed to have become philosophically utterly irrelevant. Only since the 1970s, in the wake of increasing historiographical interest in the Reform movement, did the radical reformer reappear in scholarly publications. Apart from a short article by Georg Salzberger, who summarized Holdheim's rabbinical career and thought, concluding with the retrospective rhetorical question "how far the assimilation accompanying the political and intellectual emancipation of the Jews should be allowed to go without compromising the essence of historical Judaism,"[22] the most important publication was Jacob J. Petuchowski's article on "Abraham Geiger and Samuel Holdheim: Their Differences in Germany and Repercussions in America," which contrasts Geiger's insistence on an organic-evolutionary path to reform to Holdheim's plea for a revolutionary break and compares their ideological dissent to that between David Einhorn and Isaac M. Wise in the American context.[23]

Michael Meyer, in his magisterial *Response to Modernity* (1988), emphasized the significant role Holdheim played within the early German-Jewish Reform movement as well as the enormous influence he exerted particularly as a "model for radical Reform Judaism in nineteenth-century America."[24] He anticipated the image portrayed in this volume of a highly complex intellectual figure, whose intellectual development from an all-embracing talmudism to a radical Reform ideology was full of tensions, sometimes contradictions. The most valuable contribution of Meyer's passage on Holdheim is his clear interpretation of the reformer's "protracted quest for an

---

[20] Wiener, *Juedische Religion*, 98 and 103.

[21] Ibid., 104.

[22] Georg Salzberger, "Samuel Holdheim. Ein Vorkämpfer der Reform im Judentum," *Emuna* 7 (1972), 254-259, here 259.

[23] Jacob J. Petuchowski, "Abraham Geiger and Samuel Holdheim: Their Differences in Germany and Repercussions in America," *LBIYB* 22 (1977), 139-59.

[24] Michael A. Meyer, *Response to Modernity: A History of the Reform Movement in Judaism* (New York: Oxford University Press, 1988), 80.

acceptable religious authority" that would legitimize the practical reforms he had in mind.[25] While at the beginning Holdheim perceived the entire rabbinical tradition as normative, he later postulated the right to distinguish between the divine and non-divine in the Talmud, and eventually ended up in denying the entire Talmud, since he saw it as the expression of an outdated interpretation of biblical revelation. At this stage, Holdheim believed for a while that the entire Bible (at least its religious and moral teachings, whereas the destruction of Israel's national existence had revealed God's will to abolish civil and ceremial law) had to be ascribed the authority of divine revelation, but finally, by the end of his ideological development, he came to the opinion that even the Bible "was but the human reflection of divine illumination"[26]—which means that, in his eyes, eventually modern Jewry, or its religious leadership, became the final authority of tradition. This attitude, from Meyer's point of view, characterizes both the unique radicalness of his ideology and the limits of his influence, since he never succeeded in persuading his reform-minded colleagues to entirely abandon the Talmud instead of reading their own modern views into rabbinical tradition. Meyer's interpretation of Holdheim provides also a most valuable orientation for future research in that it points to the "discordant notes [...] in his universalist rhapsodies,"[27] thus emphasizing the need to look very carefully at the inherent tensions in his theoretical universalism instead of attributing him an attitude that excluded each kind of particular Jewish identity.

Recently, Holdheim was given renewed attention in Andreas Gotzmann's thorough analysis of the history of halakhic thinking in nineteenth-century Germany. In a chapter on his Reform system within the context of the struggle between Reform and Orthodoxy, Gotzmann characterizes Holdheim as "one of the most interesting and innovative religious thinkers of the nineteenth century" and presents the internal dynamic of the Reform controversies as reflected in the process of his theoretical radicalization.[28] In another book,

---

[25] Ibid., 81.
[26] Ibid., 81.
[27] Ibid., 84.
[28] Andreas Gotzmann, *Jüdisches Recht im kulturellen Prozeß. Die Wahrnehmung der Halacha im Deutschland des 19. Jahrhunderts* (Tübingen: J.C.B. Mohr, 1997), 198-250, here 000.

Eigenheit und Einheit, he treats Holdheim within the context of nine-teenth-century discussions about the relationship between religion and nation, highlighting Holdheim's idea that it was only the purifi-cation of Jewish tradition from its national elements that enabled Judaism to regain its religious essence and that it was the aim of divine Providence to transform it into a bourgeois confession.[29] Gotzmann is also the first who devoted his attention in more detail to Holdheim's confrontation with the contemporary ideology of the Christian state as formulated by Friedrich Julius Stahl and empha-sized the irony inherent in the fact that in the same moment in which the Reform movement endeavored to liberate Judaism from its national components, conservative Protestantism embraced a pro-grammatic anti-liberal agenda of Christian "theocratic" dominance over the affairs of state and society.[30] Even more recently, Benjamin M. Baader, in his chapter on "The Women's Question at the Rabbinical Conferences of the 1840s," described the prominent role played by Holdheim during the debates on the status of women within Jewish tradition. Holdheim's sharp criticism with regard to some of his reform colleagues who tried to make a case for women's rights on the basis of rabbinical tradition reveals a fundamental dis-sent within the Reform movement regarding the authority of the Talmud. In the context of the long, protracted discussions within German and American Reform, Holdheim's position was, as Baader shows, the most radical, since he was the only reformer for whom "the emancipation of women in Judaism formed part of the eman-cipation of Judaism from Halakhah" and who refused to import the Talmud into the modern religious consciousness.[31]

The mentioned elements of Holdheim's Reform ideology are just a few among the complex aspects of his thought that are being explored in this volume. These include his eventually radical denial of the authority of the Talmud and the validity of ceremonial laws, the universalistic reinterpretation of the concept of Israel's chosen-ness by means of the notion of a universal messianic "mission" of

---

[29] Idem, *Eigenheit und Einheit. Modernisierungsdiskurse des deutschen Judentums der Emanzipationszeit* (Leiden: Brill Publishers, 2002), 225ff. and 237ff.

[30] Ibid., 237ff. See Samuel Holdheim, *Stahl's christliche Toleranz beleuchtet* (Berlin: Julius Abelsdorff, 1856).

[31] Benjamin M. Baader, *Gender, Judaism, and Bourgeois Culture in Germany, 1800-1870* (Bloomington, IN: Indiana University Press, 2006), 64-73, here 72.

the Jewish people, the de-nationalization of Messianism, the concept
of separation of politics and religion as a basis for a full integration
into non-Jewish society, practical reforms concerning Jewish rituals
(including circumcision, liturgy, the status of women, and intermarriage), and the relationship toward Christianity. The contributions of
the present volume are the best expression of both the necessary dif-
ferentiations of the image associated with Holdheim's name as a radical iconoclast and the variety of different perspectives from which
his intellectual profile and his work as a practical reformer can be
illuminated, thus shedding light on an intriguingly multi-faceted figure within the broader context of the Reform debates in Germany.
By thoroughly reconstructing Holdheim's intellectual path as a scholar,
practical reformer and political thinker, by analyzing his attitude
toward the specific contested questions that dominated the agitated
Reform controversies during the 1840s, and by comparing him to
other—equally radical or more moderate—reformers and scholars of
this time, the articles assembled in this volume provide most valuable elements for a future intellectual biography of Holdheim himself and a differentiated interpretation of the complex intellectual and
social phenomenon of "radical Reform."

Further differentiating his earlier interpretation of Holdheim, Michael
A. Meyer characterizes him as a highly complex thinker, even a
"divided personality," whose biography included a process of religious self-emancipation from his traditional background as an Orthodox
scholar and gifted Talmudist, a stage in which these inner struggles
led to his a-historical iconoclastic critique of Jewish tradition and to
polemics directed not only against his opponents but against his own
past, and finally, during his tenure as rabbi of the Berlin Reform
Congregation, to a new element—the role as a committed advocate
of Jewish loyalty. This intellectual development reveals two opposite
poles of his thought: a radically universalistic interpretation of Judaism
that made him the severest critic of any element of Jewish tradition
and practice which contradicted the morality of modern society as
well as of any half-hearted aesthetical reform and reinterpretation of
institutions and customs, and a strong determination to counter the
anti-religious consequences of Enlightenment and secularization in
order to preserve Judaism and its universal religious-ethical mission.
Meyer emphasizes the irony inherent in the fact that by the end of
Holdheim's life, when serving as a rabbi and teacher of the most

radical Reform congregation in Germany, his radicalism diminished, apparently due to a thorough disillusionment of his messianic enthusiasm in the face of reactionary German politics after the failed revolution of 1848. The result of this gradual shift was, as Meyer shows (in an implicit contradiction against David Philipson's rather sweeping judgment), a stronger attempt to link the Reform movement to Jewish history, the willingness to respect at least the historical authority of tradition, and the constant emphasis on the necessity of resisting the temptation of abandoning Judaism.

Andreas Gotzmann illustrates Holdheim's ideological position within the broader context of the 1830s and 1840s—a period in which the invention of radical new ideas reflects the way German Jews embraced the newly developed bourgeois concept of religion and religiosity. Comparing him with other reformers who were content to introduce isolated changes of the Halakhah while preserving the legal system, he describes the protracted process in which Holdheim, one of the most ingenious ideologues among the scholars of his age and the "halakhist of the Reform," eventually attempted to overcome the entire system, replacing it by a more flexible ideological system which included both legal and historical arguments and which tended to emphasize what Gotzmann calls a humanistic-interdenominational approach. Describing the tension between the emergence of Holdheim's new concept of the biblical law as the normative center of Judaism and the fact that, as an extremely skilled Talmudist who always maintained the legal discourse as a basic argumentative system even where he radically questioned the authority of rabbinic tradition, he sheds light on the unique phenomenon of a reformer who appears at the same time traditionalistic and radically anti-traditional.

Ken Koltun-Fromm's article explores the interesting relationship between Jewish scholarship and religious politics in the nineteenth century by demonstrating that Holdheim, despite his resolute separation of religion (as the realm of universal, necessary truths) and politics (as a purely human endeavor), was a clear-sighted political thinker who was very much aware of the political implications of his Reform ideology. The separation of the two realms served as a strong argument against the concept of the Christian state and an excellent means to reverse Christian supersessionism, since it helped to attribute universalism to Judaism, while Christianity with its political implications appeared as a particularistic, even theocratic tradition. Apart from

this advantage, however, Koltun-Fromm argues, Holdheim's constricted image of religion as an eternal set of religious ideas untouched
by particular and historical forms, presented in his strict distinction
between the "Mosaic religion" and the "Mosaic state," implies a
problematic a-historical view of religion that tends to create a dichotomy
between the "religious idea" and any human activity and ritual. On
the basis of an analysis of Holdheim's biblical hermeneutics, Koltun-
Fromm characterizes him as a "categorical thinker," whose theoretical interpretation of Judaism (though to a certain degree relativized
by his later sermons) caused him to exclude the richness and complexity of Jewish identity—an echo, as it were, to Philipson's critical
judgment quoted above.

Instead of focusing on Holdheim's published work, Carsten Wilke
devotes his article to an analysis of his tenure as the *Landesrabbiner* of
the Grand-Duchy of Mecklenburg-Schwerin, who was responsible for
the implementation of reforms in the context of rather conservative
congregations in that region of Germany. In contrast to contemporary accusations according to which Holdheim's activities amounted
to a radical reformist dictatorship, Wilke demonstrates that exactly during the period in which he had his intellectual breakthrough as a
reformer and became an influential part of the radical Reform movement, the relationship between his theological system and his reform
practice was much more complex: on the one hand, Holdheim tried
rather cautiously to inspire reforms by fostering a process of spiritualization of Jewish life, based on a reform of the school system, and,
by aiming at compromises that were likely to reconcile the ambitions
of modernists and conservatives, avoided endangering the unity of the
congregation; on the other hand, Wilke points to Holdheim's growing inclination to emphasize the need of a uniform Jewish ritual authorized by the state that should be imposed on the congregations instead
of allowing a certain degree of liturgical pluralism. Despite this tendency, however, Wilke emphasizes Holdheim's will to preserve the religious unity of German Jewry, thus characterizing him not as the
"Luther of Judaism", but rather as an Erasmus, i.e. as a radical reformer
as far as his thought is concerned, but as a realistic thinker who was
aware of the fact that life demanded compromises.

Katrien de Graef, whose article stands at the end of the first part
which explores Holdheim's profile as a scholar, rabbi and
political thinker, is devoted to his last work, *Ma'amar ha-Ishut* which,

interestingly enough, allows to perceive him as a highly skilled Hebrew writer and Talmudist, and to the scholarly discussion between Holdheim and the conservative scholar Salomon Juda Loeb Rapoport on the origins of Karaism. Based on a scholarly analysis of the history of the Karaites and on Abraham Geiger's theories on the difference between Sadducees and Pharisees in relation to the Torah of the Karaites, this book, according to de Graef, reflects a new dimension in Holdheim's work, namely a strong historical interest combined with the search for a "usable past" that would serve as a justification of his reform theory. The fact that, during the Reform controversies, reformers like Holdheim were accused of being Karaites because of their rejection of rabbinical tradition, challenged Holdheim to demonstrate that Karaism, instead of being rooted in non-Jewish traditions, for instance in Shiite Islam, as Rapoport maintained, was an originally Jewish phenomenon that can be traced back to the split between Sadducees and Pharisees. In this context de Graef shows how Holdheim proceeded to clarify his hermeneutical attitude toward Scripture, emphasizing that the Bible as the human reflection of the unchangeable divine revelation of ethical monotheism is ultimately subject to the authority of modern religious consciousness that provides the categories for its constant reinterpretation.

The second part of the volume sheds more light on the distinctiveness of Holdheim's reform concept by analyzing his attitude toward specific aspects of the heated controversies on practical reforms. Robin Judd differentiates the image of Holdheim as a radical determined to abandon the rite of circumcision, despite its profound rootedness in Jewish identity. Within the broader context of the circumcision debates of the 1840s which reflect the attempt to rethink the rite's significance in the modern era, Holdheim's agenda was not so much aiming at encouraging the widespread abdication of circumcision, as in the case, for instance, of the radical Frankfurt *Reformfreunde*; rather, as Judd demonstrates, his pamphlet *Ueber die Beschneidung zunaechst in religiös-dogmatischer Beziehung* (1844), one of the most radical interpretations of the circumcision question, was much more concerned with traditional authority and leadership: as a response to the polemical disputes concerning the rite's significance for questions of religious belonging and the Jewish community's attitude toward men who rejected religious customs like circumcision, Holdheim vehemently rejected any attempt of Conservative or Orthodox thinkers to use the circumcision debates in order to retail their authority. Although

Holdheim held the opinion that circumcision was no longer a central ritual, since it belonged to the realm of religious law, which is open to historical interpretation, and not to the eternally binding realm of religious truth, he never openly encouraged its abandonment, but focused mainly on the ritual's political character. By pointing to this accent of Holdheim's argument, Judd emphasizes that these questions of an appropriate definition of the community's civic authority and the separation between politics and religion were much more significant for him than the actual reform of the system of Jewish rites and customs itself. The radical aspect of his attitude was, according to Judd, that the potential consequences of a general abandonment of circumcision for Jewish identity were less important to him than his ideal of a Jewish community that consistently refrained from acting as a political entity.

Klaus Herrmann's article on Holdheim's contributions to the debate on liturgical reforms provides another example of the peculiar mixture of theoretical radicalism and practical conservativism that characterized his activity as a reformer both in Schwerin and in the Berlin Reform congregation. Comparing Holdheim's and Abraham Geiger's reaction to the prayerbook of the Hamburg Temple congregation, Herrmann shows that Holdheim was—much more than the historian Geiger—inclined to accept certain inconsistencies as long as the general aim of revitalizing the prophetic spirit of Judaism and of eliminating liturgical elements that were counterproductive when it came to express a universalistic interpretation of Jewish tradition was achieved. Despite his increasingly radical theoretical views, the reforms Holdheim introduced within the context of his new Synagogue Order for his congregation in Schwerin were far from radical, since he was willing to take the feelings of more conservative members of the congregation into consideration. But even during his tenure as a rabbi of the radical Berlin Reform congregation, Holdheim's position, despite his support for the latter's decision to transfer the Sabbath service to Sunday, included some surprising conservative elements, including his strong critique of the protestantizing character of the chorals that had been included into the Reform congregation's prayerbook.

As far as the Berlin Reform congregation is concerned, Margit Schad's contribution on the moderate reform of the religious service within the larger context of the Berlin Jewish community describes the theoretical and practical alternative provided by Holdheim's Berlin

adversaries, especially the conservative reformer Michael Sachs. Schad
emphasizes the interesting phenomenon that while there was a certain agreement between the Orthodox and the radical Reform to
tolerate each other, an agreement that was apparently based on their
respective self-understanding as separate circles, the moderate reformers were strong rivals of both camps and rejected this kind of tacit
toleration as a threat to the unity of the congregation. Although
focusing on the conflict between moderate Reform and Orthodoxy,
Schad's article demonstrates why the strongest attacks against Holdheim
were launched by the camp of the Positive-Historical school: from
the point of view of Zacharias Frankel, Michael Sachs and later
Heinrich Graetz, the radical reforms implemented by Holdheim,
despite their sometimes rather cautious and conservative character,
destroyed the creative potential of Jewish self-understanding, based
as they were on the adoption of forms that were not grounded in
the historical essence of Jewish tradition.

   David Ellenson's article deals with the subject of Holdheim's attitude toward questions of marriage and divorce, one of the most controversial aspects of his Reform concept since the publication of his
Ueber die Autonomie der Rabbinen und das Princip der juedischen Ehe (1843).
Analyzing Holdheim's halakhic argument in his famous work and
Zacharias Frankel's thorough critique, he places the controversy into
the historical context of the general controversy with regard to the
question of rabbinical authority. While Holdheim, basing his views
on Talmudic reasoning, argued that marriage, according to Jewish
law, had to be understood as a purely civil act instead of a religious
act, thus attributing the state ultimate sovereignty over Jewish law
in relation to marriage, Frankel understood marriage as a holy religious-moral act that cannot be viewed solely from a secular legal
perspective. In his article, Ellenson strongly emphasizes the political
motivation behind Holdheim's views and interprets them as a response
to the contemporary debates on emancipation: challenged by Bruno
Bauer's argument that the Jew, by the very nature of his eternal
separateness, cannot be emancipated, Holdheim embraced classical
nineteenth-century liberal political theory and attempted to demonstrate that the distinction between the domain of politics and the
realm of religion, including the obligation to observe the law of the
state (*dina de-malkhuta dina*) was rooted in Jewish tradition itself. The
fact that Frankel, who wanted the Jews to fully participate in modern German society as well, felt it an unnecessary, opportunistic act

to assign marriage to the political sphere in an effort to demonstrate that Jews were worthy of emancipation (a charge that Holdheim would, of course, have rejected), best illustrates, from Ellenson's point of view, the process of division that took place within the different currents of German Liberal Judaism in the mid-nineteenth century.

The final part of this book is devoted both to the attempt to thoroughly look at the intellectual relationship between Holdheim and other scholars, and to an interpretation of Holdheim's approach in comparison to contemporary intellectuals who can also be counted among the radical reformers. Andreas Brämer's article on Holdheim and Zacharias Frankel sheds more light on the fierce antagonism between these two figures who embodied extremely different Reform concepts. He thoroughly analyzes the process of mutual estrangement that begun in the 1840s when both started to perceive each other as competitors. The main divisive issue, according to Brämer, was both scholar's divergent use of "nation" and "history" as central concepts of their reform agenda. While Frankel demanded that the state should refrain from interfering with religious matters and concede that Judaism be allowed to preserve some—however de-emphasized—national elements, Holdheim emphasized the national elements of traditional Judaism, characterizing them as anachronistic relics that had to be overcome by a consistent confessionalization. And while Frankel perceived religious law as fundamentally compatible with modern ethical standards and demanded only minor modifications, Holdheim, for whom, at a later stage of his ideological development, the destruction of the Second Temple had to be understood as a symbolic divine revelation pointing to the loss of validity of the halakhah, perceived Frankel as an insincere, apologetic thinker whose attitude was likely to confirm anti-Jewish prejudice and prevent full emancipation. Holdheim's own strategy, however, which consisted in uncompromisingly naming the flaws of Jewish tradition, from the point of view of moderate reformers like Frankel, threatened the status of Judaism and was likely to legitimize potential state interventions into Jewish religious affairs. By pointing to this aspect, Brämer demonstrates that the division between radical and moderate Reform was not only rooted in the difference between a philosophical and an historical approach, but also implied important political and strategic responses to the problem of Jewish emancipation.

Céline Trautmann-Waller's comparative article on Holdheim and Leopold Zunz describes the indirect dialogue and controversy between these two very different thinkers, whose relationship was originally actually characterized by a clear affinity with regard to the historical-critical basis of their reflections upon Judaism and their critical judgment on issues like rabbinic authority or the validity of the rituals and ceremonial laws. Trautmann-Waller emphasizes the ironic fact that Zunz, whose anti-rabbinism and critique of religious tradition had strongly influenced Holdheim, eventually became much more conservative than the latter as far as religious practice was concerned. She thus confirms the phenomenon already seen in the comparison to Abraham Geiger that scholars engaged in historical studies on Jewish history and culture like Zunz tended to develop a much stronger feeling for the cultural, symbolic power of Jewish tradition than Holdheim with his a-historical approach. As a scholar of *Wissenschaft des Judentums*, Zunz became very sceptical about Reform, since, in his eyes, the Reform rabbis were instrumentalizing scholarship for their ideological purposes instead of taking it seriously as a philological-historical endeavor, and Holdheim, in particular, seemed, from his point of view, to neglect the historical elements that were likely to legitimate tradition and ceremonial laws in favor of general moral laws. Furthermore, Trautmann-Waller sheds light on Holdheim's and Zunz's diverging concepts of Jewish nationality and universalism: while Holdheim called for radically overcoming any concept of Jewish national identity and for divesting Jewish religion of its particular forms, Zunz, who was equally critical with regard to Jewish exclusiveness, nonetheless aimed at preserving what was particular and unique in Jewish history, since he assumed that a certain degree of particularity did not exclude a universalistic interpretation of Judaism within a democratic, tolerant Europe.

Ralph Bisschop's comparison of the rabbi Holdheim to the layman, historian, theologian, political activist, and member of the board of the Berlin Reform congregation, Sigismund Stern, attempts to define the specific form of radicalness in Holdheim. Contrasting Stern, who represents the "protestantizing" tendency in Reform Judaism and who was extremely sceptical about the rabbinate's ability to create a radically new interpretation of Jewish tradition, with Holdheim's continuing "Orthodoxy," Bisschops, despite the many shared convictions of the two intellectuals, identifies several areas in which they strongly disagreed. The most important result of this comparison is that, in contrast to the dominating image designed by previous research, it is inappropriate and overly simplistic to identify

Holdheim with the radicalism of the Reform congregation. Bisschops accentuates the difference between Stern's opinion that, in the age of emancipation, full participation in Gentile life was an ethical duty of the Jewish people, and Holdheim's reluctance to relate reforms to external political circumstances. Emphasizing the thoroughly rabbinical character of Holdheim's thinking, he maintains that, rather than emancipation, his main concern was the question of how an emancipated Jew could still be a religious Jew and preserve loyalty to his tradition. By the end of his life, as this article shows, the reformer had found a balance between his strong commitment to universalism and a fundamental respect for the traditionalism of earlier interpretations of Judaism, and he even tended toward a traditionalist way of understanding the Jewish mission that seemed to imply the notion of an indelible particularity of the Jewish people. Finally, Bisschops demonstrates that Stern's and Holdheim's attitudes toward Christianity were diametrically opposed, with Stern praising Christianity—and particularly Protestantism—as a model for liberating ethical monotheism from national exclusiveness, while Holdheim resolutely refuted the notion of Christian superiority and emphasized Judaism's role as the religion of the future, thus expressing his distinctive loyalty to his religious convictions and the importance the idea of a universal mission of the Jewish people had for him.

Judith Frishman presents a comparison between Holdheim and another radical reform ideologue, Samuel Hirsch. Focusing on both reformer's attempt to present a philosophical middle-ground between Bruno Bauer's polemical rejection of Jewish Reform and the radical reform concept of the *Reformfreunde* in Frankfurt am Main, which was characterized by a strong denial of any authority of Jewish tradition, she illustrates how Holdheim's and Hirsch's respective philosophical-theological systems developed into different directions. The image emerging from this comparative analysis is that both thinkers had a different vision of the essence of Judaism and the implications of the "Jewish mission" with respect to Jewish rites and ceremonies: Hirsch, from whose point of view circumcision was one of the most important ceremonies which could not be abandoned without violating the essence of Judaism, countered Bauer's views by insisting that, as long as the Jewish mission was not fulfilled, the Jewish communities needed symbolical rites and ceremonies—they should, therefore not be sacrificed simply in order to placate non-Jewish polemicists like Bauer. In contrast to this, Holdheim, who denied the importance of circumcision and other rites, focused on a different aspect of Bauer's polemics, rejecting the latter's argument that the Jews are a nation and emphasizing Reform Judaism's strictly religious identity. Interestingly enough, as Frishman points out, Hirsch, who was at first rather conservative with respect to the preservation of rites, became more and more radical, particularly after his emigration to the United States, while Holdheim, who had initially expressed much more radical ideas, became much more cautious toward the end of his life and eventually tended to emphasize at least the symbolical and historical value of Jewish tradition.

Another comparative perspective is provided by my own article on David Einhorn, Holdheim's "closest ally in conviction," who shared many aspects of Holdheim's intellectual profile, including the protracted path from an Orthodox Jeshiva student to a radical Reform rabbi. Following in detail the development of the—first ambivalent and then increasingly strong—friendship between those two radical reformers, the focus is on David Einhorn, who had developed his own independent Reform philosophy in Europe, and later, with his uncompromising radicalism, was to mould the Reform movement in America into the later nineteenth and early twentieth centuries—at a time when Holdheim's influence in Germany had already faded. The conflicts described between Einhorn and Holdheim include initial theoretical differences with regard to the authority of the Talmud and Einhorn's more cautious, historical approach, but since the rabbinical conferences both scholars became close allies in nearly all the relevant issues of practical reform. The main aim of the article on Einhorn, however, is a systematic comparison of Einhorn's, Holdheim's, and Samuel Hirsch's closely related, albeit distinctive philosophical interpretation of Jewish universalism. With regard to Holdheim and Einhorn, it leads to the conclusion that, while they may have shared the same enthusiastic faith in a universalistic Jewish mission in modern times, for Holdheim this faith entailed the demolition of the barriers between Jews and non-Jews (including the acceptance of mixed marriages), whereas Einhorn's characteristic concept of the Jews as God's "priestly people" with a mission to all humankind necessitated the survival of the Jews as a distinct group. The analysis of the dissent between Einhorn and Holdheim on this issue and of a conflict between Einhorn and Hirsch on the question of mixed marriages shows that, although these three radical reformers could be perceived as sharing almost the same convictions, even within the radical wing of the Reform movement theoretical and philosophical assumptions varied and led to sometimes surprisingly different practical conclusions.

This volume is based on an international conference on *Samuel Holdheim (1806-1860). Reformer oder Häretiker? Leben, Werk und Wirken* that took place in Germany on April 17-20, 2001 under the auspices of the Salomon Ludwig Steinheim-Institute for German-Jewish History at Duisburg University. This first comprehensive academic conference ever devoted to Holdheim owed very much to the initiative and inspiration of Ralph Bisschops, who convincingly argued that it was important to finally go beyond traditional clichés and stereotypical—polemical as well as apologetic—representations of the reformer and to explore his work in more detail. Under the academic supervision of Ralph Bisschops, Michael Brocke, and Robert Platzner, the conference succeeded in bringing together scholars from Germany, the USA, France, Belgium, and the Netherlands, who provided a fresh look at Holdheim from different perspectives, in a contextual analysis, and in comparison to other intellectual figures and movements of his time. The publication of the contributions of such an academic event is always an adventure that depends on the willingness of the participants to develop and rethink their papers and to submit substantial articles. I would, therefore, like to thank all the participants of the conference, including those authors who did not originally participate but agreed to contribute to this volume, for their fine articles. Furthermore, I am indebted to Michael Brocke and Ralph Bisschops for offering me to edit this volume and for their support. As it is not easy to find a publisher for such a specialized collected volume, I would like to thank Giuseppe Veltri for accepting it for his Studies in European Judaism-series, and Michiel Swormink for his enthusiastic interest in the project. Igor Nemirowsky and Michael J. Mozina have been extremely helpful in producing the manuscript—I owe them special thanks for their patience. I would also like to thank the Buber-Rosenzweig-Foundation in Bad Nauheim, Germany, for its generous and substantial financial support of the translation of some of the German articles into English. Finally, I would like to express the hope that this volume will contribute to strengthen the scholarly interest in the phenomenon of

the nineteenth-century (radical) Reform movement and inspire additional research in some of its leading representatives as well as the
important links that exist between the German and the American
Reform movement.

Brighton, United Kingdom
October 2006

PART I

REFORMER, SCHOLAR, POLITICAL THINKER

"MOST OF MY BRETHREN FIND ME UNACCEPTABLE": THE CONTROVERSIAL CAREER OF RABBI SAMUEL HOLDHEIM[1]

Michael A. Meyer

1

During his relatively brief lifetime, Rabbi Samuel Holdheim (1806-1860) was arguably one of the most prominent, and certainly the most controversial, of the Jewish religious reformers in Germany, but his legacy has received remarkably little attention. In contrast to his contemporaries, Rabbis Abraham Geiger and Zacharias Frankel, none of his works was fully reprinted or translated in the twentieth century. He has been discussed only within the context of larger subjects, such as the history of the Reform movement or the history of Judaism in Germany.[2] A fresh look at Holdheim, dwelling on the contradictory images that he presented to his contemporaries, his development from ahistorical iconoclast to advocate of Jewish loyalty, his interpretation by later historians, and his significance in the subsequent history of modern Jewish religion and scholarship, reveals a complex individual of considerable daring, whose concerns and objectives continued to be relevant long after his death.

There is probably no personality in German-Jewish history regarding whom the views of contemporaries were so sharply divided. It is as if friends and enemies were not describing the same person. The most prominent among his admirers was Geiger, who developed

[1] This chapter on Holdheim, based on my opening lecture for the conference entitled "Samuel Holdheim (1806-1860). Reformer oder Häretiker? Leben, Werk und Wirken" in Germany, April 17-20, 2001, is reprinted here from *Jewish Social Studies* 9 (2003), 1-19.
[2] See, e.g., the treatments in Michael A. Meyer, *Response to Modernity: A History of the Reform Movement in Judaism* (New York: Oxford University Press, 1988), 80-84, and Michael A. Meyer and Michael Brenner, eds., *German-Jewish History in Modern Times*, vol. 2 (New York: Columbia University Press, 1997), 142-150.

a deep friendship with Holdheim that lasted for more than a quarter of a century and culminated in two visits, the second of longer duration, during the last months of Holdheim's life.[3] Geiger wrote of Holdheim after his death:

> Seldom was a man regarded with so much suspicion and animosity, defamed and treated with such forced disregard as this, my dear departed friend. [....] His whole life was a continuous struggle because his steadfast working toward the future was an eternal protest against the decadence of beatifying the past.[4]

In Geiger's view, Holdheim's consistent concern was for truth. To Leopold Zunz, Geiger wrote in 1845:

> I'll admit to you, I love Holdheim with all my heart, even if I don't subscribe to all of his claims and can't regard every one of his actions as appropriate. I love him because I recognize in every word the enthusiasm of honest conviction, of an elevated moral outlook.[5]

Geiger greatly admired Holdheim's daring and uncompromising willingness to accept and act upon conclusions that could only make him enemies within the Jewish community. Like Holdheim a radical in theory, but less so in practice, Geiger may well have seen in his contemporary a consistency that, because of his desire to gain broader support within the Jewish community, Geiger could not himself represent. By contrast, Holdheim pressed forward "to the furthest point of all reform."[6] Geiger also recognized not only that Holdheim was more willing to carry ideas to their logical conclusion but that his approach to Jewish tradition differed from Geiger's own. Whereas Geiger described his relation to Judaism as predominantly historical, Holdheim, he claimed, remained dogmatic and dialectical.[7]

Geiger was not alone in his admiration for Holdheim. A number of his contemporaries were impressed by the radical reformer's lack

---

[3] David Einhorn, "Samuel Holdheim," *Sinai* 5 (1860), No. 10, 289-297, here 296.

[4] Samuel Holdheim, *Gott siehet! Predigt für den Neujahrstag des Jahres 5621 (1860), als Entwurf aus den hinterlassenen Papieren des kurz vor dem Neujahrsfeste verstorbenen Dr. Samuel Holdheim: Nebst einem Vorworte von Dr. Abraham Geiger, Rabbiner in Breslau* (Berlin: Im Selbstverlage der Wittwe des sel. Verfassers, 1861), v.

[5] Abraham Geiger, Brief an Leopold Zunz, in *Nachgelassene Schriften*, vol. 5 (Berlin: Louis Gerschel, 1878), 182.

[6] Ibid.

[7] Abraham Geiger, review of Samuel Holdheim, *Sein Leben und seine Werke*, by Immanuel Ritter, *Jüdische Zeitschrift für Wissenschaft und Leben* 3 (1864/65), 216-218, here 216.

of fanaticism—that, despite the fervor expressed in his writings, as a person he was mild mannered, even shy.[8] Rabbi David Einhorn, himself a radical reformer both in Europe and the United States, called Holdheim "a star of the first magnitude" and a "gadol-be-yisrael [a great Jewish scholar]." For him, as for Geiger, Holdheim was an honest seeker after truth and a genuinely religious personality whose lifelong concern was the ennoblement of Judaism.[9]

An almost totally different image of Holdheim emerges from the moderate reformers, who saw in Holdheim's thinking what they regarded as the disastrous results of a religious reform not held in check by the countervailing force of tradition. Frankel, the founder of the Positive-Historical School, and Heinrich Graetz, the historian at Frankel's seminary in Breslau, could not be content with a refutation of Holdheim's writings. They insisted on repugning his motives. In its original version, Frankel's review of Holdheim's *Ueber die Autonomie der Rabbinen und das Princip der jüdischen Ehe* was so filled with personal invective that the censor insisted on revisions.[10] In Frankel's view, Holdheim was not at all a seeker after truth but was playing "a dishonest game" with it; his use of *Wissenschaft* was in fact a misuse. Frankel may have disagreed with Geiger, but he believed that the latter was at least an honest scholar. Holdheim, by contrast, was an enemy of Judaism, intent on purchasing emancipation for the Jews at the price of Judaism.[11]

In his *Geschichte der Juden,* Graetz was no more sparing in his condemnation of Holdheim than was Frankel. He too questioned Holdheim's truthfulness, adding epithets like "sophist" and "spirit of negation" and besmirching his early personal life.[12] Writing earlier about Holdheim in his diary in 1845, however, Graetz was both more balanced and also more revealing. He recognized that the feverish criticism then reigning in Jewish literature was the sign of

---

[8] Anonymous, "Personalzeichnungen aus der Braunschweiger Rabbinen-Versammlung," *Der Israelit des neunzehnten Jahrhunderts* 5 (1844), 297-300, here 297.

[9] Einhorn, "Samuel Holdheim," 289, 293, 296.

[10] Immanuel Heinrich Ritter, *Samuel Holdheim, Sein Leben und seine Werke. Ein Beitrag zu den neuesten Reformbestrebungen* (Berlin: Peiser, 1865), 129.

[11] Zacharias Frankel, review of *Ueber die Autonomie der Rabbinen und das Princip der jüdischen Ehe* by Samuel Holdheim, *Zeitschrift für die religiösen Interessen des Judenthums* 1 (1844), 204-208; 244-248; 273-288; 321-328, here 205, 207, 208, 327.

[12] Heinrich Graetz, *Geschichte der Juden von den ältesten Zeiten bis auf die Gegenwart,* 2nd edition, vol. 11 (Leipzig: O. Leiner, 1900), 512, 514, 515.

a beneficent crisis and that the dominant talmudism, which Graetz himself did not cherish, could only be brought down through "terrorism." But, like Frankel, Graetz possessed an emotional attachment to Judaism that made him detest Holdheim as a critic who lacked his own appreciation for Jewish historical achievements. He wrote:

> O what impertinence, what shamelessness! This Holdheim! All historical reminiscences, which grip my heart with tremendous force and make the full glory of the Jewish past come alive within me and shine radiantly for me, and which instill the ecstasy of pain—all of this to the impudent Kempner [from the town of Kempen] is a horror, a fable.[13]

A third virulent critic was Pinchas Menachem Heilprin, who anonymously published a work in Hebrew that was largely devoted to a sustained attack on Holdheim. In language even less restrained than that of Frankel and Graetz, Heilprin called Holdheim "a sinner in Israel," compared him to the wicked Haman of the Book of Esther, and accused him of *Schadenfreude*, of deriving pleasure from causing anguish to his fellow Jews. Heilprin's most serious and revealing charge was to brand Holdheim as a *moser*, one who by revealing Jewish faults makes the Jews odious to gentiles.[14] Holdheim was, in short, a dangerous traitor analogous to the *malshin*, the stool pigeon who is condemned in the daily traditional Jewish liturgy. Frankel had expressed the same view when he referred to Holdheim's work repeatedly as "denunciations" and compared Holdheim to Johann Andreas Eisenmenger, the notorious seventeenth-century Christian scholar whose severely critical *Entdecktes Judentum* Jews had attempted unsuccessfully to keep from being published.[15]

It seems clear from this brief review of Holdheim's strikingly contradictory image in the eyes of his contemporaries that, even as he aroused admiration among those who could agree, at least theoretically, with his radicalism, he struck a raw nerve among those who feared the destructive consequences of his writing. Although

---

[13] Idem, *Tagebuch und Briefe*, ed. Reuven Michael (Tübingen: J.C.B. Mohr, 1977), 146.

[14] [Pinchas Menachem Heilprin], *Teshuvot be-anshe aven: Holdheim ve-reav be mikhtavim sheloshah asar* (Frankfurt am Main: s.n., 1845), 1, 2, 22.

[15] Frankel, review of Holdheim's *Ueber die Autonomie der Rabbinen*, 277, 328n; idem, review of *Teshuvot be-anshe aven* by Pinchas Menachem Heilprin, *Zeitschrift für die religiösen Interessen des Judenthums* 2 (1845), 159-160; 241-248; 278-284; 363-368, here 368. Holdheim himself was not averse to defending Eisenmenger when he believed his translation and understanding of a talmudic text to be correct. See Samuel

conservative reformers themselves employed the techniques of modern scholarship to weed out what they regarded as outdated customs and ceremonies, they set limits to their enterprise, being careful
to leave intact a chain of tradition from ancient times to the present. Even though they did not fully accept the talmudic view of
the world, they refused to see it as failing utterly to reach the moral
standards of the present age. By sharply differentiating Jewish past
from German present, Holdheim was implicitly raising questions
about whether Judaism in any recognizable form was worthy of
continuation. But no less troubling to them was the effect they
assumed Holdheim's critique of rabbinic Judaism would have on
the Jewish struggle for emancipation. Would not the enemies of
the Jewish claim that the adherents of a legal tradition that did
not treat non-Jews in the same manner as it treated Jews and that
possessed legal means to avoid fulfilling an oath were not worthy
of Jewish political equality? Holdheim must have called to mind
the medieval apostate who, using his knowledge of Judaism, took
the Christian side in disputations directed against his former com-
rades. They could not look with equanimity upon this talmudist
who attacked the Talmud, this rabbi who raised moral questions
about the rabbis of old. In their eyes, he was an underminer not
only of the Jewish past but also of the Jewish future. Both Graetz
and Zunz (as early as 1839) called him a second Paul, comparing
him to the New Testament figure who had cast aside a Judaism
based on law in favor of a new faith entirely liberated from it.[16]
In Graetz's unsparing words: "Since Paul of Tarsus Judaism had
not experienced such an enemy from within, who tried to shake

---

Holdheim, *Gemischte Ehen zwischen Juden und Christen. Die Gutachten der Berliner
Rabbinatsverwaltung und des Königsberger Consistoriums beleuchtet* (Berlin: L. Lassar, 1850),
36-37.

[16] Graetz, *Geschichte der Juden*, 515; Nahum N. Glatzer, ed., *Leopold Zunz: Jude—
Deutscher—Europäer* (Tübingen: J. C. B. Mohr, 1965), 209, note 1. According to
Ritter, *Samuel Holdheim*, 80, Zunz and Holdheim remained on good terms until 1842.
In a letter from Holdheim to Zunz, dated January 18, 1842, preserved in the Zunz
Archives at the Hebrew University in Jerusalem (40792 g14), Holdheim expresses
doubt that contemporary rabbis and laity are prepared to make even minor changes
in the liturgy and sends him, along with the letter, his published opinion on the
new Hamburg Temple prayer book (1841). It is likely that it was precisely Zunz's
reading of his pamphlet affirming radical liturgical reform that led to a severing of
the ties between them. There is no indication that Zunz answered the letter.
Holdheim's biographer, Immanuel Heinrich Ritter, in a positive sense, likewise called
his subject "der Paulus des reformirten Judenthums" (Ritter, *Samuel Holdheim*, 273).

the entire structure down to its foundations." Yet that was not at all the way that Holdheim understood himself.

2

The young Samuel Holdheim was by all accounts an *ilui*, a genius in the study of Talmud, destined for a prestigious rabbinate in his native Posen. But during his early twenties he began to stray from the closed world of Polish Orthodoxy to the point that his first marriage broke up, and he went to study at the University of Prague. A surviving document shows that among the subjects he studied there were empirical psychology and moral philosophy. He attended the lecture for both subjects most diligently and on the examinations given in June 1833 received for each course the mark of "first class with merit."[17] While in Prague, Holdheim also undertook rabbinical studies with the leading rabbis of the city, among them Samuel Landau, later dedicating a sermon "to the memory of his unforgettable teacher and benefactor."[18] After further studies in Berlin, Holdheim undertook his first rabbinate in the city of Frankfurt an der Oder in 1836.

The few sermons that survive from his early years already attest both to the universalism and to the desire to preserve Judaism that would come to the fore during the later stages of his career. The very first printed sermon was delivered in his native Kempen while he was still a "candidate for the rabbinate and a student of philosophy" in Berlin.[19] It is self-admittedly a sermon that lacks reference to the "characteristic pecularities" of Judaism, dwelling instead very generally on the close connection between morality and religion. Although Holdheim cites rabbinic literature and speaks of the need for public spiritedness in Israel, the burden of the sermon is to defend the importance of religion as such, not of Judaism per se. Similarly, a later sermon finds the particular celebration of Jewish holidays of

---

[17] I received a copy of the *Zeugniß*, dated June 20, 1833, from the late Jacob Rader Marcus in 1980. I do not know how it came into his possession.

[18] Aron Tänzer, "Samuel Holdheim als Rabbinatskandidat," *AZJ* 62 (1898), 19-20, here 19; Samuel Holdheim, *Die Einsegnung des Neumondtages: Rede gehalten an den beiden Sabbathen vor dem Gedächtnißtage der Zerstörung Jerusalems des Jahres 5597 (5. August 1837) in der Synagoge zu Frankfurt an der Oder* (Frankfurt an der Oder: F. W. Koscky, 1837), dedication page.

[19] Idem, *Rede verfaßt und gehalten in Kempen* (Berlin: Julius Sittenfeld, 1836).

value for strengthening and rejuvenating religious life in general.[20]

However, the most remarkable sermon from this period addresses a very particular imperative to the listener: "concern for preserving the ancestral religion so that it not perish in the stream of time." Here Holdheim complained of those many Jews who had deserted the House of Israel, failing to remain true to their tradition. The structure of the house, he claimed, was still sound and not antiquated, even if it was "dreadfully neglected by many of those who dwelled in it."[21] Although during the following six years of his life, as rabbi in Mecklenburg-Schwerin and advocate of radical religious reform, Holdheim came to believe that that house was indeed antiquated and that only the stream of time could rejuvenate it as a universal religion, he never abandoned his belief that the desertion of the House of Israel was morally despicable. During the Mecklenburg-Schwerin years, Holdheim became the leading polemicist for a thoroughgoing transformation of Judaism; during the last 13 years of his life, as rabbi and preacher of the Reform Congregation in Berlin, the note of loyalty to the Jewish faith is again sounded more loudly.

3

By the time he left Frankfurt an der Oder, Holdheim had come to view what he called the present-day *Zeitbildung*, the contemporary cultivation of mind and character, as the criterion by which historical Judaism was to be judged and modified. In his first major tract in favor of religious reform, he argued that Judaism could survive only if it attached itself to the Zeitbildung, which was already embodied in a large portion of the German-Jewish population.[22] This Zeitbildung, however, as Holdheim would repeatedly make clear, was for him neither Christian-Germanic nor Christian-European, but universally human. What Holdheim set out to do in the following years was to [pour Jewish tradition through the filter of universally human moral principles, removing all those elements that he believed to be in contradiction with them.] Not only did his efforts bring him

---

[20] Idem, *Die Einsegnung des Neumondtages*, passim.
[21] Idem, *Ob es Pflicht jedes Israeliten für die Erhaltung der Religion seiner Väter zu sorgen: Rede gehalten am I. Sabbath Chanukka .... 23. Dec. 1837* (Frankfurt an der Oder: F. W. Koscky, 1838), 11.
[22] Idem, *Der religiöse Fortschritt im deutschen Judenthume* (Leipzig: F. W. Koscky, 1840).

into conflict with all but the most radical reformers but they also involved a <u>severe struggle with himself</u>. Holdheim told a visitor to his home in 1845 that Jews were reluctant to abandon the Talmud "because the Talmud still sticks in people's limbs, because they are still chained to it by invisible bonds, still unable with complete freedom and self-consciousness to position themselves opposite in the way that Christian theologians do with regard to equally reprehensible church teachings of earlier times."[23]

⌈The Talmud seems to have stuck in Holdheim's bones as well.⌉ Contemporaries and later writers noted that Holdheim—ironically, for a critic of the Talmud—himself remained a talmudist, even a pilpulist, in his style of writing. But perhaps it was not simply a matter of style. Holdheim engaged himself in a struggle to liberate German Judaism from what he believed to be the dead hand of the Talmud, a struggle that was energized by his personal quest for self-emancipation from it. We gain some insight into his inner emotional turmoil when Holdheim refers angrily to the "rotten principles of talmudic-orthodox Judaism" or writes of the "progressive inner self-liberation from the legal bonds of Judaism."[24] <u>Compromises, which Holdheim consistently rejected, at least in theory,</u> would have meant <u>to him compartmentalization into a Jewish self and an incompletely self-emancipated one</u>. It seems not unfair to Holdheim to suggest that his unmitigated critiques of Jewish tradition were motivated, at least in part, by his need to justify rationally his own emotionally difficult abandonment of it. His polemics were not solely directed against his opponents but also against himself.

It was this *religious* <u>self-emancipation</u> from a system that he believed both dated and morally deficient, for himself and his fellow Jews, that was primary for Holdheim. Political emancipation, his critics notwithstanding, was secondary. Much as Holdheim saw no lasting value in the Jewish ceremonial law, he expressed his severe opposition to any German state's requiring Jews to give up dietary and ceremonial laws in order to gain civic equality.[25] He also

---

[23] Anonymous, "Holdheim und die rabbinische Lehre vom Eide," *Der Israelit des neunzehnten Jahrhunderts* 6 (1845), 118-119, here 118.

[24] Holdheim, *Gemischte Ehen*, v; idem, *Moses Mendelssohn und die Denk- und Glaubensfreiheit im Judenthume* (Berlin: J. C. Huber, 1859), 55; see also idem, *Die religiöse Stellung des weiblichen Geschlechtes im talmudischen Judenthum* (Schwerin: C. Kürschner, 1846), 3.

[25] Idem, *Das Gutachten des Herrn L. Schwab, Rabbiners zu Pesth, über die Reformgenossenschaft daselbst* (Berlin: J. Sittenfeld, 1848), 14.

believed that the state did not have the right to force Jewish school-children to write on the Jewish Sabbath.[26] Even less did he toler-ate an offer of emancipation made conditional on Jews giving up elements of their belief. But what indicates most clearly that Holdheim was concerned with religion first and political status only second is his refusal to abandon his severe moral critique of talmudic Judaism although he realized that it might very well be used by state authorities as an excuse for withholding emancipation. The sharp opposition to Holdheim was motivated in no small measure by his critic's fears that Holdheim was undermining their struggle for political equality.

Holdheim explicitly agreed with the champion of Jewish political rights in Germany, Gabriel Riesser, that Jewish emancipation could be gained only when German states were established on a "solid foundation of justice," not by religious concessions.[27] "The unfree fatherland," he writes in the wake of the 1848 Revolution, "was unable to grant us liberty."[28] This is not to deny that the state does indeed play a very important role in Holdheim's thought. But it is for him *ideally* a moral entity that should embody the principle of freedom for all of its subjects. In the years leading up to the 1848 Revolution, Holdheim believed that such a state was developing in Germany. He firmly rejected the idea of the Christian state, as advo-cated by the Jewish apostate Friedrich Julius Stahl, believing it to be a violation of the principle of freedom of conscience. Such a state was not based on a common morality but on a particular religious faith, on the world-to-come rather than this world. He termed it a "dogmatic and missionary institution."[29] But the state founded on the rule of law possessed religious sanctity on a higher level, and hence, in the area of civil and criminal law, Jews were religiously obligated to accept its laws, even when they stood in conflict with rabbinic or even biblical legislation. Jew and Christian, he believed, would meet

---

[26] Simon Bernfeld, *Toldot ha-reformatsyon ha-datit be-yisrael*, 2d ed. (Warsaw: Tushiyah, 1923), 177.

[27] Samuel Holdheim, *Das Religiöse und Politische im Judenthum: Mit besonderer Beziehung aufgemischte Ehen* (Schwerin: C. Kürschner, 1845), iv-vi.

[28] Idem, *Die geprüfte Vaterlandsliebe: Predigt am Tage vor Eröffnung der Preußischen Kammern (25. Februar 1849)* (Berlin: L. Lassar, 1849), 7. See also idem, *Der Kampf bis zum Anbruch der Morgenröthe: Eine Predigt gehalten am 2. April, dem Stiftungstage der Genossenschaft für Reform im Judenthume zu Berlin* (Berlin: L. Lassar, 1848), 11.

[29] Idem, *Ueber die Autonomie der Rabbinen und das Princip der jüdischen Ehe*, 2d ed. (Schwerin: C. Kürschner, 1847), xi-xii.

in the "universally human," which the state must represent.[30]

During his years in Schwerin, Holdheim became the severest critic of all those Jewish institutions that he believed to be in conflict with the underlying morality of this idealized modern state. Unlike other Jewish religious reformers, he was not content to argue merely for aesthetic changes in the synagogue or for the reinterpretation of traditions. To his mind, there was an unbridgeable gulf between the values and the institutions of traditional Judaism, on the one hand, and a universal, higher morality, on the other. His attacks were so painful because they lashed out mercilessly at one of the most central institutions in Judaism—circumcision—and unsparingly revealed to the world the embarrassing truths about traditional Judaism.

[For Holdheim, circumcision possessed no higher status than other ceremonial laws.] Like them, it has ceased to have religious significance once Israel ceased to be a nation. In addition, as symbol of an ancient, exclusive covenant with Israel, it was objectionable because it set the Jews apart from the rest of humanity. He noted—correctly—that according to Jewish law, a male child was a Jew by birth, not by circumcision.[31] Yet for his fellow Jews, circumcision was much more than another ceremonial law. It was a historically significant and emotionally laden symbol of Jewish identity. To abandon it meant more than a violation of dietary laws, for example; his opponents could see it as an abandonment of Judaism itself.

In direct opposition to the apologetic strain in nineteenth-century Judaism, which served the purpose of emancipation, Holdheim focused on Jewish sources that revealed a moral gap between Jewish law and contemporary values. He called attention to the biblical law (Deut. 23:20-21) that prohibited taking interest from fellow Israelites but permitted it with regard to the foreigner as an instance of a double moral standard, understandable in the light of a particularistic theology that elevated the Jews as the people of God, but unacceptable in terms of the universalistic Judaism that Holdheim advocated. Similarly, Holdheim revealed that, according to Jewish law, in some instances, an oath can be withdrawn without the consent of the party

---

[30] Ibid., 1st ed. (Schwerin: C. Kürschner, 1843), ix; see also Max Wiener, *Jüdische Religion im Zeitalter der Emanzipation* (Berlin: Philo-Verlag, 1933), 97-98.

[31] Idem, *Ueber die Beschneidung zunächst in religiös-dogmatischer Beziehung* (Schwerin: C. Kürschner, 1844), 8 and 87; David Philipson, "Samuel Holdheim, Jewish Reformer," *Central Conference of American Rabbis Year Book* 16 (1906), 305-329, here 328-329.

to whom it is sworn.[32] Although he readily admitted that contemporary Jews took oaths seriously, Holdheim was determined to show that there was a gulf between rabbinic attitudes and modern ones. His opponents regarded these writings as a defamation of Judaism that gave ammunition to the enemies of emancipation. Perhaps one could not trust the Jews, after all. Holdheim told an acquaintance regarding his articles on this subject in the *Israelit des neunzehnten Jahrhunderts:* "You can see that nothing else the *Israelit* has published as clearly cast the firebrand into the enemy camp and jolted the sleeping watchman into taking defense measures as did the discussion of the oath."[33]

Holdheim's treatment of the status of women in Judaism belongs in the same category as his discussion of interest and oaths. Here too Holdheim was seeking to show that the talmudic view was far removed from contemporary conceptions. What sets this subject apart from the others, however, is not only the repeated attention Holdheim gave to it but also his specific suggestions for reform. Indeed, in retrospect, Holdheim appears to be a pioneer of Jewish feminism. In contrast to his contemporaries, both the Orthodox and the more moderate reformers, Holdheim insisted that Jewish laws pertaining to marriage were unacceptable by contemporary moral standards.[34] It was not possible to avoid the conclusion "that women in talmudic Judaism occupy a religious status far beneath that of men, and that only the transformed religious consciousness of the present, standing in opposition to that of the Talmud, has liberated them from it."[35] Although the medieval authority Rabbenu Gershom had forbidden polygamy, as allowed by the Bible, his decision was not a permanent revision. Whereas married women were guilty of

---

[32] Ritter, *Samuel Holdheim*, 202.

[33] Anonymous, "Holdheim und die rabbinische Lehre vom Eide," 118-119. In 1850 Holdheim published anonymously *Denkschrift der Genossenschaft für Reform im Judenthum zu Berlin, wegen Abänderung des von den jüdischen Staatsbürgern zu leistenden Eides* (Berlin: J. Draeger, 1850). Here he argued that the Prussian state should finally abolish the demeaning and highly particular manner in which Jews were still required to swear legal oaths. Instead of a swearing ceremony conducted in the synagogue during which the rabbi gives warning that oaths demanded by Christian authorities are binding and the man swearing the oath wears a head covering and holds a Torah scroll, Holdheim proposed a common oath for Jews and gentiles that would be taken in the court room.

[34] Holdheim, *Ueber die Autonomie der Rabbinen*, 1st ed., 215, 258-260.

[35] Idem, *Die religiöse Stellung des weiblichen Geschlechtes*, 77.

violating Jewish law if they had relations outside marriage, the same was not true for a married man who had a relationship with an unmarried woman. Holdheim's critics insisted that, in fact, Jewish mores had advanced beyond such conceptions. Holdheim agreed, but held that, nonetheless, the laws on which they were based had not been permanently abrogated. Jewish law made marriage a civil act in which the husband acquires the wife much in the same manner in which he acquires other property. Although religious sentiments might be involved, the act itself was not a religious one.[36] Similarly, Holdheim attacked the inequality in Jewish law between husband and wife with regard to divorce, which grants validity to a husband divorcing his wife without moral cause and denies the right of the wife to force a divorce from her husband even on the most substantial grounds.

Geiger had preceded Holdheim as a critic of the status of women in Judaism. As early as 1837, he had denounced the persistence of Orientalism and pointed to various legal and religious disabilities that Jewish women were forced to suffer. He urged reforms in such areas as divorce and levirate marriage, and he wanted to give validity in Jewish law to the state's declaration of a husband's death, allowing the widow to remarry. But Geiger's more encompassing historical approach had also called attention to the improving treatment of women in actual fact: despite the legalities, Jewish men did not regard their wives as a commodity. Geiger was also more moderate with regard to sexual equality. He wrote that he was opposed to any "elevation of women above their natural limits, as some in recent times have been."[37] And he did not favor a wedding ceremony in which the bride was allowed to speak more than her consent, believing that nature had made men active and women passive.[38]

Holdheim, by contrast, proposed that bride and groom should play identical roles and that, as a result of this mutuality, women

---

[36] David Ellenson, "Samuel Holdheim on the Legal Character of Jewish Marriage: A Contemporary Comment on His Position," in *Marriage and its Obstacles in Jewish Law: Essays and Responses*, ed. Walter Jacob and Moshe Zemer (Tel Aviv: Freehof Institute of Progressive Halakhah, 1999), 1–26.

[37] Abraham Geiger, "Die Stellung des weiblichen Geschlechtes in dem Judenthume unserer Zeit," *Wissenschaftliche Zeitschrift für jüdische Theologie* 3 (1837), 1–14, here 6.

[38] Michael A. Meyer, "German-Jewish Identity in Nineteenth-Century America," in idem, *Judaism Within Modernity: Essays on Jewish History and Religion* (Detroit: Wayne State University Press, 2001), 323-344, here 337.

should necessarily enjoy equal rights with men in cases of divorce. In keeping with his objection to symbolism, Holdheim proposed an abandonment of the wedding ring altogether. The oral pledge was, to his mind, sufficient, just as prayer, for Holdheim, was a sufficient substitute for ritual. In place of the traditional "Be sanctified to me with this ring according to the law of Moses and Israel," Holdheim wanted to substitute a new formula to be spoken by both bride and groom: "I will be sanctified to you according to the laws of God."[39] Aside from its mutuality and its omission of the ring, this formula was radical in two other respects. First, for the particular laws of Moses and Israel, which Holdheim rejected not only for much of their content but also because he believed all lawhould pass into the hands of the state, he substituted the universal—and very vague— "laws of God," rendering the ceremony nonsectarian. And, second, he changed the text whereby the husband committed the wife to be sanctified (wedded) to him to words whereby each partner sanctified himself or herself to the other.

During the seven years he spent in Mecklenburg-Schwerin, from 1840 to 1847, Holdheim wrote his most important radical tracts. But, like Geiger, he remained convinced that religious progress in German Jewry should be collective. Those Jews who were ready for more radical steps should not abandon those who were not. In a sermon delivered at the synagogue in Schwerin on June 29, 1844, he urged solidarity: "Moving ahead *slowly* but *together*—let that be our motto."[40] Yet only a little more than two years later he had decided to accept a position as rabbi and preacher of the separatist Reform Society in Berlin. Ironically, during the last 13 years of his life, spent preaching and teaching within a circle of German Jews whom he earlier defined as "a small band of the elect, standing upon the highpoint of the age,"[41] Holdheim's radicalism diminished. It did not disappear, but his concern seems progressively to have been less oriented to pressing for reform and more for Jewish preservation.

During the late 1840s, Holdheim was possessed with messianic enthusiasm. He was convinced that a new age was dawning for the German Jews in which they would participate together with non-Jews

---

[39] Samuel Holdheim, *Vorschläge zu einer zeitgemäßen Reform der jüdischen Ehegesetze* (Schwerin: C. Kürschner, 1845), 25.
[40] Idem, *Der glaubensvolle Muth des israelitischen Volkshirten dem Murren seiner Gemeinde gegenüber* (Schwerin: C. Kürschner, 1844), 13.
[41] Ibid., 12.

in the liberal state. He argued that immediate complete abandonment of the Jewish ceremonial laws would present a living example
of the messianic kingdom wherein all religious particularism, both
Christian and Jewish, would yield to messianic universalism.[42] Holdheim
celebrated the 1848 Revolution as the end of the "bondage of the
German Israelites," which had lasted as long as the bondage of the
German people. Now a "new dawn" was breaking all over the fatherland. Holdheim prayed to God that henceforth the state would no
longer favor one religion over another, that it would destroy the special relationship between Christianity and the state.[43]

4

The 1850s, the last decade of his life, must have been a great disappointment to Holdheim. The years of messianic hopefulness gave
way to a new period of reaction. The idea of the Christian state,
as expounded by Stahl, gained its greatest influence in Prussia during the decade from 1848 to 1858.[44] Holdheim had earlier written
against what he called the new "Christian theocracy," comparing it
unfavorably with the theocracy of ancient Israel, which insisted only
on comformity of praxis, not of belief.[45] Now he attacked Stahl
directly at a time when the liberal state, and along with it Jewish
emancipation, were again in question.[46] Holdheim's messianic fervor
began to ebb. To be sure, he remained a universalist. As before, he
preached that all human beings who acknowledged and loved God,
and not the Jews alone, were to be counted among the chosen and
the holy.[47] He continued to believe that the covenant between God
and Israel was destined to be superseded by the covenant between

---

[42] Idem, *Das Ceremonialgesetz im Messiasreich* (Schwerin: C. Kürschner, 1845), 70,
72. And see Jakob J. Petuchowski, "Abraham Geiger and Samuel Holdheim: Their
Differences in Germany and Repercussions in America," *LBIYB* 22 (1977), 139-159,
here 146.

[43] Holdheim, *Der Kampf bis zum Anbruch der Morgenröthe*, 11, 12, 14.

[44] Hans-Joachim Schoeps, "Friedrich Julius Stahl und das Judentum," in *Vergangene
Tage: Jüdische Kultur in München*, ed. Hans Lamm (Munich: Langen Müller, 1982), 152.

[45] Holdheim, *Ueber die Autonomie der Rabbinen*, 1st ed., viii.

[46] Idem, *Stahls christliche Toleranz* (Berlin: J. Abelsdorff, 1856).

[47] Idem, *Die wesentlichen Erfordernisse eines ächt jüdischen Gottesdienstes: Predigt gehalten
am zweiten Tage des Neujahrsfestes 5611 (8. September 1850) im Gotteshause der jüdischen
Reformgemeinde zu Berlin* (Berlin: L. Lassar, 1850), 13.

God and humanity.[48] [He celebrated the Jewish Sabbath on Sunday, and he officiated at weddings between Jews and non-Jews in the belief that they could share a common religious faith devoid of all particular beliefs and practices] Nonetheless, a careful examination of his writings during the Berlin period reveals a shift in emphasis. Holdheim, who had long stressed the inward religious life of the individual Jew, now increasingly turned to the relationship of Jews to their tradition and to their fellow Jews.

In his inaugural sermon in Berlin in 1847, Holdheim had defined his role as that of teacher rather than priest and, in his circle of educated Jews, looked forward to "reciprocal instruction."[49] However, increasingly, he acted out a different role vis-à-vis this congregation, which required no urging in the direction of religious reform. Paradoxically, he became the universalistic preacher who urged them not to abandon their relationship to their particular tradition.

Holdheim was no less concerned to argue for religious reform on rational grounds and more to find historical precedent for it, thereby linking the Reform congregation to Jewish history. During this period he adopted Geiger's positive view of the Pharisees, explicitly rejecting the image of them presented in the New Testament. Unlike the Sadducees and their later descendants, the Karaites, they had been willing to adjust Judaism to changing times and therefore had been able to accomplish the task that Holdheim now placed before his congregation: "the preservation and progress of Judaism in its conflict with the age." Holdheim, who had earlier made the case for historical discontinuity, stressing how different modern religious consciousness was from that of the ancient rabbis, now attempted to find an anchor in the past. He told his congregants: "As old as Judaism, that old is the history of its development, that old is the reform of Judaism."[50]

---

[48] Idem, *Moses Mendelssohn*, 76; Ralph Bisschops, "Metaphor as the Internalisation of a Ritual: With a Case Study on Samuel Holdheim (1806-1860)," in *Metaphor, Canon and Community: Jewish, Christian and Islamic Approaches*, ed. Ralph Bisschops and James Frances (New York/Bern: P. Lang, 1999), 284-307, here Behr's Buchhandlung.

[49] Samuel Holdheim, *Antrittspredigt des Dr. Samuel Holdheim bei dessen Einführung in sein Amt als Rabbiner und Prediger der Genossenschaft für Reform im Judenthum zu Berlin am 5. September 1847* (Berlin: 291. 1847), 13.

[50] Idem, *Die Erhaltung des Judenthums im Kampfe mit der Zeit: Ein Bild aus der Vergangenheit belehrend für die Gegenwart. Predigt gehalten im Gotteshause der jüdischen Reformgemeinde zu Berlin (am 11. Mai 1851)* (Berlin: L. Lassar, 1851), 5 and 11. It should be noted,

In general, [Holdheim during his last years became more appreciative of both the history of Judaism and the history of the Jews] Although he continued to deny the dogmatic authority of the Talmud, he now claimed that it was "indisputably an unshakeable *historical* authority."[51] And he began to glorify the Jewish past. Like Graetz, his severest critic, he extolled the history of Jewish martyrdom, recommending that it be taught to Jewish children so that its deep impact would prevent them in later life from engaging in the "faithless denial of Judaism for the sake of external advantage."[52] Loyalty to Judaism, set against apostasy, now became a leading theme in Holdheim's writings and sermons. On one sermonic occasion he was even willing to compare the present unfavorably to the past, complaining that the present "enervated time" with all of its "much praised *Bildung*" was far removed from the spirit of sacrifice that characterized the spirit of Moses. In the 1850s, it continued to be true that remaining Jewish required a measure of sacrifice, and Holdheim declared that the unwillingness to accept that sacrifice was a moral offense. He referred to the Reform Congregation as an "association against apostasy."[53] Earlier his arguments for liberation from traditional Judaism had reflected his own quest for self-liberation from it; now he spoke of the abandonment of Judaism as an abandonment of self.[54] Holdheim had always had a special interest in Jewish education.[55] Surprisingly, the Reform Congregation's religion school, which was under his direction, offered instruction both on the significance of the ceremonial law and, on voluntary basis, in the Hebrew language.[56]

---

however, that in his sermons Holdheim was not averse to giving his own meanings to historical texts. For example, Torah was rendered in German as "Religion" (ibid., 4, 10).

[51] "Briefe zur Charakteristik der Zeit und der Zeitgenossen; Holdheim an [Leopold] Löw (11 Juli 1859)," *Ben Chananja* 8 (1865), 490-491, here 491.

[52] Idem, *Geschichte der Entstehung und Entwickelung der jüdischen Reformgemeinde in Berlin: Im Zusammenhang mit den jüdisch-reformatorischen Gesammtbestrebungen der Neuzeit* (Berlin: Julius Springer, 1857), 252.

[53] Ibid., 251, 253; idem, "Der verbesserte Religionsunterricht," *Programm zur öffentlichen Prüfung der Zöglinge der Religionsschule am 2. April 1858* (Berlin: Friedländer, 1858), 10.

[54] Idem, "Das wahre Opfer: Gehalten den 10. Oktober 1857 (5618)," in idem, *Sechs Predigten* (Berlin: Im Selbstverlage der Wittwe des sel. Verfassers, 1863), 63-72, here 71.

[55] Bernfeld, *Toldot ha-reformatsyon ha-datit*, 171.

[56] Anonymous, "Schulnachrichten," *Programm zur öffentlichen Prüfung der Zöglinge der Religionsschule*, 12.

This does not mean, however, that Holdheim abandoned his opposition to symbolic religion. The children in the school were to learn
how to celebrate the religious and moral message of Jewish holydays, for example, without employing any of the symbols connected
with them. The word, too, Holdheim wrote, was only a form, "but
the purest, noblest, most transparent and spiritually permeated form
of the divine."[57] In the sermons he delivered during the last years
of his life, Holdheim used the spoken word to defend Judaism against
its cultured critics, who believed that Christianity or modernity superseded it. Reading traditional texts selectively and nonhistorically, he
equated the essence of Judaism with truth and morality. Distinguishing
Judaism from Christianity, he declared the former a religion whose
messianic goal lies in the future, not in the past.[58]

In the last months of his life, Holdheim was occupied with writ-
ing his first and only book in the Hebrew language, *Maamar ha-ishut*
(A Treatise on Personal Status), which was published only after his
death. The otherwise critical Jewish nationalist historian Simon
Bernfeld believed that this work, in which Holdheim referred to
Hebrew as "our language," should have entered the canon of
Wissenschaft des Judentums.[59] A year before his death, Holdheim
expressed to his friend and disciple Rabbi David Einhorn in the
United States his hope that this book would introduce the efforts for
religious reform into the circles of the Hebrew-reading public.[60]

In large measure Holdheim's last major work returns to the subject of the status of women in Judaism. The tone this time is less
polemical and more historical. He takes his stand within the tradition, not outside of it: "It is not my purpose, God forbid, to
desecrate the honor of our ancestors in the eyes of our generation, but to cherish and to honor them."[61] Yet once again Holdheim

---

[57] Samuel Holdheim, *Ha-emunah veha-deah: Jüdische Glaubens- und Sittenlehre. Leitfaden
beim Religionsunterricht der jüdischen Jugend. Zunächst für die Religionsschule der jüdischen
Reformgemeinde zu Berlin* (Berlin: Julius Springer, 1857), 123.

[58] Idem, *Licht im Lichte! Oder das Judenthum und die Freiheit: Eine Festpredigt gehalten
am Wochenfeste Schabuoth 5519 (8. Juni 1859) im Gotteshause der jüdischen Reformgemeinde
zu Berlin* (Berlin: W. J. Peiser, 1859), 7.

[59] In this connection only, Bernfeld refers to Holdheim using the form Ra"SH
Holdheim, thus placing him within the traditional chain of rabbis; see Bernfeld,
Toldot ha-reformatsyon ha-datit, 181).

[60] Einhorn, "Samuel Holdheim," 296.

[61] Samuel Holdheim, *Maamar ha-ishut al tekhunat ha-rabanim veha-karaim* (Berlin: s.n.,
1861), 22.

castigates the inequality between men and women in talmudic law, especially with regard to the marriage ceremony, to infidelity and to divorce. In this instance, basing himself on what he believed to be a Sadducean conception—and in florid Hebrew—he also paints a picture of the ideal Jewish marriage, concluding that in such a marriage faithfulness is as incumbent on the husband as on the wife.[62]

5

In his introduction to *Maamar ha-ishut,* Holdheim admitted that most of his Jewish brethren found him unacceptable. Empirically that was an accurate statement, both during his lifetime and after his death. When the Jewish community informed its elderly *Rabbinats-Verwalter,* Jacob Joseph Oettinger, of Holdheim's death, he is supposed to have replied: "Holdheim is dead? *Boruch dajin emmes*—he was a great *lamdan;* whatever else he did and his turn of thought —for that he will now have to render account to God. Death blots out everything. I have nothing against his being buried in the row of the rabbies."[63] However, the conservative preacher of the community, Michael Sachs, was so upset by the decision to bury Holdheim in the so-called "first row" that he temporarily resigned his position. Frankel, too, was unwilling to make peace with Holdheim even after his death.[64]

In contrast to Graetz's work, later general histories of the Jews have been relatively kinder to Holdheim. The secular Jewish nationalist Simon Dubnow called him "the most significant theoretician of the reformation next to Geiger" but criticized him for failing to recognize the continuing value of Jewish autonomism.[65] The twentieth-century Marxist-Zionist historian Raphael Mahler was the first to call attention to Holdheim's championing the rights of women and gave him credit for his honesty and daring, but he insisted on

---

[62] Ibid., 40-41.
[63] Anonymous, "Die letzten Vorgänge in Berlin," *AZJ* 24 (1860), 573-575, here 574.
[64] Moritz Güdemann, "Zacharias Frankel: Von ihm und über ihn," *MGWJ* 45 (1901), 243-253, here 248-249.
[65] Simon Dubnow, *Weltgeschichte des jüdischen Volkes,* vol. 9 (Berlin: Jüdischer Verlag, 1929), 100-102.

reducing his motives to the quest for emancipation. Mahler also recognized that the later Holdheim had become more Jewishly oriented,
but he very questionably explained this shift by reference to an
alleged achieved emancipation.[66]

In the perspective of almost two centuries since his birth, Holdheim
seems in some respects very much in tune with the present. Jewish
scholarship today is increasingly liberating itself from apologetic considerations. It is less concerned with potential ill consequences for
the Jews that could arise from an honest examination of their past.[67]
Holdheim's call for religious equality between men and women in
Judaism remains an issue in Orthodox circles. The question of the
adequacy of Jewish law to deal with matters of personal status has
become especially relevant in the State of Israel, where such matters are given over to religious courts.

Within the perspective of his own life, however, Holdheim appears
more as a divided personality than as a pioneer. Geiger believed
that Holdheim's inner development paralleled the stages of the Reform
movement in Germany.[68] Geiger was right for the nineteenth century. But Holdheim's trajectory from the mentality of a talmudist
within the closest orthodoxy of a small Posen town to a universal,
"reformed" faith in the Prussian capital was neither easy nor complete. His early inner struggle for self-emancipation was driven by
both mind and heart, but with his achievement of it the two became
divided.[69] The Nobel-Prize-winning Hebrew writer S. Y. Agnon relates
the following anecdote:

> Samuel Holdheim was the preacher of the reform house of worship in
> Berlin. Those were the reformers who shifted the holy Sabbath to the
> first day of the week. On the Day of Atonement, between the morn-
> ing and afternoon prayers, when they would take a long recess, Holdheim
> was accustomed to visit the café close to the synagogue. People were
> of the opinion that he had gone there to eat and drink, but in fact he

---

[66] Raphael Mahler, *Divre yeme yisrael: Dorot aharonim*, vol. 2 (Merhavjah: Sifriyat
Po'alim, 1980), 153-155.

[67] See, e.g., Israel Yuval, "Ha-nakam veha-kelalah, ha-dam veha-alilah (me-alilot
kedoshim le-alilot dam)," *Tsiyon* 58 (1993), 33-90, and Elliot Horowitz, "Ve-nahafokh
hu': Yehudim mul sonehem be-hagigot ha-purim," *Tsiyon* 59 (1994), 129-168, which
exposed different aspects of medieval Jewish vindictiveness. The Yuval article did,
however, unleash a fierce debate in Tsiyon. Horowitz attacked Graetz, in particular, as an apologist.

[68] Geiger, review of Ritter's *Samuel Holdheim*, 216.

[69] See Petuchowski, "Geiger and Holdheim," 149.

went there only to read all those prayers and liturgical poems that he had excised from the High Holyday prayer book of his congregation.[70]

In thus bowing to the force of nostalgia, or perhaps tacitly recognizing the role of highly particularized emotions in religion, Holdheim may have been closer to contemporary Judaism than to that of his own time.

---

[70] S. Y. Agnon, "Sipurim shel ashkenaz ve-agapehah," in *In zwei Welten: Siegfried Moses zum fünfundsiebzigsten Geburtstag*, ed. Hans Tramer (Tel Aviv: Verlag Bitaon, 1962), Hebrew Section, 10. Also cited in Petuchowski, "Geiger and Holdheim," 147.

FROM NATIONALITY TO RELIGION:
SAMUEL HOLDHEIM'S PATH TO THE
EXTREME SIDE OF RELIGIOUS REFORM

Andreas Gotzmann

The German-Jewish religious Reform was more than just the starting point of the later world wide movement. It rather became the
intellectual origin of a new religious concept of Judaism. The main
development of these new ideas took place in the first half of the
nineteenth century, while later the reformers, having succeeded to
acquire the title and the authority of the rabbinate, tried to introduce the given models into the communal structures. The most extreme
reform concepts had been proposed especially in the 1830s and 1840s,
a period shaped by radically new ideas and a growing reform spirit
in Germany. During this period the Reform movement tried to establish itself on a larger scale within the organizational structures of the
Jewish communities, which generally remained rather conservative.[1]
The main factors determining this process were the same that had
shaped the Haskalah. Important was particularly the support by a
first rather small but very progressive class of acknowledged Jewish
personalities, quite often community leaders who were striving for an
adequate religious setting for their new social position. Together with
the influence of the state authorities, which either denied any change

---

[1] I am most grateful to Christian Wiese for his extensive revision of the English
text, a toiling work he performed, as always, with exquisite and meticulous expertise. This article is based on lectures given at the Van Leer Institute in Jerusalem
and at the *Institut zur Erforschung der Geschichte der deutschen Juden* in cooperation with
the University of Hamburg. The major works about the developments described
are Max Wiener, *Jüdische Religion im Zeitalter der Emanzipation* (Berlin: Philo Verlag,
1933); Michael A. Meyer, *Response to Modernity: A History of the Reform Movement in
Judaism* (New York: Oxford University Press, 1988); Andreas Gotzmann, *Jüdisches
Recht im kulturellen Prozeß, Die Wahrnehmung der Halacha im Deutschland des 19. Jahrhunderts*
(Tübingen: J.C.B. Mohr, 1997). See also Michael A. Meyer and Michael Brenner,
eds., *German Jewish History in Modern Times*, vol 2: *Emancipation and Acculturation, 1780-
1871* (New York: Columbia University Press, 1997).

or supported a rather conservative reorganization of the inner Jewish organizational structure and German Jewry's religious character, they played a paramount role in the protracted process in which the communal institutions gradually—over approximately 40 years—opened for a certain degree of change within the Jewish ritual.[2]

To understand the dynamic the religious development gained, it has to be considered that the idea of a change or a reform of the old structures was further spread than the initially small circles of reformers might indicate. A short look at the public perception of some rabbis who were perceived as a bulwark against Reform is quite telling. Many of those rabbis were at the same time seen as representing a new era that certainly had to be met by changes or reforms. The idea of reform was quite widespread and could therefore be applied to Orthodox rabbis as well.[3] More than that, the term actually included definite progressive factors like the university

---

[2] The politics of the German states covered the whole range from preventing any changes (in Prussia and Bavaria) through the reform-oriented politics pursued in Baden, Sachsen-Weimar or in Mecklenburg-Schwerin. Nevertheless, the establishment of the first reform services and congregations was characterized by the combination of three factors: the very conservative, yet pragmatic reaction of the rabbinate, the determined support by economically independent and quite active reformers in the community board as well as by the state (in Baden, Hamburg, Mecklenburg-Schwerin; not exactly in Prussia); the latter's politics were influenced by conservative considerations concerning the preservation of the central Jewish community's religious unity and by the needs of the centralized tax administration and the welfare institutions. At least in the first decades of the nineteenth century the reforms were limited to questions of the aesthetic appearance of the services. Furthermore, it is interesting to see that the rabbinate's reaction was usually directly linked to the public, institutionalized break with the existing Halakhah, thereby jeopardizing the rabbinical authority. See Ismar Schorsch, "Emancipation and the Crisis of Religious Authority: The Emergence of Modern Rabbinate," in idem, *From Text to Context, The Turn to History in Modern Judaism* (Hanover, NH: Brandeis University Press, 1994, 9-50; Steven M. Lowenstein, "The 1840s and the Creation of the German-Jewish Religious Reform Movement," in *Revolution and Evolution, 1848 in German-Jewish History*, ed. Werner E. Mosse, Arnold Paucker, and Reinhard Rürup (Tübingen: J.C.B. Mohr, 1981), 255-297; Michael A. Meyer, "The Religious Reform Controversy in the Berlin Jewish Community, 1814-1823," *LBIYB* 24 (1979), 139-155; idem, *German Political Pressure and Jewish Religious Response in the 19th Century* (LBI Memorial Lectures 25) (New York: Leo Baeck Institute, 1981). Gotzmann, *Jüdisches Recht im kulturellen Prozeß*, 107-160.

[3] A guiding element was the conservative contemporary connotation of the term *reform*, for instance the idea of the necessary evolution of social structures. Well-known rabbis from the older generation like Samuel Levy Eger, Ascher Löw Wallerstein, and certainly the next generations with Isaac Bernays, Jakob Ettlinger, (with some restrictions even Seligmann Bär Bamberger), Samson Raphael Hirsch, Michael Sachs, Marcus Lehmann, and Esriel Hildesheimer were definitely inclined to accept changes. Neither the emancipation of the Jews nor the education of the

education now demanded for the rabbis, their ability to deliver "German Sermons," their occupation with children's education, sometimes even the expectation that they would teach Rabbinical Studies in High German. All these were innovations based on the general assumption that particularly the rabbinate should be a decisive factor in creating a new, bourgeois culture. Even Orthodox rabbis were, therefore, regarded as innovative and progressive. Fundamentalism was not approved by any part of German Jewry; rather, any tendency to close one's mind to the strong social and political changes was rejected as backwardness.

It was on the level of the highly polemical discussions that the term *reform* gradually gained a negative taste and was first, at the turn of the century and still under the influence of the Enlightenment, regarded as a name for free-thinkers and, later, during the 1840s, as a term for revolutionary tendencies.[4] In contrast, almost the entire German Orthodoxy rejected their designation as *Orthodox* as an inadequate term since it implied backwardness and outmoded views. One rather chose terms like *religiös-gesetzlich, traditions-* or *gesetzestreu* [loyal toward tradition or the law] in order to underline the major ideological factor, namely the unbroken continuity of tradition. The representatives of this current of Judaism did not want to risk being

---

youth nor even the reform of the religious practice was questioned. The controversies were not based on the idea of rejecting any change at all, but merely referred to the question how far these changes should be allowed to go; See David Ellenson, *Tradition in Transition: Orthodoxy, Halakhah and the Boundaries of Modern Jewish Identity* (New York: University Press of America 1989); idem and Richard Jacobs, "Scholarship and Faith, David Hoffmann and his Relationship to Wissenschaft des Judentums," *Modern Judaism* 8 (1988), 27-40. The closeness between the Orthodox and the Reform position concerning the idea of change is illustrated by the Orthodox author Leopold Donath's highly critical remarks about Holdheim's reforms in Mecklenburg and his own idea of religious development; see Leopold Donath, *Geschichte der Juden in Mecklenburg von den ältesten Zeiten (1266) bis auf die Gegenwart (1874), Auch ein Beitrag zur Kulturgeschichte Mecklenburgs* (Leipzig: Leiner, 1874, reprint Walluf: Sändig, 1974), 232, 252. He asks for the change of "misuses and prejudices" ("Mißbräuche und Vorurtheile") which accumulated because of the oppression since medieval times; the very same formula was an important part of the *Synagogenordnung* introduced by Holdheim and criticized by Donath.

[4] The descriptions of the early reformers by the rabbinates depicted them not merely as "reformers" but with the very negative contemporary terms "a-religious" and "free-spirits," while the rabbinate of Hamburg used the positive connotation of these same terms for themselves and proclaimed that there should be certain "reforms," albeit without saying which reforms they were actually considering; see *Ele Divre Ha-Berith [....] Beit Din Zedek de K"K* (Hamburg-Altona, s.n., 1819), VIIIff., XII. Interestingly enough, this part of the text is missing in the Hebrew translation since there it could have been misunderstood.

identified with the negative implications of the term *Orthodoxy*. It was just the very small group around Samson Raphael Hirsch that adopted this pejorative name as a banner of pride. Only at the end of the century this term was gradually accepted as an appropriate self-description, as indicated by the name assumed by the *Freie Vereinigung für die Interessen des orthodoxen Judenthums*, founded in 1885.[5]

It is important to see that the development of the German-Jewish culture at the beginning of the modern era never had a fundamentalist character. There was no place for the concept of rejecting the ongoing social changes and distancing oneself from the surrounding world in order to avoid or at least to delay the cultural change, although the Orthodox ideology continued to embrace the idea of retaining a supposedly timeless way of life.[6] When looking for the reasons of this innovative character displayed by German Jewry, there is no point in asking whether or not Jewish culture opened to outward influences: it obviously did. But on the level of the symbolic transactions of cultural identity it remained a closed, segregated entity.[7] The contacts were manifold and the external pressure on the

---

[5] This took place in the 1870s as a part of the debate about the strict separation of the Orthodox community from the communal organisations dominated by the Reform; see Matthias Morgenstern, *Von Frankfurt nach Jerusalem. Isaac Breuer und die Bedeutung des Austrittsstreits für die deutsch-jüdische Orthodoxie* (Tübingen: J.C.B. Mohr, 1995), 42, 120ff., 182ff.

[6] Such fundamentalism can only be found within some of the Hasidic groups of Eastern Europe. This excursus aims at demonstrating that historical research on complex cultural structures cannot easily resort to models already established by the scholarly discourse. This example shows that the perception of the religious development of the nineteenth century based on a biased concept of a strong opposition between Reform and Orthodoxy inevitably misses characteristic structures of the religious process. In this specific case, the historical research on German Judaism is, moreover, restricted by its own tradition because these models were created by contemporaries of the nineteenth-century debates. Present historical thinking does not have to be limited by such structures that seem to be imposed by the sources as well as the historiographic tradition. Restrictions like these make it very difficult to describe the inter-subjective processuality of cultural structures and their dynamics. As the deconstruction of the accepted biased interpretation of the relationship between Orthodoxy and Reform demonstrates, the idea of "reform" was not restricted to the movement bearing its name. For a comparative view on different Jewish cultures see Jacob Katz, *Ha-Halakha be-Mezar. Makhsholim al Derekh Ha-Orthodoxia Be-Hitavuta* (Jerusalem: Magnes Press, 1992); idem, ed., *Toward Modernity: The European Jewish Model* (New Brunswick, NJ: Transaction Books, 1987); David Ellenson, "The Orthodox Rabbinate and Apostasy in 19th Century Germany and Hungary," in idem, *Tradition in Transition*, 161-184.

[7] For the question in which way and to what extent external developments were included and transformed by German-Jewish culture, see Steven M. Lowenstein,

Jewish minority too overwhelming to allow the scattered and generally very small Jewish communities in the German territories to really seclude themselves from the overall cultural developments.[8] This inevitable close relationship to external processes proved to be a good prerequisite when the legal conditions began to thoroughly change for the German Jews. Regardless of the ideological structures, in the nineteenth century *change* and *renewal* were always deliberately accepted aspects of a new era to come. The German-Jewish Reform movement adopted this trend and programmatically presented itself as the "religion in progress" and as the most adequate religious expression of a new society that implied new challenges not only for the Jewish minority but for general society as well. This self-representation can merely be understood on the basis of the insight into the fundamentally progressive character of the religious development during the nineteenth century.[9]

The Berlin Jewish Community: Enlightenment, Family, and Crisis (1770-1830) (New York: Oxford University Press, 1994).

[8] This perception of the relation between external forces and the reaction of the minority does not deny the distinct character of German Jewry as an amazingly differentiated and concise cultural system. Yet the "own" space was primarily created on a symbolic level nurtured by the sphere of religious life. The character of this sub-cultural entity nevertheless was predominantly defined by the "outside" culture. This is clearly shown by the typical pragmatism; see Gotzmann, *Jüdisches Recht im kulturellen Prozeß*, 70ff., 86ff. The moment the idea of cultural systems as continually evolving structures is accepted, rigid models dealing with closed and rather independent entities are not convincing any more. This is certainly true for the discussion started by Jacob Katz and Esriel Shochat about the period or the point when the Jewish sphere allegedly opened up for external developments as well as for the question of assimilation; see Esriel Shochat, *Al Khilufe Tekufot. Reshit HaHaskalah be-Yahadut Germaniya* (Jerusalem: Mossad Bialik, 1960); Jacob Katz, *Tradition and Crisis: Jewish Society at the End of the Middle Ages* (New York: New York University Press, 1993).

[9] The general ideas depicted on the following pages should also be seen in the context of the latest development in the study of German-Jewish history. Like many others, even the very interesting social-historical study of Till van Rahden, despite its quite critical approach to previous research, nevertheless supports the old concept; see Till van Rahden, "Weder Milieu noch Konfession. Die situative Ethnizität der deutschen Juden im Kaiserreich in vergleichender Perspektive," in *Religion im Kaiserreich. Milieus—Mentalitäten—Krisen*, ed. Olaf Blaschke and Frank-Michael Kuhlemann (Gütersloh: Gütersloher Verlagshaus, 1996), 409-34. As meritorious as this article certainly is, it mainly analyses the historical meta-level projected on German-Jewish culture. If one applies descriptive structures like "milieu" or "ethnicity" (here defined in a very restricted way) to the phenomenon of German Jewry, i.e., definitions crafted for fundamentally different social entities, the conclusion that they are not really suitable should not come as a surprise. Furthermore, there is another logical circle which is created by the misunderstanding of the analytical process: All these constructs are rigid and stable by definition, which means that they always repro-

This article focuses on the most extreme version of this general reform-spirit in the guise of a religious-cultural program, namely the radical Reform. The extreme religious ideologies of its representatives do not only embody the most radical culmination of the German-Jewish Reform movement, they are also likely to define the transition between the rather vague systematic entities of normativity and divergence. They thus point to the potential directions the cultural system could take and to its heretical extreme, which provided the possibility of transcending the boundaries of the given system. Moreover, the clarification of the emergence and development of an extreme Reform concept provides further knowledge about the nature of the Reform movement as a whole. At the same time, it illustrates the manifold possibilities created by these newly forged ideological structures as well as the internal restrictions they caused.[10]

1

The transition from the early efforts of individual reformers to the public recognition as an actual Reform *movement* was accompanied by suggestions of an extremely radical reinterpretation of Jewish tradition and practice. But even from the perspective of the then dominating cultural perception of Judaism as a closed self-referential legal system, these public discussions remained rather conservative.[11] Most of the reformers actually felt that the reform-process led to a

---

duce a diachronic fractured image of religious life on the one hand and a bourgeois lifestyle on the other. Cultural history should, therefore, be approached by a much more complex thinking, given the fact that cultural developments are not only constructs themselves. Cultural topoi, I would like to suggest, have, at the same time, to be understood as meta-texts evolving in an inter-subjective process.

[10] This article applies the cultural-semiotic analysis of complex structures to Holdheim's writings, especially to the cultural structure of authorization, the religious law as represented thereby. Only the knowledge about the use and the redefinition of general factors of such central normative elements of Jewish culture enables us to assess the question concerning the renewal, the redefinition, and the independence of such new ideologies. The dialectic discussion of contemporary perceptions of Holdheim's work has, however, to be restricted to short remarks. For further discussion see Gotzmann, *Jüdisches Recht im kulturellen Prozeß*, 251-302.

[11] This static concept of Jewish culture is still very influential. Another good example for an outstanding work which combines socio-historical analysis with a cultural-historical approach is Steven M. Lowenstein, *The Berlin Jewish Community* (see footnote 7 in this article). Although most of the various analyses are quite convincing, the overall concept of the book suffers from its ideological assumption of

fundamental change of the traditional religious culture since it opened it to the developments within general society. Their reform ideas represented, however, nothing else than a change of the public appearance of the Jewish religion. The dynamic force underlying this change had been the wish to embrace the newly developed bourgeois concepts of religion and religiosity which soon became common convictions. The inherited approach to religion with its predominant legal character seemed to be especially outmoded. In view of the anti-Talmudic trends of the German Haskalah movement, e.g. in the philosophy of Jewish Kantians like Saul Ascher, Lazarus Ben-David or David Friedländer, the rabbinic tradition was now seen as the ideological antipode to the new conception: the legally defined religious ceremony was now confronted with the ideal of "religious feeling." In close dialogue with contemporary Romanticist Protestant theology as formulated, for instance, by Friedrich Schleiermacher, religion was now rather perceived as an intimate individual conviction closely related to contemplation than as collective ceremonial practice. The religious service was supposed to lead to the moral advancement of the believer instead of the fulfillment of divine laws.[12] The rather conservative way through which these conceptual changes were integrated into the own tradition, however, at least slowed down the progressive dynamics of this cultural change. With regard to the early reforms it can certainly be said that the very fact that these

---

cultural stability and the leading idea of closed cultural spheres which define any change as a crisis of the whole system. A transition other than a *break* can impossibly be described from this point of view.

[12] This shift was described by Michael A. Meyer, "'How Awesome is this Place!', The Reconceptualization of the Synagogue in Nineteenth-Century Germany," *LBIYB* 41 (1996), 51-63; and see Andreas Gotzmann, "The Dissociation of Law and Religion in Nineteenth-Century German-Jewish Education," *LBIYB* 43 (1998), 103-126. The question whether this is an "assimilatory" or, to be less ideological, an "acculturative" adjustment to Christian, especially Protestant views, is likely to distort the idea standing behind these changes. Unquestionably, the incentive for changes came in general from external developments, including assimilatory pressure. The fact that Christian models were picked up results primarily from the dominance of Christianity as the majority's cultural background. However, even if the development is characterized by acculturation, the basic idea of these changes was certainly not the adaptation of the Jewish religion to Protestant religious forms. On the contrary: the newly developed ideas of religiosity were seen as a common ground and not as specific Christian. From the perspective of cultural history, such questions are irrelevant anyway; not the change (or in the case of minority cultures the adaptation) is central but the question in which way new ideas were incorporated into the framework of the existing cultural system and whether this led to its opening.

new concepts of religion and religiosity were projected unto the given scheme of authorization and legal discourse strongly limited their revolutionary potential for Jewish culture. As the pivotal aspect of the cultural system, the central structure of legitimization was only criticized instead of being abolished altogether; the system itself continued to work as a self-induced one. The acceptance of any changes remained closely linked to and dependent on their legal assessment. This made it necessary, with regard to any reform idea, to prove either that it implied nothing but minor changes within the framework of the given system, or that it was an integral part of tradition that was just to be restored by the reformers. This was exactly the way the first reforms were understood and presented: The changes of the religious ritual, whether it was the inclusion of another language than Hebrew into worship or the accompaniment of the liturgy by organ music, were based on legal discussions of marginal questions that were either presented as yet undecided matters or as questions that had some support in the halakhic literature.

At the same time, there were voices accentuating a general opposition against the basic structure of the pre-emancipatory Jewish culture, the Halakhah] From the first decade of the nineteenth century on, but increasingly in the 1830s and 1840s, a smaller part of the reformers recognized that the striving for reform could not be satisfied by the criticism of some marginal laws and the inclusion of changes into the given system, avoiding a thorough change of the system's structures. In order to gain authority as an influential movement promoting a new religious idea, Reform Judaism had to be aware of the dynamics already created by the first attempts to reform the own tradition. By now, the representatives of the rabbinate were already alarmed and rejected all the changes proposed by the reformers.[13] If the latter wanted to promote more fundamental reforms, the basic idea of reconstructing the tradition had to be taken seriously. They had to face modifications of the given system itself, something the numerous sketches of reform systems tried to introduce in the 1830s and 1840s. Simultaneously, they had to define the goal of all those reforms and to create an own independent code of legitimization

---

[13] The well known first Reform debates pertained to the problem of early burial, the change of the laws for Passover, and the prayerbook-controversy associated with the *Hamburger Tempelverein* in 1818; see Gotzmann, *Jüdisches Recht im kulturellen Prozeß*, 107-54.

for them. From the manifold reform systems, however, only very few conceptualized a new normative system that superseded the cultural idea of Halakhah.[14] [The development of Samuel Holdheim's radical thought illustrates this general tendency and embodies the transition from the legal discourse to a newly defined one.]

It has to be noted that these changes of the religious ideology were characterized by specific social structures. Through the decades from 1780 to 1840, the *maskilim*, the members of the early Reform movement, and finally the representatives of its radical wing, were all individuals who were not able to claim any authoritative position as legitimate keepers of tradition. In the German Haskalah and among the first reformers almost no German rabbis can be found.[15] Even when the second generation of reformers succeeded in gaining the rabbinical title and some rabbinical seats, again most of the spokesmen for an extreme reform—like the two "Associations for the Reform of Judaism" in Frankfurt and Berlin (*Reformfreunde*)—did not belong to the camp of those with religious authority. At the beginning, obviously the social control within the German rabbinate did not allow such deviations. Later on, the reformers' self-definition and intellectual independence changed in view of their often quite problematic integration into the given organizational structures. The basic

---

[14] This does not mean that the pre-emancipatory or the Orthodox understanding of the Halakhah was accepted. Rather, the question is whether basic structures changed, whether there were definite breaks with the ideological concept of religious law, and when the system ceased to uphold its (fictitious) autopoietic structure and opened to external entities. Although the crossing of such imagined boundaries is very difficult to be clearly defined, the process itself can be described.

[15] This is certainly not true for Shaul Berlin. But it is revealing that he had to publish his works anonymously and eventually even lost his rabbinate; see Moshe Pelli, "Ha-reforma ha-datit shel ha-rav 'haredi' Shaul Berlin," *HUCA* 42 (1971), 1-23 (Hebrew section). At the same time, the first reforms were all promoted by rabbis from other countries than Germany like Eliezer Liebermann, Aron Chroin, or the rabbis voting for the changes discussed in the Hamburg Temple Controversy. It should be marked that those were to quite a percentage natives from Hungary. Some of them, for instance like Eliezer Liebermann and Moses Brück, got in contact with the new thoughts during a rather short stay in Germany. The few German rabbis, like Samson Wolf Rosenfeld or Samuel Levi Eger, cannot really be compared to them; see Meyer, *Response to Modernity*, 102. The comprehension of norm, radicalism, or heresy does not only change with the time, it is also bound to the very perspective. To speak of a "general radicalism" one has to construct a cultural representation of the line between the vague entities of norm and deviancy. In the nineteenth century most of the different religious groups nevertheless regarded changes—like the shift of the Sabbath to the Sunday, the abolishment of the circumcision, or the acceptance of mixed marriages—to be outside of the normative frame.

message that can be identified in these recurring structures is that
the cultural background even in the small camp of the Reform ideologues always remained rather conservative.

Furthermore, the mostly small Jewish communities scattered over
the countryside provided a tight system of social control that made
any deviation from the established ways extremely difficult. And
although some of the large communities, from the 1840s on, accepted
a certain degree of religious pluralism, this leniency was again
slowed down by the heated public controversies over the appointment of Abraham Geiger in Breslau and Leopold Stein in Frankfurt.
The breach caused in both communities by the appointment of
these reformers as communal rabbis made a strong impact on the
general attitude. At least after the establishment of a few separate
Orthodox communities, this trend toward a more pluralistic spectrum of differing religious convictions organized in independent
religious congregations came to an end because the majority of
German Jews still upheld the idea of a greater unity.[16] The diver-
sification of German Jewry very often also met harsh opposition
from the side of the government: first of all, many states rejected
any religious diversity or radicalization, and secondly, most of them
still insisted on the coercive community bond for taxation, regulation and for the funding of a separate school-system, health care
and public welfare.

Whatever the reasons for the upholding of a general unity, the
organization of all religious groups in a unified congregation
[*Einheitsgemeinde*] that was common toward the end of the century, is
characteristic of the rather conservative attitude with regard to extreme
views.[17] Before the Reform movement even reached the peak of its

---

[16] One should not forget that the states' intervention against separation and in
favour of a strong general Jewish communal organization made such a diversifica-
tion extremely difficult.

[17] This model presupposed either an Orthodox chief-rabbinate that could also
allow liberal or conservative rabbis to work in separate spheres of the same congregation, or a rather conservative Reform rabbi who did not question the Orthodox
institutions. There are many variations of this basic model. The establishment of
the *Allgemeine Synagogenverband* in Hamburg shows that this weak pluralism was nothing but the pragmatic toleration of opposite attitudes in order to avoid the financial breakdown and to prevent a breach in the community. Single parts of the
general union nevertheless always tried to prove their superiority, at least in ideological terms. In Hamburg, the Orthodox part of the community hesitated to put
down its own regulations which would have reduced its ideological standing to the
reality to be one further part of the whole union; see Ina Lorenz, "Zehn Jahre

radicalization, its pace was already slowed down. In 1844, even a staunch reformer like the district rabbi of the Bavarian town of Landau, Elias Grünebaum, complained about the still very strongly restricted pluralistic outlook of Judaism:

> The distress of our days definitely is that religion has gained such a multi-coloured appearance in everyday life and that all conformity of the religious act is lost; from this comes the urgent challenge for us to go to work and regain the lost unity.[18]

Only few of the radical rabbis succeeded in being offered and, even more important, in keeping a position in Germany. Many of them had to emigrate to the United States, where—under more liberal conditions—they promoted a much more progressive kind of reform. Among those are well known rabbis like the named Elias Grünebaum, Samuel Hirsch, David Einhorn, Samuel Adler, Bernhard Felsenthal, Marcus Jastrow, and Kaufmann Kohler. As the latter had said at the beginning of his career, radical thinkers did not have a real chance to be accepted as a rabbi by his community:

> In present day Germany [the Jewish congregations] are not supposed to support or even to encourage the demands and the views of a sincerely liberal minded and uncompromisingly truth loving young man who wishes to pursue a theological career. Unprincipled indecision and political connections are the conditions for a theological calling even among liberals in Germany. With the slogan "the coachman must be sober" they convert the spiritual guides into dissembling hypocrites so as to be all the better able to laugh at priestly deception and the like. [....] There is no sympathy for any one who, following the insistent urge of his heart, desires to break through the obstacles which surround a great and free Judaism and prevent its development [....].[19]

Although this statement is unquestionably characterized by Kohler's personal disappointment, the general image of a Reform that had to accommodate itself with the conservative conditions within the

---

Kampf um das Hamburger System, 1864-1873," in *Die Hamburger Juden in der Emanzipationsphase, 1780-1870*, ed. Peter Freimark and Arno Herzig (Hamburg: Christians-Verlag, 1989), 41-82.

[18] Elias Grünbaum, [name misspelled], "Gutachten des Bezirksrabbiners....zu Landau in der Pfalz in der Frankfurter Reform-Angelegenheit, Abgegeben an Sr. Hochwürden, den Herrn Rabbinen Salomon Trier in Frankfurt a.M.," *Israelit des neunzehnten Jahrhunderts* 5 (1855), no. 16, 121-125; no.17, 129-132, here 131.

[19] David Philipson, "Some Unpublished Letters of Theological Importance," *HUCA* 2 (1925), 418-33; reprint 1968, 427-30; see the printed letter of Kaufmann Kohler (Fürth) to Samuel Adler (New York) (6 April 1869).

Jewish communities and with the anti-liberal situation in general seems to be quite accurate.

While the Reform movement was rather effective regarding the integration of their new ideas about religion into the new, fast spreading educational system, thus securing a new foundation for the next generation's ideological outlook, its general representation and acceptance as a legitimate religious denomination was strongly contested for a long time.[20] Throughout the nineteenth century, the Reform movement never really succeeded in establishing its claim to be a legitimate heir and interpreter of the common tradition.[21] According to Kaufmann Kohler, the conviction was wide-spread that religious authority demanded a much more conservative attitude and demeanor than that expected from a "normal" person. If a rabbi did not want to endanger his authority, he better stayed on safe-ground, i.e. the Orthodox Halakhah.

This general expectation of the Jewish population in Germany was not only the result of the quite late change from an Orthodox lifestyle to a greater leniency in everyday religious life.[22] It was primarily an outcome of the very conservative standing of the Reform movement itself, which had never really abandoned the Orthodox Halakhah but accepted it at least as the argumentative point of reference of their reform ambitions.

2

The question concerning the extreme side of the development of the German Reform movement in the nineteenth century leads to

---

[20] See Gotzmann, "The Dissociation of Religion and Law in 19th Century German-Jewish Education"; idem, *Eigenheit und Einheit. Modernisierungsdiskurse des deutschen Judentums der Emanzipationszeit* (Leiden: Brill Publishers, 2002), 28-113.

[21] Under the ideological premise of unity there existed the bare necessities of a common organization and of everyday life that furthered the mutual toleration of the different religious camps. This development with its many different pragmatic truces created something like a rather unloved and weak pluralistic religious culture. There is no need to underline that Orthodoxy never accepted the Reform movement as an equivalent partner. Nor did the Reform movement accept the Orthodox conviction as a legitimate attitude. In general it refuted the Orthodox claim to be the only legitimate bearer of tradition, relegating it to a backward way of Jewish life that seemed unable to grasp the very idea of religiosity.

[22] This change most probably took place during the last third of the century, the period of the geographical re-location of major parts of German Jewry. The numbers often cited as a proof for a definite change toward Reform at the beginning

the interesting ideas of Samuel Holdheim, one of the most radical reformers. Against the background of a strong, albeit intrinsically conservative change of the religious culture, Holdheim stands out as an uncompromising figure, as a zealot for reform. He was the ultimate extremist among the German rabbis and the German Reform movement. While sketching reform plans like the other reformers, his contribution to the heated ideological debates and his views of the political developments grew more and more radical. [Aiming at the definition of new normative structures, he created a concise reform system that took the increasing external pressure toward an assimilation of Judaism into consideration.] In contrast to earlier radical reformers, Holdheim was eventually offered rabbinical seats that enabled him to actually implement his plans within congregations, later in his career even within an outspoken Reform community. As a result, he was not forced, at least in the last third of his life, to refrain from radical changes and to be considerate of conservative opposition to his ideas.

Samuel Holdheim is one of the most intriguing figures in the history of German Jewry in the nineteenth century. So far the only detailed biographical data are provided by his student Immanuel Heinrich Ritter, who cooperated with Holdheim as a co-preacher of the *Berliner Reformgemeinde* and published a history of the Reform movement.[23] The list of scholarly literature about Holdheim is short, most probably because of the close link between post-war research about German-Jewish culture and its predecessor, the historical scholarship

---

of the Kaiserreich should not be trusted. The predominance of reform-oriented communal boards in the large cities does not allow any judgment about the religious outlook of the majority of their members. The same can be said about the diminishing numbers of people attending the synagogue services. The definite change from an Orthodox lifestyle to a conservative one shows the same conservative, albeit lenient process of secularization that can be discovered among the Protestant and the Catholic population. This religious conservative outlook and self-definition was, however, much closer to Orthodoxy than to a pronounced Reform; see Mordechai Breuer, *Jüdische Orthodoxie im Deutschen Reich 1871-1918* (Frankfurt: Jüdischer Verlag bei Athenäum, 1986), 6-7; Thomas Rahe, "Religionsreform und jüdisches Selbstbewußtsein im deutschen Judentum des 19. Jahrhunderts," *Menora* 1 (1990), 89-121, here 92ff.; Marion Kaplan, *The Making of the Jewish Middle Class* (New York: Oxford University Press, 1991), 64-83; Andreas Gotzmann, "Koscher und Trefe; die Veränderung der religiösen Praxis im Deutschland des 19. Jahrhunderts," *LBI Informationen* 7 (1997), 85-109.

[23] Immanuel Heinrich Ritter, *Geschichte der jüdischen Reformation*, vol. 3: *Samuel Holdheim. Sein Leben und seine Werke, Ein Beitrag zu den neuesten Reformbestrebungen im Judenthum* (Berlin: W. J. Peiser, 1865); idem, "Samuel Holdheim, The Jewish Reformer," in: *JQR* 1 (1889), 202-15; Donath, *Geschichte der Juden in Mecklenburg*, 226ff.

within the larger frame of *Wissenschaft des Judentums*.[24] Holdheim was born 1806 in Kempen (Poznan) and died already in 1860, at the age of 54, in Berlin. His education was typical for the pre-emancipation period. After divorcing his first wife, he attended the Yeshivah in Prague. Following the general trend fostered by the governments, he simultaneously studied humanities and philosophy at Prague University and, after having finished his rabbinical studies, was offered the prestigious post as a rabbi in Frankfurt an der Oder in 1836.[25] At this time, no one thought of him as a reformer but rather as one of the modern Orthodox rabbis. This is best illustrated by the fact that, earlier on, his famous teacher Samuel Landau of Prague, clearly a defender of the old views, had written him a praising letter of recommendation for the rabbinical post at Vorarlberg.[26]

Four years later, however, Samuel Holdheim accepted the seat of the chief rabbi of Mecklenburg-Schwerin on the condition that he was permitted to introduce thorough changes of the Jewish ritual and to rebuild the school-system.[27] During the following seven years he tried, together with the main Jewish community board, to implement reforms which were then—at least partially—rejected by the small rural communities. Under the auspices of a pro-reformatory government they introduced changes to the liturgy that were, despite of constant controls, more or less disregarded at least by some of the congregations.

This strategy of defying the prescribed reforms turned into open opposition when the general board of the Jewish communities and Holdheim installed new regulations for the service and for the religious conduct adopted from the so-called *Württembergische Synagogenordnung* that had been composed by the chief rabbi of Württemberg, Joseph Maier, who was known as a notorious reformer. The vehement

---

[24] Wiener, *Jüdische Religion im Zeitalter der Emanzipation*, 87ff. Jakob J. Petuchowski, "Abraham Geiger and Samuel Holdheim: Their Differences in Germany and Repercussions in America," *LBIYB* 22 (1977), 139-159, here 147-149. For an interesting analysis of Holdheim's work see Meyer, *Response to Modernity*, 80-84.

[25] Although he began his university studies in Prague, it is not clear whether he received his Ph.D. from the University of Frankfurt an der Oder or from Berlin University.

[26] Aron Tänzer, *Die Geschichte der Juden in Hohenems und im übrigen Vorarlberg*, (Meran: Elmenreich, 1905; reprinted Bregenz: Lingenhöle, 1982), 597ff.

[27] Donath, *Geschichte der Juden in Mecklenburg*, 230ff. depicts Holdheim as someone who destroyed Judaism. He suspects that he betrayed the state and the communities by introducing himself as an Orthodox rabbi. The archival records of the *Landeshauptarchiv Schwerin*, still without entry numbers, show that the government had looked for someone who would promote reforms.

protest voiced by an Orthodox group caused the government to slow down the pace of the reform process. It led to the establishment of one of the very first separate Orthodox communities and eventually clearly weakened the reform spirit.[28]

Before Holdheim accepted the new position offered to him by the "Association for the Reform of Judiasm" in Berlin [*Berliner Reformverein*], he had already visited the congregation in order to preach at one of its services; at this time he assured the government in Schwerin that he had no intention to abandon his post. However, when the opposition grew stronger and even the state authorities tended to prevent or slow down further innovations, he decided to become the rabbi of the newly founded *Reformgemeinde* in Berlin.[29] In retrospect Holdheim described his years in Schwerin as a time of toiling work for the betterment of Judaism that did not, unfortunately, bear many fruits. The new position he assumed in this extreme Reform congregation had, earlier on, been rejected even by Abraham Geiger, who also had the reputation of being a religious radical. Geiger's reason for not accepting the call had to do with the status of this association that was just a small group of radicals merely tolerated by the state and the Berlin Jewish congregation; he wanted to establish the Reform as a broad movement of at least the majority of the Jewish population and not as the altered religious behaviour of a small group seen as heretics.

---

[28] See Ritter, *Samuel Holdheim*, 41ff.; Donath, *Geschichte der Juden in Mecklenburg*, 230ff., gives a one-sided but nevertheless rather accurate description of the development. It has to be added that after David Einhorn—the sucessor of Holdheim in Schwerin—had to leave his post in 1851, the newly employed Orthodox rabbi tried to abolish the established reforms without any formal resolution. To his own astonishment he met strong resistance in some of the larger communities that wanted to keep at least some of the reforms, arguing that by now they had got used to the new style and didn't want to miss it. Holdheim's vision of his own role is illustrated by the title of a published sermon given in Schwerin; see Samuel Holdheim, *Der glaubensvolle Muth des israelitischen Volkshirten dem Murren seiner Gemeinde gegenüber, Predigt gehalten in der Synagoge zu Schwerin am Sabbath Chukkath (29. Juni 1844)* (Schwerin: C. Kürschner, 1844).

[29] The government withdrew its already cautious support after the scandal that erupted when a Jewish father in Teterow refused to circumcise his son and the following public controversy between the Christian scholar Franz Delitzsch and Holdheim's successor David Einhorn (see Christian Wiese's contribution to this volume, particularly 331-344). On 17 February 1853 it decreed that from now on no Reform rabbi should be elected any more and that the contested *Synagogenordnung* had to be revised. The election of new members into the *Oberrat* was strongly restricted by the government and subject to its approval; see Donath, *Geschichte der Juden in Mecklenburg*, 247-249.

When the members of the *Reformgemeinde* attempted to be officially accepted at least as a partly independent association, i.e. as one separate synagogue among others, the Berlin congregation refused to give its consent. It had only accepted the existing arrangement as long as the members of the private association, apart from taking care of their own institutions, kept paying taxes to the main congregation as well. When some members stopped doing so, the *Reformgemeinde* was forced back, with the aid of the state, into the status quo which it never managed to alter later on.[30]

In the thirteen years spent in Berlin Samuel Holdheim made his strongest move toward more extreme reforms, for instance [the famous "transfer" or—to be more accurate—the prolongation of the Sabbath to the Sunday.] However, apparently not all of the reforms implemented by his congregation met Holdheim's personal religious feelings. Nevertheless, he was one of the outstanding spokesmen of the *Reformgemeinde*, and the public opinion perceived him as one of the most radical German rabbis of the nineteenth century. The general judgment outside of his congregation was rather negative. When Holdheim died in 1860, his burial caused some turmoil. His critics, especially the conservative preacher of the Berlin Jewish community, Michael Sachs, were strictly opposed to honor someone whom the majority of German Jews regarded as heretic. After Sachs had denied Holdheim an honorable burial in the row reserved for the rabbis, it was probably only the conciliatory consent of the deputy chief rabbi, Jakob Joseph Öttinger, that eventually led to his being buried at the cemetery of Berlin-Weissensee in this very place.[31]

Among contemporary observers and in the later scholarly literature Holdheim was remembered as the "worst enemy, Judaism has seen since Paul," to quote Heinrich Graetz's famous judgment.[32]

---

[30] Meyer, *Response to Modernity*, 131. For this development and the nevertheless very close ties between the *Reformgemeinde* and the Berlin Jewish community, expressed by the personal union of many leaders of this group in the administration board of both communities, see Samuel Holdheim, *Geschichte der Entstehung und Entwickelung der jüdischen Reformgemeinde in Berlin: im Zusammenhang mit den jüdisch-reformatorischen Gesammtbestrebungen der Neuzeit* (Berlin: Julius Springer, 1857), 227ff.

[31] Franz D. Lucas and Heike Frank, *Michael Sachs, Der konservative Mittelweg, Leben und Wirken des Berliner Rabbiners zur Zeit der Emanzipation* (Tübingen: J.C.B. Mohr, 1992). The Orthodox tradition, however, as Mordechai Breuer told me, knows a much less positive version of this story: Öttinger supposedly had said: *Nor bagroben* (Just bury him)!

[32] Heinrich Graetz, *Geschichte der Juden von der ältesten Zeit bis auf die Gegenwart, aus den Quellen neu bearbeitet*, 2nd edition, vol. 2 (Leipzig: O. Leiner, 1900), 533; vol. 11

Although his name became synonymous with a Reform abandoning tradition and becoming almost "un-Jewish," this excessive polemic hardly meets the point. It is, however, certainly true that his radical reform plans were among the most extreme in Germany. The Berlin *Reformgemeinde* and the more conservative *Tempelverband* in Hamburg always remained the only separate Reform congregations in Germany. The Berlin congregation had been established in 1845 with around 600 persons attending its services. But the regular members of the "Association for Reform of Judaism" (Reformverein) from which the *Jüdische Reformgemeinde Berlin* originated in 1850, counted only 327 families in Berlin and an additional 426 supporters from elsewhere. And if we take a look at the first decade of the twentieth century, it never exceeded the number of 500 members.

Interestingly enough, the congregation was apparently quite stable in terms of its membership. According to Holdheim, it neither lost the generation of the founders nor that of their children to conversion, which is quite telling with regard to the religious power of the extreme Reform. On the other hand, this current never gained any nationwide influence, nor was it able to compete with the main Berlin community. The simple comparison between its total number of members and the numbers of the entire Jewish population of Berlin (in 1871 about 36000 and almost 173000 people at its peak in 1925) illustrates how weak the support for a radical Reform in Germany was throughout the nineteenth century and in the early decades of the twentieth century.[33]

(Leipzig: O. Leiner, 1900), 561ff.; idem, *Volkstümliche Geschichte der Juden*, vol. 3 (Leipzig: O. Leiner, 1888), 733. The reassessment of Graetz's dictum can be easily seen, e.g., in Heinz Moshe Graupe, *Die Entstehung des modernen Judentums. Geistesgeschichte der deutschen Juden 1650-1942*, 2nd edition (Hamburg: Leibniz Verlag, 1977), 217; Wiener, *Jüdische Religion*, 93; Donath, *Geschichte der Juden in Mecklenburg*, 229-231; the judgment voiced by Donath, who was Esriel Hildesheimer's student, is devastating: "Holdheim hatte aber keine urwüchsigen Gedanken, die er als Hebel zum Umsturz des Judenthums hätte anlegen können; er hatte nur talmudisch geschliffenen Scharfsinn. [....] Sein Scharfsinn diente ihm aber dazu, diese wenigen halbwahren Voraussetzungen anwendbar zu machen, sie mit einem Schein von Wahrheit zu umgeben. [....] Nur die Leichtfertigkeit konnte eine ebenso hohle, wie unwürdige Theorie aufstellen, oder die Sucht etwas ganz Neues, was noch nicht dagewesen auszuklügeln. Holdheim, der Sohn des Talmud, schlug das talmudische Judenthum todt mit den Waffen, die er ihm gereicht hatte."

[33] Meyer, *Response to Modernity*, 129ff.; Gabriel E. Alexander, "Die jüdische Bevölkerung Berlins in den ersten Jahrzehnten des 20. Jahrhunderts: Demographische und wirtschaftliche Entwicklungen," in *Jüdische Geschichte in Berlin. Essays und Studien*, ed. Reinhard Rürup (Berlin: Edition Hentrich, 1995), 117-48, particularly 141.

This is also reflected by the harsh rejection of Holdheim's writings among his contemporaries. He was not only attacked by the Orthodox and the Conservative reformers. Even liberal intellectuals from the Reform camp tended to dismiss his ideas.[34] It suffices, however, to compare his numerous writings—he published 15 books and countless essays, articles, and sermons—to the work of other Reform and Orthodox thinkers in order to show that he was not only a prolific writer but one of the most ingenious ideologues of his time. [He was one of the few reformers who succeeded in creating a concept of reform characterized by a rare degree of freedom from the inherited cultural model.] Although his reform system continued to preserve a link to the given structures, its strength consisted in the ability to outline a genuinely new and concise idea of Jewish religion that was unquestionably aiming at acculturation, but remained thoroughly aware of its distinct Jewish identity.

3

At the beginning of Holdheim's career, the evolution of his reform concept followed the general path of the German-Jewish Reform movement. This is certainly true for the period until 1843, when he published his major work, a book about the question of mixed-marriage entitled *Ueber die Autonomie der Rabbinen und das Princip der jüdischen Ehe.*[35] In contrast to the vast majority of other German-Jewish

---

[34] Abraham Geiger, however, while keeping a certain distance to Holdheim, was one of the few who appreciated Holdheim's radical concepts; see, for instance, his review of Holdheim's *Ueber die Autonomie der Rabbinen* published in *Zur Judenfrage in Deutschland. Vom Standpunkte des Rechts und der Gewissensfreiheit, im Vereine mit mehreren Gelehrten herausgegeben* von Wilhelm Freund (Berlin: Veit, 1843), 164-74.

[35] Samuel Holdheim, *Ueber die Autonomie der Rabbinern und das Princip der jüdischen Ehe, Ein Beitrag zur Verständigung über einige das Judenthum betreffende Zeitfragen,* 2nd edition (Schwerin: C. Kürschner, 1847). His most important earlier writings are: idem, *Ueber das Gebetbuch nach dem Gebrauche des neuen Israelitischen Tempelvereins zu Hamburg, Ein Votum* (Hamburg: B. S. Behrendson, 1841); idem, *Verketzerung und Gewissensfreiheit. Ein zweites Votum in dem Hamburger Tempelstreit mit besonderer Berücksichtigung der Erwiderung eines Ungenannten auf mein erstes Votum* (Schwerin: C. Kürschner, 1842); idem, *Ueber die Beschneidung zunächst in religiös-dogmatischer Beziehung* (Schwerin: C- Kürschner, 1844); idem, *Vorträge über die mosaische Religion für denkende Israeliten* (Schwerin: C. Kürschner, 1844); idem, *Zweite Mittheilung aus dem Briefwechsel über die neueste jüdische Literatur. Ein Fragment von Samson Raphael Hirsch, Landrabbiner zu Emden* (Schwerin: C. Kürschner, 1844); idem, *Vorschläge zu einer zeitgemässen Reform der jüdischen Ehegesetze, der nächsten*

reformers, Holdheim did not only sharpen the newly defined norms when confronted with Orthodox and conservative criticism, he also consistently took into account their dynamic implications for a fundamental alteration of the traditional cultural concept. Compared to him, most of the other reformers, at least until the last third of the nineteenth century, stopped at the first step of reform and were content to introduce isolated changes of the Halakhah. As a consequence, they remained tied to the legal system of the pre-emancipatory period, at least insofar as it was the foundation on which their reforms were based and usually also the background against which they had to be legitimized.

Holdheim's first writings, which are characterized by the endeavor to mainly change Judaism's aesthetic appearance by reinterpreting rather marginal laws, show that originally he shared this approach. Shortly after that he adopted typical concepts that were also supported by many other reformers. Authors like Peter Beer, Aron Chorin, Moses Brück, and Michael Creizenach changed the given halakhic concept of Judaism, redefining certain legal structures or altering the authoritative methods for the interpretation of the law.[36] This resulted into new legal systems which, although reduced in their scope, nevertheless preserved the legitimatory structures of a theonomous law, including the concept of a legal religious culture.

Rabbinerversammlung zur Prüfung übergeben (Schwerin: C. Kürschner, 1845); idem, *Das Ceremonialgesetz im Messiasreich. Als Vorläufer einer größeren Schrift über die religiöse Reform des Judenthums* (Schwerin: C. Kürschner, 1845). An analysis of his earlier writings can be found in Gotzmann, *Jüdisches Recht als kultureller Prozeß*, 198-250.

[36] Ibid., 161-83; Meyer, *Response to Modernity*, 120, 152ff., 160-161; Peter Beer, *Geschichte, Lehren und Meinungen aller bestandenen und noch bestehenden religiösen Sekten der Juden und der Geheimlehre der Cabbalah*, 2. vols., (Brünn: Trassler, 1822-1823); Moses Brück, *Das mosaische Judenthum, In einer Andachtsstunde als Predigt vorgetragen am Wochenfeste 5597 und durch Anmerkungen erläutert* (Frankfurt am Main: J. C. Herrmann, 1837); idem, *Der mosaische Gesetzescodex* (Ofen: s.n., 1847); idem, *Pharisäische Volkssitten und Ritualien in ihrer Entstehung und geschichtlichen Entwicklung* (Frankfurt am Main: J. C. Hermann, 1840); idem, *Rabbinische Ceremonialgebräuche in ihrer Entstehung und geschichtlichen Entwicklung* (Breslau: Schulz, 1837); idem, *Reform des Judenthums, in 100 Thesen dargestellt* (Nagy-Becskerek: Bettelheim, 1848); Aron Chorin, *Iggeret Elassaph, Oder Sendschreiben eines afrikanischen Rabbinen an seinen Collegen in Europa, hg. mit einem deutschen Vorworte, Nachworte und Noch-Etwas von A. Chorin* (Prag: Landau, 1826); idem, *Der treue Bothe an seine Religionsgenossen gesendet* (Prag: Selbstverlag, 1831); Michael Creizenach, *32 Thesen über den Talmud* (Frankfurt am Main: Jäger, 1831); idem, *Schulchan Aruch oder encyclopädische Darstellung des Mosaischen Gesetzes wie es durch die rabbinischen Satzungen sich ausgebildet hat, mit Hinweisung auf die Reformen, welche durch die Zeit nützlich und möglich geworden sind*, 4 vols. [with changing titles] (Frankfurt am Main: Andreäische Buchhandlung, 1833-1840).

From the point of view of Orthodoxy these new legal interpretations were certainly far away from being legitimate, and very soon the reformers actually started to change the mode of interpretation. But although these new concepts indeed successfully introduced far reaching changes, their basic characteristic, i.e., being part of a legal discourse, always forced them to cling to the very model they tried to abolish. Despite of the limits imposed by this approach, it can be observed that they increasingly confined the practical influence of the religious law on everyday life.

(3)   The next important step within the general development of the reform idea could be characterized as the attempt to define the "truly religious" parts of the Talmudic law. After having redefined parts of the Talmudic tradition and after having excluded vast amounts of the legal corpus, the reformers turned their attention to the foundation of the rabbinical legal system.

Like other equal-minded Jewish intellectuals, Holdheim came to challenge the authority of the very source of the halakhic system, i.e. the laws preserved in the Pentateuch itself. Here again, the changes were implemented based on the redefinition of legal elements that allegedly anticipated or at least seemed to tend toward the intended reforms. The basic idea remained the same: the destruction of the legal tradition by means of a legal argument was to lead the reformers to a Jewish religion that contained nothing else than the norms directly revealed by God himself.[37]

All these popular steps that reflect quite an astonishing progress of the Reform ideology were adopted by Holdheim as well. (4) Around 1843, however, some reformers became aware that the constant reference to the basically rejected idea of a divine law, the Halakhah, as the normative center of Judaism, would inevitably

---

[37] Almost until the year 1842 Holdheim held fast to the position of the "halakhic" redefinition of marginal laws. It was during the dispute about the revised prayerbook of the Hamburg *Tempelverein* that he began to reconstruct the "truly divine laws" embedded in the Rabbinic tradition; see Holdheim, *Verketzerung und Gewissensfreiheit*, 2-3, 24, 43-44, 50, here 82; "Für Alles, was im Talmud im Namen des einen oder anderen Gelehrten als dessen eigene, von ihm selbst nicht auf höhere Quellen zurückgeführte Ansicht vorkommt, *traditionelle Autorität* in Anspruch zu nehmen, hieße *Menschliches* mit *Göttlichem* verwechseln, jeden auf Unkosten dieses zu erheben." It is hard to define the exact point at which the transition from the change of the traditional Halakhah to the construct of the biblical law as the only binding normative text took place. In any case it seems clear that in 1845 it formed already a basic assumption of Holdheim's ideology; see idem, *Vorschläge zu einer zeitgemässen Reform der Ehegesetze*, 41.

paralyze any further development. The fundamentally new aspect of the reform systems was the introduction of historical research into the given discourse. This historicization of the religious tradition with its universalistic core mostly served just to make the old system more flexible, thus contributing to modernizing Judaism's religious outlook.

But while Holdheim's more radical colleagues, particularly Abraham Geiger and Samuel Hirsch, began to detach themselves from the legal discussion in order to generate a truly fundamental reform of the religious idea, turning to a theology strongly indebted to historicist concepts, Holdheim, like the vast majority of the reformers, maintained the conviction that only the *legal* destruction of the given law was likely to bring about an intrinsically religious reform that would widen the holistic frame of the religious law. 1842, in a public statement aiming at Zacharias Frankel, one of his strongest opponents who was to become the leader of the conservative wing of the Reform Movement, Holdheim expressed his views quite frankly: "Abandoning the standpoint of the law and denying its authority when deciding religious questions" would definitely mean leaving the "framework of the Orthodox legitimate church."[38] It was the knowledge about the *misinterpretations* of the Talmud and the differentiation between *human interpretations* and *truly divine* parts of the law that would, according to his view, harmoniously lead to a *re-formation*, or a re-construction of the inherited tradition.[39] Nevertheless, Holdheim's normative structure did not differ that much from Frankel's romantic historical construction of a *positiv religiös-gesetzliche Reform* or from Geiger's idea of a *spirit of the historical evolution*. As in the case of his contemporaries, Holdheim's ideas were rooted in the historicism of the nineteenth century, and like them he developed

---

[38] Holdheim, *Verketzerung und Gewissensfreiheit*, 93; den "Standpunkt der Satzung und der Regel [= the Halakhah] aufgeben, ihm die Competenz, in religiösen Sachen zu entscheiden, entschieden absprechen, hieße das nicht, [....] aus der orthodoxen Kirche heraustreten?" He argued against Frankel's "positive-historical" concept, strengthening the idea of a legal discussion of the law. These "legal discussions," however, already implied the historicization as a kind of internal factor of the legal discussion.

[39] Ibid.; according to Holdheim, this legal reconstruction of the truly divine parts provided the only option an "Orthodox rabbi" had. At this time, Holdheim's self-perception was still shaped by the idea of the reformer being a part of the Orthodox rabbinate, the legitimate keeper of tradition; this idea is certainly absent in Holdheim's later ideology.

the humanistic idea of an outstanding character of Judaism or even
of its specific providential mission to humankind. Although Holdheim
later discarded his self-conception as an "Orthodox rabbi" expressed
in the remark quoted above, he remained, to some extent, the
halakhist of the Reform for the rest of his life, or, as his contemporaries put it, someone who defeated the Orthodox Halakhah by
its own means.[40]

4

I will leave the question of the inclusion of contemporary philosophical
trends as well as the idealistic concept of history aside and, instead,
concentrate on the aspect of the development and change of given
structures. This seems to be the only way to understand and assess
the dynamic transformation of the cultural system, but also the element of breaking with it.[41] We are not talking about the Halakhah
as perceived by Orthodoxy, nor are the following deliberations devoted
to the idea of the Jewish law presented by Holdheim himself. Rather,
they aim at analyzing his Reform ideology by looking for the change
of basic systematic structures and—most interesting—for the ideological means by which he maintained the assumption of Jewish distinctiveness. At least from 1843 on Holdheim argued that his distinction
between the "national" and the "religious" parts of the rabbinic tradition inevitably led to the destruction of the religious law, because,
according to his concept, the legal parts were nothing else than those
"national" elements, while the religious obligations were part of the
religious moral system.[42] From the perspective of system analysis,

---

[40] Meyer, *Response to Modernity*, 81; Donath, *Geschichte der Juden in Mecklenburg*, 229ff.

[41] The discussion about the change of the cultural system should not only rely
on the semiotic analysis of the ideology itself but also on the dialectic discussion of
its cultural discourse. I have, however, to refrain from discussing the latter aspect
in this article.

[42] Holdheim, *Ueber die Autonomie der Rabbinen*, 10-12, 158-159. Although the following analysis shows how close this—supposedly anti-halakhic—Reform model
maintained and transmitted even basic structures of the Halakhah, another rather
feeble trend shows that, to a certain extent, Holdheim changed to the "other side,"
away from Halakhah. Like many others, for instance, he began to prefer Aggadah
to Halakhah as the religious norm; see, e.g., Samuel Holdheim, *Moses Mendelssohn
und die Denk- und Glaubensfreiheit im Judenthume* (Berlin: J. C. Huber, 1859), 53:
"welches Hagada genannt, damals noch von keinem talmudischen Schiffer befahren,

however, even these "religious" parts maintain the characteristics of the former legal system; it seems, therefore, adequate to understand them, as the traditional Halakhah would have done as well, as parts of a concept defined by religious law.

While the majority of the Reform systems were hampered by their own conservative link to the legal concept of Judaism, it is quite interesting to observe that it were exactly these bonds which helped Holdheim to create a Reform system that was far more independent from the pre-emancipatory and the Orthodox standpoint than most of the other models. Moreover, if we take a glimpse at the outcome, he almost succeeded in achieving the seemingly impossible, namely to change the given structure while, at the same time, opening it in a self-referential process. It is this aspect that makes Holdheim's idea so unique and outstanding, particularly compared to Reform concepts which saw no other choice than to create an entirely new theological system that, again, could hardly be legitimized by historical patterns alone.[43]

A genuine understanding of all the steps Holdheim had to take in order to create a concise system has to take into account his apologetic wish to reconcile the Jewish tradition with the expectations of the non-Jewish majority and the spokesmen of emancipation. This was certainly not a motivation that was solely characteristic for him. Confronted with the anti-Jewish allegation that the Jews, as a foreign cultural minority, could not possibly be included into the German Nation, reformers and Orthodox alike felt constantly forced to prove that Judaism did, indeed, not display a single characteristic that would prevent it from perfectly fitting into the legal frame of the state.[44]

It is quite obvious that it had been the legal-religious Jewish culture that, since the late eighteenth century, encountered strong suspicion and was regarded, at first, as a non-religious, later even as

---

und obgleich es die eigentlichen Glaubens- und Sittenlehren des Judenthums, seine ethischen Ideen und sittlichen Grundsätze in sich schließt."

[43] For other such concepts, see Meyer, *Response to Modernity*, 84-99; Wiener, *Jüdische Religion*, 118-39; Ismar Schorsch, *From Text to Context: The Turn to History in Modern Judaism* (Hanover, NH: Brandeis University Press, 1994), 319, 323, and many other passages. Schorsch claims that the "scholarly" criteria stood against the halakhic norms regarding the determination of reforms. This factor appears in Holdheim's system—as in many others as well—as an integral part.

[44] See Jacob Katz, "A State within a State, The History of an Anti-Semitic Slogan," in idem, *Zur Assimilation und Emanzipation der Juden. Ausgewählte Schriften* (Darmstadt: Wissenschaftliche Buchgesellschaft, 1982), 124-54.

foreign national cult. In the eyes of non-Jewish critics, this kind of Judaism displayed all aspects of a separate state and was, therefore, not considered to deserve integration into the German state and nationhood. The efforts of the Jewish minority to refute these ideological reservations sometimes even went as far as to try to demonstrate that it was the justice and the moral obligations demanded by the Jewish religion that made Jews the better citizens.[45]

From the very beginning of the public debate about whether the Jews should be granted equal rights or not, there had been severe doubts. Granting civil rights and religious freedom implied that the Jewish law with its dominating influence on religious life had to be changed or abandoned: Didn't these laws disqualify the Jewish citizen as soldiers because of the Sabbath, and didn't the dietary and matrimonial laws separate the Jews from their Christian neighbours? It is not even necessary to refer to open anti-Jewish prejudice to understand that the non-Jews—and even many Jews– actually saw a conflict of interests that could not be solved unless the Jewish law was altered. The allegation that Jews formed a separate state within the state, and particularly Bruno Bauer's anti-Jewish writings prompted Holdheim to adopt a Reform idea that can already be traced back to the writings of the first generation of reformers.[46]

To Holdheim the halakhic rule of *mizvot shetaluyot ba'aretz*— the laws concerning the existence of the Jewish state in Palestine—seemed to prove that the rabbinical legal tradition already provided a solution to this question of the relation between church and state.[47]

---

[45] For Orthodox and conservative reactions see, e.g., Zacharias Frankel's review of Holdheim's *Ueber die Autonomie der Rabbinen*, published in the *Zeitschrift für die religiösen Interessen des Judentums* 1 (1844), 206-207, 274-277, or Samson Raphael Hirsch, *Zweite Mittheilung aus dem Briefwechsel über die neueste jüdische Literatur, Ein Fragment* (Altona: Hammerich, 1844), 33ff.; for further material see Gotzmann, *Jüdisches Recht im kulturellen Prozeß*, 218ff.

[46] Holdheim's major work *Ueber die Autonomie der Rabbinen* was first published in March 1843, but the two articles put together for this book had already been written in 1841. Nevertheless, Holdheim claims that the book was already in print, when Bruno Bauer's pamphlet came out and that this is why he could include only three lengthy annotations. Bauer's first publication was published in 1842; see Bruno Bauer, "Die Juden-Frage," *Deutsche Jahrbücher für Wissenschaft und Kunst* 5 (1842), 1093-1126; see Samuel Holdheim, *Das Religiöse und Politische im Judenthum. Mit besonderer Beziehung auf gemischte Ehen. Eine Antwort auf Frankel's Kritik der Autonomie der Rabbinen und der Protocolle der ersten Rabbiner-Versammlung in Betreff der gemischten Ehen* (Schwerin: C. Kürschner, 1845) 10ff.

[47] Philipp Biberfeld, "Dina DeMalkhuta Dina," in *Schriftenreihe des Bundes Jüdischer Akademiker*, vol. 2 (Berlin: Menorah, [1925]), 31-37; Leo Landman, *Jewish Law in the*

The traditional background of this law is quite simple: After the destruction of the Jewish state it had been impossible to enact the laws concerning the land or the temple service because of the lack of any state or temple. Therefore, generations of rabbis perceived these laws as being irrelevant for the present. But while the Orthodox Halakhah regarded these laws just as inoperative and not as invalid, Holdheim tried to show that the above mentioned legal rule actually meant nothing else than the simple fact that all civil legal acts of the Jewish law were abolished.[48]

Moreover, this Talmudic decision also seemed to prove that the difference between the civic and religious element of Judaism was known to the legal tradition. Holdheim came to the conviction that the "national" elements of the rabbinic tradition, i.e. those connected to the Jewish state, were the actual Jewish law, while defining all the other regulations of the Halakhah as the truly religious norms. Apart from following halakhic structures, this argument is also supported by a historical model.[49] On the basis of a teleological concept the ideological strategy to abolish parts of the law *in actu* but not *de jure* was exposed as a historical misinterpretation that contradicted the *inspired progress of Jewish history*. According to Holdheim's reading, the first destruction of Jerusalem and its Temple and the Babylonian Exile were immediately followed by the abolishment of the law of the destroyed Jewish state.[50]

While this had been the consistent result of the divine purpose of the history of the Jewish people, the leaders of the Jewish nation misinterpreted the divine law after the second destruction of the Jewish state by the Romans and tried to preserve the national legal system by defining them as a temporarily inactive, albeit still valid

---

Diaspora: Confrontation and Accomodation. A Study of the Development, Composition and Function of the Concept of Dina D'Malkhuta Dina—The Law of the Kingdom—the State—is the Law (Philadelphia: Dropsie College for Hebrew and Cognate Learning, 1968); Gil Graff, *Separation of Church and State: Dina d'Malkhuta dina in Jewish Law, 1750-1848* (Alabama: University of Alabama Press, 1985), 120ff., gives only a cursory glance at the center of Holdheim's Reform system. Graff is after all more concerned with the legal history of this concept.

[48] Holdheim, *Ueber die Autonomie der Rabbinen*, 22.

[49] Ibid., 81ff.; almost every legal argument includes some historical construct.

[50] Holdheim adopted these somewhat strange ideas from Isaak Markus Jost; see Holdheim, ibid., 23ff; idem, *Das Religiöse und Politische im Judenthum*, 17-22; citation 83: "Gott selbst hat es ja durch die Geschichte deutlich genug ausgesprochen [....]; er selbst hat ja die stärkste Schutzwehr desselben, nämlich die Existenz des jüdischen Volkes, vernichtet, den Jahrhunderte lang bestandenen Damm durchbrochen!"

part of the religious regulations. But, Holdheim argued, if the religious idea already aimed at separating or purifying the religious law from its national elements and had, therefore, never demanded their reactivation, why should this historical error of the Talmudic sages not be corrected in the present era, since the Jews were now integrating into the German nation and deliberately leaving their own nationality behind?[51]

With such historicist arguments and lengthy legal reflections upon the Talmudic "misinterpretation" of Jewish tradition Holdheim radically questioned all "national elements" of the religious law. Thus he did not only de-construct an essential element of the Halakhah, namely the equality of all laws, including the sacredness of the divine law itself, but also replaced halakhic categories by modern ones, equating the meaning of the categories indicated by the Geonic rule of *dina demalkhuta dina* with the nineteenth century categories of *civil law (Staatsgesetz)* or *state*.

However, even if the norms according to which the Jewish tradition was reinterpreted were partly non-legal, Holdheim kept integrating them into the rabbinical legal discourse.[52] He did everything

---

[51] Holdheim's concept of nationhood and state relies on the liberal idea that the state as a secular entity is not bound to any specific religion. By being accepted as equal citizens and adopting the laws of the state, the Jews became a part of the nation; see Holdheim, *Ueber die Autonomie der Rabbinen* 4-5, 17-24, 57-58; by emancipation alone "the oriental is transformed to a native European, the Jew who partially obeys alien laws but carries all duties of the citizen was transformed into a native, an equal participant of the highest possession of a state, the civil law" (5). At the same time his idealistic historicist theology proclaims: "Der Jude ist angewiesen, mit anderen Völkern ein gemeinsamens Volks- und Staatsleben zu bilden" (idem, *Das Religiöse und Politische im Judenthum*, 83). From Holdheim's point of view, the Jewish national character is closely connected to the idea of a unique sanctity of the Jewish people. This idea of *Volksheiligkeit* is, by means of a historicist construct, transmitted into the humanistic ideal of Judaism as the guardian of the moral idea for humanity. See, e.g., Holdheim, *Ceremonialgesetz im Messiasreich*, 28, 33-34, 40-42; idem, *Gemischte Ehen zwischen Juden und Christen, Die Gutachten der Berliner Rabbinatsverwaltung und des Königsberger Consistoriums beleuchtet* (Berlin: L. Lassar, 1850), 76-77. Due to the increasingly problematic debate about the character of German nationhood, Holdheim's rather simplistic concept turned out to be outdated very soon—a process that prompted him to further develop and strengthen his idea; see idem, *Gemischte Ehen zwischen Juden und Christen*, 54-55: according to his argument, the *Volksgemeinschaft* based on common citizenship is more important than the nationality which is dependent on a citizen's descent.

[52] This is also true for the historical argument which is not at all an entirely new factor in halakhic discussions. In Holdheim's "legal" reasoning, however, it assumed an essential importance. Although this is certainly a change compared to the pre-emancipatory period, Holdheim applied the historical argument in a way that con-

to establish his argument as a "halakhic" one. This is illustrated by the way, he projects the modern meaning of civil law on the Talmudic interpretation of the legal concept "Laws of the Land." While Holdheim tried to prove from the authoritative sources that the meaning of *eretz* (land) corresponds to state, the Talmudic discussion had defined it as *karka*, which simply means soil.[53] The traditional meaning was thus restricted to questions like the *shmita*-year and the laws concerning harvesting. According to Holdheim's interpretation, the legal concept could be broadened to the extent that it embraced all the legal entities that, in the nineteenth century, were ascribed to the authority of the state. Such meticulous legalistic procedures helped to establish the idea of an intrinsic "halakhic" argument. Thus the reformers invested their own ideas with the authority of the given tradition, creating a new link in the old chain of the interpretation of the divine law.

Holdheim's adversaries, especially the Orthodox rabbi Samson Raphael Hirsch, were clearly aware of this intrusion of modern ideas into the Talmudic literature. Not only did he reject Holdheim's "talmudic" reasoning, he also challenged his opponent arguing that the Halakhah would never tolerate any inclusion of alien factors and that, therefore, the latter could absolutely not be granted the status of a normative part of tradition.[54] From a semiotic perspective, such criticism cannot be simply dismissed. However, the problems Holdheim's Reform concept entailed had still another—even more serious—dimension. As it turned out, the traditional categories he used were not as stable and well-defined as he needed them to be. In his controversy

---

tinued to be in accordance with the legal system; one could almost describe its function as that of a supporting argument whose inclusion does not touch the system itself. This is even more important, since we are dealing here with the aspect of the ideological constructs that preserved the effectiveness of the closed autopoietic system; see Schorsch, *From Text to Context*, 149-388.

[53] Holdheim, *Ueber die Autonomie de Rabbinen*, 25-31; reflecting bT Kidushin 37a.

[54] See Hirsch, *Zweite Mitteilung*, 17: "[Es ist ein] bodenloses Beginnen, Begriffe die in einem andern Gebiete erzeugt sind und dort ihre Geltung haben, ohne Weiteres auf ein anderes Gebiet, in gebieterischer, normgebender Stellung zu übertragen, wo sie fremd sind und weder Werth noch Geltung haben"; and see Frankel, Review of Holdheim's "Autonomie", 205: Holdheim "befindet sich auf einem den rabbinischen Judenthume ganz entgegengesetzten Standpunkte, aber er will auch aus diesem selbst die Rechtfertigung seiner Behauptung demonstriren; [....] Es liegt dem ganzen Verfahren des Verf. ein so unredliches Spiel mit der Wahrheit zu Grunde, [....] die willkürliche Unterschiebung von Ideen, die dem Geiste derjenigen, denen sie aufgebürdet werden, ganz fremd waren."

with Hirsch, Holdheim made a definite step forward and reacted to
the latter's harsh judgment by openly redefining his method as a scholarly historical-legal research that clearly differed from the process of
interpretation characteristic of rabbinical tradition.[55]

At the same time, Holdheim held fast to all the elements of the
earlier reform discussions, for instance the strategy of re-evaluating
traditional arguments that had no normative meaning, as well as the
inclusion of historical explanations, or the reference to a "plain meaning" of the text. Important, however, is his claim that the legal discussion of the sources should include a historical perspective: "One
has to put oneself in the position of the rabbis, ask the same questions again und answer them according to our point of view."[56]

Although this is a rather accurate description of how the general
process of legal interpretation actually works, Holdheim clearly challenged the traditional ideology of an unchangeable, eternally valid
law as well as the idea that the divine law already provides an answer
to all the potential legal cases that might come up. By integrating
the contemporary assessment of a problem into the Reform debate,
Holdheim emphasized his basic idea of a Jewish Reform movement
as it was already depicted by the title of his book. [The center of
any harmonious change of the tradition was the freedom of the modern rabbi to interpret the law according to the contemporary needs
and religious convictions.] However, while he replaced the ideological assumption of an eternal stability of tradition by a concept of
dynamic change, he nevertheless re-established his "Halakhah," i.e.
the remaining religious norms, as the center of Jewish religion and
the "legal" discussion as the only way to redefine them.[57]

---

[55] All the reformers encountered the same problem. The fact that the traditional
legal categories were not established as exclusive logical and systematic entities was a
major challenge to their Reform systems. The same is true for Holdheim: Since, according to the Talmudic law, the term "land" (understood by Holdheim as state) did not
include all the entities he considered to be part of the "civil" law, he had to refer to
a medieval perception, namely to Maimonides' list of the laws concerning the temple
service, the kingdom, the laws for war, and the laws regarding capital crimes. This
difficulty was clearly seen by Mendel Hess in his review of Holdheim's *Ueber die Autonomie
der Rabbinen;* see *Israelit des Neunzehnten Jahrhunderts* 5 (1844), 1-4; 9-12; 17-21; 25-28; but
see Holdheim, *Das Religiöse und das Politische im Judenthum,* 32-33, 35, 39-40.

[56] Idem, *Ueber die Autonomie der Rabbinen,* 49: "[Man muß sich] auf jenen Standpunkt
der Rabbinen zurück versetzen, und dieselben Fragen von Neuem aufwerfen und
sie nach unsern Gesichtspunkten beantworten."

[57] Ibid., 63. Like most of the other reformers, Holdheim claimed that this "freedom" was historically true for the Talmudic rabbis as well. He was still convinced

While Holdheim did, in fact, undermine the holistic ideal of a religious system enclosing all aspects of life, even without refuting its theoretical basis, he definitely destroyed the ideology of stability upheld by Orthodoxy. The strategy of holding fast to the rabbinic idea of a legal and yet a historical legitimization enabled him to create a flexible ideological system. This model had to match the demands of a state that tended to fight even the last resorts of German Jewry's religious legal autonomy, for instance the laws of marriage and divorce. At the same time, it had to be self-conscious and self-referential in order to make sure that the Reform concept did not jeopardize the ideological stability of a distinct Jewish identity.

As Holdheim re-modelled the Jewish law according to his idea of the two separate spheres of state and religion, the ongoing public discussion that defined Germany as an intrinsically Christian state forced him to take the other side into consideration as well. A positive vision of the relationship between state and Judaism as presented by Holdheim presupposed that the state, too, accepted the new interpretation of Judaism as a middle-class religious conviction. Therefore, Holdheim found himself challenged to specify his concepts of state and nation. His initial liberal and legalistic conviction that the acceptance of the civil law formed the national bond between all its citizens was now strongly questioned.[58] To accommodate this model, the ideal state had to consciously avoid being exclusively connected to one specific religious tradition instead of incorporating the

---

that the old Halakhah could only be defeated by the rabbinic discussion, these "peculiar rabbinical weapons [eigenthümliche rabbinische Waffen], whose [....] sharpness alone can penetrate it [i.e., the Halakhah]." Geiger had left this Reform concept behind much earlier and tended to a historical-theological reassessment of Judaism; see Abraham Geiger, "Die religiösen Thaten der Gegenwart im Judenthume," *Wissenschaftliche Zeitschrift für jüdische Theologie* 6 (1847), 1-16, particularly 14-15. Nevertheless, their methods were not that different, because both of them used the knowledge about the historic development of the law to abolish the ideological structures of the holistic cultural myth. At the same time, these historical constructs slowly created an altered, albeit not really independent structure of authorization.

[58] This is illustrated by the additions Holdheim included in the second edition of his *Ueber die Autonomie der Rabbinen* in 1847, where he made it very clear that the Christian side was just embracing the argument of the anti-emancipationists, according to whom the alleged "special character" of the Jews prevented the state from granting them equality. While Judaism, Holdheim claimed, had now reached the level of a religion that had left all national bonds behind, striving for the unity of all citizens, Christianity seemed to decline to the level of an exclusive nationality; see Holdheim, *Ueber die Autonomie der Rabbinen*, VIII, X-XIV, 13-14; idem, *Gemischte Ehen*, 3-4.

minorities' religion as well. This did not mean, however, that the state had to be completely secular or a-religious. Like other Orthodox and Reform authors, Holdheim now defined the state as an over-arching supra-religious entity guaranteeing the unity of its citizens. Apart from leaving the religious system unharmed and accepting dif-fering religious beliefs, the state, according to the conviction of the differing religious camps, served as a humanistic meta-level, and both "state" and "religion" ultimately embraced the same aims, striving toward the ethical norms of morality, humanity and justice.

While Zacharias Frankel or Samson Raphael Hirsch also had to keep these two entities apart, at least ideologically, lest the religious system be endangered, Holdheim followed a more radical path.[59] For him, both were not simply separate spheres: By virtue of the reli-gious idea of public welfare which, from Holdheim's perspective, was a religious demand, the state gained an almost religious quality. Furthermore, he regarded the dissolution of the Jewish people into the European *national life* as the providential outcome of Judaism's religious idea. According to this concept, only the ideal harmony between the state and the Jewish religion was likely to lead to an

---

[59] Confronted with the problem of mixed marriages, Holdheim again tended to describe the ideal relation between state and religion as a tolerant but clearly sep-arated one; see Holdheim, *Gemischte Ehen*, 76. Typical contemporary ideas are: Josef Aub, "Die Rabbinerversammlung und ihre Gegner," *Sinai* 1 (1846), 357-62, par-ticularly 361; Samuel Hirsch, review of Holdheim's *Ueber die Autonomie der Rabbinen*, printed in the *Literaturblatt des Orient* 44 (1843), 696-699, particularly 698: "Der Staatsorganismus ist als das Höchste anzuerkennen, in den das Religiöse niemals hindernd eingreifen darf [....]. Staat und Religion stehen für das Bewußtsein unserer Zeit nicht mehr nebeneinander, als zwei sich nicht berühren sollende Gebiete, son-dern sie verhalten sich, wie Inneres zum Aeußeren, wie Wesen und Form"; anony-mous, "Das Wesen des Judenthums," *Der Treue Zionswächter* 5 (1849), 366-367, 371-373, particularly 366; anonymous, "Der Staat in seinem Verhältnisse zur Kirche," *Der Treue Zionswächter* 5 (1849), 225-227, 233-234, 243, particularly 226-227; Hirsch, *Zweite Mittheilung*, 20-26, 33; here the common zeals are the ideas of "the Useful and Good [des Nützlichen und Guten]," "the Divine and True [des Göttlichen und Wahren]," and of "justice and love on earth [Gerechtigkeit und Liebe auf Erden]." Similarly, Frankel adds the "sense of justice, love of freedom, and dignity of man [*Gerechtigkeitssinn, Freiheitsliebe und Menschenwürde*]," these being universal moral aims which demand from the Jews to strive for their own eman-cipation. Only then will they be able to devote all their strength to the well-being of the state and all its subjects; see Frankel, Review of "Autonomie," 208. Both Frankel and S. R. Hirsch saw the aims of the religious individual matching the interests of the modern state. Nevertheless, they had to set definite limits to the influence of the state on the realm of religion and vice versa. It is very interest-ing to see that these restrictions have a primarily ideological character rather than being relevant for reality.

achievement of their common aims, namely the realization of the humanistic ideal.

Critics like Frankel or Hirsch condemned this attitude as the expression of a religious system based on "a dog's obedience.".[60] From their point of view, Holdheim did not only accommodate the religious sphere to the demands of the modern state, but suggested the total subordination of the religion to the will of the state. This criticism was actually quite clear-sighted, as shown by the fact that with regard to some of the critical points in the debate about emancipation, Holdheim's model always granted absolute priority to the interest of the state. This is, for instance, illustrated by his discussion of the state's acceptance of the Jewish matrimonial laws as well as in his solution for the question of military service on the Sabbath. Here the conflict between the loyalty of the Jewish soldier to the state and his loyalty to the regulations of the Jewish law was solved by Holdheim's decision that, according to the religious law, the interest of the state was considered to be more important than the Sabbath laws.

From an analytical point of view, Holdheim integrates this question into the frame of the internal concept and thus provides a clear solution which leaves the ideological system intact. Thanks to this legitimatory gesture, the religion doesn't appear to stand back against the interests of the state, although this is exactly what happened. His critics were, therefore, right, at least with regard to the factual outcome of this procedure. Zacharias Frankel ridiculed Holdheim, claiming that he simply gave religious sanction to the quite questionable motto: "Obedience [to the civil law] is every citizen's first duty."[61] To Frankel, Holdheim's harmonization of the two spheres transformed the state into a religious idol and citizenship into a kind of idolatry.

Samson Raphael Hirsch was even more aware of the ideological risks involved in playing with legal arguments which created a special dynamic that invested the state almost with a religious character. Holdheim's solution, for instance, for the question whether or not the state should accept the autonomy of the Jewish laws of marriage and divorce, transformed the state into an intrinsic part of the religious sphere. Holdheim stated that, from the point of view of the Halakhah, these were legal acts with a clear monetary

[60] Ibid., 207-208.
[61] Ibid.; "Gehorsam ist die erste Bürgerpflicht."

character which, according to his basic distinction, were civil and
not religious elements of tradition. In this context, he referred to
the well-known halakhic principle *dina demalkhuta dina*, which means
that "the law of the kingdom is law," or, to put it in modern
words, the civil law is recognized by Jewish law as legally binding
transaction.

The pre-emancipatory and the Orthodox Halakhah used this fictitious assumption to keep the legal system unharmed. Monetary
transactions that were agreed upon on the basis of civil law were
accepted by Jewish law, which actually means that the external legal
act is redefined as an internal one. By this gesture the rabbis had
kept the holistic system of the Halakhah at least ideologically intact,
given the fact that the latter was unable to compete in this field
with the overwhelming pressure of the civil law. It is very interesting to see that Holdheim, time and again, used the same ideological "trick." In his eyes, this Geonic decision actually meant that
the state seized the religious power to decide in such matters. By
using the same self-referential gesture he, too, maintained the validity of the religious "legal" system. Radicalizing the original idea,
Holdheim followed the dynamics of the ideological process and sym-
bolically "included" the state's decision into the frame of religion.
Now it is clearly the state that contracts and separates marriages,
because religion invested it with the same qualification the rabbinical
courts once had.

To a profound ideologue like Samson Raphael Hirsch these logical, but utterly "un-religious" thoughts were clearly heretic. For him,
the boundaries of legitimate interpretation was already transgressed
with the "legal" discussions of reforms, as they altered traditional
interpretations and made selective use of the rabbinical sources. It
is not quite clear whether Samson Raphael Hirsch, like other defenders of Orthodoxy, for instance Jakob Ettlinger, just wanted to convince his audience that the legal arguments of the reformers distorted
the authorized ways of legal interpretation. It is, however, clear that
the above-mentioned conservative trait of the Reform Movement was
extremely challenging for the representatives of Orthodoxy because
it directly affected their authority to be the guardians of the law.
This is certainly one of the major motives for the strong attacks on
the "legal" Reform model.

Hirsch's concerns about the dynamic created by the use of the—
intrinsically "halakhic"—self-assuring gesture to keep the legal

ideology intact seems rather contestable.[62] Moreover, the development of Holdheim's Reform concept shows that it was rather the ideological "inclusion" or, to put it more precisely, the "legitimization" of elements grounded in another sphere than the Jewish tradition that enabled him to create a flexible system that, nevertheless, remained "closed." Holdheim's ability to reconcile the unavoidable with tradition by giving in to the changes imposed on Judaism by the external political development, the appearance of a clearly independent decision makes him an example of the degree of ideological virtuosity needed to promote acculturation without giving up Jewish identity.

5

Even though Holdheim's model may not have been very sophisticated, it nevertheless proved to be stable when it came to counter the problems created by its own newly defined structures. There is one example from the realm of marital laws that is likely to illustrate in which way Holdheim managed to meet the necessities imposed by his own system by means of the same self-referential move. His basic idea consisted in giving the state the opportunity to issue civil marriage-laws that was not tied to any specific religious conviction. The question emerged because several states, for instance Prussia or Mecklenburg-Schwerin, decreed that some Jewish ceremonies like the wedding act would be recognized in order to establish the bond of marriage, while the divorce act would be restricted to a civil lawsuit.[63]

From Holdheim's point of view this mixing of the two spheres was doomed to failure. According to the Halakhah, he argued, marriage

---

[62] For the so-called "neo-Orthodox" Samson R. Hirsch, the deviation from the Orthodox legal argument was sufficient to reject Holdheim's perspective. Although he discussed the systematic argument in order to show the inconsistency of the Reform model, the "reconstruction" of the legal process on the basis of the assumption of a Talmudic "misunderstanding" provoked Hirsch's rejection early on; see Hirsch, *Zweite Mittheilung*, 16-17, 21.

[63] For example Jeremias Heinemann, *Sammlung der die religiöse und bürgerliche Verfassung der Juden in den Königlichen Preussischen Staaten betreffenden Gesetze, Verordnungen, Gutachten, Berichte und Erkenntnisse: Mit einem Anhang, welcher Gesetze fremder Staaten enthält*, 2nd enlarged edition (Glogau: Heymann, 1831; reprint Hildesheim: Olms, 1976), 233ff., 241ff., 248, 264ff.; Holdheim, *Gemischte Ehen*, 78ff.

and divorce were nothing else than monetary civil transactions, i.e. actually just the "acquisition" of a wife. As we have already seen, Holdheim projected this internal concept into the state, providing it with the religious authority to decide such cases. Here again some relevance is granted to the civil law within the religious system, because the Jewish regulations could no longer be applied to such "civil" cases.[64] Now the same had to be achieved with regard to the acts of marriage and divorce. But at this point another parallel discussion interfered.

At the Rabbinical Conference in Frankfurt am Main in 1845, some reformers tried to redefine the role of women in Judaism. The halakhic idea of an "acquisition" of the wife by her husband made it impossible for the Jewish woman to actively divorce her husband by herself. This underlying legal concept had caused many problems since medieval times, and Holdheim decided to eliminate it once and forever. In order to exclude all these matters of family law from the religious sphere, however, he had strengthened the idea of a one-sided act of acquisition.[65] He was, therefore, confronted with the same problem the halakhists had encountered in the past. In order to gain more flexibility within the logic of the system, Holdheim cited a decision that had provided the rabbinical courts the possibility of doubting the validity of the marriage and thus to dissolve it.

This rather questionable legal procedure was now taken as a precedent. Since the Halakhah only knows the possibility of the husband divorcing his wife, rabbinical courts in the past had sometimes seen no other chance to protect the wife's interests but to relativize the act of marriage itself, particularly the act of acquisition by the symbolic price of a *pruta*—since antiquity by a ring. By virtue of the

---

[64] To Holdheim this would have been an inadequate description, because he intended this division to be a total one. The legal act could not be perceived as the symbolic inclusion it was, but actually had to be considered as an act of separation of the couple.

[65] Here we can see that Holdheim is not satisfied with splitting up the religious law. Time and again he returns in a conservative gesture to the older concept the way he does here. According to his system it would have been sufficient to leave the divorce act to the state, without worrying about the way the state would regulate it. Instead, Holdheim recurs to the realm of the "Halakhah" in order to provide a solution before eventually shifting the responsibility to the state courts. Apart from the fact that the procedure invests the state with qualities originally restricted to the religious law, it does not seem very consistent; see Holdheim, *Vorschläge zu einer zeitgemässen Reform der jüdischen Ehegesetze*, 12-13.

court's right to expropriate goods *hefker beit din hefker* it was possible
to dispossess the ring's owner, i.e. the groom. According to Holdheim,
this procedure made the act of marriage doubtful and invalid. He
referred to this quite complex legal argument because he wanted to
grant women the right to actively divorce her husband.[66]

But here the necessities implied in Holdheim's initial argument
proved to be counterproductive: since he generally considered these
acts to be of civil nature, i.e. restricted to the decision of the state,
the rabbinic court as a religious institution was no longer able to
interfere. Otherwise, both spheres that he wished to be strictly separated would have to interact, which, according to Holdheim, would
have been an almost "un-religious" development. Hence it could
not be the rabbinical court that expropriated the ring. In theory,
Holdheim claimed, the solution to this problem could consist in
the state granting the right to perform this act again to the Jewish
courts; however, while this solution would have kept the normative structures of the Reform system intact, it would have undermined Holdheim's basic conviction according to which the civil
and the religious spheres had to be rigidly separated. To disregard
this aspect would have meant to negate the very core of the whole
concept. In this case, the rabbinical court would again have decided
civil, i.e. non-religious matters, this being a clear contradiction to
Holdheim's religious Reform concept and a return to pre-emancipatory times. In order to solve these tensions within the system,
Holdheim ascribed the state the halakhic right of the Jewish courts
to expropriate goods. According to this interpretation of the Jewish
law, the state had to be the only legal forum for all civil matters.
This certainly included all questions of property and thus also the
expropriation of the ring.

Holdheim's solution did not contradict the norms of his Reform
model; in fact, both strictly separated spheres appear to merge into
each other again. The only difference seems to be that, from an
external point of view, it was now the state court which decided
these matters because it had gained its authorization from the religious law. Like in the traditional gesture, the civil judge would apply
a civil law that had been sanctioned by the Jewish law and thus
appeared to be an integral part of the religious legal system. Again,

---

[66] Idem, *Gemischte Ehen*, 74-75; idem, *Vorschläge zu einer zeitgemässen Reform der jüdischen Ehegesetze*, 16-17.

the system was saved by a symbolic act that transformed the factual
state of affairs into an internal and thus legitimate procedure.

From an outside perspective, the boundaries of the two spheres
were blurred by this interpretation, since it granted the state a certain degree of religious authority. Nevertheless, Holdheim had managed to keep his religious system intact. However, the necessities
imposed by the contemporary perception of the sanctity of the marital bond forced him to admit that Judaism understood marriage not
just as the monetary "acquisition" of the wife but also as a profound
religious act. Interestingly enough, he confined the religious aspect
of the marriage to the morality of the union of two persons.[67]

At the same time, the traditional ceremony by which the couple
is married appears to be nothing more than the historical garb of
this moral idea, as a symbol that could be changed according to its
contemporary perception. This shows that, while Holdheim's Reform
concept itself actually worked, transforming the former system in a
concise way into something quite different, it was unable to satisfy
all the expectations nurtured by the profound general change of the
concept of religion and religiosity. Even Holdheim began, therefore,
to define a somewhat paralleling level of moral convictions, a realm
enclosing the progressive factors of the cultural change and basic
normative entities for his Reform model. For the first time, it is obvious that the otherwise concise system had to be opened, because the
legalistic approach would not allow the inclusion of such independent values. Nevertheless, the importance attributed to the inherited
religious sphere and the extent to which the older model was reshaped
while upholding the legal discourse, was unique in nineteenth-century Germany.

This basic construct might seem rather simplistic and even arbitrary, but Holdheim proved that it was not only sufficiently flexible
to meet the challenges by competing systems, but also an extraordi-
narily consistent model that was able to overcome the problems created by the system itself. There were only few new concepts that
achieved such an inner stability despite the contradictions caused by
the strong link to the inherited legal tradition. One last example, again
in the realm of marriage, is likely to illustrate how Holdheim's system tried to handle such internal tensions: Although Holdheim stated

---

[67] Ibid., 19-20; idem, *Das Religiöse und Politische im Judenthum*, 55ff.; idem, *Gemischte Ehen*, 75ff.

that the Halakhah interpreted the acts of marriage and divorce as civil acts, the traditional Halakhah obviously knew—according to the norms he projected onto the ancient law—also "religious" aspects of the family law. Unfortunately for his approach, the rabbinic tradition accepts the *un-religious* behavior of the wife as a reason to divorce her.

However strange this idea might have appeared from the point of view of Holdheim's categories, this law obviously proved that the Halakhah, at least partly, held the idea of a "religious" character of the marriage. Holdheim's solution is rather weak: he merely cites the decision of a medieval commentary, according to which this decree was not coercive but voluntary. This argument probably solved the practical problem from a legal point of view, but it did not answer the question concerning the religious quality the traditional Halakhah attributed to the marriage. Obviously the internal tensions could somehow be handled by internal procedures. But since the whole concept relied strongly on norms that were not fully integrated into this legalistic model, it could not possibly overcome or exclude such self-imposed problems; the reason for this inability can be traced back to the origin of the Reform system. It was unable to really integrate such new concepts like morality and religion, because the traditional structures were not familiar with these factors that were now declared to be the foundation of the entire system. Like most of the extreme reformers, Holdheim had, therefore, no other choice than altering his ideological approach and moving from the realm of religious law to a new theology.

He now stated that the religious character of marriage was not dependant on the ritual, which was bound to change with the passage of time. The religious meaning was created by the morality [*Moralität*] of the union of man and woman, an ideal that was not characteristic for a specific denomination but was rather supposed to be true for all human beings. Holdheim defines this extra-systemic level as a meta- structure. [This universal humanistic idea became an important ideological tool of Reform Judaism, which represented itself as the ideal guardian of these thoughts and as a paradigm for all the other religions.] Whereas this somewhat apologetic gesture was quite often used by religious ideologues from all camps, Holdheim was, again, one of the very few rabbis who followed the dynamic of its idea without avoiding its consequences, for instance the acceptance of mixed-marriages.

Holdheim's latest writings show that he also liberated himself from

the constraints created by his legalistic system and was increasingly
inclined to embrace a humanistic inter-denominational approach.
After abandoning the "national character of the Jews," the divine
religious law, as Holdheim defined it, lost its binding force which
was based on its being revealed exclusively to the Jewish people.
Although the rabbinic tradition had lost its value, the written tradition of the Torah and the prophets was preserved. By now the concept of the "scholarly" interpretation of their ethical value formed
the center of his religious thinking; as a result, even biblical laws
like the Sabbath laws or the circumcision had to be reconsidered.
[Nevertheless, there had to be a clear limit to these radical changes
of the tradition. Without such a line of demarcation it would not
have made any sense to maintain a separate Jewish identity or even
to be a rabbi any more] None of the reformers, not even Holdheim,
wanted to cross it. Holdheim repeatedly had to define this line which
he found in a rather vague entity that comprehended all the truly
moral laws revealed to Moses by God:

> [Any] advance that went beyond the religious thinking and feeling of
> biblical times, i.e. the biblical idea of God and of morality as an immutable
> foundation of Judaism—would not be a development, but the destruc-
> tion of Judaism. [....] The biblical teaching of God and morality is the
> absolute limit for any advancement. [....] The strong and immutable
> basis of any historical development within Judaism is the biblical reli-
> gion, the pure and genuine Jewish teaching of God and morality.[68]

While this definitely strengthened the idea of a separate, distinctly
Jewish tradition, Holdheim had—already in 1850—rejected such a
detachment from the rest of humankind:

---

[68] Idem, *Geschichte der jüdischen Reformgemeinde*, 115-116: "Ein Hinausgehen über das
religiöse Denken und Fühlen des biblischen Zeitalters, nämlich über die biblische
Gottes- und Sittlichkeitsidee als die unverrückbare Basis des Judenthums, wäre keine
Entwicklung, sondern eine Zerstörung des Judenthums. [....] Die biblische Gottes-
und Sittenlehre ist die Schranke, an welcher jede Fortbildung sich brechen muß. [....]
Die feste, unverrückbare Basis aller historischen Entwickelungen im Judenthum ist die
biblische Religion, die reine, unverfälschte Gottes- und Sittenlehre des Judenthums";
see idem, *Das Religiöse und das Politische im Judenthum*, 80-81; and see idem, *Moses
Mendelssohn*, 47: "Auf religiösem Gebiet stellen wir allen Ernstes die Autorität über
jede Majorität und meinen, daß auch die jüdische Gesammtheit sich weder von der
wesentlichen Basis des Judenthums [which is the biblical teachings about God and
moral] entfernen, noch von seiner Geschichte im Ganzen losreißen dürfe, es wäre
denn, daß sie darauf verzichtet, noch ferner eine jüdische Gesammtheit zu heißen."
Holdheim rejects the criticism according to which contemporary humanism is an
inappropriate external norm; see idem, *Das Religiöse und Politische im Judenthum*, 58.

The reformed Judaism [....] denies the idea of an exclusive holiness of the Jewish people, the idea of its chosenness and its covenant with God. [....] In the same way the reformed Judaism transcends the tight boundaries of salvation by which Orthodox Judaism fenced in the holy people of Israel and expands them to include the entire humankind.[69]

Whereas it had been the separate divine law that was first binding for the Jewish people, [Holdheim now creates the concept of a universally valid holy moral law.] This development could be characterized as the transition from the legal norm of Halakhah to the Kantian idea of a general moral norm governing human existence.[70] On its way to universalism, Judaism nevertheless appears to be the guardian of this idea, the prophetic mirror reflecting the relationship between God and man, a religion that ignores and rejects all national and religious boundaries in order to create a moral "nationality of humankind."[71] Although Holdheim's statements sometimes still refer to the legalistic model, here the legal complex has definitely lost its normative character as a closed system and was replaced by a general meta-level of humanism.

It is to be hoped that these complex religious and, even in quite a traditional sense, also legal discussions convey an impression of the very distinct character of Holdheim's ideological concept of the Jewish religion. While he always maintained the legal discourse as a basic argumentative system, he eventually overcame the structures of the older concept. At the beginning, he reinterpreted the ideology that saw the Halakhah as a perfect, eternal law in terms of a new view that included the aspect of interpretative growth. Later, he defined the idea of a *religious spirit of the legal evolution* as the new normative structure.[72] The legal discourse was nevertheless seen as the only possible expression of the spirit of a divine order, or as the only way

---

[69] Idem, *Gemischte Ehen*, 64.

[70] See ibid., 64-65: "statt eines besonderen heiligen Ceremonialgesetzes für Israel ein heiliges Sittlichkeitsgesetz für alle Menschen"; idem, *Moses Mendelssohn*, 71: "Nicht soll das nationale Gesetz Mose zur neuen Fessel für die Völker werden, sondern das von ihm selbst befreite Israel soll seinen reinen und freien Glauben den Völkern im Lichte der freien Erkenntnis zeigen, das sie ihn als sanftes Joch auf ihre Schultern legen."

[71] See ibid., 65: "und setzt statt dieser künstlichen Nationalitäten die Eine natürliche Nationalität des Menschenthums. Es kann ihm ein verbesserter Partikularismus, eine Verwandlung der jüdischen Geburtsaristokratie in die christliche Aristokratie des Glaubens nicht genügen, und will es aufrichtig den Universalismus."

[72] It refers to his historical model; see, e.g., idem, *Moses Mendelssohn*, 22-23: "auf dem Princip der historischen Fortbildung fußende religiöse Reform, eine

to reach the higher religious level of *morality* and *humanity*.

With this traditionalistic and yet radically anti-traditional approach Holdheim's Reform concept differentiates itself from almost all those defined by other reformers. It created an ideological system that kept the structures of the old norm and at the same time gained enough independence to radically change the inherited Halakhah, to the extent that it was eventually transformed into another theological system. Only on the basis of this standpoint was Holdheim able to respond to Samson Raphael Hirsch, who had pointed out that his arguments did not meet the traditional ways of legal interpretation: "But you will have to accept that the results of my work show that something can be made out of it!"[73]

Uebereinstimmung mit der Bibel, die weder eine logische Identität, noch eine mathematische Congruenz, sondern eine historische Uebereinstimmung sein will."

[73] Idem, *Zweite Mittheilung*, 12: "Die Resultate meiner Schriften [...] zeigen doch, daß sich aus ihm [i.e., the argument] etwas machen läßt."

THE POLITICS OF RELIGION IN THE THOUGHT OF SAMUEL HOLDHEIM

Ken Koltun-Fromm

In the current academic climate of religious studies, we often hear terms of the sort "religious politics," or "the politics of religion," and find even within liberal protestant circles a new call for integrating the religious life within political discourse—what Ronald Thiemann and Stephen Carter refer to as "public religion."[1] Though the terms are contemporary, the debates are certainly not, for students of nineteenth-century German religious thought have labored to understand how the profound challenges of the Enlightenment (and in the Jewish context, emancipation) have formed complex religious and political identities. For German Jews the problem was particularly acute, for together with such challenges came new optimism for a vibrant and respected political life, where Jews could enter as partners in establishing a unified Germany, and participate as competitors in every profession and civil service. The history of this progressive optimism, together with its disappointments and failures, have been well documented and discussed, and they need not detain us here. But I do want to emphasize how integrated the debates really were over religion and politics in nineteenth-century Germany. For many of the early Jewish academic (*Wissenschaft*) scholars, political acceptance would arise out of renewed investigation and respect for Jewish history. The academic study of Judaism (*Wissenschaft des Judentums*) developed and encouraged religious politics, and its many practitioners understood the value of this practice. Religious discourse carried political meaning and weight.

This is no less true for Samuel Holdheim. He forcefully and resolutely separated religion from politics, but in so doing clearly

---

[1] See Stephen Carter, *The Culture of Disbelief: How American Law and Politics Trivialize Religious Devotion* (New York: Basic Books, 1993), and Ronald Thiemann, *Religion in Public Life: A Dilemma for Democracy* (Washington, D.C.: Georgetown University Press, 1996).

understood the politics of religion, even if, for Holdheim, that meant no politics at all. Questioning the justice of a public religion at a time when debates over a Christian state were then raging, Holdheim revealed a keen sense of his contemporary political environment, and respected the power of religious discourse to inform political debates.[2] Indeed, Holdheim's concern over marriage law in Jewish practice witnesses to the significance of religious politics for his thought. So even as Holdheim claims that religion maintains an ideal innocent purity outside the ravages of political intrigue, we should still recognize in that very claim a strong political voice and interest.

Holdheim's political voice, I want to argue, comes to the fore most forcefully when he discusses the meaning of the religious and the political. I state it in this way because I want to understand religion and politics as general categories of Holdheim's thought, as I believe he himself considered them to be. So it is not quite right to speak of religion and politics, but rather what counts for Holdheim as religious or political thought and activity. To be sure, scholars of Reform Judaism have already made much of this distinction,[3] leading one to quickly sum up: "In short, the absolute and pure *religious* elements of the revealed Mosaic legislation remain eternally binding; the rest no longer applies."[4] But this summary resists a more textured analysis of what Holdheim really means by the religious and the political. Andreas Gotzmann, in his work on Jewish law,[5] has offered the most nuanced and detailed account of Holdheim's more complicated picture of the religious and political spheres, and he helps us to appreciate the cultural dilemmas that resonate in much of Holdheim's thought. We require a more textured account of religious politics to better appreciate Holdheim's liberal Judaism.

I hope to provide that kind of thick analysis to unearth Holdheim's account of the religious and the political, one that parses out the distinctions among religion, Judaism, tradition, and Mosaic religion. We will see how Holdheim erects a protective barrier to thwart

---

[2] Andreas Gotzmann, *Jüdisches Recht im kulturellen Prozeß* (Tübingen: J. C. B. Mohr, 1997), 207.

[3] See Michael A. Meyer, *Response to Modernity: A History of the Reform Movement in Judaism* (Oxford: Oxford University Press, 1988), 82.

[4] Jay M. Harris, *How do we know this?: Midrash and the Fragmentation of Modern Judaism* (Albany, NY: SUNY Press, 1995), 166.

[5] See Gotzmann, *Jüdisches Recht im kulturellen Prozeß*, passim.

religious critique and interpretation. This protective strategy[6] shields religious ideals from the turmoil and complexity of political discourse and action. [For Holdheim, religion inappropriately slides into the realm of politics when it expresses human, contingent, and material relations.]

In Holdheim's view, the interpretation of religion always yields a political reading of events because it is this-worldly, material, and historical. Religion, for Holdheim, only contains pristine, universal, and necessary truths. It conforms to God's will and action. Politics, on the other hand, is a human endeavor and activity. So it is wrong to argue, as some do, that religion supports moments of freedom, while politics constricts the will through civic law. Precisely the opposite, Holdheim argues, for only eternal necessity exists within the religious sphere. Holdheim's biblical exegesis reveals a severely constricted view of the religious as a necessary and eternal promise by God to all human beings, and a view of the political as the realm of human free response to this covenantal promise. Holdheim dismisses entirely what many of us recognize as religious activity—the human response to a perceived divine initiative. This human reaction is always political, and must be so for Holdheim to safeguard the timeless purity of religious truth. Even in this radical displacement of the religious from the political, Holdheim plays the game of the politics of religion.

Holdheim formulates the religious and the political as general categories in his *Rabbinic Autonomy and the Principle of Jewish Marriage* (1843). As the title suggests, Holdheim limits the juridical capacity of Jewish rabbis in order to firmly place all marriages within the public, political sphere of civic law. To defend such a claim Holdheim must distinguish between proper and improper religious authority, one that separates political concerns from religious ones. Although his argument appeals to the contemporary scene, in which Jews simply desire a national identity within their country of residence, it becomes increasingly clear that Holdheim targets Jewish tradition and its representatives. He turns to sources within the Jewish tradition that suggest a strong contrast between religious and political goods. He recovers the "religious moment in Judaism" and returns

---

[6] A term borrowed from Wayne Proudfoot, *Religious Experience* (Berkeley, CA: University of California Press, 1985).

it to its "natural borders or limits."[7] [By restricting this religious moment to God's relation to humanity, Holdheim treats person-to-person encounters as part of the wider public realm of civic life.] One enters the province of the state in a "pure human capacity" rather than from a religious standpoint or concern. This sharp division between private religion and public virtue, identity, and space suggests that altogether different relations exist in the two spheres, with little continuity or dissonance. Jews could live their private, religious lives in the confines of their home and God, but then check that baggage at the door as they enter professional and communal activities. The state maintains a "universal human standpoint" because all particular standpoints express private relations unencumbered by political concerns. And this, according to Holdheim, is what Judaism teaches us. But Germany takes on the particular form of a Christian state. Even as this poses significant barriers to Jewish emancipation, it harms Judaism less and undermines more Christian claims to universality. A Christian state, for Holdheim, unites two fundamentally different categories, and so restrains both religious expression and political life. Judaism, however, recognizes this categorical distinction between politics and religion, and thereby remains within the private sphere where it belongs. Indeed, throughout his *Rabbinic Autonomy* Holdheim reverses Christian supercessionism. Judaism now becomes the universal religion and Christianity the particular, insular community that has yet to free itself from the stain of political power. Only when Christians no longer maintain political aspirations will they become more universal, and thus more Jewish. As Amos Funkenstein has suggested, the particularity of Judaism now resides in its universality.[8] To Holdheim, the separation of the religious from the political in Judaism speaks to its superiority and destined triumph over Christianity.

This separation is clearly expressed by Holdheim in the forward to his *Rabbinic Autonomy:* the religious contains "that which is eternal and unchanging," while the national and political "has to be considered according to its essence as that which is transient."[9] Statements

---

[7] Samuel Holdheim, *Ueber die Autonomie der Rabbinen und das Princip der jüdischen Ehe* (Schwerin: C. Kürschner, 1843), viii.

[8] Amos Funkenstein, *Perceptions of Jewish History* (Berkeley, CA: University of California Press, 1993), 20.

[9] Holdheim, *Ueber die Autonomie*, vii.

such as this suggest that Holdheim really thinks in terms of general categories, where the religious stands for all that is universal, ever-present, and unmoving (in short, being), while the political repre-sents all that the religious is not: particular, ephemeral, and changing (in short, becoming). This also suggests that the inner life, as the residence of spirit, corresponds to all that is universal and unchang-ing in us, while our political bodies decay in the world of change and progress. These categorical distinctions are clearer still in Holdheim's *Lectures on the Mosaic Religion for Thinking Israelites* (1844), a text published a year after *Rabbinic Autonomy* and one that I will return to later in this article. In these popular sermons, Holdheim distinguishes "the Mosaic religion" as "the revelation of divine Providence" from "the Mosaic state" as a "worldly government." All states, together with their laws and orders, "are transient as every-thing else that is human," but religion, in contrast, "can alone eter-nally remain unchangeably itself."[10] Public activity is as ephemeral as the state within which it resides. But religion overcomes the lim-its of historical contingency. The religious constitutes not the sphere of freedom, but a realm of eternal necessity immune to human pow-ers. Bodily performances are always ephemeral and limited by his-torical contingency; Mosaic religion as divine revelation eternally remains itself beyond history.

To be sure, the state enforces laws as obligations to civic norms of justice, and so they are not as fleeting as specific political acts. Even more, those political acts can endure to yield consequences well beyond the more limited historical event. But we should dis-tinguish this sense of law from an unchanging force or prescription. Civic laws still remain within historical time, and not beyond it. Mosaic religion, that "revelation of divine Providence," moves within history without being subject to it. With the abandonment of Jewish autonomy in civic affairs (symbolized by the "moral death" of the right to excommunicate), the proper groundwork for the separation of law and religion had been established: "Religion has to do with faith and religious customs, the state with laws."[11]

Yet faith and customs are as historically conditioned as state laws and, given Holdheim's definition of the religious, should remain

---

[10] Samuel Holdheim, *Vorträge über die Mosaische Religion für denkende Israeliten* (Schwerin: C. Kürschner, 1844), 38-39.
[11] Holdheim, *Ueber die Autonomie*, 10.

outside the restricted scope of divine revelation. The religious is really
a category of monotheistic exclusiveness, a kind of unmoved idea
that excludes all particular and historical forms—and so the important gap between the eternity of religious ideas and the contingency
(perhaps fallenness) of the historical and human. But within which
category do faith and religious customs reside? Are they closer to
Holdheim's understanding of law, or more like the eternal and
unchanging character of divine truths? So too, we could ask, of biblical interpretation and the hermeneutical enterprise. There appears
to be a number of human pursuits that fall somewhere between these
two extreme categories of pure truths and tainted forms.

But Holdheim will have none of this, and we can see this forcefully in his reading of a Talmudic passage in *Kidushin* 37a, where
the *gemara* distinguishes obligations to the body (גוף) from those to
the land (קרקע). Rashi notes those obligations to the body (including Sabbath, circumcision, and Tefillin) as well as to the land (a list
that includes the mixing of different fruits and the growth at the
end of fields). In the *gemara*, Rabbi Jehuda claims that all obligations
to the body remain duties for those inside and outside the holy land,
while obligations to the land pertain only to those in Palestine.
Holdheim offers this reading of the *gemara* and Rashi:

> The subject of obligation is and can be at all times only the person,
> that is, his moral personality. The object of obligation is either his
> own body or something other outside of it. Obligations to the land
> [חובת קרקע] can only have the sense that the ground or its prod-
> ucts are the object of obligation, and if obligations to the body [הגוף
> חובת] should make up the other category, then it can similarly have
> no other meaning than the human body is the object of obligation.[12]

Gotzmann reads this paragraph too and concludes that obligations
to the body are "religious obligations."[13] But this cannot be so if we
take into account Holdheim's distinction between the religious and
the political. Note how Holdheim reduces all obligations, to land as
well as to body, to objects of duty. The proper subject of duty is
the moral personality. I have a duty toward my body and those
things outside of it, but we should distinguish the object of that commitment from the person actually performing or intending to

---

[12] Ibid., 26-27.
[13] Gotzmann, *Jüdisches Recht im kulturellen Prozeß*, 208-209.

perform that duty. Human acts exist independently, as it were, from the persons or personalities who perform them. This is why Kant suggested that we can never know a moral act when we see one because the actor's intentions remain obscure—did she rescue him from drowning to save a life or to steal his wallet? For Kant as well as Holdheim, morality has more to do with human intentions (what Holdheim here calls "moral personality") than with external acts. And it is not difficult to understand why, for if morality were to reside in external acts, then it becomes as ephemeral and contingent as all historical and material bodies. If a great many of Jewish commandments concern objects of obligations (body and land) but not their subject (the moral personality), then they too become as fleeting and as temporary as material bodies and land, and therefore cannot be *religious* obligations at all, but only political ones. What Holdheim has done in his reading of *Kidushin* 37a is quite radical: he has turned apparent religious duties into political ones by exposing their focus on objects rather than human subjects. Religion has to do with faith and religious needs—the stuff of the moral personality. Jewish *mitzvoth* concern material objects, and so too the political laws of civic life.

Yet if not religious, the duties to the body fit uneasily within the category of political laws. How should we understand, for example, the Sabbath and laying Tefillin as political or historical acts? Perhaps Holdheim's bifurcation of human activity cannot account for all contingent and historical endeavors. It seems reasonable, then, to seek out a mediating sphere to negotiate between the two excluding categories of the religious and the political. One candidate to do such work is the notion of tradition. Traditions can be religious in Holdheim's sense by continuing or embodying eternal religious truths while still being fully embedded in the historical process. But will that embeddedness stain the pristine ideal of religious truths? Holdheim confronts this issue in his *Rabbinic Autonomy*, but his answer is far from clear:

> What in the Mosaic law and in the later historical development of Judaism, what some might call spiritual *tradition* or human progress, is of an *absolute religious* nature, of *pure religious* content, and refers to the relation of human beings to God as their holy father, is given by God to Jews for eternity.[14]

---

[14] Holdheim, *Ueber die Autonomie*, 49-50.

Holdheim recognizes only the "pure religious content" as an eternal divine gift. Not all of the Mosaic law and its later development
count as religious. So features of a "spiritual tradition" might be of
a religious nature, while other parts would remain on this side of
eternity, more closely aligned with human progress and historical
development. The status of a tradition still remains unclear in this
rather murky mediating ground between historical development and
the pure, eternal religious nature.

This confusion continues in his *Lectures on the Mosaic Religion* (1844).
Note how Holdheim distinguishes religion proper from human relations to God:

> Religion itself, as a being of divine origins, is not capable of being per-
> fected, educated, or developed. It is as its author, as perfect as God is
> perfect. But the *relationship* of human beings—as more limited and imper-
> fect beings—to religion is indeed capable of progress and perfection.[15]

Holdheim again contrasts the eternal and divine origins of religion to other more limited and historical relations. Persons stand in
relation to religion, but they do not embody it. Religion, like God,
is monotheistic, and excludes all other challengers to its eternal
authority. Yet for all that, we *do* relate to religion, and in this sense
may move closer to, although never become one with religious sources.
But the status of this movement toward religious perfection remains
unclear. Is it a political, religious, or some other kind of activity?

However we may describe these human encounters and movements, Holdheim has severely curtailed the nature of religion to better conform to a perfect God. In Zacharias Frankel's reading of
Rabbinic Autonomy, Holdheim reduced religion to an empty shell, wholly
subsuming and subordinating it to the state.[16] That certainly did not
fit Holdheim's intentions, and in his reply to Frankel, published in
1845 as a separate book entitled, *The Religious and the Political in
Judaism*, Holdheim illustrates well the restrictive purity of the religious sphere. Religion, Holdheim argues, never conflicts with the
common civic good because that common good itself expresses religious ideals. Yet the civic sphere in no way tampers with or impairs
the eternal and pure nature of the religious:

---

[15] Idem, *Vorträge über die Mosaische Religion für denkende Israeliten*, 41.
[16] Gotzmann, *Jüdisches Recht im kulturellen Prozeß*, 205.

Only the *positive form* and *shape* of every religious *idea* will be removed in its conflict with the civil law, which likewise has as its ground the promotion of the common welfare and is a pure religious idea, but not the *religious idea itself,* which under various situations in life gains another form. The command to love your neighbor is certainly a pure religious command; the positive laws, which have as their foundation the love of neighbor, are only civil laws which are formed in different ways in different states, both ancient and modern.[17]

Holdheim protects the religious idea from any marking or "forming." All positive expressions of the religious idea change with altered historical and political circumstances. They remain political, not religious laws, however rooted they are in religious truths. But those truths recoil from historical work. Even as religious ideas underwrite all true political goals, those ideas are neither sullied nor changed by the political. I am deliberately invoking the language of purity to describe Holdheim's account of religion because so much of it draws upon the [Gnostic or platonic sense that historical forms represent a falling away from true ideas] Holdheim seeks to protect the religious idea from all human response, activity, ritual, and textual reading. True ideas belong to the religious sphere; everything else resides within the political. Religion has no history. But how do we relate to a category so removed and beyond human response? Can we, as Hermann Cohen once famously suggested, only love an idea?

These are troubling questions, in no small part because much of the Jewish tradition concerns human responses to a sacred text composed of human struggles, fears, miscalculations, narratives, laws, and, to be sure, ideas. Holdheim's constricted picture of religion as *only* an eternal set of religious ideas is, to my mind, incoherent. Witness, for example, Holdheim's discussion of biblical interpretation in his 1840 essay, *Religious Progress in German Judaism.* The title itself proves ironic, for Holdheim dismisses the notion of religious progress. He claims quite early in the essay that, "religion does not change with the times because it is the most unchanging of elements." Only "the kind and way" of religion (its "form" or "vessel") "is conditioned and dependent on the times," and can thus form itself "according to various needs of the times and in many

---

[17] Samuel Holdheim, *Das Religiöse und Politische im Judenthum* (Schwerin: C. Kürschner, 1845), 13.

different ways."[18] Eternal religion presents an ahistorical body of religious ideas. But historical forms never damage, touch, or alter the divine purity of religion.

The incoherence of this position comes to the fore in Holdheim's discussion of the biblical text. The Bible, says Holdheim, contains "the active seed for the many-faceted designs and expressions of religious life," for it is "the unchanging divine expression for human beings." As a "holy text," the Bible manifests the eternal nature of religious truths. The text itself remains the only material object that corresponds perfectly to the divine ideas. The Bible is unchanging, but not the way in which readers interpret it:

> The *use* and *application* of the Bible covers only a *particular time*. Religious instruction, in its most all-encompassing meaning, always searches and draws out of the Bible the most fitting expression for a particular period and formation of religious life.[19]

Readers apply biblical truths to historical circumstances, but in doing so they leave religion alone—they only "use" it. But then what is the force of Holdheim's claim that the Bible is an "unchanging divine expression"? If all *reading* is conditioned by history, then what claim does a pristine, unread, and unusable text have upon me? Holdheim's biblical text, untouched by human hands, embodies religious truth. But once I place my hands upon it, read and thus "use" the text, it becomes a feature of a particular time and of various religious needs. So all biblical interpretation is *political* (or what we might call *historical*) in the sense that it remains dependent upon and influenced by changing circumstances and concerns. Judaism, however we wish to define it, produces for Holdheim but one of many political readings of the biblical text. The Jewish tradition, like all other religious traditions, reflects a tainted form of contingent and ever-changing activity.

Holdheim consistently invokes a notion of *religion* as the ground of all becoming, as the source of the religious life, as the eternal idea of divinity. Judaism is but one form of it. And so the title, *Religious Progress in German Judaism*, may not be ironic after all, for Judaism can indeed develop and progress as an "application" or "use" of the biblical text

---

[18] Idem, *Der religiöse Fortschritt im deutschen Judenthume* (Leipzig: E.L. Fritzsche, 1840), 9.
[19] Ibid.

according to the times. But what cannot change is "Mosaic religion." In his *Lectures on the Mosaic Religion for Thinking Israelites* (1844), Holdheim criticizes the Frankfort Reform community for their statement that, "we acknowledge in the *Mosaic religion* the possibility of unlimited progress."[20] Holdheim contends that "Mosaic religion" cannot progress, for it reveals perfection itself. There are better and worse Judaisms, but only one eternal Mosaic religion. The rabbis of the Talmud accommodate Mosaic religion to the needs of the time. Their Judaism, to echo Frankel's criticism of Holdheim, blatantly subordinates religion to political concerns.[21] Rabbinic Judaism proposes yet another political reading of eternal religion. Thinking Israelites, as Holdheim's title suggests, would do better to return to a biblical Mosaism. Religion is not religion, Holdheim says here, "when it allows itself to be degraded as the handmaid of the times and its needs."[22] This the rabbis had done, but thinking Israelites must return to the Mosaic religion of the Bible and its pristine holiness.

Holdheim's reading of biblical covenants reasserts this incoherent view of the Bible. Let me restate here, before we move to a more detailed reading of his biblical exegesis, the incoherency in Holdheim's account. Holdheim argues that the Bible is eternally unchanging as a principle or ground that allows for and makes possible all interpretive acts. But as soon as we seek to clarify that principle or ground —when we ask for some content or substance to the claim—we reside in the realm of interpretation. The letters on the page appear eternal and unchanging, but once read they become enmeshed in historical contingency. *That* the words exist is an eternal fact, but *what* they do or mean is a historical question. But this is to purchase divinity at the price of obscurism. The biblical text escapes all historical contingency, change, and meaning. By insulating the text from such impurities, Holdheim wins back religion from political upheavals but loses all sense of religious content. Surely the motivations for such a project are compelling, and I will say more about them in the conclusion to this article. But this kind of politics of religion suppresses identifying markers of religious practice that inform modern Jewish identity. To see this, let us turn to Holdheim's

---

[20] Holdheim, *Vorträge über die Mosaische Religion für denkende Israeliten*, xii.
[21] Ibid., xiv.
[22] Ibid.

biblical interpretation and the ways in which his reading ruthlessly constricts religious meaning.

In the first of his *Lectures on Mosaic Religion for Thinking Israelites*, Holdheim deciphers the meaning of the rainbow in the covenant announced by God to Noah. The lecture's title, "The oldest Covenant of God with all Humanity and the Sign of the Covenant," suggests that "oldest" confers the priority of a universal covenant for all persons. Thinking Israelites recognize immediately that ⌈God chooses humanity, and not only Israelites, to form an eternal bond⌋ God enacts all future biblical covenants with Israel, but these covenants reflect only a more intense form of this first and most universal covenant: "the oldest covenant with Noah and his progeny is always the first foundation upon which all later covenants are established."[23] The rainbow is both sign and command (*Gebot*), for it addresses human ethical power (*sittliche Kraft*) and free will. One can indeed choose to fulfill the covenant or deny it altogether. Yet Holdheim distinguishes this human freedom from the natural sign of the rainbow, emphasizing how the latter remains thoroughly independent from the former.[24] The rainbow's status as an independent, eternal, and necessary divine sign perfectly conforms to its nature as the oldest and most universal divine covenant. Here again we witness Holdheim's strong distinction between the religious as the eternal, unchanging, and independent truth, and the political as the arena of free will and human powers. Like its "author," religion cannot be moved, altered, or in any way influenced by human concerns or actions. Religion marks the realm of divine necessity and activity.

Note, however, the tension in Holdheim's biblical exegesis, for he offers a reading of covenant unencumbered by human endeavors. The rainbow covenant remains eternal, universal, and unchanging, and thus so very distant from human desires, concerns, and responses. Holdheim's reading, then, marks the covenant as beyond marking. To make sense of this, Holdheim cannot really be interpreting the text at all, for all biblical interpretation, in his schema, would begin from this side of the political divide. Hermeneutics is a human enterprise, but God's rainbow covenant hovers above all in its unchanging universality. The covenant with Noah as a "natural law of

---

[23] Ibid., 5.
[24] Ibid., 3.

necessity" requires not interpretation but pure translation: reason does not interpret necessary laws so much as reveal them. Holdheim merely uncovers a law of nature written into a text. Rather than a political reading, it denotes a rational acceptance of the way things are. Textual interpretation, the political sphere, and Judaism indicate human activities that require judgment, concern, and freely chosen acts and thoughts. Reason and its laws, the religious realm, and Mosaic religion are pristine, eternal and unchanging, and thus remain forever beyond human concerns and influence. This either/or typology illustrates one of the more striking features of Holdheim's thought. Either eternal or contingent, pristine or impure, divine or human, universal or particular.

To be sure, it is better to reside on the far side of eternal necessity than on this side of interpretive play. So Holdheim will not read the special covenants following Noah's as anything but "fruits" that grow out of the "roots" of the rainbow covenant. The later covenants with Abraham are neither particular nor special, but rather intensifications of the more universal and original covenant with Noah.[25] Human beings remain eternally bonded to each other through their participation in the original covenant, specified now by Holdheim as God's love for all human beings[26]—a love that remains eternal and unchanging. Holdheim claims that the sign of the rainbow existed from the very beginning, before history and the flood (*vom Uranbeginn*), and it alone constitutes the essence of the Mosaic religion.[27] But not all of us recognize God's love or the eternal bonds that connect us to God. This human failure points the way to Israel's divine calling, for God says to Abraham: "through you all the families of the earth shall be blessed" (Genesis 12:3). The covenant between God and Abraham restates the original covenant to Noah, only this time with an additional command for all nations of the earth to recognize God's love for humanity. All will be blessed through Abraham and his descendants because through them the nations will accept God's blessing of love:

---

[25] Ibid., 6 and 13.

[26] Ibid., 7. Of course, the biblical text does not speak of love at all, and could certainly be construed otherwise (for example, one could understand the covenant with Noah as a sign of God's guilt for destroying the earth and most creatures— and not, as Holdheim claims here, as a sign of God's love).

[27] Ibid., 10.

> So long as the whole human world does not yet possess this divine
> blessing, does not yet possess this pure faith and pure ethical teach-
> ing, so long as humanity does not yet worship in a purified voice the
> one and only God and serve him with heart and soul, so long then
> has the divine covenant with Abraham not yet come to an end. The
> special position of Israel to God as a ring in the great covenant chain
> with all humanity begins with Abraham and ends with the Messiah.[28]

Israel's vocation as a "holy people" makes real the universal divine
covenant with Noah. Chosen for universal ends, Israel safeguards
the eternal religious truth that God loves humanity. The "purely
religious" contains no other positive content than God's love.

This covenant bestows a divine promise without regard to human
failings and without recourse to a second party that agrees to the
terms. Holdheim recognizes how detached this covenant may appear
to believing Jews, and because he knows his audience, he turns to
what rabbis all turn to when caught in a dilemma—rhetorical flourish! The sign of the rainbow, Holdheim now tells his listeners, also
signifies "the divine light of wisdom and knowledge, of faith, virtue,
hope, love" and the power to overcome the darkness of disbelief and
idolatry.[29] To bring the divine covenant closer to home, Holdheim
turns to human concerns and desires, to human psychology and pain,
to human love and hope for clearer understanding and ethical direction. In other words, he turns to all that he has defined as beyond
the religious. For Holdheim grounds biblical covenants in an eternal
time *beyond* history and human freedom. By upholding those covenants
we return to that original time and exercise our freedom. But our
covenantal response cannot really be a feature of the covenant itself.
Even Holdheim recognizes this as a far too minimalist picture of
covenantal relationships. So he appeals to human desires and fears,
and thereby blurs distinctions between the religious and political spheres.

This is not, then, mere rhetorical flourish, but a breach in
Holdheim's strong distinction between religious eternal purity and
stained political human actions. Yet this conflation of categorical
opposites points to something more as well. If reading biblical texts
recovers divine laws and truths, it also supports a politics of religion
where human acts move ever closer to or distant from God's love.
In the end, Holdheim must interpret the text, because like religion,

---

[28] Ibid., 25.
[29] Ibid., 9.

the text must speak to more than eternal laws. It must be political too, and speak in a human voice about faith, virtue, hope, love, and the human struggle against darker forces.

Holdheim is a categorical thinker. He boldly divides life between political activities and religious truths, contingent and eternal factors, history and divine promise, human response and necessary laws, impurity and purity. When he turns to subtle variations on these categorical barriers, his voice sharpens to raise deep human concerns and fears above trivial passions, and he sweeps those concerns into a grand vision of messianic ends. Human struggles with superstition and faith, together with the strong passions of hope and love, fall somewhere between ethereal religion and mundane life. They are mixed emotions, revealing those contingent, precious, yet most essential features of our lives. This is murky ground, and Holdheim seems all too aware of it. When he rhetorically appeals to the powerful emotions of hope and despondence, he resides in a space between political and religious discourse. His categories fade, and in their place stands the preacher who recognizes how faith and hope too easily fall into despair, and how grand claims to eternal religion ring hollow for a community besieged by competing social, political, and religious duties. This, even as Holdheim's religion offers divinity outside time, beyond and untouched by historical currents.

The categorical limits of the religious and political spheres cannot bear the rhetorical weight for his reform communities. And Holdheim knows it. In the forward to his *Lectures*, he admits to the homiletical and popular tone of his sermons. He writes a forward to these lectures in order to state the "ground principles and ideas" that underlie his popular appeals.[30] But those popular statements do not always conform to Holdheim's grounding principles. His appeals to human emotions and responses to religion tend to soften his sharper dichotomy between purely religious and contingent political life.

Yet even in those popular lectures, Holdheim returns to the safe ground of categorical imperatives. He protects religion from the vulgarities and insecurities of everyday life, and the state need not fear dual loyalties from its citizens, nor a politics sullied by religious beliefs. As Gotzmann has persuasively argued, the politics of nineteenth-century German emancipation form the background to

---

[30] Ibid., vii.

Holdheim's account of religion. There were real goods to be won in public life, and Holdheim desired them, as did many of his contemporaries, for their universal and human value. [But to enter into the uncharted waters of social and political life, not as a Jew but as an equal German citizen, Holdheim required an anchor to moor his Jewish identity. If public life represented progress with uncertainty, politics with intrigue and power, and history with competing visions and goals, then religion supplied the unchanging ground of purity, eternity, and identity] There the Jew was always and forever a Jew stamped by the eternal covenant of divine promise. No political deceit or human error could overturn that bedrock. Eat their food, marry their daughters and sons, live among them and prosper. God's promise is eternal, and so too Jewish identity founded upon it.

I am moved by this vision of purity and commitment, and I imagine others in Holdheim's community were far more profoundly inspired by this vision of innocence and integrity. But the price Holdheim must pay for this purified vision is high, indeed too high for those who understand Jewish identity as richer, and more complex, than Holdheim admits or wants to recognize. As much as Holdheim champions a modern, reformed Judaism, he is also fearful of it: fearful that it will lose its moorings, fearful that it will destroy the foundations of Mosaic religion, fearful that public political life will swallow up even the most whittled down Jewish community. Progress is a universal human good, but it can be deformed, debased, run off track. Holdheim's religion, as the eternal divine promise of God's love, can offer guidance and stability for Jews in the modern world. Yet for religion to be both universal and foundational, Holdheim must discourage complex interchanges between social life and religious observance, between political power and religious pursuits, between mundane and noble passions. He must, in the end, undermine interpretation that complicates life on this side of the divide, in order to rationally retrieve the divine laws from the other. The interpretive move is a human one, unclear in motivation and poisoned by influence, history, and passion. Yet the hermeneutical enterprise testifies to the complexity of human identity as persons work through the meaning and significance of their values, commitments, and fears. Holdheim's account of the religious and the political reveals an interpretive act of protection, one that constricts the religious sphere in order to safeguard its purity from political influence and poison. Holdheim's strategy fails, and not only because it reflects a political act of defiance and retreat. It fails because Holdheim's categories of the eternal and contingent cannot fully account for the religious significance of the interpretive act. Interpretation is a human enterprise, one that empowers persons to uphold their side of the eternal covenant of God's promise. The politics of religion, for Samuel Holdheim and the rest of us, is a religious act of interpretive boldness.

HOLDHEIM'S SEVEN YEARS IN SCHWERIN:
THE RABBI AS AN ECCLESIASTICAL COUNCILOR*

Carsten Wilke

The rationalistic theology of the Enlightenment created a paradox in the cultural history of the clergy of all religious orientations: as a result of their studies, it was precisely the *homines religiosi* who often adhered to a secularized conception of religion, that is, they were in a traditional sense less religious than the average member of their congregations. The first generation of academically trained rabbis was also intensely aware of the contradiction between the demands of critical scholarship and the demands of the congregational consensus. For young Abraham Geiger, for example, this posed such a virulent ideological and social conflict that he unburdened himself in two special essays, the titles of which are telling: "Hypocrisy, the first requirement of the young rabbi in our time" (1835), and "Two different perspectives: The writer and the rabbi" (1838).[1] The pioneering thinkers of modern Jewish theology, for whom no specialized institutions of training as yet existed, were forced to resolve the paradox of personal conviction and the duties of their office within the framework of their cultural environment and using the tools of their individual philosophy of life. Their respective answers to this crucial question were thus part of their most intimate personality traits.[2]

---

* Translated from the German by Thomas Dunlap.

[1] "Heuchelei, die erste Anforderung an den jungen Rabbiner unserer Zeit," *Wissenschaftliche Zeitschrift für jüdische Theologie* 1 (1835), 285-306; idem, "Die zwei verschiedenen Betrachtungsweisen. Der Schriftsteller und der Rabbiner," *Wissenschaftliche Zeitschrift für jüdische* Theologie 4 (1839), 321-333. The second essay is dated 13 June 1838.

[2] Gustav Karpeles was referring to Geiger's essay as late as 1894 when he wrote about Levi Herzfeld: "For him, the dangerous conflict between the writer and the rabbi did not exist. [....]He has the courage to profess as a rabbi what he has learned as a writer." Krakauer added the revealing comment: "It was lucky for Herzfeld that he had a teacher like [Sabel] Eger[s] and a community like Braunschweig. The struggles that split communities elsewhere had long since been decided in

As I propose to examine, from this perspective, the question of whether (and if so, how) Samuel Holdheim sought to put his theological system into practice in the years between 1840 and 1847 during his time as *Landesrabbiner* in Schwerin, what is striking is the lopsided attention that this question has heretofore received, since the interest in Holdheim has been directed almost exclusively at his published work. That is already true of Immanuel Heinrich Ritter's monograph, even though it dealt largely with the Schwerin years,[3] and the same holds for Heinrich Graetz, whose polemical account presumably became the most important source of the black legend against Holdheim.[4] Leopold Donath, a student of Esriel Hildesheimer, drew a disastrous inference about Holdheim the rabbi from Graetz's caricature of the anti-Jewish theorist and thinker: in his *History of the Jews in Mecklenburg*, Donath claimed that in Schwerin, Holdheim, after a brief initial period of hypocrisy, raged as an "apostle of the most extreme reform, which entirely negated religious Judaism."[5] Donath had not bothered to even consult the files of his own Schwerin rabbinate; instead, he drew his

---

Braunschweig." See "Biographische Einleitung," in Levi Herzfeld, *Handelsgeschichte der Juden des Alterthums. Aus den Quellen erforscht und zusammengestellt* (Braunschweig: Johann Heinrich Meyer, 1879; 2nd ed., 1894), VIII, XXIII.

[3] Immanuel Heinrich Ritter, *Samuel Holdheim* (Berlin: W. J. Peiser, 1865), 43-265. Ritter thus devoted more than two-thirds of his biographical study to Holdheim's rabbinate in Schwerin, a period of almost exactly seven years (he delivered his inaugural sermon on 19 September 1840 and left on 28 August 1847). However, on his activities as rabbi see only ibid., 45-48, 258-63.

[4] Heinrich Graetz, *Geschichte der Juden*, vol. 11 (Leipzig: Leiner, 1869; edition Berlin: Arani, 1998), 528-536.

[5] Leopold Donath, *Geschichte der Juden in Mecklenburg* (Leipzig: Leiner, 1874), 228. Although Donath's chapter about Holdheim's time in Schwerin (227-236) offers a tendentious treatment of the topic, it is more detailed than the more recent publications on regional history, where only passing references can be found. See Heinz Hirsch, *Spuren jüdischen Lebens in Mecklenburg*, 2nd ed. (Schwerin: Friedrich Ebert Stiftung, 1997), 21-22; Hans-Michael Bernhardt, *Bewegung und Beharrung: Studien zur Emanzipationsgeschichte der Juden im Großherzogtum Mecklenburg-Schwerin 1813-1869* (Hannover: Hahn, 1998), 198-201; Irene Diekmann, ed., *Wegweiser durch das jüdische Mecklenburg-Vorpommern* (Potsdam: Verlag für Berlin-Brandenburg, 1998), 230-231; Heinz Hirsch, "Aspekte jüdischen Lebens in Mecklenburg im 19. und 20. Jahrhundert," in *Antijudaismus Antisemitismus Fremdenfeindlichkeit. Aspekte der Geschichte der Juden in Deutschland und Mecklenburg*, publ. by the Verein für Jüdische Geschichte und Kultur in Mecklenburg und Vorpommern (Schwerin: s.n., 1998), 113-135, here 123; Ursula Homann, "Juden in Mecklenburg-Vorpommern, Geschichte und Gegenwart," *Tribüne* 151 (1999), 186-196, here 190. The illustrated volume *Zeugnisse jüdischer Kultur: Erinnerungsstätten in Mecklenburg-Vorpommern, Brandenburg, Berlin, Sachsen-Anhalt, Sachsen und Thüringen* (Berlin: Wichern-Verlag, 1992), 60, has a photograph of Holdheim's official residence in the house Großer Moor 12.

picture of Holdheim's reformist dictatorship from the murkiest possible source: he accepted at face value the charge to that effect which the reactionary government of Mecklenburg had used in 1853 to strip its Jewish population of their civic rights and self-government over religious affairs.[6] Donath's partisan and sloppy research, along with the postulate that Holdheim must have performed his official duties much as he wrote, seem to have made a crucial contribution to the consensus view that today still surrounds the thesis formulated so concisely by Michael Meyer: "Unlike Geiger, Holdheim demanded full consistency between belief and practice."[7]

In the case of Holdheim, the question about the relationship between his reform theology and the reality of his rabbinic activities is made all the more complex by the fact that he worked on his religious ideas throughout his life and that the environments of his practical work changed no less radically. Holdheim was a Talmudic scholar of the Polish school, then a conservative congregational rabbi in Frankfurt a. d. Oder, then an employee of the state in Mecklenburg-Schwerin, and finally a preacher of the reform community in Berlin, an institution under civil law. The developments in Holdheim's theological system and the stations of his work environments as a rabbi[8] were not always in conformity; indeed, as we shall see, during his years in Schwerin they diverged considerably for most of the time.

As the *Landesrabbiner* of Mecklenburg-Schwerin, Holdheim ministered to the religious needs of about 3,000 Jews.[9] Measured against

---

[6] Donath, *Geschichte der Juden in Mecklenburg*, 247-257. See also the expert opinion by two members of the Oberrat, Lewis Jacob Marcus and David Assur in LHA Schwerin, LR 10, dated 17 February 1852.

[7] Michael A. Meyer in *German-Jewish History in Modern Times*, ed. Michael Meyer, vol. 2 (New York: Columbia University Press, 1997), 144.

[8] Concisely summarized by Meyer Kayserling, *Gedenkblätter: Hervorragende jüdische Persönlichkeiten des 19. Jahrhunderts* [Leipzig: Grieben, 1892], 34: "Er hat verschiedene Phasen der religiösen Richtung durchgemacht: als Rabbiner in Frankfurt a. d. O. huldigte er dem Herkömmlichen, in Mecklenburg-Schwerin der Reform, bestritt dann das bestehende historische Judenthum, wie es sich in Lehre und Leben ausgeprägt hatte, leugnete die Gültigkeit des Ceremonialgesetzes." On Holdheim's biographical data see *Biographisches Handbuch der Rabbiner*, ed. Michael Brocke and Julius Carlebach, vol. 1: *Die Rabbiner der Emanzipationszeit in den deutschen, böhmischen und großpolnischen Ländern, 1781-1871*, ed. Carsten Wilke (München: K.G. Saur, 2004), 454-456.

[9] The Jewish population of Mecklenburg-Schwerin hit its highest historical level in 1845 when it stood at 3,318; see Bernhardt, *Bewegung und Beharrung*, 37. A contemporary statistic is given by Liepmann Marcus, *Kurze Uebersicht der Verhältnisse der Einwohner mosaischen Glaubens in den Großherzogl. Meckl. Schwerinschen Landen* (Güstrow: J. M. Oeberg, 1833).

what was considered the ideal ratio at the time of one clergyman for 1,000 faithful, his district was relatively large, but at the same time provincial. Then as now, Mecklenburg was one of the most rural regions of Germany; it was only during the age of mercantilism that a Jewish settlement was allowed to take root again; moreover, Jews continued to be barred from the economic center of Rostock. The Jews of Mecklenburg were dispersed among rural communities, they lacked dominant centers and indigenous traditions and were dependent on outside cultural influences. Three geographic vectors need to be distinguished with respect to the latter: western Poland sent both the holders of the only rabbinate, which had its seat in the capital city,[10] as well as the lower religious officials who performed the office of both shohet and teacher in the countryside under difficult conditions. Meanwhile, religious modernizing tendencies radiated into this eastern periphery early on from Hamburg. Finally, the governing elites derived their political model of modern Jewish congregational organization from south-western Germany.

Following the relatively early onset of interference in the autonomous rabbinical jurisdiction,[11] Mecklenburg pursued a process of subjecting Jewish communal organization to an ecclesiastical organization that was quite different from its Prussian neighbor. It culminated in the statute of 1839,[12] which placed the religious affairs of the Jews under the authority of a religious office that stood under the immediate oversight of the government and was composed of one *Landrabbiner,* five community delegates, and two non-Jewish councilors (*Regierungsräte*). The administrative structure of this *Oberrat* (High Council), which had its earliest model in the *consistoires* of Napoleonic France,[13] offered in fact a poor imitation of Protestant ecclesiastical

---

[10] On the history and legal status of the territorial rabbinate (*Landesrabbinat*) in Mecklenburg-Schwerin see *AZJ* 3 (1839), 349-351.

[11] See in LHA Schwerin, MfU No. 9022, the expert opinion from *Ministerialreferent* Buchholz, dated 24 June 1853. According to this document, the autonomous Jewish jurisdiction of the duchy had already been suspended temporarily on 29 October 1755 and permanently on 23 September 1769. Until the statute of 1839, the rabbi was elected and paid by the board of the community in the capital; the rural communities called on him only for specific official actions.

[12] "Statut für die allgemeinen kirchlichen Verhältnisse der israelitischen Unterthanen Mecklenburgs," 14 May 1839; printed in AZJ 3 (1839), 332f., 349-51, and in Donath, *Geschichte der Juden in Mecklenburg*, 223-226.

[13] Andreas Brämer, *Rabbiner und Vorstand: Zur Geschichte der jüdischen Gemeinde in Deutschland und Österreich 1808-1871* (Wien: Böhlau, 1999), 21-37; on Mecklenburg see 33-35.

organization, in that the self-government of local congregations was abolished, and the now centralized decision-making was given state backing and subjected to state oversight. As a civil servant of the state, the *Landesrabbiner* of Mecklenburg was thus neither a mere employee of the community as in traditional Judaism, nor the holder of true political power as the clergy in Catholicism; rather, he was the approximate counterpart to a Protestant General Superintendent.

Holdheim's agency, the personnel composition of which did not vary during his tenure, included, in addition to himself, two lawyers with doctoral degrees and one doctor of medicine; only the two remaining members of the *Oberrat* came from the merchant class.[14] Although Holdheim had to coordinate his measures and decisions with the body already in the preliminary stages, he visibly dominated the deliberations and at times even opposed the collegial decision-making by trying to present his *Landesrabbinat* as an office that was independent of the *Oberrat*.[15] A particular target seems to have been the merchant Liepmann Marcus, who took the most conservative position among the six men on matters of faith, and whom Holdheim appears to have dismissed with sarcastic outbursts about his lack of knowledge.[16] Still, against the backdrop of what were otherwise often clouded relationships between rabbis and lay leaders, it must be noted that the six members of the *Oberrat* were generally on good, professional terms.[17]

---

[14] The communities elected to secular councils the two Jewish advocates of the land, Dr. Lewis Jacob Marcus in Schwerin and Dr. Nathan Baruch Aarons in Güstrow, along with physician Dr. Israel Behrends in Grevismühlen and two merchants, A. J. Kauffmann in Schwerin and Liepman Marcus in Malchin. State oversight over the decisions of the *Oberrat* was exercised by two commissioners, namely the *Geheime Kanzleirat* Friedrich Christian Müller and the *Schulrat* Christian Friedrich Meyer. See the list of names in *Großherzoglich Mecklenburg-Schwerinischer Staats-Kalender*, Schwerin (1841), 177; (1842), 177; (1843), 174; (1844), 173; (1845), 171; (1846), 170; (1847), 170; (1848), 170.

[15] LHA Schwerin, LR 68, letter of Holdheim to the government, dated December 1845: "With respect to Jewish-ecclesiastical affairs, the Israelite *Oberrat* and the *Landes-Rabbinat* form two offices side by side."

[16] LHA Schwerin, LR 62, letter from Liepmann Marcus to the Oberrat, 2 January 1843: his criticism of a series of deletions of prayers in the planned synagogue order had drawn from Holdheim "nothing but ironic allusions and humorous barbs about his knowledge." See LHA Schwerin, LR 62, letter from Holdheim to the commission, dated 7 February 1843. L. Marcus had requested that a letter from Holdheim dated 21 February 1842 should be removed from the files, because it allegedly "contains attacks against his *person*, specifically regarding his *knowledge*."

[17] LHA Schwerin, LR 51, submission by the *Oberrat* to the government, dated 28 August 1844, calls Holdheim "a *Landrabbiner* excellent in both mind and character, a true ornament to our fatherland."

The deliberations among the councilors, three of whom resided outside the capital city in keeping with the terms of the statute, were generally done by letter. Holdheim was unhappy with what he regarded as an "extremely slow and cumbersome way of doing business," since he would have preferred clear instructions about their tasks and a clear distribution of areas of responsibility.[18] For the historian, however, it is stroke of good fortune that the members of the *Oberrat* were forced to constantly put down in writing their personal views and how they arrived at their decisions. Because of the public status of the territorial rabbinate, its files have been preserved in the main archive (*Landeshauptarchiv*) of Mecklenburg in Schwerin. Apart from the letters of deliberation, these files contain drafts of the rabbi's detailed annual reports and other dispatches to the territorial government or the two commissioners, copies of which are in part preserved in the ministerial files. In this way, hundreds of pages of reports, expert opinions, and memoranda from Holdheim's own hand have been preserved. This material has not been studied before, and it offers a rare opportunity to glimpse the principles that informed the professional work of a prominent nineteenth century rabbi and to evaluate them against the touchstone of the life of the community at the time.[19] In addition, from the early period of Holdheim's work in Schwerin (to April 1845), about forty letters he wrote to the board of the Jewish community in Schwerin have survived in its archives, which are now at Yeshiva University in Jerusalem.[20]

We know that in Frankfurt an der Oder, Holdheim was still regarded as strictly Orthodox.[21] And the letter of introduction to the board

---

[18] LHA Schwerin, LR 22, submission from Holdheim to the *Oberrat*, 29 September 1842; vigorous protests from his colleagues J. Marcus, Kauffmann, and Behrends on 30 September 1842, and from L. Marcus on 7 and 14 October.

[19] A comparable resource exists in Germany only in the 457 files of the Württemberg consistorial body (*Konsistorialgremium*), which are kept in the Staatsarchiv Ludwigsburg; see Erwin Biemann, Wolfgang Schmierer, and Gerhard Taddey, *Israelitische Oberkirchenbehörde im Königreich Württemberg: Inventar* (Stuttgart: Kohlhammer, 1996). Such an inventory does not exist yet for the files in Schwerin.

[20] Yeshiva University, Archives Collection, MS 412. Professor Michael Brocke kindly alerted me to these documents, most of which deal with the community school.

[21] He had been recommended by leaders of Orthodoxy like Chief Rabbi Moses Sofer in Pressburg and the preacher Salomon Plessner in Berlin. See CAHJP Jerusalem, "Frankfurt/Oder," KGe 11/34, Plessner's letter to Löb Mendel, from Berlin, Tuesday of Paraschat Zaw 5596/1836 (transliteration from Hebrew script): "Sie erlauben, daß ich, theils ersucht, theils—denn ich könnte und sollte es wohl

before his arrival in Schwerin following his appointment in 1840 shows that he was trying to live up to that reputation. Composed in Hebrew script, the latter marshals a considerable body of polite rabbinic phrases, benedictions, and other traditional elements, and it revolved chiefly around the casuistic question of whether Sabbath rest prohibited the rabbi only from *reading* his oath of office or also its mere *utterance*.[22] Upon his arrival, Holdheim evidently held the view, expressed in his first annual report, that the Jews of Mecklenburg still had a thoroughly religious imprint and had been spared the phenomenon of secularization found in some of the other German states.[23] The report, however, noted cultural differences among the communities:

auch—aus eignem Antriebe, es wage, ein ohnparteiisches Zeugniß 'al ha-hu' gavra' ha-nifla' ha-mᵉfursam hä-ḥarīf k[ᵉvod] mo[renu] ha-[rav] Samuel Holdheim abzugeben, was ich auch bereits mündlich kᵉha-'alluf ha-yaqar ha-'adon Leon gethan. Herr Holdheim ist mir immer als ein sehr würdiger untadelicher junger Mann bekannt gewesen. Die letzern ihm angedichteten Beschuldigungen können daher nicht anders als theils ganz ungegründete, theils sehr unerhebliche sein, von denen 'eṣäl k[ᵉvod] mo[renu] ha-[rav] gewiß keine Notiz zu nehmen ist. Wir leben in einer Zeit, wo man selbst die namhaftesten Rabbiner durchaus nicht mehr ganz im alten Stile antrifft, vielleicht die in Russisch-Polen ausgenommen. Es ist also ungereimt, [wenn man] jemand[en], der ein ausgezeichneter Talmudist ist, gebildet ist, und nie in einem schlechten Rufe gestanden hat, bᵉšäva' hᵃqirot uviᵈdiqot 'en mispar untersuchen will. [....] Das Amt bildet erst recht eigentlich den Mann, und *eh* einer Rabbiner ist, ist es unmöglich, daß er einer sei und als Rabbiner dastehe—man kennt große Volkslehrer, auf der linken und *rechten* Seite, die erst im Amte die gehörige Würdigkeit angenommen. Wollte Gott, alle Lehrstühle des Rabbinismus wären statt mit doktorhuttragenden Geistlichen—mit solchen Holdheimen besetzt! [....] Ihrer werten Familie, sowie Herrn Holdheim, meinen Gruß."

[22] LHA Schwerin, LR 68, letter of 9 Elul 5600 (7 September 1840).

[23] LHA Schwerin, LR 10, Holdheim's annual report of 27 October 1841: "Ueber den wahrgenommenen religiösen Zustand in den von mir besuchten Gemeinden läßt sich im Allgemeinen so viel sagen, daß mit wenigen Ausnahmen einzelner Personen ein religiöser Sinn und ein religiöses Leben im Ganzen vorherrschend sei, und daß hier noch nicht wie in sehr vielen israelitischen Gemeinden des auswärtigen Deutschlands der Indifferentismus und Gleichgültigkeit für Religion und religiöse Gegenstände als öffentlicher Gottesdienst und häusliches religiöses Leben, um sich gegriffen habe. [...] In Ansehung des *religiösen Zustandes* ist es nicht zu läugnen, daß es hie und da auch nicht an betrübenden Beispielen fehlt, wie der religiöse Sinn, aus gänzlichem Mangel an *Leitung* und *Belehrung*, welche die Religion von ihrer *geistigen* und *sittlichen* Seite zeigt, sich auf *Äußerlichkeiten* geworfen und in gedankenloser Uebung von unverstandenen und unverständlichen, mitunter auch nicht einmal von der Religion vorgeschriebenen und nur vom Herkommen geheiligten mißbräuchlichen Zeremonien den ganzen Gehalt und allen Werth eines religiösen Lebens erblickt. Jedoch ist solche Wahrnehmung weniger betrübend als die des völligen Indifferentismus, da von einer besseren Gestaltung und Behandlung der betreffenden religiösen Institutionen sich wohl hoffen läßt, daß der in Ermangelung aller und jeglicher geistlichen Pflege auf falsche Richtungen irre geleitete religiöse Sinn sich wieder in die rechte Bahnen eines geistig-sittlich durchwehten Lebens einlenken

while the Jews in the countryside were still venerating their shohet as an "oracle," the board of the community in Schwerin had already adopted some of the regulations intended to discipline the religious service that had been introduced in the Hamburg synagogue.

As a result, what was still lived as a ritual life in the countryside was already experienced in Schwerin, in a cognitive split, as the doctrine of a confession. In his report, Holdheim clearly stakes out his position on these two models of Jewish tradition. He arranges the observations he made during his tour of inspection onto a linear value scale of a progressive development that is gradually freeing the Jews "from the ground of an unthinking (*gesinnungslosen*) ceremonial service" and is leading them to "a piety that is grasped and understood by the mind rather than being mechanical and unthinking." Holdheim thus formulated from the outset an explicit program of replacing halakhic with confessional piety. In actual practice, though, he wanted to accompany this process of spiritualization rather than command it, since he estimated that it would take years, indeed, decades, to change the Jewish-religious awareness or create it in the first place.

The consolidating rebuilding of the edifice of religion should most definitely not start from ritual regulations, which is where his fellow rabbis usually began, even though for Holdheim, too, "the public religious service is the *foundation* and the *pillar* of this edifice."[24] In his memoranda, as in his pamphlets,[25] Holdheim continuously dwelled on his leitmotif that all religious reform had to begin with school reform, in fact, that in its initial phase it had to be entirely limited to school reform.[26] He devoted his first year as rabbi above all to establishing religious schools in the four largest communities of the territory.[27] Holdheim believed that the religious life of the community

---

lassen wird. Es fehlt aber auch nicht an Beispielen wahrhaft erleuchteter Frömmigkeit und auf Kenntniß und Bildung ruhender Religiosität."

[24] LHA Schwerin, LR 62, first part of the "preliminary report" on the synagogue order, no date.

[25] See, for example, Holdheim's pamphlet *Der religiöse Fortschritt im deutschen Judenthume. Ein friedliches Wort in einer aufgeregten Zeit* (Leipzig: E.L. Fritzsche, 1840); on this see Ritter, *Samuel Holdheim*, 36.

[26] See his speech at the opening of the school in Schwerin (in Ritter, *Samuel Holdheim*, 46; LHA Schwerin, LR 10, Annual Report of Holdheim dated 27 Octtober 1841, where he repeatedly asserts that "the educational system is the very first and most necessary concern that must be satisfied."

[27] The school in Schwerin was ceremoniously opened on 10 January 1841, followed by similar institutions in Güstrow, Bützow, and Waren; see *Israelitische Annalen* 3 (1841), 55.

depended entirely on the men who filled the office of religious teacher and cantor.[28] Since their appointment was in his hands, he made it one of the most important duties of his office to maintain a constant correspondence with the rural communities as well as with job-seekers "from all over Germany" so he would be always be able to place the right man at the right time in the right job.[29] Holdheim placed great importance on the fact, quite unusual within a provincial setting, that as teachers for the four city communities he had hired "scientifically and theologically educated men," mostly young candidates for the rabbinate, and had also placed them under obligation to deliver a sermon in the synagogue once a month. In the countryside, no fewer than thirteen additional communities had launched a school program with certified teachers.[30] Despite his far-ranging recruitment policy, Holdheim of necessity adopted the government's demand for teachers trained domestically. Right up to the time of his departure, Holdheim tried, with the best of intentions, to mediate between the absurd demand that the small handful of Jews in Mecklenburg finance seminary training for religious officials, and the no less unrealistic demand from his colleagues, who sought to save money by putting him in charge of running the entire seminary.[31]

---

[28] LHA Schwerin, LR 10, annual report from Holdheim, 28 November 1843: "The ecclesiastical-religious life of the community depends solely on those who fill the positions of servants to the synagogue, and in the end, the greatest effect comes, more so than from any institution, from the loyal performance of his duties by an educated and conscientious religious teacher."

[29] LHA Schwerin, LR 11, Holdheim to school councilor Meyer, 2 June 1846.

[30] LHA Schwerin, LR 10, annual report from Holdheim, 27 October 1841. On the four preachers see also *Israelitische Annalen* 3 (1841), 359.

[31] Holdheim initially insisted on his known priorities. First, a new generation had to grow up in the schools, and the job of teacher had to be improved socially and materially (LHA Schwerin, LR 11, expert opinion of Holdheim dated November 1840, and vote of 7 January 1841). However, under pressure from the government, he soon tried to encourage his colleagues to establish a seminary: "Overly timid economic considerations have to yield to the importance of the matter" (ibid., Holdheim's vote on 7 November 1841). Holdheim's plans for a teacher seminary were already known to the *AZJ* 5 (1841), 279. His first project, which he wanted to finance with a special levy on the communities, was still quite ambitious: a seminary with four classes was to offer six hours of instruction a day in both religious and secular sciences (LHA Schwerin, LR 11, Holdheim's proposal of 21 January 1842). The lay members of the *Oberrat*, however, opted for thriftiness. They wanted to have the meals of the students provided by households offering free board, the secular education by the public *Gymnasium*, the religious education by the lower level class of the teacher already hired in Schwerin, and in the upper class by Holdheim himself, who was already obliged by the bye-laws to provide six hours of teaching a week. The plans was accepted by the members of the *Oberrat*; Holdheim, however,

At first glance, the priority that Holdheim gave to pedagogy reminds one of the ideals of the Mendelssohnians,[32] though it is in actuality part of the political context of the Restoration period. Not only was it easer to write on the *tabula rasa* that was children's piety; it was also easier to make the attendance of reformed schools by children legally obligatory than to compel the attendance of reform services by adults. Holdheim therefore placed great stock in the government's decree of 29 April 1842, which made attendance of religious school obligatory for Mecklenburg's Jewish children, and he wanted to see this obligation expanded to include the qualifications of teachers and the curriculum, even though he was fully aware of the material obstacles this measure faced in the countryside.[33]

Although Holdheim's school policy sought to make a complete break with the *"Schächterregiment"* (kosher butcher rule) of the cheder,[34]

---

asked them to bear in mind that the inadequate theological qualification of the teacher in Schwerin would make the hiring of a separate seminary teacher unavoidable (ibid., memorandum from Aaron dated 24 April 1842, Holdheim's minutes of the vote on 26 May 1844 and separate vote by Holdheim to school councilor Meyer on 20 March 1844). Holdheim pointed to his own tight schedule: "To be sure, the *Landesrabbiner* should provide adequate teaching in the religious sciences, and as far as I am concerned, I am happy to do so. However, given the other activities of my job, which are growing with the years, being solely responsible for the seminarians will no doubt become too burdensome." In a letter of 30 May, Holdheim held out the prospect that he would work out a teaching plan after his return from the rabbinic conference in Brunswick, but such a plan is not preserved in the files of the rabbinate of Mecklenburg. The communities should withhold their support even from the extremely thrifty plan, the only added burden of which were the extra hours for religious teachers in the two cities with a *Gymnasium*, Schwerin and Güstrow, and the meals for the students (ibid., circular from Holdheim to the Jewish communities of Mecklenburg-Schwerin dated 31 July 1844). Holdheim meanwhile continued to demand the hiring of a separate teacher and a reduction in his hours from six to four, possibly three (ibid., letter from Holdheim to school councilor Meyer dated 2 June 1846). His proposal to offer scholarships for attending the Jewish *Realschule* in nearby Altstrelitz was rejected by the government. Holdheim was busy planning the seminary right up to his departure (ibid., Holdheim's vote "concerning board for seminary students," 26 April 1847).

[32] On this see Jacob Katz, *Out of the Ghetto: The Social Background of Jewish Emancipation, 1770-1870* (New York: Schocken Books, 1978), 124. There was good reason why Holdheim praised "especially the educational institute in Seesen (Braunschweig), with respect to both its general-scientific and religious training, which was founded by Israel Jacobsohn, the president of the consistory who was also known in Mecklenburg;" LHA Schwerin, LR 16, annual report from Holdheim, 14 December 1845.

[33] LHA Schwerin, LR 10, annual report from Holdheim, 28 November 1843.

[34] LHA Schwerin, LR 51, Holdheim's petition to the government dated 11 August 1843, which invokes the time "when the *Schächterregiment* was eating away at the religious organism like gangrene." He mentions the earlier children's teacher in Schwerin, "the ex-shohet Moses Posener, a man of indescribable confusion and a

and religious instruction was given the primary task of conveying
"the beautiful teachings of God, virtue, eternity, and love of humanity,"[35] the cognitive transmission of a rationalist dogma was less dominant in the curriculum he devised than one might have expected.
Boys and girls began by learning Hebrew through the prayers followed by Biblical history using the Zunz Bible and the textbook of
the orthodox rabbi Baruch Flehinger from Baden; only the third
part of the curriculum was devoted to so-called religious instruction,
the "doctrine of faith and obligations," with the lessons based on
the most widely used religion book at the time, that of Salomon
Herxheimer. The boys were even given special Hebrew lessons with
school grammar, Bible texts, and the Medieval commentators Rashi
and Rashbam. They were also supposed to acquire the skill of being
able to "write Jewish," meaning the ability to write Yiddish or German
in Hebrew letters.[36]

We see here the dual tendency of basing the reform policy on
legal compulsion, while at the same time accommodating the traditional demands of the communities when it came to content and
substance.[37] In much the same way, Holdheim's reforms of the service internally sought to fit themselves into the historical framework.

---

corrupted way of thinking." Holdheim had one Schwerin shohet with the telling
name Dunkelmann fired, and he clashed continuously with his successor, Groß,
over the fact that the latter gave religious instruction and performed weddings and
Eidesverwarnungen (religious admonitions by a clergyman which had to precede any
serment in a law suit). See Yeshiva University, Archives Collection, MS 412, 22
October and 29 November 1842; 17 October, 4 November 1844.

[35] LHA Schwerin, LR 10, annual report by Holdheim, 28 November 1843.

[36] LHA Schwerin, LR 62, 19 September 1841; as well as the curricula drawn
up by Holdheim in Yeshiva University, Archives Collection, MS 412, vom 3. Januar
und 8. Dezember 1841.

[37] Paradoxically enough, this approach in fact helped historical Judaism to gain
ground, since the new regulations provided Hebrew lessons not only for boys, but
also for girls. Although Holdheim, unlike the majority of the members of the *Oberrat*,
did not wish to make Hebrew instruction obligatory for girls, it is evident in him,
too, that he was pursuing reform with traditionalist means: since the community
would cling to Hebrew as the language of prayer for some time yet, the reformist
call to shape a religious awareness could be pushed through only at the price of
teaching the young of both genders the Hebrew language: see LHA Schwerin, LR
68, Holdheim to the government, December 1845. Holdheim's wish to have German
songs in the service was overruled by his colleagues, and he was able to introduce
them only within the framework of the new rite of confirmation against the opposition of Liepmann Marcus; LHA Schwerin, LR 62, letter from Holdheim to the
Oberrat, 18 November 1842; letter from Holdheim to the territorial commission, 7
February 1843.

The statute of 1839 mentioned, as the first two functions of the *Oberrat*, "establishing the service order in the synagogues" and the "so-called ecclesiastical-administrative (*kirchenpolizeilichen*) decrees pertaining to the form of the Israelite service."[38] The implementation of these measures was discussed by the members of the *Oberrat* beginning in the summer of 1841.[39] The most pro-Reform position was put forth by advocate Aarons, who justified the need for authoritative steps against the manifold liturgical abuses[40] on the basis of the theory of inertia, according to which people by nature followed the same old routine "until they are given a goal through an outside impulse." The conservative Liepmann Marcus wanted to steer around the difficult terrain of the liturgy for now and improve the discipline of the service by means of a "church-regulatory order" (*kirchenpoliceiliche Ordnung*). Remarkably enough, Holdheim was the only one who came out against the immediate introduction of liturgical reforms. He cautioned that their authoritative implementation would not create the desired unity, but only strife and discord. By way of justifying his position he argued once again that [the education of the youth, sermons, and community work should first impart the necessary ethical and aesthetic values, so that the desire for a reformed liturgy would be felt on a broad basis.[41] Until such time,

---

[38] Statute § 13, Art. 1-2, in AZJ 3 (1839), 333.

[39] LHA Schwerin, LR 62, with the opinions of Holdheim (7 July 1841), Aarons (10 July), and Liepmann Marcus (18 July).

[40] His goal was to prohibit not only the so-called "disorderly yelling," the loud singing and talking during the service, but also prayer texts like the long piyutim, passages hostile to gentiles, and the so-called 'mi sheberakh,' finally the traditional leading of the prayer by mourners, and certain festival customs on 9 Av, Purim, and Simchat Torah—Aarons and not Holdheim had thus first proposed these elements of the later synagogue order.

[41] LHA Schwerin, LR 62, opinion of Holdheim, 7 July 1841: "Noch würden die entgegenstehenden Hindernisse in vielen Gemeinden zu groß sein, als daß sie auf ganz friedliche Weise überwunden werden könnten. Erst muß die wohlthätige Wirksamkeit des Statuts in immer größere Kreise dringen, ein kirchliches Leben im geistigen und edlen Sinne erzeugt werden, erst müssen in den meisten Gemeinden Religionsschulen blühen und an der Spitze der religiösen Angelegenheiten Männer stehen, die Sinn für kirchliche Ordnung haben und derselben, nicht den eingeschlichenen Mißbräuchen das Wort reden. In diesem Augenblick würde eine nach genannten Vorbildern einzuführende Synagogenordnung in vielen Gemeinden statt Ordnung nur noch größere Verwirrung erzeugen, und auf noch nicht besiegte, aber mit Gotteshülfe immer mehr zu beseitigende Mißstände bei der Abfassung der Synagogen-Ordnung Rücksicht zu nehmen, würde dieselbe mit angeborenen Fehlern behaften, die mit den vorgeschrittenen Gemeinden schon jetzt, mit der fortschreitenden religiösen Bildung der in diesem Moment noch zurückgebliebenen später in Widerspruch stehen dürften."

only "*introductory* steps" could be taken, namely one should prohibit the crude abuse of the auctioning of mitzvot, which most communities no longer tolerated, in all the remaining communities as well. But a few weeks later, when Holdheim was asked by a rural community to express his objection to this pious commerce, he declined to get involved. As long as no general order had prohibited this custom, he maintained, he did not have the legal authority to intervene in the circumstances of an individual community, nor did such intervention seem substantively justified.[42] It is hard to believe: [the man who was at that very time defending the expurgated Hamburg temple liturgy insisted in tolerating even the auctioning of mitzvot in his own jurisdiction!]

The influence of his colleagues, the developments in the rest of Germany,[43] and government requirements slowly caused Holdheim to change his position. After careful consideration, he wrote, he was now also convinced of the special urgency of liturgical regulation. He had found the Württemberg liturgical regulations of 1838 entirely acceptable in terms of religious law,[44] and he could therefore imagine adapting this text to local conditions.[45] To work out their differences of opinion, the members of the *Oberrat* went through Holdheim's annotated copy of these regulations point by point during their regular meetings in 1842.[46] On the basis of these deliberations, Holdheim drew up a handwritten draft in the Fall, which has been preserved in the files along with numerous critical comments from his colleagues.[47] The definitive and binding text, complete with

---

[42] LHA Schwerin, LR 15, Holdheim to the *Oberrat*, 30 August 1841.

[43] The first generation of synagogue regulations were written by neo-Orthodox men like Isak Noa Mannheimer in Vienna (1826; see IA 1839, p. 213), Isaak Bernays in Hamburg, Nathan Adler in Hannover (1829), and Abraham Wolff in Copenhagen, author of *Agende for det mosaiske Troessamfunds Synagoge i København, til Brug ved Gudstjenesten og andre høitidelige Leiligheder* (Copenhagen: sn., 1833), which Holdheim used in part as his model. Reform rabbis composed the synagogue regulations in Upper Franconia (1834), in Central Franconia (1836), and in Württemberg (1838).

[44] *Gottesdienst-Ordnung für die Synagogen des Königreichs Württemberg. Unter höchster Genehmigung festgesetzt von der Königl. israelitischen Oberkirchen-Behörde* (Stuttgart: Hallberger, 1838). All Württemberg rabbis had approved these regulations, but they had previously been hand-picked through state examinations, and some engaged in passive resistance to them; see *AZJ* 9 (1845), 217.

[45] LHA Schwerin, LR 62, Holdheim to the *Oberrat*, 6 December 1841.

[46] LHA Schwerin, LR 62, Holdheim to the *Oberrat*, 32 May 1842.

[47] LHA Schwerin, LR 62 and 68, in the latter file Holdheim's accompanying letter to the *Oberrat*, dated 17 November 1842.

the approval of the Grand Duke of 19 April 1843, was disseminated in the printed version.[48]

The synagogue regulations thus appeared shortly after Holdheim's *Ueber die Autonomie der Rabbinen* (The Autonomy of the Rabbis), whose foreword is dated March 1843. While Holdheim had already justified the elimination of the liturgical professions of national content in his opinions to the Hamburg temple, in *Autonomie* he declared that the disappearance of national elements from Judaism was a fundamental precondition for its "thorough and modern (*zeitgemäße*) reform of religious law"—in this regard, historical-literary criticism could "render a *practical* service to Judaism."[49] It is thus much more remarkable that Holdheim did not try to implement anywhere his own call "for a *thorough* and *decisive* reform, not merely a *moderate* and *watered-down* one"[50] in his synagogue regulations of 1843. On the contrary: his "preliminary report" dismissed any thought of an original, consistent, or scientific reworking of the liturgy; he was concerned solely with a pragmatic compromise, one that was supposed to reconcile on a legal basis the claims of modernists and conservatives.[51] So that

---

[48] *Synagogen-Ordnung für die Synagogen des Großherzogthums Mecklenburg-Schwerin unter allerhöchster Genehmigung festgesetzt von dem großherzoglichen israelitischen Oberrath in Schwerin* (Schwerin: Kürschner, 1843).

[49] Samuel Holdheim, *Ueber die Autonomie der Rabbinen und das Prinzip der jüdischen Ehe. Ein Beitrag über einige das Judenthum betreffende Zeitfragen* (Schwerin: C. Kürschner, 1843), vii and 35, note.

[50] This is how Holdheim later summarized the thrust of *Autonomie;* see Samuel Holdheim, *Das Religiöse und Politische im Judenthum* (Schwerin: C. Kürschner, 1845), 3.

[51] LHA Schwerin, LR 68, second part of Holdheim's "introductory report" to the synagogue regulations: "Das größere Publikum, für welches diese S. O. nicht bestimmt ist, wird uns dessen ungeachtet noch so manche Inconsequenz vorzuwerfen haben, und die in solchen Fällen kitzlichste Frage vorlegen, warum wir hier das 'bis dahin', dort das 'nicht weiter' gesetzt haben? und vielleicht gar wegen wissenschaftlicher Mangelhaftigkeit in der Durchführung der Principien den Reformirungen solcher Art nothwendigen Ernst nothwendig absprechen. Wir können solchen Einwürfen im Voraus begegnen mit der Betheurung, daß wir weder streng consequent sein wollten, noch sein konnten, daß wir keine wissenschaftlich durchgeführte Ansicht unserem Entwurf zu Grunde gelegt, sondern den factischen Zustand unserer Gemeinden genau und ernst berücksichtigt. Wir fühlten uns von dem heiligen Streben durchdrungen, die auffallendsten Mißbräuche, die dem Gottesdienst die heilige Weihe und Andacht rauben, zu entfernen, und ihm so viel als möglich Würde und Wirksamkeit auf Leben und Gesinnung zu verleihen. Unsern Gemeinden aber können wir die Versicherung geben, daß Ernst, heiliger, religiöser Ernst überall unsere Schritte geleitet, daß Achtung und Ehrfurcht gegen die heiligen gottesdienstlichen Gebräuche unsere Führerin gewesen, daß wir nicht gegen diese, sondern gegen ungesetzliche Mißbräuche anzukämpfen suchen, und überall auf das religiöse Gewissen oder mehr auf die Gewohnheit der Einzelnen, in so fern dies mit der

the educated and the conservative could continue to worship together,
Holdheim noted that "the Jewish-legal, so-called orthodox position"
was consistently "retained and placed at the foundation";[52] most of
all, no changes had been made to the doctrinal content of the prayers,
in fact, the expressed wish for the restoration of the temple and the
sacrificial cult, which was so alien to the sensibilities of the modern
Jew, had been left untouched.[53] The changes were purely external,
their tendency was "*preparatory* and *educational,* and to stimulate the
feeling of devotion and propriety."[54] Holdheim summed up the
approach of retaining strict halakhic legality while simultaneously
exhausting the modern means of exerting religious-psychological influence in his motto: "permissibility and suitability," which is in fact
an apt description of the thrust of the synagogue regulations.[55]

---

dem Gottesdienst und der Andacht der ganzen Gemeinde schuldigen Ehrfurcht
vereinbar ist, schonende und zarte Rücksicht genommen." Ibid., LR 51, Holdheim's
submission to the government of 11 August 1843 sums up the goal of the synagogue order: "To bring about a union of the existing with the needs and demands
of the majority and of the learned of Israel on a *legal* foundation."

[52] LHA Schwerin, LR 62, Holdheim to the *Oberrat,* 6 December 1841.

[53] LHA Schwerin, LR 51, Holdheim's submission to the government, 3 June
1844: "Von einer *inneren Reform* der Gebete, von einer *Kritik* der dogmatischen
Auffassungsweisen in denselben, war bei der Feststellung der Synagogen-Ordnung
nicht im Entferntesten die Rede. Hätte man solchen kritischen Gesichtspunkten eine
Berücksichtigung im mindesten verstatten wollen, was läge näher, als so viele Gebete
um Wiederherstellung des blutigen Opferdienstes in Jerusalem, woran kein vernün-
ftiger Jude mehr glaubt, geschweige denn einen solchen der heutigen Bildung im
höchsten Grade widerstrebenden Dienst wünscht, zu modificiren? Aber auch nur
die leiseste Berührung der dogmatischen Linie des Judenthums lag unserem Bestreben
ferne. Man hätte hierdurch so viele in ihrer religiösen Bildung vorangeschrittene
Israeliten noch inniger und enger mit dem Gottesdienste befreundet, man hätte der
Jugend viele Verwirrung, die aus einem Mißverhältniß des öffentlichen Gottesdienstes
mit dem Religionsunterricht nothwendig hervorgeht, erspart, aber man hätte
zugleich viele in ihrer Bildung zurückgebliebene in ihrem religiösen Gewissen
unangenehm berührt und sie gehindert, das, was sie Pflichtgebet nennen, mit uns
gemeinschaftlich zu beten. Solch *innere* Reform der Gebete, bei der eine kritische
Läuterung der dogmatischen Auffassung zur Sprache käme, muß der Zukunft überlassen bleiben, nachdem Religionsschule und würdiger Gottesdienst auf der einen,
eine wissenschaftliche Behandlung der jüdischen Theologie auf der andern Seite,
mehre Decennien ihre wohlthätige Wirksamkeit entfaltet haben werden."

[54] LHA Schwerin, LR 10, annual report from Holdheim, 10 February 1847.

[55] LHA Schwerin, LR 51, Holdheim's submission to the government, 3 June
1844: "Auch die Beschwerdeführer haben in ihrem Protest gegen die Confirmation
sich selbst das Urtheil gesprochen. Sie wissen keinen Grund gegen dieselbe anzuführen,
als *daß sie nicht früher gewesen.* Auf die *innere Zulässigkeit und Zweckmäßigkeit* reflectiren
sie nicht, sondern ob sie *alt* oder *neu* ist. Sie eifern *für* die Beibehaltung *augenfälliger
Mißbräuche* aus keinem andern Grunde, als weil sie *alt* sind, und *gegen* neue Gestaltungen
wiederum aus keinem andern Grunde, als weil sie *neu* sind."

Although their pretext was the *political* ideal of standardizing the ritual,[56] [the primary substantive concern of the synagogue regulations—as of most synagogue regulations at that time—was an *aesthetic* one focused on the basic bourgeois values of solemnity, dignity, and orderliness] The authors of the synagogue regulations were suffering from the stigma of the "Jewish school" (*Judenschule*) with its spontaneous individual expressions by voice and body movement;[57] they had no less strongly internalized completely an ideal of religious service derived from their Protestant environment, an ideal that may seem alien to us today with its stiff and compulsive ceremonialism, but which was shared back then by representatives from across the religious spectrum. It was thus Holdheim's declared goal "to *restrict* the excessive participation of the individual in the acts of the service, which strikes us as abusive," and to focus the liturgy hierarchically on "the cantor as the sole organizer and leader of the whole."[58] It was typical of Holdheim, however, that he offered new forms that continued to guarantee some participation by the individual.[59] The political and aesthetic motivations behind the new liturgy were joined by the *practical* concern to free up more time by shortening the prayers. It was especially some portions of the *piyutim* that were sacrificed; however, Holdheim emphasized that in shortening what he called "songs composed during the Middle Ages by self-styled would-be

---

[56] LHA Schwerin, LR 10, annual report from Holdheim, 28 November 1843, sees the main accomplishment of the synagogue regulations in "generalizing the progress in Jewish ritual and sanctioning it legally."

[57] Holdheim wished to see "public respect restored" to Jewish ritual (LHA Schwerin, LR 68, second part of the "prefatory report" to the synagogue regulations), since "the word *Judenschule*' was used as a proverbial way of expressing the highest degree of confusion and impropriety" (LHA Schwerin, LR 51, Holdheim's submission to the government, 3 June 1844).

[58] LHA Schwerin, LR 62, first part of Holdheim's "introductory report" to the synagogue regulations.

[59] For example, regular choir practice should "enable a large part of the congregation to participate in the responsoria;" LHA Schwerin, LR 10, annual report from Holdheim, 28 November 1843. On 9 Av, Holdheim would provide low stools on which the faithful could assume the prescribed mourning pose in a seemly manner, and he noted especially that in this case he was dealing with an old custom with greater tolerance than the Württemberg synagogue regulations; see Synagogue Regulations Chap. I, § 11e, and justification, LHA Schwerin, LR 51, Holdheim's submission to the government, 3 June 1844. The symbolic liturgical recitation of the Talmud section *eizehu m'qoman* would be dropped, in its place "the cantor would read aloud a meaningful [*inhaltsreiche*] passage from the Talmud following the prayer" (Synagogue Regulations Chap. II, § 6, with marginal comments against L. Marcus, and defense ibid.).

poets,"[60] he had proceeded more cautiously than his Württemberg model. On one issue, though, he had gone further:[61] some liturgical cuts reflected *moral* concerns, since some Jewish prayers were purged of traces of a conflictual relationship with the surrounding non-Jewish world.[62]

[Holdheim's change to the 12th benediction in the Prayer of Eighteen Petitions, the so-called "blessing of the slanderers," was the most daring innovation in the latter category. Through a minor alteration of Hebrew morphology, the liturgical curse was now directed at "evil," and no longer at the "evildoers."[63]] Holdheim's hope that this

---

[60] LHA Schwerin, LR 51, Holdheim's submission to the government, 11 August 1843. The synagogue regulations prohibited the recitation of *piyutim* on the Sabbath (§ 18 [2]) and reduced them on feast days (§ 21f, 26f, 30f). The goal of the synagogue regulations, to standardize local variations and create a "*unity* and uniformity of the service in all communities of the land," justified additional cuts in the prayers, since the shorter text was consistently preferred. What was abolished, therefore, was the daily *Šomer Yisrael* (Chap. II, § 9), the *šir ha-yiḥud* on the Sabbath (§ 11), the psalms at the beginning of the service (§ 12), the monthly *Yom Qippur Qatan* (§ 15), and the sixteen fast days *ŠOVaVIM TAT* in the leap year (§ 17).

[61] LHA Schwerin, LR 51, Holdheim's submission to the government, 11 August 1843: "Nur in der Ausmerzung menschenfeindlicher, antisocialer Stellen ist unsere S. O. weiter als ihr Vorbild gegangen. Dieses ist aber kein *Weitergehen* im *Princip*, sondern eine Folge *größerer Aufmerksamkeit* und Umsicht in der kritischen Sichtung und Aufsuchung aller betreffenden Stellen, in welche während des Mittelalters aus bekannten Ursachen solche gehässige Elemente sich einschlichen, die mit dem Geiste der Religion, der da ist ein Geist der Duldung und der reinen Nächstenliebe, unvereinbar sind. Da dieser Punkt uns besonders am Herzen lag und für uns eine heilige, religiöse Gewissenssache ist, da die *Heiligung des Göttlichen Namens* in unserer Religion tief begründet ist und von ihr als die *höchste Pflicht* des Israeliten gelehrt wird, da aber der göttliche Namen durch uns entheiligt wird, wenn wir es veranlassen, daß unsere Religion als eine *menschenfeindliche*, ungöttliche verschrieen wird, so glaubten wir es für unsere Schuldigkeit, besonders darauf unser Augenmerk zu richten."

[62] The changes concerned especially the desire for revenge as found in the 12th benediction of the '*Amidah* against the calumniators (Chap. II, § 7), in a line from the prayer *wehu' Raḥum* (§ 8), in a line in the prayer of repentance *Avinu Malkeinu* (§ 10; in Sidur, 237), in three passages of the Yom Kippur liturgy (§ 18), and in the entire closing section of the martyrs' prayer *Av ha-Raḥamim* (§ 20). Complaints about afflictions suffered at the hand of the nations were deleted from the *Taḥanun* (§ 9), although the remembrance of the martyrs in '*El Male' Raḥamim*, which had been cut from the Württemberg synagogue regulations, was retained in its entirety (§ 23).

[63] LHA Schwerin, LR 62, Holdheim's submission to the government, 4 October 1842: "Sämmtliche *nomina appellativa* in dem gedachten Gebetsstück, als *ula-malšinim* 'den Verläumdern', '*ośé rišʿah* 'den Boshaften', *wʿha-zedim* 'den Uebermüthigen', '*oyʿvim* 'Feinde', sollen [....] in *abstracta* als *ula-malšinut* 'der Verläumdung', *ha-rišʿah* 'die Bosheit', *wʿha-zadon* 'der Uebermuth', '*evah* 'Haß' verwandelt werden [....]. Die vorgeschlagene *materiell* geringfügige, *geistig* aber höchst bedeutsame Aenderung der verrufenen Formel erlaube ich mir um so mehr der ernstesten Berücksichtigung

suggested change might be adopted throughout Germany would be fulfilled—the fact that it went back to his Mecklenburg synagogue regulations was passed over in silence whenever possible. Historians have attributed the revision of the 12th benediction to either Zacharias Frankel, who appropriated the idea the following year and introduced it in his Dresden congregation without any evidence of opposition,[64] or to Abraham Geiger, who ensured that it would be widely noticed by incorporating it into his Siddur of 1854.[65]

Largely *identical* reforms would thus be rated "conservative" in Frankel, while coming from Holdheim they were already considered radical by his contemporaries. Shortly after the introduction of the Mecklenburg synagogue regulations, nine members of the Schwerin congregation filed a complaint about the violation of their freedom of conscience. It would appear that the synagogue regulations provided them above all an occasion to protest Holdheim's ideological direction and to nurse ancient communal conflicts.[66] For the leader of the protest party was none other than the merchant and rabbi's son Esaias Markus Jaffé, who thirty years earlier had already schemed against Holdheim's Polish predecessor and had established himself as a counter-rabbi.[67] Jaffé had seen the handwriting on the wall, as

---

meiner verehrten Herrn Collegen im Oberrathe anzuempfehlen, als sie einerseits die *Consequenz* und die religiösen Grundsätze mit der Praxis in Einklang bringt, und andererseits mir wenigstens die Ueberzeugung gewährt, daß sie von sehr vielen israel. Gemeinden Deutschlands Nachahmung finden würde, wodurch immer größere Conformität in den Verbesserungen des Cultus erzielt werden möchte."

[64] Michael A. Meyer, *Response to Modernity. A History of the Reform Movement in Judaism* (New York: Oxford University Press, 1988), 107; Andreas Brämer, *Rabbiner Zacharias Frankel: Wissenschaft des Judentums und konservative Reform im 19. Jahrhundert* (Hildesheim: Olms, 2000), 144-145.

[65] Jakob J. Petuchowski, *Prayerbook Reform in Europe: The Liturgy of European Liberal and Reform Judaism* (New York: World Union for Progressive Judaism, 1968), 223-225.

[66] Holdheim seems to have become the target of attacks—rising to the level of insults—In the Schwerin synagogue early on; Yeshiva University, Archives Collection, MS 412, 21 February 1841. At times the Schwerin rabbi himself used harsh language: he had to apologize for an "unseemly" statement contained in a letter to the board of the community; ibid., 23 and 27 October and 15 December 1844.

[67] LHA Schwerin, LR 51, letter from Holdheim to the *Oberrat*, 2 October 1843; Behrend commented on 5 October that Jaffé "lives in quarrel and discord with every acting rabbi." On Jaffé see *Biographisches Handbuch der Rabbiner*, vol. 1, 475. As he had done in 1814-1816, Jaffé issued his own ritual decisions and separated himself from the public prayer along with his supporters; see LHA Schwerin, LR 10, annual report from Holdheim, 28 November 1843, who confirms that "the compatriots who are not friendly toward these—even if only formal and external—

this time he also sought to draw an ideological line of separation. He solicited an expert opinion from Samson Raphael Hirsch, and while the latter supported him, the only thing objectionable he could find in Holdheim's synagogue order was the change to the curse on the slanderers.[68] Fearful of a lawsuit, the officials gave the group permission on 22 May 1844 to hold its own service in the old style.[69] This triumph by the orthodox sent a powerful signal. As the *Oberrat* complained, many rural communities were emboldened to engage in passive resistance to the synagogue regulations, the reputation of the *Oberrat* was in ruins, its income had been reduced,[70] indeed, after the abolition of compulsory membership in the community in 1849, even the post of the *Landesrabbiner* was in jeopardy.[71] Holdheim had every reason to see this oppositional minority as "driven by the impure spirit of opposition," but he did take their challenge remarkably seriously, as is evident already by the number and scope of the memoranda he penned against them.

---

improvements are not participating in the service in the synagogue." After 1845 there were also efforts by this group to perform weddings on its own or with rabbis outside the state: LHA Schwerin, LR 20, Holdheim's submission to the government, 4 July 1845, "regarding the petition by E. M. Jaffé to personally perform his daughter's wedding in his residence," and LR 51, Holdheim's submission to the government, 20 October 1845, "regarding the permission requested by E. M. Jaffe himself to have his daughter marry outside the state."

[68] LHA Schwerin, LR 51, Holdheim's submission to the government, 11 August 1843: "So ist in dem anliegenden Schreiben des Rabbiners zu Emden nirgend von einem Verstoße gegen das mosaische Gesetz die Rede, und von allen Bestimmungen der S. O., die er theils weise lobend anerkennt u. zu derer Annahme ermahnt, weiß er keine einzige zu tadeln als die Modification des Ketzergebetes, und auch weniger die Modification selbst als vielmehr das bei Gelegenheit derselben im Vorbericht ausgesprochene Princip, daß, wenn sich uns kein geeignetes Auskunftsmittel dargeboten hätte, wir uns durch *moralische Gründe* genöthigt gesehen haben würden, das Ketzergebet ganz zu streichen. Dieses Princip mißbilligt der Emdener Rabbiner und will die *moralische Nöthigung*, die hier nichts anderes sind, als der *Geist der Liebe und der Duldung*, nicht gelten lassen. [....] Es gibt gewiß keinen besseren Maßstab, die Querulanten zu beurtheilen, als ihre Vertheidigung des Ketzergebetes. Daß auch ein deutscher Rabbiner für dasselbe—freilich nur mit Rodomontaden—ficht, darin wird er unter den wissenschaftlich gebildeten deutschen Rabbinen wol schwerlich einen Genossen finden."

[69] LHA Schwerin, LR 62, Government rescript to , 22 May 1844; on this see Ritter, *Samuel Holdheim*, 257f. Holdheim's protest notwithstanding, the authorized private synagogue was allowed to admit members crossing over from the larger congregation; indeed, it was later given permission to hire a ritual officer; see LHA Schwerin, LR 62, Government rescript to Rabbi Dr. David Einhorn, 9 December 1947.

[70] LHA Schwerin, LR 51, submission by the *Oberrat* to the government, 28 August 1844.

[71] LHA Schwerin, LR 10, Lewis Jacob Marcus to the *Oberrat*, 17 February 1852.

These texts are an exceedingly interesting source on Holdheim's quest for new foundations of authority for a Jewish religious praxis that wanted to move beyond the criterion of simply preserving tradition. Holdheim initially protected his synagogue regulations with formal authorities from within the Jewish community: the acceptance of the regulations' precursors, especially in Württemberg, the good reception in "the public organs of Jewry," the recommendation they received from the rabbinic conference in Brunswick, their emulation in various communities in Germany and the United States,[72] the support from the majority or at least the "educated" at home—all authorities, of course, that the opposing camp did not accept. With one important exception, namely the moral condemnation of the prayer against slanderers and the prayers for revenge,[73] Holdheim's apologia were dominated by halachic argumentation which tried to bring out the objective orthodoxy of the ritual regulations by way of several of his typical Talmudic deductions,[74] not infrequently with reference to ideas he had developed previously in sermons and

---

[72] LHA Schwerin, LR 10, annual report of 28 November 1843, mentions the "rituals of the Israelite communities in Frankfurt am Main, Breslau, Saxony-Meiningen, which are based on our local synagogue regulations, with partial modifications." LR 51, submission from the *Oberrat* dated 28 October 1844, points to its "approval on the part of the rabbinic conference in Brunswick and its wide diffusion—even as far as North America."

[73] LHA Schwerin, LR 51, submission from Holdheim to the government, 3 June 1844. Here Holdheim did not wish to acknowledge his critique of Jewish values explicitly as such; at least he insists on identifying the spiritual foundation of Judaism also with the historic foundation (Biblical teachings). He points to one of his publications in which he had "clearly and thoroughly demonstrated the reprehensible nature of such curses on slanderers on the basis of the Mosaic and rabbinic tradition" (he was referring to his *Verketzerung und Gewissensfreiheit. Ein zweites Votum in dem Hamburger Tempelstreit, mit besonderer Berücksichtigung der Erwiederung eines Ungenannten auf mein erstes Votum* (Schwerin: s.n., 1842). In service to this backward-looking reform model, he attributed, for example, the liturgical invocations of revenge he had deleted—although in the case of the *Av ha-Raḥamim* they were all literal quotes from the Bible!—essentially to "the distortions and creations of a dull-witted and confabulating rabbi of the Middle Ages."

[74] Just as his work *Autonomie* reads a secularized separation of religion and civil law into the Talmud, Holdheim projected a modern concept of a state-controlled public sphere into the Talmudic definition of "public" prayer, that is, prayer performed by at least ten men; the main idea in LHA Schwerin, LR 51, submission from Holdheim to the government, 3 June 1844. It would appear that he read the bourgeois ideal of "devotion" into the Talmudic ideal of *kavanah;* see LHA Schwerin, LR 62, first part of Holdheim's "introductory report" to the synagogue regulations. He was also not lacking for rabbinic authorities in support of his halakhic justification for eliminating piyutim. And he derived the justification of his alteration of the prayers against slanderers and for revenge from the rabbinic statement in

pamphlets.[75] The most important point in his argument seems to be that the reformed service, as well, retained all collective prayers (*barchu*, kedusha etc.) in their strict halakhic form, and that everyone who attended service could adopt the other liturgical forms in keeping with his conscience. [While the dogmatic modernist had to tolerate the songs about the messiah and Zion, he could "conceive of this redemption in a material or spiritual sense"; the conservative, meanwhile, could no longer force the *piyutim* and curses against the gentiles upon his fellow celebrants, but he could pray them silently by himself.[76]] Elements of prayer and other ritual forms were metaphors open to individual interpretation, Holdheim maintained, only the respect for the dignity of the communal service had to remain obligatory for all.[77]

The fundamental distinction between inviolable, inner dogmatic content, and the external form in terms of ecclesiastical regulations, which could be revised in keeping with political, psychological, and aesthetic suitability,[78] is, of course, not a halakhic distinction but one of state law, for it clearly reflects the political claim to the *jus circa sacra*. As Holdheim noted with growing emphasis in his memoranda, the highest criterion of authority was the government's education policy, whose instruments included also the disciplining of the synagogue service. It prepared the Jews for the maturity of the citizen and therefore served the common good. According to Holdheim,

---

Berakhot 10a that it was not the sinner, but the sin that should be destroyed; on this see LHA Schwerin, LR 62, Reason for Holdheim's emendation of the prayer against slanderers, 4 October 1842.

[75] LHA Schwerin, LR 51, letter from Holdheim to the Jewish community board in Schwerin, 12 December 1841, with reference to two recent sermons on the unworthiness of the medieval prayers of revenge.

[76] LHA Schwerin, LR 51, submission by Holdheim to the government, 3 June 1844.

[77] LHA Schwerin, LR 51, submission by Holdheim to the government, 11 August 1843: "Die S. O., die kein *Ritualgesetzbuch* sein und nur den Gottesdienst mit *Würde* und *Anstand* regeln will, konnte keine andere Fassung wählen, als die, welche jedem die Freiheit des Gewissens läßt. [....] Nur die Würde des Gottesdienstes, worin alle übereinstimmen, muß für alle Norm und Regel sein; nur die *sittliche Reinheit* und moralische Würde der öffentlichen Gebete könnten Viele mit Recht fordern. Uebrigens kann ja jeder für sich still und leise dasjenige beten, was er für gut und recht hält."

[78] LHA Schwerin, LR 51, Holdheim's submission to the government, 3 June 1844, justifies reformulating the prayer for the territorial ruler: "Wir halten den Gesichtspunkt fest, daß man bei solchen formalen Gestaltungen, wo weder der dogmatische noch der gesetzliche Gehalt des Judenthums in Betracht kommt, nicht durchaus nach dem *Alter*, sondern nach dem innern Werthe einer Form zu fragen nöthig habe."

the uniformity of Jewish ritual and the prohibition against any liturgical pluralism was so essential to reform that the recognition of the
separate Orthodox synagogue had "*in principle* and *factually* repealed"
the synagogue regulations.[79]

Holdheim maintained that communities may—indeed, must—establish basic norms, secure them by political laws, and impose them on
recalcitrant fellow believers. That is precisely what earlier, autonomous
rabbinates and community boards had also done, and in an even
far more authoritarian fashion. Modern Jewish religious authorities
had inherited these powers, Holdheim argued, they were merely
exercising them in a more reasonable way since their decision-making processes were transparent and no longer interfered in the private lives of individuals.[80] However, some kind of restriction on
individual freedom is the condition of any legal order; and the religious conscience could not possibly complain about coercion, because
obedience to authority was not only a religious duty, but the *highest*
of all religious duties.[81] The synagogue regulations were thus binding

---

[79] LHA Schwerin, LR 51, submission from Holdheim to the government, 3 June
1844. Holdheim maintained that the prohibition against any prayer meeting (*minyan*)
outside of the communal synagogue was a principle and foundation of the synagogue regulations, without which they could not exist.

[80] LHA Schwerin, LR 10, annual report by Holdheim, 10 February 1847: "Wer
historische Kenntniß vom Judenthum hat, weiß, daß in den frühern Zuständen der
Juden, solange die Staatsregierungen von denselben keine Notiz nahmen,
Gewissensfreiheit so wenig dem Namen als der Sache nach existirte, daß man den
Uebertreter eines ritualen Gesetzes mit den härtesten und infamirendsten Strafen
verfolgte. Erst seitdem die Humanität deutscher Regierungen ihrer verlassenen jüdischen Unterthanen sich annahmen [!], der Autonomie der Rabbinen und dem Reiche
der Willkühr ein Ende nehmend, die Verhängung und Ausübung der Kirchenstrafen
den Juden verboten, erfreuen sich auch die Juden der Wohlthat der Gewissensfreiheit
gegen den Fanatismus im Schoße der eigenen Gemeinde. [....] Ich kann aber hoher
Landes-Regierung auf Ehre und Gewissen die feierlichste Versicherung geben, daß
nur unter dem Einflusse derjenigen Grundsätze, nach welchen ich das Rabbinat
verwalte und der Oberrath seine Wirksamkeit entfaltet, für alle Juden der Genuß
der Gewissensfreiheit gesichert ist, und daß wenn die Grundsätze und Tendenzen
derer, welche gegen die gegenwärtige Gestaltung der Dinge protestiren, wieder zur
Herrschaft kämen, der große Theil der mecklenburgischen Juden, welcher durch
Bildung, Humanität und Sittlichkeit auf ihre Glaubensgenossen einen sittlich
bildenden und veredelnden Einfluß ausüben—von denen ich beispielsweise nur
sämmtliche Ärzte und Advokaten anführen mag—sich dem gröbsten Gewissenszwang
unterworfen, von der jüdischen Kirche sich excommunicirt sehen und daher von
dieser sich äußerlich lossagen würden."

[81] LHA Schwerin, LR 51, submission from Holdheim to the government, 3 June
1844: "Die Freiheit des Gewissens als species der Freiheit im Allgemeinen als *genus*,
die natürliche Freiheit des Bürgers, sein religiöses Gefühl, seine sittlich-religiöse

simply by virtue of the state approval they received, and had the right to impose themselves authoritatively on all opposing religious tendencies in the interest of the "general welfare." For his work in the province of Mecklenburg, Holdheim invoked the same civilizing mission that characterized the rule of the European colonial powers in their overseas dominions: the *Oberrat* was prohibiting the Jewish mourning customs of 9 Av with the same right by which the English colonial lords in India were outlawing the custom of widow burning that was hallowed by tradition.[82]

Lebensanschauung durch äußere Handlungen kund zu geben, wird nothwendig wie die Freiheit überhaupt, *derjenigen Beschränkung* unterliegen müssen, welche das *Wohl des Ganzen* erheischt, und in dem bürgerlichen Rechte, dem Staatsgesetz im weitesten Sinne des Wortes seine Norm findet. Das religiöse Bewußtsein ist wesentlich ein individuelles; sollten nun aber die im Interesse der Gesammtheit vom Staate getroffenen Maßregeln dem religiösen Bewußtsein jedes Einzelnen weichen müssen, so würde die Wirksamkeit der Gesetzgebung im Staate so gut wie vernichtet sein. [....] Soll daher im Staate eine gesetzliche Norm, und nicht vielmehr individuelle Willkür herrschen, so wird sich jeder Bürger den im Interesse für das Gesammtwohl getroffenen Anordnungen fügen müssen, ohne daß man darin eine Beschränkung der Gewissensfreiheit finden dürfte [....], denn in jedem Collisionsfalle wie z. B. die Leistung des Militärdienstes an Sabbath und Festtagen, geht das Staatsgesetz dem Religionsgesetz vor, oder vielmehr richtiger gesprochen: Jedem Bürger muß die Beobachtung der Staatsgesetze *gänzlich* und zwar *vorzugsweise* als religiöse Pflicht erscheinen. Daß der Staat mit seinen Gesetzen nur allgemeine Wohlfahrt beabsichtige und darum nicht ohne Noth dem Bürger die Beschränkung seiner individuellen religiösen Anschauung zumuthen würde, das muß jeder Unterthan von seiner Staatsbehörde voraussetzen."

[82] Ibid.: "Bei der Anwendung des Begriffes der Gewissensfreiheit auf den vorliegenden Fall kommt es nach meiner unmaßgeblichen Ueberzeugung lediglich auf den einen Gesichtspunkt an, daß die Synagogen-Ordnung aus Rücksicht auf die allgemeinen moralische und etwa daraus hervorzugehende bürgerliche Wohlfahrt der israelitischen Unterthanen Mecklenburgs als *Gesetz* von hoher Landes-Regierung anerkannt und erlassen worden ist. Ist dies der Fall, so muß sie jedem Unterthanen, der zu ihr im Verhältniß steht, heilig und unverbrüchlich sein. Wenn die Supplicanten aber dessen ungeachtet vorgeben, in ihrem religiösen Gewissen verpflichtet zu sein, am Gedächtnißtage der Zerstörung Jerusalems mit unbekleideten Füßen im Gotteshause zu erscheinen und auf der Erde zu sitzen [....], oder wenn sie es für religiöse Pflicht des Israeliten halten, alle ihre im Glauben von ihnen abweichende Nebenmenschen zu *verfluchen* und die blutige Rache des Himmels auf das Haupt derjenigen herabzuflehen, deren Vorfahren vor vielen Jahrhunderten den Israeliten einen Märtyrertod bereiteten [....], so haben sie eben so wenig ein Recht, über Verletzung der Gewissensfreiheit sich zu beklagen, als Jemand darin eine Gewissensverletzung finden wird, wenn die Engländer in Ostindien es nicht zugeben, daß die braminischen Frauen bei dem Tode ihrer Männer auf einem Scheiterhaufen sich selbst verbrennen, obwohl sie hierdurch eine religiöse Pflicht zu erfüllen vermeinen und hieran verhindert werden. Für das, was sie in Gedanken oder in stiller Andacht beten, sind sie nur dem Allwissenden verantwortlich; äußere, nach Außen hin sich kundgebende Handlungen kann das Staatsgesetz [blotted out: 'verbieten'] beschränken und jeder Unterthan muß sich jeder Beschränkung fügen, die der Staat

It is astonishing to see how [Holdheim, the supposed champion of religious liberalization, is here trying to position himself to the right of the authoritarian politics of a small German state.] Do these hand-written documents confirm Graetz's verdict that Holdheim saw the state as a "Moloch" who had the right to demand the strictest "denial of autonomy, freedom, and every religious sensibility"?[83] That one should beware of resorting too quickly to the arsenal of polemic stereotypes is shown by Holdheim's emphatic protest against the spiteful Mecklenburg Jewish oath with which he ended nearly all of his annual reports. In fact, when he was asked in 1842 to affirm an expert opinion with this formula, he refused until the interested party was willing to accept the usual oath for experts.[84] Three years later he explicitly informed the authorities of the Grand Duke: "Should I find myself in the position of having to swear an oath *more judaico*, I would loudly protest against the violation of my conscience before the eyes of all of educated Germany."[85] For Holdheim, the emphatic identification with the state-mediated will of the community also allowed for vigorous political criticism which did not rule out the beginnings of civil disobedience.

The problem of the oath points to one of the sharpest clashes between Holdheim the writer and Holdheim the rabbi. It is well known that in 1844, Holdheim penned his famous treatises about the dis-solvability of an oath and about mental reservation (*reservatio mentalis*) in Talmudic law in response to Zacharias Frankel's attempt to accom-modate Talmudic law to modern concepts of morality.[86] At the same time, in a memorandum opposing the Mecklenburg oath, he empha-sized that the oath "had complete legally binding force," and on this point "there is in the Jewish religious texts no conflict of opinion but complete unanimity."[87] This is the only place where Holdheim, in the interest of politics, contradicts his scholarly conclusions, while his posi-tion on all other occasions employs purely civic and ethical principles.

---

um dessen willen was *er* nach *seiner* Einsicht als das allgemeine Beste anerkennt, für nothwendig hält, unbekümmert um das, was der Einzelne, nach seinem individu-ellen Bewußtsein, mit der allgemeinen Wohlfahrt übereinstimmend glaubt."

[83] Graetz, *Geschichte der Juden*, vol. 11, 533.

[84] LHA Schwerin, LR 16, Holdheim's expert opinion about the oath, 14 October 1845, recounts the case under item 8.

[85] LHA Schwerin, LR 16, annual report from Holdheim, 14 December 1845.

[86] On this controversy see Brämer, *Rabbiner Zacharias Frankel*, 308-312.

[87] LHA Schwerin, LR 16, expert opinion from Holdheim about the oath, 14 October 1845.

For he draws the conclusion from the postulate of the complete abolition of the autonomous Jewish law that [the legal doctrines of the
Talmud were irrelevant to the political treatment of a Jewish citizen.[88]]
As soon as the Jews assumes a direct relationship to the state, the
credibility of his oath in fact no longer depends on whether or not
the tossafists at one time permitted mental reservations. However, with
this call for civic equality that did not have to be purchased at the
price of an apologetic, blinkered view of the Jewish past, Holdheim
was ahead of his time by more than a century.[89]

We can see that the new, direct relationship of the Jewish citizen to the state removes him from his once autonomous tradition,
while at the same time it is supposed to subordinate him to a consensus in religious reforms mediated by religious policy. In this argumentation on the basis of state church law we detect the common
intellectual foundation of Holdheim's substantive moderation in his
reforms and his vehement justification of political repression on their
behalf. In the interest of a consensus that was objectively adapted
to the time and place, Holdheim accepted constraints on himself,
but he demanded that his opponents make the same concession.[90]

---

[88] LHA Schwerin, LR 16, expert opinion from Holdheim about the oath, 28
March 1844: "Diese Formel [i. e. the *reservatio mentalis*], weil sie im Talmud erwähnt
wird, ist zwar wie viele andere Gesetze mit unkritischer Einseitigkeit in die Rechtslehre
der Juden aufgenommen worden. Diese Rechtslehre ist aber ohne alle vernunft-
gemäße Entwickelung in die engen Grenzen des Talmuds eingeschränkt und darum
ohne alle Rücksicht auf Zeit- und Lebens-Verhältnisse stereotyp geblieben. Aber was
kümmert uns die *jüdische* Rechtslehre, da nicht diese sondern die *Landesgesetze* für uns
normiren, da nicht die Rabbinen, sondern die landesgesetzlich competenten Richter
unser Forum bilden? Die jüdische *Rechtslehre* ist nicht mit der jüdischen *Religion*, die
absoluten Rechtsbegriffe der Rabbinen nicht mit dem *Glaubensbewußtsein* der Juden
zu verwechseln."

[89] Holdheim's idea—scandalous at the time—that medieval Jewish law knew the
dissolution of the oath and mental reservation has been confirmed by historians like
Jacob Katz, *Exclusiveness and Tolerance: Studies in Jewish-Gentile Relations in Medieval and
Modern Times* (London: Oxford University Press, 1961), 50, 62. It is only the more
recent period that has allowed scholars to escape the circle of anti-Jewish and apologetic value judgments in pursuing the question about the historical contexts of such
phenomena.

[90] It is revealing that he waited to delete the Kol Nidre until his protest against
the separatist synagogue had been turned down. This "purification of our service
so urgently demanded by our honor," too, he would have sacrificed to a forced
unification with the separatists. See LHA Schwerin, LR 62, letter from Holdheim
to the commission of the territorial ruler, 15 September 1844. The Kol Nidre had
been outlawed in all Mecklenburg synagogues since Yom Kippur of 1845; see LHA
Schwerin, LR 16, Schwerin, LR 16, expert opinion from Holdheim on the Jewish
oath, 12 October 1845. Zacharias Frankel, who prohibited the recitation of the Kol

From this non-partisan political perspective, Holdheim even defended the Prussian prohibition against private religious communities.[91] When he opened the synagogue of the Berlin Reform Association in 1846, while he was still *Landesrabbiner* of Mecklenburg, he assuaged the local authorities—and no doubt himself—with the flimsy assurance that this association was recognized by the ministry and was not interested in pursuing a separate liturgical path.[92] It was therefore anything but consistent when a man with such ideas a year later lent his voice to the de facto liturgical separatism of this very same community.

Holdheim's project of a uniform community that was guided with gentle coercion from reform to reform would be fundamentally challenged by the proclamation of civic rights in 1848,[93] but it had failed even before that in Mecklenburg. None of the rural communities Holdheim visited during the last year of his rabbinate had

---

Nidre that same year, was thus wrong in maintaining that his scruples were greater than those of the *Landesrabbiner* of Schwerin; see Brämer, *Rabbiner Zacharias Frankel*, 231-232. Incidentally, the spokesman of Orthodoxy, Samson Raphael Hirsch, had abolished the prayer even earlier: Petuchowski, *Prayerbook Reform*, 337-338.

[91] LHA Schwerin, LR 51, 3 June 1844: "Im Königreiche Preußen, wo für die israelitischen Kirchen-Angelegenheiten von Seiten der Staatsbehörde bis jetzt wenigstens nichts geschehen, werden gottesdienstliche Zusammenkünfte außer in den Synagogen polizeilich nicht gestattet. Dieser einen Maßregel der Regierung ist die *Einheit* der israelitischen Kirche in Preußen ausschließlich zu verdanken; nur durch sie ist die Spaltung und Zersplitterung derselben in Sekten bis jetzt verhütet worden. Wäre diese polizeiliche Maßnahme von der Regierung nicht mit aller Strenge festgehalten worden, es würden sich die Partheien dermaßen zerklüftet haben, daß selbst die jetzt in Berathung begriffene Kultusordnung der Verwirrung nicht mehr hätte steuern und die Einheit retten können. Jetzt ist noch möglich, daß eine zeitgemäße Ordnung in den gesunkenen Verhältnissen wieder Lebensfrische wird einhauchen können."

[92] LHA Schwerin, LR 68, letter from Holdheim to the *Oberrat*, 20 February 1846: "Die Genossenschaft für Reform im Judenthum hat bis jetzt in dem ganzen Verlaufe ihrer bisherigen Entwickelung durchaus keinen *schismatischen* Charakter angenommen und ist ihr ein solcher auch von keiner Seite her zum Vorwurf gemacht worden. Das einzige Actenstück, welches sie bisher veröffentlicht, das von ihren *dogmatischen* Tendenzen Kunde giebt, ist der Aufruf vom 2. April v. J., in welchem aber, von Glauben, von positivem Judenthum die Rede ist neben dem dringenden Bedürfniß einer Reform, welche durch eine Synode erst erzielt werden soll. [....]; 2) ist das Bestreben der Genossenschaft von der 2. Rabb.-Versammlung als ein *ächt religiöses* anerkannt und der Wunsch ausgesprochen worden, daß ,es bei seiner allmähligen Ausbreitung nur solche Wege einschlagen möge, *wodurch die Einheit unserer Glaubensgenossen nicht gefährdet werde*' (2. Bericht, 5). [....] 4) ist der gedachten Genossenschaft der öffentliche Cultus von Seiten des hohen Ministerium (ibid., 13) gestattet worden, was schwerlich der Fall gewesen sein dürfte, wenn schismatische Tendenzen vorgelegen hätten." Similar Holdheim's letter to the government, 1 March 1846 (ibid.).

[93] See the government rescript of 3 May 1849; printed in *AZJ* (1849), 554.

implemented the synagogue regulations, while the board of the community in Schwerin was introducing German songs, a three-year cycle of reading, and additional cuts to the prayers in the service.[94] A government rescript now made it possible to introduce any reform with a three-fourth majority of community members.[95] Against all subsequent defamations, it is important to note that the fragmentation of Mecklenburg's Jewry proceeded apace in spite of, not because of, Holdheim's tenure as rabbi;[96] and when an Orthodox rabbi was appointed in 1853, ostensibly to repair the damage done by Holdheim, he caused such acrimonious discord that he had to be dismissed after only four years in the most disgraceful way.[97]

Holdheim drew the consequences from a general trend toward pluralism when he did not claim any ecclesiastical authority from the outset in his new office in Berlin, but referred to it as a "pure teaching position." The sole "undoubted revelation" of Jewish religion was not a consensus theology, but subjective conscience.[98] While

---

[94] LHA Schwerin, LR 10, annual report by Holdheim, 10 February 1847.

[95] LHA Schwerin, LR 51, notification from Holdheim to the *Oberrat*, 22 February 1847.

[96] His colleagues on the *Oberrat* later defended Holdheim against this accusation; LHA Schwerin, LR 10, Lewis Jacob Marcus to the *Oberrat*, 17 February 1852: "Ist der Zwiespalt in der Gemeinde durch die H. Dr. Holdheim u. Einhorn hervorgerufen, oder hat er nicht schon lange vor ihnen nach Innen u. Außen existirt? Die Divergenz der religiösen Ansichten unter den Juden hat schon lange, nicht blos bei uns, sondern überall existirt; sie ergreift nicht das Dogma, sondern hauptsächlich nur die Gränzen der Anwendung des Ceremonialgesetzes; bei uns, wie in vielen anderen Ländern, hat diese Divergenz zu einer Trennung der Gemeinde bedauerlichst geführt." David Assur, an *Oberrat* since 1848, added under the same date that "the distortions and defamations of the smaller local party of dissidents have succeeded in bringing about a completely false understanding of the work of Dr. Holdheim and Herr Einhorn, as well as of the *Oberrat*, even in the most influential circles."

[97] *Biographisches Handbuch der Rabbiner*, vol. I, 606-607, s. v. "Lipschütz, Baruch-Isaak." In an official gazette (*Sämmtlichen israelitischen Gemeinden hiesiger Lande....*, dated 10 October 1853), this rabbi repealed most of the reforms introduced by Holdheim and his successor, David Einhorn. Holdheim, then in Berlin, received a call for help from some members of the community in Waren, who said "that our innermost being balks at listening to the prayers of revenge and those against the slanderers;" Holdheim papers in CAHJP Jerusalem, P 43, 17 October 1853. In his letter of dismissal dated 26 September 1857, Lipschütz confessed that he had not moderated "the discord that existed among the Israelites of Mecklenburg," but had exacerbated it. Since he had become "an inexhaustible source of neverending troubles," the community wanted to get rid of him; LHA Schwerin, Meckl.-Schw. MfU 9022. Donath is dishonest enough to omit this episode entirely: *Geschichte der Juden in Mecklenburg*, 257.

[98] Samuel Holdheim, *Antrittspredigt [....] bei dessen Einführung in sein Amt als Rabbiner und Prediger der Genossenschaft für Reform im Judenthum zu Berlin* (Berlin: B. Behr's Buchhandlung,1847), 8.

a conventional view has Holdheim's biography heading toward this post of preacher in Berlin with a kind of inexorable inner logic,[99] the archival documents from Schwerin appear to me to suggest the opposite conclusion—namely, that [the move from Schwerin to Berlin was also, and above all, a break, a break that anticipated almost emblematically the path of "Reform Judaism" of the German *Vormärz* [1830-1848] to modern Liberal Judaism.] Modern day Reform Judaism is developing in states which either have no church privileges to distribute or reserve them for other religious currents, and it has good reason to look for its historical roots in the Reform Associations rather than in the Jewish ecclesiastical council in Schwerin. However, there is at least one reason why Holdheim's failed and forgotten attempt should interest us today: his Reform Judaism, which was anything but liberal, describes the ambitious as well as arduous endeavor to preserve the religious unity of all religious Jews in the storms of modernity.

This persistent political ideal of the *Kelal Yisrael*[100] explains why Holdheim during his years in Schwerin could be a radical thinker, but by no means a radical reformer.[101] The sources about his work there do not show us anywhere a Luther of Judaism, but rather an Erasmus. Precisely because Holdheim was more than the pugnacious dogmatic of his writings, and precisely because the maxim of his action was based on an ethic of political responsibility, he could, on the one hand, deny tradition (or in his language, "customs") any truth content, while, on the other hand, demanding emphatically that they were binding for the life of the community. In science and scholarship (*Wissenschaft*), as Holdheim put it in a sermon, there was no mercy for errors and half-truths, but life in the midst of history constantly demanded it. Preservation of the community

---

[99] For example, Salomon Samuel in his preface to Immanuel Heinrich Ritter, *Die jüdische Reformgemeinde zu Berlin und die Verwirklichung der jüdischen Reformideen innerhalb derselben* (Berlin: W. J. Peiser, 1902), 28: "Die ersehnte Ernte reifte in der jüdischen Reformgemeinde; da war das neue ceremoniebefreite Judentum, das ihm vorgeschwebt hatte, und das er in Gottesdienst, Schule und Haus verwirklicht sehen wollte."

[100] LHA Schwerin, LR 10, 27 October 1841, with a telling account of the successful reforms in Bützow: "Gotteshaus, Vorbeter, Knabenchor und Predigt bilden in gedachter Gemeinde ein schönes harmonisches Ganze, dessen schönster Schmuck der *Friede* ist."

[101] More accurate is the *Encyclopaedia Judaica* (vol. 8: col. 818), which speaks of "slight reforms."

of Israel ranked higher than the zeal for truth, he concluded on the pulpit in Schwerin: "it is better that we proceed forward *slowly* but in unison."[102]

---

[102] Samuel Holdheim, *Der glaubensvolle Muth des israelitischen Volkshirten dem Murren seiner Gemeinde gegenüber* (Schwerin: Kürschner, 1844), 12-13. While the present paper was in print, its topic was dealt with by Dirk Drewelow, *Das Landesrabbinat des Reformers Samuel Holdheim in Großherzogtum Mecklenburg-Schwerin (1840–47)*, Phil. Diss, University of Rostock, 2003. I am grateful to Dr. Klaus Hermann for calling my attention to this unpublished study. Drewelow ackowledges the gap between Holdhiem's ideas and his actions (240), but he argues that the *Landrabbiner*'s redicality was hampered by mainly by the opposition of the Mecklenburg government, which became more conservative during the reign of Friedrich Franz II (208). In February 1846, Holdheim indeed demanded that the synagugue order should include twenty far-reaching liturgical reforms recommended by the Frankfurt Rabbinical Assembly; the government, however, turned down his proposal and left the realization of these reforms to the decision of each community (198-199).

HOLDHEIM'S ATTITUDE TOWARDS KARAISM AS EXPOUNDED IN THE *MA'AMAR HA-'ISHUT*

Katrien de Graef

Apart from many works in German, Holdheim wrote only one work in Hebrew, *Ma'amar ha-'Ishut* ("Essay on Personal Status"), a historical work, published in Berlin posthumously in 1861. Although known under the short title *Ma'amar ha-'Ishut*, it bears a rather long title and subtitle: *Ma'amar ha-'Ishut. 'Al Tekhunat ha-Rabbanim ve-ha-Kara'im—kolel Khakirot Shonot be-Makhalkot ha-Tsedokim ve-ha-Perushim ha-Kara'im ve-ha-Rabbanim 'al Zmanem ve-Sibbot Toldotem* ("Essay on Personal Status. On the Habits of Rabbanites and Karaites—including Various Studies on the Controversies between Sadducees and Pharisees (on the one hand) and Karaites and Rabbanites (on the other) on their Time and Causes of their History"). Indeed, it is not a treatise on the matter of *'ishut* in Jewish Law only. The first part deals in one way or another with "Personal Status," but in the final chapters, Holdheim explores the different opinions and practices within the Rabbanite and Karaite traditions in general, which, in turn, leads him to a discussion of the controversy between Sadducees and Pharisees as the basis of the differences between Rabbanites and Karaites. In these last chapters, we are witness of a discussion between Samuel Holdheim and a contemporary scholar, Salomon Judah Loeb Rapoport (1790-1867) on the origins of Karaite religion. Further on, we shall have a closer look at the difference of opinion between Holdheim and Rapoport on the origin of Karaite Judaism, a divergence of views which is to be situated in the greater discussion on Karaism within the "reformation" of Judaism in nineteenth-century Germany.

1. *Holdheim and the* Ma'amar ha-'Ishut

The *Ma'amar ha-'Ishut* is the only book Holdheim wrote in Hebrew.
Nobody knows exactly why he did that. One year before his death,
Holdheim expressed to his friend and former disciple David Einhorn[1]
the hope that with this Hebrew work, he would reach the Hebrew-
reading public[2]; this might certainly have been a reason. Whatever
the case may be, it shows us Holdheim as a highly-skilled talmudist, who had acquired an extraordinary command of the Talmud
and Rabbinical literature, and a remarkable versatility in dialectics
and the art of discussion. This does not surprise us: being born in
the pre-modern closed world of Polish Jewry,[3] Holdheim received
an exclusively talmudic education and remained untouched by the
ideas of the *Haskalah* during his youth. Nevertheless, although he
started as *yeshivah bokher* from the East, Holdheim became Germany's
most revolutionary and controversial Reform rabbi.[4]

Holdheim's main thesis was the separation of the binding religious-ethical content of Judaism from its political and national content, which should not be binding since Jews are citizens of the
countries in which they are living.[5] According to Holdheim's view,

---

[1] David Einhorn (1809-1879) succeeded Holdheim in 1847 as Chief Rabbi of
Mecklenburg-Schwerin; in 1852 he became Rabbi of the Reform congregation of
Budapest, which was closed two months later by the government. Denied any
chances in Europe, Einhorn emigrated to America. See Christian Wieses's article
in this volume; and see *EJ* sub Einhorn, David.

[2] See David Einhorn, "Samuel Holdheim," *Sinai* 5 (1860), 296, cited in Michael
A. Meyer, "'Most of My Brethren Find Me Unacceptable': The Controversial
Career of Rabbi Samuel Holdheim," *JSS* 9 (2003), no. 3, 1-19, particularly 13.

[3] Holdheim was born in 1806 in Kempno near Poznan in Poland, which became
part of the East Prussian province of Posen shortly before his birth in 1793.

[4] For Holdheim's life, works and views in general, see Immanuel Heinrich
Ritter, *Samuel Holdheim, sein Leben und seine Werke (= Geschichte der jüdischen Reformation
III)* (Berlin: W. J. Peiser, 1865); Georg Salzberger, "Samuel Holdheim. Ein
Vorkämpfer der Reform im Judentum," *Emuna* 7 (1972), 254-259; Jacob J.
Petuchowski, "Abraham Geiger and Samuel Holdheim. Their Differences in
Germany and Repercussions in America", *LBIYB* 22 (1977), 139-159; Maurice H.
Hayoun, "Samuel Holdheim (1806-1860), un rabbin adversaire du Talmud," *Revue
des Études Juives* 105 (1992), 283-288; Michael A. Meyer, *Response to Modernity. A
History of the Reform Movement in Germany* (Detroit: Wayne State University Press,
1988), 77-84; idem, "'Most of My Brethren Find Me Unacceptable"; and see *EJ*
sub Holdheim, Samuel.

[5] This idea is already expressed in *Mishnah Kiddushin* 1,9: "Every precept which
is dependent on the land (Palestine); and that which is not dependent on the land
is practised both within and without the land (in the diaspora), except 'orlah and

rabbinic Judaism was based on an error, viz. the misunderstanding of the destruction of the Temple in 70 CE. To show that the talmudic view was far removed from contemporary conceptions, Holdheim tried to create a "usable past," in order to justify his own program of reform. From its very start, Judaism had been a developing and progressive phenomenon, undergoing various stages of transformation in response to environmental and historical challenges, i.e. what Geiger called "Tradition," the second period in the evolution of Judaism after the "Revelation" that brought the Bible into being.[6] Yet, until the eigteenth century, Jews regarded their religion as eternal and unchanging, especially since the codification of Jewish Law by Joseph Caro – the *Shulḥan 'arukh* – in the sixteenth century. Holdheim, therefore, questioned the unity of Written and Oral Law as equal components of Revelation, and insisted on restoring the Jewish chain of adaptation and evolution of the Written Law according to the needs of contemporary society. Nevertheless, although a severe critic of the Talmud, Holdheim himself remained a talmudist, as appears not only from the *Ma'amar ha-'Ishut*, but also from his sermons which are richly illustrated with *halakhic* and *aggadic* Talmud passages, quoted in the original Aramaic and Hebrew.[7]

It goes without saying that the *Ma'amar ha-'Ishut* is of great importance for the understanding and analysis of both Holdheim's ideology and person. Simon Bernfeld, in his 1900 *Toledot ha-Reformatsion ha-Datit be-Yisrael*, expressed his conviction that Holdheim's *Ma'amar ha-'Ishut* should be considered to be part of the canon of *Wissenschaft des Judentums;* consequently, he referred to Holdheim using the acronym Ra"Š (=Rav Šmu'el) Holdheim (ר"ש האלדהים), thus placing him within the traditional chain of Rabbis.[8] Moreover, this work contributes largely to a reconsideration of the so called "mephistophelian temperament" of a man who was, by some

---

kilayim. R. Eleazar said: *hadash* too" (translation taken from *Soncino Classics Collection* [Chicago: Davka Corporation, 1991-1996], *Talmud Kiddushin* 36b-37a). For Holdheim, however, the Rabbinic discussion on this *Mishnah* passage (*Talmud Kiddushin* 37b-39b) was not very consistent and did not go far enough, as he stated in his *Ueber die Autonomie der Rabbinen* (Schwerin: C. Kürschner, 1843); see Petuchowski, "Abraham Geiger and Samuel Holdheim," 144.

[6] See ibid., 141 and Meyer, *Response to Modernity*, 3-9.

[7] See Petuchowski, "Abraham Geiger and Samuel Holdheim," 148.

[8] Simon Bernfeld, *Toledot ha-Reformatsion ha-Datit be-Yisrael* (Cracow: Achiasaf, 1900), 181; and see Meyer, "'Most of My Brethren Find Me Unacceptable'", 12-13.

contemporaries, considered "the greatest enemy of Judaism since Paul of Tarsus."[9]

Before focusing on some specific passages in chapter IX, in which Holdheim treats Rapoport's views in the debate on the Karaites, we shall give a short survey on the content of Holdheim's only Hebrew work.

As a good historian, Holdheim starts at the very beginning, dealing first with the meaning of matrimony and celibacy in the Laws of Israel and the descendants of Noah.[10] In the second chapter, he deals with the controversy between the *Beth Shammai* and the *Beth Hillel* on divorce (מחלוקת ב"ש וב"ה בנרושין). Here, we are witnesses of Holdheim's "feminist" character,[11] since he reflects upon the historical dispute between the two aforementioned schools of exposition of the Oral Law on the exact meaning of the rabbinical statement that *"whosoever divorces his first wife, even the altar shed tears"* and therefore she should not be divorced unless *"he found something obnoxious about her."*[12] At the same time, he treats divorce on the grounds of adultery by the wife in matters of *'ervah* (nakedness, incest, shame and prostitution) and her rights to remarry as stated in the Law, and brings up a new argument on the intention of the Law which binds the man to set free his divorced wife to remarry.

In his third chapter, Holdheim declares himself clearly an opponent of the Talmud, the Oral Law. He discusses the topic (God's) Word *versus* the Will of (God's) Word (דבר נגד רצון ד') within the existing practice, and puts the principle of the Talmud against his own. He also deals with the separation of "Traditional Law" (*Halakha*) and "Practice," confronting the vision of some of the wise men of his generation in this matter with his own. In the fourth chapter, Holdheim

---

[9] Heinrich Graetz, *History of the Jews*, vol. 5: *From the Chmielnicki Persecution (1648 CE) to the Period of Emancipation in Central Europe (c. 1870 CE)* (Philadelphia: JPS, 1895), 680: "Since Paul of Tarsus, Judaism had not experienced such an enemy from within, who tried to shake the entire structure down to its foundations."

[10] *'inyan ha-'ishut ve-ha-she'ar ba-sar le-yisra'el u-li-vney noaḥ.*

[11] Holdheim can indeed be seen as a pioneer of Jewish "feminism." Also from his earlier German works it becomes clear that he considered Jewish laws pertaining to marriage unacceptable to contemporary moral standards because of the lower religious status of women in talmudic Judaism, compared to that of men. See Meyer, "'All my Brethren Find Me Unacceptable," 8-9 with references to the original passages by Holdheim.

[12] See Talmud tractates Gittin 90b and Sanhedrin 22a.

sheds further light on the theories, opinions and practices of the
Sadducees on the one hand, and the Christians on the other, in the
matter of divorce.[13] Hereafter, he discusses the debates of Rabban
Johanan ben Zakkai, the leading *tanna* at the end of the Second
Temple Period and the years following the destruction of the Temple,
who clashed openly with the sons of high priestly families who had
concentrated in their hand communal and political power.

Chapter five discusses the testimony of Karaite Law on the Law
of the Sadducees in the matter of matrimony and divorce and explains
the difference between the Karaite Law and the Rabbanite Law as
shown in their writings.[14] In addition to these reflections on marriage, divorce and celibacy in Jewish Law, where the opinions and
convictions of various traditions—Rabbanite, Karaite and Sadducean
—are confronted, Holdheim delves deeper into the fundamental differences between and practices within the Rabbanite and Karaite
traditions, which leads him to a discussion of the controversy between
Sadducees and Pharisees as the basis of these diverging views.

In his sixth chapter, he deals with the opinions of the Sadducees on
the one hand, and the Pharisees on the other, in the matter of revival
and reprisal of "The World to Come" (העולם הבא), treating at the same
time the distribution of the visions of the Oral Law. In the seventh
chapter, this subject is continued with a discussion of *Tosafot* stating
that it was the controversy in the "Tradition" (*Qabbalah*)[15] that caused
the Pharisean belief in and the Sadducean denial of the resurrection
of the dead and the recompense in "The World to Come"; this then
leads Holdheim to treat the appearance of old customs of the Sadducees
in the Pharisean theology[16] as well as the testimony of the Italian his-
toriographer, physician and philologist Joseph ha-Kohen (1496-1578)
about the leanness of the Sadducees with regard to the supervision or
restriction of God's Word upon humankind.[17] In chapter eight, Holdheim
discusses the history and origin of the controversy between both sects.

---

[13] *da'at ha-tsedoqim ve-ha-notsrim be-'inyan gerushin.*

[14] *'edut torat ha-qara'im 'al torat ha-tsedoqim be-'inyan 'ishut ve-gerushin ve-ha-hevdel she-yesh
'odotem ben torat ha-qara'im le-torat ha-rabanim.*

[15] *Qabbalah* is here to be understood as "post-Mosaic Scriptures" in contrast to
the *Torah* or *Torat Mosheh.*

[16] *hemshekh ha-'inyan ba-tosafot be'ur, she-ha-mahaloqet ba-qabalah haytah ha-sibah le-'emunat
ha-perushim u-li-khfirat ha-tsedoqim bi-thiyat ha-metim u-bi-gmul la-'olam ha-ba'.*

[17] *'edut yosef ha-kohen 'al kehush ha-tsedoqim ba-hashgahah 'o bi-gzerah me-et davar 'al bney'
adam.*

He also comes up with a new commentary on the *Baraitha ha-Kiddushin* 66-71, describing the practice of the wise men during the reign of Yannai the king, i.e., Johanan Hyrcanus, the high priest.[18]

In his ninth chapter, Holdheim discusses the history of the Karaites in great length and comments upon their theology, essence and origin from the Second Temple Period onwards. Further on, he expounds Rabbi Judah ha-Levi's view on Karaite history[19] and subjects the latter's work to a thorough research. Finally, he discusses the opinion of a contemporary scholar, Salomon Judah Loeb Rapoport, on the renewal of Karaite religion by 'Anan and responds to Rapoport's ideas.[20] In his tenth and last chapter, he again discusses the opinion of a contemporary scholar, Abraham Geiger, on the importance of the differences between Sadducees and Pharisees in relation to the Torah of the Karaites.[21] Holdheim attempts to refute Geiger's opinion on the nature of the controversy between the Sadducees and the Pharisees, and defends the traditional thesis that the principle in dispute was whether interpretation of the Bible should be based on the primary meaning (Sadducees) as opposed to midrashic exegesis (Pharisees). After examining some peculiarities of Karaite doctrine, Holdheim ends this chapter with a new commentary on the controversy between *Hillel ha-Bavli* (Hillel the Babylonian[22]) and the *Bne B'terah* (Sons of B'terah[23]).

---

[18] *be'ur ḥadash 'all ha-baraytah ꜣꜣ-zḥyu ba-ma'aseh she-'era' la-ḥakhamim 'im yana'i ha-melekh hu' yoḥanan hurqanus kohen gadol.*

Johanan Hycarnus, son of Simeon the Hasmonean, was ethnarch of Judea and high priest from 135 till 104 BCE.

[19] The poet and religious philosopher Judah ha-Levi's (before 1075-1141) views on Karaism are written in his Arabic volume entitled *Kitab al-Hujja wa-al-Dahl fi Nasr al-Din al-Dhalil* (The Book of Argument and Proof in defense of the Despised Faith), which was translated into Hebrew in the middle of the twelfth century by Judah ibn Tibbon. This work is more commonly known as *Sefer ha-Kuzari* (Book of the Kuzari), called after the king of the Khazars whose conversion to Judaism provides the literary framework of the work. In one of his letters, Judah ha-Levi states that he was prompted to write this book by having to answer questions posed by a Karaite; see Masha Itzhaki, *Juda Halévi. D'Espagne à Jérusalem 1075-1141* (Paris: Michel, 1997), 83-100. See *EJ* sub Judah Halevi.

[20] *khaqirah bizman ve-sibot toldot ha-qara'im. da'at ha-qara'im 'etsmem 'al qadmutem mi-yemey bet sheni. shitat rabbi yehudah halevi ve-khaqirotenu 'al davrav. da'at ḥoqer 'eḥad mi-ḥoqrey zmanenu 'al ha-hithadshut dat ha-qara'im me-'anan u-tshuvatenu 'alav.*

[21] For the difference in opinion between Samuel Holdheim and Abraham Geiger in different matters, see Petuchowski, "Abraham Geiger and Samuel Holdheim."

[22] I.e. *Hillel ha-Zaken* (Hillel the Elder), one of the greatest *tannaim* (end of first century B.C.E—beginning first century C.E). Since he was a native from Babylonia, he is sometimes referred to as "Hillel the Babylonian." See *EJ* sub Hillel (the Elder).

[23] The *Bne B'terah* were members of a scholarly Jewish family, prominent from

2. Holdheim and Karaism

For a full understanding of the discussion on Karaism within the nineteenth-century German Reform movement in general and Holdheim's ideas hereon in particular, we shall dwell shortly upon the origin and history of Karaism in general. Of special importance for us is the nineteenth-century Karaite separatist movement in Russia and Lithuania—the latter being Holdheim's spiritual homeland—which led to a general integration and even assimilation of the Karaite Jews in their Christian environment, a status which surprisingly resembles the status Holdheim envisioned for the Jewish population of Germany.[24]

As a result of various heterodox trends in Babylonian-Persian Jewry, the Karaite sect, originally known as 'Ananites, was founded in the eighth century CE by 'Anan ben David.[25] Yet, Holdheim and other nineteenth-century scholars trace the origin of the sect to the first split among the Jewish people at the time of Jeroboam (ca. 928-907 BCE), where the foundation of the schism between Sadducees and Pharisees was laid. This schism was mainly based on their attitudes toward the Torah. The Pharisees assigned to the Oral Law a place side by side with the written Torah, whereas the Sadducees refused to accept any precept as binding unless it was based directly on the written Torah. After the destruction of the Temple in 70 CE, the Sadducees—whose whole power and *raison d'être* were bound up with the Temple cult—ceased to exist as a group.

The Karaites saw themselves partly as descendants of the Sadducees: *"The true Law had subsequently been preserved by the Sadducees, whose leader*

the first century BCE to the second century CE. The family, much favoured by Herod, is said to be named after the city of Bathyra, a place in the toparchy of Batanea (i.e. Bashan, east of the Golan), founded by Jewish military settlers from Babylonia. See *EJ* sub Bathyra, sons of.

[24] See Nathan Schur, *History of the Karaites* (Frankfurt am Main: Lang, 1992), 13-76. See *EJ* sub Karaites.

[25] Following Yoram Erder, "Early Karaite Conceptions about Commandments given before the Torah," *Proceedings of the American Academy for Jewish Research* 60 (1994), 101-140, particularly 102-103, Karaism is to be considered as one of the important results of the cultural encounter between Judaism and Islam: as it came to face with Islam in the eighth century, Jewish thought developed new concepts. It appears from various writings that the early Karaites were aware of this Muslim influence: writing in Judaeo-Arabic, they borrowed terms from Muslim theology. For the interpretation of Karaism having its origin in Islam (or more particularly in Shi'ism as stated by Rapoport), see *infra*.

Zadok had discovered a portion of the truth, while the discovery of the whole truth was the achievement of the exilarch 'Anan ben David," thus Al-Qirqisānī.[26] Indeed, the basic doctrine of Karaism is the recognition of the written Torah as the sole and immediate source of religious Law, to the exclusion of the Oral Law. Since a religion based on revelation cannot tolerate the complete exclusion of a tradition, either in principle or in practice, the Karaite demand for a return to Torah should be taken as a theoretical watchword, directed not against all tradition, but specifically against the rabbinical tradition. The Karaites themselves also developed a tradition, described by them as *Sevel ha-Jerushah* (סבל הירשה), or "Yoke of Inheritance," consisting of doctrines and usages which, although not always found in the Bible, were accepted as binding by the entire community, i.e. the *'edah* (עדה)—corresponding to the Muslim term *ijmā* (consensus). At the end of the eleventh century, Karaite activity in Israel came to an abrupt end as the result of the First Crusade (1099 CE), with the centre of Karaite intellectual activity shifting to Europe. In the second half of the thirteenth-century, Karaism in the Byzantine Empire entered a new period of spiritual florescence. In the fifteenth and sixteenth centuries, even a rapprochement took place between Karaite and Rabbanite Jews due to the conquest of the Byzantine Empire by the Turks.

In the seventeenth and eighteenth centuries, Karaite activity shifted at first to Crimea[27] and Lithuania, and from there Karaites spread to other towns in Volhynia, Podolia and Galicia.[28] These Polish-Lithuanian Karaites benefited from their contact with the Rabbanite Jews in that area, which led to a period of spiritual renaissance. In the same period, treaties on Karaism and its major differences with Rabbanite Judaism, as well as polemics against Rabbanite Judaism and Christianity were written by Karaite scholars such as Solomon ben Aaron Troki and Mordecai ben Nisan Kukizow. Yet, at the

---

[26] Abū Yūsuf Ya'qūb ibn Ishaq Al-Qirqisānī in his *Kitāb al-Anwār wa-'l-Marāqib* (The Book of Lights and Look-outs), tenth century C.E.

[27] Cf. Schur, *History of the Karaites*, 104-107. The existence of individual Karaites—sectarians among the Turkish nomads occupying parts of southern Russia—in Crimea—is traced back to the twelfth century. At the end of the fourteenth century, Grand Duke Witold of Lithuania, after defeating the Tatars in 1392, carried a large group of Tatar prisoners, including some Karaite families, to Troki (near Vilna), Lutsk and Halicz, and settled them there.

[28] On Karaite presence in Galicia, see Philip E. Miller, "Evidence of a Previously Undocumented Karaite Presence in Galicia," *Studies in Bibliography and Booklore* 17 (1989), 36-42.

time of the Chmielnicki massacres in 1648, the Karaites, for the most part, suffered the same fate as the Rabbanite Jews.

A new epoch in the history of the Karaites, leading to the Karaite *Haskalah* and the legal separation from the Rabbanites under Russian rule in the nineteenth century[29] was opened by the incorporation of Crimea (in 1783) and Lithuania (in 1793) into Russia. Until then, the external history of the Karaites had been similar, and parallel, to that of the Rabbanite Jews. Both considered each other as Jews and regarded even the most violent polemics between them as an internal Jewish quarrel. It was only at the end of the eighteenth century, when Russia conquered Crimea, that a difference in the legal status was made between Rabbanite and Karaite Jews. In 1795, Empress Catherine II relieved the Karaites of the double tax imposed upon the Jews and permitted them to acquire land. Thus the 1795 law created a wall of separation between Rabbanite and Karaite Jews, each group enjoying civil rights to a different degree.

Inequality before the law of the two groups was further expanded in 1827, when the Crimean Karaites, like the Crimean Tatars, were exempted from the general military draft law enacted by Czar Nicholas I, a privilege that was not extended to the Rabbanite Jews. In 1828, exemption from military service was also granted to the Karaite Jews of Lithuania and Volhynia. In their attempts to improve their legal status, Russian Karaite leaders, such as Simḥah ben Solomon Babovich, had at first refrained from resorting to attacks upon Rabbanite Jews. This policy was changed in 1835, when the Karaite Jews, in appeals and memoranda to the Russian Government, began to stress their fundamental difference from the other Jews, namely their refusal to accept the validity of the Talmud. Influenced by the Lithuanian Karaite scholar and communal leader Abraham Firkovich, Karaites believed their "racial" origins not to be Jewish, but saw themselves as descendants of the Khazars.[30] They also achieved a change in

---

[29] See Schur, *History of the Karaites*, 112-118; Warren P. Green, "The Karaite Community in Interwar Poland," *Nationalities Papers* 14 (1986), 101-109; Philip E. Miller, *Karaite Separatism in Nineteenth-Century Russia: Joseph Solomon Lutski's Epistle of Israel's Deliverance* (Cincinnati: Hebrew Union College Press, 1993); idem, "A Speculation on External Factors in the Formation of the Crimean Karaite (National) Identity," in *Judaism and Islam: Boundaries, Communication and Interaction. Essays in Honor of William M. Brinner*, ed. Benjamin H. Hary, John L. Hayes and Fred Astern (Leiden: Brill Publishers, 2000), 335-342.

[30] Note that since the seventeenth century, Protestants had considered the Karaites to be "rational" Jews—in contrast to the Rabbinic Jews whom they considered

their official designation: instead of Karaite *Jews*, they became to be
called Russian Karaites *of the Old Testament Faith*, or simply Karaites.
In 1840, the Karaites were put on an equal footing with the Muslims,
and were granted an independent church statute. In 1863—only
three years after Holdheim's death—the Karaites were given rights
equal to those of the native Russian population.

3. Holdheim versus Rapoport on the Origin of Karaism

Here, we shall treat some passages of the ninth chapter of the *Ma'amar
ha-'Ishut* in detail. In these particular passages, we are confronted
with one of the main issues in the nineteenth century discussion on
Karaism, namely the origin of Karaism and the role of 'Anan ben
David. Important for the Reformers accused of being Karaites by
the Orthodox was to pinpoint the original Jewish character of Karaite
religion or even the *more original* Jewish character of Karaite religion
as compared to Rabbanite Judaism.

In the last part of the ninth chapter subtitled "The opinion of
one scholar out of the scholars of our time on the renewal of Karaite
religion by 'Anan and our answer on it"[31] we are witness of Holdheim's
reaction to an article by Salomon Judah Loeb Rapoport,[32] published
in the fifth volume of the Hebrew annual (*Sefer*) *Kerem Khemed* ([The
Book of the] Vineyard of Delight).[33]

"superstitious"—since they rejected the Talmud; see Emanuela Trevisan-Semi, "A
Brief Survey of Present-day Karaite Communities in Europe," *Journal of Jewish
Sociology* 33 (1991), 97-106, particularly 97. In the nineteenth and early twentieth
century, the "racial" origin of the Karaites was studied by Italian and German
scholars (see e.g. the Nazi racial theoretician Peter Heinz Seraphim who wrote in
his book *Das Judentum im osteuropäischen Raum* (Essen: Essener Verlagsanstalt, 1938)
that Karaites, although practising the Mosaic religion, were not of Jewish racial
descent). These debates played a significant role in influencing the Nazi government's policy towards Karaites: they were considered a distinct ethnic group of non-
Jewish origin by decree (January 5, 1939), and as a result, the lives of about 12,000
Karaites living under Nazi domination were saved (see Green, "The Karaite
Community in Interwar Poland," 108-109).

[31] Samuel Holdheim, *Ma'amar ha-'Ishut. 'Al Tekhunat ha-Rabbanim ve-ha-Kara'im—
kolel Khakirot Shonot be-Makhalkot ha-Tsedokim ve-ha-Perushim ha-Kara'im ve-ha-Rabbanim
'al Zmanem ve-Sibbot Toldotem* (Berlin: s.n., 1861), 130-135.

[32] In Holdheim's book, Rapoport is never mentioned by name, he is always
referred to as ש"ר הב החכם שי"ר being the acronym of Shlomo Yehudah Rapoport.

[33] Hebrew annual of the Galician *Haskalah*, published in Vienna, Prague and
Berlin from 1833 to 1856. See *EJ* sub Kerem Ḥemed

Like Holdheim, Salomon Judah Loeb Rapoport received a traditional education in Lemberg, Galicia, where he was born. Yet,
influenced by Nahman Krochmal, he took an early interest in
Haskalah and secular learning, studying classical, Semitic and modern languages as well as science. Although respected for his contribution to modern Jewish scholarship (*Wissenschaft des Judentums*),
Rapoport was known for his criticism on Reform and especially
rabbinical synods. As a "man of the middle," devoted to both the
preservation and progress of Reform, he became an object of the
radical Reformers blistering satire.[34]

Holdheim repeats his thesis, stated earlier in this chapter, that
"Karaite religion still continues from the time of the Second Temple
onwards." Despite the fact that the name of the Karaite religion,
i.e. *Bne Miqra'* (Sons of the Scriptures) or simply *Qara'im*, did not
exist before 'Anan, Holdheim sees in this "no contradiction to the
truth that the controversy between Karaites and Rabbanites is to be
found in the old Oral Law from the Second Temple period onwards,
namely from the controversy between Sadducees and Pharisees." The
Karaites were right to define their religion from then on as *Dat
Qara'it:* "they believed in the written word without explanation."
Hence, this religion was not new: "it had disappeared in the eyes
of all who lived before 'Anan, but is was not dead until 'Anan came
to clear it up and define it."[35]

In this context, Holdheim cites Salomon Judah Rapoport's considerations in this matter, as expounded in the fifth volume of *Kerem Ḥemed:*

> Every deed of 'Anan did not stand on its own, in presence of its
> essence it was linked to the course of the history of the peoples in
> these days. Like the reason of the controversy of the Arabs in the
> ways of their religion between those who attached merit only to the
> Qur'an and to what Muhammad handed over to his son-in-law Ali
> and nothing more (they are called Shi'ites) and those who attached
> merit to the tradition that was delivered by Muhammad to his wife
> and his son-in-law, as well as to his children and his many students
> (they are called Sunnites in the Mishna); and as it became known,
> this controversy entered as poison between the Jews, and it put 'Anan

---

[34] See Meyer, *Response to Modernity*, 136, 140 and 196. A good example of this
blistering satire can be found in Holdheim's commentary on Rapoport's *Auflösbarheit
der Eide* from 1845; see *Ueber Auflösbarkeit der Eide von S. L. Rapoport, beleuchtet von
Samuel Holdheim* (Hamburg: Hermann Cobert, 1845).

[35] Holdheim, *Ma'amar ha-'Ishut*, 130-131.

and his son Saul to the renewal of a sect similar to this one (i.e. the Shi'ites), and they thought that the leaders of the Ismaelites would support them, since they were alike in the foundations of their religion, namely to attach merit only to that what is written, apart from the explanation, and to not accept all changes from men to men.[36]

The parallel between Judaism and Islam quoted here by Rapoport with regard to the controversy between two religious groups concerning the acceptance of the Oral Law in addition to the Written Law is an interesting point. Indeed, like in the case of Karaite ideology and the Torah, Shi'ite doctrine is principally based on the Quranic texts. Like the Karaites, the Shi'ites did not reject the Oral Law completely: they developed also a tradition consisting of doctrines and usages that were accepted as binding by the entire community. This Shi'ite *hadith* literature includes all the sayings of the Prophet accepted by the Shi'ites as well as the traditions of the twelve Imams from Ali to the Mahdi. Ja'far al-Sadiq, the sixth Imam (702-765 BCE), once declared that "every *hadith* which is in contradiction with the Qur'an is but a beautiful lie."[37]

Salomon Judah Rapoport's consideration is based on two assumptions:

And the ideas that found favor in the eyes of the king of the Arabs coming from the Shi'ites fulfilled the heart of every man and leader in Israel to do the same among the Jews, namely to persuade the people to reject the belief in the Tradition and the Oral Law, and to accept only what was written. And the Covenant of the Almighty that raised such a favor to test the leader and the head of his people to do such a nasty thing like this in Israel and to separate the heart of the people from God and his Law.[38]

Holdheim, however, answers:

Look, it is true and right when this great wise man says that everything 'Anan did does not stand on its own in the presence of its essence, without a link to and connection with all that was and that was made before him. Anyhow, he was not involved in the history of those days in the camp of the Arabs, only in the history of the first days in the camp of the Hebrews as he made clear for us.[39]

---

[36] Ibid., 131.
[37] See Mohammad Ali Amir-Moezzi, *Le guide divin dans le shî'isme original: aux sources de l'ésotéricisme en Islam* (Lagrasse: Verdier, 1992), 200 and William C. Chittick, *A Shi'ite Anthology* (London: Muhammadi Trust, 1980), 5ff.
[38] Holdheim, *Ma'amar ha-'Ishut*, 131.
[39] Ibid., 132.

By tracing the origin of Karaism back to the first split among the Jewish people at the time of Jeroboam, which laid the foundation of the schism between Sadducees (Written Law only) and Pharisees (Written and Oral Law), Holdheim assigned Karaism a place in the history of Judaism.[40] He describes Karaism as part of the evolution of early Judaism: "[....] the Sadducees did not die out after the destruction of the Second Temple, but only became pauperized, until 'Anan, blessed be his memory, stood up and strengthened them." This seems to be a very important element in the legitimization of some of the innovations Holdheim and other nineteenth-century reformers had in mind.

Indeed, apart from the rejection of the Talmud, a number of other innovations proposed by Holdheim and other nineteenth-century reformers can be traced back to Karaite tradition. It goes without saying that this needs a thorough analysis of both Karaite and nineteenth-century German Reform ideology, which is, off course, not the purpose of this article. Yet, as mentioned above, Holdheim examines some peculiarities of Karaite doctrine in that last chapter of the *Ma'amar ha-'Ishut*. I will, therefore, single out two aspects of Holdheim's ideology which are found in Karaite tradition.

First of all, there are some aspects of the liturgy, such as the introduction of the local non-semitic Karaite dialect as well as national languages (Tatar) in the prayerbook and synagogue worship.[41] As mentioned earlier, in the seventeenth century Karaite activity shifted to Crimea and Lithuania. Karaites who were settled in these areas and soon assumed the leadership of the whole sect, spoke Tatar and Karaimsk, a Cunamo-Karaimic dialect.[42] Some of the Karaite

---

[40] Note that the Egyptian Karaites (a part of them live in France nowadays) claim till today "to be true and original (unmixed) descendants of the Jews from the era of Jeroboam the first" (see Trevisan-Semi, "A Brief Survey of Present-day Karaite Communities in Europe," 98).

[41] Even till today, there exists a close affinity between the Karaite and Reform liturgies: both diversify the prayer for each occasion trying to avoid stereotypic repetition. However, there is one serious difference: where Karaite prayer is Zion-centered, all hope of "rebuilding Jerusalem" was eliminated from Reform liturgy (see Meir Ydit, "Karaite and Reform Liturgy," *CCAR Journal* 18 (1971), 53-61, particularly 61.

[42] Karaimsk or Judeo-Crimean Turkish belongs to the Kipchak-Polovtsy group of Turkic languages. Karaimsk divides into a number of dialects: the Crimean dialect, the Trakai dialect (Lithuanian) and the Galich-Lutsk dialect (western Ukraine); the dialectal differences are mostly phonetic and in vocabulary. Yet, the slavic (Polish, Ukrainian, Belorussian, Russian) influence on the Trakai and Galich-Lutsk dialects began early: the syntax is slavic, but Turkic origins are still evident in the vocabulary. The Trakai dialect had been influenced by Lithuanian. The Karaite

religious writings, and especially their *Siddur*, were translated from
Hebrew in Tatar and Karaimsk. Following their Karaimsk Siddur,
attempts were made to introduce the use of Karaimsk to the synagogue worship—unfortunately without success.[43]

Secondly, it seems appropriate to point at some principles established by the Karaites as norms for the determination of the Law:
the "consensus of the community" (*'edah kibbuts*) and the "knowledge
based on human reason and intelligence" (*Hokhmat ha-Da'at*). Similar
principles are certainly present in Holdheim's ideology. For Holdheim,
Scripture represented but the human reflection of the divine illumination, which means that modern Jewry, especially its religious community and leadership, became the ultimate authority, the judge of
tradition. Authority was no longer ascribed to the texts, but to reason and conscience. In his *Das Ceremonialgesetz im Messiasreich*, Holdheim
stresses the enormous difference between the elements and conditions of his age and those of rabbinic Judaism. Indeed, Judaism was
fixed once and for all by the revelation at Sinai, which means that
its ideal content as monotheism and morality was present from the
very beginning, but at every turning point in history, it had to be
given normative form and substance again by the religious consciousness of the present age.

4. Conclusion

In this article, we tried to shed some further light on the difference
of opinion on the origin of Karaism between two scholars belonging to the nineteenth-century German Reform movement. Salomon
Judah Rapoport was convinced that Karaism had its origin in Shi'ite

---

dialect itself has not had any effect on neighbouring languages, due mainly to the
small number of Karaites and their historical isolation. In any case, Karaites have
always been multilingual; apart from Karaimsk, they spoke the closely related
Crimean Tatar language, Russian and Polish or Ukrainian and Polish (information
compiled from the SIL Ethnologue database, cf. www.sil.org). In its written form,
the Karaite dialect used Hebrew characters until the end of the nineteenth century; later on it made use of the roman alphabet. See also Paul Wexler, "Is Karaite
a Jewish Language?," *Mediterranean Language Review* 1 (1983), 27-54; Ananiasz
Zajaczkowsky, *Karaism in Poland* (Warsaw: Panstwowe Wydawn, 1961); Trevisan-
Semi, "A Brief Survey of Present-day Karaite Communities in Europe."

[43] See Nathan Schur, *The Karaite Encyclopedia* (= Beiträge zur Erforschung des Alten
Testaments und des Antiken Judentums 38) (Frankfurt am Main: Lang, 1995), 78.

Islam, while Samuel Holdheim traced the foundation of the Karaite sect back to the first split among the Jewish people at the time of Jeroboam, where the foundation of the schism between the Sadducees and Pharisees as the basis of the differences between Rabbanites and Karaites was laid. In doing so, Holdheim created a usable past to legitimate his reforms. As he gave Karaism a crucial place within the early history of Judaism and stressed the importance of the original Jewish concept of reinterpreting the Written Law according to contemporary evolutions in society, he cleared the way to reject the unity of Written and Oral Law—the latter became "eternal and unchangeable" after its codification in the sixteenth-century—as equal components of Jewish Revelation.

Like the Karaites, Holdheim did not reject the idea of "tradition" *an sich*, but simply refused to consider rabbinical tradition compatible with contemporary moral standards. Following the Karaite idea of "consensus" (עדה), he proposed to start reinterpreting the Written Law according to contemporary civil society—an originally very Jewish concept which would result in a continuously developing and progressive tradition.

PART II

HOLDHEIM IN THE CONTEXT OF THE
REFORM CONTROVERSIES

SAMUEL HOLDHEIM AND THE GERMAN
CIRCUMCISION DEBATES, 1843–1876

Robin E. Judd

During the 1840s, Samuel Holdheim and other Jews in the German speaking lands witnessed a series of overlapping conflicts concerning the Jewish rite of circumcision.[1] In 1844, Holdheim responded to these acrimonious circumcision debates with his eighty-eight-page pamphlet, *Ueber die Beschneidung zunächst in religiös-dogmatischer Beziehung*. Holdheim's study immediately began with a condemnation of his fellow participants in the debates concerning the Jewish rite. According to the ideologue, the discussions about circumcision had thus far been guided by the mythology associated with *brit milah* and by the intensity of the times. Holdheim thus challenged his colleagues to go deeper and pursue a more thoughtful understanding of the rite's historical, religious, and doctrinal character. "This is not a simple discussion," he warned. Identifying the deliberations about circumcision as a moment when German-speaking Jews had "raised the trumpets of war," he urged his readers to think seriously about the rite's significance in the modern era.[2] Despite his plea, it was not only circumcision's place in modernity that framed Holdheim's study or attracted attention to his pamphlet. Instead, *Ueber die Beschneidung* also rested on whether it was appropriate for the Jewish community to determine the significance and timeliness of the rite. Holdheim's challenge of Jewish communal

---

[1] I am grateful to the Salomon Ludwig Steinheim-Institute for German-Jewish History at Duisburg University, Germany and to the conference's organizers for allowing me this opportunity to look closely at Holdheim's position in the circumcision debates and I deeply appreciate for the feedback I received at the symposium. Before the symposium, my understanding of Holdheim had been greatly influenced by the works of Michael A. Meyer, *Response to Modernity: A History of the Reform Movement in Judaism* (New York: Oxford University Press, 1988) and Andreas Gotzmann, *Jüdisches Recht im kulturellen Prozeß. Die Wahrnehmung der Halacha im Deutschland des 19. Jahrhunderts* (Tübingen: J. C. B. Mohr, 1997).
[2] Samuel Holdheim, *Ueber die Beschneidung zunächst in religiös-dogmatischer Beziehung*, (Schwerin: C. Kürschner, 1844), 4 and 1.

authority and his challenge of the viability of Jewish rites circumscribed his pamphlet and shaped its long lasting reputation.

For over a century after its publication, scholars heralded or lambasted Holdheim's pamphlet as one of the most radical interpretations of the circumcision question. According to the mythology surrounding Holdheim, the ideologue's 1844 text promoted the abandonment of the ritual.[3] Holdheim certainly had the opportunity to promote such a revolutionary view before his second short statement on circumcision in 1857.[4] Yet, in 1844 the scholar did not encourage the rite's widespread abdication. Instead, his pamphlet was more concerned with issues of leadership and authority.

This study examines Holdheim's position on the circumcision question and his influence on the deliberations more generally. Holdheim's 1844 pamphlet did not flatly reject circumcision, but it intimidated contemporaries because of the challenge it posed. Holdheim demanded a reconsideration of the political status quo. Envisioning a Jewish community under a different kind of leadership, *Ueber die Beschneidung* threatened the traditional and emerging Jewish communal authorities. It also presented a challenge in its form. Holdheim's prose was murky and at times he was unable to articulate the pragmatics of the moral religion he embraced. In addition, he frequently insisted on his own indifference to the consequences of the debates concerning Jewish rites. Such blatant disregard shaped his text's reception and his own reputation. Yet, despite these flaws and despite Holdheim's polemical maneuvers, his text should not be ignored. Instead, *Ueber die Beschneidung* illustrates a sophisticated understanding of the political and religious environment in which he lived.

---

[3] See, for example, the description in Zvi H. Kalischer, "Einiges zur Widerlegung der Ansichten des Herrn Dr. Samuel Holdheim in seinem Werkchen: 'Ueber Die Beschneidung' enthaltend," *Der Orient* 6 (1845), no. 1 (supplement), 1-4; Abraham Glassberg et al., eds., *Die Beschneidung in ihrer geschichtlichen, ethnographischen, religiösen und medicinischen Bedeutung: Zum ersten Male umfassend dargestellt* (Berlin: Boas, 1896); Ludwig Löwenstein, *Die Beschneidung im Lichte der heutigen medicinischen Wissenschaft, mit Berücksichtigung ihrer geschichtlichen und unter Würdigung ihrer religiösen Bedeutung* (Trier: Commissionsverlag von Heinrich Stephanus, 1897), 77-82. For a later reading see David Philipson, *The Reform Movement in Judaism*, revised ed. (New York: Ktav Publishing House, 1967), 136-137.

[4] Holdheim, *Geschichte der Entstehung und Entwickelung der jüdischen Reformgemeinde in Berlin*, 46-49.

1. The Circumcision Debates

Between 1843, when a few fathers rejected circumcision for their sons, and 1857, when the circumcision disputes appeared to come to a close, over one hundred German-speaking Jews and non-Jews participated in two sets of discussions concerning the Jewish rite of circumcision.[5] Responding to charges that circumcision posed a risk to society's health, one set of deliberations, *Die Circumcisionsfragen*, interrogated the medical and scientific character of the Jewish rite. These debates considered the few, but well publicized, cases when circumcision seemed to negatively affect the health of newborns. Instances of severe disfigurement, disease, and death provoked participants to consider a paradox that would characterize the modern age. In written correspondence, conference meetings, and published medical and popular treatises, they weighed the necessity of government intervention against the protection of Jewish communal autonomy and religious practices. Participants in these debates asked: should the safety of society trump the preservation of the Jewish rite or, conversely, should the religious significance of the ritual be sufficient to override anxieties concerning its potential risks?[6]

---

[5] For a closer examination of this question, see chapter one in my *Cutting Identities: Jewish Rituals and German Politics, 1843-1933* (forthcoming, Cornell University Press). Also see the discussions in Jacob Katz, "Die Halacha unter dem Druck der modernen Verhältnisse," in *Judentum im deutschen Sprachraum*, ed. Karl E. Grözinger (Frankfurt am Main: Suhrkamp, 1991), 309-324; idem, "The Controversy over *brit milah* during the first half of the Nineteenth Century" (Hebrew), in *Jewish Law in Conflict* (Hebrew), ed. Jacob Katz (Jerusalem: Magnes Press, 1992), 123-149; Robert Liberles, *Religious Conflict in Social Context: The Resurgence of Orthodox Judaism in Frankfurt am Main, 1838-1877* (Westport, Conn.: Greenwood Press, 1985); Michael A. Meyer, "Alienated Intellectuals in the Camp of Religious Reform," *AJS Review* 6 (1981), 61-86; idem, *Response to Modernity*, 119-123. On the latter scholarship, see Sander L. Gilman, *The Jew's Body* (New York: Routledge, 1991); idem, "The Indelibility of Circumcision," *Koroth* 9 (1991), 806-817; idem, *Freud, Race and Gender* (Princeton, NJ: Princeton University Press, 1993); idem, *The Case of Sigmund Freud: Medicine and Identity at the Fin de Siècle* (Baltimore: The Johns Hopkins University Press, 1993).

[6] Participants included Jewish and non-Jewish reformers, governmental authorities, physicians, academics, and community members. See Moritz Gustav Salomon, *Die Beschneidung. Historisch und medizinisch beleuchtet* (Braunschweig: Friedrich Vieweg und Sohn, 1844), 79-80; Ben Rabbi, *Die Lehre von der Beschneidung der Israeliten, in ihrer mosaischen Reinheit dargestellt und entwickelt* (Stuttgart: Hallberger'sche Verlagshandlung, 1844), 45-48, 63, and 70; Klein, "Die rituelle Circumcision: eine sanitätspolizeiliche Frage," *Allgemeine Medicinische Central Zeitung* (11 June 1853), 365-366; Joseph Bergson, *Die Beschneidung vom historischen, kritischen und medicinischen Standpunkt mit Bezug auf die neuesten Debatten und Reformvorschläge* (Berlin: Verlag von Th. Scherk, 1844), 115-116;

As one group of discussants considered circumcision's medical benefits and shortcomings, another contemplated another set of questions concerning the Jewish rite. The *Beschneidungsfragen* concerned the acts of over a dozen Jewish fathers. Between 1843 and 1857, these men spurned the Jewish rite of circumcision, but affirmed their own and their sons' Jewish affiliations.[7] Their simultaneous rejection of circumcision and demand for inclusion challenged traditional methods of recording Jewish membership. Historically, German Jewish communities—like many other Jewish communities in Europe—registered male children after their circumcisions. This timing was appropriate. Jewish custom dictates that parents not divulge a male child's name until after his circumcision. Moreover, the child's survival of his first week of life (and of his circumcision) suggested likelihood that he would endure infancy. When a few fathers clamored for the inclusion of their uncircumcised children, they pressured Jewish communal institutions to reconsider their processes of registration. Some communities registered the uncircumcised boys after their naming, similar to the process through which they recorded the names of newborn girls. Others refused. The result was a decades long dispute concerning the rite's relationship with religious belonging and the community's responsibility toward men who rejected religious customs like circumcision. It was specifically to this discussion that Holdheim responded.

What was it about the mid-nineteenth century and the Jewish rite of circumcision that resulted in the deliberations' intensity?

Gideon Brecher, *Die Beschneidung der Israeliten, von der historischen, praktisch-operativen und ritualen Seite zunächst für den Selbstunterricht. Mit einem Approbationsschreiben von Herrn Rabbiner H. B. Fassel* (Wien: Selbstverlag, 1845), iii; idem, "Die Beschneidung vor dem ärztlichen Forum," *AZJ* 52 (1857), 709-10. Since I originally presented this work, John M. Efron has published his helpful *Medicine and the German Jews: A History* (New Haven: Yale University Press, 2001). Also see, Eberhard Wolff, "Medizinische Kompetenz und talmudische Autorität : jüdische Ärzte und Rabbiner als ungleiche Partner in der Debatte um die Beschneidungsreform zwischen 1830 und 1850," in *Judentum und Aufklärung; jüdisches Selbstverständnis in der bürgerlichen Öffentlichkeit* edited by Arno Herzig, Hans-Otto Horch and Robert Jütte (Göttingen: Vandenhoeck & Ruprecht, 2002), 119-149; Bernard Homa, *Metzitzah* (London: [s.n.] 1960).

[7] The *Beschneidungsfrage* also included discussions concerning the possibility of burying uncircumcised children and the rights of Jewish communities to circumcise dead infants despite the parents' refusal. On this, see Robin Judd, "Circumcision and the Modern German-Jewish Experience" in *My Covenant in Your Flesh: Circumcision, Gender, and Culture across Jewish History*, ed. Elizabeth Mark (Hanover, NH: University Press of New England, 2003), 142-155 and "German Jewish Rituals, Bodies, and Citizenship" (PhD dissertation, University of Michigan, 2000), 36-84.

Circumcision's religious significance partly explains why Holdheim and other discussants leapt into the debates. Within the Hebrew Bible, circumcision serves as an embodied mark of the covenant. "You shall," commands Genesis 17:11 of Abraham, "circumcise the flesh of your foreskin, and that shall be the sign of the covenant between me and you. And throughout the generations, every male among you shall be circumcised at the age of eight days."[8] Because of this relationship between the covenant and the rite of circumcision, Jewish law historically has insisted upon the centrality of the rite to the Jewish tradition. Yet, the ritual's religious and communal import only partly contributed to the intensity and widespread nature of the mid-century deliberations, something illustrated by the minimal interest paid to those few men who had refused to circumcise their sons before the 1840s. Instead, the mid-century discussions about circumcision gained a national audience because they lent themselves to the contemporaneous phenomena affecting Jews and their relationship to the communities among whom they lived. This historical confluence did not escape Holdheim and his contemporaries. Holdheim recognized that the circumcision debates highlighted contemporary concerns. According to the scholar, they reinforced the clash between the "binding nature" of Judaism and a "belief in progress."[9]

As Holdheim suggested, the mid-century discussions about circumcision served as arenas in which Jews (and non-Jews) wrestled with the confluence of several important historical changes, including emancipation, religious reform, and the growth of the centralized state. In reflecting on some of these historical changes and their influence on Jewish religious behavior, Holdheim offered a unique formulation of his ideal Jewish community. His *Ueber die Beschneidung* provided a template for the kinds of relationships possible among Jewish communities and non-Jewish authorities. He also used the deliberations to set out the boundaries and limits of Jewish communal jurisdiction and authority.

---

[8] The commandment for circumcision can be found in Genesis 17:10-15. This translation stems from David L. Lieber, ed., *Etz Hayim Torah and Commentary* (New York: JPS, 2001), 91. The Talmudic understanding of its importance can be found in the Babylonian Talmud, Nedarim 32 a.

[9] Holdheim, *Ueber die Beschneidung*, 2. Also see his similar comments ibid., 12-13, 22, and 24-31.

2. Playing a "Trumpet of War":
Holdheim's Interpretation of the Circumcision Questions

Holdheim was drawn to the circumcision questions during a moment when internal and external historical phenomena were on the cusp of fundamentally altering—or already had altered—the Jewish communities of Western and Central Europe. During the first half of the nineteenth century, the different territorial states, manorial demesnes, and free imperial cities in the German-speaking world slowly intervened in Jewish communal life. These intrusions changed Jewish communal life considerably. German governments modified Jewish communal structures and assumed jurisdiction over previously autonomous spheres. Pre-emancipatory Jewish communities had acted as autonomous units. Over the course of the nineteenth century their status diminished as state and local governments demanded certain changes in exchange for rights, gradually extended their jurisdiction over religious communal life, and abolished much of the political authority of the Jewish courts.

It was within this context that Holdheim wrote his 1844 pamphlet. His text posed three questions:

> (1) Is circumcision so necessary that an uncircumcised child born to Jewish parents should not be considered Jewish? (2) Should the father, who fails to circumcise his son, or the Jewish-born, who comes of age [bar-mitzvah] and remains uncircumcised, be excommunicated? (3) And when should Jewish religious authorities intervene in this conflict or turn to the secular authorities for assistance, if at all?[10]

Holdheim's responses to these queries reflected his deep commitment to understanding the definition and limits of Jewish communal authority and character. Like many of his contemporaries, Holdheim was invested in the future of the Jewish community and recognized how emancipation and the growth of the nation state would change and already had changed the society in which he lived. *Ueber die Beschneidung* therefore raised questions and responses that allowed him to formulate a vision of the character and limits of the Jewish community.

Unlike most of his colleagues, Holdheim expressed the least interest in the first question he posed. His response to that query was

---

[10] Ibid., 6.

clear. Disputing the assertion that circumcision was a standard of Jewishness, Holdheim emphasized that Jewish law dictated that matrilineal descent—and not a boy's circumcised state—determined a child's Jewish identity. In his view, "religious law mandated that an uncircumcised child born to Jewish parents was to be considered an Israelite."[11] Jewish birth-parents, and not a surgical act, served as the prerequisite for one's Jewishness. The Jewish community, wrote Holdheim, should follow these standards and register children born to Jewish parents as Jews. In the cases that already had occurred, communities should take on the responsibility of acknowledging the youngsters as Jewish children.

Holdheim forcefully argued that Jewish communities register, as Jews, the uncircumcised children born to Jewish parents. However, his analysis of the fathers' actions and their repercussions was a bit more complicated. During the 1840s, a number of Jewish communal leaders had demanded punishment for the fathers who refused to allow for their sons' circumcisions. These rabbinic leaders expressed frustration that these men had flagrantly ignored their responsibility to arrange for their newborns' circumcisions. They were even angrier that the fathers had appealed to non-Jewish authorities in order to enforce their sons' registrations as Jews. As such, these Jewish leaders called for the repeal of these men's positions in communal organizations and, in some cases, their excommunication. In a case that preceded the release of Holdheim's pamphlet, for example, the chief rabbi of Frankfurt threatened a local father in the Jewish court, newspaper, and published anthology for refusing to circumcise his son.[12] Seven years later, a rabbi in Bavaria remained so furious at an ex-congregant for acting similarly that even after the father moved away, the rabbi fervently broadcast the father's failure to have the boy circumcised. In letters to nearby Jewish authorities and advertisements in German-Jewish newspapers, the rabbi urged local Jewish leaders to exclude the Landauer family. "Robert [the child]'s status as an *aral* should not be concealed," he wrote to the Jewish community council of a neighboring town, "The

---

[11] Ibid, 49-51.

[12] 1844 statement issued by the Frankfurt Jewish Court (*bet din*), found in *Neue-Synagoge Berlin Centrum-Judaicum Archiv* (NSBCJ) 75 B An1 1-2; Salomon Abraham Trier, *Rabbinische Gutachten über die Beschneidung, gesammelt und herausgegeben* (Frankfurt am Main: Druck der J. F. Bach'schen Buch- und Steindruckerei, 1844).

Jewish community should not care for them [Robert and his father]. Instead, it should turn away from them."[13]

Holdheim renounced such counsel, but he acknowledged that the fathers had indeed deviated from Jewish law. Early in his pamphlet he agreed with his traditional colleagues that the fathers had transgressed. As a biblical ritual, circumcision was obligatory. "The fact at hand," wrote Holdheim, "is that there [....] is no uncertainty that this is against Mosaic law. The simple biblical text of more than a thousand years lends no doubt."[14] Yet, in Holdheim's schema, violation of Jewish law was not sufficient grounds for punishment. Allowing for (if not endorsing) what Gotzmann has termed "tolerated deviance," Holdheim deemed that the parents were not to be punished for abandoning the biblical rite.[15] To arrive at this somewhat contradictory conclusion, he examined the father's motivations, the viability of religious law and ritual in the modern period, and the character of the Jewish community as a political entity.

In his discussion of the father's censure, Holdheim devoted much attention to the way in which the Talmud treated men who did not fulfill their obligations of circumcising their sons. The Talmud is deeply interested in the motivations of these men, distinguishing between the *mumar le'hahis* and the *mumar le'aralot*—fathers who reject circumcision to anger others and those who do so because of their children's health or out of fear.[16] While Holdheim also examined the *mumar* closely (in part because the Talmud calls for such an inquiry), he did not exonerate the fathers based on their motivations. Instead, he allowed for transgression because they had violated a law that Holdheim deemed to no longer be significant. In Holdheim's view, the ritual of circumcision was no longer central and thus a rejection of the rite could be overlooked.

Holdheim rested his interpretation on a number of grounds. First, the ideologist held that circumcision could be rejected without

---

[13] 3 June 1853 letter Jewish community of Speyer (no. 2119) *Central Archives for the History of the Jewish People* (hereafter referred to as CAHJP) Inv 6941. Also see 3 June 1853 letter to the Jewish Community of Breigshaben (no. 2120) CAHJP Inv 6941; 3 June 1853 letter to the Jewish Community of Durkheit (2121) CAHJP Inv 6941.

[14] Holdheim, *Ueber die Beschneidung*, 4.

[15] Gotzmann, *Jüdisches Recht*, particularly 280-286.

[16] Here, Holdheim strongly disputed Isaak Noah Mannheimer's and Trier's discussion of the *mumar le'aralot*; see Holdheim, *Ueber die Beschneidung*, 52-70. My thanks to Joel and Shaul Epstein for offering their assistance in the study of the different rabbinic and exegetical contexts in which the *mumar* appears.

repercussion because it belonged to the sphere of religious law and not that of religious truth. In his view, religious law was ever changing, open to interpretation, and historically inconsistent. To Holdheim, legalities belonged within the realm of the state, a sphere completely distinct from the religious community. "Today," wrote Holdheim, "we are governed by the laws of the state and church [....]. That the Shulhan Arulch should serve as a code of law is legally finished."[17]

While Holdheim allowed for the disavowal of religious law, he did not permit the abandonment of religious truth, which he defined as moral, unchanging, universal, and deeply significant. In his view, the goodness of religion encouraged the renewal of religious conscious-ness, and he criticized the rite of circumcision for having little rela-tionship to one achieving a moral state. According to Holdheim, Jews practiced the ritual out of a sense of religious obligation, because of its assumed centrality to the Jewish religion, or because of its role as a standard for membership, all motivations guided by the past or by politics. Interested in moral goodness and religious renewal, the scholar compared circumcision with baptism, a sacrament that served to renew the bonds between Christian children and Christianity. Holdheim rejected the suggestion that the two were parallel, although he recognized that each rite was intended for a limited audience, thus openly defying what was central to religious truth, universal-ity.[18] Yet, while Holdheim accepted that baptism allowed for reli-gious renewal for the case of some Christians, he rejected the notion that circumcision represented the covenantal relationship for all time. In his view, the covenant made between God and Abraham was—like other aspects of religious law—lodged in the past and he insisted that later redaction had mistakenly transformed the Jewish rite to represent the covenant for eternity.[19] Driven by a desire to expunge rabbinic additions from what he envisioned to be proper religion, he insisted that man did not need to rely on the removal of a new-born's foreskin to forge a link between god and man.[20] He thus had

---

[17] Holdheim, *Ueber die Beschneidung*, 62.
[18] Ibid., 11-22.
[19] While some of his colleagues (and predecessors) had interpreted the talmudic injunction mandating the performance of circumcision on the Sabbath (Nedarim 31b) to substantiate the elevation of circumcision over other rites, Holdheim did not.
[20] See, for example, Holdheim, *Ueber die Beschneidung*, 22.

no tolerance for the suggestion that circumcision was more significant than other Jewish rites because it physically represented the
covenant. In his view, not only did that specific representation no
longer have meaning, but Judaism also did not endorse a system in
which one set of laws was more important than another group.[21]

Holdheim also allowed for the father's deviance because he believed
that the laws concerning circumcision were contradictory. According
to the reform ideologist, if circumcision was fraught with contradiction—evidenced by the transgression of Jewish communities when
they declared that uncircumcised children born to Jewish mothers
were not themselves Jewish—its real truth could not be accessed. In
other words, contradiction confirmed that it belonged to the realm
of law and not truth. Many aspects of Jewish law governing circumcision were irreconcilable to him. Mosaic law mandated the circumcision of non-Jewish slaves, but did not imagine that such an
act converted them. Nor did it require the circumcision of daughters who, if born to Jewish mothers, were considered Jewish.[22]

Furthermore, the scholar's analysis of the character and limits of
Jewish communal membership similarly exonerated fathers who
rejected the Jewish rite. Holdheim's third question posited whether
Jewish communal leaders could enforce circumcision; punish the
fathers who rejected the rite; or request governmental intervention
to mandate compliance.[23] Here too, Holdheim was influenced deeply
by the contemporary context. By the 1840s, the nascent European
nation-state had abolished much of the political authority of the
Jewish court. Rabbinic leaders also had seen a diminution in their
authority to emerging confessional leaders. Holdheim was acutely
aware of the sensitivity rabbinic leaders had to their own political
predicaments. He acknowledged that the Talmud had granted the
Jewish communal court the sanction to intervene if a father refused
to circumcise his son. Yet, Holdheim insisted that this authorization
no longer was applicable. In Holdheim's view, the power of the community to punish members was limited to the historical past when
the Jewish community was an autonomous corporation. The birth
register, he claimed, was a civil document, not a religious source;
furthermore, only the state, and not the Jewish community, had the

---

[21] Ibid., 25.
[22] Ibid., 4-7
[23] Ibid., 71.

right to punish individuals. The Jewish community thus had no right to censure those who wished to interpret religious law as they saw fit. Holdheim had entered into similar analyses elsewhere, asserting, for example, that marriage was to be under the jurisdiction of civil authorities, not the Jewish community.[24]

Holdheim also rejected the notion that the Jewish community could serve as a political entity because he believed that his contemporary rabbinic community and that of the past (to which he referred as rabbinism) were insufficient to cope with the significant task of reflecting upon divine law. Too influenced by political and religious dogmatic beliefs and orientations, they could not be considered to have the reason or conscience to understand religion's moral laws, civil needs, or essence. For Holdheim, authorities used the circumcision controversies to position themselves politically and retain their authority. He was most critical of the Viennese rabbi, Isaak Noah Mannheimer, who called to exclude uncircumcised Jewish boys from the *Bund* and to drive out radical reformers from the Jewish community. In Holdheim's view, Mannheimer simply was motivated by his desire to reassert his authority, not by any attachment to Jewish law.[25] Interestingly, unlike some of his colleagues, Holdheim identified both the rabbis and the Jewish community as actors in this schema, perhaps recognizing the growing authority of the Jewish council as opposed to rabbinic leaders.

As Holdheim berated the community that imagined itself to have the power to discipline its members, he denounced their strategies to turn to state authorities for support. Other scholars from across the religious continuum had encouraged their fellow rabbis to turn to governments for assistance in the circumcision dispute. After two Frankfurt fathers had abdicated the Jewish rite, for example, both Isaak Noah Mannheimer and Salomon Trier ruled that the Jewish community had the responsibility of intervening in the *Beschneidungsfrage* by appealing to state authorities. Holdheim sharply criticized them.[26] While he agreed that the civil authorities were to govern all of the corporations within their jurisdictions, he did not believe that intervention was called or that it should have been invoked. The fathers, Holdheim reminded his leaders, still embraced Judaism; there was

---

[24] See, for example, Meyer, *Response to Modernity*, 81-84.
[25] Holdheim, *Ueber die Beschneidung*, 70.
[26] Ibid., 69-73.

no reason to turn to the authorities, and even if the fathers had rejected the rite, no one should be enforced to exercise religious customs. Furthermore, he charged that the rabbis had petitioned the civil authorities for political and not religious reasons. In his view, rabbis cast circumcision as an organizing standard for membership in the Jewish community because they wished to retain their diminishing control.[27]

3. *Holdheim and His Critics*

It is not surprising that Holdheim's defiant reading attracted attention from fellow Jewish ideologues soon after his text's publication. Many of his contemporaries, like Moritz Steinschneider, referred to Holdheim's controversial arguments, and even fifty years later, Jewish physicians who recommended state regulation of circumcision (or its abolishment) invoked Holdheim in their works and heralded his pamphlet as one of the most radical interpretation of the circumcision question.[28] Yet his text tended to allude categorization. It did not easily conform to the form or content driving the circumcision-literature of the 1840s.

Holdheim's pamphlet was physically dissimilar from other circumcision texts of the period. Much of the literature of the 1840s followed a similar format. Divided neatly into chapters examining the origins, medical dangers, reforms, and significance of the rite (or its possible replacements), most texts were organized around the question concerning the uncircumcised boy's membership in Jewish society. In contrast to this, Holdheim's *Ueber die Beschneidung* contained three intersecting chapters that analyzed the significance of religious customs, the characterization of religious and political spheres, and the role of Jewish texts and authority. Its central question did not concern the boy's registration, but dealt with the father's possible punishment. Furthermore, his language was distinct as well. Holdheim

[27] Ibid., 70-88
[28] Moses Dreifuß, "Eine ganz neue Erklärung über das Gebot der Beschneidung," *Der Orient* 6 (1845), no. 39 (supplement), 611-15; Kalischer, "Einiges zur Widerlegung;" Moritz Steinschneider, *Die Beschneidung der Araber und Muhammedaner, mit Rücksicht auf die neueste Beschneidungsliteratur. Sendschreiben an Herrn Gideon Brecher* (Wien: Gedruckt bei Franz Edlen von Schmid und J. J. Busch, 1845); and see Philipson, *The Reform Movement in Judaism*, 136-137.

expressed frustration with other reformers who, he thought, relied too frequently on aggadic literature and romantic prose and misread rabbinic and biblical texts. Instead, he called for rigorous and thorough exegesis, himself writing in an extremely technical, complicated, and heady fashion.[29] The reformer also was unlike many of his contemporaries in that he seemed completely indifferent to fashioning his analysis so that it could be available for a larger audience, something that Gideon Brecher and Josef Johlson advocated in their works.[30] His murky text might account for the fact that his nineteenth century contemporaries tended not to cite his reflections beyond the pamphlet's introduction. It is interesting that Holdheim, a supposed antagonist of the Talmud was himself a Talmudist, relying heavily on its language, style, and analytical tools.

In addition to its form, Holdheim's text diverged from those of his coreligionists in content. Much of the reform-leaning corpus tended to embrace one of three positions: (1) that circumcision be abandoned; (2) that the ritual be reformed and practiced, but not formally used as a standard for membership; and (3) that the rite be regenerated and legally utilized as an organizing system of Jewishness. Many reformers embraced the second model; while they acknowledged that circumcision did not dictate one's Jewishness, they were loath to surrender it. They defended their difficult position by highlighting circumcision's role in fashioning one's private relationship with God (what many referred to as being an *Israelit*) or conversely its role as a standard for communal organization.[31] Holdheim did neither. In his view, circumcision had no relationship with one's Jewishness and he never differentiated between communal or private Jewishness. Interestingly enough, Holdheim never embraced the Jewish rite, nor did he encourage its abandonment.

Furthermore, unlike Holdheim's text, most reform leaning works concerning circumcision clearly articulated emancipatory aspirations and called upon members of the Jewish community to regenerate Jewish rites presumably to achieve that end. Reform-leaning scholars tended to advocate that Jews shed circumcision to

---

[29] See, e.g., Holdheim's discussion in *Ueber die Beschneidung*, 22.

[30] Brecher, *Die Beschneidung der Israeliten;* Josef Johlson, *Ueber Die Beschneidung in historischer und dogmatischer Hinsicht: Ein Wort zu seiner Zeit. Den Denkenden in Israel zur Prüfung vorgelegt von Bar Amithai* (Frankfurt am Main: J. E. Hermann'sche Buchhandlung, 1843).

[31] See Judd, "Circumcision and the Modern German-Jewish Experience," passim.

resemble their gentile compatriots physically,[32] or at least to reform the rite in order to illustrate their respectability and worthiness.[33] Describing the ritual as intolerant, for example, the Berlin-based physician, Joseph Bergson encouraged Jews to reform circumcision because it would always be seen as an irreversible divide.[34] If he was motivated by similar concerns, and I think he was, Holdheim did not express them. He did not call for the dramatic reform of the Jewish rite, nor did he articulate an anxiety that circumcision posed the final barrier to emancipation. Yet, he too was not free from a political agenda. His text clearly illustrates that he was interested in the ritual's political character and the community's civic authority.

Third, while reform scholars of the 1840s intently examined circumcision's medical character, Holdheim did not.[35] Drawing upon contemporary issues in medical science and by social scientific discussions concerning deviance within German society, participants in this debate argued over the desirability of medical regulation of the Jewish rite. They feared that circumcision might lead to impotence, to the spread of disease, or even to death.[36] They charged that the *mohelim* spread contagion because they had "unsatisfactory" training, used their fingernails for *periah* (the uncovering of the corona of the penis), and practiced *metsitsah be peh* (the sucking of the wound by the *mohel*). Holdheim visited the topic of medical character only when he described the rationalizations employed by fathers who refused to circumcise their sons or when he refuted hygiene as an explanation for the origin of the rite. In his view, medical concerns were sufficient to explain why a father would abandon the Jewish rite; they were not, however, adequate to explain its origins. Never did he use the rite to encourage medical reforms or regulation.

---

[32] Johlson *Ueber die Beschneidung;* Salomon, *Die Beschneidung,* 79 and 89.

[33] Bergson, *Die Beschneidung,* and Brecher, *Die Beschneidung.*

[34] Bergson *Die Beschneidung,* 1. Also see Ben Rabbi, *Die Lehre von der Beschneidung,* 18.

[35] See, e.g., Ben Rabbi, *Die Lehre von der Beschneidung* and Salomon, *Die Beschneidung.*

[36] See, e.g., the criticism in Bergson, *Die Beschneidung;* Salomon *Die Beschneidung;* Theodor Friedrich Balz, *Die schädlichen Folgen der Beschneidung: Ein Sendschreiben an die hocherwürdige Versammlung der Herren Rabbiner in Frankfurt A.M* (Berlin: Als Manuscript gedruckt und privatim vertheilt, 1845); Eugen Levit, *Die Circumcision der Israeliten. Beleuchtet vom ärztlichen und humanen Standpunkte von einem alten Arzt* (Wien: Druck und Commissions-Verlag von Carl Gerold's Sohn, 1874).

Finally, while Holdheim agreed with his reform colleagues that circumcision was unnecessary for determining membership in the Jewish community, he differed in his formulation concerning governmental intervention in communal affairs. Most reformers did, in the end, call for governmental intervention of some kind—whether it was to force the father to have the circumcision or to force the more traditional rabbi to enforce the registration of the uncircumcised child. Holdheim did not, in part because he was less concerned with the pragmatic elements of the circumcision controversy, though he too desired that civil authorities oversee birth registers.

Why, then, was Holdheim's pamphlet regarded as radical? First, Holdheim's early discussion of baptism, combined with his reputation, dramatically shaped future readings of his text. His comparison of baptism to circumcision sounded alarm bells to his opponents who already feared his radical philosophies. Many of the debates had their origins in the decisions of fathers to choose registration in the Jewish community; these men had made a conscious judgment not to baptize their sons. Baptism was a rite that few Jewish participants in the circumcision disputes wished to cross and Holdheim's reference to it alarmed them. Furthermore, Holdheim seemed indifferent to the consequences of the debates. While he did not encourage the rite's abandonment, he gave little thought to what would occur if Jews rejected the rite universally. Most participants in the debates were desperate to retain the religious character of the Jewish community, and even if they allowed for the registration of uncircumcised boys, they still warned of the importance of the Jewish rite to Jewish life and to the community at large. Holdheim included no such caveat, nor did he follow the path of other more radical reformers who proposed alternative visions to the rite of circumcision.[37] Moreover, he was a polemicist and frustratingly ambivalent, frequently endorsing one side and then the other. He chided his contemporaries who supposedly used the controversy to "declare war" on one another, but he lambasted a number of scholars by name.[38] He also expressed little tolerance for those solely motivated by an intense opposition to traditional "rabbinism," a category that

---

[37] Johlson, *Ueber die Beschneidung*.
[38] He also pointed to the conflicts concerning the publication of a new prayerbook and the pursuit of research that challenged Talmudic authority; see Holdheim, *Ueber die Beschneidung*, 1.

included many of his reform leaning colleagues.[39]

In his response to the mid-nineteenth century circumcision deliberations, Samuel Holdheim positioned himself as an intellectual observer of the Jewish rite. He did not recommend reforms or set out the rite's social history; nor did he consider what might happen if individuals followed his arguments to their linear conclusions. Perhaps that was because Holdheim, an acute observer of the community and times in which he lived, understood that circumcision was a line that Jews would not cross, but that it allowed for a convenient springboard for crucial discussions concerning Judaism during the period of emancipation. Using the circumcision deliberations to define the significance of religious customs, he differentiated between law and truth and between sacraments of the past and contemporary acts of religious consciousness. While his fellow ideologists set out specific platforms for action, Holdheim was less interested in the day-to-day pragmatics and instead was occupied with a desire to understand the foundations of Mosaic religion and religious progress. Yet his alleged occupation reveals a preoccupation with the political environment in which he lived. His analysis of circumcision was deeply interested in delineating the limits of religious authority and casting the relationship of future religious leaders with their congregants and the authorities that rule them.

---

[39] Ibid. Zunz had made a similar complaint; see Leopold Zunz, "4 Mai 1845 Letter to Geiger," in Abraham Geiger, *Nachgelassene Schriften*, vol. 5 (Berlin: Gerschel, 1875), 184-185, here 184 and idem, *Gutachten über die Beschneidung* (Frankfurt am Main: Druck der J. J. Bach'schen Buch- und Steindruckerei, 1844).

SAMUEL HOLDHEIM AND THE PRAYERBOOK REFORM IN GERMANY

Klaus Herrmann

Samuel Holdheim happened to turn to prayerbook writing just shortly before his death in 1860. His first and only prayerbook, *Gebete und Gesänge für das Neujahrs- und Versöhnungsfest*, was published in 1859 for the Reform Congregation in Berlin, whose rabbi and preacher he had been since 1847. In the preface to this book, Holdheim declared that his actual intention was to publish soon—"God willing"—a prayerbook ultimately for all the festivals and the weekly Shabbat, or better "Sunday service," together with the guidelines underlying his prayer collection.[1] Unfortunately, God was not willing and Holdheim was unable to carry out this task. Nevertheless, though not the famed author of a prayerbook (and the one that he did publish was, as we shall see, not even accepted by his own community) he made significant contributions to the debate on liturgical reforms. By describing some major events in the prayerbook reform of the nineteenth century, this article intends to mark Holdheim's position in these matters.

1

Everyone working in the field of Reform prayerbooks has to start with Jakob Petuchowski's pioneering book, *Prayerbook Reform in Europe*,

---

[1] See Samuel Holdheim, *Gebete und Gesänge für das Neujahrs- und Versöhnungsfest zum Gebrauche für die öffentliche und häusliche Andacht jüdischer Reformgemeinden* (Berlin, J. E. Huber's Verlag, 1859), VIII: "A more thorough account for sources, agenda and tendency of this collection as well as an attempt to deal with the reasons prompting the author to undertake this work and to present them to the audience for examination and assessment is reserved for the preface to a complete collection encompassing all the holydays of the year and the Sabbath prayer, which the author, God willing, is determined to publish within the next time."

published in 1968,[2] which Michael A. Meyer has accurately called a "milestone" in its field.[3] As far as I know, his work has not been continued over the last decades despite its great influence on many publications dealing with the Jewish Reform movement. While writing this book, Petuchowski decided to choose the most instructive and illuminating examples to describe the development of Reform prayerbooks over one and a half centuries from the 1817 publication of *Die Deutsche Synagoge* in Berlin through *Service of the Heart*, published in 1967 by the Union of Liberal and Progressive Synagogues in London. In following his method, I would like, in this much more modest article, to cite a few specific textual examples in order to illustrate some of the main liturgical perspectives of the Reform movement. I will deal with the *Shema Yisrael* and its blessings, which—together with the *Amidah*—forms the basic pillar of Jewish liturgy, concentrating mostly on the *Shema* in the morning service. Since the major focus is on the prayerbooks used by the Reform Congregation in Berlin, the *Amidah* would not be a suitable prooftext, because, unlike the *Shema*, only fragments of the *Amidah* were preserved in the process of reformulating its *Siddur*.

As is well-known, the *Shema* contains three biblical passages, the first beginning with the basic statement of belief: "Hear, O Israel: The Lord our God, the Lord is One." These three biblical passages are framed by three "blessings," two before and one after the biblical quotations, in which God is praised for various aspects of his dealing with the world in general, and with Israel in particular.

The first blessing before the *Shema* in the morning service, called *Yotzer Or*, praises God as the Creator of light, who continously renews the work of creation. The second blessing, *Ahavah Rabbah*, praises God for the great love He has shown to Israel—a love manifest in Israel's being given the Torah. The blessing following the *Shema* affirms its message as "true and enduring," *Emet ve-Yatziv*, and the theme of the Exodus from Egypt, mentioned in the third biblical text of the *Shema*, is further developed, both in terms of the events of the past and the hope for the future.

"The Shema and its Blessings," thus contains the basic confession within the Jewish service. It proclaims the monotheistic faith and

---

[2] Published by the World Union for Progressive Judaism, New York.
[3] See Michael A. Meyer "Recent Historiography on the Jewish Religion," *LBIYB* 35 (1990), 3-16, here 14.

Israel's loyalty to the divine commandments, and it links that proclamation—to speak with Franz Rosenzweig—with an affirmation of the doctrines of Creation, Revelation, and Redemption.

At first glance the *Shema* does not seem to have been the object of far-reaching reforms, which would make it a quite unlikely object for an essay intending to describe the reform of Jewish liturgy. · However, closer analysis of the *Shema* reveals elements which prove to be problematical in the context of the prayerbook reform envisoned by nineteenth-century reformers in Germany.

The last paragraph of the first benediction speaks of the new light, in Hebrew *Or Hadash*, which will shine over Zion: "Cause a new light to shine upon Zion, and may we all be speedily worthy to behold its brightness." Was this still relevant in a post-Enlightenment world where Jews were struggling for emancipation and equal political rights? Might not the new light be rising over Europe instead?

The second *Berakhah Ahava*—Love—praises not only God's love in giving His Torah and the laws of life to Israel, but also implores God to gather the people of Israel from all corners of the world to their land so that they may sanctify His Name there, an element called *Havienu*, according to the blessing's first Hebrew word: "And bring us in peace from the four corners of the earth, and lead us upright to our land." Was the seemingly narrow nationalism and particularism of such prayers not directly opposed to the Reform movement's goals? To quote Samuel Holdheim: "Zion and Jerusalem we celebrate as the planting sites of the Kingdom of God, as the cradle of religion, but not as divinely consecrated earth to which the life and existence of religion is bound."[4] And immediately after the quoted passage the text reads: "Thou who hast chosen us from all the nations and tongues." Is this expression of an awareness of Israel's separateness from other nations still justified, when equality of civil rights is being demanded and the Holy Language has been largely replaced by the vernacular? Instead, as one of the reformers pointed out, it seemed much more appropriate to express joy over the gradual overcoming of such barriers.[5]

The third blessing, *Emet ve-Yatziv,* recited after the biblical passages,

---

[4] Samuel Holdheim, *Geschichte der Entstehung und Entwicklung der jüdischen Reformgemeinde in Berlin. Im Zusammenhang mit den jüdisch-reformatorischen Gesammtbestrebungen der Reform* (Berlin: Julius Springer, 1857) 197.

[5] See Abraham Geiger's statement below.

praises Israel's redemption from Egypt in the past, culminating in a plea for redemption in the future. But should worshippers still say: "Thou slaughtered all (Egypt's) firstborn" and "split the Red Sea, sank the overly arrogant [....] (so that) the waters covered their enemies and none remained"? Does this part of the blessing match the necessity of "political correctness" in a Christian society where Judaism had always been accused of being the religion of revenge (*Vergeltung*)? "A Jewish heart should be soft, gentle, mild, conciliatory and peaceable, and it should forgive the Egyptian today and tomorrow the anti-Semite!"—these are the original words of a Passover sermon by a Reform Rabbi in the nineteenth century.[6]

The new service was supposed to embody both true devotion and edification, and the reformers were concerned that this could not be achieved if prayers consisted of a torrent of words as illustrated by the passage at the beginning of the third *Berakhah:*

> True, constant, well-founded, everlasting, upstanding, of proven value, sweet, dear, gracious, splendid, awful, mighty, well-ordered, pleasing, good and beautiful is this word to us forever and ever.

Did these phrases not tend to tempt people to just reel off the prayers instead of experiencing inspiring true devotion and edifying feelings as Protestantism has succeeded in doing in such an exemplary manner? Thus is how many Jewish reformers viewed the Protestent culture of their time. Didn't the service have to undergo a complete reformation from an aesthetic point of view by introducing the organ, German chorals and well-shaped sermons?

2

We will now turn to several selected Reform prayerbooks from the beginning of the Reform movement and try to determine to what extent Holdheim was involved in these affairs.

The outset of the Reform movement is closely connected with the

---

[6] This sermon was in 1880 in Vienna by Adolph Jellinek, one of the most talented nineteenth-century Jewish preachers; quoted in Moritz Kayserling, *Die jüdische Litteratur von Moses Mendelssohn bis auf die Gegenwart, in Die jüdische Litteratur seit Abschluß des Kanons. Dritter Band: Die Poetische, Kabbalistische, Historische und neuzeitliche Litteratur,* ed. Jakob Winter und August Wünsche (Berlin: Poppelauer, 1897), 819.

figure of Israel Jacobson (1768-1828), who in the chapel of his school in Seesen began to conduct a modernized service characterized by an abbreviated liturgy, some prayers in German, German sermons, a choir and an organ for the embellishment of the service.[7] When Jacobson moved to Berlin in 1815, this kind of liturgy was continued in private homes, and a prayerbook for this liturgy was published by Eduard Kley (1789-1867) and Carl Siegfried Günsburg (1784-1860) in 1817, entitled: *Die Deutsche Synagoge*. The Introduction to the prayerbook seems to justify its title by pointing out:

> Holy is the language in which God once gave the Torah to our fathers. [....] But seven times more holy to us is the language which belongs to the present and to the soil whence we have sprung forth, [....] the language in which a mother first greets her new-born child, [....] the language which unites us with our fellow-men in happy fellowship or in serious business, the language, finally, in which our philanthropic and just king speaks to us, in which he proclaims his law to us [....].[8]

The title and the introduction, however, are misleading. From a remark on the following pages of this prayerbook ("The subsequent prayers are recited in Hebrew, of which the following is the translation") it becomes clear that *Die Deutsche Synagoge* contains the German translation of prayers, most of which are meant to be said in Hebrew.[9] The German translation is more or less literal with one exception: In the second blessing of the *Shema*, the *Havienu* ("And bring us in peace from the four corners of the earth, and lead us upright to our land") was omitted, but it is not clear to us whether this phrase was left out in the Hebrew reading as well. Thus the basic structure of the service and even the Hebrew language are preserved.

The Hamburg Temple congregation was the first to have been founded on a declared Reform basis. Established in 1817 under the name "Neuer Israelitischer Tempelverein" (New Israelite Temple Association), it published the first edition of its prayerbook two years later under the title: *Ordnung der öffentlichen Andacht für die Sabbath- und*

---

[7] For the whole ceremony see the standard work to the Reform movement by Michael A. Meyer, *Response to Modernity. A History of the Reform Movement in Judaism* (New York: Oxford University Press, 1988), 28-43.

[8] Quoted from the introduction to *Die Deutsche Synagoge oder Ordnung des Gottesdienstes für die Sabbath- und Festtage des ganzen Jahres zum Gebrauche der Gemeinde, die sich der deutschen Gebete bedienen*, Part I (Berlin: In der Mauerschen Buchhandlung, 1817), XI-XII.

[9] Ibid., 6.

Festtage des ganzen Jahres. Nach dem Gebrauch des Neuen-Tempel-Vereins in Hamburg. Attacked by Orthodox opponents, one of its publishers, Isaac Fränkel, felt the need to explain the general tendency of this prayerbook which, incidentally, was opened like a German book, i.e., from left to right.[10] On the one hand, he defended the dominant use of the Hebrew language, arguing that abandoning it would lead to the suspicion that the reformers wanted to abandon Judaism as well. On the other hand, he insisted on deleting those passages which had to do with the sacrificial cult and its restitution or with the hope of returning to Jerusalem.

The Temple should not be awaited in a future Jerusalem, but, let's say, joined in contemporary Hamburg; in Europe, the Jews were struggling for their emancipation and integration into European societies; the messianic hope was being transferred to the present, thus contradicting the traditional messianic expectation of a return to the Holy Land. How did this general orientation of the Hamburg prayerbook affect the shaping of the *Shema?*

As one might expect, the *Or Hadash*, "The new light upon Zion," in the first blessing is omitted. Should a new light begin to shine, then over Hamburg, not over Zion. The *Havienu* ("And bring us in peace from the four corners of the earth, and lead us upright to our land") in the second blessing is changed and translated as follows: "Provide us with Thy blessing in all parts of the earth, for Thou, Almighty, alone bringeth about blessings and salvation". Here the Hamburg prayerbook follows the Sephardi rite, which fits the universalistic orientation of the Hamburg prayerbook much better than the Ashkenazi does; however, in the Sephardi rite, too, this phrase is linked to the traditional hope to return to Israel: "and break off the yoke of the nations from our necks; and lead us speedily upright to our land." No question about it, this wording was omitted in the Hamburg prayerbook.

The torrent of words marking the traditional beginning of the third *Berakhah* is replaced here by choral singing in German, paraphrasing the Hebrew original:

> Eternal truth remain as such for us: He is always His throne—
> His word living for the entire human race. Eternal truth is His

---

[10] The third edition, published in 1868, reintroduced the traditional Hebrew book pattern.

commandment—this holy belief remains as such for us: He only is God to us, no one but Him.[11]

Following a decision by the constitutive assembly, the prayer was accompanied by numerous choral songs. As we shall see, Holdheim was not in favor of Protestant church music.

In 1841 a second edition of the Hamburg prayerbook was published. This revised version finely illustrates the fact that the Reform movement did not develop in a linear fashion. This edition stirred up even more reactions than the first one; this time, however, objections were not only raised by the Orthodox, as in 1819, but also from within the newly emerging Reform movement itself.

In that same year Samuel Holdheim published an article in Isaak Markus Jost's *Israelitische Annalen* under the title "Der neue Israelitische Tempel zu Hamburg," in which he expressed his personal impression of the service.[12] To summarize it in a few words: Holdheim was overwhelmed by the "lively and definitely agreeable impression" it made and praised its "festive and truly elevating" character. The Temple has to be seen as "the most important moment in the cultural history of Judaism."[13] From his point of view, the service has a quasi-messianic character and could be seen as the anticipation of a new, still utterly unachieved ideal that had become the aim of "the aspirations, rooted in deep yearning, brought about from within Judaism." Then, however, Holdheim raised some basic questions:

> What is the Temple, what does it want to be and what is it supposed to be? Is it a Jewish institution or an institution for Jews? Does it stand within Judaism, outside of it, or between it and Christianity?[14]

These questions clearly mark a specific stage in Holdheim's personal development: it was a time when he was feeling torn to a certain extent between the unrestrained positive experience of the worship service on the one hand and quite fundamental reservations and

---

[11] *Ordnung der öffentlichen Andacht für die Sabbath- und Festtage des ganzen Jahres. Nach dem Gebrauch des Neuen-Tempel-Vereins in Hamburg*, ed. Seckel Isaak Fränkel and M. J. Bresslau (Hamburg: Fränkel und Bresslau, 1819), 40; see also the second edition *Gebetbuch für die öffentliche und häusliche Andacht, nach dem Gebrauch des Neuen Israelitischen Tempels in Hamburg* (Hamburg: B. S. Berendsohn, 1841), 62.

[12] Samuel Holdheim, "Der neue Israelitische Tempel zu Hamburg," *Israelitische Annalen* 45 (1841), 353-355.

[13] Ibid., 354.

[14] Ibid., 355.

doubts about the Reform efforts on the other. The reader had to wait for Holdheim's answer until the next issue of the *Israelitsche Annalen*,[15] but then his answer was clear:

> I dare say that the Temple stands not only in Judaism—in whose innermost sanctum it has its center of gravity, from whose heart-chambers it pulsates all over with movement warm with life and about whose inner life it furnishes the liveliest proof—but also in the synagogue, in its most concrete meaning, [where] it is rooted with all its fibres, having emerged out of the synagogue together [with it], and [where], while ennobling, purifying and erecting it, it leads to a much higher, perhaps even to the highest development stage.[16]

Holdheim gave real proof of his opinion in his report, *Ueber das Gebetbuch nach dem Gebrauche des neuen Israelitischen Tempelvereins zu Hamburg. Ein Votum*, published in the same year in Hamburg.[17] It is interesting to note that his defense of the Hamburg prayerbook is thoroughly based on the Talmudic tradition. To give two examples: the recitation of some prayers in German is in accordance with *Mishnah Sotah* VII,1, where it is said that the *Shema* could be recited "in every language" (*bekhol lashon*). The inclination of the prayerbook to eliminate the sacrificial cult corresponds with the Jewish tradition, above all with Maimonides' statement that sacrifices were, according to Holdheim, "an accommodation of divine wisdom to the low level of ritual observance [*Cultus*] among the Israelites at that time and a temporarily necessary prayer in the light of the sacrificial and idolatrous worship then widespread throughout the world."[18]

It is interesting to compare Holdheim's opinion with Abraham Geiger's statement, published in 1842 under the title *Der Hamburger Tempelstreit, eine Zeitfrage*.[19] At first Geiger condemned the critique of the Hamburg prayerbook by the Orthodox Hamburg Chief Rabbi, Isaac ben Jacob Bernays (1792-1849), who had banned it. In face of this attack, one would expect Geiger to have gone on to defend

---

[15] Idem, "Der neue Israelitische Tempel zu Hamburg," *Israelitische Annalen* 46 (1841), 362-365.

[16] Ibid., 363.

[17] *Ueber das Gebetbuch nach dem Gebrauche des neuen Israelitischen Tempelvereins zu Hamburg. Ein Votum von Dr. S. Holdheim* (Hamburg: B.S. Berendsohn, 1841).

[18] Ibid., 15.

[19] First published in Abraham Geiger, *Der Hamburger Tempelstreit, eine Zeitfrage* (Breslau: F. E. C. Leuckart, 1842); reprinted in idem, *Nachgelassene Schriften*, ed. Ludwig Geiger, vol. 1 (Berlin: Gerschel, 1875), 113-196.

the prayerbook against its critics and to praise its merits as Holdheim did. However, although his criticism is by no means less radical, it points, of course, in the opposite direction:

> But the most severe reproach concerning the Hamburg Temple, which deprived and deprives it of the position which it would have inevitably occupied in the Jewish community, is *that it did not understand how to make itself the advocate of scientific, correctly recognized religious progress in the new Judaism.*[20]

Thus Geiger misses a "scientific approach" in the prayerbook, and it is interesting to note, in this context, that Geiger combines his critique with the general demand for the establishment of a Jewish Theological Seminary at a German university.[21] In relying on his own critical scholarship, it was easy for Geiger to find inconsistencies in the wording of the *Shema* in the Hamburg prayerbook. In the first edition of the Hamburg prayerbook, for instance, the *Or Hadash* was omitted, but taken up again in the second one, albeit not in its full "brightness"; it was printed in smaller letters, enclosed in parentheses and not expressed in the translation. In the second edition, the phrase "his firstborn killed and yours saved" was removed.

Holdheim was certainly aware of these inconsistencies as well, even naming some of them in his report. The main difference between Holdheim and Geiger, however, is their different point of departure. Geiger tried to base his opinion on a strictly historical-scientific approach which did not allow him to tolerate any inconsistencies, whereas Holdheim, still dependent on the Talmudic way of argumentation, can afford to overlook these shortcomings, hereby envisioning a rebirth of Judaism in the future. This becomes even more evident in Holdheim's second statement on the Hamburg prayerbook,[22] in which he revealed himself to be a master of Talmudic discourse. He was forced to write this second statement after his first one had been attacked by an anonymous writer in the pamphlet, *Jude und Nicht-Jude, eine Erwiederung auf die Schriften der Triple-Allianz der Herren Doctoren Holdheim, Salomon und*

---

[20] Ibid., 176.

[21] On this subject see also idem, "Die Gründung einer jüdisch-theologischen Fakultät—ein dringendes Bedürfnis unserer Zeit," *Wissenschaftliche Zeitschrift für jüdische Theologie* 2 (1836), 1-21; idem, *Über die Errichtung einer jüdisch-theologischen Facultät* (Wiesbaden: L. Riedel, 1838).

[22] Samuel Holdheim, *Verketzerung und Gewissensfreiheit. Ein zweites Votum in dem Hamburger Tempelstreit, mit besonderer Berücksichtigung der Erwiederung eines Ungenannten auf mein erstes Votum* (Schwerin: C. Kürschner, 1842).

Frankfurter, von einem Ungenannten.[23] He strongly rejected the anonymous writer's charge that he was now to be identified with those reformers who had abandoned the Talmud "on their journey toward equal civil rights."[24] On the other hand, he argued "that the worship service has now been made to accord with the Talmud, i.e., it has been brought back to an older stage."[25] Despite its general orientation we can find in Holdheim's second opinion some quite telling nuances, hinting already at his later intellectual development. Thus he praised the Hamburg prayerbook as a work "that seeks its main focus in the prophets and to revitalize the prophetic spirit of Judaism in and amongst us as its noblest goal."[26] Moreover, he pointed out that his argument was based on the Bible and the Talmud and that it revealed "the true spirit of the Israelite religion."[27]

Over the next years Holdheim became more and more radical in claiming that the doctrines, both religious and ethical, of biblical Judaism were the positive contents of Judaism and that a truly historical reform must, for the sake of these positive doctrines, liberate Judaism from Talmudism. When Holdheim radicalized his opinions during his tenure as *Landesrabbiner* of Mecklenburg-Schwerin, he introduced for the synagogues of his province a Synagogue Order (*Synagogen-Ordnung für die Synagoge des Großherzogthums Mecklenburg-Schwerin unter allerhöchster Genehmigung von dem Großherzoglichen israelitischen Oberrath in Schwerin*), published in Schwerin in 1843 and based, with only a few deviations, on the Synagogue Order drafted by the Württemberg *Landesrabbiner* or, as he was called, "Ecclesiastical Councilor" ("Kirchenrath") Joseph von Maier (1797-1873).[28] This set of rules focuses more on the outer decorum of the service than on the wording of the prayers. It only renders the texts of those prayers that had been repeatedly cited in anti-Jewish propaganda, especially the *Birkat ha-Minim* and comparable prayers. The other paragraphs deal

---

[23] Anonymous, *Jude und Nicht-Jude, eine Erwiederung auf die Schriften der Triple-Allianz der Herren Doctoren Holdheim, Salomon und Frankfurter, von einem Ungenannten* (Amsterdam: s.n., 1842).

[24] Holdheim, *Verketzerung und Gewissensfreiheit*, 50.

[25] Ibid., 40.

[26] Idem, *Ueber das Gebetbuch nach dem Gebrauche des neuen Israelitischen Tempelvereins zu Hamburg*, 13.

[27] Idem, *Verketzerung und Gewissensfreiheit*, 43.

[28] *Gottesdienst-Ordnung für die Synagogen des Königreichs Württemberg, unter Höchster Genehmigung festgesetzt von der königl[ichen]] Israelitischen Ober-Kirchen-Behörde* (Stuttgart: Hallberger, 1838).

with fixed prayer times, the avoidance of gestures, or the dignified manner of prayer recitation, among others. Nevertheless, the Synagogue Order caused a tremendous debate among the Jewish congregations and was criticized or, rather, rejected by most of them. Though far removed from the "revolutionary" character of the Hamburg Reform prayerbook, even the slightest variant rendering of the traditional prayer text provided severe criticism. For instance, the Synagogue Order prescribes in the second section "Prayers" ["Gebete"], §7, as follows: "the twelfth benediction of the Amidah should have the following form." The Hebrew text which follows differs from the traditional wording of this *Berakhah* in this sense that the personal form "the slanderers," "all doers of wickedness," "all the arrogant" and so on, who should be annihilated by God (an idea always claimed by Christians as being directed against themselves), has now been changed to a neutral one: according to the new phrasing, "the slander," "all wickedness," and "arrogance" should disappear from the world.[29]

Fortunately, in the case of Holdheim's endeavors to modernize the religious service and the reactions of the Jewish congregations in Mecklenburg-Schwerin to his policy, all the documents dealing with these affairs are still extant. One only has to take a brief look at the newly published index of these documents housed in the *Mecklenburgisches Landeshauptarchiv Schwerin* to realize that severe limitations put a damper on the modernization endeavors.[30] Ultimately, Holdheim had thus to concede the holding of private services following the traditional form.[31] Hence it is clear that he could not

---

[29] Some nineteenth-century Reform prayerbooks skipped the twelfth Berakhah (like the Hamburg Reform prayerbook of 1841; the 1819 edition contains no weekday service which includes only the middle Berakhot of the Amidah) or renders the text in a similar way; see Petuchowski, *Prayerbook Reform in Europe*, 223-225.

[30] See *Quellen zur Geschichte der Juden in den Archiven der neuen Bundesländer*, vol. 4: *Staatliche Archive der Länder Mecklenburg-Vorpommern, Sachsen und Thüringen*, ed. Stefi Jersch-Wenzel and Reinhard Rürup (Munich: K. G. Saur, 1999), particularly 134ff. ("Israelitischer Oberrat") and 142ff. ("Landesrabbinat"). I would like to thank Ms. Christel Schütt, who worked on this part ot the *Quellen zur Geschichte der Juden*, for her kind hospitality during my stays in Schwerin. For this subject which is beyond the scope of the present paper, see Carsten Wilke's contribution in the same volume and the dissertation by Dirk Drewelow, "Das Landesrabbinat des Reformers Samuel Holdheim im Großherzogtum Mecklenburg-Schwerin (1840-47)", Rostock University, 2003.

[31] See the documents LH 10.72-2 Nr. 51 (*Quellen zur Geschichte der Juden in den Archiven der neuen Bundesländer*, vol. 4, 146, No. 2486), in which the establishment of services for traditionalists ("Altgläubige") in Schwerin, Güstrow, Teterow, Ludwigslust, Hagenow, Grevesmühlen and Rehna is documented.

even begin to think about prescribing extensive substantive changes in the prayers, e.g., altering the *Havienu* text in line with the tenor of the Hamburg prayerbook (and in so doing, about admitting a Sephardi tradition into the Ashkenazi prayerbook!) or even deleting the *Or Hadash* altogether.

The Synagogue Order has to be seen as part of a general tendency in the nineteenth century to standardize and unify the services by insisting on a strict adherence to the worship-service regulations, especially to those of Prussia, Saxony, Bavaria and Baden; furthermore, it should not be forgotten that within the context of the Protestant churches, too, strong reactions to any innovation were quite usual. Expressing it somewhat ironically, we could say that what the parade meant to the army, this is what the liturgical order meant to the Church worship-service, all aiming at the strengthening and glory of the provincial "landesherrliche" government. Thus, in full conformity with the spirit of his time Holdheim demanded "that the Israelites in those German lands where their church has obtained a legal constitution from the state should strive for a uniformity that would be appropriate to their changed needs and conditions in any regulation [*Ordnung*] of their ecclesiastical relationships, and particularly in the improvement of their rites."[32]

In accordance with this maxim, at the beginning of the first rabbinical conference in Brunswick in 1844 Holdheim asked for and secured the approbation of the Synagogue Order of Mecklenburg-Schwerin to which the assembly acceded.[33] At this conference as well as at the following ones in Frankfurt am Main in 1845 and in Breslau in 1846, Holdheim played a prominent role in most of the debates. For our purpose some of his statements on the discussed liturgical reforms will be briefly summarized.

With regard to the question of the legitimacy of introducing German into the service Holdheim now claimed:

---

[32] *Synagogen-Ordnung für die Synagogen des Großherzogthums Mecklenburg-Schwerin unter allerhöchster Genehmigung festgesetzt von dem israelitischen Oberrath in Schwerin* (Schwerin: C. Kürschner, 1843), 5.

[33] *Protocolle der ersten Rabbiner-Versammlung, abgehalten zu Braunschweig vom 12ten bis zum 19ten Juni 1844* (Brunswick: Vieweg, 1844), 21: "Eine Hochwürdige erste Rabb.-Versammlung wolle die Synagogenordnung des Großherzogth. Mecklenburg-Schwerin prüfen und dahin begutachten, daß dieselbe dem jüdischen Glauben und Ritus gemäß sei, und daß jeder rechtgläubige Jude an dem nach dieser Synagogen-Ordnung abzuhaltenden Gottesdienst Theil nehmen darf."

There is no strictly Talmudic Judaism. Scholarship has concluded that practically and dogmatically the Talmud has no authority. Even those who do not want to acknowledge this ignore the Talmud. The question is: Who gives us the right to alter a liturgy?[34]

Here we can clearly observe a departure from his earlier argumentation in the Hamburg Temple debate, when the authority of the Talmud was still unquestioned.

The question of the language to be used in the service was one of the most controversial themes at the *Rabbinerversammlungen*. At the second assembly, held in Frankfurt in 1845, Holdheim strongly advocated the vernacular in the service:

There is no need to fear being pushed out of one's religious persuasion through removing the Heb[rew] language from the service [....] [using] the national language in the service, where required, would exert a most beneficial influence on the purification of religious ideas and, instead of harming Judaism, would, on the contrary, bring about a strengthening of its mission internally and recognition externally.[35]

Abraham Geiger argued in a similar way, confessing "that a German prayer stimulates deep worship more than a Hebrew one does."[36]

Holdheim's objection to the Talmud coupled with his insistence on a biblically grounded Judaism became clear when he demanded that the reading of the Torah be kept in Hebrew: "The Torah should continue to be read in Hebrew. Young people must get to know the Pentateuch in the original language!"[37] In questions concerning the reform of the worship service, for instance with respect to prayers for the return to Israel, any decisions had to adhere to a strict division between the religious and the political spheres. The question about the holy nature of the Sabbath led Holdheim to the following basic idea: "For once we cannot adopt the view of the Sabbath held by the rabbis. Rather we must ask our conscience what the Sabbath celebration should be like."[38]

---

[34] Ibid., 55.

[35] *Protokolle und Aktenstücke der zweiten Rabbiner-Versammlung, abgehalten zu Frankfurt am Main, vom 15ten bis zum 28ten Juli 1845* (Frankfurt am Main: E. Ullmann, 1845), 31.

[36] Ibid., 33. For Holdheim's criticism on Geiger's first prayerbook, published in 1854, which was composed mainly in Hebrew with a German paraphrase, see below.

[37] Ibid., 68.

[38] Ibid., 90.

The problem of the Sabbath was the main theme at the third
rabbinical conference in Breslau. For this assembly Holdheim delivered the introductory paper, using as his starting point the basic biblical idea of the Sabbath, that of God resting after completing the
Creation—as the symbol of God's absolute eternity and elevation
over everything created by Him, who sought to present the resting
of human beings on this day as the symbolic representation of this
idea. In this manner Holdheim could draw the following "bold conclusion," as he himself put it:

> All of our efforts to restore a dignified Sabbath celebration have been
> in vain and there is unfortunately no way to reconcile the Sabbath
> celebration in detail with the demands of civic [*bürgerlich*] life other
> than moving the first to a ferial [*bürgerlich*] day. I protest against any
> concession that would have us believe that this move has been done
> in accordance with Christian beliefs; I am only concerned about the
> chance to celebrate a dignified Sabbath.[39]

The way in which Holdheim's views became increasingly more radical reveals all too clearly that his position as *Landesrabbiner* of
Mecklenburg-Schwerin was not the ideal base for trying to carry out
his reformist ideas. It is, therefore, no surprise to learn that in 1847
Holdheim left this post to become the rabbi and preacher of the
Berlin *Genossenschaft für Reform im Judenthume*, which had been established in 1845; it should be emphasized that it was Holdheim's
explicit wish to have the title of rabbi alongside that of preacher.
To a certain degree this step seems already to have been prefigured
by his behavior at the third assembly: when the assembled rabbis
decided not to respond to the "declaration of solidarity" by the Berlin
Genossenschaft, Holdheim vehemently dissented. On the other hand,
he explicitly requested that it be recorded that in the Sabbath question the Berlin *Reform Genossenschaft* and the rabbinical assembly did
not differ from each other. In the beginning, the Berlin Reform
Congregation held their services on both Saturday and Sunday, but
under the auspices of Holdheim Sunday became the day of worship.

---

[39] *Protokolle der dritten Versammlung deutscher Rabbiner, abgehalten zu Breslau vom 13. bis
24. Juli 1846* (Breslau: Leuckart, 1847), 70-71.

4

The following passages are devoted to the analysis of prayerbooks of the *Genossenschaft für Reform im Judenthume*. Before the appearance of the first complete prayerbook of the Berlin Reform Congregation in 1848 (in two volumes, Part One being entitled *Allwöchentliche Gebete und häusliche Andacht* and Part Two *Die Festgebete*) seven experimental prayer leaflets had been published in 1845 and 1846, starting with the services for Rosh ha-Shanah and Yom Kippur. In the preface to the Rosh ha-Shanah service the preliminary character of the arrangement is stressed,[40] but the experimental leaflets became the basis for all the following prayerbooks, with one exception, namely Holdheim's own prayerbook, as we shall see. The Berlin Reform Congregation formulated its service in the German language; only the first verse of the *Shema* and the *Kedushah* and a few similar verses were recited in Hebrew. This tendency was, as we have seen, in accordance with Holdheim's demand for reforming the service. The prayer texts were radically shortened, the German sometimes paraphrasing more than translating the Hebrew, and new prayers in the spirit of the period and choral singing were introduced.

The biblical text of the Shema is limited to the first quotation from Deuteronomy 6. In accordance with the general tendency of these leaflets to universalize the prayers, the phrase with "Israel's redeemer" at the end of the third blessing is altered as follows: "Praised be Thou O Lord, Eternal Savior." In none of the prayers does the *Havienu* appear, nor are the firstborn of Egypt killed and the Pharaoh with his soldiers is not sunk in the sea. But, most striking, the *Or Hadash*, the New Light over Zion, which had been disputed since the Hamburg prayerbook, appears in the Reform service for the first time in the service of the second day of Rosh ha-Shanah in the following form: "Then, like Thy sun, Thou hast allowed a new light from Zion to shine; o let us all walk soon in this light." Also, the Reform prayerbook completely ignores the utopian character of the original wording, the hope to return to Zion. Moreover,

---

[40] *Gebete und Gesänge zu dem von der Genossenschaft für Reform im Judenthum eingerichteten Gottesdienst in Berlin, für das Neujahrsfest des Weltjahres 5606* (als Manuscript gedruckt) (Berlin: Im Selbst-Verlage der Genossenschaft, 1845), preface (n.p.): "Die ganze Einrichtung ist nur für diese Tage und macht keineswegs darauf Anspruch, für folgende Jahre in Geltung zu bleiben."

it is highly questionable whether the new form is a good choice in order to illuminate the tremendous changes in nineteenth-century Europe. Most of the reformers would not have accepted "the New Light over Zion" as an adequate symbol to express this ongoing process: to put it in visual terms, if a new light appeared to be rising, then it should do so from and over Europe, not from Zion. Here the Reform congregation's prayer leaflets are indeed inconsistent (and there are other examples like this one).[41]

Despite its very radical character in remolding the whole service, the prayerbook is boldly reactionary in some parts. This becomes even more evident when we compare it with the demands uttered by certain reform-oriented rabbis that the main body of the service had to be conducted in Hebrew and the traditional wording and form of the standard prayers had to be more or less retained. A very fine example of this more balanced position within the reform movement is the prayerbook which Joseph von Maier published in 1848. While the German translation is, for the most part, a paraphrase of the Hebrew original, there is no question in Maier's mind that "the Hebrew language represents [....] a holy bond which one should never sever completely."[42] In his prayerbook the *Or Hadash* of the first benediction is missing, and in the second *Berakhah* the *Havienu* was adopted from the Hamburg prayerbook. Most of the Reform prayerbooks in the nineteenth century are shaped like Maier's edition; in particular, the *Or Hadash* is omitted in most of them.

Thus we may ask how Holdheim intended to handle all the inconsistencies in the prayerbook of the Berlin Reform congregation when he became its rabbi and preacher in 1847. As already mentioned, only one year after he assumed office the experimental leaflets were transformed into the first official prayerbook of the community; it offers nine cycles in order to add some variety to the regular Sunday service.[43] Indeed, as Holdheim pointed out in his *Geschichte der Entstehung und Entwicklung der jüdischen Reformgemeinde in Berlin*, published in 1857, he was by no means a friend of this liturgy, as the following quotation

---

[41] See Petuchowski's analysis of the service of the Berlin Reform congregation in his *Prayerbook Reform in Europe*, 58ff.

[42] Quoted from the introduction to Maier's prayerbook *Israelitisches Gebet- und Andachtsbuch, zum Gebrauche bei der häuslichen und öffentlichen Gottesverehrung* (Stuttgart: Zu Guttenberg, 1848), VI.

[43] This reminds us of the last edition of the American liberal prayerbook *Gates of Prayer*, which offers a choice of four different arrangements for the service.

demonstrates, in which he tries to excuse its various insufficiencies:

> The prayerbook based on the service and now in the hands of the Jewish Reform community has come into being by way of a slow and gradual development; not, however, in the sense of working on it by slowly examining and carefully pondering it, but in the sense of always working only on the most immediate burning needs, from hand to mouth, so to speak, but then quite quickly and hurriedly.[44]

The situation in the revolutionary year 1848 was even worse: "That quite turbulent period of summer 1848 was the most unfavorable time imaginable to do a calm and thorough revision of a prayerbook."[45] According to his own testimony his major contribution to the prayerbook was the preface. Indeed, this text does not even try to evaluate the underlying concept of the prayerbook, but makes only some very general remarks. Nevertheless, the first prayerbook of the Reform congregation does show some differences to the earlier prayer leaflets, and we may ask whether this happened on Holdheim's request. The theme treated at first by Holdheim in the preface is "Israel's chosenness," characterized as a "subjective fact in the religious consciousness of the Jewish people," so that Holdheim can state: "In this sense it is still a truth, even for us, that Israel was a chosen nation." But there is also an "objective fact" ["Objektive Thatsache"], defined as follows: "The human characteristic and dignity, being the image of God, is for us the exclusive sign of being chosen." Against this background it is interesting to note some textual changes in our prooftext, the *Shema*. Instead of the statement, "Thou hast chosen us from all tongues and nations and brought us close to the truth of Thy essence in order to praise and acknowledge Thee as the only one. Blessed be Thou, o Lord, who has chosen Israel in love, to glorify Thy name" ["Denn uns hast Du erwählt von allen Zungen und Nationen und uns nahe geführt der Wahrheit Deines Wesens, um Dich zu preisen und als den Einzigen zu bekennen. Gepriesen seist Du Herr, der Du Israel erkoren hast in Liebe, um Deinen Namen zu verherrlichen,"], we now read: "Thou hast called us from all tongues and nations and brought us close to the truth of Thy essence in order to praise and acknowledge Thee as

---

[44] Holdheim, *Geschichte der Enstehung und Entwicklung der jüdischen Reformgemeinde in Berlin*, 193.
[45] Ibid., 194.

the only one. Blessed be Thou, o Lord, who has called Israel in
love, to glorify Thy name among all the sons of the earth" ["Und
uns hast Du berufen von allen Zungen und Nationen und uns nahe
geführt der Wahrheit Deines Wesens, um dich zu preisen und als
den Einzigen zu bekennen. Gepriesen seist Du Herr, der Du Israel
berufen hast in Liebe, um Deinen Namen zu verherrlichen unter
allen Erdensöhnen."].[46] By adding the phrase "among all the sons
of the earth," ["unter allen Erdensöhnen"] the idea of the chosen
people is universalized by avoiding any particularistic understanding
of the prayer. Thus the latter could have been changed under
Holdheim's influence. Elsewhere we read in the preface: "Everywhere
the national and dogmatically stifling imprint had to give way to the
vital flow of purely human, truly religious thought."[47] As might already
be expected by now, in the 1848 edition of the prayerbook the *Or
Hadash*, the new light over Zion, disappeared entirely. Here again I
would suggest that Holdheim's influence is visible.

In his aforementioned history of the Reform congregation, Holdheim
listed all his reservations about the prayerbook of his own community.
Before coming to this point, however, let us have a brief look at Geiger's
prayerbook, published in 1854. As we have seen, Abraham Geiger was
one of the most severe critics of the Hamburg Temple Prayerbook.
We might, therefore, expect that his own 1854 prayerbook for the
Breslau congregation would be as radical as his criticism. But on the
contrary: his prayerbook follows the structure of the traditional prayerbook very closely. Therefore Holdheim criticized him for being inconsistent and accused him of contradicting his own statements during the
rabbinical conferences.[48] The conservatism of Geiger's prayerbook is

---

[46] *Gebetbuch der Genossenschaft für Reform im Judenthum. Erster Theil: Allwöchentliche Gebete
und häusliche Andacht* (Berlin: Im Selbst-Verlag der Genossenschaft, 1848), 44.

[47] Ibid., X.

[48] See particularly the statement in Holdheim, *Geschichte der Entstehung und Entwicklung
der jüdischen Reformgemeinde in Berlin*, 197: "Geiger (schreibt) in der Vorrede zu dem
von ihm im Jahre 1854 herausgegebenen Gebetbuch S. VII. [....]: 'Das Ansehen
der Gebete knüpft sich aber nicht blos an deren Inhalt, sondern an die ganze
überkommene Gestalt, an das Wort, in dem sie sich zu uns vererbt haben, also auch
die hebräische Sprache. Sie bleibe also, mit wenigen Ausnahmen, die Sprache des
Gebetes.' Wir vermögen nicht diese Ansicht mit seinem eigenem in der 2.
Rabbinerversammlung 1845 (Protokoll S. 32. 33) so laut und öffentlich ausge-
sprochenem Urtheil zu vereinbaren, nach welchem er es für wünschenswert hält,
daß in der Muttersprache gebetet werde, in welcher unsere tiefsten Empfindungen
und Gefühle, unsere heiligsten Beziehungen, unsere höchsten Gedanken ihren Ausdruck
finden; ja nach welchem er es für die tiefste Verletzung des Judenthums erklären

above all a concession to the familiar traditional wording of the prayers, which he did not want to change. But this wording is clearly not meant to be understood literally at all, as is evidenced by Geiger's German translation, or rather paraphrase, which is much more radical.

Thus we find in Geiger's 1854 prayerbook the *Or Hadash* in the first *Berakhah*, but the German translation allows no light to rise over Zion: "So let also the light of the spirit, the sun of truth and of salvation rise over us all, so that we can enjoy it in clarity and fervor!"[49] The same holds true for the phrases "Thou hast killed all their firstborn and saved all Thy firstborn," "The arrogant Thou hast sunk," "the waters covered their enemies, no one was left" in the third *Berakhah*, which are paraphrased in German as "du hast der Aegypter Uebermuth versenkt" ["Thou hast sunk the over exuberance of the Egyptians"].[50] In spite of the conservative character of the Hebrew wording, here too, there are two subjects about which Geiger made no compromises and in which he always wanted to have changes made whenever they turned up in a prayer: these are the restoration of the sacrificial cult and the ingathering of the exiles. Thus the *Havienu* in the second *Berakhah* of his version is missing. Moreover, there is a further textual change, which, as far as I know, is found for the first time in his edition and illustrates very nicely his attitude in this question. Immediately after the *Havienu* the traditional prayerbook reads: "For Thou art a God who brings about salvation and Thou hast chosen us out of all the nations and tongues and brought us closer to Thy great name." This sentence was adopted without any change in all the prayerbooks discussed so far, while different accentuations are definitely noticeable in the German translations.

The Hamburg prayerbook of 1819 reads:

> "Thou hast brought us, from all the people, closer to Thy holy name" ["Du hast uns von allem Volk deinem heiligen Namen nähergebracht"].[51]

The revised edition of the Hamburg prayerbook (1841) reads more literally:

---

müsse, wenn man dieses auf der Krücke einer Sprache einhergehend denke und es als ein nationale Religion darstelle, die mit der Sprache auf's Engste verknüpft sei."

[49] *Israelitisches Gebetbuch für den öffentlichen Gottesdienst im ganzen Jahre: mit Einschluß der Sabbathe und sämmtlicher Feier- und Festtage, geordnet und mit einer neuen deutschen Bearb[eitung] ver[sehen] von Abraham Geiger* (Breslau: Hainauer, 1854), 33.

[50] Ibid., 43.

[51] *Ordnung der öffentlichen Andacht für die Sabbath- und Festtage des ganzen Jahres,* 37.

"Thou hast chosen us out of all sorts of people and languages" ["Du hast uns aus allerlei Volk und Sprache erwählt"].[52]

Kirchenrath von Maier in 1848 translates this phrase in the following way:

"We are the ones Thou hast chosen out of all peoples and tongues" ["Uns hast du erkoren aus allen Völkern und Zungen].[53]

Even the radical Berlin Reform Congregation took, as we have seen, no basic offense at this phrase, which was changed from the literal translation "For Thou hast chosen us from all the tongues and nations" ["Denn uns hast Du erwählt von allen Zungen und Nationen"] into "Thou hast called us from all tongues and nations" ["Du hast uns berufen von allen Zungen und Nationen"].[54]

The Hebrew phrase *mikol am ve-lashon* ("out of all nations and languages") was struck out for the first time in Geiger's prayerbook. In German this section appears as follows: "Thou hast called Israel to Thy holy Torah, to glorify Thy name throughout the world" ["Du hast Israel zu deiner heiligen Lehre erkoren, daß es deinen Namen verherrliche durch alle Welt."] However minor this textual alteration may appear at first glance, it implies a whole worldview as far as Geiger is concerned. This he formulated in the *Denkschrift* which he submitted to the Frankfurt congregational authorities in 1869, as follows:

Concerning, in particular, the position of Israel in world history, this must be strongly articulated in the following direction: Judaism is the religion of truth and of light [....]. Consequently, the national aspect of Israel must recede into the background: the once existing separation between Israel and the other peoples has no right to be expressed in prayer. Rather there ought to be an expression of the joy that such barriers are increasingly falling.[55]

Geiger published these principles several times, including them in the revised version of his prayerbook printed in 1870 for the congregation

---

[52] *Gebetbuch für die öffentliche und häusliche Andacht, nach dem Gebrauch des Neuen Israelitischen Tempels in Hamburg,* 59.

[53] *Israelitisches Gebet- und Andachtsbuch, zum Gebrauche bei der häuslichen und öffentlichen Gottesverehrung,* 35.

[54] *Gebetbuch der Genossenschaft für Reform im Judenthum. Erster Theil: Allwöchentliche Gebete und häusliche Andacht,* 44.

[55] Quoted according to the reprint of the *Denkschrift* in the introduction to his prayerbook *Israelitisches Gebetbuch für den öffentlichen Gottesdienst im ganzen Jahre* (1870), VIII.

in Frankfurt, although by this time Geiger had already moved to Berlin. The main difference to the 1854 edition is that in the Hebrew text of the revised version Geiger expressed his basic standpoint much more strongly than before. For example, in the first *Berakhah* the *Or Hadash* is now omitted.

As pointed out above, Holdheim was by no means a friend of the prayerbook of his own community. In his history of the Reform Congregation he reduced his verdict on this book to the simple formula: "Apart from the language, the restructuring of the messianic idea is the only positive feature, therefore the only reform in the prayerbook."[56] This sounds indeed like a devastating critique. Holdheim sees the real reason for the deficiencies of the work in the fact "that as our Reform first got started, it had to make its way through the revolution, whose very nature is always negation, and that the positively creative and formative forces can become effective only by [plowing] the ground liberated by the revolution."[57]

Here Holdheim formulates his positive-constructive criticism of the prayerbook in the context of the discussion of ten motions, which a commission, established in 1856 by the community board on Holdheim's request, had proposed, summarizing it as follows:

> We must thank God for the higher spiritual and moral education and, even more, for the religious standpoint purified and transfigured in the light of this education, a religious stance which reveals the moral-religious liberation from the binding nature of that law to which our fathers had once been bound. This is the essence of the positive reform which the prayerbook is supposed to express![58]

What does this mean in concrete terms? Not to ignore and repress things at any rate. This is true for the omission of the shofar blasts on Rosh ha-Shanah and the Four Species bouquet on Sukkoth, as well as for the Tefillin, Mezuzah and Kippah, which were no longer in use in Holdheim's community. He declared that "Not oblivion, but only the further construction of Judaism have we recognized and proclaimed as our goal." The task he envisioned consisted in "fulfilling and penetrating the historical memories with our reformatory

---

[56] Holdheim, *Geschichte der Entstehung und Entwicklung der jüdischen Reformgemeinde in Berlin*, 198.

[57] Ibid. 198.

[58] Ibid., 205.

spirit, in purifying and transfiguring them, in placing that aspect in the foreground which is a worthy object of the festival and in creating the fitting form for it."[59] Thus Holdheim could not help but admit that the prayerbook then being used was not entirely incorrectly criticized as "half-Jewish" or even "unhistorical" because of its a-historical nature. While the new prayers of the prayerbook contained too many fashionable clichés, they lacked the "biblical spirit," namely "in the form of biblical simplicity and language." However, he wrote, this diagnosis should definitely not be interpreted as a call for falling back into a "dogmatically rigid biblical viewpoint," best offset by the "historical authority of post-biblical Judaism, the Talmud." Among the fashionable innovations that Holdheim did not like at all were the—let's call a spade a spade—Protestant-like opening chorales, which he felt could be replaced by psalm recitations: "If Christians return to the original and organic nature of the Jewish psalms, why should we seek our refuge in Christian art? Whatever in our chorales is found to have been lifted from Christian hymnals must be removed."[60] But it was not before the 1885 revision and edition of the prayerbook of the Berlin Reform Congregation that the introductory chorals were replaced by psalms.

Two really significant community achievements definitely worth retaining, according to Holdheim, were the general use of German in the worship service, which was singularly effective in promoting the edification and religious devotion of the participants, and the switching of the weekly worship service to Sunday. German must only be used for the prayers, however, whereas the reading from the Bible should be in Hebrew, "because only the Bible composed in this language, not in some other translated language, Hebrew can be valid as the source of knowledge of religion." With respect to Sunday as the true day of the Sabbath festival and rest in the community, it ought "to be called by its name so that the most courageous and most decisive of our deeds will not seem to have been illusory and futile."[61] Holdheim's reflections on the worship service seem extremely sophisticated, yet fully consistent in their peculiar crosshatching of radicalism and conservativism. How did Holdheim then put his theories about the worship service into practice?

---

[59] Ibid., 200.
[60] Ibid., 207.
[61] Ibid., 209.

As mentioned at the very beginning of this article, he published his only prayerbook, *Gebete und Gesänge für das Neujahrs- und Versöhnungsfest*, only one year before his death. Without going into details, the whole service clearly expresses his above-mentioned theories of the service. Now how did he render our prooftext—the *Shema* and its blessings? Interestingly enough, the *Shema* is by no means very suited for evaluating Holdheim's book, for in his prayerbook it is transmitted in a strongly abbreviated, fragmentary form. The reason is simple enough, since Holdheim criticized the older book for including the everyday prayers more or less unabridged in the festival service, but neglecting those prayers which are typical for the holidays: "You just need to take one look at the two morning services of the Rosh Ha-Shanah festival and note how long it takes to wind your way through the welter of the everyday-prayer section before encountering a real holiday prayer, appearing like a flowering oasis in the desert!"[62] As a consequence, Holdheim did just the opposite: he minimized the everyday prayers and focused more on those prayers which would arouse "festive feelings and moods" ["festliche Gefühle und Stimmungen"] among the visitors of the service. Nevertheless, I would argue that, at least to some extent, we can reconstruct his prayerbook for the weekly service. I even like to imagine that he may have completed a handwritten version of his book before his death. Admittedly, I have no idea what was in his estate and it is, of course, quite daring to speculate about it, but it seems worthwhile to do it.

To be sure, the biblical part of the *Shema* is included in the festival service as well and the quotation is limited to the first section from Deuteronomy 6 as before. It is interesting to note a slight change in the translation. The 1848 prayerbook tried to skirt the issue of wearing *tefillin* by translating this passage in a very literal way: "Wear them to bear witness on your hands and as a reminder before your eyes"; whereas, by following his principles, Holdheim had no intention of disguising the traditional behavior: "Bind them on your arm to bear witness and wear them between your eyes as a memorial."[63] As far back as 1848, in the preface to the prayerbook then being published, Holdheim had stated:

---

[62] Ibid., 202.
[63] *Gebete und Gesänge für das Neujahrs- und Versöhnungsfest*, 4.

Even if this sensorial marking is missing from our arms, this conspicuous feature from our foreheads, yet we still bear the thoughts and
feelings connected with it in our minds and our hearts and we like to
remember that our fathers sought to express the same thoughts and
feelings through symbols appropriate for their period and their whole
spiritual view of life."[64]

What happened to the phrase "Thou who hast chosen us from all
the nations and languages" in the second blessing? As we have seen,
Geiger strongly opposed the phrase "from all the nations and languages," which was eliminated from his prayerbook. Not so Holdheim,
in whose prayerbook we find the following:

Thou hast chosen Israel from all the nations, hast blessed it with Thy
love, sanctified it with Thy commandments, consecrated it to Thy service, so that it may worship Thee with a pure heart in the truth and
bear Thy great and holy name through all the ages in the whole world.

According to Holdheim, the idea of the chosen people is a historical fact that cannot be ignored. But it has to be transformed and
universalized; thus the aforementioned passage continues as follows:

Out of paternal graciousness Thou hast granted us this day of commemoration (jom ha-zikaron), on which we become aware that Thou,
Almighty, thinks of mankind, that Thou, Infinite, respects the earthly
son, tests him every day, purifies him every moment and watches over
him with Thy all-loving Providence.[65]

In another prayer Holdheim expresses this universalization idea
as follows: "And as Abraham was the model for Israel, so is the
image of the purest mankind reflected in the fate of Israel. Thou,
O God, hast chosen men for salvation."[66] In this regard Holdheim
is more consistent than Geiger and true to his maxim—not to forget, not to ignore, but to reform positively. I would even like to go
one step further. I would not be surprised, if, despite all the expected
cuts and renderings, Holdheim would have included the *Havienu* in
the second blessing of the Shema ("And bring us in peace from the
four corners of the earth, and lead us upright to our land"). Indeed,
in the Rosh ha-Shanah service the same idea is expressed in the

---

[64] *Gebetbuch der Genossenschaft für Reform im Judenthum. Erster Theil: Allwöchentliche Gebete und häusliche Andacht,* X.
[65] Holdheim, *Gebete und Gesänge für das Neujahrs- und Versöhnungsfest,* 3.
[66] Ibid., 51.

prayer *Ata nigleta*. In the older prayerbook this prayer is transmitted in a very fragmentary and unsystematic way. Holdheim criticized this kind of deficient citation. When we look at the end of the prayer with the *Havienu*-phrase, we will easily understand why this prayer was not cited in its entirety:

> Our God and God our father, blow the great shofar to our freedom and raise a banner to gather our exiled and bring close our scattered people out of the midst of the nations and collect our dispersed people from the ends of the earth, bring us with jubilation into Thy city Zion and with eternal joy to Jerusalem, the site of Thy sanctum. There, before Thee, we want to prepare the sacrifice of our duty.

How did Holdheim handle this phrase? He universalized the whole text in the following manner:

> Our God and Father! Let Thy consolatory promises, which you have pronounced through the mouth of Thy servants, the Prophets, be fulfilled and let the time draw near when Thy exalted divine voice shall ring out mightily, like the resounding of trumpets in the mountains, in the hearts of all men, when Thou shall gather the exiled in the land of error and all the banished in the realm of superstition and lead them back into the holy land of truth and of faith in Thee, the one eternal God.[67]

Here we clearly can see that, according to Holdheim, an outmoded historical commemoration could be, or better, should be transformed into a new universalistic understanding of religion, whereas a falsely placed utopian hope—the return to Zion and the reestablishing of the offerings in Jerusalem—needed to be replaced by a new one. Therefore we should probably not expect to find in his weekly prayerbook the *Or Hadash*, unless the text was changed, as in the above-mentioned example, in the Rosh ha-Shanah liturgy. But, as we have seen, this phrase had been already deleted in the 1848 prayerbook and, as suggested before, this might have been done at Holdheim's request. In any case, if Holdheim had been able to publish a prayerbook for the whole liturgical year, his own community would hardly have appreciated it. Indeed, Holdheim's successor, Immanuel Heinrich Ritter, in his biography on Holdheim, praised most of his works and activities without any hesitation—except his prayerbook. Here we read:

---

[67] Ibid., 32.

It will also have been said of them (the prayers in Holdheim's prayerbook) [....] that they contain much that is sound and eminently use-
able details, that by and large, however, they fail to strike the right
note and [respect] the limits which are imperative for a simple solemn
worship service.[68]

---

[68] Immanuel Heinrich Ritter, *Samuel Holdheim. Sein Leben und seine Werke. Ein Beitrag
zu den Reformbestrebungen im Judenthume* (Berlin: W. J. Peiser, 1865), 288.

THE PROBLEMS OF MODERATE REFORM:
THE HISTORY OF THE BERLIN
LITURGICAL REFORMS, 1844–1862*

Margit Schad

When scholars speak of reform in Berlin, they usually refer either to the controversy over the reform of religious services by Israel Jacobson and Jacob Herz Beer between 1814 and 1823, or to the Reform Association. Scholarship has generally overlooked the fact that the years between 1844 and 1858 saw a struggle over, and the eventual implementation of, a moderate reform of communal religious service in Berlin. The reason for this neglect may be the moderate nature of the reform, but also the problematic situation of source material. The flow of sources is, unfortunately, quite sparse. What has been passed down, in Ludwig Geiger, for example, is contradictory, and in some cases only fragments are still extant.[1] Missing primary sources must be supplemented and replaced with secondary sources, chiefly press reports and private accounts. In this hitherto unwritten story of the reform of religious service in Berlin, Rabbi Michael Sachs (1808-1864) played a central role.[2]

Sachs was an ardent opponent of the Reform movement, even though he shared, in principle, the notion that regeneration and reform were necessary in the religious service and the school system. His opposition was born not only from divergent opinions about the scope and nature of the needed changes. His assessment of the motivations that drove the reformers—"emancipation mania" (*Emanzipationssucht*), which went hand in hand with an internalization

---

* Translated from the German by Thomas Dunlap.
[1] Ludwig Geiger, *Geschichte der Juden in Berlin*, 2 vols. (Berlin: Guttentag, 1871-1890; reprint Berlin: arani, 1988), vol. 1, 204-205.
[2] A detailed account can be found in my monograph on Michael Sachs; see Margit Schad, *Judentum als Lebensanschauung und Literatur. Michael Sachs (1808-1864) —Rabbiner, Prediger und Übersetzer* (Hildesheim: Georg Olms Verlag, 2006).

of anti-Jewish arguments, and a "presumption" that was aimed at the founding of a "new Judaism,"[3]—did not allow any rapprochement.

Sachs had been a keen observer of conditions in the Prussian capital during his years at the University of Berlin (1827-1835). In the third great wave of conversions, which convulsed Berlin Jewry on its path into modernity, he experienced the last aftershocks of the governmental ban on any reform and the breaking off of the reform controversy in 1823.[4] Resignation and stagnation, the split of the community into hostile camps of traditionalists and supporters of reform, the "epidemic of baptism," and a growing indifference and apathy, especially toward the religious concerns of the community, conveyed to the young Sachs a sense that Judaism was in a profound spiritual crisis. What he saw and experienced in Berlin led him to search for a third way, one that would draw the consequences from the "insensibility" (Bewußtlosigkeit) and "passivity" (Tatenlosigkeit) of Orthodoxy, on the one hand, and the "arbitrariness" of a reform that was oriented exclusively toward the needs of a present celebrated with inappropriate euphoria, on the other hand, and would win back the indifferent. But first he succeeded Leopold Zunz as the preacher of the "Temple" in Prague, where he gathered experience with the model of moderate reform adopted from Vienna.

On 25 March 1844, Sachs was elected third Rabbinic assessor in Berlin, after years of negotiations with Zacharias Frankel had ended in failure. Eighty-six Orthodox and reform-minded members of the community lodged a protest against his election, objecting not only to Sachs himself, but also to the election procedure and to the holding of new elections as such.[5] Supporters of radical reform could not expect that Sachs, whose position was suspect to them, would pursue the sort of reforms they had in mind. Orthodox opponents, meanwhile, rejected the establishment of the post of preacher who was rewarded as a Rabbinical assessor as an inadmissible innovation;

---

[3] Michael Sachs, *Festpredigten und Sabbatpredigten zum ersten und zweiten Buch Mose* (Berlin: Louis Gerschel, 1866/67), 41, 427, 469.

[4] On the reform controversy between 1814 and 1823 see Michael A. Meyer, "The Religious Reform Controversy in the Berlin Jewish Community, 1814-1823," *LBIYB* 24 (1979), 139-155.

[5] See the letter by Carl Lehfeldt to Michael Sachs, dated 21 April 1844, in Central Archives for the History of the Jewish People, Jerusalem (CAHJP), P 41/4; Simon Bernfeld, *Mikha'el Zaqs. Me'ora'ot hajjav u-fe'ulato ha-sifrutit* (Berlin: s.n., 1900), 47; Geheimes Staatsarchiv—Preußischer Kulturbesitz, Berlin (GStA PK) I. HA, Rep. 76 III, Sekt. 12, Abt. XVI, Nr. 2.

they were suspicious, and not without reason, that this would bring further reforms in its wake. However, Rabbi Jakob Josef Oettinger (1780-1860), had agreed to work with Sachs—whom he knew since 1827, when Sachs began his studies in Berlin—on the condition that he would only deliver German sermons and provide religious instruction. As a result, when Sachs assumed his post in October 1844, he was able to introduce the German sermon into the service of the Old Synagogue without any meaningful opposition. Shortly thereafter, on 11 November, the board asked him to draw up the basic principles and concrete elements of a reform of the religious service.

For years, the religious service of the Berlin community had been the subject of criticism and wishes for reform even from the side of religious conservatives. The banker and wholesale merchant Aron Hirsch Heymann (1802-1880), a longtime leader of the community and a synagogue warden, strove for moderate changes corresponding to the norms and rules of bourgeois life style. According to critical observers, the communal service of the synagogue in the Heidereuter Gasse was sparsely attended even on the Sabbath and holydays, and it offered "a depressing sight of abandonment and desolation."[6] Many members of the community attended smaller "*Winkelsynagogen*" (unofficial synagogues), since the service there was shortened through the elimination of the *piyutim*, and only came to the Alte Synagoge afterwards.[7] The constant coming and going, public conversation, and offering of tobacco were seen as incompatible with "dignity" and "solemnity." R. Oettinger showed little interest in the service of the community; instead, he held his own private service. In 1838, Heymann introduced a code of synagogue regulations (*Synagogenordnung*), a small men's choir, and official vestments for the cantor.[8] These innovations must not have lasted long, however, for in 1844 there were efforts to combat the same conditions that Heymann had sought to change.

Sachs presented his proposals for a reform of the service on 2 December 1844.[9] As he saw it, this reform should not proceed from

---

[6] See *AZJ* 4 (1840), 637.

[7] See Aron Hirsch Heymann, *Lebenserinnerungen*, ed. Heinrich Loewe (Berlin: Poppelauer, 1909), 250.

[8] Ibid., 249-251. See also Michael A. Meyer, "'Ganz nach dem alten Herkommen'? The Spiritual Life of Berlin Jewry Following the Edict of 1823," in *Bild und Selbstbild der Juden Berlins zwischen Aufklärung und Romantik*, ed. Marianne Awerbuch (Berlin: Colloquium-Verlag, 1992), 229-243, here 241.

a clash between historical Judaism and the Judaism of the present, or that between ritual law and "life." Rather, it should be based on the realization (1) that religious self-awareness, history, and law, on the one hand, and the "legitimate" needs of the present, like that of a reform of the service, on the other hand, have always had and continue to have a living coexistence, and (2) that the current crisis must be blamed on the *Zeitgeist* ('nihilism,' 'materialism,' 'indifference,' and 'selfishness'), and not on historical Judaism. Sachs positioned his reform projects distinctly between Reform movement and Orthodoxy. Radical reforms, he believed, destroyed the creative potential of self-understanding and self-cleansing; the Orthodox side, meanwhile, placed every tradition and custom as holy and inviolable in the way of the living development. For the results are "petrification" ("Erstarrung"), "spiritlessness" ("Geistlosigkeit") and "religious indifference"; a reform which deserves its name must reopen the staunched process of life and the inner potentials of self-cleansing and self-development.

Thus, the principles of moderate reform were to restore what was pristine and original, "give shape to the shapeless," "invigorate the spiritless and lifeless," and reorganize the "external" that it might become the "bearer of the inner":

> Everything that disturbs the quiet and devotion of the synagogue, and that goes against its elevated and holy meaning, must be removed. Everything that elevates the dignity and meaning of prayer, that is suitable to imparting solemnity and holiness to the synagogue, must be introduced. The formless must be given shape, that which is merely disfigured and distorted must be returned to its original shape and form, the spiritless and lifeless must be invigorated, the external must be ordered in such a way that it can become the bearer of the internal, that the synagogue may present itself as the place of assembly of a religious, educated community [....].[10]

According to Sachs, the regeneration must occur out of its own substance, without the adoption of alien forms that are not grounded in the nature and historical essence of the Jewish service:

> Ordering and shaping the religious service requires not so much the

---

[9] "Gesichtspunkte, die bei der gottesdienstlichen Ordnung in der Synagoge als leitend festzuhalten sein dürften," 21 Kislev 5605, copy in CAHJP, P 17/549, from which the following quotes are taken.

[10] Ibid., 23.

introduction of new components that are foreign to it, than the elimination and removal of those that have taken away its original character and have been detrimental to its dignity; the point is less to support or prop it up by means external to it, than to bring out the elements that are inherent in it, that form and sustain it.[11]

A code of synagogue regulations was intended to put a stop to the "walking around," the "chaotic yelling," and the "chats with neighbors" during the service, to restore "dignity" and "solemnity," and to eliminate "abuses."[12] The auctioning off of *mitzvoth* was to be abolished, the *mi she-berakh* blessings restricted, while other customs, such as the kaddish prayer and the priestly blessing, would be regularized and coordinated. The traditional performance of Torah reading was to be retained, but more emphasis would be placed on the meaning of the words and context; the chanting of the *haftarah* (a passage from the Prophets) should be given up in favor of a new, simplified version.

The synagogue regulations prescribed a manner of praying that was regularized by the cantor and the choir. The cantor, as the *shaliah ha-zibbur*, formes the center of the service: "Although every person performs the prayer for himself, he presents it out loud in the name and at the behest, as it were, of all."[13] He unites the individual worshippers into a community, only he made private worship into a public service. Henceforth, the community was supposed to follow him in a quiet and regulated manner. The task of the choir was "to push the immoderate yelling back within the boundaries of propriety."[14] He represents the community, which joins him in quiet devotion, for example, in the *Shema Jisrael*, the *Kadosh*, and the antiphonies of the *Hallel*. The choir, used since the beginning of the 1840s, was to receive more intensive musical training following Salomon Sulzer's *Shir Zion;* in addition, a second cantor was to be hired. The musical form of the service should *not* be seen as a separate musical performance, but should always be subordinated to the content and purpose of the prayers. These stipulations disempowered the traditional, independent, loud praying of the community in favor of bourgeois norms like "order" and "dignity." If these norms

---

[11] Ibid., 4.
[12] Ibid.
[13] Ibid., 10.
[14] Ibid., 11.

were to be installed in the synagogue, however, older authorities like the "sacred minhag" or the "sacred community" would have to be violated.

With respect to the shortening of the liturgy, Sachs established the "inviolable" principle "that in the *tefillah* proper, in so far as it is obligatory—that is, prescribed—prayer (*tefillat Torah*), no changes be made, either to the number or arrangement of the prayers, nor in their form and wording."[15] The "actual framework of the prayers must be preserved as inviolable."[16] Only the "elaborations" and "additions," in particular the *yozerot, qinot, selihot,* and a number of *piyutim* for the pilgrimage festivals should be shortened or left out entirely.[17] Most members of the community did not understand them, and they were largely responsible for the thoughtless recitation of prayers and the chatting during the service.

No mention is made of German prayers, of the elimination or revision of prayers whose theme is the messianic promise of Zion or the restoration of the sacrificial service of the Temple, or of an organ.

The board accepted the proposed changes. Still in the winter of 1844, a commission was formed to work out the regulations for the future musical design of the service. Abraham Jakob Lichtenstein was hired as a second cantor alongside Ascher Lion.[18] In July 1845, twenty-three year-old Louis Lewandowski was hired, first as temporary choir conductor and singing teacher, later as choir director. A four-part choir with forty singers was set up. In the years to come, Lewandowski would compose new, epochal pieces for this choir.

On 23 December 1944, the board asked R. Oettinger and Elhanan Rosenstein to express their opinion on the planned reform.[19] Both men categorically rejected it on 20 January 1845.[20] Their decision was prompted by the not unjustified fear that any change, no matter how

---

[15] Ibid., 22.

[16] Ibid. For Sachs that included the *musaf* prayer, among others.

[17] Sachs wanted to postpone special regulations for the High Holy Days, the days of atonement, and *tisha be-av*. Of the *piyutim* for the pilgrimage festivals, only the prayers for dew (*tefillat tal*) and rain (*tefillat geshem*) would be preserved in the *musaf* prayer for Passover and Sukkot, though they should be limited to "characteristic pieces."

[18] See E. Ehrenreich, "Der erste Synagogenchor in Berlin," *Gemeindeblatt der Jüdischen Gemeinde zu Berlin* 19 (1929), 66-68, 107-111, here 108.

[19] See the copy of the letter of the board in CAHJP, KGe 2/30.

[20] The vote is printed in the circular of the board dated 1 September 1845, in CAHJP, P 17/584.

small, would bring other reforms in its wake. How, they asked, was one to determine the limits of change? The reason behind their opposition was not the reforms themselves, but the risks and dangers of reform as such. Neither the current state of the service at the Old Synagogue, which they did not attend, after all, nor the justified call for change, played any role in their vote.

The progress of the reform efforts was paralyzed not only by the opposition from the Orthodox rabbis. In a sermon on 15 February 1845, Sachs called the reform of the service one of the "most urgent and imperative demands" of the present time. He criticized the community's lack of interest and lamented the delay of all necessary changes.[21] That same sermon speaks of "ever-widening decay," of "ever deeper upheaval," of "strife that is becoming ever more serious," and of "selfishness," "laxity," and the "lack of strength and will."[22] On 2 April 1845, twenty-eight members of the community came out in favor of radical reforms with their "Appeal to our German coreligionists." On 8 May, the Berlin Reform Association came into being with around 300 members.

Also in May of 1845, Sachs drew up a code of synagogue and prayer regulations.[23] After "repeated oral and written discussions," the decision was made to implement the synagogue regulations "gradually."[24] But its mere announcement led to "dozens of petitions" that promised to vigorously fight even the smallest change.[25] The prayer code discussed further by Sachs and a liturgical commission was presented to R. Oettinger and Rosenstein on 27 June 1845 with the question whether "it contains regulations that go against the prescriptions of religious law." Both men reiterated their absolute opposition and now invoked the principle of the inviolability of the "sacred minhag."[26] Nevertheless, in July 1846, R. Oettinger, after initial protest, approved the performance of marriage ceremonies in the synagogue and performed them together with Sachs.

---

[21] Michael Sachs, *Festpredigten und Sabbatpredigten*, 433.

[22] Ibid., 433, 443.

[23] See the circular of the board, ibid., and Magnus Davidsohn, "Die Umgestaltung des Gottesdienstes in der Alten Synagoge," *Israelitisches Familienblatt* 38 (1926), 11ff. Neither code of regulations is extant.

[24] See "Denkschrift für eine Gottesdienstreform," drafted by Moritz Veit, 19 August 1845, in CAHJP, KGe 2/151.

[25] See Davidsohn, "Die Umgestaltung des Gottesdienstes," 11ff.

[26] This vote is also printed in the circular of the board, ibid., Insert C.

That same summer, the orthodox opposition was able to celebrate a victory. Plans to eliminate some *qinot* on *tisha be-av* were thwarted by the "incitements" (*Aufreizungen*) it instigated—evidently the opponents of reform no longer relied solely on their petitions.[27] The board addressed the community with a multi-page pamphlet on 1 September 1845, published all rabbinical opinions, and promoted the reform.[28]

Only parts of the synagogue regulations were implemented. The unexpectedly vigorous resistance prompted the board to postpone the introduction of the prayer regulations entirely. In his opinion of 1844, Sachs had made it a condition that the liturgical changes be undertaken only after the community had approved the synagogue regulations. Moreover, the question of who had the right to make changes to the service—the board, the rabbi, or the representatives—was unresolved.[29] The Minister of Culture asked the parties to wait for the revision of the Prussian laws concerning the Jews, which had been in preparation since 1845, and they did so.[30] As long as there were neither community statutes nor regulations pertaining to the religious situation of the Jews (as had been announced in the Edict of 1812), there was no legal basic of any kind for the implementation of reforms.

As a result, the only thing the reformers were able to introduce was the German sermon.[31] The musical design of the service was limited by the space in the synagogue, which had been built in 1714; the necessary renovations dragged on until 1855. It was precisely

[27] See *Der Orient* 7 (1845), no. 35, 273, and "Die Verhältnisse der israelitischen Gemeinde zu Berlin,"*AZJ* 9 (1845), 657-659. See Abraham Ehrlich, "Ele toledot rabbenu Jehiel Mikha'el Zaqs," *Ha-Maggid* 40-46 (1866), 317-318, 341-342, 349-350, 357-358, 365. According to Ehrlich, 349 there was also considerable opposition to the shortening of the *mi she-berakh*. Bernfeld, *Mikha'el Zaqs*, 50 indicates—without any date—that the elimination of the *jequm purqan* had to taken back. It does not appear in Sachs's reform program of 1844. However, it could have been part of the no longer extant prayer code or the result of joint deliberations.

[28] See the circular of 1 September 1845, in CAHJP, P 17/584. According to this circular, a special order for the High Holidays with a few German prayers and songs had also been worked out.

[29] According to Zunz, who was asked about this particular issue by the Ministry of Culture in 1844, liturgical changes should be decided jointly by the board and the rabbi. For "substantial changes," however, the approval of the community was also necessary. See Leopold Zunz, *Kurze Antworten auf Kultus-Fragen* (Berlin: J. Springer, 1844), 9.

[30] See Geiger, *Geschichte der Juden in Berlin*, vol. 1, 204.

[31] The almemor had been dismantled in August 1844 and a pulpit had been erected in front of the Torah shrine. See *Orient*, 10 September 1844, 283.

the introduction of new elements—German sermon and choir—that were tolerated or accepted by Orthodoxy, even if there were groups that rejected them. By contrast, moves to abbreviate or drop prayer insertions, to eliminate customs, and to regularize the traditional form of prayer ran into strong opposition, which would block the implementation of reform for an entire decade.

After 1848, the board of the community and synagogue carried out certain cuts, especially with regard to the holiday services; protest against it was mild. For example, the shortening of the *mi she-berakh* ceremony on Yom Kippur in 1849 elicited only scattered protests. However, the Royal City-Court (*Königliches Stadt-Gericht*) did get involved.[32] The shortening of the same service (and previously for *tisha be-av*) through the elimination of several *piyutim* was received without any protests; R. Oettinger had voted in favor.[33]

Since the space in the Old Synagogue was no longer sufficient and halls had to be rented for the High Holidays, the board eventually took over the private synagogue of the joiner Albert Fränkel, located in the rear courtyard of Große Hamburger Straße 11, and expanded it.[34] It was solemnly consecrated as interim synagogue on 1 September 1850, in the presence of all three rabbis.[35] Here, too, there was no meaningful opposition to the religious service that was based on the proposals of 1844/45.

In September 1851, the newly elected board presented to the rabbinate proposals for a new prayer order for Yom Kippur and Rosh Hashanah and a new code of synagogue regulations for the Old Synagogue. R. Oettinger protested emphatically against them.[36] Sachs also spoke out against any further changes to the service for the High Holidays. The plans for reform were shelved again.

The service was shortened once again on *tisha be-av* in 1852 with-

---

[32] See Sachs's expert opinion for the Royal City-Court of 1 November 1849, in CAHJP KGe 2/30.

[33] See Heymann, *Lebenserinnerungen*, 318. Heymann gave no exact date, but based on the chronological context, it must have been 1849/50.

[34] See the report by the board for the years 1849 to 1853, in GStA PK, I. HA. Rep. 76-III, Sekt. 12, Abt. XVI. The half-timbered building designed by the architect Tietz comprised 1,700 to 2,000 seats. The synagogue existed until 1866. See also *Synagogen in Berlin. Zur Geschichte einer zerstörten Architektur*, 2 vols. (Berlin: Arenhövel, 1983), vol. 2, 14.

[35] See *Der Orient* 11 (1855), no. 37, 145, and *Der Orient* 11 (1850), no. 40, 157-158.

[36] See *AZJ* 15 (1851), no. 37, 437-438.

out eliciting any protest.[37] So far, Orthodoxy had thus tacitly accepted the smaller, unconnected changes or cuts in the service and the reform service in the interim synagogue.[38] However, one could also assume that the religious energies for or against reforms were absorbed by the political events of the Revolution of 1848 and the period of reaction that followed in its wake. In any case, as long as the community was not calling for reform, rabbi Sachs, who did not have the right to initiate reforms, could not resurrect his proposals. As a response to the failure of reform in 1844/45, he had been calling for the building of a second communal synagogue since 1846. Only this synagogue could be the "free space" for a "comprehensive and far-reaching arrangement" of the service.[39]

With the first direct communal election in 1854, the conservative majority on the board was lost for the first time since 1838. It survived in the assembly of the representatives, though weakened.[40] The new board prepared a synagogue and prayer order in the spring of 1855 and presented it to the rabbinate.[41] R. Oettinger and Rosenstein voted against the draft, Sachs voted for it.[42] Sachs's approval was not unconditional, however. In principle, every reform of the service in the Old Synagogue should be undertaken "carefully and gently." If possible, the service for Rosh Hashana and Yom Kippur should remain unchanged.[43] After all, the synagogue was very well attended on the High Holidays, the community was voting for the

---

[37] See the prayer order of 1855, in CAHJP, P 17/549.

[38] See also *Vossische Zeitung* of 24 February 1856.

[39] "Ein Schreiben des Vorstandes an die Repräsentanten vom 29. Januar 1862," in CAHJP, KGe 2/26, quoted from Sachs's expert opinion of 18 July 1855, of which only the last page is extant, in Centrum Judaicum—Neue Synagoge Berlin, Archiv (CJA) 1, 75 D Sa 1.

[40] See Heymann, *Lebenserinnerungen*, 329f., and Moriz Türk, "Das erste Gemeindestatut und die Genossenschaft für Reform im Judentum," in *Festschrift zum 70. Geburtstage von Moritz Schaefer* (Berlin: Philo-Verlag, 1927), 241-257, here 253. The college of the board and representatives now included also several members of the Reform Association: Carl Heymann, Moses Simion, Jean Benda, and Ph. Marckwald.

[41] Copy of the "Synagogen- und Gebetordnung, 6. April 1855" in CAHJP, P 17/549.

[42] See David Cassel, *Die Cultusfrage in der jüdischen Gemeinde von Berlin* (Berlin: Adolf, 1856), 1, and Geiger, *Geschichte der Juden in Berlin*, vol. 1, 205.

[43] See Ehrlich, "Ele toledot rabbenu Jehiel Mikha'el Zaqs", 357. In 1844, Sachs had argued in favor of drawing up a separate order for the High Holidays, and he probably submitted such an order in 1845. Any further changes should be reserved for future experience. In 1851 he rejected additional alterations to the service for the High Holidays.

traditional service. Even the many secondary or so-called *Winkelsynagogen*, who had banished all *piyutim* on the Sabbath and festival days, retained them for Rosh Hashanah and Yom Kippur. But what Sachs chiefly criticized in the board's reform proposals was their underlying motivation and principle of reform—the "interests of the time." This, Sachs believed, opened the door wide for arbitrariness and a lack of principles.[44]

On the whole, though, Sachs's proposals from 1844/45 formed the basis of the new synagogue and prayer regulations. Additional cuts involved prayer insertions after the reading of the Torah,[45] special insertions for Purim, and the *piyutim* of the Rosh Hashanah and Yom Kippur liturgy. The *mi she-berakh* blessings were dropped entirely. The only German prayer that is mentioned is the one for the ruler. However, it was precisely Sachs's translation of this prayer, which "suppressed" the messianic connotation in the second part, that aroused the greatest wrath of the opponents of reform.

The liturgical changes concerned especially the service on the Sabbath and the pilgrimage festivals. These changes, too, hardly went beyond the proposals of 1844/45. The weekly service, the service for the new moon, and the middle days of the festivals and the evening service were retained in their traditional form, the service for the minor holidays of Purim and Chanukkah, the fast and atonement days, as well as of Rosh Hashanah and Yom Kippur was slightly modified or fixed in its already modified form. The introduction of a synagogue order, the elimination or shortening of *piyutim* and other insertions, and the abolition of certain customs continued to constitute the clear limits to reform.

The synagogue and prayer code of regulations was published on 3 September 1855. Five days later, the Old Synagogue, renovated and redesigned according to plans by Eduard Knoblauch, was reopened.[46] The service was conducted in accordance with the new

---

[44] See Sachs's expert opinion in CJA 1, 75 D Sa 1.

[45] *ba-me madliqin*, the first *jequm purqan*, and the *av ha-raḥamim*.

[46] See Cassel, *Die Cultusfrage in der jüdischen Gemeinde von Berlin*, 32, 70. There was enough room for a choir on one of the expanded upper galleries. It was now possible to use Lewandowski's compositions for multi-voice choir. The number of seats for women had been expanded. The new interior design of the synagogue—colored glass windows, a new lighting system, new synagogue decorations, and so on—was rejected by some as "wasteful ostentation," as "pomp and glitter." See *Vossische Zeitung*, 7 September 1855, 1st Insertion, and *AZJ* 19 (1855), no. 30, 386, and *AZJ* 19 (1855), no. 38, 486.

synagogue and prayer code. While one part of the conservative members of the community, represented by the long-time Elder and *Geheimer Kommerzienrat* Joel Wolff Meyer (1794-1869) and Aron Hirsch Heymann, welcomed the reform, its introduction led to outburst of protest from another part of the Orthodox wing of the community, which was vented in newspaper articles, pamphlets, booklets, petitions, and memoranda to officials and the Berlin public.[47] Once again, the protest was aimed against the enactment of changes and the abolition of *minhagim* and *piyutim*, but it also questioned whether the board had legitimate authority to alter the service.[48] Opponents identified by name were Moses Pinner, Gustav Liepmannssohn, Louis Jolenberg, and a group around Dr. Jacobius.

Liepmannssohn, publisher of the short-lived magazine *Volksvertreter des Judentums*[49] and a "Sachsian" until 1854, represented the quasi "democratic" element of the opposition. He protested against the new manner of prayer that was regulated and dominated by the choir and the cantor, and against the disempowerment of the community, which—as Liepmannssohn decried—was no longer able to participate actively in the service. He demanded a general participatory right for the community, a clarification of the authority of the board and the representatives, and proposed that the rabbi be given a suspensive veto on matters relating to the service.[50] He argued that reforms could be carried out only with the consent of the entire community or in a second synagogue.[51]

---

[47] See particularly GStA PK, I. HA, Rep. 76-III, Sekt. 12, Abt. XVI—"Akte, betr. die Angelegenheiten der jüdischen Gemeinde zu Berlin und insbesondere die gottesdienstlichen Einrichtungen derselben." The *Vossische Zeitung* in Berlin emerged in the summer and fall of 1855 as the stage on which the struggle between supporters and opponents of reform was fought out.

[48] See also *AZJ* 19 (1855), no. 44, 562; Geiger, *Geschichte der Juden in Berlin*, vol. 1, 205, and Ehrlich, "Ele toledot rabbenu Jehiel Mikhael Zaqs," 357. In 1855/56, Sachs, in the nine-volume *Festgebete der Israeliten*, presented the complete Ashkenazi liturgy, on a philologically secure textual basis and, with few exceptions, translated and provided with commentary. See Michael Sachs, *Festgebete der Israeliten* (Berlin: Veit & Co, 1855/56).

[49] It appeared only for a few months in 1847.

[50] See Liepmannssohn's letter in the above-mentioned file of the GStA PK and his article in *Publicist. Zeitung für Recht und Gerichtswesen*, 29 July 1856. In a letter to the police president on 18 October 1859, the minister of the interior rejected a veto right for the rabbi, because this had neither backing from "tradition" nor a basis in law; the rabbi was an official of the community, which was self-governing.

[51] See Liepmannssohn's letters in the *Vossischen Zeitung*, 22 August 1855, 1st insert, and 4 September 1855, 1st insert.

The merchant Louis Jolenberg advocated downright reactionary positions. He proposed reviving the infamous Order of 1823 in order to protect the "old-Orthodox" position.[52] Jolenberg asserted the inviolability and sacred nature of the *minhag* and vigorously defended the *piyutim*. The moderate reform disturbed the "deepest peace" in which the old Orthodoxy and the *Reformgenossenschaft* coexist. He conveyed to the Ministry of the Interior the wish of the Territorial rabbi (*Landesrabbiner*) for Silesia, Gedalja Tiktin, to be heard in the Berlin reform controversy.

Moses Pinner (1800/1801-1880), known for his project to translate the Talmud, of which only Berakhot was published in 1842, joined the fray with three polemical tracts that attacked above all the representatives of moderate reform: Michael Sachs, Moritz Veit (1808-1864), and David Cassel (1818-1893). And Pinner did not shy away from political denunciations.[53] Moderate reform itself, he charged, was a "catastrophe," because it dissolved the Jewish service into meaningless sermons and "choral concerts."[54]

The moderate reformers—Pinner called them "fundamental" or "total"—did not, as the "radical" reformers of the *Reformgenossenschaft*, establish a closed circle, but tried to force the "true believers" ("Aechtgläubigen") into it by distorting the basic religious teachings.[55] Pinner demanded that Rabbi Sachs should be "resolutely" returned to "his true, dependent position,"[56] even though his authority was limited anyhow and he was not the real initiator of the reform. At the same time, Pinner protested against the board that had been elected in 1854.[57] However, he admitted that the opposition he represented was numerically very small.[58] His petition to hold a meeting

---

[52] See Jolenberg's memorandum for the Ministry of the Interior, "Wie ist der Conflict in der Berliner Synagogen-Angelegenheit auf friedlichem und gesetzlichem Wege zu lösen," June 1856, in GStA PK, ibid.

[53] See Mose Pinner, *Geschichte der neuesten Reformen der jüdischen Gemeinde Berlin's und deren Bekämpfung. Ein Beitrag zur Cultusgeschichte der Juden* (Berlin: Selbstverlag, 1857), 37ff.

[54] Ibid., 5.

[55] See idem, *Kol Kore. Aufruf an die orthodoxen Rabbiner Europa's und die Nothwendigkeit einer streng orthodoxen allgemeinen Rabbiner-Versammlung* (Berlin: Selbstverlag, 1858), 3 and 5.

[56] See idem, *Denkschrift für die Juden Preußens besonders für die Juden Berlins, Oder Gründliche Darstellung der den jüdischen Vorständen zustehenden Rechte in religiöser, politischer und gesetzlicher Hinsicht* (Berlin: Selbstverlag, 1856), 4.

[57] See idem, *Geschichte der neuesten Reformen*, 14.

[58] See idem, *Denkschrift für die Juden Preußens*, 33, and idem, *Geschichte der neuesten Reformen*, 45.

of Orthodox rabbis in Berlin in 1858[59] was turned down by the authorities.

Prussian government officials took the Berlin reform controversy very seriously, since "the resolution of the same must necessarily anticipate the further development of the Jews in Prussia."[60] The police president responded as early as 19 December 1855. According to his decision, because of the "considerable upheaval that the measures of the board and the representatives of the community seem to have already caused, no changes to the existing order of the service shall be put in motion that could lead to a split of the community and a disturbance of the public order."[61] On 8 April 1856, in keeping with the provisions of the law concerning the condition of the Jews (*Gesetz über die Verhältnisse der Juden*) of 1847, a commission was appointed to examine the conflict.[62] A second order put a stop to all changes of the service pending the final review of all complaints.[63] The petitions from the opposition continued and new opponents spoke up.[64] Apart from the contentious issues of *minhag* and *piyutim*, the question of what authority the board, the rabbi, and the representatives had to alter the service was of central importance. The law of 1847 had put decisions over ritual matters into the hands of the board and the representatives, as long as there were no community statutes to the contrary. Opponents of reform like Liepmannssohn argued that the revolution had rendered the law obsolete, and that this question had to be revisited. The authorities, however, had delayed the implementation of the provisions of the 1847 law for years, had rejected drafts of statutes from the Berlin community and obstructed their adoption over many years.[65]

---

[59] See idem, *Kol Kore*, passim.

[60] GStA PK, ibid., fol. 224.

[61] Ibid.

[62] In cases of quarrels over ritual and conflicts of secession, paragraph 53 provided for the establishment of a commission composed of nine "ritual officials" or other trusted men. I do not know whether this commission was ever formed, and if so, who was on it.

[63] See also *AZJ* 20 (1856), no. 22, 295.

[64] W. Goldschmidt and Dr. Simon.

[65] A draft from 1850 envisaged a community decision with a simple majority vote for all questions relating to the service (see "Entwurf der Statuten der Jüdischen Gemeinde zu Berlin," in CAHJP, KGe 3/9, printed in *Der Orient* 11 (1850), no. 25, 99-100; no. 26, 102-103; no. 27, 105-106; and no. 28, 109-110). The statutes that were eventually enacted in 1860, however, transferred all decisions on ritual matters to the representatives (two-thirds majority with a quorum of at least 17

On 7 July 1856, the board sent a lengthy memorandum to the police president defending "the internal autonomy of the synagogue community" and the reform project.[66] It is highly probable that Sachs penned this memorandum, in spite of the tensions that existed between him and the board. The submission explained that the actual prayer order had not been touched. Only prayers that no longer reflected the religious awareness, later additions, or "unintelligible" interpolations, which interrupted the "essential part of the real service" especially on Shabbat and the pilgrimage festivals, had been abolished, while other interpolations, like many *piyutim*, which enjoyed greater interest from the community and whose elevated "poetical power and depth" promoted devotion, had been retained. The choir was not taking the place of prayer by the community, but where the latter was acting "otherwise in a loud and irregular manner," it was leading it to "regular joining and participation."

The public defense of the reform was taken on by the literary historian and teacher David Cassel. On 15 July 1856, he presented to the Minister for Spiritual Affairs, Friedrich von Raumer, his "The Ritual Question in the Jewish Community of Berlin" (*Cultusfrage in der jüdischen Gemeinde von Berlin*). The reform, Cassel maintained, violated neither ritual law nor the community's religious sense. In fact, it was better to speak of "inner transformation," that is, of a "simplification and shortening of the service that is as much in accord with the times as with Jewish law," than of "reform."[67] Historically, the *piyutim* had, "in a certain sense," taken the place of the "instructional sermon that could not be arranged always and everywhere."[68] Following the model of Sephardic ritual, reformers had limited themselves to retaining the *piyutim* of Rosh Hashanah and Yom Kippur. "For all their beauty," the *piyutim*, "because of the frequently dominant haggadic element, are not suitable, after all, as public prayers, which they truly are not."[69]

On 23 July 1856, the police president recommended that the minister solicit an expert opinion not only from Gedalja Tiktin, but also from Isaak Noa Mannheimer and Samson Raphael Hirsch.

---

members). Disagreements over ritual matters were explicitly *not* to be decided by a community vote. See GStA PK, I. HA, Rep. 76, III, Sekt. 1, Abt. XVI Titel IV.

[66] Letter of the board to the police president, in GStA PK, I. HA, Rep. 76, III, Sekt. 12, Abt. XVI. The following quotes are taken from there.

[67] Cassel, *Die Cultusfrage in der jüdischen Gemeinde von Berlin*, 50.

[68] Ibid., 13-14.

[69] Ibid., 28.

On 14 October 1856, he proposed "protective measures on behalf of the integrity or restitution of the old-faith community association." In his statement of 13 February 1857, Hirsch took the side of the complainants and branded the elimination of prayer insertions as apostasy from the Jewish religion.[70] By now, Dr. Jacobius had filed a petition to establish a separate community.[71] Additional expert opinions were requested from Natan Adler and Salomon Juda Rapoport in August 1857.[72] It is possible that Rapoport's opinion tipped the scale for the decision by the authorities.[73] The latter had in the meantime determined that the opponents were not backed by the majority of the community. The conflict was finally settled in the Summer of 1858 in favor of the reform. Henceforth, however, all service matters were to be regulated by community statutes.[74]

During the reform controversy, the rabbinate had agreed on a policy of neutrality and mediation. Although R. Oettinger and Rosenstein had rejected the reform in 1855, they did participate in the reformed service of the reopened synagogue.[75] In fact, Oettinger had approved a few earlier, specific cuts. During the subsequent years of the conflict, the rabbinate negotiated with the "quarreling parties" and distanced itself publicly from "cliquishness."[76] Finally, in the spring of 1858, Rosenstein and Oettinger consented to the reform.[77] There was also agreement to leave the role of the official expert to Sachs. When the Ministry for Spiritual Affairs asked the rabbinate in the early Summer of 1858 whether "changes in ritual and liturgy" constituted reasons for a split, Sachs gave a differentiated and neutral account of the Berlin reform conflict in his response.[78] The reform consisted in the elimination of "abuses," the introduction

---

[70] *AZJ* 20 (1856), no. 50, 670-71.

[71] See GStA PK, I. HA, Rep. 76, III, Sekt. 12, Abt. XVI.

[72] None of the expert opinions was found in the relevant file of the GStA PK.

[73] Rapoport had proposed a reform model that should be realized after the construction of a second synagogue. See the letter from the Ministry of the Interior to the police president, 18 October 1859, in GStA PK, ibid. See also Geiger, *Geschichte der Juden in Berlin*, vol. 1, 205.

[74] See the letter to Dr. Jacobius, 17 August 1858, in GStA PK, I. HA, Rep. 76, III, Sekt. 12, Abt. XVI.

[75] *AZJ* 19 (1855), no. 40, 514.

[76] *Vossische Zeitung*, 24 February 1856, 6.

[77] *AZJ*, 12 April 1858, 214.

[78] Hand-written draft of an expert opinion from Sachs, addressed to the Ministry of Spiritual and Instructional Affairs "in the name of the rabbinate," no date [early Summer 1858], in CAHJP, Salomon Herxheimer collection, P 46.

of a service order, and the shortening of interpolations with a preservation of the core prayers. A few of the additional changes and cuts
made after 1855 "are at least in part in explicit contradiction to the
prevailing ritual laws" (like the prohibition against waving the lulav
and removing the shoes during the priestly benediction.) "Nevertheless,
these innovations are not in and of themselves of the kind that they
run counter to the essence of the Jewish religion or explicitly contradict dogma."[79] The reform itself thus constituted no reason for a
separation from the ritual life of the community. "However, if one
looks at the way in which these innovations came about, the opposition of the old-faith part of the community must appear as not
without justification." The community had not been asked, the reform
had been imposed from the top. The board was the "administrative
representation of the material interests of the community." It could
not be the bearer of religious changes and "introduce the direction
it liked into the synagogue and drive out those who cling to the
old." The current changes were "in and of themselves permissible,"
but they lacked "trust, and the resistance by the so-called old-faith
party is directed less against the changes themselves as against the
motives behind them."[80]

Sachs had approved the 1855 proposals of the board in substance,
though he criticized them on individual points and with respect to
the overall principle of reform. He rejected any imposition of the
reform from above. Only the community itself, not the board, could
decide on a reform,

> for in a time like the present one, in which the service, tradition, and
> what has been passed down from antiquity are seen as running counter
> to the spirit of the time, [....] in which piety and inhibition in reli-
> gious matters are counted as foolishness which the emancipated spirit
> should rid itself of, the community and the foundation are done for
> if the current handling of the community's religious interests is handed
> over to the board without the consent of the community.[81]

In 1861, the controversy over the introduction of the organ
launched the struggle over the New Synagogue, whose foundation
stone had been laid in 1859.[82] The board decided in favor of an

---

[79] Ibid.
[80] Ibid.
[81] Ibid.
[82] On the issue of the organ see also *Synagogen in Berlin*, vol. 1, 75-76, 81.

organ service in October 1861.[83] To obtain the approval of the assembly of representatives for the necessary funds, the board solicited opinions not only from rabbis Sachs and Rosenstein (Rabbi Oettinger having died in 1860), but also from five outsiders, among them emphatic reformers like Abraham Geiger, Ludwig Philippsohn, and Joseph Maier.[84] On 14 November, the board of the community was presented with a petition signed by about 1,200 members of the community and demanding an organ, additional shortening of the ritual, and more German prayers for the service in the new synagogue.[85]

Sachs and Rosenstein rejected the organ. The board, however, invoked the opinion of R. Simon Löwe (d. 1881) in Ratibor, who provided halakhic backing for organ music. It disqualified Sachs's opinion as "unrabbinical," for Sachs had derived his objections not from Halakha, but had argued "in very general, rational terms."[86] While Sachs's opinion left no doubt that Halakha prohibited the playing of instruments on the Sabbath, his main objection against the organ was that it fundamentally altered the nature of the service. Instead of true—that is, spiritual—religious devotion, it created an ecstasy of emotion and the illusion of devotion, thus leading to passivity and externalization instead of spiritual deepening and internalization.[87]

The Jewish organ service, Sachs maintained, imitated the Christian one and denied the richness of Judaism's own ritual material. A new, living, religious awareness could not develop with the organ:

> No external attractions or stimulations are needed for those who attend the service out of a religious sense [....]. We have found our very own, autonomous expression of our religious awareness, without imitation and parroting, we stand on our own ground, we know and appreciate our ancient heritage, we know that we are connected to and in harmony with the spirit of the present, without denying our past or giving up our future.[88]

---

[83] *AZJ* 25 (1861), no. 41, 591.

[84] Copies of the opinions from all the rabbis as well as from music director Stern and from Lewandowski can be found in CAHJP, P 17/585.

[85] Petition in CAHJP, KGe 2/26.

[86] See the circular of the board in CAHJP, P 17/585.

[87] See Sachs's opinion of 13 November 1861 in *Zur Lehr' und zur Wehr. Über und gegen die kirchliche Orgel im jüdischen Gottesdienste*, ed. Abraham Berliner (Berlin: Nathansen & Lamm, 1904), 12-22, here 13-14.

[88] Ibid., 17.

The attempt "to infuse life and interest into the service with external, alien means" was a "step backward," "a sign of inadequacy," and self-denial.

The board, however, saw in the organ "no innovation, but a return to the original ritual forms [....], unless one wished to regard this instrument, because of its use in Christian churches, as a specifically Christian one and therefore impermissible in synagogues. However, there is no reason whatsoever for this kind of opinion [....]." For the organ, and here the board was basing itself on Geiger's opinion, "was already used in the Temple in Jerusalem, even if not in its current, perfected form."[89]

In April 1862, a second petition for an organ was submitted to the board, this time signed by 1,695 members of the community. The assembly of representatives, however, rejected the organ with a bare majority.[90] The organ supporters threatened to break away from the community. In September 1862, it seemed that a compromise was emerging on the organ issue. Although Sachs had rejected even limited organ playing in his opinion, he was willing to accommodate the large group of the community that wanted an organ. A compromise was worked out, whereby the organ would be allowed to play at weddings and on similar occasions as well as on kabbalat Shabbat, but not on the Sabbath and feast days.[91]

The compromise, however, was not implemented. Although the necessary two-thirds majority for an organ was still missing in the assembly of representatives, the board presented it with a new proposal, which seemed to accommodate some of the opponents to the extent that it left the question of the use of the organ to future decisions by community representatives and separated the question of acquiring an organ from the question of how it would be used. On 18 January, 15 representatives voted to procure an organ, the opposition had shrunk to 4 votes.[92] Once the organ had been obtained, no one spoke of limited use any longer.

The organ in the new community synagogue did not arouse strong

---

[89] Circular of the board, in CAHJP, P 17/585.
[90] *AZJ* 26 (1862), no. 31, 426.
[91] As reported by Sachs to his wife, Henriette Sachs, on 7 September 1862, in Staatsbibliothek Berlin—Preußischer Kulturbesitz (StBPK), Sammlung Autographa, Michael Sachs, Mappe I/43-44.
[92] See *AZJ* 27 (1863), no. 5, 70, and Heymann, *Lebenserinnerungen*, 341.

opposition—at least that much can be inferred from the absence of any traces of resistance in the sources. The supporters of moderate reform retained the status quo of the service in Heidereutergasse. Sachs died on 31 January 1864. Shortly thereafter, the board probably commissioned Moritz Steinschneider with working out a liberal service for the synagogue in Oranienburger Street.[93]

The self-positioning of moderate reform beyond Orthodoxy and the Reform movement was connected with the claim that it stood above all currents, and that it demonstrated the compatibility of a religious self-awareness grounded in history and ritual law with the education and culture of the present day. De facto, however, moderate reform was one current among others, without defining or organizing itself as such. The claim to be embracing the totality stood in the way of doing that, as did the rejection of pluralization, which was rightly linked with the process of secularization and seen as an additional centrifugal force that threatened Judaism.

Strict traditional Orthodoxy made its peace even with moderate reform only very reluctantly and after a long struggle, or it withdrew into private services and private religious associations. The radical reformers were from the beginning not satisfied with a moderate reform but set up their own religious community.

In the 1840s, the Berlin community found itself in the midst of a process of transformation. By 1846, immigration, especially from the Prussian eastern provinces (particularly Posen, Silesia, and East and West Prussia), as well as from Mark Brandenburg and the adjoining provinces, had more than doubled the number of Jews who had been counted in 1825 (3,500). By 1864, the number nearly tripled again to over 24,000.[94] In the 1850s and 1860s, these new arrivals formed a large part, if not the majority, of the Berlin Jews and their communal representatives. They fundamentally altered the social and religious composition and the balance of power within the Berlin

---

[93] On this see Ismar Schorsch, "Moritz Steinschneider on Liturgical Reform," *HUCA* 53 (1982), 241-264.

[94] 1846: 8,243, 1864: 24,280, see Herbert Seeliger, "Origin and Growth of the Berlin Jewish Community," *LBIYB* 3 (1958), 159-168, here 163. In 1854, by way of implementing the law of 1847, 60 smaller, surrounding villages were incorporated into the synagogue district of Berlin. See Eugen Wolbe, *Geschichte der Juden in Berlin und in der Mark Brandenburg* (Berlin: Verlag Kedem, 1937), 274, and Ludwig Geiger, *Michael Sachs und Moritz Veit. Briefwechsel* (Frankfurt am Main: Kauffmann, 1897), XXII.

community.[95] The large, pluralistic city had a centrifugal, secularizing, and liberalizing effect. Although some continued to cling to the traditions and religious ties they brought with them, the religious needs and religious practice of most changed under the pressure, but also prospects of new economic and cultural conditions. This large group within the community did not have the personal relationships, experiences, or memories of the modernization crisis through which the old Berlin community had passed. With its rapid economic integration and acculturation, it was closer to a liberal stance than to a moderate model of reform and its considerations, limits, and loyalties, from which the new group was in the process of disconnecting. The sort of sense of crisis that Sachs shared and which formed the basis of moderate reform could hardly be integrated into economic and social success and advancement.

The old Berlin elites receded into the background, the prospering classes of the new Berliners set the tone of the community after 1854.[96] The Orthodox, strict-traditional opposition became a minority. Although the moderate reform was carried out in 1858 under the auspices of a liberal board, a few years later it was overtaken and pushed aside by the liberal reform. Although the service of the Old Synagogue acquired a new attraction under Sachs, Lichtenstein, and Lewandowski and became a "focusing mirror and symbol of renewed classical Judaism,"[97] moderate reform was not able to become a community model. For that, it would have needed a leadership figure who charted a programmatic course. Moderate reforms most important representative in Berlin, Sachs, would not and could not be that figure.

Supreme authority over the service belonged to the board and the representatives. The board had the right to initiate reforms, the representatives the right to vote on them. By contrast, the rabbis had merely an advisory function. The relationship between the board and Sachs was tense. Moreover, the situation within the Berlin rabbinate was more than problematic. Sachs faced two orthodox rabbis who rejected the reform project of their younger, academically trained colleague and approved it only at the last moment. A strong

---

[95] See *AZJ* 9 (1845), no. 5, 59, and *AZJ* 18 (1854), no. 20, 247.
[96] See Moritz Kalisch, *Berlins jüdische Reformatoren nach der Thronbesteigung Friedrich Wilhelms III. und IV. Eine religionsgeschichtliche Betrachtung* (Berlin: C. Feister, 1845), 132.
[97] James Jaakov Rosenthal in Max M. Sinasohn, *Die Berliner Privatsynagogen und ihre Rabbiner* (Jerusalem: Sinasohn, 1971), 35

rabbinic authority was not wanted in Berlin, nor could it have emerged under these conditions.

Moderate reform had taken the risk that the old Orthodoxy had deliberately avoided: justifying and legitimizing reforms and drawing boundaries. To justify the dropping of *piyutim* and other prayers, as well as the elimination or change of customs, moderate reformers used—and had to use—arguments similar to those put forth by more emphatic reformers: the restoration of "dignity" and "devotion," the needs of the present, an altered religious awareness, "alienation," or a "scientific" and "historical" perspective. The formula common to all was "restoration of correct customs and practices" and "return to a form full of vitality." Zunz had articulated this formula in 1832.[98] Every reform, moderate or radical, employed it. More difficult, however, was the problem of drawing boundaries. It was the neuralgic point of moderate reform. No matter how much it conceived of itself as conforming to the law, it did not derive its self-understanding from Halakha. Thus moderate reform was abandoning traditionalist patterns of argumentation when Sachs marshaled above all concepts like "self-confidence," "essence," and "one's own ground and foundation" in opposition to the organ. What was demanded, however, was formal halakhic arguments.

Moderate reform was strenuous, it required reflection on various level and called for limits and a willingness to sacrifice. It appealed for restraint and self-reflection where "progress" and "success" were the order of the day.

Sachs was the religious and spiritual leader of the community. A programmatic stance in favor of moderate reform would have reduced the claim of being above all parties to absurdity. As a result, however, moderate reform was denied any larger effectiveness and future in Berlin. Without a programmatic platform and organization, it was unable to develop into a model for the community. Moreover, it could not adequately protect its boundaries and stabilize the entire endeavor as a model. The victory of moderate reform in Berlin was the beginning of its supersession by liberal reform.

---

[98] "Wiederherstellung des rechten Gebrauchs, Rückkehr von dem Mißbrauche zu dem Brauch, welches die Rückkehr von der erstarrten zu der lebenskräftigen Form ist"; see Leopold Zunz, *Die gottesdienstlichen Vorträge der Juden, historisch entwickelt. Ein Beitrag zur Alterthumskunde und biblischen Kritik, zur Literatur- und Religionsgeschichte*, 2nd ed. (Frankfurt am Main: Kauffmann, 1892), 479.

SAMUEL HOLDHEIM AND ZACHARIAS FRANKEL ON THE LEGAL CHARACTER OF JEWISH MARRIAGE: AN OVERLOOKED DEBATE IN NINETEENTH-CENTURY LIBERAL JUDAISM[1]

David Ellenson

Samuel Holdheim (1806–1860) was the preeminent spokesman for radical Reform during the nineteenth century. He assessed the *Halakhah* as a transitory element within Judaism and abjured law as an enduring dimension of the Jewish religion. Nevertheless, in his most famous work, *Ueber die Autonomie der Rabbinen und das Princ̦ip der jüdischen Ehe* (On the Autonomy of the Rabbis and the Principles of Jewish Marriage, 1843)[2] he offered a serious and insightful analysis of *kinyan* (the legal act of acquisition) as it related to *dinei kiddushin* (laws of marriage) in Jewish law. The reasoning he employed in this analysis can be seen as supplying a base for comprehending the stance he adopted at the Brunswick Rabbinical Conference of 1844 regarding the question of Jewish-Christian intermarriage.

In contrast to Holdheim, Rabbi Zacharias Frankel (1801–1875) was the champion of the traditional wing of Liberal Judaism in nineteenth-century Germany. Committed to the centrality of *Halakhah* in Jewish life, Frankel became a great scholar of *Wissenschaft des Judentums* and, in 1854, was appointed head of the Breslau Jewish Theological Seminary. Disturbed by the stance Holdheim adopted in his 1843 work, Frankel felt constrained to respond to the halakhic analysis Holdheim had put forth. This essay will delineate Holdheim's arguments on these matters as well as Frankel's critique. By placing this debate within its historical context, we will see how the diverse

---

[1] This chapter is reprinted from David Ellenson, *After Emancipation: Jewish Religious Responses to Modernity* (Cincinnati: HUC Press, 2004), 139-153.

[2] Samuel Holdheim, *Ueber die Autonomie der Rabbinen und das Princ̦ip der jüdischen Ehe: Ein Beitrag zur Verständigung übereinige das Judenthum betreffende Zeitfragen* (Schwerin: C. Kürschner, 1843).

positions of these two men on the subject of marriage and Jewish
law sheds light on the history of an incipient Jewish religious denom-
inationalism.

1. Holdheim's Analysis of Kinyan in Relation to Dinei Kiddushin

Holdheim's halakhic analysis of *dinei kiddushin* focused on the nature
of *kinyan* in Jewish matrimonial law. In offering his analysis, Holdheim
set for himself the task of determining whether *kinyan* as it related
to marriage was distinct from the mechanism of *kinyan* in other cases
of acquisition.[3] In the first half of *Ueber die Autonomie der Rabbinen*,
Holdheim noted that Jewish law used the term *kinyan* to refer to a
variety of acts in which a person voluntarily obtains legal rights—
both proprietary and contractual. *Kinyan*, for example, was the legal
mechanism whereby one could acquire legal right to ownerless (*hefker*)
or neglected (*yei'ush*) property. It was also the means through which
one acquired ownership over property through sale or gift, and it
referred as well to contractual or personal rights one party held in
relation to another, such as servitude (*shi'bud*) or debt. Holdheim
noted that for *kinyan* to be legally valid and binding in Jewish law,
in every instance the person or party who obtained legal rights had
to affirm the acquisition by his or her own free will. Secondly, in
cases where a previous person or party held legal rights, he or she
had to consent freely to the transmission of those rights. If these
conditions were met, then *kinyan* could be effectuated. This was true
of every mode of *kinyan* in Jewish law. As the act of *kinyan* was a
standard part of virtually every act of acquisition in Jewish law,
Holdheim argued that *kinyan* was a civil act.[4]

   In light of these observations concerning the overarching nature
of *kinyan*, Holdheim went on to address the question of whether
kinyan in connection with the institution of Jewish marriage also constituted a civil act. In other words, did the act of marriage transform the character of *kinyan* in such a way that the *kinyan* of marriage

---

   [3] For the *locus classicus* of his discussion on the nature of marriage as a civil act
in Jewish matrimonial law, see Holdheim, *Ueber die Autonomie der Rabbinen*, 137-165.
   [4] Holdheim delineates the different modes of acquisition in Jewish law in ibid.,
85ff. For an excellent English language treatment of the details and complexities of
kinyan in Jewish law, see *Encyclopedia Judaica*, s.v., "Acquisition."

could be regarded as so qualitatively distinct from *kinyan* in other cases of legal acquisition that it no longer constituted a civil act? He ultimately concluded that it did not accomplish this transformation. Jewish law regarded the act of *kinyan* in relationship to marriage as a civil act, just as in any other instance of acquisition. As long as all the conditions of the acquisition were known to all involved in the transaction, *kinyan* was established and a state of *kiddushin* (marriage) obtained between the husband and his wife. Though the sentiments of love and trust may well have existed between the man and woman, in his view they were of no legal relevance in establishing a state of *kiddushin* between them as husband and wife. Even if these sentiments were lacking, the *kiddushin* between them was valid and binding as long as the parties involved gave their consent and the husband gave his bride a coin worth at least a *perutah*.[5]

Holdheim buttressed his logical but admittedly novel contention by comparing Jewish legal sources that dealt with the process of acquisition in the case of slaves and real estate with the stipulations put forth concerning the act of *kinyan* in regard to marriage. In the instance of slaves and real estate, the Talmud asserted that legal title could be acquired in one of three ways: money, contract, and usucaption (*kesef, shtar, ve-'azakah*).[6] Holdheim pointed out that a husband acquired a wife in a parallel fashion. As the Talmud states in *Kiddushin* 2a, "A woman is acquired in three ways: money, contract, and intercourse."[7] The first two modes of acquisition—money and contract—provided the normative means whereby title was

---

[5] Holdheim, *Ueber die Autonomie der Rabbinen*, 139ff. See *Mishnah Kiddushin* 1:1.

[6] Holdheim, *Ueber die Autonomie der Rabbinen*, 137ff. Holdheim cites the famous passage in *Kiddushin* 26a (ibid., 86) that lists these three modes of acquisition and on the previous page in his footnote lists the various types of *kinyan* that exist in Jewish law along with their Roman equivalents. For the mishnaic sources that prescribe the same modes of acquisition for a wife as for Cannanite slaves and real property, see *Mishnah Kiddushin* 1:1, 3, and 5. Judith Romney Wegner, a modern scholar, offers the following commentary upon these sources in her outstanding book *Chattel or Person? The Status of Women in the Mishnah* (New York: Oxford University Press, 1988), 42. Wegner writes, "The procedure for acquiring a wife (set forth in tractate *Kiddushin*) treats marriage as a formal sale and purchase of a woman's sexual function—a commercial transaction in which a man pays for his bride's virginity just as for any other object of value." For a comprehensive English-language treatment of the many sources involved in the Jewish laws of matrimony and divorce, see Elliot N. Dorff and Arthur Rosett, *A Living Tree: The Roots and Growth of Jewish Law* (Albany, N.Y.: SUNY Press, 1988), 442-545.

[7] Holdheim, *Ueber die Autonomie der Rabbinen*, 138.

established in Jewish law, and Holdheim stated that these modes
were absolutely identical whether the object of acquisition was a wife
or anything else.

Interestingly, Holdheim observed that the third way—*bi'ah*, here
meaning consensual intercourse—seemingly distinguished the act of
kinyan in marriage from (and perhaps even elevated it above) the act
of acquisition in other types of property transactions. He even conceded that the foundation of this mode of acquisition was the love
and trust that existed between the couple. Furthermore, he acknowledged that in Jewish marriage law the bride and groom had each
freely pledged to sanctify their union. Nevertheless, he contended
that neither these sentiments nor the sanctity involved in the couple's union distinguished *kinyan* in marriage from *kinyan* in regard to
other contractual arrangements between two parties. Interestingly,
he compared *bi'ah* as a mode of *kinyan* in marriage to the act of
akhilat ha-peirot (the eating of fruits) as a means for establishing ownership in the case of a field. Just as *bi'ah* constituted an act sufficient to establish ownership, so *akhilat ha-peirot* was an act sufficient
to establish *'azakah* (*usucapio*). *Bi'ah*, from this point of view, was formally no different a mechanism. Just as possession or investment of
labor could give rise to title in the domain of the ordinary civil law
of property, so too could intercourse give rise to possession in the
case of a wife. *Bi'ah*, in Jewish law like *kesef* and *shtar*, was a civil
mode of acquisition.[8]

---

[8] Ibid., 86 and 137ff. Of course, as my friend and colleague Nomi Stolzenberg
has pointed out to me, Holdheim's analogy here is quite problematic from a logical standpoint. For *'azakah* in relation to an ownerless field displays no contractual
features. Absolute title to the field is established by possession of the property for
an uninterrupted and specified period of time (three years—on this point see *Mishnah
Baba Batra* 3:1). There is no contractual element here, nor are there two persons
involved as there would be in the case of marriage. As stated in the body of the
paper itself, *bi'ah* must be consensual if *kinyan* is to be established. It is impossible
to imagine how one could speak of a field in these terms. In light of this point, it
is significant that in *Baba Batra* 48b there is a discussion in which the betrothal of
a woman is compared to the acquisition of a field, the sale of which is valid even
if the sale occurs under coercion. However, the rabbis ultimately reject this position. Consent remains a vital component of the marriage process. I am aware of
only two exceptions to this requirement. The first is where a father designates the
betrothal of his minor daughter without her consent. *Bi'ah* is not at all involved
here. The second exception concerns the case of levirate marriage. In *Mishnah
Yebamot* 6:1, it is written that a state of marriage is established between the *yabam*
(the brother of the deceased husband) and the *yabamah* (the widow) when intercourse takes place between them even when the intercourse is unintentional (mis-

Holdheim further bolstered his argument by citing two other Jewish precedents: proscribed activities on Sabbath and holidays and *dina de-malkhuta dina* (the law of the land is the law). He first pointed out that Jewish law would not permit any type of *kinyan* to take place on either the Sabbath or the holidays. As these were designated as days of rest in *Halakhah*, many forms of work and all civil transactions were proscribed on them. Yet Holdheim noted that certain actions, which would normally have been forbidden as violations of the interdiction against proscribed forms of labor on these days of rest, were permitted if these actions were defined as religious ones. Hence, Jewish law ruled that *milah* (ritual circumcision) and *avodah* (Temple worship), *as religious acts*, superseded the Sabbath.[9] Since marriage, though possessed of religious import and meaning, did not, Holdheim took this as a clear indication that marriage and the act of *kinyan* associated with it remained an act of civil law—*ein civil-rechtlicher Act.*[10]

Holdheim immediately expanded and elaborated upon the line of reasoning used to support this conclusion. His argument can be summarized as follows: inasmuch as the Talmud forbade *kinyan* of any type to take place on the Sabbath or Jewish holidays, the talmudic prohibition that specified that a marriage ceremony could not be held on these days of rest demonstrated that *kiddushin* and the act of *kinyan* associated with it were not defined primarily as religious

---

taken identity) or involuntary by either party. Here *bi'ah* is involved, but it is the only place in Jewish law where a marriage is established by non-consensual intercourse. In sum, there are two instances in Jewish law where a woman may be married despite her lack of consent. In the case of a male, there is only one.

One more point of distinction is to be made concerning the analogy Holdheim drew between the *kinyan* of a wife and the *kinyan* of an ownerless field. In the case of a wife, *bi'ah* establishes the absolute right of the man to the woman only in an instance where the woman is unmarried. A married woman who willingly has intercourse with a man other than her husband is simply an adulteress. The consensual intercourse in which she has engaged with a man other than her husband does not effectuate *kinyan* in such a circumstance. *Chazakah* is distinct from *bi'ah* then on the grounds that the former establishes absolute, not relative, title. Even if the original owner of the property should return to claim title after three years, that person could not do so. However, *bi'ah*, in contrast to *chazakah*, can be said to establish only a presumptive right. Even if the woman has honestly assumed that her first husband was dead, if the first husband is alive and there has been no divorce, then *bi'ah* could not establish *kinyan* between the "adulteress woman" and the man other than her presumably dead husband with whom she engaged in consensual intercourse.

[9] Holdheim, *Ueber die Autonomie der Rabbinen*, 107-8.

[10] Ibid., 159.

acts. If Jewish law had regarded marriage as a religious and not a civil act, then *kiddushin*—like *milah* and *avodah*—would have superseded the Sabbath and *kinyan* could have taken place. In Holdheim's opinion, the failure of Jewish law to do so constituted a warrant for the position that the *kinyan* of marriage was not distinct in this way from the civil character with which *kinyan* was invested in other transactions. Thus Judaism regarded marriage as a civil-legal transaction, not a religious-moral act. Holdheim supplemented this argument by pointing out that the autonomy accorded the husband in biblical law to divorce the wife he had acquired through *kinyan* was identical to the right of any owner of any object to dispose of that object at will;[11] *kinyan* in Jewish matrimonial law was a civil, not a religious, deed.

Holdheim's analysis led him to conclude that marriage properly fell under the category of civil law, *dinei mamanot*, and not Jewish religious law, *dinei issura*. After all, *kinyan* in marriage constituted no less a commercial transaction than would *kinyan* in any other business matter. Holdheim was thus able to contend that just as Jewish law—through the principle of *dina de-malkhuta dina*—accorded state law sovereignty over Jewish law in civil matters, so too should state law have dominion over Jewish law in relation to marriage. In short, marriage came within the jurisdiction of the state, and civil law in this area superseded Jewish law. As Holdheim put it:

> That which is of an absolutely religious character and of a purely religious content in Mosaic legislation and in the later historical development of Judaism [....] and which refers to the relationship of man to God [....] has been commanded by God to the Jew for eternity. But whatever has reference to interhuman relationships of a political, legal, and civil character [....] must be totally deprived of its applicability everywhere and forever when Jews enter into relationships with other states.[12]

---

[11] Ibid., 138.

[12] Ibid., 49ff . The translation is taken from Jakob J. Petuchowski, "Abraham Geiger and Samuel Holdheim: Their Differences in Germany and Repercussions in America," *LBIYB* 22 (1977), 139-159, here 143.

2. The Response of Zacharias Frankel

Holdheim's position met with swift and critical response. Samson Raphael Hirsch immediately published *Zweite Mitteilungen aus einem Briefwechsel über die neueste jüdische Literatur* (A Second Set of Information on the Exchange of Letters Regarding the Most Recent Jewish Literature) and fulminated against Holdheim's abdication of rabbinic authority in Jewish matrimonial law. Hirsch contended that the application of *dina de-malkhuta dina* to this area was unnecessary and unwarranted.[13] Another polemical work issued by Orthodox rabbis thundered:

> I ask you, Holdheim! Tell me, where has your heart gone? And if, according to your word, you would say, "All who are sanctified in marriage are sanctified according to the authority of the rabbis,"— "according to the authority of the rabbis" we have heard! "According to the authority of heretics and non-believers like you," we have not heard! [....] "According to the law of Moses and Israel," we have heard in connection with *kiddushin*. We have never heard, "According to the law of the king and the customs of the nations."[14]

Other Orthodox leaders joined in the chorus against Holdheim as well.[15] It was left to Zacharias Frankel, however, to produce the chief legal arguments against Holdheim's assessment of *kinyan* in relationship to *inei kiddushin* (the laws of marriage).

Frankel had initially attacked Holdheim's position immediately after the publication of *Ueber die Autonomie der Rabbinen*, and, again, shortly after the Brunswick Rabbinical Conference of 1844.[16] In his initial responses to Holdheim's work, Frankel was full of invective; he accused Holdheim of being a traitor to the Jewish religion.[17]

---

[13] *Zweite Mittheilung aus einem Briefwechsel über die neueste jüdische Literatur: Ein Fragment von Samson Raphael Hirsch, Landesrabbiner zu Emden. Beleuchtet von Dr. Samuel Holdheim* (Schwerin: C. Kürschner, 1844).

[14] [Pinchas Menachem Heilprin], *Teshuvot be-anshe aven—Holdheim v-re'av be mikhtavim sheloshah asar* (Frankfurt am Main: s.n., 1845), 71.

[15] Zvi Hirsch Chajes, Jacob Ettlinger, and others joined the chorus of protest against Holdheim and his followers. An account of the ire Holdheim aroused can be found in David Ellenson, "Traditional Reactions to Modern Jewish Reform," in idem, *After Emancipation*, chapter 7.

[16] Holdheim's response to Frankel's initial critique can be found in Samuel Holdheim, *Das Religiöse und Politische im Judentum, mit besonderer Beziehung auf gemischte Ehen* (Schwerin: C. Kürschner, 1845).

[17] For Frankel's critique of Holdheim at this juncture, see Frankel's several articles on this issue in his *Zeitschrift für die religiösen Interessen des Judenthums* 1 (1844), issues 5-8.

Nevertheless, it was in an article Frankel published fifteen years later, *Grundlinien des Mosaisch-talmudischen Eherechts* (Outlines of Mosaic-Talmudic Marriage Law), that he explicitly advanced a strong argument against the interpretation of Jewish law Holdheim had put forth.[18] Although Frankel did not mention Holdheim explicitly, his essay put forth a case for refutation of the claims Holdheim had made in *Ueber die Autonomie der Rabbinen* and provided a more elaborate response to them.

Frankel agreed that the means whereby *kinyan* was established in regard to *kiddushin*—*Geld oder Geldeswerth, Urkunde, oder Beischlaf (kesef, shtar, u-bi'ah)*—were parallel to those modes whereby *kinyan* was effectuated in other civil matters.[19] The *kinyan* of marriage, however, diverged from the *kinyan* of objects immediately after the act of *kiddushin* was performed: the love and trust that obtained between the couple transformed the *kinyan* of marriage from a matter of acquisition into a matter of holiness and ethics.[20] Frankel pointed out that in Judaism the institution of marriage had developed in accordance with the principles of morality (*der Sittlichkeit*) and the act of acquisition (*Handlung*) itself had to be accompanied by the words, "*Du seiest mir geheiligt*—You are sanctified unto me."[21] Furthermore, the holiness accorded to marriage in Jewish tradition led the rabbis to frown upon intercourse as a proper mode for establishing *kiddushin*. Indeed, Frankel cited a passage in the *Mishneh Torah of Maimonides, Hilkhot Issurei Bi'ah* 21: 14 ("Any man who sanctifies his wife by means of intercourse [....] lashes are applied to him")—to support the view that the rabbis condemned *bi'ah* as "*Unsittlichkeit*—immoral."[22]

Holdheim, too, had stated that *kiddushin* involved an understanding that love and trust existed between the couple. He had argued, however, that these factors of sentiment were not legally actionable; they neither effectuated nor annulled the *kinyan*. Frankel considered

---

[18] Zacharias Frankel, "Grundlinien des mosaisch-talmudischen Eherechts," *Jahresbericht des jüdisch-theologischen Seminar* (Breslau, January 27, 1860), i-xlviii.

[19] Ibid., xi and xxv.

[20] Ibid., xliii.

[21] Ibid., xxv.

[22] Ibid., xxvi. Frankel also cited the talmudic passage (*Kiddushin* 12b) upon which Maimonides based his ruling. In that passage, Rav, a third century rabbinic authority, sought to discourage betrothal through intercourse by imposing lashes upon men who betrothed women in this way.

this position incorrect. The recitation of the words, "You are sanctified to me," indicated that marriage was marked by more than a
legal (*rechtlicher*) act. It had a religious (*religiöse*) dimension,[23] and this
dimension meant that the *kinyan* of marriage could not be equated
with *kinyan* in other transactions; it was *sui generis*.

Frankel further supported this contention on two other grounds.
He noted that in the case of marriage, an act of infidelity on the
wife's part required the husband to issue a *get* (a divorce) to her.
The authority of the husband to do with his wife what he might
wish in such an event was abrogated; by the same token, he had
no license to forgive her. Jewish law provided no other option.
Divorce was unavoidable. From this, Frankel concluded that *kiddushin*
and the act of *kinyan* associated with it could not be equated with
other instances of *kinyan:* the wife was a person in her own right;
she was not simply an inanimate piece of property over whom the
husband could exercise total domination. If marriage was simply a
civil act and if his wife was simply akin to a piece of property, then
the husband could retain or dispose of his wife according to his will.
The institution of marriage, however, was viewed from a religious-
moral, not simply a legal, perspective; thus the act of *kinyan* that
established it had to be regarded as unique and therefore distinct
from every other type of *kinyan*. The adulterous act of the wife was
a "moral abomination—*sittlicher Abscheu*." It violated both culture and
modesty and represented a rupture in the moral order of society.[24]

In categorizing the laws of marriage as matters of religion, Frankel
believed that he undermined Holdheim's position on the matter.
Marriage was not simply a civil affair. Judaism could not surrender
its right to regulate marriage through an unwarranted application of
dina demalkhuta dina as Holdheim had proposed.

Frankel continued his case against Holdheim's stance by pointing
out that a husband could not in every instance do with his wife as
his heart desired. Indeed, the wife retained the right not to have
intercourse with her husband if she so chose. Moreover, if she found
her husband repulsive, then Jewish law held that the rabbinic court
had the power to compel him to issue her a divorce. Citing
Maimonides, *Hilkhot Ishut* 14: 8, Frankel held that the wife was not

---

[23] Ibid., xxxi.
[24] Ibid., xliv.

a "*Kriegsgefangene*—a captive."[25] Once more, he held that in Jewish law, she was a person possessed of rights, not an object subject to the caprice and whim of her husband.

The husband's control over his wife in the Jewish marriage relationship was circumscribed in other ways as well. Frankel observed that in other ancient cultures the husband could terminate his relationship with his wife at any time; she was identical to any other object he owned. He had no need to issue his wife a divorce should he desire to rid himself of her. This situation did not obtain in Judaism. If the husband wished to terminate their relationship, he had to issue his wife a get and recite the words that allowed her to remarry.[26]

For Frankel, the phrase, "*Harei at mekudeshet li—Du seiest mir geheiligt*," uttered by the husband when he betrothed his wife under the *khuppah*, elevated the act of marriage in Jewish religious law as well as the act of *kinyan* which accompanied it to a level of holiness. The external acts associated with the process of marriage within Judaism might appear identical to those acts that accompany civil transactions, but *kedushah* (holiness) was an integral part of the relationship established between the bride and groom at the Jewish wedding ceremony. It transformed the mechanism of *kinyan* with regard to marriage from a civil to a religious act. Marriage, from the perspective of Judaism, was a religious affair. Frankel, unlike Holdheim, refused to reduce it to a civil matter.

In assessing Frankel's critique of the position Holdheim advanced, one must bear in mind that Frankel's essay was intended as more than a narrow, albeit interesting, disagreement with Holdheim about the character of *kinyan* in Jewish marriage law. Rather, Frankel's assault on Holdheim betrays a different perception about the character of Judaism in the modern world. To understand precisely what was at stake in this halakhic debate as well as to ferret out the meaning of this last statement, we need to place this entire argument within the historical context of the mid-1800s.

---

[25] Ibid., xlviii.

[26] Ibid., xi ff. See especially xliv-xlv and xlvii-xlviii. Of course, one could look at the institution of divorce in Judaism from another perspective as well. For one could maintain that the divorce simply renders the women "unowned." In this way, the institution of divorce might be said to make the woman more rather than less akin to other forms of property.

3. The Historical Context for Holdheim's Position and Frankel's Response

The argument advanced by Holdheim in *Ueber die Autonomie der Rabbinen* was prompted by the continuing political struggle for Jewish emancipation that marked the Germany of his day. Holdheim's immediate target was Bruno Bauer. A Protestant theologian, Bauer published his "Judenfrage" ("Jewish Question") in 1842 in the *Deutsche Jahrbücher* and reissued it as a pamphlet in 1843.[27] In it, he argued that the Jew, by his very nature, could not be emancipated. "As long as he is a Jew," he wrote, "his Jewishness must be stronger in him than his humanity, and keep him apart from non-Jews. He declares by this segregation that this, his Jewishness, is his true, highest nature, which has to have precedence over his humanity."[28] For this reason, "the Jews as such cannot amalgamate with the nations and cast their lot with them."[29] They must "always remain a foreign element."[30]

Bauer, in effect, argued that the "Jewish Question" in the modern political order could not be resolved because the Jew, by his very nature, placed fidelity to religion over allegiance to a state characterized by a putatively neutral public sphere. Emancipation could be granted the Jew in the modern political order only when he was prepared to surrender the imperatives of his religion—when he was willing, for example, "to go to the Chamber of Deputies on the Sabbath and participate in public discussions."[31] In short, the condition modernity established as a prerequisite for Jewish emancipation and Jewish participation in the modern political order was for the Jewish people to agree voluntarily to surrender their particularity—their language, the initiatory rite of circumcision for their sons, and their observance of the dietary and Sabbath laws. Only then could the Jew become a full member of the nation. Until that time, the nature of Judaism made full citizenship an impossibility for the Jew.[32]

---

[27] Bruno Bauer, "The Jewish Problem," trans. Helen Lederer (Cincinnati: HUC Press, 1957).

[28] Ibid., 22.

[29] Ibid., 47.

[30] Ibid., 55.

[31] Ibid., 67.

[32] Ibid., 110ff.

Bauer pressed this point by devoting an entire section of his pamphlet to an analysis of the transactions of the Paris Sanhedrin.[33] He dismissed as a lie the distinction the delegates to the Sanhedrin had made between the political and the religious obligations Judaism imposed upon its adherents, and he observed that many of the major addresses the delegates delivered to the Assembly were offered in Hebrew and only afterwards translated into French. This was emblematic of the primacy the Jews accorded their own nation. Bauer wrote:

> It would be fine if the Jew openly declared, "I want—since I wish to remain a Jew—to keep only that much of the Law which seems to be a purely religious element. Everything else which I recognize as anti-social I shall weed out and sacrifice." But instead he pretends to himself, and wants to make others believe that in this distinction between political and religious commands he remains in accord with the Law, that the Law itself establishes this distinction [....] Judaism cannot be helped, the Jews cannot be reconciled with the world, by the lie.[34]

Dina de-malkhuta dina was at best an illusory remedy to the dilemma of the Jew. The nationalist component in Judaism could not be eliminated. The Jew *qua* Jew could not be made fit for participation in the modern political order.

Bauer's argument garnered a great deal of attention. Indeed, Karl Marx himself issued a response to it. He criticized Bauer for failing to take the implications of his argument to their logical conclusion. Marx charged that Bauer, in singling out the particularity of Judaism as he had, neglected the particularity of the State itself and the role assigned to religion in it. He argued that present-day Jews and Christians could be free only when society was emancipated from religion altogether. The essential "species-being" of humanity demanded nothing less. There could be no distinction between political and private spheres. People could not be regarded as communal beings in the arena of politics while acting as private individuals in the realm of civil society.[35]

Holdheim disagreed, and his *Ueber die Autonomie der Rabbinen* was no less a response to Bauer than was the work of Marx. Holdheim's book can be seen as an expression of classical nineteenth-century

---

[33] Ibid., 114ff.
[34] Ibid., 122.
[35] Karl Marx, *On the Jewish Question*, trans. Helen Lederer (Cincinnati: HUC Press, 1958).

liberal political theory. It attempted to distinguish between public and private spheres and sought to carve out a position for particularistic religious commitments in the private realm. Indeed, Holdheim advanced the position that religion continued to possess a legitimate right to exist in the setting of the modern nation-state. It simply had to demonstrate that it could be confined to the private sphere and would not interfere with the individual citizen's performance of duties for the modern nation-state in the public realm. Bauer, Holdheim contended, was wrong not to recognize that Judaism allowed for these civic responsibilities no less than Christianity in the setting of the modern nation-state. A Jewish soldier, for example, was no less obligated to serve in the military on the Sabbath than was his Christian counterpart to serve on Sunday. Nor would a Jewish bureaucrat neglect his duties as a citizen on the Sabbath. Indeed, the dictum of *dina de-malkhuta dina* provided a religious sanction for these acts. It directed the Jew's actions in the political realm and made the Jew fit for life as a citizen in the modern political setting.[36]

In short, the Jew's obligation to observe the laws of the state sprang from meaningful religious warrants contained in Judaism itself. Moreover, the doctrines of Judaism directed the Jews to an appropriate role in the emancipated world of nineteenth-century Germany.

Holdheim's argument concerning the nature of marriage in Judaism as well as his analysis of *kinyan* in relation to *dinei kiddushin* were intended to further complement his brief on behalf of the suitability of Judaism in the present-day political order. His position was informed in large measure by instrumental considerations and was designed to advance the cause of Jewish political emancipation by demonstrating that Judaism recognized and affirmed a distinction between the domain of politics and the realm of religion. His stance on this matter comported with the distinction he drew between the transitory national-ritual-legal dimensions of Judaism and the eternal ethical-religious sentiments he claimed informed its core.[37]

---

[36] Holdheim, *Ueber die Autonomie der Rabbinen*, 96ff.; and see especially 100.

[37] In making this argument, Holdheim was taking a stance in direct opposition to Bauer, who had branded the distinction made between political and religious commandments in Judaism "a lie." See n. 31 above. On the distinction Holdheim drew between the "perishable" ritual and national elements within Judaism, and the "eternally valid" religious teachings that comprised the essence of the Jewish religion, see David Philipson, *The Reform Movement in Judaism* (New York, 1967), 252-53.

In asserting that Judaism did distinguish between civil and religious spheres, Holdheim was arguing that Jews, without abandoning their religion, were therefore fit for citizenship in the modern order. Meeting Bauer's challenge, he was prepared to "weed out and sacrifice" the "antisocial" elements in Judaism that were incompatible with that order. The distinction drawn in Judaism between religious and political commands was not, as Bauer had charged, an illusory principle. It was a vital component of the teachings and ethos of Judaism, and thus they were not incompatible with the contours of a contemporary secular order that attempted to confine religion to a private sphere. Holdheim's position on the nature of *kinyan* in Jewish matrimonial law was designed to support this stance. It is not surprising, then, that one year later, at the famed Brunswick Rabbinical Conference, he led the proponents of a measure that stated:

> Members of monotheistic religions in general are not forbidden to marry if the parents are permitted by the law of the state to bring up children from such wedlock in the Jewish religion.[38]

Indeed, his advocacy of this measure in 1844 was totally consistent with the posture he adopted in his *Ueber die Autonomie der Rabbinen* in 1843. His actions on behalf of this resolution reflect more than an alleged comment upon and affirmation of sentiments expressed by the rabbis of the Paris Sanhedrin in 1807.[39] They bespeak a heartfelt longing for Jewish political emancipation and the articulation of a posture designed to accomplish this goal. Holdheim's views on *kinyan* in connection with *dinei kiddushin*, as well as the open stance he took in regard to intermarriage, are paradigmatic of the efforts made by some Jews to be deemed worthy of enfranchisement in the modern state.

Nothing in Frankel's writings indicates that he was not an advocate of classical liberal political theory: he also wanted the Jew to be a full participant in modern society. But unlike Holdheim, Frankel did not believe that for such enfranchisement to take place, it was necessary to assign marriage to the public sphere as opposed to the private realm. Indeed, given Frankel's own views, not only was Holdheim's application of the principle of *dina de-malkhuta din*a to the

---

[38] W. Gunther Plaut, *The Rise of Reform Judaism* (New York: World Union of Progressive Judaism, 1963), 222.
[39] Ibid., 220.

area of Jewish laws of marriage unprecedented from an halakhic standpoint, but it also marked Holdheim, in Frankel's eyes, as an opportunist who would destroy the religious integrity of Judaism for "a mess of pottage." Frankel not only disagreed with Holdheim's characterization of Jewish marriage as an exclusively civil act, but he could not, in effect, understand why Jewish participation in the modern political order was dependent upon the assignment of Jewish marriage to the civil realm. Further research may shed light on the historical factors that caused Holdheim to disagree. For our purposes, it is enough to observe that the setting of the 1840s and the struggles for Jewish political emancipation that this decade witnessed provide a context for understanding some of the factors that motivated the positions adopted by both Holdheim and Frankel in their debate over the civil and religious nature of Jewish matrimonial law. Their stances surely illuminate the divisions that distinguished the Positive-Historical and radical Reform wings of German Liberal Judaism at this juncture.

PART III

RADICAL REFORM IN COMPARATIVE PERSPECTIVE

SAMUEL HOLDHEIM AND ZACHARIAS FRANKEL: COMPARATIVE PERSPECTIVES[1]

Andreas Brämer

The embourgeoisement of German Jewry was accompanied by radical changes that affected both the social as well as the religious sphere of German Jewish culture. As liturgical reforms increasingly permeated the synagogue, German Jewry lost much of its former unity, at least inasmuch as this unity had been based on a general consensus concerning halakhah and its importance for everyday life. Within a growing number of communities, tensions grew as a consequence of the increasing pluralism of religious opinions. Furthermore, a wide variety of local reforms exposed the lack of a central authority that would have been necessary for deciding on liturgical matters and coordinating religious progress. Many rabbis of the new generation came to the conclusion that mere cosmetic measures in the synagogual service were insufficient as a means for countering the phenomenon of increasing religious alienation. Basing their ideas on contemporary concepts and terminology, these scholars sought to create a new Jewish theology capable of resolving the tensions between traditional religious practices and a modern middle-class lifestyle.

Samuel Holdheim and Zacharias Frankel were certainly outstanding representatives of the modern rabbinate. Frankel was born in 1801 in Prague, where—unlike Holdheim in Kempen—he learned German from the early days of his childhood. It is important to note, however, that Frankel did not receive a thorough secular education until early adulthood, ultimately attaining his Ph.D. in 1830. After completing his studies, Frankel first served as a rabbi in Teplitz (Bohemia) from 1832-1836, where he established a reputation as a moderate reformer. Then, in 1836, the Jewish community of Dresden

---

[1] Translated from the German by William Templer.

selected him as its chief rabbi. During his long tenure in Dresden,
Frankel engaged in a wide range of public activities, thereby creating a name for himself well beyond the frontiers of the kingdom
of Saxony.

Frankel was appointed to his office during a period of fundamental transition: for the first time in its history, the Jewish community
had gained legal recognition as a corporate body. Within the Dresden
Jewish community, both education and communal worship were placed
under Frankel's supervision. He established a new Jewish elementary
school that combined both religious and secular instruction in a curriculum that succeeded in meeting the expectations of both the state
and the Jewish minority. In addition, Frankel devoted considerable
energy in pushing forward the construction of Dresden's first synagogue, which was completed in 1840 and replaced a number of private prayer circles. Frankel considered public prayer to be a pivotal
component of his own pastoral work. He introduced regular German-
language sermons, a male choir and moderate liturgical changes within
the framework of the new synagogue, and within a short period of
time, the Jews of Dresden came to view the new place of worship as
the centre of their religious community.[2] As in numerous other loca-
tions, the synagogue acquired a status it had not possessed in traditional Jewish society.

Like all their colleagues, Frankel and Holdheim were active first
and foremost within the institutions of their own rabbinical district.
And just as processes of disunification and isolation went hand-in-
hand with the modernization of German Jewry, these processes also
strongly influenced developments within the rabbinate itself. For
despite widespread agreement among young rabbis and preachers
that faith and religious practice must be made compatible with
modernity, no consensus could be reached with regard to the direction and speed of this process. On the contrary: Jewish theologians
elaborated a wide range of divergent concepts. Very often they
combined their "doctrine of salvation" with an attitude of intoler-
ance that appears to be a characteristic of younger movements.
These manifold developments within Judaism emerged from a widespread perception of crisis that all parties eagerly sought to overcome. In their efforts, they viewed their opponents as misguided

---

[2] See Andreas Brämer, *Rabbiner Zacharias Frankel. Wissenschaft des Judentums und konservative Reform im 19. Jahrhundert* (Hildesheim: Olms, 2000), 77-156.

competitors who either perpetuated the errors of the past or allowed reform processes to reel out of control. Uncertainties and a lack of self-confidence merely exacerbated the difficulty of arriving at a consensus.

Moreover, Frankel and Holdheim were never friends. Their mutual disaffection increased over time and went beyond the difference of opinions, venting itself even in occasional personal insults.[3] Despite the fact that both rabbis discontinued their quarrelling as of the late 1840s, they were far from achieving reconciliation. Frankel publicly confirmed his aversion to Holdheim one last time when the latter died in Berlin in 1860, expressing that he considered it a sacrilege when the Berlin community's council of elders provided Holdheim with an honorary burial alongside the graves of famous talmudic scholars. He commented on the events as follows:

> Dr. Holdheim, the reform community's rabbi, passed away in Berlin, and the community board arranged for his burial in a row of the cemetery reserved for rabbinical scholars. This was a severe mistake. Let us disregard Holdheim's character as it revealed itself during his lifetime, let us remain silent about his denunciations of Jews and Judaism, and let us ignore his public declaration that, according to the teachings of the Talmud, a Jew was permitted to commit perjury and allowed to kill Gentiles. In these cases it is acceptable to apply the expression: death reconciles. But if death reconciles, it does not elevate, it does not turn an enemy of positive Judaism into its friend, and it does not transform a person for whom the foundations of Judaism lacked all binding nature into a believer. To bury him alongside those old teachers shows contempt both for the deceased as well as for the beliefs they maintained.[4]

---

[3] The Reform periodical, *Israelit des 19. Jahrhunderts*, spread the rumour that censors had reprimanded Frankel for his abusive language against Holdheim; see *Israelit des 19. Jahrhunderts* 6 (1845), 48, 56.

[4] "Zu Berlin verstarb Dr. Holdheim, Rabbiner der Reformgemeinde, und der Gemeindevorstand liess ihn in der auf dem jüdischen Gottesacker für Rabbiner bestimmten Reihe beerdigen. Der Missgriff war arg. Sehen wir ab von dem Charakter Holdheim's, wie er sich im Leben zeigte, schweigen wir davon, dass er Juden und Judenthum denuncirte, öffentlich erklärte, der Jude dürfe nach talmudischer Lehre einen Meineid ablegen, der Jude dürfe nach talmudischer Lehre den Nichtjuden umbringen. Hierfür mögen die Worte angewendet werden: ‚Der Tod versöhnt.' Aber versöhnt der Tod, so erhebt er nicht, wandelt nicht den Feind des positiven Judenthums in dessen Freund um, macht nicht Denjenigen, für den die Grundsäulen des Judenthums nichts Verbindliches enthalten, zu deren Bekenner: ihn nun in der Reihe jener alten Lehrer begraben ist ein Hohn gegen die Verstorbenen, wie gegen den von ihnen bewahrten Glauben"; see Zacharias Frankel, "Der Rückblick," *MGWJ* 10 (1861), 1-19, here 17.

Their process of mutual estrangement had begun two decades earlier, in the early 1840s, and was linked to contemporary reform debates as well as personal experiences connected to the ideological search for religious truth. In contrast to Frankel, whose theological principles remained essentially the same throughout his life, Holdheim increasingly turned toward more radical positions during his tenure as chief rabbi in Schwerin. Both in 1839 and 1840, Holdheim declared that his Dresden colleague stood as an exemplary representative of the new spirit among German rabbis.[5] However, a chasm between both thinkers began to develop in 1841 when Holdheim cited Frankel's critique of the Hamburg Temple prayer book as evidence that his colleague's nebulous arguments did not express a sufficiently consistent position. Holdheim nevertheless felt obliged to uphold traditions of utmost collegial politeness when he apologized for any expressions that might have hurt Frankel's feelings.[6]

Even before both scholars met personally for the first time in 1845, during the second rabbinical conference convened in Frankfurt am Main, previous polemical statements from both rabbis had created a climate in which rapprochement was unlikely to occur. Holdheim's work on "rabbinic autonomy," which appeared in 1843, was the primary reason for their dispute. While focusing chiefly on the promulgation of a new vision of Judaism and its history, Holdheim's book once again referred to Frankel's report on the Temple *siddur*. A comparison with the ideas that Frankel elaborated in his short-lived monthly *Journal for the Religious Interests of Judaism* (*Zeitschrift für die religiösen Interessen des Judenthums*)[7] may contribute to

---

[5] Jonathan Alexandersohn, *Ehrenrettung und auf Dokumente gestützte Widerlegung aller gegen mich vorgebrachten Beschuldigungen und Verunglimpfungen. Meine durch öffentliche Blätter einigermaßen schon bekannte Verfolgungsgeschichte. Ein merkwürdiges Aktenstück in den Annalen des Judenthums*, 2nd ed. (Frankfurt am Main: J. F. Bach, 1847), 141-142 (German part); Samuel Holdheim, *Der religiöse Fortschritt im deutschen Judenthume. Ein friedliches Wort in einer aufgeregten Zeit* (Leipzig: E. L. Fritzsche, 1840), 19.

[6] Zacharias Frankel, "Erwiderung auf das von Herrn Dr. Salomon, Prediger am neuen israelitischen Tempel zu Hamburg, an mich gerichtete Sendschreiben," *Literaturblatt des Orients 3* (1842), 353-68, 377-84; idem, "Schreiben des Oberrabbiners Dr. Frankel an die Direction des Tempelvereins zu Hamburg," *Orient 3* (1842), 53-56, 61-64, 71-72; Samuel Holdheim, *Verketzerung und Gewissensfreiheit. Ein zweites Votum in dem Hamburger Tempelstreit, mit besonderer Berücksichtigung der Erwiederung eines Ungenannten auf mein erstes Votum* (Schwerin: C. Kürschner, 1842), 89-111; Frankel did not respond to Holdheim's reproach.

[7] "Unter Mitwirkung mehrerer Gelehrten," Berlin and Leipzig 1844-1846.

a better understanding at least of the rational aspects of the dispute. In the following, Holdheim's and Frankel's divergent use of "nation" and "history" as central concepts of their respective reform platforms will be examined in order to provide an assessment of the conflict.

It was considered a major task of Jewish theology to formulate potential reconfigurations of religious faith that would allow Judaism to remain compatible with bourgeois identity. Zacharias Frankel followed in Moses Mendelssohn's footsteps when he insisted on separate spheres for the church and state. The state, he made clear, must limit its purview to the practical affairs of everyday life and had no right whatsoever to interfere in matters of religious conscience.[8] Frankel sought to demonstrate that a religion whose ethical standards remained in harmony with bourgeois morality could neither positively nor negatively affect the legal status of its adherents.[9] He opposed the concept of a "Christian state" that upheld the principle of a strong linkage between religion and politics.[10] Seeking to resolve the discrepancy between cultural integration and legal discrimination, he demanded the full participation of Jews as citizens of the state.[11] The German patriotism that underlay his argument remained questionable, however, since it basically emphasized a cultural sense of belonging. While Frankel exercised restraint in his national sentiment, it nevertheless influenced his religious thinking because it interfered with the essential "national" characteristics of the Jewish religion. Expectations both of the coming of the Messiah as well as the *kibbuts galuyot* in Eretz Israel appeared

---

[8] Zacharias Frankel, "Die Symptome der Zeit," *Zeitschrift für die religiösen Interessen des Judenthums* 2 (1845), 3-21, here 4-5; idem, *Die Eidesleistung der Juden in theologischer und historischer Beziehung*, 2nd edition (Dresden and Leipzig: Arnold, 1847), 136-137, note 172; see Michael A. Meyer, *Response to Modernity: A History of the Reform Movement in Judaism* (New York: Oxford University Press, 1988), 104.

[9] Frankel to Joseph Muhr, 26 January, 1842, in Simon Bernfeld, "Zacharias Frankel in Berlin," *AZJ* 62 (1898), no. 29-31, 33-34, 37, 39, 41, 45, 48-51, here no. 37, 437-439, quotation at 438.

[10] Zacharias Frankel, *Der gerichtliche Beweis nach mosaisch-talmudischem Rechte. Ein Beitrag zur Kenntniss des mosaisch-talmudischen Criminal- und Civilrechts. Nebst einer Untersuchung über die Preussische Gesetzgebung hinsichtlich des Zeugnisses der Juden* (Berlin: Veit, 1846), 14 and 90; idem, *Anzeige und Prospectus einer Zeitschrift für die religiösen Interessen des Judenthums* (Dresden: Simion, 1843), 2.

[11] See idem, *Historisch-kritische Studien zu der Septuaginta. Nebst Beiträgen zu den Targumim. Erster Band. Erste Abtheilung: Vorstudien zu der Septuaginta* (Leipzig: Vogel, 1841), VIII.

to link ethnic views with religious concepts. The ultimate goal of a Jewish homestead forced the questions of whether and under what circumstances Jews could fulfil their duties within a national society.[12]

Frankel was no harbinger of Zionism.[13] His efforts to justify particularistic Jewish hopes for independence without taking refuge in national categories reflected the Jewish dilemma as a minority within history. Frankel characterized Jewish nationality as a consequence of oppression and discrimination, as a mere invention imposed on the Jews by their environment. He was prepared to blend German nationalism and national Judaism, thereby weakening the concrete nature of the latter:

> We have a fatherland that we do not want to leave. Once we were an independent people. Religion and history are witnesses to this fact. Who could hold against us our proud, uplifting wish that our name may once again stand out independently? Holy memories tie us to the land of our forefathers. To those of us who have found a home, the wish to regain this land is merely an idea, an indulgence in a nostalgic dream. When we look at it soberly, we abandon the desire to achieve it.[14]

As a matter of fact, Frankel at times did confuse issues that he wanted to keep separate. Holdheim proved to be a keen observer

---

[12] Ibid.

[13] See Rivka Horwitz, "Zacharias Frankel's 1842 Idea of Jewish Independence in the Land of Israel" (hebr.), *Kivvunim 6* (1980), 5-24; idem, *Hashpa'at ha-Romantiqa 'al Chochmat Jisrael* (Jerusalem: Merkaz Zalman Shazar, 1984), 16-17; Isaak Heinemann, *Ta'ame ha-Mitsvot be-Sifrut Jisrael*, vol. 2 (Jerusalem: s.n., 1956), 177-180; Aron Kleinberger, "Peraqim be-Toldot ha-Chevrah ha-yehudit bi-Yme ha-Beynayim u-va-'Et ha-chadashah," in *Tesisah le'umit be-Jahadut Germanyah ba-Machatsit ha-rishonah shel ha Me'ah ha-19*, ed. Emanuel Etkes and Yosef Salmon (Jerusalem: Magnes, 1980), 225-247, particularly 237 and 246; Michael A. Meyer, "Recent Historiography on the Jewish Religion in Modern Germany," *LBIYB* 35 (1990), 3-16, particularly 11, note 35; Saul Pinchas Rabinowicz, *R. Zecharjah Frankel* (Hebrew) (Warsaw: s.n., 1898-1901), 78-81, 307-314; David Rudavsky, "The Historical School of Zacharias Frankel," *JSS* 5 (1963), 224-244, particularly 232-235.

[14] "Wir haben ein Vaterland, das wir nicht verlassen wollen: einst waren wir ein selbstständiges Volk; Religion und Geschichte sprechen davon: wer kann uns den stolzen erhebenden Wunsch, daß unser Name einst wieder selbstständig hervortrete, verargen? An das Land unserer Väter knüpfen uns heilige Erinnerungen: der Wunsch es wieder zu erlangen ist uns, die eine Heimath gefunden, nur eine Idee, ein Schwelgen in früherer Zeit, bei nüchterner Betrachtung geben wir das Verlangen nach ihrer Verwirklichung auf'"; Frankel, "Erwiderung auf das von Herrn Dr. Salomon, Prediger am neuen israelitischen Tempel zu Hamburg, an mich gerichtete Sendschreiben," 362.

who confronted Frankel's occasional inconsistencies with a strictly denominational perspective. In 1844, when the chief rabbi of Dresden publicly defended the circumcision ceremony as an essential rite of religious initiation, Holdheim accused him of formulations that appeared to ascribe an ethnic component to Judaism that stood alongside and primary to its religious character.[15] Holdheim was correct in this case, as can be concluded from a letter Frankel sent years later to the Saxon ministry of education. In this letter, Frankel described the *brit mila* as the true sign of a child's entry into the religious community. According to Frankel, a boy who was not circumcised might be considered a fellow member of the Jewish people, but he did not belong to the religious community. In Frankel's view, along with all of its essential religious characteristics, Judaism also contained the element of common heritage. While baptism might transform a Jew into a Christian, he remained a Jew according to his heritage.[16]

Generally, however, Frankel set forth his arguments more carefully. In order to preserve certain national elements of Jewish identity, he tended to de-emphasize their significance. Like Holdheim, he sought to establish Judaism as a confession whose status was equivalent to that of the Christian faith. Holdheim's efforts, however, took the opposite direction: he elaborated a theory that underscored the national aspects of traditional Judaism while simultaneously singling out these aspects as anachronistic relics. For him, Frankel's plea for a moderate course of reform repeatedly served as the negative foil for his own radical proposals.

Holdheim postulated a close integration between modern citizenship and Judaism and grounded his theory on the sacred texts of Jewish literature. At the same time, he employed history to turn it against *halakha*, arguing that it was an urgent task of the present to break with a misdirected past. His central idea rested upon the assumption that, during the Second Temple period, the Jewish state had merged religious commandments and general laws into a *corpus*

---

[15] Samuel Holdheim, *Ueber die Beschneidung zunächst in religiös-dogmatischer Beziehung* (Schwerin: C. Kürschner, 1844), 86-88; cf. Zacharias Frankel, "Nachbemerkung des Herausgebers," *Zeitschrift für die religiösen Interessen des Judenthums* 1 (1844), 60-73, particularly 67.

[16] Frankel to the Ministry of Education, 27 January, 1852, in Sächsisches Hauptstaatsarchiv (SächsHSTA) Dresden, Ministerium für Volksbildung (MfVb) 11134.

juri in force at the time. He concluded that, since the Jews no longer constituted a unified national entity following their loss of political independence, *halakhah* could no longer claim ubiquitous validity and must therefore be revised. Viewed in this way, the destruction of the Temple attained the status of a divine revelation: all reform measures that sought to filter out those rules and prohibitions that putatively had no religious foundation, but were solely directed toward maintaining the order of the Jewish community, thereby received divine sanction.[17] Furthermore, in Holdheim's theories, even admittedly religious customs were to be sacrificed for the welfare of the modern state whenever they interfered with the sphere of civic life. Ultimately, the Jewish believer was called upon to adhere to an unspecific set of moral commitments which possessed "absolute and categorical" authority but which were no longer distinguishable from bourgeois ethical standards.[18]

Holdheim's book on "rabbinic autonomy" emerged within the general context of Jewish efforts toward social integration but paid particular attention to Bruno Bauer, who had offered his own answer to the Jewish question one year earlier. Bauer, a leading member of the Young Hegelians, delivered harsh polemics against the Jewish faith; however, his polemics were situated within his overall vision that postulated the disappearance of all religions as a basic precondition for universal emancipation. From this point of view, all efforts of Reform Judaism to reinterpret the concept of messianism were insufficient: as long as Jews lived as Jews, they would remain estranged from their fellow men, unable to find their place within society.[19]

Rather than simply refuting Bauer, Holdheim made occasional attempts to accommodate his arguments. Frankel, on the other hand, had begun to elaborate a conservative conceptualization of Judaism,

---

[17] Samuel Holdheim, *Ueber die Autonomie der Rabbinen und das Princip der jüdischen Ehe. Ein Beitrag zur Verständigung über einige das Judenthum betreffende Zeitfragen* (Schwerin: C. Kürschner, 1843), 14-51; and see Andreas Gotzmann, *Jüdisches Recht im kulturellen Prozeß. Die Wahrnehmung der Halacha im Deutschland des 19. Jahrhunderts* (Tübingen: J.C.B. Mohr, 1997), 207-218.

[18] Holdheim, *Ueber die Autonomie der Rabbinen*, 109-111; see Gil Graff, *Separation of Church and State. Dina de-Malkhuta Dina in Jewish Law, 1750-1848* (Alabama: The University of Alabama Press, 1985), 121-124.

[19] Bruno Bauer, *Die Judenfrage* (Brunswick: Otto, 1843); see Nathan Rotenstreich, "For and against Emancipation: The Bruno Bauer Controversy," *LBIYB* 4 (1959), 3-36.

which Holdheim interpreted as a hindrance toward integration within bourgeois society. Frankel persistently held fast to ideas that integrated national elements into the realm of faith, thereby appearing to confirm accusations levelled by opponents of Jewish emancipation. Frankel's perspective thus also called into question Holdheim's argument that messianic hopes and German patriotism comprised incompatible opposites. In 1842, Frankel publicly expressed the desire "that our name should once again spring forth free and independent." Without naming names, Bauer cited Frankel's formulation as evidence to prove his assertion that the Jews would never be prepared to surrender their national particularism.[20] Holdheim looked upon Frankel as a champion of antiquated ideas, and he held these ideas responsible for Bauer's anti-Jewish prejudices.[21] In fact, Holdheim was not far removed from accusing Frankel of impeding Jewish emancipation. Although Holdheim argued passionately against Bauer, it was nevertheless possible to gain the impression that he did not merely acknowledge the decline of ritual observance among the Jewish middle class, but that he even accepted the expectations of the Christian majority as a standard for restructuring Jewish religious life.

Frankel scrutinized Holdheim's theories but at first refrained from criticism—for tactical reasons, as he made clear to rabbi Michael Sachs:

> What is the use of attacking Geiger and Holdheim and revealing their unfortunately completely reprehensible character? Do you believe that we can defeat them in this manner? The public will perceive it as quarrelsomeness and particularly as a sign of intellectual weakness that has to resort to insults as a means of attack. And when it is over [....], what is to follow? We will simply have made our opponents our equals; because once we attack our opponent, it is his right to attack us in return, and it will ultimately be a question of whose lungs can hold out longer. Why not behave calmly and prove the justice of our cause with sound arguments? We can certainly mount a sufficient attack in this manner; once we believe we have won over the public, or at least convinced them of our sincere intentions, we can tear off the mask of our wretched adversaries. Then we can declare to the public: choose between us and them, who represent not you, nor your

---

[20] Bauer, *Die Judenfrage*, 29-30; see Frankel, "Schreiben des Oberrabbiners Dr. Frankel an die Direction des Tempelvereins zu Hamburg," 63.

[21] Holdheim, *Ueber die Autonomie der Rabbinen*, 54-56.

belief, nor your cause, but merely themselves and their utterly disgraceful egoism. So have no concern. The time for quarrelling will
come [....].[22]

Even before Frankel, Rabbi Samson Raphael Hirsch in Emden sought
to refute Holdheim's treatise on "rabbinic autonomy" as anti-
Talmudism in disguise.[23] Although Frankel had labelled Hirsch a
champion of "harsh and rigid Orthodoxy"[24] as early as 1839, he did
not hesitate to cite Hirsch as a source when he published his own
critical response to Holdheim.[25] However, there can be no doubt
that Frankel was far removed from Hirsch's modern Orthodoxy.
Frankel had recognized that the problematic relationship between
revelation and tradition needed to be examined. According to the
beliefs of normative Judaism, both tradition and revelation (which
tradition sought to explain) were of divine origin and jointly

---

[22] "Was wird es nutzen, wenn wir mit Zank und Geschrei über Geiger und
Holdheim herfallen und sie nach ihrem leider! ganz verwerflichen Charakter
schildern? Sie meinen, wir werden hierdurch sie besiegt haben? Das Publicum legt
es für eine Zanksucht aus, erblickt gerade hierin eine geistige Schwäche, die nur
des groben Geschützes der Beleidigungen sich zum Angriff bedienen kann: und ist
dieser verdampft (und hierin gibt es doch in der That gerade keinen gar zu großen
Spielraum für Dialectik und logische Entwicklungen) was dann? Wir selbst haben
den Gegner ebenbürtig gemacht; denn haben wir geschimpft, so hat er das Recht
dagegen zu schimpfen und es wird nur darauf ankommen, wessen Lunge länger
aushält. Warum denn nicht gelassen auftreten und mit Gründen die Gerechtigkeit
unserer Sache nachweisen? Man kann wahrhaftig! auch hier genug Hiebe anbrin-
gen; und glauben wir das Publicum gewonnen oder es wenigstens von unserer
redlichen Absicht überzeugt zu haben, dann diesen elenden Gegnern die Larve
heruntergerissen; dann werde gezeigt: wählet zwischen uns und Jenen, die nicht
den Glauben, nicht Euch, nicht Eure Sache, sondern sich, den schändlichsten
Egoismus meinen. Seien Sie demnach unbesorgt: die Zeit des Zankens wird kom-
men [....]"; Frankel to Michael Sachs (1844), in Central Archives for the History
of the Jewish People, Jerusalem (CAHJP), P41/8; see Immanuel Heinrich Ritter,
*Geschichte der jüdischen Reformation. Dritter Theil: Samuel Holdheim. Sein Leben und seine
Werke. Ein Beitrag zu den neuesten Reformbestrebungen im Judenthume* (Berlin: W. J. Peiser,
1865), 126-133.
[23] Samson Raphael Hirsch, *Zweite Mittheilungen aus einem Briefwechsel über die neueste
jüdische Literatur. Ein Fragment* (Altona: J. F. Hammerich, 1844); see Noah H. Rosenbloom,
Tradition in an Age of Reform. The Religious Philosophy of Samson Raphael Hirsch (Philadelphia:
JPS, 1976), 80-82.
[24] Frankel's report, 15 October 1839, in: SächsHSTA Dresden, MfVb 11133.
[25] Zacharias Frankel, Review of S. Holdheim, Ueber die Autonomie der Rabbinen,
Zeitschrift für die religiösen Interessen des Judenthums 1 (1844), 204-208, 244-248, 273-288,
321-328, here 328; see Gotzmann, *Jüdisches Recht im kulturellen Prozeß*, 221-223, 238-
246; Frankel had originally planned to ask a friend—probably rabbi Salomon J.
Rapoport—to review Holdheim's book; see Frankel to Michael Sachs (1844), in
CAHJP, P41/8.

constituted the Jewish religion. Since the early nineteenth century, historical analysis had gained currency in every field of the humanities; as a result, tradition was no longer perceived as a rigid system but rather as a product of historical developments over time.[26] Frankel at times referred to "positive-historical Judaism" but spoke more frequently of "positive" Judaism to circumscribe his theological outlook.[27] Frankel was interested in depicting both the revelation at Mount Sinai (as a unique and direct message from God) as well as historical tradition as complementary aspects of Jewish religion. He explicitly distinguished between biblical and talmudic Judaism—terms he used as synonyms for revelation and tradition—without, however, seeking to rank one higher than the other.[28] He achieved an approximate parity between the two by enhancing the status of the historical elements of Jewish religion—elements which had actually been relegated to a secondary level of importance. By ascribing to tradition the status of a second and to some extent immanent revelation, Frankel removed tradition from the mundane area of human passions without, however, succumbing to a static conception of the world. For Frankel, it was this view of Judaism as the result of an organic process of growing and becoming that opened up concrete possibilities for moderate reform.

Certainly, Frankel was far removed from the radical determination of Holdheim, against whose arguments he strove to prove that Jewish religious law did not contain the justification for its own self-limitation within the modern state. In opposition to Holdheim, Frankel defended *halakhah* as compatible with contemporary ethical standards, especially in the area of marriage and divorce. Holdheim had not only advocated a thorough adaptation of Jewish marital laws to

[26] See Nathan Rotenstreich, *Tradition and Reality. The Impact of History on Modern Jewish Thought* (New York: Random House, 1972), 7-18; Gershom Scholem, *Über einige Grundbegriffe des Judentums* (Frankfurt am Main: Suhrkamp, 1970), 90-105; Michael A. Meyer, "Ob Schrift? Ob Geist?—Die Offenbarungsfrage im deutschen Judentum des neunzehnten Jahrhunderts," in *Offenbarung im jüdischen und christlichen Glaubensverständnis*, ed. Jakob J. Petuchowski and Walter Strolz (Freiburg: Herder, 1981), 162-179.

[27] Frankel, *Anzeige und Prospectus einer Zeitschrift für die religiösen Interessen des Judenthums*, 4-5; idem, "Über Reformen im Judenthume," *Zeitschrift für die religiösen Interessen des Judenthums* 1 (1844), 3-27, particularly 9, 13, 24; idem, "Die Symptome der Zeit," 12, 16; *Protokolle und Aktenstücke der zweiten Rabbinerversammlung abgehalten in Frankfurt am Main vom 15ten bis zum 28ten Juli 1845* (Frankfurt am Main: Ullmann, 1845), 19, 89; *Der Orient* 6 (1845), 253, 322, 342.

[28] Frankel, "Die Symptome der Zeit," 15-16.

common notions of morality,[29] he had also contested the religious context of divorce and recommended that divorce be subject to the purview of state legislation.[30] While this was an entirely secular point of view, it was a perspective through which Holdheim simultaneously appeared to accept and condone the Christian-religious bias of state matrimonial laws. Frankel did not intend to hold fast to rabbinic jurisdiction in matters of civil law, yet he demanded that rabbinical authority be preserved in matters of Jewish matrimony.[31] German bishops, too, resisted Prussian state interference in the realm of religious institutions. In general, however, the Catholic Church recognized no dissolution whatsoever of marriage. Frankel drew his conclusions from an opposite, more liberal point of view, inasmuch as he defended the breakdown of a marriage as a sufficient reason for divorce; this perspective accorded with Jewish tradition but was opposed to state matrimonial laws. Against the background of increasing state intervention, Frankel's fear that Holdheim's writings might provoke and legitimate legal intrusions into religious affairs was not altogether unfounded. Nevertheless, Frankel did not call processes of modernization fundamentally into question; rather, he sought to orient himself toward both, *halakhah* as well as the norms and values of bourgeois society and the state.

Frankel too acknowledged that contemporary Judaism was in need of regeneration. For him, the terms "public will" and "scholarship" ("Gesammtwille und Wissenschaft") were the guiding concepts for determining the course of religious progress. In accordance with his understanding of tradition as both historical and sacred, Frankel viewed the continuation of the Oral Law not as a strict reconstruction of God's will but as the independent and creative unfolding of Sinaitic revelation. The fact that tradition, as a manifestation of human existence, could not lay claim to absolute validity lent justification to certain religious reforms. Frankel maintained that tradition was established according to the religious needs of the Jewish

---

[29] Holdheim, *Ueber die Autonomie der Rabbinen*, 221, 260.
[30] Ibid., 157.
[31] Frankel, Review of S. Holdheim, *Ueber die Autonomie der Rabbinen*, 277-278; see Frankel's report, 21 January, 1842, in Stadtarchiv Dresden, RA C.XLII 240e; Frankel's report, 28 January, 1842, in: SächsHSTA Dresden, MfVb 11145; see also David Ellenson, "Samuel Holdheim and Zacharias Frankel on the Legal Character of Jewish Marriage," in idem, *After Emancipation. Jewish Religious Responses to Modernity*, (Cincinnati: Hebrew Union College Press, 2004), 139-153.

people as a whole, who then decided on the validity of legal interpretations.[32] In essence, the public will that Frankel outlined clearly
tended to uphold the status quo rather than manifesting itself as a
creative force and initiating change. Indeed, Frankel interpreted resistance to change as a guarantor of religious devoutness—devoutness
that had developed organically. Only those changes that succeeded
in asserting themselves against the conservatism of the general public could provide sufficient guarantee for the future. On the other
hand, however, reform efforts also required a creative element in
order to overcome passive opposition.[33] Frankel hoped that the necessary momentum would be provided by theologians who synthe-
sized critical scholarship and religious *vox populi*.[34] However, Frankel's
plans did not have an immediate effect on the everyday religious
life of German Jewry, due especially to the fact that he exercised
conspicuous restraint in proposing concrete reforms. Unlike Holdheim,
Frankel contented himself with the modification of a number of
minor details within Jewish religious law and did not question the
corpus as a whole.[35]

Aside from their differences in matters of theoretical and practical reform, Holdheim also diverged from Frankel in his approach
to tactical measures. Holdheim was uncompromising in his choice
of tactics. He allowed no consideration of the political interests of
the religious community if it meant exposing the supposed faults of
Judaism:

> We cannot ignore the fact that the enemies of emancipation can and
> will misuse many of our statements and arguments to further their
> own hostile causes. However, this consideration must not lead us to
> engage in the smallest disguise or minutest ambiguity in our comments
> on the spirit, essence and contents of the Talmud or of rabbinic
> Judaism. For this reason, we have never hesitated to call things by
> their real names, nor have we ever tried to cover up any weaknesses,
> no matter how embarrassing they might have seemed. [....]. In order
> to purify our religious convictions, we must succeed in a difficult and

---

[32] Frankel, "Über Reformen im Judenthume," 19-21; see Talmud Bavli, Avoda
Zara 36a.
[33] Frankel "Über Reformen im Judenthum," 22.
[34] Ibid., 24.
[35] Zacharias Frankel, "Über manche durch den Fortschritt der Medicin im
Judenthum bedingte Reformen," *Zeitschrift für die religiösen Interessen des Judenthums* 2
(1845), 265-269, 289-301, 342-349, 369-380; idem, "Die Symptome der Zeit," 16.

sacred fight against antiquated prejudices. Hence, from our point of view, we would be committing a sin if we were to ignore the strict requirements of truth and religion for the sake of emancipation, or if we were to permit any postponement of our search for religious truth for fear that ruthless criticism of any false propositions in our earlier religious ideas and feelings might harm our efforts to achieve emancipation.[36]

Holdheim launched his attacks against tradition in public, since otherwise his radical reform proposals would have lacked legitimation. Frankel viewed Holdheim not as an untiring seeker of true knowledge but rather as a traitor. In response, Holdheim accused Frankel of manipulative insincerity.[37] Frankel was not an overly pious hypocrite; rather, he felt pressed to act as a defender of Judaism in the face of both the Christian world as well as the emergent reform movement. In order to avoid the danger of being misinterpreted and serving as a bridge to more radical positions, Frankel tended to exercise extreme caution, a fact that strengthened his inclination to occupy conservative positions.

In early 1845, Frankel indicated that he would consent to the abolition of the second day of festivals if such a measure were to be recommended after careful debate. Pressed by rabbi Salomon Judah Loeb Rapoport in Prague not to make any concessions to the reformers,

---

[36] Samuel Holdheim, *Das Religiöse und Politische im Judenthum. Mit besonderer Beziehung auf gemischte Ehen. Eine Antwort auf Hrn. Dr. Frankel's Kritik der Autonomie der Rabbinen und der Protocolle der ersten Rabbiner-Versammlung in Betreff der gemischten Ehen* (Schwerin: C. Kürschner, 1845), IV-V: "Obwohl wir es uns nicht verbergen können, daß Emancipationsfeinde so manche unserer Aussprüche und Nachweisungen für ihre feindlichen Zwecke mißbrauchen können und werden, so haben wir uns von dieser Rücksicht dennoch nicht bestimmen lassen dürfen, in unsern Aeußerungen über Geist, Wesen und Inhalt des Talmuds oder des rabbinischen Judenthums die kleinste Verhüllung, die mindeste Zweideutigkeit zu gebrauchen, und haben wir uns deshalb niemals gescheuet, die Sachen bei ihrem rechten Namen zu nennen und keine noch so starke Blöße zu verdecken gesucht. [....] so würden wir auf unserem Standpunkte, wo wir für die innere Läuterung der religiösen Ueberzeugung einen nicht minder schweren und heiligen Kampf mit dem verjährten Vorurtheil zu bestehen haben, es als gleiche Versündigung halten, wenn wir aus Rücksicht auf die Emancipation den strengen Forderungen der Wahrheit und der Religion im mindesten vergeben, wenn wir aus Furcht, es könnte aus der rücksichtslosen Kritik der oder jener falschen Vorstellungen in unserem bisherigen religiösen Denken und Fühlen ein Nachtheil für die Emancipationsbestrebungen erwachsen, uns in dem Streben nach Wahrheit auf dem Gebiete der Religion aufhalten lassen wollten."
[37] See ibid., 5; idem, *Die erste Rabbinerversammlung und Herr Dr. Frankel* (Schwerin: C. Kürschner, 1845), passim; *Israelit des neunzehnten Jahrhunderts* 6 (1845): 89f., 97; Ritter, *Geschichte der jüdischen Reformation*, 133-144.

he quickly abandoned the thought and did not consider it again even in later years.[38] As a participant at the second rabbinical conference in Frankfurt am Main, he refused to enter any compromises with his more radically reform-minded colleagues. On the contrary, he used the first opportunity to stage his departure as a demonstration of resistance. Superficially, his protest was directed toward the neglect of Hebrew as the language of synagogual prayer; in reality, however, he questioned the whole "tendency" of the reform movement. The majority of participants, including Holdheim, had voted against the objective necessity of the Hebrew language in Jewish liturgy. Frankel voted with the minority—even though he himself had recently predicted that synagogues would turn to German-language prayer in the near future.[39] Through his unyielding conduct, he sought to counteract the unrestrained modernization of Jewish liturgy that, in his perception, was being given higher sanction by members of the conference.

An episode involving the *Kol Nidre* prayer provides an additional illustration of Frankel's careful efforts to avoid the impression that he had any association whatsoever with Holdheim's faction. The Aramaic chant, which is part of the liturgy on the eve of the Day of Atonement, was the subject of increasing dispute among German Jews because it contained a passage referring to the annulment of personal vows and therefore aroused doubts as to whether the promises of Jews could be trusted. Already in Brunswick, where the rabbis had congregated for their first conference in 1844, the *Kol Nidre* had been discussed in connection with the Jewish oath.[40] Frankel, who had written a detailed review of the discussions at the conference, omitted—of all issues—the debate over the *Kol Nidre*. While Holdheim did not fail to notice the omission, he was unsure how to interpret it. He simply accused Frankel of lacking the strength to counter

---

[38] Frankel, "Die Symptome der Zeit," 16; see Salomon J. Rapoport to Frankel, 8. Tammus (1845), in Ben Zion Dinaburg, "Iggrot Shir'," *Kiryat Sefer* 3 (1926/27), 222-35, 306-19, particularly 227-228; Jacob Katz, "The Orthodox Defense of the Second Day of the Festivals," in idem, *Divine Law in Human Hands: Case Studies in Halakhic Flexibility* (Jerusalem: Magnes, 1998), 255-319.

[39] Protokolle und Aktenstücke der zweiten Rabbinerversammlung, 54; see Frankel's report, 2 May 1835, in SächsHSTA Dresden, MfVb 11131; idem, "Schreiben des Oberrabbiners Dr. Frankel an die Direction des Tempelvereins zu Hamburg," 54.

[40] *Protocolle der ersten Rabbiner-Versammlung abgehalten zu Braunschweig vom 12ten bis zum 19ten Juni 1844* (Brunswick: Vieweg, 1844), 33-41.

outdated beliefs among the Jewish people.[41] However, Holdheim was mistaken on this point; in fact, Holdheim himself had motivated Frankel's tactical restraint. In 1844, Holdheim had published a brief article on the oath according to rabbinical precepts in the radical reformist Jewish weekly *Israelit des 19. Jahrhunderts,* that was edited by Mendel Hess, the dedicated reformer and chief rabbi of Saxe-Weimar. In his essay, Holdheim challenged the thesis that halakhic principles fully committed a Jew to uphold his oath. In actual fact, he explained, Jewish oaths could be dissolved even if they contained obligations toward one's fellow man. Holdheim's argument also took issue with Frankel, who had published a study in 1840 expounding on the harmlessness of *Kol Nidre* and the overall trustworthiness of the Jewish oath. In his essay, Holdheim accused Frankel of engaging in biased and unscholarly research in his written defence of Jewish honor.[42]

It is interesting to note that the *Kol Nidre* disappeared from the liturgy of the Dresden synagogue in the autumn of 1845.[43] Frankel had long contemplated the possibility of omitting the prayer but at first had avoided making a final decision:

> During the time when this slander against the *Kol Nidre* arose, I strongly discouraged its elimination. In an epoch such as ours, this kind of action would have been viewed as an admission that scandalous breaches of faith had indeed occurred among the Jews. What a disgrace to our ancestors, what a disgrace to those Jews who are still alive and who still keep the 'kol nidre'! Last year—the thought still causes me great pain—when such slanderous remarks were made by an anti-Semitic rabbi [*author's note: this refers to Holdheim*], I also expressed my opinion that 'kol nidre' should not be abolished. These slanderous statements, one may hope, have been completely disproved [....].[44]

---

[41] Holdheim, *Die erste Rabbinerversammlung und Herr Dr. Frankel,* 10-11.
[42] Idem, "Was lehrt das rabbinische Judenthum über den Eid?," *Israelit des neunzehnten Jahrhunderts* 5 (1844), 277-280, particularly 178-280; see idem, "Der Eid nach dem rabbinischen Judenthume," *Literaturblatt des Orients* 6 (1845), 164-69, 197-204, 215-20, 229-34.
[43] *AZJ* 9 (1845), No. 43, 661; *Israelit des neunzehnten Jahrhunderts* 6 (1845), 382.
[44] "Hingegen rieth ich gerade zu jener Zeit, wo diese Verläumdung [gegen das Kol Nidre] sich erhob, dringend von der Abschaffung ab, weil in solcher Epoche dieses ein Geständniß ist, daß bisher in der That ein solcher empörender Treubruch unter den Juden stattgefunden: welche Schmach wird also hierdurch auf die Vorfahren, welche Schmach wird auf die noch lebenden Mitbrüder gewälzt, die 'kol nidre' beibehalten!—Als im vorigen Jahre—wir gedenken dessen nur mit tiefem Schmerze—von einem judenfeindlichen Rabbiner [d.h. Holdheim] diese Verläumdung erhoben wurde, hielt ich ebenfalls dafür, daß 'kol nidre' nicht abgeschafft werden dürfe.—Die Verläumdung ist, wie man hoffen darf, vollständig widerlegt [....]." Frankel

The debate over the abolition of the *Kol Nidre* simultaneously illustrates that agreements and decisions with respect to concrete matters of reform were not necessarily based on shared motives. While Frankel took the view that *Kol Nidre* failed to satisfy the spiritual needs of those attending the public service of Yom Kippur, Holdheim sought to eliminate both the *Kol Nidre* prayer as well as the theory it supposedly rested on. However, he succeeded in rallying only a few comrades-in-arms, at least among German rabbis, who wished to follow his extreme views.

Holdheim's polemics fell short when he insinuated that Frankel was a populist. In no way did Frankel regard rabbis as mere mouthpieces for pious formulas that were then embraced by the masses. Moreover, he was aware of the fact that the religious practices of the majority were only rarely based on an explicit profession of faith in a particular religious credo.[45] In this respect, from a rational point of view he might have agreed with Holdheim when the latter declared that the general public all too frequently possesses only a vague understanding of religious issues:

> Religion is popular but theology is not. And it is not religion but theology that is represented by the rabbis, the teachers of religion. With regard to religion, the essence of which is so difficult to explain, there is no distinction between the people and its teachers. The simplest man among the people often has more religion than the most learned theologian. In order to think and act piously and religiously, it is not always necessary to possess scholarly knowledge on the essence of piousness and religion. This is the popular consciousness, which lays no claim to theological erudition.[46]

If Holdheim was correct in his assertion that the majority of

---

suggested psalm 103 as a substitute for the *Kol Nidre; Zeitschrift für die religiösen Interessen des Judentums* 2 (1845), 400; see also Rapoport to Frankel, 8th Tammus (1845), in Dinaburg, "'Iggrot Shir'," 228; Frankel, *Die Eidesleistung der Juden*, 63-64.

[45] See idem, "Gutachten des Oberrabbiners Dr. Z. Frankel, Directors des jüdisch-theologischen Seminars in Breslau," *Mittheilungen vom DIGB* 2 (1875), 26.

[46] Holdheim, *Die erste Rabbinerversammlung und Herr Dr. Frankel*, 9: "Die Religion lebt im Volke, aber nicht die Religionslehre, und nicht jene, sondern diese wird von den Rabbinern, den Religionslehrern, vertreten. Hinsichtlich der Religion, deren Wesen so schwer zu erklären ist, waltet kein Unterschied zwischen dem Volke und seinen Lehrern ob. Der schlichteste Mann im Volke hat oft mehr Religion als der gelehrteste Theologe. Um fromm und religiös zu denken und zu handeln, ist es nicht immer nothwendig, wissenschaftlich darüber aufgeklärt zu sein, worin das Wesen der Frömmigkeit und der Religion ruhe. Das ist das populäre Volksbewußtsein, das auf theologische Durchbildung keinen Anspruch macht."

community members were not critical intellectuals[47] but rather everyday individuals who were not preoccupied with ideological questions,
then theoretical models of religious progress and modernization could
achieve only a limited effect. The search for a modern understanding of traditional teachings was limited to a scholarly elite that was
unable to reach an agreement. The "positive-historical" middle ground,
which Frankel sought to establish both ideologically and institution-
ally, underwent a development whereby pragmatic adaptability acquired
a higher priority than dogmatic commitments to a "confession of
faith." In order to retain their internal unity, Jewish communities
often pursued a policy of compromise when it came to reshaping
religious institutions in accordance with contemporary criteria. A
middle-of-the-road course was actually followed that made no explicit
reference to Frankel's guiding theories. Even the founding of the
Jewish Theological Seminary in Breslau, which appointed Frankel as
its first director in 1854, did not lead to a fundamental resolution
of this ambiguous situation.

Holdheim was confronted with even greater obstacles—his system
of reform demanded practical consequences that few if any Jewish
liturgical communities could justify to their members. Holdheim
escaped his personal dilemma when in 1846 he assumed his rabbinical office at the *Reformgemeinde*—a private reform association that
had been established within the greater Jewish community of Berlin.
However, he confronted restrictions even in his new position—not
because the association's members were opposed in principle to his
desire for reform, but because he could not claim any rabbinical
prerogative with regard to decisions on liturgical matters.[48]

Despite the controversies, a comparison between Holdheim and
Frankel supports the conclusion that those rabbis who deviated from
the path of normative Judaism confronted a common problem: The
principle of religious self-determination had inspired new models of
Judaism, yet at the same time it hindered their claims to validity in
everyday life. In many places majority opinion carried more weight
than the expertise of rabbis whose decision-making authority was
subordinated to democratic procedures. Halakhic authorities were

---

[47] See also Amos Funkenstein, *Perceptions of Jewish History* (Berleley, CA: University
of California Press, 1993), 256.
[48] See Ritter, *Geschichte der jüdischen Reformation*, 264-265.

replaced by pastoral advisors who at best succeeded in spreading a popularized version of their theologies. While both Holdheim and Frankel were prominent figures within the German Jewish community, most of its members associated their names with diffuse notions of radical or moderate reform. Viewed in this way, both rabbinical scholars exerted an influence on the narrative of both intellectual and general German Jewish history.[49] However, both failed to achieve a direct, widespread influence on the religious perceptions of their Jewish contemporaries. Reality shaped the minds that it then used for its own legitimation.

---

[49] The ideas of both Holdheim and Frankel had considerable resonance within American Jewry; see, e.g., Jakob J. Petuchowski, "Abraham Geiger and Samuel Holdheim. Their Differences in Germany and Repercussions in America," *LBIYB* 22 (1977), 139-59; Ismar Schorsch, "Zacharias Frankel and the European Origins of Conservative Judaism," *Judaism* 30 (1981), 344-54.

HOLDHEIM AND ZUNZ:
FROM THE QUESTION OF RABBINIC AUTHORITY
TO A NEW DEFINITION OF CEREMONIAL LAWS*

Céline Trautmann-Waller

Several reasons seem to justify a joint, comparative study of Leopold Zunz (1794–1886) and Samuel Holdheim (1806–1860), regardless of the fact that they hardly knew each other, that one was a rabbi and the other was not, and that they never belonged to the same organizations. What unites them is a shared experience of preaching in German, the historical-critical basis to their reflections on Judaism, its past, present, and future, and, finally, the path—as indicated in the title of the present essay—that led both men from questioning rabbinic authority to examining the validity of ritual and ceremonial laws. Both scholars shared similar experiences and were confronted with similar problems. Not least, there was an indirect dialogue between the two, expressed in the reciprocal reception of their scholarly writings: first, Holdheim—like many others of his generation—read, as we will see, Zunz's *Gottesdienstliche Vorträge* and incorporated the historical perspective they defended in his own argumentation for reform; later, Zunz defended certain Jewish institutions like circumcision and *tefillin* against Holdheim and other reformers, to which Holdheim responded in his *Das Ceremonialgesetz im Messiasreich* by confronting Mendelssohn's definition of ceremonial laws, that Zunz, as many others, used at this date as an argument against reform.

Already in the first half of the nineteenth century, the accelerated social development and the acculturation of the Jewish community, in conjunction with Mendelssohn's philosophical legacy, gave rise to a Jewish modernity that raised a myriad of questions. The partly similar, partly divergent answers by Zunz and Holdheim illuminate each other and make it possible to recognize more clearly Zunz's

* Translated from the German by Thomas Dunlap.

historical and Holdheim's philosophical-theological position. It is interesting that Zunz, in whom anti-rabbinism and the critique of tradition were much more pronounced than in Holdheim, in a sense newly appropriated the various elements of Jewish tradition through his historical studies (like the Talmud, whose importance he originally questioned), and essentially became much more conservative than Holdheim as far as religious practice was concerned. By examining the elements of Jewish tradition historically, Zunz acquired a feeling also for their cultural, symbolic power. He sacralized them—so to speak—as the legacy of Jewish history and its suffering, while Holdheim, whose definition of the Jewish religion became increasingly more abstract, was intent on preventing excessive emphasis from being placed on these elements.

Where Holdheim called for giving up any concept of Jewish nationality, for Zunz, the critical paradigm of culture pointed in a new way to the nation (he considered that the notion "Judentum" was to be interpreted through the analogy with "Deutschtum" and "Griechentum"[1]), which in his eyes presupposed—scientific universalism nothwithstanding—tradition in the sense of a necessary preservation of what was particular and most unique to Jewish history. For both, criticism of Jewish exclusiveness led to a new interpretation of messianism. In Zunz, however, it expressed itself—in a far more secularized form than in Holdheim—above all in his political engagement for a radically democratic Europe during the revolution of 1848 and afterwards, while Holdheim envisioned, not only socially but also in the religious sphere, a fusion of the various confessions in the messianic age, that for him had already begun.

1. The Questioning of Rabbinic Authority and Anti-rabbinism

Holdheim's frequent references to Isaak Markus Jost's *Geschichte der Israeliten*[2] at strategic points of his argument against the authority of rabbis and in favor of the separation of religion and politics show

---

[1] See his notes for a series of conferences on *Wissenschaft des Judentums* in Zunz-Archiv 4° 792 D 33, f° 1 (JNUL), in Céline Trautmann-Waller, *Philologie allemande et tradition juive. Le parcours intellectuel de Leopold Zunz* (Paris: Cerf, 1998), 218-19.

[2] Isaak Markus Jost, *Geschichte der Israeliten seit der Zeit der Makkabäer bis auf unsere Tage* (Berlin: Schlesinger, 1820-1828).

how important the recourse to history was to him. When Jewish writers first began to study the history of Judaism at the beginning of the nineteenth century, one result was the realization of the degree to which "rabbinism" represented merely a phase in the long history of the Jewish people, though a phase that extended into the present. For most writers of this generation, historical study overlapped with the legacy of Mendelssohn's *Jerusalem:* his clear separation between religion and the state, between religion and any exercise of power, and between those laws that were part of Israel as a state created by God in ancient times, and those laws Mendelssohn defined as "ceremonial laws" and which "must [....] be observed strictly according to the words of the law, until it shall please the Most High to set our conscience at rest and to make their abrogation known in a clear voice and in a public manner."[3] As we shall see, this sentence would give Holdheim a lot of trouble.

In the wake of Mendelssohn, whom Holdheim liked to count among the "opponents of rabbinism,"[4] the fusion of religion and the state could be characterized solely by the negative term "theocracy," which he cleverly applied also to the modern Christian state[5] if it made the admission and equal treatment of individuals dependent on religious belief—a distant response to theoreticians like Jakob Friedrich Fries and Friedrich Rühs, whose ideal of the Christian state Zunz, too, had opposed.[6]

The questioning of rabbinic authority had an exceedingly stimulating effect in the first decades of the nineteenth century, as is also evident from—among other things—Zunz's beginnings in the "Science of Judaism" (*Wissenschaft des Judentums*) and the entire enterprise of the *Verein für Cultur und Wissenschaft der Juden* that was founded in 1819, which were characterized by a strong anti-rabbinic sentiment. In the eyes of the young Zunz and his friends, the rabbis stood for

---

[3] Moses Mendelssohn, *Jerusalem, or, On Religious Power and Judaism* (Hanover, NH: University of New England Press, 1983), 134.

[4] Samuel Holdheim, *Ueber die Autonomie der Rabbinen und das Princip der jüdischen Ehe. Ein Beitrag zur Verständigung über einige das Judenthum betreffende Zeitfragen* (Schwerin: C. Kürschner, 1847), 48.

[5] Ibid., VIII–X.

[6] See *Das Buch Zunz: künftigen ehrlichen Leuten gewidmet*, ed. Fritz Bamberger (Berlin: Soncino-Gesellschaft, 1931), 19 and 26; and Leopold Zunz, *Etwas über die rabbinische Literatur nebst Nachrichten über ein altes bis jetzt ungedrucktes hebräisches Werk* (Berlin: Maurersche Buchhandlung, 1818), 31, note 1.

authority against freedom, for Talmud against Spanish-Jewish philosophy, for death against vitality, for the closing off of the law against life, development, and regeneration. In this circle of Jewish intellectuals we therefore encounter especially vividly the notion of a possible, imminent extinction of Judaism. These young students at Berlin University—inspired by Hegel's philosophy, Herder's cultural pluralism, and the philological methodology of August Boeckh and Friedrich August Wolf—felt that in a time when the beginning emancipation seemed to be dissolving the unity of nation and religion, when the general secularization was weakening the binding force of religious practice, and acculturation was making certain elements of tradition appear irreconcilable with life, "rabbinism" meant the certain death of Judaism.

Zunz had planned an especially combative book about what he called the "spirit of the rabbis," announcing it in the papers,[7] and his first publication—*Etwas über die rabbinische Literatur*[8]—was already a declaration of war against the traditional methods of textual interpretation, against Talmud and Orthodoxy. While the questioning of rabbinic authority could thus be a spur to scientific investigation, it also—and often simultaneously—represented one of the most important starting points of reform. Using as an example Zunz's *Gottesdienstliche Vorträge* and Holdheim's adoption of many of the positions advocated there, I will examine more closely how the Reform movement in its early stages based itself on history.

2. *Zunz's Gottesdienstliche Vorträge: Science and Reform*

We have no direct testimony of the effect that Zunz's *Gottesdienstliche Vorträge* had on Holdheim, but we may assume that it was similar to what Joseph Derenburg, for example, reported in a letter to the aged Zunz: "For us elders the memory of 1832 remains alive, when we, my unforgettable Geiger and I, devoured your book about the sermons (*gottesdienstliche Vorträge*), taking delight in the rich content of this work."[9]

---

[7] See Ludwig Geiger, "Geist der Rabbiner, Ein geplantes Werk von Leopold Zunz," *AZJ* 35 (1916), 413-414.

[8] Zunz, *Etwas über die rabbinische Literatur*.

[9] Letter from Derenburg to Zunz, 21 January 1879, in Zunz-Archiv 4° 792 G11 (JNUL); printed in Trautmann-Waller, *Philologie allemande et tradition juive*, 314-315.

For the first time, this book provided an example of the possibilities that a non-dogmatic, historical study of certain areas of Jewish traditions had to offer, in this case the sermons that were found first in the Temple and than in the synagogues alongside the reading of the Torah, the commentaries, and the interpretations. The historical viewpoint, which naturally asserted itself also in the *Geschichte der Israeliten* by Zunz's former fellow student Jost, though with a less close reference to religious practice, would remain decisive for Holdheim's perspective, as is evident from his frequent demand not to act "in defiance of history."[10]

In Zunz's book, which wanted to deal a "death blow" to the "sliphshod way in which Jewish literature is being treated,"[11] the account of the rich diversity of changes and accommodations that had made the survival of Jewish traditions possible throughout the centuries was intended to discredit any dogmatism from the outset. This made the reforms that were called for or introduced in some places since the beginning of the ninteenth century seem like the natural result of a long line of similar "reforms," whose goal had always been to preserve tradition by adapting it to the situation the communities found themselves in. Through this historical description, Zunz wanted to free up Jewish religion for a new development: a dynamic which naturally established a close link between the beginnings of the Science of Judaism and the Reform movement, especially clearly in Zunz and Abraham Geiger. This made the *Gottesdienstliche Vorträge* also into a manifesto in favor of reform, the first steps of which in the areas of the rabbinate, religious instruction, and the religious service Zunz celebrated in the last chapter of his book, which was devoted to the present. Holdheim was mentioned very briefly here for his positive view of the new rituals of the reformist synagogues.[12]

That Zunz picked sermons to prove his point had something to do with his own practice as a preacher, and with the fact that sermons

---

[10] See, e.g., Holdheim, *Ueber die Autonomie der Rabbinen und das Princip der jüdischen Ehe*, V and XIII.

[11] In the words of Zunz, in Ismar Elbogen, "Leopold Zunz zum Gedächtnis," *Fünfzigster Bericht der Lehranstalt für die Wissenschaft des Judentums* (Berlin: s.n., 1936), 14-32, here 24.

[12] Leopold Zunz, *Die gottesdienstlichen Vorträge der Juden historisch entwickelt. Ein Beitrag zur Altertumskunde und biblischen Kritik, zur Literatur- und Religionsgeschichte*, 2nd ed. (Frankfurt am Main: Kauffmann, 1892), 474.

in German had given umbrage to certain representatives of Orthodoxy as well as the Prussian government, which had eventually prohibited them. But his choice can also be explained by the fact that this clear accentuation of the role of the sermon highlights the pastoral elements much more emphatically than the judicial one, an important point that must have appealed strongly to Holdheim, and which he then elaborated upon in his own struggle against the "purely legal conception of religion" he claimed was characteristic of the rabbis.[13] The sermon represented the part of the synagogue service that had the most vitality and was most open to development, a part that had always adapted itself to the needs of the community in a language it could understand.

Zunz's own experience with preaching at the Beer Temple in Berlin, however, had not been very satisfactory. His letters reveal that he was constantly venting a certain anger over the petty scheming within the community and the religious indifference of the listeners. And this eventually led to a rupture of the relationship. In 1836 he accepted a post at the newly established reformed synagogue in Prague, which now offered him an opportunity to implement his ideas about the service.[14] This episode of his biography is little known, probably because it was entirely unsuccessful and Zunz left Prague, a city he disliked and where he longed for the libraries of Paris and Oxford, before his contract was up. His only comment later was: "I never saw it as my task to be the direct educator of the Jews."[15]

At the heart of Zunz's efforts was not really the Jewish religion, but what he had tried to define as Jewish culture already since his first publications, even if it was thoroughly pervaded by religion and its treatment by Zunz, too, was characterized by a deep religiosity. This also explains, then, why Holdheim and Zunz pursued such different paths in the subsequent years, as I will presently show by looking at the controversy over ceremonial law.

---

[13] Samuel Holdheim, *Das Ceremonialgesetz im Messiasreich. Als Vorläufer einer größern Schrift über die religiöse Reform des Judenthums* (Schwerin: C. Kürschner, 1845), 44.

[14] See Ludwig Geiger, "Zunz' Synagogenordnung für Prag (1836)," *AZJ* 41 (1916), 485-487.

[15] Leopold Zunz, quoted in Sigmund Maybaum, "Aus dem Leben Leopold Zunz'," *Zwölfter Bericht der Lehranstalt für die Wissenschaft des Judentums* (Berlin: s.n., 1894), 1-63, here 55.

3. The Question of Ceremonial Law

At the beginning of the 1840s, Zunz gave his last public demonstration of sympathy for an enterprise that was close to the Reform movement by assuming for a time the leadership over a newly established *Kulturverein*, whose board also included Aaron Bernstein, Sigismund Stern, Moritz Veit, and Heymann Steinthal.[16] The Association, whose name was the abbreviated revival of that of the *Verein für Cultur und Wissenschaft der Juden*, sought to promote scientific and artistic endeavors among the Jews.[17] In 1841, it made the "historical discussion of the rabbinate" the topic of its first prize essay contest. Since no submissions were received, it posed a simpler task: "A historical survey of the institution of the rabbi and the preacher from 1782 until the most recent time, combined with an introduction about the earlier state of affairs and an account of the needs of the present."[18] One can sense in these questions, as well as in the general cultural focus, the influence of Zunz, and yet he distanced himself increasingly from the Association, until the majority of its members participated in 1845 in the founding of the *Genossenschaft für Reform im Judentum* (Association for Reform in Judaism), whose preacher Holdheim would become in 1847. Did Zunz sense the radical direction that support for reform was taking through the members of the *Kulturverein*, or did he feel that the chosen guiding concept of culture was being neglected in favor of religious questions? Did the texts of synagogal poetry that he was studying in those years (he had announced as early as 1838 in a letter that he was preparing a work on synagogal poetry) bring about a change in attitude? One is inclined to say that it was all of these factors simultaneously. Zunz became unmistakably critical toward Reform with the beginning of the rabbinic conferences (*Rabbinerversammlungen*) in the 1840s. Unlike many of his friends, he expected nothing from them for the future of Judaism. In letters he referred to them as

---

[16] On this see Zunz's entries in his diaries, in Trautmann-Waller, *Philologie allemande et tradition juive*, 136-138. When the Association was founded in 1839, Zunz was elected a representative, in 1840 he was elected secretary, and in 1841 director. In 1843 he submitted his resignation from the board, though he remained vice-director for some time.

[17] See *Statuten des Cultur-Vereins* (Berlin: sn., 1841).

[18] "Jahresbericht des Culturvereins. Berlin 1842," *Orient* 18 (1842), 139-141.

"rabbi procession" (*Rabbineraufzug*)[19] and maintained that nothing good could ever come from a meeting of rabbis, it "reeked of priestliness (*Pfaffentum*) and hierarchy."[20] Reform as an assertion of the freedom of development, of closeness to the needs of the changing community, of the recognition of historical evolution and especially of a new age beginning with emancipation, was appropriate to his way of thinking. But from the moment the reformers themselves became a new authority, he could only accuse them. All the more so since most of the reformers based their authority—just as he had once done with the *Gottesdienstliche Vorträge*—in part on a historical view of Judaism and therefore were guilty in his eyes of instrumentalizing the Science of Judaism. This was the thrust, for example, of the charges that Zunz leveled against Geiger, who as early as 1838 had published a call for the founding of a Jewish-theological faculty,[21] and of whom he now said: "People who defend a party lose their capacity for understanding."[22] He also criticized Zacharias Frankel for putting the Science of Judaism in the service of theology, as was evident in the transition from his first journal to the famous *Monatsschrift*: In the year 1841, Frankel moves from "religious interests" to the "History and Science of Judaism."[23] He branded Frankel's notion of the Science of Judaism as "science of faith"(*Glaubenswissenschaft*).[24]

We have seen that Zunz's plan for a Science of Judaism as a philology directed explicitly against theology had emerged out of a certain anti-rabbinism. Intent on continuing the defense of unencumbered research against any kind of dogmatism, and as late as 1873 still provoking many Jewish readers with a series of articles about the Bible, Zunz was probably thinking of Geiger and Frankel, among others, when he wrote into his diary: "But the rabbis assume

---

[19] Letter from Leopold Zunz to Philipp Ehrenberg (3 May 1844), in Nahum N. Glatzer, ed., *Leopold Zunz. Jude, Deutscher, Europäer. Ein jüdisches Gelehrtenschicksal des 19. Jahrhunderts in Briefen an Freunde* (Tübingen: J.C.B. Mohr, 1964), 229.

[20] Letter by Zunz to Ehrenberg (5 July 1844), in ibid., 124.

[21] Abraham Geiger, *Ueber die Errichtung einer jüdisch-theologischen Facultät* (Wiesbaden: Riedel, 1838).

[22] Letter from Zunz to the Ehrenberg family (28 December 1845), printed in Nahum N. Glatzer, "Some of Zunz's Letters to the Ehrenbergs," *Proceedings of the American Academy of Jewish Research* 25 (1956), 63-90, here 66.

[23] See the excerpt from *Das Buch Zunz*, "Meine Schriften," in Ismar Elbogen, "Zum Andenken an Leopold Zunz 2," *JJGL* 30 (1937), 140-172, here 141.

[24] Ibid., 156.

the posture as though they had actually founded this science, although it was, quite the opposite, achieved in a struggle against them."[25]

Zunz's distancing from Reform took the form of defending two important elements of tradition: circumcision, which was intensely debated at that time, and the *tefillin* or phylacteries. The argumentation is similar in both cases; especially striking is the pathos, which was so pronounced in this instance that Jost told him in writing that he had gone too far, and one could easily, "especially in connection with [the] essay about the tefillin, misinterpret the nature of [Zunz's] conviction, which [he, Jost] believes [he] know[s]."[26]

As for Geiger, he wrote to Zunz: "To take the side of circumcision with such resoluteness because it was always and still is held in high esteem, is, I must confess, not something I can do."[27] But Zunz saw in circumcision, in particular, a "sign of the unity and eternal duration of Israel, a visible act of transmitting and inheriting the divine law,"[28] which is why:

> The ceremony of circumcision has captivated the poets; in the old synagogal poetry, the symbol of the blood is surrounded by the images of the sufferings that Israel has born and still bears for the sake of its faith, and the impressions it leaves behind in the soul are more elevating than the impression of modern invitations on which circumcision is turned into a breakfast. [....] An abolition of circumcision that entails the denial of the Talmud and the Messiah, that is, the abandonment of the past and the future, cuts the life of Judaism straight down the middle; a suicide is not a reform.[29]

Precisely the aspect of Reform he had defended in the *Gottesdienstliche Vorträge* he now criticized in the sharpest terms when he spoke of those who "presume to prepare the eternal content for transitory purposes."[30] Rituals were defended for the sake of their symbolic power: "As often, then, as the symbol becomes visible on our external self,

---

[25] Ibid., 141.

[26] Ludwig Geiger, "Zunz' Gutachten über die Beschneidung (1844)," *AZJ* 80 (1916), 449-452, here 452.

[27] Ibid., 452.

[28] Leopold Zunz, *Gutachten über die Beschneidung* (Frankfurt am Main: J. F. Bach, 1844), printed in idem, *Gesammelte Schriften*, vol. 2 (Berlin: Gerschel, 1875-76), 191-203, here 199.

[29] Ibid., 197-198.

[30] Leopold Zunz, "Thefillin," *Jahrbuch für Israeliten* 2 (1843-44), 133-138; printed in idem, *Gesammelte Schriften*, vol. 2, 172-176, here 172.

the old love stirs inside and pulls all into its consecrated circle."[31] Addressing the reader in person, Zunz finally asked: "The symbolic act has ceased to be something merely external, do you wish to dismiss as an empty ceremony something that moves you deeply?"[32]

Zunz emphasized here something he would later sharply condemn as Mosaism in a book intended for Jewish religious instruction:[33] anyone who neglected the historical elements of Judaism in favor of general laws of love for humanity was threatened by "the lack of everything positive, of history and concrete figures, or by an Eternal, that is an ideal of religious life recognized by all humans."[34]

This charge can be seen as a response to Holdheim's conception of Jewish religion. Holdheim himself considered that "Zunz's witty remark that circumcision and Sabbath are institutions and not mere ceremonies, reduces itself to nothing,"[35] but he was very sensitive to the fact that the opponents of the radical reform he advocated always invoked Mendelssohn. For example, he said in regard to Mendelssohn's statement quoted earlier:

> Mendelssohn did in fact make this statement, which is such an obstacle to reform. Mendelssohn is for our time a greater authority than the Talmud. Men like Reggio, Zunz, Luzzato, who—at least the first two—do not think they are sufficiently defended by the shield of the Talmud, invoke this statement by Mendelssohn; it must therefore be refuted. [....] Today, one cannot advance a single step as long as this fortress behind one's back has not been captured.[36]

Here it becomes clear how much Holdheim returned to the debate on philosophical-theological grounds, resuming it where it had ground to a halt. Among other things, this debate revolved around the concepts of the particular and the universal, in the tension between which loyalty to Judaism was to be defined.

---

[31] Ibid., 174.

[32] Ibid., 174.

[33] "Beurtheilung von 'Die mosaische Religion. Catechismus für den israelitischen Religionsunterricht in Schule und Haus', von Julius Löwenheim, Lehrer an der Stadtschule in Lengsfeld, Eisenach, 1864," *Rheinische Blätter* 16 (1865), 73-77; printed in idem, *Gesammelte Schriften*, vol. 2, 236-240.

[34] Zunz, *Gutachten über die Beschneidung*, 201.

[35] Holdheim, *Das Ceremonialgesetz im Messiasreich*, 144.

[36] Ibid., 54.

4. Loyalty to Tradition

When Zunz speaks of "consecrated (*geheiligt*) memory" and the loyalty it demanded, one understands the extent to which history, as a sign of love, had also become a religious authority for him. The concept of institution he used to prove that circumcision was inviolable reveals just how much historical study, which was initially intended to legitimize change to the service, could now turn tradition into authority. Zunz's Science of Judaism, just like the historiography and philology of his day in general, seems to be constantly moving in the field of tension between a critical study of the past and the establishment of this past as a model and a foundation.

It was precisely this legitimizing of tradition and ceremonial laws by history that Holdheim opposed, and he was surely thinking of Zunz when, in the preface to the new collection of his sermons, he defended his own notion of a "spiritualized ritual law," and offered a definition of loyalty for which the memory of vanished institutions is sufficient:

> The author regards it as the task of the Jewish sermon to study, with a serious and holy attitude, the ethical spirit of Judaism's oldest institutions which, though vanished from life, proudly, as the immortal monuments of the Jewish spirit, look down upon the millennia that pass by them, and with this torch of the mind to illuminate and warm the spirit and heart of the Jewish community and to awaken in its bosom a lasting love of and attachment to the inexhaustible legacy of the religion of their fathers. It is only the firm belief in the immortality of this ethical spirit, for which the national-religious institutions once served as the material shell, that gives rise to a feeling of comfort over the disappearance of these institutions themselves—and from this faith in immortality is born a piety for the great dead that is deeper, healthier, and more vital than the sickly, desolate piety which, because it is without a future and becomes already extinct in the next generation, clings to the de-spirited dust itself and denies it its grave.[37]

This description of the cultivation of memory is reminiscent of Zunz's works on synagogal poetry, the study of which Holdheim seems to have accorded a positive influence on the community. On the other hand, Holdheim sensed very clearly where this veneration of the past

---

[37] Idem, *Neue Sammlung jüdischer Predigten worunter über alle Feste des Jahres gehalten im Gotteshaus der jüdischen Reform-Gemeinde zu Berlin* (Berlin: Carl David, 1852), VII.

could lead. With respect to the explanation of ceremonial law as a genre of writing (*Schriftart*) in Mendelssohn, Holdheim remarked that "it was still today held in such high esteem also by the learned Zunz that we may surely expect from him a study of the ceremonial laws of the Jews that Mendelssohn left incomplete."[38] And, as we know, he was right about this.[39]

The dynamic of the particular and the universal appeared very different in this indirect dialogue between the two men. For Holdheim, the universal is religion, the religious feeling, which can also live on without its physical casing—or, to put it more accurately: it is precisely by shedding the physical form that religion can free itself from a dangerous particularism which has often stood in the way of the Jews "participating in all forms of life," "in the promotion of the social and political common good."[40] Confessionalization was thus a step in the direction of universalism, which at first meant a "reciprocal relationship" of Judaism with the "total development of the human mind,"[41] and which would then lead in the messianic vision to the dissolution of the particular. Zunz, on the other hand, tried to articulate the universal and the particular in a different way: for him, the one was not the negation of the other, but in every particularity there was also revealed the universal, which means that a "suicide," like the one he feared, would at the same time harm the universal. These contrary notions explain the different definitions of loyalty, though for both Zunz and Holdheim, loyalty was closely tied to the notion of love. Of course, the central question is always that about the awakening and preservation of the religious feelings, for both drew upon a conception of religion—inspired by Schleiermacher —as a religion of feeling. Thus, in both Holdheim and Zunz, the recourse to love served to fill up the empty spaces that had been created because religion was understood less and less in the form of laws, and because the authority of the rabbis and the normative nature of the de-canonized texts was not infrequently being questioned.

---

[38] Idem, *Das Ceremonialgesetz im Messiasreich*, 61.

[39] See Leopold Zunz, *Der Ritus des synagogalen Gottesdienstes, geschichtlich entwickelt* (Berlin: J. Springer, 1858).

[40] Holdheim, *Ueber die Autonomie der Rabbinen*, V.

[41] Ibid.

5. Conclusion

By trying to define for the community the foundations of a renewed loyalty, Zunz and Holdheim indirectly also recounted the path that had taken them, on the basis of general concepts that were determinative at the time, to a new definition of their own bond to tradition. These two, in many ways contrary, paths intersected most obviously around the *Gottesdienstliche Vorträge*, when Reform was still reflecting the hopes of both men and Zunz's Jewish philology did not yet appear to be consolidating tradition.

The example of Jewish tradition in the dialogue between Holdheim and Zunz that I have traced reveals a set of questions that shaped the nineteenth century in general: how to deal with the past—or, in other words, the collective memory—in the tension between the freedom to think and authority, between tradition and development, the relationship between nation, religion, and history. As far as the Jews were concerned, these questions were posed in a particularly complicated, heightened form: on the one hand because of the originally especially close connection between nation and religion, on the other hand because there was—even more so than in other cases—the lack of a unity of place, language, and culture. This situation could lead to an extreme "inhibition" as a withdrawal into oneself, or to a very expansive "opening up." Both Holdheim and Zunz, each in a different way, sought a path toward opening up, one in which what was universal and common to humanity could be articulated together with the loyalty to one specific tradition, the past together with the present—even if it was only in a dreamed-for future that blended the messianic hope with a faith in progress typical of the nineteenth century.

SAMUEL HOLDHEIM AND SIGISMUND STERN: THE CLASH BETWEEN THE DOGMATIC AND HISTORICIST APPROACH IN CLASSICAL GERMAN REFORM JUDAISM[1]

Ralph Bisschops

The few studies devoted to Holdheim to this day portray him as a representative of the extreme side of German Reform Judaism, i.e., its utterly heterodox and assimilationist tendency. However, there may be several ways of being a radical. In this respect a comparative analysis of the personality and attitude of Sigismund Stern, another figurehead of classical German Reform Judaism, promises to shed further light on this question. In comparing Holdheim to Stern we attempt to gain a more adequate appreciation of the peculiarity and subtleness of his position. To Holdheim, as well as to Stern, reforming religious practice was not going far enough. Instead, both aimed at transforming the heart of Jewish life itself. However, while Holdheim in his temperament and argumentation was "Orthodox" to the core,[2] Stern represents the so called "protestantizing" tendency in German Reform Judaism.

1. Sigismund Stern and the Program of the Berlin Reform Movement

It is common knowledge that a synagogue is too small to embrace two great personalities among its leadership. However, that was precisely the case with the Berlin *Genossenschaft für Reform im Judenthum*. This congregation which became the final harbor in Holdheim's itinerary after his years in Frankfurt an der Oder and in Schwerin,

---

[1] I would like to thank Professor Robert L. Platzner and Dr. Peter Oliver for their incisive readings of earlier drafts and their helpful remarks.
[2] See Michael A. Meyer, *Response to Modernity* (Detroit: Wayne State University Press, 1995), 83, who observes that "ironically, at his most extreme, Holdheim in some ways comes to resemble his polar opposite, Samson Raphael Hirsch."

was founded and until 1855 chaired by a layperson with great scholarly and theological ambitions, Dr. Sigismund Stern (1812-1867). He was the very embodiment of German "Bildung," a universal man who pursued intellectual careers as varied as those of a poet, a linguist, a historian, a theologian and an educational theorist. The appearance of Sigismund Stern as a personality on the scene of German Jewish life in the 1840s marked a new phase in the history of Reform Judaism and can easily be compared to that of Israel Jacobson forty years earlier. Both Jacobson and Stern were laypersons who set into motion a process of religious reforms only subsequently carried on by the rabbis. Both were involved in the history of their time, Jacobson on an international scale as a banker, Stern as an intellectual and as a political activist, and both developed a sort of seismographic awareness of the needs of their time through their many connections with the Gentile world. However, where Jacobson was merely attempting to adapt Orthodox Judaism to a changing world, unaware himself that he would enter history as a reformer,[3] Stern's programme was radical in every respect. Unsatisfied by the rabbinical attempts to accommodate Judaism to the needs of sociologically and economically emancipated Jews, and highly sceptical about whether they would be of any benefit to their political emancipation, which had not yet come about, he advocated a radically new conception of how to deal with the heritage of traditional Judaism. The present time, Stern argued, demands more than occasional modifications of Talmudic law. What the rabbis had done until then was to present a modernized Judaism more oriented toward the Bible and—in the best case—toward the Prophets, but not a Judaism of the nineteenth century.[4] True, there was the *Wissenschaft des Judenthums*, Stern concedes, but he also sardonically notes that its

---

[3] Jacob Rader Marcus, *Israel Jacobson: The Founder of the Reform Movement in Judaism* (Cincinnati: Hebrew Union College Press, 1972), 84.

[4] See Sigismund Stern, *Die Aufgabe des Judenthums und des Juden in der Gegenwart* (Berlin: W. Adolf & Co, 1853), 114-115: "Daher jene merkwürdigen Widersprüche in den Reformbestrebungen der meisten Rabbinen, jenes ängstliche Bemühen, sich für jede Konzession die von der Zeit unabweisbar gefordert wird, die Erlaubnis aus dem Talmud zu suchen. [....] Sie bieten uns, je nachdem sie mehr oder weniger freisinnigen Ansichten huldigen, ein modernisiertes Judentum, ein biblisches, oder gar ein prophetisches Judentum, aber kein Judentum unserer Zeit, kein Judentum des 19th Jahrhunderts, kein Judentum [....], welches das Bewusstsein an der Stirn trägt, seinen Anteil an der Entwicklung der Weltgeschichte wieder gewonnen zu haben."

paramount representative, Leopold Zunz, was not a rabbi and that he even proved loath to take part in any rabbinical discussions. However, even toward the emerging Science of Judaism Stern was far from appreciative. This new discipline only widened the gap between the rabbis and their community and paradoxically has led to a new rabbinical clergy, he complains.[5] Stern voices the position of the new Jewish burghers who felt attracted neither by Talmudic Judaism nor by the academic discourse of the new academically trained rabbis. They wanted a new doctrine which affirmed both their Jewish identity and their new role in German society in a thorough way. To this effect Sigismund Stern pleaded for the creation of a Jewish "Church" charged with resolving all halakhic issues arising out of the clash between rabbinical Judaism and the involvement of modern Jews in the Gentile world. Stern was aware that such an undertaking required theological and philosophical assumptions independent of ancient biblical and rabbinical lore, and he found it in Hegel's philosophy.[6] Hegel's basic idea was that the absolute was time-bound, that God himself was progressively becoming aware of himself across history. The history of humankind was also the history of God's own being. The theological consequence of this axiom was that all that was felt as the most absolute moral and religious truth was merely the reflection of the awareness reached by humankind at a particular time. Hegel's paradigm was highly attractive to liberal German-Jewish circles of the nineteenth century precisely because it enabled them to do away with the traditional and canonical settings of their faith and identity and yet allowed them to appreciate them as the most genuine expressions of Judaism in previous times.

It thus becomes obvious that Stern wanted a Judaism built up from scratch and not made up of re-contextualized pieces of rabbinical lore; he wanted it to be a faith and a practice designed for modernity, "tailor-made" as one might suspect. It was part of the philosophy of the Berlin *Genossenschaft* that Judaism is much too important to be left to the rabbis, and that its principles should be established by laymen who knew much better what it is to be a Jew in the nineteenth century.

---

[5] Idem, *Geschichte des Judenthums von Mendelssohn bis auf die Gegenwart* (Frankfurt am Main: Literarische Anstalt, 1857), 236.

[6] On Stern's Hegelianism see Arthur Galliner, *Sigismund Stern, der Reformator und der Pädagoge* (Frankfurt am Main: Englert und Schlosser, 1930), 95.

2. Holdheim and the Berlin Reform Congregation

Scholars have quite uncritically assumed that, in Berlin, Samuel Holdheim had eventually found a circle of like-minded fellows. However, Holdheim's biographer, Immanuel Ritter, leaves no doubt about the fact that his impact on the board members was almost non-existent.[7] Everything pertaining to principles of faith, to liturgy and to the religious practices of the Reform congregation was decided by the board before Holdheim's assumption of office as the first rabbi of the Berlin Reform community. Holdheim's forte, the most important skill he could bring into the position for which he seemed to be destined, namely the elaboration of guidelines for Reform Jewish life and worship, were of no use. Apart from the fact that Holdheim had no business in a congregation which wanted Judaism without rabbis, there are also elements which indicate that cooperation between him and Sigismund Stern must have been problematic at best.

It is significant that Holdheim was not the first candidate who was asked to become the rabbi of the newly founded Berlin reform community, but Abraham Geiger. He declined, of course, since he wanted to reform Judaism step by step and from within its own ranks; he was, therefore, absolutely not interested in leading a community which, right from the outset, was branded as a splinter group.[8] In addition, he was one of the figureheads of the *Wissenschaft* and therefore not at all the person to support Stern's ideas, even supposing that he was familiar with them. Samuel Holdheim was only the third choice of the *Genossenschaft* (the second one being Naphtali Frankfurter) and the fact that Sigismund Stern indicates this explicitly in his *History of Judaism*, which, quite offensively, appeared during Holdheim's lifetime, indicates that there were some reservations toward Holdheim on the part of the Berlin community.[9] This becomes unambiguous when, in the same book, Stern expresses resentment at Holdheim's disapproval of the board's decision to regard circumcision

---

[7] Immanuel Ritter, *Samuel Holdheim, sein Leben und seine Werke* (Berlin: W. J. Peiser, 1865), 265.

[8] Ibid., 246-247

[9] Stern, *Geschichte des Judenthums von Mendelssohn bis auf die Gegenwart*, 298: "Die Wahl für diese bedeutende Stellung fiel, nachdem längere Verhandlungen mit Geiger und Frankfurter ohne Resultat geblieben, auf [....] Samuel Holdheim, der am 1. September 1847 sein Amt antrat."

as obsolete.[10] In addition, Stern continues, Holdheim was a weak orator,[11] which, understandably, is a great disadvantage for a Reform-rabbi, who, above all else, is expected to deliver captivating sermons.[12] Yet, even as a writer Holdheim could not find favor in Stern's eyes, who in a childish reflex alleged that everything Holdheim had written was contained in a nutshell by his own essays.

As to Holdheim, he did not spare Stern from public attack either. He calls Stern's public lectures wherewith he set into motion the Berlin movement "of only minor importance" ("von nur geringer Bedeutung")[13] and deplores that Stern had been elected chairman of the *Genossenschaft*. The fact that these remarks appear in a historiographical context, i.e. the book Holdheim devoted to the history of the Berlin Reform movement, makes clear that both personalities disputed each other's right to be considered as a founding father.

The least one can say is that an ego-clash occurred between these two men. However, in their thinking Holdheim and Stern were very similar in many respects, and it is possible to explain their mutually disparaging remarks—very unusual for members of the same synagogue who generally avoid bringing internal dissents before the public—as the expression of a love-hate relationship typical of persons who share some basic convictions and who, precisely because of their intellectual kinship, are particularly sensitive to the other's peculiarity.

3. Holdheim's and Stern's Basic Common Assumptions

In fact, both, Stern and Holdheim, were concerned with the perception of Judaism by the Gentile world. Holdheim claims that a genuinely Jewish religion should be capable of attracting people of a different faith.[14] Stern even regarded this as a political necessity.

---

[10] Stern, *Geschichte des Judenthums von Mendelssohn bis auf die Gegenwart*, 273.

[11] Ibid., 298.

[12] In their written form, however, Holdheim's sermons enjoyed great success. Jacob A. Fränkel devoted a series of articles intending to prove that Holdheim's Frankfurt sermons were the most perfect ones ever to be delivered; see Jacob A. Fränkel, "Zur Geschichte der Homiletik," *Literaturblatt des Orients* 37 (1840), 590-592.

[13] Samuel Holdheim, *Geschichte der Entstehung und der Entwicklung der jüdischen Reformgemeinde in Berlin* (Berlin: Julius Springer, 1857), 57.

[14] Idem, *Die wesentlichen Erfordernisse eines ächt jüdischen Gottesdienstes* (Berlin: L. Lassar, 1850), 5.

He believed that, contrary to France, the emancipation of the Jews in Germany was dependent on the recognition of Judaism as a religion by the Christians. Both regarded ethics as the core of Judaism and denied any validity to laws and customs which have no intrinsic ethical significance.[15] This attitude culminates in Holdheim's claim that all which is inconvenient cannot possibly be religious.[16]

Both regarded the cessation of the cult of the Temple and the downfall of the ancient Jewish State as the unambiguous signals that the Jews should no longer regard themselves as a nation but as the bearers of religious truth which they ought to spread through all parts of the world.[17] Independently of each other, both made a distinction between the intrinsic religious and ethical messages of the Sinaitic revelation, which they regarded as the eternal core of Judaism, and the laws pertaining to the Mosaic state, whose significance they regarded as bound by historical circumstances. Both respected Talmudic and medieval Judaism as a means of preserving Jewish life throughout eighteen centuries of hatred and persecution, but denied its validity now that with the (gradual) emancipation a new era in Jewish history was dawning.

The most important characteristic, however, which Stern and Holdheim had in common, was that both appealed for a genuine Jewish Reformation similar to the Lutheran one, built up on a new theological basis, instead of the hesitating and occasional reforms effected until then by rabbis of liberal persuasion. Stern regarded them as highly dangerous to political emancipation since they had led to a great variety of religious practices and had made it much more difficult for the German authorities to deal with Jewish issues

---

[15] See Stern, *Die Aufgabe des Judenthums*, 185: "Wenn sich aber einzelne Handlungen als religiöse Forderungen geltend machen, ohne sich als sittliche Taten zu dokumentieren, so muss die Religion den Boden verlieren, dessen sie bedarf, um als die höchste sittliche Macht das ganze Leben in gleicher Weise zu durchdringen."

[16] See Samuel Holdheim, *Der religiöse Fortschritt im deutschen Judenthume* (Leipzig: E. L. Fritzsche, 1840), 21: "In der Ästhetik gilt der Grundsatz, dass das Unanständige nie ein Gegenstand der Kunst sein könne, wenn er auch nach ästhetischen Gesetzen künstlerisch behandelt wird. Ebenso, nach der Analogie, kann das Unanständige nie ein Gegenstand des Religiösen sein, wenn es auch religiös gebraucht würde, und eben darum kann es auch nicht religiös geboten sein, wie das Ungerechte, wenn es religiös geboten wäre, nicht gerecht sein könnte, und darum auch nicht religiös geboten sein kann."

[17] On the cessation of the cult of the Temple see Stern, *Die Religion des Judenthums*, 211-213, where he takes up Holdheim's positions as they have been set down in *Das Zeremonialgesetz*.

because they no longer knew exactly what it meant to be a Jew. Holdheim, less political in temperament, was particularly opposed to the Conservative and Neo-Orthodox movements whose attitude toward the modern world he branded as "half-hearted" or to use a word of the twentieth century which renders quite accurately his accusations: schizophrenic. Both, Holdheim as well as Stern, shared a basically Hegelian view of history from which they derived the claim that the ethical consciousness of the Jews of the nineteenth century exists in its own right and permits them to question traditional beliefs and customs. In this respect, Holdheim appears more cautious when he states that one ought to apply the Talmud as long as it is possible but that there are issues where this is no longer possible and where one has overtly to admit that Judaism has reached a higher level of ethical awareness.[18]

However, there also are differences and they are more than accidental. The aim of the present article is to lay them bare. The main reason for this contrastive approach is that the Holdheim imago has been distorted because scholars tend to identify him with the positions of the *Genossenschaft*, the most notorious being that on circumcision, while actually he firmly disagreed with some of them. The radicalism of the *Genossenschaft* has impacted on the interpretation of Holdheim who, as their rabbi, has uncritically been supposed to have supported or even to have initiated all most extreme decisions.

4. Methodological Considerations

It cannot escape the reader's attention that Stern's essays present a general overview of the aims and scope of Reform Jewish thinking.

---

[18] Samuel Holdheim, *Das Ceremonialgesetz im Messiasreich* (Schwerin: C. Kürschner, 1845), 9; see also idem, *Ueber die Autonomie der Rabbinen und das Princip der jüdischen Ehe*, 2nd edition (Schwerin: C. Kürschner, 1847), 165: "Der uns leitende Grundsatz ist: den Geist der Rabbinen, in dem wir mit so vielen Zeitgenossen ein tiefbegründetes Streben, den Buchstaben des Gesetzes mit späteren Zeitverhältnissen in Einklang zu bringen, erblicken, der also an sich ein Erzeugnis des Fortschrittes ist, so lange als Mittel des zeitgemäßen Weiterschreitens für unsere Verhältnisse anzuwenden, bis das Judentum auf einem höheren Stadium einer selbständigen, über die Grundanschauung der Rabbinen sich erhebenden und auf einer freien und selbständigen Erfassung des in der Bibel offenbarten religiösen Geistes ruhenden Entwicklung gelangt sein wird, also einem höheren als dasjenige ist, auf welches der Entwicklungsprozeß des Talmuds es gebracht hat."

That can be explained by the fact that he was much less concerned with the halakhic consistency of his writings. He had to present a manifesto for the synagogue he was going to found and this had to be, above all, affirmative. Stern aimed at making clear what Reform Judaism generally should be about. Holdheim, in contrast, was much more concerned by the issue of how this new movement could be presented to the audience as a genuinely Jewish one. In addition, Holdheim remained attached to the rabbinic genres of *teshuvah* (legal responsum) and *derasha* (homily), the former being mostly used in his work for polemic purposes, the latter being the attachment of a religious or ethical message to a given biblical pericope. However, despite the fact that the authors compared each used different genres which may have impacted on the nature of their messages and the items discussed, there are still many issues on which Holdheim's and Stern's positions are sufficiently specific or typical to be compared. Among these issues I have chosen the most charged ones, i.e. those which generally are brought up when people are discussing about whether Reform Judaism has still anything to do with Judaism:

1. Are the motives which have triggered Reform Judaism merely of political or sociological nature?
2. Should Reform Judaism be regarded as a positive religion or not? In other words: Has it a delineated body of principles of faith and religious prescriptions?
3. How does Reform Judaism define itself vis-à-vis Christianity?

5. The Motivation of Reform Judaism

On the usual and more popular view, the rise of Reform Judaism is seen as an attempt to face the new sociological conditions of the Jews in the nineteenth century. The same way the rabbis of the Talmud responded to the changed political conditions of the Jewish community after the destruction of the Second Temple and the downfall of national sovereignty, Reform Judaism responded to the civil emancipation of the Jews eighteen centuries later. Jewish law and religion had to be adapted to the socio-economical challenges going along with (gradual) emancipation. The problem with this view is that it matches precisely that what the detractors of Reform Judaism want to hear. They find that Judaism has not to respond to anything at all. The Torah has been given once and forever, not one single word should be added or removed. Every attempt to alter rabbinical law can only be inspired by lesser motives such as the greed for profit or fame. Of course it is attractive to behave like the Gentiles, engaging in Gentile professions and pursuits, they argue, but being a faithful Jew is a commitment of whose consequences one ought to be aware. Nobody can be forced to remain within the Jewish community, but the least that can be demanded of those who abandon the yoke of law is that they cease claiming to be Jews.

It is no accident that the German reformers in general, and Stern and Holdheim in particular, were particularly anxious not to be regarded as opportunists. There are numerous passages and phrases expressing their belief that those who scoff at their endeavours also fail to behave like Jews. It is highly important to note that in their apology of Reform Judaism Holdheim and Stern focused on the ethical problems arising out of the closer coexistence between Jews and Gentiles.

The idea of the "messianic age" plays a pivotal role in both Holdheim's and Stern's elaboration of a Reform Jewish ethos. They believed that the era, prophesied by Isaiah, where all nations of the world will worship the same God was getting closer. Idolatry was no longer of this world, at least the Western one, and ethical monotheism had become a common spiritual property. In the light of this, Jewish self-reclusion, though perfectly justified in biblical and medieval times, lacked the conditions of its necessity and even of its acceptability in modern times. The attachment to the ceremonial laws ceased to be compatible with the ethical inspiration of the Hebrew Bible. Yet, two different types of Reform Jewish ethics appear to emerge out of these basic assumptions. They will be discussed in the following paragraphs.

6. Stern's Historicism

Sigismund Stern regarded Reform Judaism as inspired by motives of an absolutely ethical character. In his view, the history of humankind is driven by a force and a spirit which lie far beyond that which the historical agents, i.e. the individuals or groups, perceive as right and truthful. In this genuinely Hegelian view, all historical events are bestowed with sense. Accordingly, the event of emancipation is a phenomenon which urges the Jews to reconsider the validity of their traditional beliefs. The fact that Jews are no longer locked up in their ghettos and can

play a role in human history also indicates that it is their ethical duty
to take up that new challenge and to do everything possible to become
a vector in the development of the modern world. Hence the historical facts become automatically messages of what men and women ought
to do. That which is, is altogether that which *must* be, a thesis which
Hegel applies to the smallest details of history. Therefore emancipation to Stern is not only a phenomenon which triggered Reform Judaism,
even more than that it is a clear signal that Jews ought to do away
with the beliefs of the past, which as long as Jewish life was confined
to the ghetto were also perfectly justified. History itself has the right
to impact upon religious life.[19] The new era invites a new truth and
altogether a "Reformation" in the Lutheran sense which radically calls
into question inherited beliefs and practices. The emancipation is a task
which Judaism as a religion has to carry out.[20]

Up to this point, Holdheim's view does not differ fundamentally
from Stern's position, insofar as he also sees Reform Judaism as the
result of a general spiritual development in Western humanity. Judaism,
also Holdheim says, must acknowledge the fact that both materially
and spiritually it owes a great deal to the Gentile world, especially
since the advent of Enlightenment. The specific character of Stern's
position is that he regards it as an *unconditional ethical duty* of the
Jewish people to actively participate in Gentile life. Now that the
time has come that Judaism can spread its messages throughout the
world, it would be an unpardonable mistake to maintain Jewish self-
reclusion. What makes Talmudic Judaism so specific, Stern argues,
is not the peculiarity of its laws, but the fact that in obeying these
laws Jews fulfilled *all* their duties.[21] Presently, however, new duties
have arisen and Jews are growing aware of the fact that they have
a decisive role to play in the history of humanity. This fact in itself
indicates that modern Jews have abandoned the Talmud's basic
assumptions, whether they are aware of it or not. Jews *are not only*

---

[19] Stern, *Die Aufgabe des Judenthums*, 104.

[20] Ibid., 155: "Die Emanzipation der Juden ist eine Aufgabe, welche das Judenthum
als Religion zu verwirklichen hat."

[21] Ibid., 30: "Was war es, was den Talmud so bedeutungsvoll, so einflussreich
auf die Gestaltung des Judenthums machte? Nicht dass es gerade diese oder jene
Vorschriften waren, welche er festsetzte, und denen sich der Jude unterwarf, sondern sein Einfluß war in dem Bewußtsein begründet, welches der Jude empfand,
mit der Befolgung aller dieser Vorschriften seine ganze Lebensaufgabe erfüllt zu
haben."

allowed to take part in Gentile life, Stern argues, it is *their innermost duty* to do so.[22] The so-called wish to engage in Gentile pursuits only echoes the call of humanity which appeals to the Jews and urges them to take part in a broader destiny. It is precisely this ethical imperative of joining the Gentile world in striving for a better world which makes for Stern's firm rejection of all previous attempts made by enlightened rabbis to reform Judaism over the past decades. Their endeavors, Stern argues, consisted in making a few concessions to modern life, without any awareness of the new tasks Jews had to fulfil and without any overall perception of the new goal toward which both Jews and Gentiles were striving. Now that Christians have abandoned particularism, Jews should be absorbed by the "nationhood of the people to which they belong"[23] and Jewish religion should leave behind all national (i.e. particularly Jewish) influences. Judaism should be a nation without the particularity of a State which had vanished two thousand years before and be grounded in the essence and the spirit of the peoples who are carrying contemporary history.[24]

Against the backdrop of these concerns, Holdheim's position is definitely more cautious. In Stern's eyes he, too, must have belonged to the rabbis who tried to justify changes by appealing to talmudic lore; the few sardonic lines he wrote about Holdheim leave no doubt about it.

7. Holdheim's Dogmatic Approach

To Holdheim external circumstances cannot provide the final reasons for alterations of Jewish law. The most appropriate response to

---

[22] Ibid., 31: "Das Verlangen nach einer Thätigkeit für die Mitwelt ist in dem Herzen eines jeden Menschen nur das Echo des Anspruchs, den diese an unsere Wirksamkeit macht und zu machen berechtigt ist. Der erste Ruf der Art im Herzen der Juden war also das sichere Zeichen, dass die Zeit gekommen sei, in denen es ihnen nicht nur zustehe, sondern in der es ihre Pflicht sei, wieder mitzuarbeiten an dem großen Werk der Menschheit und der Weltgeschichte."

[23] Ibid., 82: "Nur wo der Jude mit seinem Leben und Streben in die Nationalität des Volkes aufgeht, dem er gegenwärtig angehört, kann er mit seinem gesamten Bewusstsein auf der Höhe der Zeit stehen [....]."

[24] Ibid., 116: "Eine Nationalität, welche nicht mehr an der Besonderheit eines längst untergegangenen Staates festhält; sondern im Wesen und Geist der Völker wurzelt, von denen die Geschichte der Gegenwart getragen wird [....]."

the modern world from a strictly sociological viewpoint was not religious reform but indifference, he argued. Holdheim even goes so far
as to say that Reform Judaism is a child of Restoration[25] and not
of Enlightenment.

If alterations of the ancient code appear to be necessary, they
ought to be motivated from within Jewish theology. True, the changed
socio-economic circumstances can trigger reforms, but these must
eventually be sustained by Jewish lore. Holdheim's approach was
dogmatical and therefore diametrically opposed to Stern's historicism. To Holdheim, Reform Judaism is both more authentic *and*
more adapted to the modern world.

One thing that makes Holdheim so different from Stern, despite
the most striking agreements on many points, is that the former was
much more aware than the latter of the challenge by Neo-Orthodoxy
and Conservative Judaism. Both movements claimed that the increasing social interaction between Jews and Gentiles could go along with
a maximum of ritual observance. In addition, they appeared to be
much more successful among German Jewry than Reform Judaism.
Contrary to Stern, who believed that this revival of traditionalism
was doomed to disappear soon,[26] Holdheim regarded them as important enough to discuss their positions in nearly all his polemical
essays. More particularly, Holdheim was vehemently opposed to
Zacharias Frankel, who adopted a similar position toward the Talmud,
regarding it as the work of men and not of God, but who claimed
nonetheless that it had acquired legitimacy by centuries of observance and by the fact that most Jewish communities regarded it as
an integral part of their religious life.[27]

Accordingly, adapting Jewish tradition to the needs of the time was
not the first point on Holdheim's agenda, since that was precisely the
programme of the Conservative movement. To Holdheim, Reform
Jewish theology was intrinsically the most ethical form of Judaism; its
validity was not a matter of sociology. Holdheim's dogmatical and
timeless position may have been reinforced by the fact that the Berlin
Reform Congregation—Holdheim's synagogue—only represented a
tiny minority. In the light of this, the sociological motivations which

---

[25] Holdheim, *Geschichte der Entstehung und Entwicklung der jüdischen Reformgemeinde zu Berlin*, 10.
[26] Stern, *Die Aufgabe des Judenthums*, 114-115.
[27] See Meyer, *Response to Modernity*, 87.

inspired the early reformers in large part had to make place for a more intrinsically theological approach. Holdheim became increasingly aware that the Berlin Reform movement did not meet any social needs, since Conservative and Neo-Orthodox Judaism offered a much more successful response to the issue of how to behave as faithful Jews in a modern world. While indulging in socio-political considerations in his earlier writings and incurring the reproach that his thinking was marked by social opportunism (e.g. a dubious concern about what Christians might think about Jewish faith) Holdheim appears in his later writings as a religious visionary, aware that the vast majority of his coreligionists turned a deaf ear to his teachings but profoundly convinced of having seized the essence of Judaism and the deepest impulses of its historical development.

8. *"State" versus "History"*

This spiritual orientation—much more turned toward the inward religious experience—makes for the fact that emancipation never played an important role in Holdheim's thinking. Nowhere does Holdheim state—as Stern did—that the participation in world history has come to supersede religious observance. To be sure, to Holdheim the new status of the Jews and their involvement in Gentile pursuits must be affirmed in a thorough way and not half-heartedly. The essays he wrote to that effect earned him the reputation of being a "mephistophelic personality" and the "greatest traitor of Judaism since Paul of Tarsus."[28] One of Holdheim's most notorious statements in this respect is that, in a State governed by reasonable laws, there is no need for two legislations, a rabbinical one and an official one.[29] The Jews should thoroughly identify themselves with the State in which they live; it is their religious duty to strive for its prosperity (which was also Stern's position). They must acknowledge the fact that they are members of a much vaster community and that their well-being depends on it.

It is noteworthy that, where Stern shows a greater predilection for the word "history," the focus on the State *as a legal institution* is

---

[28] Heinrich Graetz, *Geschichte der Juden vom Beginn der Mendelssohnschen Zeit (1750) bis in die neueste Zeit (1848)* (Leipzig: Oskar Leiner, 1870), 565.

[29] See Holdheim, *Ueber die Autonomie der Rabbinen und das Prinzip der jüdischen Ehe*, passim.

peculiar to Holdheim's thinking. This focus on the relationship between
the Jews and their State (and *not* their role in history) accounts for
the thoroughly rabbinical character of Holdheim's thinking. He
remains a declared legalist, which becomes particularly clear when
he says that the State would benefit from Jewish emancipation,
because the Jews would be much more valuable citizens than the
Gentiles on account of the legalistic nature of their faith.[30] Holdheim's
focus on the state, according to his own sayings, reflects the high
esteem in which State affairs were held in biblical times.[31] According
to Holdheim, Judaism does not distinguish between man's duties
toward God and his duties toward his fellow men, but only between
his obligations toward God and toward the state.[32] Holdheim explains
the great reluctance of the rabbinical authorities to share this claim
by the fact that after the first exile, Jews lost the notion of a commonwealth so explicitly present in Mosaic Judaism. During the Second
Temple Period the State lacked the most secure foundation it could
have, namely self-awareness (*das Bewußtsein seiner selbst*). The idea of
a commonwealth as such, of its essence and its conditions, was no
longer present in the minds of the Jews of that time. They only perceived single features, such as a land, a temple, a high priest, a king
and a Sanhedrin, but the idea of a State as a spiritual organism,
transcending all these single phenomena, was beyond their grasp. In
contrast to the Jews of the Babylonian exile who knew too well that
they had lost a commonwealth, those after the destruction of the
Second Temple did not even realize that they had lost a state,
because they had never had one.[33] The fact that Jews are the members of a non-Jewish State does not restrict their duty as citizens,
not even from a religious viewpoint.[34]

---

[30] True, from a present viewpoint it is absolutely horrific to read Holdheim's
statement that a Jewish soldier loyal to his State should not be loath to kill Jewish
soldiers of the hostile nation, even if this nation is entirely made up of Jews; see
ibid., 137.

[31] Of course there is also the rabbinic adage that "the law of the kingdom is the
law" (*dina de-malkhuta dina*), often invoked by Holdheim, but everybody knows—first
and foremost he himself—that the consequences Holdheim derives from this verse
are illicit in any respect.

[32] Ibid., 20.

[33] Ibid., 42-43.

[34] Ibid., 15: "Mit dem Untergang(e) des jüdischen Staates hörte der Jude auf
Bürger desselben zu sein, und alle bürgerlichen Verpflichtungen gegen denselben
sind von selbst außer Kraft getreten. Mit dem Eintritt des Juden in einen anderen

In the light of all of this we may conclude that Holdheim still defines the duties of the modern Jew in terms of notions drawn from Jewish religious history, a thing which Sigismund Stern expressly refused to do. This becomes even clearer when we consider the way Holdheim responds to the question whether the Sabbath must be observed by civil servants (a profession to which Holdheim pays much attention, contrary to Stern who seems particularly interested in the free professions). He answered that the same way as the priests, who where the government officials in the Mosaic state, had to carry out their duties and to bring the offerings even on Sabbath, civil servants are exempt from the duty of keeping the Sabbath.[35]

9. *Wholeness as a Core Principle in Holdheim's Thinking*

Holdheim's most typical argument in favor of absolute loyalty toward the State, however, is that the presence of two separate rulings in private law for Jews and non-Jews within the same State would have an unfavorable impact on Jewish morality. The presence of two legislations would make for a schizoid state of mind, in which two value-systems compete with each other. This brings us to another and highly characteristic aspect of Samuel Holdheim's personality and thinking. While Stern was fretting about Jewish reclusion and exclusivism, which he felt inappropriate in a modern world, Holdheim was particularly worried by the ambivalence of feelings going along with the emancipated status of the Jews. His main attention goes not toward emancipation itself, which he regarded almost as a fait accompli, but toward the issue of how an emancipated Jew could still be a religious Jew without feeling at odds with himself. What Holdheim wanted to preserve is the ancient biblical ideal of wholeness, where one acts according to one's beliefs and feelings. In traditional ghetto life wholeness was not threatened, but with the entrance into Gentile life Jews risk adopting an ambivalent attitude both toward their fellows and toward the Gentile world. Holdheim devoted many pages to the relationship between Jews and Gentiles, not however with the purpose of encouraging the Jews to

---

Staat kann er zwar nicht, wie einst in Palästina, die Landesgesetze als religiöse Satzungen betrachten; gleichwohl muß er sich durch seine Religion zur Erfüllung aller seiner Bürgerpflichten verbunden fühlen."

[35] Ibid., 104-105, note 71

take part in Gentile pursuits, as Stern did, but to make evident that any ambivalence toward the Gentiles is deeply unethical and thoroughly irreligious. Like Stern, Holdheim opposed all rabbinical laws which aimed at separating the Jews from the Gentiles,[36] but this first and foremost because it is ethically inconvenient and even abhorrent ("*ein Unding*") merely to obey the laws of the State to which one belongs and not to take part in its life. Holdheim accused the Orthodox of having misunderstood Mosaic faith in their exclusivism, which was only justified in times when the surrounding peoples were pagan.[37]

Holdheim's universalism is formalist and not emotional, as in Stern's case, which becomes clear in the passage of *Das Zeremonialgesetz* where he deals with the notion of ethical teaching. It is absolutely unacceptable, Holdheim points out, to contend that Jewish ethics are valuable in themselves and that only their exclusive character can be subject to criticism. So-called ethics which are confined to a limited circle of beneficiaries do not deserve that name, because, by definition, ethics have no limits in their application.[38] It is out of this Kantian conception of morality that Holdheim opposed the unconditional observance of ceremonial law, and not because it was an obstacle for the Jews to meet their impending status as emancipated citizens. Even in Gentile circles there was no sympathy for Jews who

---

[36] Idem, *Vorträge über die Mosaische Religion für denkende Israeliten* (Schwerin: C. Kürschner, 1844), X, note 1: "Den Gesetzen des Staates gehorchen, ohne in die Volkstümlichkeit des Staates einzugehen, ist ein Unding, da diese Gesetze die Förderung und Entwicklung des volkstümlichen Lebens und der volkstümlichen Gesinnung eben zum Zwecke haben. Daher muß die Jugend klar und deutlich belehrt werden, daß alle Absonderungsgesetze der mosaischen Staatsverfassung, welche die Rabbinen im mißverstandenen Interesse der mosaischen Religion auf völlig veränderte Zustände übertrugen und durch Weinverbote etc. vermehrt haben, wegfallen müssen._"

[37] Idem, *Das Ceremonialgesetz*, 28: "In dem Augenblick, als alle übrigen Völker durch eine Sintflut vom Schauplatz der Erde vertilgt würden und Israel allein übrig bliebe; oder in dem Augenblick, als die übrige Menschheitswelt den patriarchalischen Glauben Abrahams annähme und zu wahrhaften Monotheisten bekehrt würde, in demselben Augenblick müßte das Zeremonialgesetz in seiner Verbindlichkeit auch für Israel aufhören, da es dadurch, daß seine vorausgesetzten Beziehungen zu heidnischen Völkern aufhörten, zu gänzlicher Bedeutungslosigkeit herabgesunken sein müßte."

[38] Ibid., 85: "Eine Morallehre, die ihre Anwendung auf einen bestimmten Kreis von Menschen einschränkt, ist schon deshalb, weil sie engherzig ist, mit ihrer Ausübung gewissen egoistischen Volks- und Religionstendenzen dient, alles andere, Politik, Staatsklugheit etc., ja selbst Religion, wenn man will, aber freilich nur im missverstandenen Sinne des Wortes, nur keine Moral, deren Wesen eben in der Schrankenlosigkeit besteht."

had left ritual observance behind, and Holdheim was aware of that.[39] To Holdheim maintaining ceremonial law posed a problem on a formal ethical level, namely that it would lead to a clash between religious ethics and secular ethics.[40] As members of a larger society composed by Gentiles, Jews naturally and automatically committed themselves to values and duties, which, albeit non-halakhic, are also to be regarded as binding from a Jewish viewpoint.[41] When a civil servant does not appear at his work-place on Sabbath he behaves in a harmful way towards the State and his colleagues, and such behaviour would be unethical, all the more since it expresses the belief that harming Gentiles is a lesser transgression. Of course, there is still the ancient solution that Jews stay within the walls of the Ghetto, and contrary to Stern, Holdheim occasionally seemed all but prepared to admit that this might still be the best thing to do. Reform Judaism was of no use in Poland, he expressly said, but was entirely appropriate to Germany. However, as soon as one leaves the Ghetto, one is bound to the ethical consequences of one's choice. In the light of this it is imperative to stress that Holdheim wants this ethical position to be understood as a genuinely religious (albeit not rabbinical) one.[42] Those who, invoking biblical and Talmudic law,

---

[39] Holdheim's awareness of anti-Semitic sentiments among the German population is documented in his *Geschichte der Entstehung und Entwicklung der jüdischen Reformgemeinde zu Berlin*, 83.

[40] Stern is even more explicit and expressly states that Judaism has emphasized the duties toward God at the expense of the duties toward our fellow human beings ("Sittlichkeit"). Then, however, he plain and simply states that, in Judaism, man has no other duty toward God than the fulfillment of his ethical duties ("[....], dass das Judentum seinem Bekenner keine besonderen Pflichten gegen Gott vorschreibe, keine besonderen Handlungen des Gehorsams gegen Gott demselben auferlege, sondern ihn die Aufgabe der Sittlichkeit, als einen Ausdruck seiner Gehorsams gegen de göttlichen Willen erkennen lehre"); see Stern, *Die Religion des Judenthums* (Berlin: W. Adolf & Co, 1853), 258. In similar statements of his Holdheim never claimed to be in accordance with Judaism, but only with the moral awareness of his time.

[41] This becomes manifest in the following passage from Holdheim, *Ueber die Autonomie der Rabbinen*, 61: "Da sie (die Religion) dem Israeliten gestattet und gestatten muß, in andere Staatsverhältnisse zu treten, so muß dies ihm sittlich möglich sein, d. h. es muß ihm von der Religion gestattet sein, alle bürgerlichen Pflichten dieses Staates, welche die moralischen Bedingungen der Aufnahme in seinen Verband sind, ohne Ausnahme zu erfüllen."

[42] Idem, *Vorträge über die mosaische Religion*, 129: "Aber es ehrt und adelt unser religiöses Denken und Fühlen, dass wir das Reinmenschliche nicht etwa als etwas besonderes von der Religion geschiedenes betrachten, sondern es in den Kreis unseres religiösen Lebens hineinziehen und als ein Religiöses unserem innersten Wesen einverleiben."

argue otherwise have not understood the essence of Mosaic faith, Holdheim argues, which teaches the love of humanity ("Menschenliebe").

10. Wholeness (Holdheim) versus
Work Ethic (Stern) in the Sabbath Controversy

It is with this ideal of wholeness in mind that we should appreciate the fact that Holdheim advocated moving the Sabbath ceremony to Sundays. In actual fact, Holdheim argues, most Jews worked on the Sabbath in any event but felt guilty about it. He feared that such a state of permanent conflict would lead to moral insensitivity.[43] Blaming the violation of the Sabbath in official religious discourse and yet tacitly accepting it as an economic necessity is a smuggler's system ("Schmuggelsystem") one should finish with.[44] Stern's position is exactly the same as far as the naked claim is concerned, but he goes much farther and calls into question the very notion of Sabbath-observance. Stern argues that the Sabbath is God's gift to the Jewish people, not a commandment. A gift, however, should be deserved. Only those who fulfil the biblical commandment that one should work during six days are granted the divine present of the sabbatical rest. Those who have not yet finished their work should go on fulfilling their duties.[45] Obviously Stern's lenient and even restrictive view on Sabbath observance is inspired by the work ethic while Holdheim seems to be concerned by the soundness of moral and spiritual life. Both positions are heterodox, but they still reflect two totally different worlds of thinking and feeling. Both invoke Rabbi Akiva's saying that it is better to "treat the Sabbath like a weekday rather than to be (economically) dependent on man" (*Pesachim* 112a), but Holdheim regards the non-observance of the Sabbath as a deplorable but sociologically accomplished fact,[46]

---

[43] Idem, *Das Ceremonialgesetz*, 142.

[44] Ibid., 143.

[45] Stern, *Die Religion des Judenthums*, 234-235: "Wer also soll den Sabbath feiern? Wer in den Tagen der Arbeit durch dieselbe seiner Pflicht genügt hat, und den Tag der Ruhe zu begreifen und zu würdigen weiß."

[46] With respect to the move of the Sabbath-ceremony on a Sunday Holdheim writes: "Das Religionswidrige kann also nicht in der Gottesdienstfeier am Sonntage, sondern in der Nichtfeier des Sabbaths am Sonnabende bestehen. Diese Nichtfeier wird aber nicht erst jetzt proklamiert, sondern steht als Tatsache einmal da [....]"; Samuel Holdheim, *Das Gutachten des Herrn L. Schwab, Rabbiners zu Pesth, über die Reformgenossenschaft daselbst* (Berlin: J. Sittenfeld, 1848), 16.

while Stern even fosters the laxness of his contemporaries with arguments expressing an attachment to the Prussian work ethic much more than to the biblical heritage.

11. The Shepherd versus the Entrepreneur

To summarize Holdheim's and Stern's positions respectively, one could say that, while Holdheim confined himself to stating that the non-Jewish world should in no way be excluded from Jewish life, Stern was much more affirmative and claimed that it should radically be *in*cluded. Philosophically speaking, Holdheim was closer to Immanuel Kant, despite the Hegelian tonality of some passages,[47] while Stern was Hegelian through and through. Holdheim regarded the State—and even the Gentile one—as an institution hallowed by Jewish teaching,[48] while Stern regarded it as a tool of history. From a sociological viewpoint, Holdheim remained more focused on the Jewish people and Jewish affairs, while Stern had the sake of whole humankind in mind, which, as he seemed to believe, expected the Jews to join them in their great adventure. While Holdheim behaved like a shepherd, above all preoccupied with the mental state of his flock, Stern voiced the entrepreneur's awareness of life. Both are driven by a deep ethical concern, but Stern's ethics contain an additional premise, typical of the nineteenth century, namely that participating in the endeavors of humankind is an ethical imperative and that men and women ought to make their capacities useful for the sake of humanity.

It is no coincidence that, when talking about the Jewish professions,

---

[47] I am grateful to Michael A. Meyer for having convinced me that my initial claim that Holdheim was a Hegelian (cf. Ralph Bisschops, "Metaphor as the Internalisation of a Ritual—With a Case Study on Samuel Holdheim (1806-1860)," in *Metaphor, Canon and Community—Jewish, Christian and Islamic Approaches*, ed. Ralph Bisschops and James Francis [Bern et al.: Peter Lang, 1999], 284-307, particularly 297) should be nuanced.

[48] The term "hallowed" is appropriate because Holdheim writes: "Hat das Judentum, welches nach dem Untergang des israelitischen Staatslebens und der israelitischen Volkstümlichkeit nebst den daran geknüpften Ordnungen nur die mosaische Religion in ihrer Reinheit festzuhalten berufen ist, aus der theokratischen Form seines ehemaligen Daseins den religiösen Grundgedanken von der Heiligkeit des Staatsverhältnisses als einer göttlichen Anstalt vor allen anderen Religionen voraus"; see Holdheim, *Vorträge über die mosaische Religion für denkende Israeliten*, X-XI.

Stern mentions in the first place the banker. Holdheim, on the contrary, when dealing with the question of which profession would be the most suitable one for the Jews, answers that it is agriculture. This again, illustrates the timeless character of his thinking. Holdheim felt estranged from the sophistication of the emancipated Jew, which he deplored as the inevitable result of his urban existence. He pleaded for the return to peasant existence, possibly echoing Berthold Auerbach's celebration of rural life. Unfortunately, the time for labouring the soil has not yet come for the Jews, Holdheim complains. Only in a time when the Gentile world will reward the intellectual—i. e. the most visible—achievements of the Jews, can they then turn to the noble work of cultivating the soil. But then, and only then, Holdheim says, shall the Jew become a *whole man*.[49]

12. Should Reform Judaism be Regarded as a Positive Religion?

A great clash between Samuel Holdheim and Sigismund Stern occurred in 1850 when the Berlin Reform Congregation had to provide some convincing arguments to the Prussian authorities for splitting from the officially recognised Jewish community of Berlin ("Gesamtgemeinde"). The ministry for religious affairs ("Ministerium des Innern und der geistlichen Angelegenheiten") expected this secession to be explicitly motivated by religious considerations. Eventually, the synagogue of the Berlin *Genossenschaft* (which called itself "jüdische Reformgemeinde" from 1850 onwards) failed to become recognized by the Prussian authorities because of Stern's unwillingness to view Reform Judaism as a positive religion and to present an overview of the beliefs and practices which defined his congregation, even though Holdheim urged him to do so. Indeed, Stern wrote to the Ministry Department that there had never been any general consensus in Judaism about articles of faith or binding norms pertaining to religious practice.[50] He even showed reluctant to present monotheism as a fundamental Jewish

---

[49] Idem, *Dibre Chaj. Worte Gottes oder Gottesdienstliche Vorträge gehalten in der Synagoge zu Frankfurt a/O* (Leipzig: E. L. Fritzsche, 1840) 270: "[....] erst dann wird ihm [Israel] der ganze Mensch da sein."
[50] Idem, *Geschichte der Entstehung und Entwicklung der jüdischen Reformgemeinde in Berlin*, 219.

belief, but finally gave way to the pressure of his board.[51] Holdheim was all but disappointed that Stern even refused to hand in the 1845 manifesto of the Berlin *Reformgenossenschaft*. It was precisely this paper, Holdheim contended, which presented Reform Judaism as a positive religion in contrast to the manifesto of the *Frankfurter Reformfreunde* (1843), according to which Judaism is "capable of an endless development."[52]

Actually, reading Stern's books we are presented with the evidence that he unambiguously stood on the side of the *Frankfurter Reformfreunde*. He explicitly states that Judaism is amenable to the laws of any living organism, the most basic of which is the undisrupted, progressive development of one and the same principle.[53] The Mosaic State was the embodiment of "the idea of morality" (*Sittlichkeitsidee*) in its time, and yet, Stern says, the idea of morality itself is susceptible of a development which goes far beyond the limits of Mosaic Law.[54] In its messianic form the knowledge of God, which Stern regards as the source of ethics, shall not be inspired by "external teachings," but "emerge from our soul."[55] To those who argue that the messianic age has not arrived yet, Stern replies that it actually has begun. The hope itself for a messianic future indicates that the ethical commitment which characterizes this era is already present, which in turn is a sign that the messianic era is dawning.[56] In a tacit reference to Sanhedrin 98b, Stern states that the messianic age is the result of the endeavors of men and women; it can be hastened or delayed by their doings. For those who perfectly conceive the messianic idea with their ethical consciousness and realize it within the realm of their activity, the messianic age

---

[51] Ibid., 231.

[52] Ibid., 57. The manifesto of the Frankfurter Reformfreunde is also quoted in Meyer, *Response to Modernity*, 122.

[53] See Stern, *Die Aufgabe des Judenthums*, 130: "die ununterbrochen fortschreitende Entwicklung eines und desselben Lebenskeimes."

[54] Idem, *Die Religion des Judenthums*, 154: "Dessen ungeachtet erkennen wir hier die Grenze und die Beschränkung des positiven mosaischen Sittengesetzes, und darum die Entwicklungsfähigkeit der Sittlichkeitsidee im Judentum über das mosaische Gesetz hinaus."

[55] Ibid., 172.

[56] Ibid., 189: "Ich wiederhole es, die Verkündigung der Messiasidee ist der Beginn der Messiaszeit, wie die Morgenröte die Verkünderin und zugleich die Bringerin des Lichtes ist, [....]; die Hoffnung auf die messianische Zukunft ist das erste Erscheinen derselben in der Gegenwart, wie die Blüte die Frucht bereits in sich trägt, die sie uns verspricht."

has already come.[57] The prophetic promise that in the days of the Messiah the Jews would return to Palestine already came true with the Second Temple.[58] Therefore this idea should be given up, particularly since the hope for a return to Palestine is no longer living in the hearts of modern Jews.[59]

Like Holdheim, Stern states that religion should not conflict with life—or to put it in his specific vocabulary—with the duties of life. This requirement, however, makes the idea of a positive religion problematic, Stern argues. The *duties* of life vary with social class, profession and country, while religion always tends to impose one single and unchangeable system of beliefs.[60] Stern champions the creation of a Jewish "church" ("Kirche") charged with reconciling the discrepancies between life and faith. This church should, in principle, embrace all Jews of the world, the way the Roman Catholic Church embraces all Catholics, but Stern admits that this is unrealizable given the striking national differences between Jewish communities. Therefore he recommends starting with the creation of national churches, such as a German-Jewish, French-Jewish or English-Jewish church.[61] Stern concedes that he could also have chosen the more usual word "synagogue," but it becomes obvious why he has not used this word, burdened as it is with significance, once we read how he outlines the authority of his "church." Among other things, it consists in establishing the forms of worship, abrogating ancient laws and legislating new ones, and this independently of any existing, i.e. traditional law or custom.[62] This makes sufficiently clear that Stern does not regard Judaism as limited to any canonical settings. The rules

---

[57] Ibid., 190: "Und wer die Messiasidee mit seinem sittlichen Bewusstsein vollkommen zu erfassen, und mit seinem sittlichen Tun in dem Kreise seines Wirkens zu verwirklichen vermag, für den ist die Messiaszeit bereits gekommen."

[58] Ibid., 192: "Und wenn wir also an den Worten des Propheten festhalten wollen, und die Wiederherstellung des jüdischen Reichs als ein wesentliches Moment der messianischen Bestimmung anerkennen, warum wollen wir nicht zugeben, dass dieselbe bereits durch die Zeit des zweiten Tempels in Erfüllung gegangen sei."

[59] Ibid.: "Ich wenigstens will mich unverhohlen zu der Überzeugung bekennen, dass die Hoffnung auf eine Rückkehr der Juden nach Palästina im Bewusstsein des Judentums der Gegenwart erloschen und aufgegeben ist [....]."

[60] Idem, *Die Aufgabe des Judenthums*, 161.

[61] Ibid., 147.

[62] Ibid., 144: "Wir erkennen ihr (der Kirche) die unbeschränkte, von keinem Gesetz und keinem Gebrauch abhängige Befugnis zu, die Form des öffentlichen Gottesdienstes und aller andern religiösen Handlungen zu bestimmen, die Befugnis, gültige Gesetze für aufgehoben zu erklären und neue festzusetzen [....]."

of the past can no longer shape the life of the modern Jew.[63] Those who have left traditional Judaism behind should no longer be branded as apostates but welcomed as the very forerunners of Judaism to come.[64] Of course, all of this begs the question as to what Stern understands by Judaism. Neither the life of the patriarchs, nor Mosaic Judaism, let alone the Talmud, can be regarded as the full expression of Judaism, Stern argues.[65] They represent great moments in Jewish history, but not Judaism itself. From a theological or dogmatic viewpoint this absolute and most intimate essence of Judaism which lies beyond any of its historical manifestations must be an empty shell. Not to Stern, who firmly believes that God's plans are carried out by the history of humankind and that the spirit of history—in the Hegelian sense—can not be so cruel and cynical as to effect the emancipation of the Jews while still demanding that they continue to live like their ancestors. Therefore there *must* be a true and authentic Judaism emerging out of the historical process, which Stern likens to a flower whose blossom is still to appear. He simply does not make it his business to ask what this true Judaism is really about and leaves this issue to the Jewish "Church," charged with making explicit that which was actually living in the hearts of Jewish men and women. The suspicion that the history of humankind can be cynical indeed, did not rise in these years marked by unbridled optimism.

13. Holdheim's Position towards the Jewish Canon

With respect to the question of whether Reform Judaism is a positive religion, Holdheim too is pretty explicit. He refused to admit that Judaism permits the generation of beliefs and practices going beyond "the biblical idea of God and morality."[66]

---

[63] Ibid., 171.

[64] Ibid., 128.

[65] Ibid., 188-189: "Das patriarchalische Familienleben der Erzväter, der Gottesstaat, das talmudische Judentum sind nicht minder solche Gestaltungen, als die Bibel; sie ist ein großes Moment in der Entwicklung des Judentums, aber sie ist nicht das Judentum selbst; denn der lebendige Organismus kann in einer einzigen Erscheinung niemals sein ganzes Dasein entfalten."

[66] Holdheim, *Geschichte der Entstehung und Entwicklung der jüdischen Reformgemeinde in Berlin*, 115: "Ein Hinausgehen über das religiöse Denken und Fühlen des biblischen Zeitalters, nämlich über die biblische Gottes- und Sittlichkeitsidee als die unverrückbare Basis des Judentums, wäre keine Entwicklung, sondern eine Zerstörung des Judentums."

Holdheim never pleaded for an overall and indiscriminate abrogation of the ceremonial laws, and his position on circumcision and the Sabbath ceremony are very illustrative of this. Holdheim did not want circumcision to be abolished; he even explicitly stated that, from a dogmatical viewpoint, such a thing is not feasible.[67] The only leniency he shows in this respect is his allegation that, again from a strictly dogmatical viewpoint, it cannot be regarded as a "sacrament" and therefore not as a prerequisite to be regarded as a member of the Jewish community.[68] Neither should the father who refuses to circumcise his son(s) be regarded as a bad Jew if his choice has been made for reasons of conscience.[69]

Moreover, in contrast to some allegations,[70] Holdheim did not transfer the Sabbath to Sunday morning. This was decided by the board of the *Genossenschaft*. Holdheim did approve of holding Sabbath services on Sunday so that those who were unable to participate on Saturdays would not be deprived of communal worship. We should not forget that, at first, there were two Sabbath services in Berlin, a regular one on Saturday and an extra one on Sunday. Due to lack of worshippers, the Saturday ones were abandoned after some time. Holdheim was obliged to accept this lack of support for Saturday services although he personally regretted this development. To him the "historical" Sabbath remained the seventh day of the week, i.e. the span from Friday night to Saturday night. However, it would have been quite easy for him to contend that the Jewish calendar is the least important thing for a community committed to the spiritual essence of Judaism. In fact, that is exactly what Sigismund Stern

---

[67] Holdheim's argumentation goes as follows: The fact that circumcision has been enjoined to *all* descendants of Abraham, and not only to Isaac and his sons (i.e. the Israelites) exhibits the strictly religious character of this commandment as opposed to the national laws of the Jewish commonwealth; see idem, *Ueber die Beschneidung zunächst in religiös-dogmatischer Beziehung* (Schwerin: C. Kürschner, 1840) 50: "Für uns liegt in der Thatsache, daß alle Nachkommen Abrahams beschnitten werden mußten und nur die von Isaak abstammenden Israeliten zur Bildung des Volkes und der Nationalität allein bestimmt waren, eben der stärkste Beweis, daß die Beschneidung nicht den politisch-nationalen Charakter an sich trage und eben darum als ein rein religiöses Gebot für immer verbindliche Kraft besitze."

[68] Ibid., 7-8.

[69] Ibid., 70-71.

[70] See entry on Holdheim in Geoffrey Wigoder, *Encyclopedia of Judaism* (New York et al.: Macmillan, 1989), 343-344.

alleged.[71] Holdheim's argumentation is totally different, namely, that a Jew who works on Saturday and celebrates the Sabbath on a Sunday cannot be regarded as a bad Jew, particularly since the one who works on Saturdays and spends his Sundays with mundane pursuits is not blamed at all by most of his fellows. (To be sure, this argument is beside the point, the major issue being whether a rabbi should say "yes and amen" to such a decisive alteration of the Jewish code.) The rationale in Holdheim's argumentation is always the same, namely that honest people should not be blamed, let alone from a Jewish angle. To be sure, and here the Orthodox opponents will always be in the right, Holdheim departs from a notion of honesty and goodness which cannot find an appropriate expression in halakhic terms. However, we should always be aware that Holdheim remained nostalgic of the *shtetl*-life of his youth. He complained that the religious fervour of Polish Jews was absolutely lacking in Germany.[72] But there may be another reason for his nostalgia, namely that there cannot be any clash between "goodness" and Jewishness as long as Jews are living in a relatively closed social and economic system. This conflict only arises as soon as Jews interact with Gentiles who also have a highly developed value-system, such as in Prussia, where honesty, correctness and loyalty were held in high esteem. The clash which occurs here cannot be solved by any halakhic means and therefore a principle should be found, which one might call "meta-halakhic,"[73] to respond to a situation which the rabbis of the Talmud have never foreseen. Holdheim found it in the notion of conscience ("Gewissen"). The Jewish laws are one thing; another thing is whether they are applicable in a given situation without violating humanism, which Holdheim regards as the most basic Mosaic value. Conscience intervenes in cases where Jewish and Gentile values *collide*. Accordingly, Holdheim does not plainly state that the halakhic commandments

---

[71] See Stern, *Die Religion des Judenthums*, 238: "Wir hielten es für angemessen die Überzeugung auszusprechen, dass nicht die Heiligung eines Tages vor anderen Tagen die Bestimmung des Sabbath sei, sondern die Heiligung des Menschen an diesem Tage, der für dieselbe bestimmt ist, dass wir nicht glauben sollen, dem Gebot der Sabbathfeier nur an diesem, und nicht an einem anderen Tag genügen zu können, dass nicht der Sabbath durch den Tag, sondern der Tag durch den Sabbath bedingt werde."

[72] Samuel Holdheim, *Die rechte Buße, Predigt gehalten am Versöhnungsfeste 5611 (16. September 1850)* (Berlin: Leopold Lassar, 1850).

[73] Andreas Gotzmann, *Jüdisches Recht im kulturellen Prozeß. Die Wahrnehmung der Halacha im Deutschland des 19. Jahrhunderts* (Tübingen: J.C.B. Mohr, 1997), 234

are to be abrogated, but that in cases of collision ("im Kollisionsfalle") each individual should have the right to assess whether they are applicable or not.[74] In this respect Holdheim is in perfect agreement with Moses Mendelssohn who stated that religious authorities should not have the right to blame or to punish. But he goes much farther than Mendelssohn, indeed: Religious authorities should not only refrain from blaming deviations from ceremonial law, neither should they tolerate them as merely permissible in extremis. Holdheim claims that ritual transgressions should even be regarded as valuable if they are committed in all truthfulness. And, of course, Holdheim expressly recommends violating the ceremonial laws as soon as they conflict with the laws of the state.

Only in one respect was Holdheim absolutely uncompromising toward traditional Judaism, namely in that (like most other reformers) he regarded the messianic hope that the Temple be rebuilt and the ancient sacrifices reinstaured as obsolete. The rabbinical saying "*Tefila bimkom korban*" (prayer replaces sacrifice) should be interpreted in the sense that prayer replaces the sacrifices *once and forever* and not only provisionally as the official reading indicates. However, even here, Holdheim never entirely gives up the notion of sacrifice and states that it should be internalized and experienced as the sacrifice of our selfish impulses.[75] Stern, in contrast, radically discarded the sacrifices as belonging to a period where Jewish religion was still inspired by fear and had not yet measured up to its true ethical dimension.[76]

A word which occurs very frequently in Holdheim's work is "higher." It is the "higher" degree of knowledge achieved during the last centuries which permits the relativization of ceremonial law. In the light of fascism's frequent use of this metaphor, and given our post-war "suspicion" of language generally, the use of spatial imagery, or references to a "higher" or "lower" level of understanding have all come to seem increasingly problematic.[77] And if we add to that

---

[74] About the use of the notion of collision ("Kollisionsfall") in Holdheim see idem, *Ueber die Autonomie der Rabbinen*, 104-105, note 71; 108, note 76. In case of collision, Holdheim argues, the general rule is that the positive commandment has priority over the negative one.

[75] I dealt with this subject extensively in my essay "Metaphor as the Internalisation of a Ritual—with a Case Study on Samuel Holdheim," passim.

[76] Stern, *Die Religion des Judenthums*, 118-119.

[77] See Ralph Bisschops, "Metapher, Wert und Rang," *Revue Belge de Philologie et d'Histoire* 68 (1990), 636-645.

the implication that somehow Reform Judaism has found a way of transcending basic Mosaic beliefs, it is easy to see why such utterances have a jarring effect on contemporary readers. Still, one must be a very astute philosopher and a great stylist as well to dissociate oneself from the vocabulary of one's time. However inappropriate it may seem today, Holdheim's use of the word "higher" is an expression of his growing presentiment that increasing interaction with other peoples naturally leads to the awareness that every human being is a link in "the great chain of humanity" ("die große Kette der Menschheit"), and to some feeling about what is ethically self-evident and what is not. Holdheim did not suggest that Judaism would be left behind as a result of this development, but he was convinced that humanity was evolving to a more unified state of moral consciousness and that in the light of this evolutionary turn it would be unacceptably parochial to adopt exclusively Jewish religious standards when talking about the value and respectability of a human being. As Holdheim observed in one of his earliest sermons at Schwerin,[78] there is the Jew, on the one hand, and the human being on the other. The Jew in a person should not be overvalued at the expense of the human being. And in the same way, just as Jews no longer adopt Jewish standards when evaluating adherents of other religions, they should also refrain from evaluating their fellows from the single viewpoint of whether or not they are behaving like good Jews. "Only the human being should be valued in each person," Holdheim says in the same sermon,[79] and not his membership in a nation or religious community. Even the religious education of a person is something external to his/her intimate relationship with God. However, Holdheim has never really made peace with the idea that this highly revolutionary shift in the ethical awareness has led him to a meta-halakhic level of thinking. In this respect Holdheim appears to be traditionalist to the core: everything, even the idea that there can be values which are not necessarily Jewish, *must* be reflected in the Scriptures. Holdheim's so-called "higher" ethical consciousness is certainly not to be understood as something which goes beyond Sinaitic revelation. It actually refers to the greater level of interaction between Jews and Gentiles which urges Judaism

---

[78] Samuel Holdheim, *Jakob und Israel. Predigt, gehalten zu Schwerin 12. Dec. 1840* (Schwerin: C. Kürschner, 1841).
[79] Ibid., 6.

to dismiss beliefs and practices fostering national and ethnical cohesion. What emerges out of this process is not a transformed Judaism but a simplified one.

Particularly by the end of his life, Holdheim reached, both in content and in tone, a remarkable equilibrium between past and present, his respect of the traditionalism of the fathers and his uncompromising commitment to Reform in its universalistic outreach. In one of his last sermons,[80] Holdheim says that the universalistic impetus of modern Jews should not cause them to forget the many stages their ancestors have gone through and should remember them with love and respect. Without these stages present-day Judaism would have been bereft of the universalistic message lying at the core of the Sinaitic Covenant. Holdheim's answer to the traditionalists who reject the Reform movement sounds much less polemic now than in his earlier writings: they also, he argues, behave according to universal ethical standards, the only difference consisting in the fact that they want the *ancient* practices to be proclaimed from the pulpit. In fact, they do not observe the ritual laws either, but they do not wish that this disobedience become a part of their doctrine. Holdheim, in contrast, argues for the concordance between teaching and practice.

Holdheim's claim that Judaism is *not* capable of an endless development will receive its most eloquent expression when he deals with Christianity, an issue we shall deal with in the next section.

14. Stern's and Holdheim's Attitude to Christianity

Many Orthodox Jews regard Reform Judaism as a movement which tries to bridge the gap between Judaism and Christianity and is even willing to embrace Christian positions to this purpose. In fact, the issue of how the Reform movement defines its position toward Christianity, is a thing everybody wants to know but nobody dares to ask, to paraphrase the title of Woody Allen's film. Over the last few decades, even in Reform Jewish circles the complaint is not unfamiliar that "one has protestantized" enough.

---

[80] Idem, "Der Bund," in idem, *Sechs Predigten* (Berlin: Im Selbstverlage der Witwe des sel. Verfassers, 1863), 49-59.

The distance from Christianity is perceived by many as a kind of litmus-test for genuine Jewishness; the closer one comes to Christian positions the less one is perceived as Jewish. This is not only due to the fact that many Christians behaved badly toward Jews, but also to the fact, observed by Jacob Neusner,[81] that rabbinical Judaism has defined itself in opposition to Christianity. The emergence of Judaism's greatest enemy out of its own ranks must have deeply traumatized the rabbis. This may be one of the reasons why they tried to present Jewish teaching as a consistent system, smoothing down all historical discrepancies such as between Torah-based and prophetic Judaism, in order to prevent such a religious rebellion ever occuring again. In the nineteenth century, prophetic Judaism, particularly as reflected in the books of Isaiah, came to be appreciated as a religious movement in its own right and as the deepest expression of Jewish religiosity. Then, however, the issue arises, of how far it is still necessary to uphold a separate identity with respect to Christianity, which also claims to be a heir of the prophets.

Comparing Stern's and Holdheim's writings appears highly interesting in this respect, since it presents us with two diametrically opposed ways of responding to this charged issue. But first we shall explore what Holdheim and Stern have in common.

If we compare the Berlin Reformers of the 1840s with the previous reformers, from Israel Jacobson onwards, one thing meets the eye, namely that they represented a self-assertive way of coping with their Jewish identity. Where Israel Jacobson was above all concerned with how Christians perceive Judaism and tried to adapt Jewish liturgy to Christian practices lest it looked too exotic, Holdheim and Stern, but also Abraham Geiger,[82] were thoroughly convinced that there is a Jewish genius and that Judaism has to teach something to the world. This self-awareness impacted upon their way of regarding the history of Christianity. Both, Holdheim and Stern, regarded Christianity as a ruse of history, spreading Mosaic monotheism and ethics throughout the world in pagan disguise. In its pure form Mosaic faith would have been uncongenial to the Greeks and the Romans, therefore the idea of a personified god was necessary to respond to the pagan need

---

[81] Jacob Neusner, *Rabbinic Judaism, Structure and System* (Minneapolis: Fortress Press, 1995), 213-214.
[82] Susannah Heschel, *Abraham Geiger and the Jewish Jesus* (Chicago: University of Chicago Press, 1998).

for a concrete representation of the divine. But this god who has become a man was only a pedagogical "trick" to raise the pagan mind to the knowledge that there is only one God and to spread the Jewish knowledge of God ("Gotteserkenntnis") to the Gentile nations. This highly inclusivist perception of Christianity —perhaps as offensive to Christians as Christian supersessionism is to Jews—is also manifest in Holdheim's and Stern's appreciation of Lutheran Reformation, which they regarded as an attempt at stripping the burdens of paganism and as the starting point of a still ongoing move Christians were accomplishing toward true ethical monotheism. Having expounded the basic assumptions of the Berlin reformers on Christianity, we now are faced with the question of whether there is still any rationale for upholding a separate Jewish religious identity. In this respect Stern appears to be much more ready to compromise than Holdheim, who pleaded for a more cautious approach.

Sigismund Stern contends that the historical mission of Christianity consists in spreading *and* developing further the Jewish message. It was Christianity, he argues, that freed ethical monotheism from nationalistic limitedness and invited all humans to join the covenant community, thereby raising Judaism to a higher spiritual level.[83] The only thing dimming Stern's eulogy of Christianity is the divinization of Christ which is a remnant of paganism. The Reformation, however, has brought Christianity much closer to Jews, having done justice to its Jewish origin and having cleared Christian faith of some (but not all) pagan relics. With the emergence of the Reformation, Jews and Christians are called to join their efforts in bringing the Jewish knowledge of God to humanity.

Finally, Stern appeals to this growing kinship between Judaism and Christianity in his claim that Judaism should become recognized as an official religion of the Prussian state, together with Protestantism and Catholicism. Albeit a state whose very principle consists in being a bulwark of Protestantism on the European continent, Prussia recognizes Catholicism as a state religion and not Judaism, Stern complains. Yet, it is the latter with which Prussia shares the most basic

---

[83] Stern, *Die Aufgabe des Judenthums*, 56: "Denn was in ihr (i.e. der christlichen Kirche) zur Erscheinung kam, war nicht nur eine Überwindung des Heidentums, sondern auch eine offenbare höhere Entwicklung des Judentums, nämlich die Befreiung der Religion vom nationalen Element, [....], die Erhebung derselben zu einem allgemeinen Besitz der Menschheit."

ideals. Both Protestantism and Judaism, Stern claims, celebrate freedom of conscience. Therefore Prussia should regard its Jewish citizens as its most precious allies in carrying out its historical mission.

The idea of a joint venture between Judaism and Christianity is certainly not to be found in Holdheim. To him the fact that Christianity has become a world religion is an accident of history much more than a historical necessity. In fact, Judaism was destined to become the universal religion. If the Jews had grasped the spiritual essence of Jewish religion and had ended the cult of the Temple hundred years earlier, then "Judaism would have poured over the Gentile nations as a spiritual flood and would not have left the honour of destroying the heathen altars to alien hands and alien names."[84]

Neither is Holdheim prepared to admit that Christianity has reached a higher level of consciousness or religiosity than Judaism. True, it has abandoned the Cult of the Temple, but at a high cost, that is to say, whilst paradoxically reinforcing the belief that sins can only be expiated by sacrifice, or to be more precise, by Jesus' blood which has been shed once and forever for the redemption of mankind.[85] Judaism, on the contrary, has overcome this archaic notion by stating that prayer replaces sacrifices.

Furthermore, unlike Sigismund Stern, Holdheim is unwilling to accept theological concessions to Christianity as a consequence of Judaism's claim to be the true religion of humanity[86] ("Menschheitsreligion"[87]).

---

[84] Holdheim, *Die wesentlichen Erfordernisse eines ächt jüdischen Gottesdienstes*, 8: "Hätte man die Idee des Judentums geistig erfaßt, geistig fortgebildet, den Opferdienst hundert Jahre früher abgeschafft und die 'Anbetung Gottes im Geiste und Herzen,' wie die Propheten sie lehrten, als das Höchste in der Vordergrund gestellt, das Judentum hätte sicherlich nicht eine neue Religion aus seinem Schoße geboren werden sehen, die eine so feindliche Stellung zu demselben einnahm, sondern hätte sich selbst wie ein Geistesstrom über die Völker ergossen, hätte den Ruhm, die heidnischen Altäre zu stürzen, nicht fremden Händen und fremden Namen überlassen müssen."

[85] Idem, *Geschichte der Entstehung und der Entwicklung der jüdischen Reformgemeinde in Berlin*, 94.

[86] Idem, *Ueber Das Gebetbuch nach dem Gebrauche des neuen Israelitischen Tempelvereins zu Hamburg. Ein Votum von Dr. S. Holdheim* (Hamburg: B. S. Berendsohn, 1841) 17: "Ich weiß nicht, woher es kommt, und es beruhet augenscheinlich auf Unkunde und Verkennung des ganzen, die Religion durchdringenden Geistes, wenn Glaubensgenossen von unserer religiösen Zukunft sprechen, als wenn wir eine besondere religiöse Zukunft hätten, als wenn die religiöse Zukunft auf die wir hoffen, nicht die Zukunft der ganzen Menschheit wäre, als wenn die Propheten (Jes 11,9. Sachar. 13,20. Zephania 3,10 u. a. m.) von einer engherzigen, Israel allein zu Gute kommenden und nicht die ganze Menschheit begreifenden Erlösung gesprochen hätten."

[87] The term appears in idem, *Ha-emuna ve-ha-deah Jüdische Glaubens- und Sittenlehre* (Berlin: Julius Springer, 1857), 109.

He makes it uncompromisingly clear that the world religion to come
will be definitely Jewish in character and not a syncretism of Judaism
and Christianity.[88]

In this context Holdheim takes up again what he stated about the
impossibility of any further development of Judaism: under no circumstances can the Mosaic covenant be regarded as the forerunner of
a new covenant. This raises the issue of how Mosaic Judaism can be
regarded as universalistic in scope while it addresses first and foremost
the Jewish nation. Holdheim answers that Mosaic Judaism is the particularistic embodiment of a more ancient and thoroughly universalistic idea in order to preserve its message through history.[89] Holdheim
has never been very consistent in his attempts to locate this "more ancient," that is to say more authentic Judaism in the Scriptures. First
he says that it is the life of the patriarchs,[90] then he points to Abrahamic
covenant,[91] finally he declares the seven Noachide laws to be the quin-
tessence of Jewish religious teaching addressing all human beings as
well.[92] One striking difference, then, between Holdheim and Stern can
be derived from the above considerations: while Stern located the essence
of Judaism in a distant future, Holdheim located it in a remote past.

15. Who is a Jew?

Suppose that, as Holdheim says, Judaism and not a syncretism
between Judaism and Christianity is called to be the religion of

---

[88] Idem, *Predigten über die jüdische Religion. Ein Buch der religiösen Belehrung und Erbauung
für's jüdische Haus, gehalten im Gotteshause der jüdischen Reform-Gemeinde zu Berlin* (Berlin:
Carl David's Buchhandlung, 1853), 164: "Noch kann es [das Judentum] nicht daran
denken; mit anderen Bekenntnissen zu verschmelzen, irgend eine seiner eigentüm-
lichen Anschauungen zum Opfer zu bringen, damit die anderen sich ihm nähern.
Es gilt vielmehr, die Kraft, die Gotteskraft des Judentums in ihrer Reinheit und
Wahrheit den Völkern als Leuchte vorzuhalten, damit sie nicht glauben und sprechen,
das Judentum sei eine seit beinahe zwei Jahrtausenden überwundene Bildungsstufe,
an welche die erleuchtete Menschheit der Gegenwart nicht anknüpfen könne."

[89] Idem, *Vorträge über die mosaische Religion für denkende Israeliten*, 51-52: "Das
beziehungsweise Alte, nämlich das alte Gesetz, war also nicht Vorbereitung eines
Neuen, sondern eine passende Umhüllung des noch Ältern; das Alte hatte also nicht
seine Begründung und Erklärung in einem Neuen, sondern im Ältesten, dem es
eine Zeitlang als äußerliches, schützendes Gewand diente, so lange diente, bis es
ihm entbehrlich und darum seines Dienstes für immer entledigt wurde."

[90] Ibid., 31.

[91] Ibid., 53.

[92] Ibid., 159.

humanity ("Menschheitsreligion"), does that mean that everyone can become a Jew? This issue presents us with a very problematic aspect of Jewish universalism as put forward by the Berlin reformers. In fact, the conversion issue was far from topical in those days. If there were any conversions to Judaism at all, they were made by the descendants of Jews who converted to Christianity.[93] For a Christian to convert to Judaism was social suicide; even his status as a German citizen would have been put at risk by such a step. True, the German reformers such as Geiger, Stern and Holdheim insisted on the fact that Judaism has always welcomed conversions, but such statements only aimed at proving that Judaism is not that exclusive as Christians generally tend to believe. In no way they can be interpreted as an encouragement to convert to Judaism. However, in the light of the growing importance the conversion issue has gained in Reform Judaism, especially over the last twenty years, one might be tempted to ask who, in Holdheim's view, is a Jew. His statements come very close to those of Stern, in that he regards anyone who loves God and walks in his ways as being part of the chosen people. The practical consequence of this open-mindedness was Holdheim's willingness to celebrate marriages between Jews and Christians.[94] However, does that mean that he regards anyone who professes ethical monotheism as a Jew? In this connection I would like to draw the reader's attention to a highly significant passage, where Holdheim discusses the *Shema Israel* and asks whether everyone who recites the *Shema* is a Jew. Holdheim's answer is unambiguously "no." Even if one who recites the verse "Hear O Israel, the Lord is our God the Lord is one" shares the basics of Jewish faith, he would never be capable of sharing Jewish *fate*. Jewish prayer, Holdheim argues, is intimately connected with centuries of persecution.[95] True, the verses of the *Shema* are destined to become the credo of the whole of humanity, nonetheless we may never forget that their message has been carried and preserved by the Jewish people throughout the ages, Holdheim argues, and that their historical mission has gone along with exclusion and suffering. Though Judaism is not limited to a national

---

[93] The Prussian law of July 28, 1848, allowed Jews converted to Christianity to re-convert to Judaism without losing their citizenship.

[94] Idem, *Einsegnung einer gemischten Ehe* (Berlin: J. A. Stargardt, 1849), 7.

[95] Idem, *Predigten über die jüdische Religion*, 148: "Wir können uns einen jüdischen Glauben ohne das jüdische Volk, welches für ihn gelitten und geduldet, welches für ihn tausend Märtyrertode gestorben ist, nicht denken."

ethnicity, it is neither something "floating in the air" ("der jüdische Glaube schwebte niemals in der Luft"). It would be a dangerous mistake to disconnect Jewish faith from its "native soil," i.e. the "spirit and the soul" ("Gemüt") of the Jewish people.[96] Jewish faith is not the result of human thinking but of Jewish life. The example of Abraham should not shake our view; his monotheism was merely an unaccomplished idea which had to be realized by his descendants.[97] Holdheim hastens to make clear that all of this does not vitiate the universal destiny of the Jewish faith. However, he also stresses that Judaism should be protected against the outside world ("die Stellung nach außen wahren"). As to the question of what Jewish universalism really means, he simply goes back to the well-known rabbinical distinction between Mosaic laws on the one hand and the Noachide laws on the other.[98] The seven Noachide laws are that part of Jewish faith which is destined to be shared by all men and women of the world. Mosaic law, on the contrary, is the exclusive property of the Jewish people ("für Israel allein und ausschließlich"). It cannot escape our notice that this surprisingly traditionalist way of viewing Israel's mission—which even the most obdurate Orthodox would agree with—conflicts with Holdheim's own theology. How could he appeal to Mosaic law, after having dismissed the largest part

---

[96] Ibid., 149: "Es ist zwar in jüdischen Kreisen sprichwörtlich geworden: wer mit dem Aufrufe 'Höre Israel' den einzigen Gott bekennt, sei ein Bekenner des Judenthums. Der Satz findet sich im Talmud und lautet 'wer es anerkennt, es gibt nur einen Gott, der ist Jude.' Aber es ist nur gesagt, der Jude, welcher den einzigen Gott bekennt, hat sich zum ganzen Judenthum bekannt, nicht aber auch, dass ein Fremder, welcher dieses Bekenntnis ablegt, ein Bekenner des Judenthums geworden. Denn Judenthum, meine Freunde, ist nicht das Bekenntnis des einzigen Gottes, wie der und jener philosophische Denker es als das Ergebnis seiner Forschung gefunden, sondern Judenthum ist dieses Bekenntnis des einzigen Gottes, wie es eine beinah viertausendjährige Geschichte im Geiste und im Leben des jüdischen Volkes bezeugt und bewahrheitet, erprobt und beglaubigt, wie sie es zum unerschütterlichen Fels des Glaubens und der inneren Überzeugung im Gemüthe der Juden ausgeprägt hat."

[97] Ibid., 150

[98] Ibid., 158: "Die alten jüdischen Weisen, obgleich hinsichtlich dessen, was innerhalb des Judenthums religiöse Geltung haben soll, einen viel beschränkteren Standpunkt einnehmend, haben doch über diese wichtige, das Verhältnis des Judenthums zur Menschheit betreffende Frage das Richtige getroffen und es glücklich wiedergegeben. Für die Völker der Erde—sagten sie—seien die sieben noachidischen Pflichten, *Bneï Noach scheva mitsvoth*, die Grundregeln des Glaubens- und der Sittenlehre, geboten, für Israel allein und ausschließlich das ganze mosaische Gesetz; jene müssen wir über alle Völker verbreiten, dieses als Israels ausschließliches Eigenthum für uns bewahren."

of it, namely all those laws which are tied up with the existence of the Jewish people as a nation dwelling on the Holy Land, and furthermore after having declared that the ritual and dietary laws are only binding in so far as they further religious devotion? Not unaware of this problem, Holdheim writes that that what the rabbis have called Mosaic law is to be redefined as the "indelible historical particularity of the Jewish people" and its "specific spiritual life."[99]

To be sure, Holdheim has not clung to this position systematically; the importance of respectively the Mosaic and the Noachide part of Jewish heritage remains problematic in his writing and to the end of his life he tends to regard the Noachide laws as the very core of Judaism. Nonetheless it remains highly significant that Holdheim uncritically takes up this ancient Talmudic distinction when he comes to discuss the charged issue of who is a Jew. It indicates that the issue of Jewish universalism, despite all solemn declarations, remains undecided in Holdheim's work.[100] The hypothesis seems to be legitimate that his universalism had a pragmatic function, opposing the inclination to ethnicism of his contemporaries, rather than representing a carefully considered theological position.

The difference between Holdheim and Stern is, of course, also one between two personalities and biographies. Holdheim was raised in an Orthodox Polish community and steeped in rabbinical Judaism. The Lithuanian orientation of his community accounts for the fact that he was inclined to the daring idea that Judaism has to teach something to the Gentile world. He was much akin to his contemporary Israel Salanter, an Orthodox rabbi who tried to convince the German authorities that Talmud should be taught in all German high schools, judging it indispensable for the development of the human mind.[101] Stern, in contrast, was brought up in Christian schools, receiving his religious education from a private tutor.

---

[99] Ibid., 159: "Was die alten Lehrer die 'sieben noachidischen Pflichten' als das Antheil der Menschheit nennen, das nennen wir den jüdischen Gottesgedanken und die jüdische sittliche Weltanschauung; was sie das ganze mosaische Ceremonialgesetz als das ewige und ausschließliche Erbe Israels bezeichnen, das nennen wir: die unauslöschliche geschichtliche Eigenthümlichkeit des jüdischen Volkes, das eigenthümliche Geistesleben des Judenthums."

[100] See also Meyer, *Response to Modernity*, 84: "Holdheim never did become a consistent universalist."

[101] Louis Ginzberg, "Israel Salanter," in *Understanding Rabbinic Judaism. From Talmudic to Modern Times*, ed. Jacob Neusner (New York: Ktav Publishing House, 1974), 362.

Both Stern and Holdheim were versed in German literature and philosophy, the former however had countless connections with Gentiles (the most renowned of which was Theodor Fontane), while Holdheim, as a rabbi, remained mainly surrounded by Jews.

16. Conclusion and Summary

Both Samuel Holdheim and Sigismund Stern regarded Judaism as the expression and the sanctification of life, which entails that the ancient codifications cannot claim to be perennial. Life changes, therefore Torah, which is first and foremost *torat chaim* (a Torah of life) should change. The present contrastive analysis reveals some aspects in Holdheim's thinking and personality which make him appear much more equilibrated than he has been depicted until now.

While Sigismund Stern argued along the lines of the "either-or"-philosophy, suggesting that a faithful Jew in the traditional sense cannot measure up to his new status in German society, Holdheim claimed that both Jewish tradition and modernity should be affirmed with *equal determination*. In the Middle Ages the religious principle was predominant, he argued, then came the centuries of Rationalism and Enlightenment which stressed universal humanity at the expense of religion. He believed that in his century, which he regarded as an era of *Restoration*, both principles, religion and universal humanism, would become reconciled.[102]

While Stern was deeply influenced by Hegelian historicism, Holdheim operated on a formal, more Kantian level. Upon leaving the ghetto and entering the Gentile world, Jews were presented with conflicting value systems, Holdheim observed, and the religious doctrines which tried to solve this conflict, i.e. the Conservative and Neo-Orthodox movements, failed to produce answers which could be felt as satisfactory from the viewpoint of ethics. Generating an ambivalent attitude toward the gentile world, they conflicted with Holdheim's ideal of wholeness. On the other hand he was unwilling to accept a merging of Jewish and Christian notions, as Stern did.

Unfortunately, the result of this cautiousness is that one of

---

[102] Holdheim, *Geschichte der Entstehung und der Entwicklung der jüdischen Reformgemeinde in Berlin*, 8-10.

Holdheim's basic claims that Jewish faith is universalistic in scope remains problematic. His distinction between the universal core message of the Hebrew Bible and its particularistic wordings has never found a positive expression in his work; that is to say, he never provided a satisfactory answer to the issue of which teachings in Jewish tradition exactly address the whole of humanity, except perhaps for the Noachide Laws and monotheism in its pure form.

Finally, I would like to stress that Holdheim's acceptance of modernity is above all rooted in his faith. It emerges out of the firm confidence that *Judaism cannot be extinguished by emancipation* and not even by assimilation. Unlike Sigismund Stern, Holdheim was unwilling to claim that Jews should play a substantial role in world history at all costs, but he firmly rejected the idea that Jews should stay away from Gentile professions out of fear of being assimilated.[103] Behaving this way, he says, is to distrust God's providence. One should commend one's ways to God and trust him instead of intervening in his plans out of exaggerated fear. Judaism is like a star, Holdheim says, hundreds of light years away. Even when it extinguishes, humanity would still benefit from its light for centuries.[104]

---

[103] Idem, *Vorträge über die mosaische Religion*, 122-123.
[104] Idem, *Licht im Lichte! oder: Das Judenthum und die Freiheit. Eine Festpredigt, gehalten am Wochenfeste Schabuoth 5519....im Gotteshause der jüdischen Reformgemeinde zu Berlin* (Berlin: W. J. Peiser, 1859), 6.

TRUE MOSAIC RELIGION: SAMUEL HIRSCH, SAMUEL HOLDHEIM AND THE REFORM OF JUDAISM*

Judith Frishman

In 1842 the first draft of a statement of principles concerning Judaism and its practice was prepared by what would later be known as the *Frankfurter jüdische Reformfreunde*. One year later, in 1843, Bruno Bauer published *Die Judenfrage* in which he linked the hotly debated issue of the emancipation of the Jews to a critique of Judaism, Christianity and society as a whole. That the two works appeared within a short period of time is hardly surprising, for the issue of religious reform in Judaism in the nineteenth century was no internal matter. Jews and non-Jews, rabbis and lay leaders, prominent theologians, philosophers, politicians and government officials took part in public discussions whereby reform and emancipation were intertwined. Without explicitly mentioning the *Reformfreunde*, Bauer attacked the radical reforms they had proposed. Subsequent proposals for reform by Jewish thinkers involved the quest for a middle ground between Bauer's rejection of Jewish religious reform and the radical reform of the *Reformfreunde*. This paper will focus specifically on the philosophical-theological solutions offered by Samuel Hirsch (1815-1889) and Samuel Holdheim (1806-1860) and the development of their thought in the 1840s.

1. The Reformfreunde and Bruno Bauer

The *Reformfreunde*'s initial statement of principles consisted of five points in which its authors 1) considered the Mosaic religion

* This article was first printed in *Religious Identity and the Problem of Historical Foundation: The Foundational Character of Authoritative Sources in the History of Christianity and Judaism*, ed. Judith Frishman (Leiden: Brill 2004), 195-222.

capable of a continuing development; 2) considered the ritual, dietary and other laws pertaining to corporal practice which originated in the ancient polity, for example, 3) circumcision, not binding as a religious act or a symbol; 4) did not recognize the Talmud as an authority; 5) neither awaited nor wished for a messiah who would lead the Jews back to Palestine, but rather regarded the land to which they belonged by birth or civil status as their sole fatherland.[1] The issues with which mid-nineteenth century German Jewry was confronted are clearly reflected in this statement, and I will briefly refer to some of these here.

The use of the term "Mosaic religion" in the first point was influenced by eighteenth and nineteenth century Protestant biblical scholarship in which a distinction was made between an earlier, prophetic mosaic-Israelite religion and a later, priestly-rabbinical Jewish religion. The later—Jewish—religion was the religion of priestly particularism, hierarchy and tyranny—characteristics not only associated with rabbinic Judaism but with Catholicism as well. It was not the rabbi but the Christian biblical scholar who truly understood the meaning of the Mosaic Law; and it was not rabbinic Judaism but Christianity that was the proper fulfilment of Jewish history. The persistence of Judaism placed Jews against the course of history, a feature that they shared with other "orientals."[2] As James Pasto has noted in a recent article:

> Two fundamental features informed and to some degree still inform Euro-Christian studies of Judaism: first, the presumption of Christian authority to define the Jewish past; and second, the assumption of immutable difference between Christianity and Judaism.[3]

In reaction, Jewish thinkers in the nineteenth century set out to prove that their religion was capable of change and equal, if not superior to Christianity. They thereby consciously and unconsciously internalised the negative judgment held by non-Jews of Judaism in general and rabbinic Judaism in particular. Thus the reference to the

---

[1] For a detailed discussion of the *Reformfreunde* see Michael A. Meyer, "Alienated Intellectuals in the Camp of Religious Reform: The Frankfurt Reformfreunde, 1842-1845," *Association of Jewish Studies Review* 6 (1981) 61-86.

[2] The term "orientalism" was coined by Edward Said in his famous book, *Orientalism. Western Conceptions of the Orient* (London: Routledge & Kegan, 1978).

[3] James Pasto, "Islam's 'Strange Secret Sharer': Orientalism, Judaism and the Jewish Question," *Comparative Studies in Society and History* 30 (1998) 437-474, here 440.

Mosaic religion was an attempt of the *Reformfreunde* to identify themselves with the earlier and more acceptable form of Judaism. At the same time it was clearly stated that this religion was capable of development so that Jews need not necessarily stand outside of history.

The re-evaluation of rabbinic authority did not derive solely from the negative assessment of Christian biblical scholars. Once the corporate identity so characteristic of the medieval Jewish communities was dissolved, the realm of jurisdiction allocated to rabbinic authority became less clearly delimited. Although since the fall of the second temple, non-Jewish law had superseded Jewish law in specific instances, growing state intervention at the end of the eighteenth century in what had previously been considered internal matters, led to a redefinition of the categories of religious and civil law. In their statement, the *Reformfreunde* explicitly denied the authority of the Talmud, thereby implicitly rejecting rabbinic Judaism and the authority of the contemporary rabbis.

The fervent hope for emancipation called the distinction between Jew and non-Jew into question. If the Jews were to be considered the members of a nation, how could they become loyal citizens of states other than their own? And if granted civil equality, should they maintain ceremonial laws that—according to some—served the sole purpose of distinguishing between Jew and non-Jew and at least hampered full integration? In answer to these questions the *Reformfreunde* denied the hope for a return to Zion and simply declared the dietary laws and circumcision as no longer binding.

Bruno Bauer (1809-1882), the biblical scholar whose radical historical critique of the New Testament led to his dismissal from the University of Bonn in 1842, was one of the most influential among those who introduced the theories of biblical scholars on Judaism into the political debates concerning the emancipation of the Jews.[4] He argued against those who claimed that the Jews had become that which they were on account of the oppression under which they lived in the Christian world. The Jews were oppressed, he countered, because of their oriental nature. They clung to their nationality and resisted the movements and changes of history, "while the

---

[4] Two and a half thousand publications concerning the emancipation of the Jews appeared between 1815 and 1850. See Michael A. Meyer and Michael Brenner, eds., *German-Jewish History in Modern Times*, vol 2. (New York: Columbia University Press, 1997), 32f.

will of history is evolution, new forms, progress, change."[5] The oriental does not know freedom because he does not maintain universal laws based on reason. To the contrary, the Jew's law demands
that he segregate himself from others:

> He sees his highest task in the performance of mindless, baseless cer-
> emonies [....]. He performs his religious ceremonies again and again
> [....] and he is content that they are just so and must be so because
> he knows of no reason other than this is so and has to be so accord-
> ing to the will of a higher, inscrutable being.[6]

The question is therefore not whether the Jews should be granted
citizenship but whether they, who do not know freedom and reason, are capable of accepting universal human rights and granting
them to others.

One might think that the reform of Judaism would help to change
the Jews' situation. Yet, Bauer notes, there are statesmen who claim
that Jews who disregard the law and introduce reforms lose the respect
of their fellow citizens (which, in Bauer's view, certainly says something about the level of the state!). The real question, however, is:

> whether the Jews are able to obey their ancient law, whether their
> present relationship to the law raises their morality, whether the rela-
> tionship can really be a moral one, since it is even doubtful what is
> really their law [....] is it the Mosaic law or the Talmud?[7]

There are those who claim that the Mosaic law contains the purest
moral doctrine and all that is necessary is to return to pure or
reformed Mosaism. But to which Mosaic law do they refer? To that
which contains the sacrificial rites, the order of priests and the distribution of property? The reformers' suggestion that these be dropped
means, according to Bauer, demolishing the centre to which all other
commandments refer. Moreover:

> [....] the Mosaic code contains, in principle, in its most important
> regulations, all the hardships of rabbinic Judaism, so that no return to
> it and no reform short of complete abolition can a mean a real lib-
> eration from the commands of the Talmud.[8]

---

[5] Bruno Bauer, *The Jewish Problem*, trans. Helen Lederer (Cincinnati, OH: Hebrew
Union College-Jewish Institute of Religion, 1958), 5. All further remarks pertaining
to Bauer's *Die Judenfrage* (1843) will refer to the English translation.
[6] Ibid., 13.
[7] Ibid., 27.
[8] Ibid., 28.

The law is impracticable, but instead of realizing that the law origi-
nates from the nature of circumstances, the Jews attribute it to the
inexplicable will of God. No universal truth could ever emerge from
such a dumb national spirit that is willing to practice arbitrary or even
unsuitable rites. Dietary matters, cooking, the home—all that which
is accidental as opposed to the true and necessary—belong to the
highest concern of life, i.e. to religion.[9] In sum, a community that sees
its salvation in the future or in heaven can't participate wholeheartedly in the affairs of the state and the events of history.[10] The only
remedy is for the Jew to give up his chimerical nationality, relinquish
belief in servitude and believe instead in freedom and humanity. The
Jew must do nothing less than cease to be a Jew, for only then would
his law not interfere with the duties toward the state and his fellow
citizens. But even this will not suffice, for "the problem of emancipation," Bauer claims, "is the problem of our age."[11] Not only does
the Jew need to be emancipated: it is only because no one is free and
privilege is the ruling power that the Jews were not granted freedom.
In a Christian state, privileges must be respected and protected because
the state is organized upon them. In the *juste milieu* the Jew should
not be emancipated as a Jew but as a human being in a society that
consists of human beings and is not based on privileges.

Bauer's extensive and harsh criticism of Judaism and religious
reform posed a challenge to those Jews desiring some form of change
in Judaism. While the methods for effectuating change were various,
a shift in orientation took place in the course of the nineteenth century. Early initiatives in the area of liturgy were undertaken by Jewish
laymen and not justified systematically. The most frequent form of
argumentation in the first half of the century was clearly located
within the halakhic framework. Support for reform was sought in
minority opinions, or in corrections of so-called faulty reasoning
which had occurred somewhere along the line. This included an historical approach that would make certain decisions irrelevant or inap-
plicable, once historical circumstances had changed.[12] The more

---

[9] Ibid., 39.
[10] Ibid., 47.
[11] Ibid., 63.
[12] For an excellent survey of reform in the beginning of the nineteenth century,
see Andreas Gotzmann, *Jüdisches Recht im kulturellen Prozeß. Die Wahrnehmung der Halacha
im Deutschland des 19. Jahrhunderts* (Tübingen: J.C.B. Mohr, 1997), esp. 129-197.

radical approaches that were to follow by the 1840s and are reflected in the draft of the *Reformfreunde*, called the authority of the Talmud and the rabbis into question and denied the revelatory nature of the oral torah. Turning at first to a "purer Mosaic" teaching, critical thinkers often went on to challenge the validity of laws, ceremonies and customs contained in the written torah. The legal system, no longer perceived to be the heart of Judaism, soon began to be replaced by diverse philosophies in which one idea or another was singled out as being central. The relationship between the philosophies and the Judaism of the past was not always clear. The place of law and ritual within these new concepts had to be worked out anew. The fact that commandments were of divine origin—if acknowledged to be so—did not suffice to legitimate their practice. Objective but also subjective criteria were to play a role. The circumcision controversy of 1843-1844, which will be dealt with in the following section is a case in point.

2. The Circumcision Controversy

The final, officially circulated version of the *Reformfreunde's* statement read as follows: 1) We recognize in Mosaism the possibility of an unlimited further development (*unbeschränkte Fortbildung* as opposed to the earlier *fortdauernde Entwicklung*). 2) The collection called the Talmud, as well as all rabbinic writings and statutes which rest upon it, possess no binding force for us, either in dogma or in practice. 3) We neither expect nor desire a Messiah who is to lead the Israelites back to the land of Palestine; we recognize no fatherland other than that to which we belong by birth or civil status.[13] A striking omission is points two and three of the first draft, i.e. "ritual, dietary and other laws of corporal practice such as circumcision" are "considered not binding as a religious act or symbol."

The *Reformfreunde*, fearing the public reaction to such radical thought, chose to act prudently. However, these points had already been leaked to the press and resulted in condemnation. Adding to the consternation was the institution of a new law by the Frankfurt city government in 1843 regulating circumcision, which was now to

---

[13] See Meyer, "Alienated Intellectuals in the Camp of Religious Reform," *passim.*

be overseen by the health department. The law opened with the words „Israelitische Bürger und Einwohner, *insofern* sie ihre Kinder beschneiden *lassen wollen* [....]" [italics J. F.]. Up to that moment all children were to be registered with the government either by baptism or by circumcision. The wording of the law seemed to imply that a Jewish father could choose whether or not to circumcise his son. Not surprisingly, two Jewish men refused to circumcise their sons. Solomon Abraham Trier (1758-1846), chief rabbi of Frankfurt, sought to exclude these children and their fathers from the Jewish community. He requested rabbis representing a broad range of positions on Jewish law, to provide responsa regarding measures to be taken against someone who refused to circumcise his child. These *Rabbinische Gutachten über die Beschneidung*, published in 1844,[14] dealt with the importance of circumcision as a rite, the Jewish status of an uncircumcised child and the authority of the rabbis to determine the membership of father and child in the Jewish community.[15] A responsum by Samuel Hirsch was included in the volume. This response was related to his earlier, more theoretical work *Die Religionsphilosophie der Juden* (1842)[16] and led to the publication of *Die Reform im Judenthum* (1844).[17] Although Samuel Holdheim chose not to participate in the edition of the *Gutachten*, he published his own reaction—*Ueber die Beschneidung zunächst in religiös-dogmatischer Beziehung* (1844)[18]—which was clearly tied to his earlier *Ueber die Autonomie der Rabbinen und das Prinzip der jüdischen Ehe* (1843).[19] He was to summarize both works and openly reject the *Reformfreunde's*

---

[14] Salomon Abraham Trier, ed., *Rabbinische Gutachten über die Beschneidung* (Frankfurt: Bach, 1844).

[15] The circumcision controversy has been dealt with at length by both Gotzmann, *Jüdisches Recht im kulturellen Prozeß*, 251-302 and Robin E. Judd, *Cutting Identities: Jewish Rituals and German Politics, 1843-1933* (Ithaca, NY: Cornell University Press, forthcoming 2007); idem, "Samuel Holdheim and the German Circumcision Debates" (in this volume, pp.127-142).

[16] Samuel Hirsch, *Die Religionsphilosophie der Juden oder das Prinzip der jüdischen Religionsanschauung und sein Verhältniss zum Heidenthum, Christenthum und zur absoluten Philosophie* (Leipzig: Hunger, 1842).

[17] Idem, *Die Reform im Judenthum und dessen Beruf in der gegenwärtigen Welt* (Leipzig: Hunger, 1844).

[18] Samuel Holdheim, *Ueber die Beschneidung zunächst in religiös-dogmatischer Beziehung* (Schwerin: C. Kürschner, 1844).

[19] Idem, *Ueber die Autonomie der Rabbinen und das Prinzip der jüdischen Ehe, Ein Beitrag zur Verständigung über einige das Judenthum betreffende Zeitfragen* (Schwerin: C. Kürschner, 1843).

statement in the Foreword to his *Vorträge über die mosaische Religion für die denkenden Israeliten* (1844).[20] Hirsch and Holdheim were of course familiar with each other's works and incorporated ideas or criticism of their colleague in their discussions of circumcision, rabbinic authority and the *Reformverein*.

3. Samuel Hirsch and Die Religionsphilosophie der Juden

Samuel Hirsch, chief rabbi of Luxemburg at the time of publication of *Die Religionsphilosophie der Juden*, was a devotee of Hegel yet disagreed with Hegel's philosophy on many points. For Hegel, religious consciousness and philosophic consciousness were divided: religion contains the truth of absolute spirit only in the form of representation. Philosophy grasps this truth in the form of a concept, changing the contents of the religious consciousness fundamentally. Religious consciousness and philosophic consciousness are divided, not only in form but also in content. Hirsch, in opposition to Hegel, attempted to show the complete identity of religious and philosophic truth. Moreover, Hirsch rejected Hegel's notion that evil was the necessary means to good. According to Hegel, man began in a state of nature and set himself in opposition to it—thereby sinning. This inescapable situation left man in a state of permanent enslavement. The philosophical negation of this situation meant freedom or virtue and was closely linked to the Christian doctrine of original sin overcome by the Incarnation. It was precisely this concept that Hirsch perceived as alien to Judaism.[21] For Hirsch the essence of Judaism is moral freedom, that is, the freedom to choose between the tendency to sin and virtue. It is this capacity for freedom that being created in God's image means. Choosing freedom entails a constant struggle against naturalness and sensuality, and the possibility of enslavement is always present. Freedom without its opposite is an abstract concept without ethical meaning; virtue and goodness have

---

[20] Idem, *Vorträge über die mosaische Religion für die denkende Israeliten* (Schwerin: C. Kürschner, 1844).

[21] For Hegel's changing views on Judaism see Hans Liebeschütz, *Das Judentum im deutschen Geschichtsbild von Hegel bis Max Weber* (Tübingen: J.C.B. Mohr, 1967), 1-42 and more recently Micha Brumlik, *Deutscher Geist und Judenhass. Das Verhältnis des philosophischen Idealismus zum Judentum* (Munich: Luchterhand, 2000), 196-249.

moral value only if their opposites—sin and evil—are real possibilities. These possibilities need not become reality, but they did when
Adam and Eve chose not for the tree of life but for the tree of
knowledge. They failed to make God's will their own conscious will
and thus did not become free but felt rather that it was impossible
for them to escape from sin. Abraham was the first to recognize his
duty to overcome sin. Therefore God chose his descendants to demonstrate in their own lives man's true destiny and to teach the world
that God is ruler over all of nature and man is to resemble God in
rising above nature. The Bible is a record of Israel's history, the
long period of education (*Erziehung*) which continued on until the
Second Temple. With the fall of the Temple and dispersion, Israel
entered its missionary phase, propagating the truth by choosing freedom instead of sin.

Judaism as an intensive form of religion, was not to spread the
truth by word. This became the task of the Church, which spread
the message to the pagans. Paganism, from which Abraham had
liberated himself, was considered by Hirsch to be passive. Believing
that human beings were subjugated perforce to nature, paganism
had to reconcile itself to its terrible fate. Only something new, from
without, brought about in a miraculous way, could save them and
that was the belief in God incarnate, a supernatural being who was
the only one not to inherit original sin. For the Jews, Jesus provided no reason to form a new religion. He had fulfilled his task,
as every Israelite must do; he was perfect only in the sense that
others were and can be.[22] But for the Church he became an intermediary, and the Church in turn became the intermediary for an
intermediary.[23] Pauline Christianity and the Catholic Church—necessary as forms of extensive religion intended for spreading the message to the heathens—could not bring them the truth.[24] The Protestant
Church negated both Pauline Christianity and Catholicism by claiming that all could come to God without the help of an intermediary by means of their deeds. While untrue to its original message,
the Protestant Church took a great step forward in bringing the
truth to the world, yet, like the Catholic Church, it mistook that

---

[22] Hirsch, *Die Religionsphilosophie der Juden*, 778.
[23] Ibid., 782.
[24] Ibid., 833.

which was proper for the heathen alone, for the absolute truth.[25] Judaism demands neither belief in dogmas nor has intermediaries. It must therefore continue—unchanged in theory and practice—to bring the truth to the world[26] so that it recognize that the essence of man is freedom and serving as God's image. While what the Jews teach is none other than the universal (*allgemein menschlich*) truth, no one born Jewish may deny this divine calling to which faithfulness was sworn on Sinai. Because the Jew's calling is eternal, ritual remains obligatory so that he will always remain conscious of his special task.[27]

The arguments Hirsch offers are aimed against Hegel but clearly would serve to refute not only Bauer's thesis—which was dependent on Hegel—but those of the Christian Biblical scholars as well. It is not the Jew, the oriental, who is not free and enslaved to a demanding God but rather the Church that demands irrational belief in its dogmas. Christianity is not superior to Judaism as its historical development and natural successor, nor is it universal, but rather a hybrid form necessary for spreading the message outward. It is Judaism that represents freedom and moral values (*Sittlichkeit*)— that which is universal and agrees with reason.

When claiming that rituals are mandatory because the Jews' calling is eternal, it would seem that Hirsch is arguing for an unchanging Judaism. Yet, his philosophy is far from traditional: he avoids using the term revelation and when he does so, he does so only circumspectly. Moreover, despite his advocacy of Israel's separate identity, he calls for obedience to the state because the present-day state is not heathen but revelation-based.[28] The law of the state is God's law, the state a divine institution. Therefore the Jews should enact everything the state demands in its own interest in so far as their religion permits. The law of the state takes precedence over Jewish law, because while both are divine, the latter is particular and the former of common interest. But should the state demand that the Jews give up their ceremonials simply in order to offend them, then the state acts not as a state but as an interested party. In that case the Jew should be willing to risk his life even for insignificant matters

---

[25] Ibid., 786f.
[26] Ibid., 864.
[27] Ibid., 865-866.
[28] Ibid., 835.

such as dress.[29] How Hirsch applied this rather vague dictum—quite close to Holdheim's position in 1843 as will be shown below—to reality becomes clear in his response concerning circumcision.

4. Hirsch on Circumcision

Hirsch opens his response found in Trier's volume of *Rabbinische Gutachten über die Beschneidung* by denouncing the *Reformfreunde:* one cannot be Jewish if one rejects important commandments, for general human duties are not sufficient. Only the Jew has received additional commandments and only by keeping them does he gain salvation. One might think that because Judaism's principle is universal it must therefore make its demands on all people. It would seem that all should be obligated to fulfil Jewish principles such as ceremonies and dietary laws, but this is not the case. Being Jewish is not the same as being human and being a good person doesn't make one a Jew.[30] Jews, priests of God for all nations, cannot choose freely, but are born into this people and have the duty to take this calling upon themselves, suffering for the false principles in the world.[31] Judaism has taken on symbols and ceremonies to fulfil this obligation—the *ḥukim*. Most Jews claim not to understand these laws and say that one must obey them blindly, but this is a half-truth. Although not equal to other godly commandments such as "Thou shalt not steal," yet the *ḥukim* are not wholly without reason: *kol ha-mizvot nitnu le-ṣaref et ha-briyot*, i.e. all of the commandments have been given for the moral improvement of humankind. The statutes keep Israel's religious duties and its national calling before its own eyes as well as those of others. While a non-Jew can please God without ceremonies, this is not true for the Jew who must always act as a teacher, recalling his history and duty by means of symbols.[32] Those who have eagerly rejected the symbols and ceremonies have left their religion so undefined as to have nothing specific to say about it— a reference to the lack of positive points on the *Reformfreunde's* agenda.[33]

---

[29] This recognition of the law of the state is based on the Talmudic principle *dina de-malkhuta dina* and is presented by Hirsch as an aside. See ibid., 838, footnote.
[30] Trier, ed., *Rabbinische Gutachten über die Beschneidung,* 50.
[31] Ibid., 51-52.
[32] Ibid., 52-53.
[33] Ibid., 53.

Circumcision, according to Hirsch, heads the list of ceremonies and, more than any other ceremony, symbolises the whole of religious thought. As such circumcision was always prohibited by those wishing to destroy Judaism. A father who refuses to circumcise his son indicates thereby that he has a formal and inimical relationship to Judaism. The community must protest and act instead of the father.[34] Are those who violate the Sabbath and dietary laws not equal offenders?, Hirsch asks, admitting to the reality of decreasing observance among his fellow Jews. No, he replies, for these violators of the commandments disagree about whether this or that pertains to the prohibition of work on the Sabbath according to Mosaic law, i.e. whether it pertains to the essence of Judaism or not. One who does not circumcise his son denies the very principle of Judaism and does not want to be considered Jewish. While the purpose of the Sabbath is to proclaim the fundamental confession of Judaism to the heathens, i.e. God created the world, working on the Sabbath nowadays in a society which has acknowledged the truth of creation does not deny this truth. Thus the Talmudic equation of one who violates the Sabbath with one who violates the whole of Judaism is no longer applicable. One must, after all, acknowledge that times have changed (*muss man den Unterschied der Zeit nicht verkennen?*).[35] But one who does not circumcise his son is not like the violator of the Sabbath, for he cannot prove that he is true to religion yet regards circumcision as somehow less essential. He commits a crime against his son's freedom of conscience, forcing *him* to decide what is or is not essential. He must proclaim which ceremonies he regards as holy, seeing that he questions the principle of ceremonies. In his hostility to Judaism he will estrange others from Judaism.[36]

Holdheim, in *Ueber die Beschneidung*, ridicules Hirsch's reference to the child's freedom of conscience and takes issue with Hirsch's interpretation of one who violates the Sabbath. Only the Jew who no longer believes in one God, he counters, is excluded from Judaism and has lost his confessional character.[37] Hirsch claims that a Sabbath

---

[34] Ibid., 54.

[35] Here we see Hirsch's acknowledgement of the role historical development may play in deciding which commandments are relevant and to be obeyed and which are of lesser value.

[36] Ibid., 55-56.

[37] Holdheim, *Ueber die Beschneidung*, 64.

transgressor simply denies God's work, i.e. that God created the world out of nothing. If Sabbath is for the affirmation of monotheism, Holdheim queries, why need not the stranger in Israel observe it, and why is it not included among the seven Noahide commandments? According to Holdheim, Hirsch singles out the Sabbath because it harmonizes with his religious-philosophical system. But he should have considered whether his argument holds water in the halakhic sphere, which is the litmus test in all cases as to what extent philosophical theories about Judaism *vom jüdischen Leben geahnt wurden und auf dasselbe von Einfluss waren.*[38] Although the Sabbath in the Bible was surely a sign of monotheism, for the rabbis this was no longer necessary; rather it was a sign of difference! This only goes to show that the rabbis were influenced by history and in order to maintain a balance between the times and scripture, came ever the more to an unnatural explanation of the Bible, Holdheim concludes.

Andreas Gotzmann, in his book *Jüdisches Recht im kulturellen Prozeß,*[39] elucidates Holdheim's critique of Hirsch. Hirsch, by linking circumcision to the Sabbath and distinguishing between one who transgresses for convenience sake and one who transgresses out of heretical principle, subsumes his independent theological construction to halakhic discourse.[40] Unlike Hirsch, Holdheim, according to Gotzmann, was an exception in being able to break down the halakhic system by conforming to his own alternate system.[41] Gotzmann's point is valid: Hirsch had not yet worked out his own criteria for selecting which ceremonies were relevant and which were not. He thus implemented halakhic discourse, his own philosophical system as well as his subjective leanings inconsistently.

Hirsch, challenged by Holdheim, subsequently searches valid criteria for reform and comes to speak of true reform and deceitful reform, as will be discussed below. Holdheim himself, however, failed to provide convincing argument for maintaining the rite of circumcision, yet never pleaded for its abolition. Why this was so remains unclear. In the debates about circumcision it becomes apparent that many contemporary Jews were transgressing the Sabbath and dietary laws. The

---

[38] Ibid., 66-67.
[39] See note 11 above.
[40] Gotzmann, *Jüdisches Recht im kulturellen Prozeß*, 278.
[41] Ibid., 198-250, esp. 228-231.

responsa show that many rabbis had clearly resigned themselves to the situation and that some, including our protagonists, even condoned this reality by justifying it within their own philosophical constructs. The historically oriented arguments that they employed in the course of their arguments were mostly pure conjecture. In any event, the borders determining what was acceptable and what was not were clearly shifting. Circumcision or its refusal, however, seems to have riled up more emotions than did the violation of other commandments.

Unlike other responsa collections, Trier's *Gutachten über die Beschneidung* included reactions from rabbis representing a broad spectrum of positions on the matter of religious reform. Why the arguments were so heated and the conclusions so inconsistent in this matter, is unclear. The circumcision debates never mention, but must necessarily reflect the changing perception of manhood in Germany in the first half of the nineteenth century. The bodies of Jewish men, which deviated from the norm, would surely have been subject to discussion in a time when greater attention was being paid to physiognomy. This, I suggest, would be a topic worthy of further investigation.[42]

5. Hirsch's Religious Reform

Weltanschauung

Hirsch's *Reform im Judenthum* (1844)—in reality more an attack on the *Reformfreunde* and an answer to Bauer than a program of reform—

---

[42] It is surprising that neither Judd nor Gotzmann make mention of the changing view of manhood in Germany at this time, although Gotzmann does note that *rites de passage* were apparently sensitive subject matter. By the beginning of the nineteenth century Johann Caspar Lavater had published his *Physiognomische Fragmente zur Beförderung der Menschenkenntnis und Menschenliebe*, 4 vols. (Leipzig/Winterthur: Weidmann und Reich, 1775-1778), and sport and bodily perfection were topical. See e.g Johann Christoph Friedrich GutsMuths, *Gymnastik für die Jugend: Enthaltend eine praktische Anweisung zu Leibesübungen. Ein Beytrag zur nöthigsten Verbesserung der körperlichen Erziehung* (Schnepfenthal: Buchhandlung der Erziehungs-Anstalt, 1793); idem, *Spiele zur Uebung und Erholung des Körpers und Geistes, für die Jugend und alle Freunde unschuldiger Jugendfreunden* (Schnepfenthal: Buchhandlung der Erziehungs-Anstalt, 1796); Friedrich Ludwig Jahn and Ernst Eiselen, *Die Deutsche Turnkunst zur Einrichtung der Turnplätze* (Berlin: Selbstverlag, 1816). For an overview of the period see George L. Mosse, *Toward the Final Solution: A History of European Racism* (London: Fertig, 1978).

is more radical than his previous works. Hirsch presents his arguments in four parts: the present-day situation or *Weltanschauung*, God, revelation and Judaism, and deceptive and true reform. He commences by condemning the *Reformfreunde* and those before them for not having reformed the ceremonial laws systematically. The founders of the Hamburg temple, for example, were in truth bearers of romantic notions. They spoke of a Temple of *Urjudenthum*, of *Urmosaismus* which would suffer no excesses. Yet everything so characteristic of Judaism was considered an excess.[43] What they should have done was reform Judaism from the inside out, so that it reflect the religious world view of contemporary Jews (*den jüdischen Kultus aus seinem innern Wesen heraus umstalten, damit er den wirklichen Ausdruck, das in Wort und Symbol gefasste, des Glaubensbewusstsein der religiösen Weltanschauung der heutigen Juden sei*). Instead, they simply imitated the Church in the hope that the Christians might grant the Jews emancipation. They concerned themselves with reforming services and public events such as funerals and weddings but they never considered reforming the entirety of the ceremonial law. Living in a transition period and being unable to specify why the old did not suffice, none—neither Jew nor Christian—was able to discover the new. Reform must be an end in itself and not simply serve as the means toward emancipation; therefore a principle must be sought.[44]

The Jewish question takes on larger dimensions: it is no longer about granting equal opportunity to the Jews, but about whether their world view accords with the changing society in which men are united in love, or whether they are a foreign element, to be rejected. Judaism, like Christianity, must subject itself to the criticism of reason. The Jews must either join society wholeheartedly or oppose it; they can't simultaneously adhere to a religion that is contrary to society and yet flirt with it. At present there are heteronomists, Hirsch explains, who artificially seek to preserve everything and there are those who are in favour of autonomy yet look to the Talmud to validate abandoning each and every custom.[45] But Talmudic Judaism cannot serve this purpose, being as wholly inappropriate for modern times as is Catholicism. The Talmud came to be in the first centuries C.E., in

---

[43] Hirsch, *Die Reform im Judenthum*, 3.
[44] Ibid., 5.
[45] Ibid., 9-11.

a time of decline, doubt and corruption. The Jews placed their hope in the future and their very being was linked to the past. The present could make no claims because there was no spiritual life. The form that Judaism took on was one foreign to itself.

While oral teaching is the true principle of development (*Fortbildung*) in every religion, once committed to writing this teaching no longer lives. The Talmud presents the traditions of the past and allows for only those of the past. Talmudic Judaism ignores the fact that while the religious principle remains constant and is eternal, every age is entitled to conceive of this religious principle in its own way and endow it with a differing physiognomy.[46] The rabbis failed to recognize that the ceremonies and rituals were intended by Moses and the prophets purely to symbolize inner religious thought. As such they only indicate the basis; each generation was to fill in the details anew. Alas, Hirsch complains of the times, ceremonies and customs have been attributed independent value and anyone who dares question their meaning is regarded as heretical. The Sabbath and dietary laws have been expanded without regard for their original purpose. They no longer ennoble the human spirit but are the incomprehensible commandments of a Higher Being. In that case, how can one talk of spiritual freedom or autonomy? Ceremonies can only be understood if they are the expression of a religious idea; they are not to be obeyed simply because God commanded them. Talmudic Judaism—like Catholicism—simply does not rhyme with freedom because in neither is there spirit. Important for contemporary Jews is moral values (*Sittlichkeit*) and living in a society born of a spirit that they comprehend. All forms that can't be justified by inner spiritual contents are empty and must leave them cold. A God who speaks in riddles is nothing more than an idol. Therefore, Talmudic Judaism no longer has the right to exist. Is Judaism then still possible?, Hirsch asks.[47]

God, Revelation, Judaism

True and perfect religion, Hirsch avers, recognizes human freedom wholly. In this sense Judaism is true religion while Christianity, which

---

[46] Ibid., 16-17.
[47] Ibid., 21-22.

relegates freedom to the next world, is a false religion. In his description of Judaism as the true religion, Hirsch goes a step further than
his philosophical work in dealing explicitly with revelation. Teachings
about God and the world are considered by him to be necessary
only in order to establish human freedom and morality. God is nothing other than a higher state of human consciousness.[48] Judaism is
a revealed religion, yet not in the sense of its being a supernatural
mystery. It proclaims only that which is clear and available to all
men through reason from the start. It is decisively unlike Christianity,
which has a revealed God, a revealed teaching and is in need of
God's grace in order to make its dogmas comprehensible. Judaism
declares its truths to be common to humanity, encouraging acceptance even without a Mount Sinai or the miraculous appearance of
God.[49] What is revealed is not a teaching but a secret of history
(*Geschichtsgeheimniss*). Judaism is neither a nationality nor a confession.
In order to be a nationality, the Jews must desire to be so, as
Holdheim rightly claims. A confession implies adhering to a confession to which others do not adhere, but Judaism is universal. It is
nothing less than history and the religion of history: the Bible is a
history book which tells of man's having been created with the ability to be free, holy and good. Humankind, however, subjected itself
to nature and was not free. Therefore a people was chosen whose
history was meant to teach men their calling. It was to serve as an
example for the world and establish God's kingdom on this earth.
This coincides with the aims of contemporary times: to realize a
kingdom of truth and virtue on earth. However, what modernity
regards as a matter of reason is a religious duty in Judaism, to be
realized in the people's own lives and in the world at large.[50]

Deceptive Reform

Even though times have changed, symbols remain necessary, Hirsch
explains. The *Reformfreunde* are right in saying that symbols must have
meaning and that disregarding certain customs is not just a matter of
convenience but a matter of conscience. Symbols must not be other-
worldly, must not make keeping the law and serving God difficult.

---

[48] Ibid., 26-28.
[49] Ibid., 31-32.
[50] Ibid., 35-38.

They should help man consider his religious life and not contradict true religion, i.e. the exercise of virtue and justice.[51] But the *Reformfreunde* are wrong in their approach. They speak firstly about a Mosaic religion: did Moses invent a religion or are they avoiding using the word "Jew"? If a man founded a religion, it must be errant. Well then, it must cease to be, rather than be built upon. And as for *unbeschränkte Fortbildung*—this would mean unlimited so that the original is no longer recognizable, no longer Mosaic. This is such a vague expression, typical of the hazy Frankfurt reformers. Their second point regards the Talmud and its lack of authority, which is simply a tautology. If Mosaism is progressive then no authority remains an authority, for an authority is that which one must accept, even when it opposes reason. If one talks of progress one must also look beyond the Talmud and even beyond the Mosaic period, but they are afraid to admit this. As far as circumcision is concerned, they are right when they say that the people regard circumcision as a sacrament, a meaning that it does not bear in Judaism. However, they are wrong in denying that circumcision symbolises purity, for it is the Jews' duty to remain pure in order to fulfil their mission. Should we abolish circumcision simply because Christians refuse to understand it and consider its symbolism hateful?[52] What they are claiming, in fact, comes very close to Christianity: the latter also acknowledges progressive revelation, rejects the Talmud and doesn't believe in a messiah who will re-conquer Palestine for the Jews. The only difference is that the Mosaic religion sanctions every form of religion that is yet to come.[53] The *Reformfreunde* are too theoretical and fail to offer practical points for the creation of a new understanding of Judaism. If they mean that man is increasingly able to understand scripture on account of better and increased knowledge of truth and nature, then it is not the Mosaic religion but we who progress. To this even the Orthodox rabbis will concede! The question they need to answer is: if we strip religion of all its customs and ceremonies, what remains and to what extent can we still speak of Judaism?[54]

---

[51] Ibid., 39-40.
[52] Ibid., 41-44.
[53] Ibid., 46-47.
[54] Ibid., 49-51.

True Reform

If one accepts Hirsch's theory that 1) man is created by a personal
God to develop his spiritual power; 2) he is not solely dependent
upon nature but has the potential to be virtuous and sanctify his life
and that 3) Jewish history serves as a proto-type for all peoples and
histories, then this may serve as the basis for a new understanding
of religion which will benefit not only the Jews but humanity.[55]
Judaism is not a confession but teaches that which is available to all
by means of reason. Because it is not a confession, it is considered
a nationality. Formerly, being a nation meant possessing a spiritual
life that is expressed in upbringing, public life, law-giving, morals,
language and communal goals. However, the term nation has taken
on other meaning and the Jews are now considered oriental, without development: a Jew will always remain a Jew. But Jews are neither a confession nor a nation. They are born witnesses to history.[56]

Present-day Judaism is permeated by the Protestant spirit and
therefore many incorrectly assume that ceremonies are unnecessary
—that sermons, choir and prayer suffice. How wrong they are! As
long as the world does not believe in history, the Jews—as witnesses
to history—must maintain a symbolic system that aids them to demonstrate ever more clearly the sanctity of history. Thus far the symbols employed were governed by medieval and Talmudic principles:
they did not serve to cleanse humankind but became a religion in
and of themselves.[57]

If the state is ordained by God for all humankind, including the
Jews (*dina de-malkhuta dina*), then a conflict between the ceremonial
laws and the laws of the state must lead to the abolition of the former. How can Jews strive for emancipation and not be willing to
fulfil the duties of the state on the Sabbath? Now that society has
become civil society (*bürgerliche Gesellschaft*), work on behalf of that
society is law. If God's kingdom is to be established on earth, then
how will it come about if not through recognition of civil society's
rights and service for the sake of the common good? Life and religion become equated and that which the times seek—truth and justice for all—is exactly the goal at which Judaism aims. All ceremonies

---

[55] Ibid., 56-58.
[56] Ibid., 60.
[57] Ibid., 62.

that obstruct the maintenance of civil society are secondary. It is a crime against the spirit of Judaism when something is preserved which obstructs the Jews from becoming full citizens. This is because they have arrived at the threshold of the future as foretold by the prophets and new and more appropriate symbols must be sought. Present-day Judaism must join in the work of the epoch because this is the true purpose of Jewish history, its final destination: that all men become free, and truth and justice enthroned. "No symbol which restrains the Jews from participation in and realization of this goal can be considered Jewish any longer."[58]

From the above it has emerged that Hirsch, having discovered the essence of Judaism, now has it serve as the basis for all reform. He thereby refutes the *Reformfreunde* who offer no principle for reform and actually deny that Judaism is a positive religion, i.e., that at its centre is something eternal and unchanging. He also writes a counter history to Bauer's conception of Judaism. He agrees that the "Jewish Question" is not simply about granting citizenship to Jews and that the Jews too must subject their religion to the criticism of reason. However, he disagrees with Bauer's description of Christianity as being on a higher level than Judaism and his description of Judaism as a religion of slaves. Hirsch inverts Bauer's arguments and insists that Judaism represents the universal and stands for human freedom. Christianity is a confession, containing dogmas that are simply to be accepted as such and remains closed for those who don't confess these dogmas. It is true that Judaism is a nation but not in the sense which Bauer employs: the Jews are a people with a mission and as such they need to remain Jews. Until the mission is fulfilled, the people need rites and ceremonies to remind them of their calling. Bauer and the *Reformfreunde* are right again when they claim that ceremonies must not be mindless. Here Hirsch has gone further than his *Religionsphilosophie* in admitting that some rites may no longer achieve the effect for which they were instituted. However, rites and ceremonies should not be abolished simply because of the pressure that non-Jews exert. Finally, Hirsch seems convinced that his own times are quite close to realizing the messianic ideal: life and religion have been equated with each other in civil society. He therefore subsumes ceremonies and even work on the Sabbath to

---

[58] Ibid., 65-69, here at 69.

service for the common good. Bauer claims that the state does not represent the *juste milieu* as long as the minority must give way to the majority in all matters such as the observance of Sunday rather than the Sabbath as the national day of rest. By identifying civil society with the ultimate, universal goal of Judaism, Hirsch seems to have resolved all conflict between Church and State.[59]

6. Holdheim on Rabbinic Authority

Samuel Holdheim, rabbi successively in Frankfurt an der Oder, Mecklenburg-Schwerin and the radical reform community of Berlin, seems to have created a clear system as an alternative to the rabbinic, halakhic one. Whether or not he was able to implement it consistently will be discussed below. In his *Ueber die Autonomie der Rabbinen*, Holdheim's central thesis is that the rabbis had committed a great historical error in failing to distinguish between national and religious law. This question, he explains, relates directly to the Jewish problem and the matter of corporate law.[60] The Jews, contrary to what others claim, have no nationality because they desire none. Thus if they are made aware of the fact that certain of the laws which they have practiced as religious law are in reality national law, they will surely relinquish these.[61] But the whole national question should also have some effect on Jewish religious consciousness and allow Jews to rethink matters. Jews should consider the essence of their religion and examine that which they consider eternal and unchanging, i.e. the religious, and that which is political and thus temporary. Only by distinguishing between the national and the religious is a true and timely reform of Judaism possible.[62]

---

[59] For the identification of the goals of Judaism with those of the state, see Andreas Gotzmann, "Zwischen Nation und Relgion: Die deutschen Juden auf der Suche nach einer bürgerlichen Konfessionalität," in *Juden, Bürger, Deutsche. Zur Geschichte von Vielfalt und Differenz 1800-1933*, ed. Andreas Gotzmann, Rainer Liedtke and Till van Rahden (Tübingen: J.C.B. Mohr, 2001), 241-261; idem, *Eigenheit und Einheit. Mondernisierungsdiskurse des deutschen Judentums der Emanzipationszeit* (Leiden: Brill Publishers, 2002), particularly 212-243.

[60] Samuel Holdheim, *Ueber die Autonomie der Rabbinen und das Prinzip der jüdischen Ehe, Ein Beitrag zur Verständigung über einige das Judenthum betreffende Zeitfragen*, 2nd edition (Schwerin: C. Kürschner, 1847), Foreword III.

[61] Ibid., IV.

[62] Ibid., V-VII.

As far as the Jews' political situation is concerned, internal improvement will only yield results if the state maintains pure human capacity as the sole condition for inclusion. But if those demanding the abolition of Jewish national identity do not themselves adhere to a universal point of view but rather to the Christian faith and a Christian state, then the specific national form with its religious garb is what is contrary to the universal, not the Jewish nationality. The Jewish national element limits the universal, but the pure religious (*rein-religiöse*) element that is stripped of its national garb, not only does not limit the universal but feels the necessity to cleanse it by providing it with a universal character. So too, the essence of Christian spirit is also the universal and thus the two—the essences of Judaism and Christianity—can never conflict. If the universal aspect of Judaism clashes with the Church, it is because the latter is not in its pure religious but in its national form that tolerates no others. It is, therefore, not their nationality that restrains the Jews but the nationality of the Christians. Thus the contradiction is not between the Jew and the human but between the Jew and the Christian, or rather, between the non-Christian and the Christian, and more correctly, between the human and the Christian.[63]

Like the *Reformfreunde*, Holdheim calls for a return to Mosaic law. Whereas in the period of the First Temple, he says, Israel was a state with no distinction between civil and religious law, during the Second Temple it did not really constitute a state. After the fall of the Second Temple the rabbis failed to realize that the destruction of the state fulfilled God's purpose and they continued to hope for its restoration, considering their situation temporary. They mistakenly considered all law, the political and religious, as religious law and proceeded to distort it. The Talmud made of Mosaism that which it wished—or better said, that which the times wished—so that the needs of times were raised to the level of religion, i.e. became the leading principle of humankind. As long as Jews lived a corporate life, rabbinic authority applied. The end of the Middle Ages meant that the state's authority increased in civil matters. The rabbis, who could no longer distinguish between the political and religious, were loath to relinquish their position. But the loss of authority, says Holdheim, should be viewed positively, as it is beneficial for the

---

[63] Ibid., VIII-X.

morality and *Bildung* of the Jews.[64] Because religion has to do with
beliefs and customs and the state has to do with law, the legal system can in no way conflict with beliefs or ceremonies.[65] The Jews'
religion demands that they fulfil all civil duties.[66] It is best when
there is one law for all, for then the Jew will not be split between
adhesion to a so-called oriental law and European law. Only the
purely religious moment that is located in the relationship between
man and God should be protected by the Jew. This influences the
relationship between man and man only in so far as it obligates men
to be honest in all things. Only by estranging Jews from the law of
the land are they forced to belong to a foreign nationality as members of a non-existent state.[67] The Jews have already taken the first
step toward civil and spiritual emancipation and the oriental has
already been reshaped into a European.[68]

Now if the Jews relinquish most of their jurisdiction to the state,
should the state not take them into account, as it does Christians?,
Holdheim asks, thereby reiterating Bauer's question. In principle yes,
but it would be impossible for the Chambers of Deputies to be closed
on both the Sabbath and Sunday because the interests of the state
would be at stake. The common good always takes precedence over
the freedom of the state's subjects, be they the Jewish minority or
the Christian majority. The choice should always be made in favor
of the interests of the majority, as long as no force is involved but
reasonable considerations. Civil duty takes precedence over the
Sabbath. A civil servant is therefore like the priests who worked in
the Temple on the Sabbath.[69] Religious customs that are obligatory
due to their eternal holiness and general validity yet which do not
detract from the religion if omitted, are subordinate to state law and
civil duty. Doctors and lawyers belonging to the Jewish intelligentsia
are considered by many to be *Freigeister* because they work on the
Sabbath. Yet they consider both the demands of Judaism and of the
civil interests of the Jews of equal importance.[70] There is relative
validity for religious customs, as opposed to moral law, which is

---

[64] Ibid., 7.
[65] Ibid., 10.
[66] Ibid., 15.
[67] Ibid., 20-21.
[68] Ibid., 5.
[69] Ibid., 101-105, n.71.
[70] Ibid., 105.

absolute, categorical and eternally valid. Just as moral law can't be obviated by civil law, so religious custom can't demand recognition by state law.[71]

It will have become apparent that Holdheim, like Hirsch has identified the German state with the strivings which represent the essence of Judaism. Whereas for Hirsch the essence was to be found in human freedom, for Holdheim it is located in morality. The latter is most extreme when identifying the civil servant who works on the Sabbath with the priest who served in the Temple. Holdheim does not agree with Bauer's claim that the Jews are a nation. It is only because the state identifies itself with Christian values and refuses the Jews entrance that they are forced to adhere to a non-extant foreign state. Like Bauer, Holdheim claims that both Jews and Christians need to rediscover the essence of their religions. For Jews this means that they must recognize the historical error made by the rabbis of the Talmud, remove all laws which pertain to the nation and retain only those which are purely religious. Insisting that the purely religious pertains only to the relationship between God and man, Holdheim eliminates further barriers between Judaism and good citizenship: Jews need not form a corporation and Jewish law need no longer judge matters which pertain to the state once the theocracy has ceased to be. Thus Holdheim, while wholly accepting Christian criticism of the rabbis, refuses to acknowledge the superiority of Christianity. He, like Hirsch, has identified Judaism with the universal, thereby reversing Christian and philosophical claims.

7. Holdheim on Circumcision

While denying the rabbi's authority, Holdheim made no comments about the status of various Mosaic laws, apart from subsuming custom to state law. In his discussion of circumcision, Holdheim opens with an affirmation of the Mosaic status of circumcision—clearly a rejoinder to the *Reformfreunde*'s rejection of circumcision as not binding, despite their acceptance of Mosaic law.[72] Although Mosaic, Holdheim says, circumcision in no way formed a mark confessional

---

[71] Ibid., 109-110.
[72] Holdheim, *Ueber die Beschneidung zunächst in religiös-dogmatischer Beziehung*, 2.

in character for the Israelite, parallel to baptism in Christianity.[73] If
one looks at the Bible carefully, one will note that the Sabbath is
regarded by Moses as a much more important sign—*ot*—than circumcision.[74] The Sabbath is incorporated in the Ten Commandments
but for Moses—if not for Joshua—no further importance is attributed to circumcision.[75] Even prior to the Mosaic system, in the story
of Abraham, it is familial descent and not circumcision which is
involved in the covenant, which includes the obligations of the Mosaic
law, whether one is circumcised or not. It is birth that is the exclusive point, as opposed to Christianity that is not determined by
birth.[76] Therefore a non-Jew who is circumcised for reasons of health
or hygiene is not a Jew.[77] Holdheim concludes that Moses maintained circumcision as an older, sanctified religious custom without
attributing to it the same meaning it had had in Abraham's time,
i.e. a mark of religious dedication and priestly sacrality. It was a
sign of God's covenant with Abraham but not a sign of God's
covenant with Israel.[78] Even if it had been commanded by God, it
was not necessarily valid for generations, and was no more important than many other commandments that had to be fulfilled.[79]

It was unthinkable to the rabbis, Holdheim writes, that someone
who refused to circumcise his son might not be a renegade but rather
did not regard the rite as a moral-religious obligation. The rabbis
only maintained two categories: he who sinned for convenience (*mumar
le-te'avon*) and he who did so because he was a heretic (*mumar le-
hakhis*). Yet belonging to the third category, a product of contemporary society, is one who is not morally depraved and does not
intend to sin or insult someone's religious opinions, but rather does
not agree with the rabbis about the eternal validity of the one law
or the other.[80] It is typical of the rabbis to consider themselves as
the sole defenders of the faith, never granting that the opposition
might have a pure motive and religious point of view. All these
judgements come forth from a life and world views which have long

---

[73] Ibid., 2, 7.
[74] Ibid., 17.
[75] Ibid., 14.
[76] Ibid., 8.
[77] Ibid., 11.
[78] Ibid., 14, 17.
[79] Ibid., 20, 22.
[80] Ibid., 53, 55-56.

been surpassed. They are tied to the authority of the hierarchical autonomy enjoyed by the rabbis which recently has had to make many concessions.[81] In fact, the rabbis, should be regarded as no more than teachers, chosen by the confidence put in them by the community, who can only try to convince others by their teaching and example. Their purely religious insights are to be valued, yet their opinions are not religiously binding. It is thoroughly ridiculous that they think of using force, of forcing someone's conscience, now that Judaism has emerged after thousands of years of battle as a purified religion in the noblest sense of the word.[82] Thus Holdheim, unlike Hirsch, rightly or wrongly denies the importance of circumcision, affirms the Jewish status of an uncircumcised child until he makes the choice himself at age thirteen, and denies the rabbis the right to exclude father or son or force the father—with or without the help of the government—to circumcise his son. As noted above, he does not suggest that circumcision be done away with, but provides no good reason for implementing it, aside from the fact that it is Mosaic.

8. A Final Synthesis

In the foreword to his *Vorträge über die mosaische Religion,* published in the very same year as his treatise on circumcision, Holdheim applies the same criteria he applied to Talmudic Judaism to Mosaic religion. As in his earlier works, Holdheim sets out to preserve the pure biblical positive religion of revelation without the troubling and rationalising rabbinic explanations and thus discover the Jewish religious duty.[83] In criticising the *Reformfreunde,* Holdheim denies that Mosaic law is so imperfect that it is in need of *unbeschränkte Fortbildung:* only mortals are in need of further explanation and development, not God. Our author surmises that having declared Talmudic authority null and void, the *Freunde* no longer knew what to do with a complete Mosaism encompassing too much of the impractical and the impossible. They had no principle, he says, with which to distinguish

---

[81] Ibid., 59-61.
[82] Ibid., 71, 74.
[83] Samuel Holdheim, *Vorträge über die Mosaische Religion für denkenden Israeliten* (Schwerin: C. Kürschner. 1844), Foreword VII-VIII.

between the eternal and the temporal, so they made use of the somewhat vague principle of development.[84] Instead of attributing the
principle of development to Talmud and subsequently declaring its
authority void, they need to see that the Talmud made Mosaism
what the times wished. Thus the needs of the times became the leading principle. The Talmudic rabbis, instead of making all law religious law, could have better distinguished between civil law and
religion. There would then be no conflict between the eternal part
of the Mosaic law and the necessities of the time. Characteristic of
religion is to reveal the light and truth of the Divine will. Therefore,
the first article of the *Reformfreunde's* statement of principles should
have read: we believe in Mosaic religion as taught in the books of
Moses and the prophets, omitting all which is related to nationhood
including laws and rites.[85] Here Holdheim has gone once step further, implying that not only rabbinic Judaism but also Mosaic law
itself should be purged of all national law.

9. Conclusions

Samuel Hirsch and Samuel Holdheim both attempted to reform
Judaism by means of newly devised philosophical-theological systems.
Within these systems the essence of Judaism was identified: for Hirsch
it was man's ability to be free and for Holdheim it was moral law.
Once these essences had been identified, Judaism could then be
reformed from the inside out. While Holdheim accuses Hirsch of
simply imposing a foreign system upon Judaism, he himself was guilty
of the same. Both men made use of categories foreign to rabbinic
thinking such as the right to conscientious objection. Having defeated
the rabbis on their own ground by means of halakhic argumentation, Holdheim subsequently introduced the distinction between
national and religious law. Despite their criticism of the *Reformfreunde's*
lack of principle, their own criteria do in turn seem vague and subjective. Hirsch, at first quite conservative as far as the preservation
of rites and ceremonies was concerned, became more and more radical in his assessment of what did and what did not properly reflect

---

[84] Ibid., XII.
[85] Ibid., XII-XV.

Judaism's lofty mission. Holdheim was more radical from the start, yet hesitated most remarkably to put his thoughts into practice when it came to circumcision. They first expressed their radical reform ideas at the rabbinical conferences in Braunschweig in 1844 and Frankfurt am Main in 1845. Their ideas were not well received because the majority of the reform oriented rabbis continued to defend change in terms of halakhic, historical development. Having identified Judaism with universalism and the state with the common good, Hirsch and Holdheim hoped to have refuted Bauer's objections and eliminated all barriers for emancipation. In the years to come Holdheim and Hirsch would be gravely disappointed in the Jewish community and its resistance to change as well as with the state and its continued identification with Christianity. Holdheim sought his solace by becoming the rabbi of the radical reform congregation in Berlin in 1847. Hirsch emigrated from Luxemburg to Philadelphia in the United States in 1866 where he was able to enact many of his radical ideas.[86]

---

[86] See Christian Wiese, "Von Dessau nach Philadelphia: Samuel Hirsch's Philosophie im Kontext deutscher und amerikanischer Reformdebatten im neunzehnten Jahrhundert," in *Jüdische Bildung und Kultur auf dem Gebiet des heutigen Sachsen-Anhalt*, ed. Giuseppe Veltri and Christian Wiese (Berlin: Metropol, 2007, forthcoming).

SAMUEL HOLDHEIM'S "MOST POWERFUL COMRADE IN CONVICTION": DAVID EINHORN AND THE DEBATE CONCERNING JEWISH UNIVERSALISM IN THE RADICAL REFORM MOVEMENT[1]

Christian Wiese

"The great master in Israel, the high priest of Jewish theological learning, the lion in the struggle for light and truth, no longer dwells on Earth."[2] It was with these words that the periodical *Sinai. Ein Organ für Erkenntnis und Veredlung des Judentums* [Sinai. An organ for the knowledge and ennoblement of Judaism], which was published between 1856 and 1863 in Baltimore by the rabbi and intellectual David Einhorn, announced the death of his friend and colleague Samuel Holdheim in 1860. Whilst in Germany there was vehement debate about whether the Berlin Jewish congregation had done the right thing in granting the radical reformer a place in the row of honor reserved for rabbis in the Jewish cemetery in Berlin, and Michael Sachs, "the arrogant fanatic in kid gloves, who in his theological poverty carried off just a little gold dust from the gold mines of Judaism," wished to deny him this honor, in an effusive obituary Einhorn accorded Holdheim a "place of honor in the foremost rank on the battlefield of the recent history of Judaism," "where his name shall continue to shine, long after the poetic blossoms of a [Michael] Sachs have been scattered by the winds!" Like his namesake the prophet Samuel, "standing on the boundary between two worlds in Israel," Holdheim had tirelessly undertaken the work of "burying what was moribund in Judaism with one hand, whilst unearthing with the other the richest treasures from the deepest shafts of its mines."[3]

Einhorn's appreciation of Holdheim's sharp-witted researcher's

---

[1] Translated from the German by Margret Vince.
[2] Death notice for Samuel Holdheim, *Sinai* 5 (1860/61), no. 9, 288.
[3] David Einhorn, "Samuel Holdheim," *Sinai* 5 (1860/61), no. 10, 289-297, quotations 297.

mind, his Talmudic learning, his striving for truthfulness, his "gentleness and mildness" that stood in contrast to "reforming boldness," his "deeply poetic nature"[4] and his enthusiasm for Judaism that made him a "*gadol be-Yisrael*" [great man in Israel],[5] demonstrates the respect and the friendship that bound the two radical reformers to one another. Conversely, in 1852 Holdheim had dedicated his first collection of sermons to "David Einhorn, the friend and kindred spirit, Rabbi of Pest," and in his *Geschichte der Entstehung und Entwickelung der jüdischen Reformgemeinde in Berlin* [History of the origins and development of the Jewish Reform congregation in Berlin] (1857), he characterized Einhorn as his "strongest ally in conviction" and as a figure of hope for the American Reform movement.[6] Einhorn could thus rightly speak of a "most intimate bond of friendship" that had lasted for 15 years.[7] This acknowledgement was all the more notable as Holdheim and Einhorn had quarreled publicly several times—no doubt most vehemently in 1844/45—in mutual polemics about the relationship of Reform and rabbinical tradition, as well as about specific questions concerning the reinterpretation of the liturgical tradition. In his obituary, Einhorn did not conceal the "literary feud," which we shall come to speak of later, but in retrospect regretted his own sometimes harsh attacks, and remembered how in 1845 Holdheim, who at the time was at the height of his renown, approached him in a spirit of conciliation at the rabbinical conference in Frankfurt and offered him his hand, with the words: "We two are, after all, fighting *le-shem shamayim*" [for the sake of God].[8]

The following remarks are devoted to the relationship between the two Reform rabbis, a companionship that was both friendly and critical, sometimes pugnacious, in a time of political upheaval, religious-cultural re-orientations, and ideological disputes. In this comparative study, the intention is to tease out the different emphases that were expressed in the then burning, topical debate about the nature and consequences of Jewish universalism in the modern era. In the course of this, besides Einhorn and Holdheim, I shall include a third radical

---

[4] Ibid., 294.

[5] Ibid., 296.

[6] Samuel Holdheim, *Geschichte der Entstehung und Entwickelung der jüdischen Reformgemeinde in Berlin: im Zusammenhang mit den jüdischreformatorischen Gesammtbestrebungen der Neuzeit* (Berlin: Julius Springer, 1857), 79 and 140, note 1.

[7] Einhorn, "Samuel Holdheim," 289.

[8] Ibid., 293.

reformer of the same generation, Samuel Hirsch, who—like Einhorn—
later emigrated to America and on whom, according to Kaufmann
Kohler, the "prophetic mantle of Holdheim" then fell there.[9] However,
the focus will be on David Einhorn, who had developed his Reform
philosophy in Europe, and later, with his uncompromising radicalism,
was to mould the Reform movement in America into the later nineteenth and early twentieth centuries—at a time when Holdheim's influence in Germany had already faded.[10] Beyond the long-term influence
of Holdheim's work in the American context, mediated by Einhorn,
the prime aim here is to highlight the specifics of Einhorn's thinking,
which made him not only the "American apostle of the teachings of
Holdheim," as Jakob Petuchowsky put it,[11] but also an important
reformer with a marked theological-philosophical profile of his own.

1. Pugnacious Companionship: Einhorn and Holdheim in the Reform Controversies in Germany

Not only in their views on the reform of Judaism, but biographically
too one can establish strong parallels between Einhorn and Holdheim,
even if Einhorn's intellectual development appears ultimately not to
be characterized by inner conflicts and tensions to the same extent
as that of his friend.[12] What they have in common, however, is the
experience of a personal turning away from the purely Talmudic education and religiosity of their youth, from which they were torn by
their immersion in the world of the university—Holdheim in Berlin

---

[9] Kaufmann Kohler, "Samuel Hirsch," in idem, *Hebrew Union College and Other Addresses* (Cincinnati: Ark Publications, 1916), 75-81, quotation 79.

[10] For a biographical study, see Kaufmann Kohler, "David Einhorn. The Uncompromising Champion of Reform Judaism. A Biographical Essay," in *David Einhorn Memorial Volume. Selected Sermons and Addresses*, ed. Kaufmann Kohler (New York: Bloch, 1911), 403-455.

[11] Jakob J. Petuchowsky, "Abraham Geiger and Samuel Holdheim. Their Differences in Germany and Repercussions in America," *LBIYB* 22 (1977), 139-159, quotation 154.

[12] See Michael A. Meyer, "'Most of My Brethren Find Me Unacceptable': The Controversial Career of Rabbi Samuel Holdheim," in: *JSS* 9 (2003), no. 3, 1-19 (reprinted in this volume), which describes the development of the radical reformer from an Orthodox Talmudist born in the small town of Kempen in Posen to a representative of a universal Reform Judaism in Berlin as that of a "divided per-sonality," whose internal tensions followed those of the Reform movement in Germany (14).

and Prague, Einhorn in Erlangen, Würzburg and Munich. Both were characterized by being originally deeply rooted in Orthodoxy, and by their natural mastery of the rabbinical texts, which interestingly is reflected in their later Reform writings too; both of them completed their renunciation of their original conceptual world in theory and practice ultimately with a radicalism and refusal to compromise which reflect the process of their personal emancipation from their own traditional origins, and which allowed them to become most controversial personalities in their respect spheres of influence.

Einhorn was born on 10th November 1809 in the small village of Diespeck in central Franconia, not far from Fürth. He grew up in an extremely traditional environment; his father, the "trader" Maier Einhorn,[13] died early, so that his mother Kehla had to see to his education. Since the village schoolmaster in Diespeck was able to quench young David's thirst for knowledge for only a short time, from the age of nine onwards he attended the *yeshiva* of the renowned rabbi Wolf Hamburger (colloquially referred to as the "high school," "Jewish university" or "Talmud faculty"), amongst whose outstanding students he was counted already in the early years of his studies. The intellectual environment in which he found himself there can be characterized as a deeply anti-modernistic one, which left no room for other paths to the Jewish tradition (such as through the philosophy of religion or biblical exegesis) than the traditional exegesis of the Talmud and the Halakhic codices.[14] In the certificate of honor issued to him by three representatives of the Fürth rabbinate—besides Wolf Hamburger, they were Josua Moses Falkenauer and Juda Loeb Halberstadter—in 1829, he was certified as having an extraordinary level of Talmudic

---

[13] According to the entry of 16 April 1844 in the register of the Bad Kreuznach register office, on the occasion of the marriage of David Einhorn and his wife Julie Henrietta Ochs.

[14] On the *yeshiva* at Fürth and on Hamburger, see Mosche N. Rosenfeld, "Talmudschule und jüdische Erziehung in Fürth," in *Kleeblatt und Davidstern. Aus 400 Jahren jüdischer Vergangenheit in Fürth*, ed. Werner J. Heymann (Emskirchen: Mümmler, 1990), 88-91; Carsten Wilke, "Bayerische Bildungspolitiker gegen den Talmud. Das Ende der 'sogenannten jüdischen Hochschule zu Fürth' (1819-1830)," in *Neuer Anbruch. Zur deutsch-jüdischen Geschichte und Kultur*, ed. Michael Brocke, Aubrey Pomerance, and Andrea Schatz (Berlin: Metropol, 2001), 113-126; on the overall phenomenon of the education of rabbis at this time, see idem, *"Der Talmud und den Kant": Rabbinerausbildung an der Schwelle zur Moderne* (Hildesheim: Olms, 2003). I am indebted to Carsten Wilke also for the reference to a record book of Einhorn's in Hebrew, from the Fürth *yeshiva* from the year 1825/26 (Hebrew Union College, Cincinnati, microfilm 126).

scholarship, which justified granting him a certificate of ordination, although he had not yet gained a name as a rabbi. On account of his learning, he received the title of *morenu* (our teacher), with the note that any Israelite could "completely trust his pronouncements, and view his decisions in religious matters as having undoubted validity."[15]

Like many of the reformers of his times who had emerged from a traditional milieu, such as for example Abraham Geiger,[16] it seems however that quite early on Einhorn found this educational horizon, from which secular subjects such as philosophy, history, literature and science were consistently excluded, much too narrow, so that from 1829 onwards he took private lessons from the head of the Würzburg *Gymnasium,* and in 1832 he obtained the "Gymnasial-Absolutorium," or higher school-leaving certificate. He had already registered at the Julius-Maximilians University in Würzburg for the winter semester of 1830/31, and for the summer semester 1832 he moved to the Ludwig-Maximilians University in Munich, where until 1833 he predominantly studied philosophy, including under Friedrich W. J. Schelling, whose thinking was to remain a lasting influence on him. During the time of his academic development, his turning away from the educational ideal of Orthodox Judaism assumed concrete form in the decision to obtain a doctorate at the Friedrich-Alexander University at Erlangen. In February 1834, he took his doctorate there with a thesis on the subject of an "Explanation of various philosophical positions in the book of *More Nefuchim (sic!)* 1st part, by Maimonides" [*Erklärung verschiedener philosophischer Stellen im Buche More Nefuchim (sic!) I. Theil des Maimonides*], in which he dealt—amongst other things—with Salomon Maimon's attempt to bring Maimonides and Immanuel Kant into discussion with one another, and himself presented a short philosophical commentary on selected passages of the "Guide of the Perplexed."[17]

In contrast to Samuel Holdheim, who persisted for several years

---

[15] This document forms part of David Einhorn's doctoral file in the archives of the Friedrich-Alexander University at Erlangen (Fasc. 257/1834).

[16] On his intellectual development, see Susannah Heschel, *Abraham Geiger and the Jewish Jesus* (Chicago: Chicago University Press, 1998), 23-49.

[17] On Einhorn's intellectual development, see Hans-Joachim Bechtoldt, *Die jüdische Bibelkritik im 19. Jahrhundert* (Stuttgart: Kohlhammer, 1995), 90-159; Einhorn's doctoral book with his hand-written dissertation is to be found in the archives of Erlangen University (Acta der philosophischen Fakultät zu Erlangen. Die Promotion des David Eichhorn [*sic!*] von Fürth. 1834. Fasces 257); on the content of the dissertation, see Bechtholdt, ibid., 115-159.

as a rabbi in Frankfurt an der Oder along rather traditional lines, before his development into a radical reformer became evident during his time at Schwerin (1840-1847), Einhorn took up his first position as chief rabbi of Birkenfeld, with his official base in Hoppstädten, not as a representative of traditional Judaism, but as a neologist who was pursued by Orthodoxy with extreme enmity. In the grand duchy of Oldenburg, which was under liberal rule,[18] he was consequently able—as a successor to the Reform rabbi Bernhard Wechsler—to implement his ideas for the reform of Judaism without any great obstacles. The fact that he did not obtain a rabbinate until 1842, eight years after his doctorate, is a result of the fact that Wolf Hamburger as well as his colleagues (with the exception of Falkenauer, who did not participate in this) and students were able, by means of intrigues and denunciations in conservative Bavaria, to consistently prevent his appointment to the post of rabbi. In 1838, Einhorn had already been elected in the congregation of Wellhausen, near Würzburg, but the government refused to confirm his election on account of his Reform tendencies.[19] Even in 1846, when he applied to succeed Holdheim in Schwerin as chief rabbi of the grand duchy of Mecklenburg-Schwerin after the latter had accepted a call to the Reform congregation in Berlin, he had to defend himself against the interventions of his former teacher who—referring to his participation in the rabbinical conferences in Frankfurt am Main and Breslau in 1845 and 1846—denounced him to the Jewish congregation as an angry young man, troublemaker, denier of revelation and an enemy of Judaism, who had deviously obtained his title of *morenu* through deception and pretence.[20] In a "declaration" in the *Allgemeine Zeitung des Judentums*, Einhorn rejected

---

[18] See the praise for liberal politics in: David Einhorn, *Gedächtniss-Predigt bei dem Trauer-Gottesdienste wegen des Hinscheidens der Großherzogin Cäcilie von Oldenburg, gehalten in der Synagoge zu Hoppstaetten am 11. Februar 1844* (Birkenfeld: C. F. Kittsteiner, 1844).

[19] See *AZJ* 7 (1843), no. 18, 269.

[20] See "Rabbi Wolf Hamburger und sein Schweif," *Der Israelit des neunzehnten Jahrhunderts* 7 (1846), no. 27, 212f. The anonymous article from Birkenfeld expresses disdain for "such disastrous hustle and bustle from a man with one foot in the grave": Hamburger, "in his heyday, honored, respected, even regarded almost as holy by students and congregations, as a light of Israel, but now in the midst of his congregation a nobody, discarded flotsam [....], only creeps out of his hiding place now and then in order to spew poison and gall at all friends of progress, whom he regards as his enemies, and to employ cunning and deception to suppress the children of the reformation wherever people know him only by name, and thus surrounded with the aura of holiness" (ibid., 212).

this as a "despicable and infamous lie," and challenged Hamburger to publicly present proof for his accusations,[21] whereupon the latter's Fürth students Joel Götz, Seligman Dinkelspühler and Menki Zimmer accused him of speaking out "with matchless frivolity against his highly renowned teacher," of denying the authority of the Talmud, and of fabricating a "new Torah in miniature," so that it was right that not only had the congregation in Schwerin been warned, but also those in Krefeld and Kassel, in order to save them "from a great danger."[22]

Despite this resistance, during his time in Hoppstädten Einhorn quickly gained a reputation as an acknowledged scholar and level-headed reformer.[23] Among the factors contributing to this reputation were his first public intervention in the ever fiercer controversies between Orthodoxy and the Reform movement concerning the legitimacy of the modernization of Judaism on the basis of a historico-scientific examination of its own tradition. Following the controversies such as those concerning the Hamburg Temple at the beginning of the 1820s,[24] this conflict reached a dramatic climax in the "Geiger-Tiktin affair," which raged in Breslau from 1842 to 1849, and led to a symbolic trial of strength between reformers and traditionalists, which played a central role in the re-orientation of

---

[21] David Einhorn, "Erklärung," *AZJ* 10 (1846), no. 18, 266.

[22] "Eingesandte Erklärung, hervorgerufen durch die 'Erklärung' des Dr. David Einhorn in Hoppsteten, in der allgemeinen Zeitung des Judenthums No. 18," *Der Treue Zionswächter* 2 (1846), no. 24, 203-205. See also the declaration by Abraham Wechsler (district rabbi in Schwabach) in *AZJ* 10 (1846), no. 23, 343-344; Wechsler refers above all to Einhorn's rejection of the concept of a personal Messiah and the reconstruction of the Temple. In one declaration, the Schwerin congregational board denied ever having made inquiries of Hamburger, as they were "completely convinced" by Einhorn's "dignity," see *AZJ* 10 (1846), no. 25, 372. The Birkenfeld congregational board too made a statement in defense of Einhorn's honor, and attested to his "level-headed, calm and pastoral effectiveness, thanks to which our synagogues, schools and congregations are blossoming to an extent lacking in many of the largest and most populous congregations of the German fatherland," see *AZJ* 10 (1846), no. 32, 472.

[23] See the article "Verhältnisse der Israeliten im Fürstentume Birkenfeld," *Der Israelit des neunzehnten Jahrhunderts* 8 (1847), no. 42, 335-336; no. 43, 342-344, which emphasizes the circumspect reforms in the area of the school system and the liturgy, in particular the new synagogue code of 1843; see also the words of praise on the occasion of his departure from Hoppstädten to Schwerin, in *Israelit des neunzehnten Jahrhunderts* 8 (1847), no. 22, 166-167; no. 35, 276-277.

[24] See Andreas Brämer, *Judentum und religiöse Reform: Der Hamburger Israelitische Tempel 1817-1938* (Hamburg: Dölling & Galitz, 2000), 23-32; on the continuation of the dispute in the 1840s, see ibid., 40-56

German Judaism.[25] When the Breslau congregational board decided to hire Abraham Geiger as a modernistic "auxiliary rabbi" alongside the traditional chief rabbi Salomon Abraham Tiktin, in order to initiate a religious change, it caused a battle for intellectual supremacy in the congregation, which ultimately led to the establishment of institutional lines of separation between the Reformers and the Orthodox. One of the core points in the controversy lay in the question as to whether a Reform-oriented scholar such as Geiger, who in his writings had questioned whether rabbinical tradition and its hermeneutics of the Bible had the quality of divine revelation, and who had applied the criteria of historical science to the sources of Judaism, could legitimately serve a Jewish congregation as rabbi.[26] Geiger himself made a distinction between the strictly scientific approach and the duty of the rabbi to keep to the ordinances and to approach customs that were suffused with religious feeling with respect, even if from a scientific point of view they seemed to him to be obsolete.[27] As regards the authority of tradition, Geiger asserted that the Talmud, in contrast to the Bible, could make no claim to canonical significance, and legitimized the renewal of religious life with the aid of the principle—based on the idea of the oral Torah—of a continual adjustment of tradition to the needs of the present.[28]

Like Holdheim, David Einhorn was one of the seventeen reformers who were called upon by the committee of senior chairmen of the

---

[25] See Michael A. Meyer, *Response to Modernity: A History of the Reform Movement in Judaism* (New York: Oxford University Press, 1988), 109-114; Andreas Gotzmann, "Der Geiger-Tiktin-Streit—Trennungskrise und Publizität," in *In Breslau zu Hause? Juden in einer mitteleuropäischen Metropole der Neuzeit*, ed. Manfred Hettling, Andreas Reinke, and Norbert Conrads (Hamburg: Dölling & Galitz, 2003), 81-98; idem, *Eigenheit und Einheit. Modernisierungsdiskurse des deutschen Judentums der Emanzipationszeit* (Leiden: Brill Publishers, 2002), 193-211.

[26] On the Reform opinion on this question, see the *Bericht des Ober-Vorsteher-Collegiums an die Mitglieder der hiesigen Israeliten-Gemeinde über die gegenwärtig vorliegende Rabbinatsangelegenheit*, 2 vols. (Breslau: H. Richter, 1842); on the Orthodox view, see Salomon Abraham Tictin [sic!], *Darstellung des Sachverhältnisses in seiner hiesigen Rabbinats-Angelegenheit* (Breslau: H. Richter, 1842) (see 25-31 there, the statements by the chief rabbi of Posen, Salomon Eiger, and of the rabbinate of Lissa); *Entgegnung auf den Bericht des Ober-Vorsteher-Collegiums der hiesigen Israeliten-Gemeinde über die Rabbinats-Angelegenheit an die Mitglieder* (anonymous) (Breslau: H. Richter, 1842).

[27] Abraham Geiger, "Die zwei verschiedenen Betrachtungsweisen. Der Schriftsteller und der Rabbiner," *Wissenschaftliche Zeitschrift für jüdische Theologie* 4 (1839), 321-333.

[28] Idem, *Nachgelassene Schriften*, ed. Ludwig Geiger, vol. 1 (Hildesheim: Olms, 1999; reprint of the edition of Berlin 1875), 1-112, particularly 14-18, 92-112.

Israelite congregation in Breslau to present a "Rabbinical opinion on the compatibility of free research with the office of rabbi" [*Rabbinische Gutachten über die Verträglichkeit der freien Forschung mit dem Rabbineramte*]. In it, they were to address the question of whether the principle of progress argued by Geiger was legitimate from a Jewish perspective; whether researchers who questioned the authority of rabbinical literature could really still call themselves Jews; whether Jewish theology could withstand the integration of free scientific research as a new religious and cultural system of interpretation; and whether those who adopted it were entitled to carry out the office of rabbi.[29] For all the differences between the individual opinions, the predominantly young, Reform-oriented rabbis defended Geiger unanimously against accusations of heresy, and spoke out in favor of the application of scientific methods, as well as—albeit with discernible reticence—in favor of a clear distinction between biblical revelation and rabbinical literature. The more radical amongst them hinted that Talmudic ethics were not in accordance with contemporary consciousness in every case, and granted the rabbi the right to initiate changes in religious practice "with the fully recognized agreement of the competent spokesmen of the times."[30] However, what is striking overall is the conservative trend of the expert opinions, that "traditionalization of the new scientific procedure," to use the words of Andreas Gotzmann, with which the rabbis attempted to integrate the categories of historico-critical research into the common religious tradition, instead of risking an open break with it.[31]

Like Holdheim, in his learned expert opinion Einhorn defended above all Geiger's right to research the Talmudic sources historically and, in his reforms of outdated practices, to invoke the principle of development. He too made use of the strategy of claiming precisely the Talmud itself, with its views that were often outdated in the opinion of the reformers, for the spirit of free research. Far more sharply and trenchantly than many other experts, with all due acknowledgement of the truthfulness of the rabbinical tradition, Einhorn condemned the Orthodox "apotheosis" of the Talmud, its "authority

---

[29] *Rabbinische Gutachten über die Verträglichkeit der freien Forschung mit dem Rabbineramte*, 2 vols. (Breslau: L. Freund, 1842/43).
[30] "Gutachten des Landesrabbiners Herrn Dr. Holdheim in Schwerin," in ibid., vol. 1, 38-83, quotation 76.
[31] Gotzmann, *Eigenheit und Einheit*, 193-207, here 195.

which transforms Judaism into a static swamp and condemns it to eternal stagnation."[32] However, if it were not to be a "frivolous game with what is holy" based on mundane laziness, deviation from the ceremonial laws must be based "in the spirit of Judaism" and on mature, scientific insight.[33] In Geiger's case, there could be no question of mocking the Talmud; rather, one found the earnest desire of a "mind and soul struggling toward light and truth," to research the sources of Judaism to discover "what elements are part of its essential nature—and what elements are accretions, how much of its divine, eternal and developing spirit, under the cloak, is prepared for breakthrough and longs for it, while the various periods of its existence have already gone out into the world, or are yet to come."[34] Einhorn's expert opinion ends with a call to Orthodoxy to drop the "whip of fanaticism" and to participate in the reform that was urgently necessary:

> Truly, what Judaism needs now is other weapons for its consolidation, weapons of love and harmony! A large, creditable part of Israel feels a lively need, one that makes itself known in all four corners of the Earth, to structure our religious circumstances better. Everywhere, the children of our holy house call to us with a thousand voices [....]: "The house has been damaged!" We would have to be deaf not to hear this call. Therefore as is fitting for priests of God, instead of steadily increasing the damage to the house, which resounds with the thunderous bombardment of mutual enmity, and instead of forcing the truth to take flight in all directions, let us rather come together in brotherly unity to examine the house, to break out the harmful rotten stones and replace them with others quarried from the holy rock of Judaism, so that the temple of God is restored to its old glory. And as we unite in the name of the Lord and the guardian of Israel, he shall also help us to build his house [....], he shall provide us with the strength to preserve his teachings on the written and spoken law, cleansed of slurry and accretions. Let us not deceive ourselves about the current standpoint of Judaism! Let us not seek to terrify with bogeymen before which these days only children tremble![35]

If in the debate with the traditional rabbis, Einhorn had fundamentally declared his support for criticism of the Talmud as a

---

[32] "Gutachten des Herrn Rabbiners Dr. David Einhorn im Fürstenthume Birkenfeld," in *Rabbinische Gutachten*, vol. 1, 125-139, quotation 127.
[33] Ibid., 131-131.
[34] Ibid., 135-136.
[35] Ibid., 136-127.

legitimate means for practical reforms, it nonetheless seems no
coincidence that he formulated the theoretical foundations of his
concept of reform and his understanding of the shape of modern
Judaism more precisely for the first time at the point where he
was overtaken in his own radicalism. The context was formed by
the lively controversy surrounding the program of the Frankfurt
association that was decisively influenced by Theodor Creizenach,
the "Verein der Reformfreunde" [Friends of Reform], that small
and short-lived movement of intellectual laymen, who in 1843 had
drafted a declaration of principles which, apart from the rejection—generally emphatic in the Reform movement—of the anticipation of a "Messiah who is to lead the Israelites back to the
land of Palestine," contested all dogmatic as well as practical
authority of the Talmud, and postulated the possibility of "unlimited further development" of the "Mosaic religion"; it ultimately
thereby also implicitly called into question the revelatory character and validity of the Bible.[36] Concealed behind the concept of
"Mosaic" religion or of "Mosaism," which was also used by Einhorn
and Holdheim, under the influence of the distinction current at
the time in Protestant biblical studies, between an earlier prophetic
Mosaic-Israelite religion and a later priestly-rabbinical one, there
lay a conscious or unconscious internalization of the negative non-
Jewish perception of the rabbinical tradition and the attempt to
demonstrate that Judaism was capable of a return to a universalism that was deeply rooted in its history. It is not without significance that also in 1843, there raged a ferocious debate about the
anti-Jewish theses of the young Hegelian Bruno Bauer, who rejected
emancipation because in his view, Judaism had no rational universal laws, but due to its "oriental nature," it was trapped in a
system of particularistic, inane and exclusive religious ceremonies.
According to Bauer, even a radical re-definition, such as the
"Friends of Reform" proposed, was not capable of lifting the barrier between the Jews and non-Jewish society—the only remedy

---

[36] Quoted after Meyer, *Response to Modernity*, 122; on the overall phenomenon of
the radical lay groups that organized themselves in cities like Breslau and Berlin
too, see *ibid.*, 119-131; on the Frankfurt Reform Association see idem, "Alienated
Intellectuals in the Camp of Religious Reform: The Frankfurt Reformfreunde, 1842-
1845," *AJS Review* 6 (1981), 61-86; David Philipson, *The Reform Movement* (New York:
The Macmillan Company, 1931), 107-139.

was, according to him, to give up all national traits and to turn toward freedom and humanity.[37]

The public debate surrounding Bauer's radical views made a clarification of the relation between Judaism, universalism and the authority of the religious sources even more urgent within the Reform movement than it was already in view of the challenge posed by the "Friends of Reform." What price were people prepared to pay in order to demonstrate Judaism's universalism and its distance from rabbinical tradition? Within the Reform camp, only Mendel Hess from Saxony-Weimar supported the position of the "Friends of Reform" "with joyful mutiny" as the basis for a "Judaism that was lively, dignified, and modern" in contrast to "rigid rabbinism."[38] The overwhelming majority of rabbis, however, rejected the idea of simply casting overboard the bulk of Jewish tradition along with rabbinical literature, and feared that the principle of "unlimited further development" would leave behind a Judaism without any revelatory basis, in which for example Ludwig Philippson could no longer see any positive Jewish religion, but at best "a mere non-Christianity."[39] In the first radical practical demands of the "Friends of Reform," the abandonment of the dietary laws and of circumcision, both of which appeared to them to be elements of an outdated Jewish particularism that were pre-Mosaic, exclusive, and which inhibited integration into non-Jewish society, many saw a sectarian radicalism which must be curbed, since ultimately it left no sacrosanct core of religious tradition untouched.[40]

---

[37] Bruno Bauer, *Die Judenfrage* (Brunswick: F. Otto, 1853); idem, *The Jewish Problem* (Cincinnati: Hebrew Union College—Jewish Institute of Religion, 1958) for Jewish reactions, see inter alia Gustav Philippson, *Die Judenfrage von Bruno Bauer näher beleuchtet* (Dessau: Fritsche und Sohn, 1843); Gotthold Salomon, *Bruno Bauer und seine gehaltlose Kritik über die Judenfrage* (Hamburg: Perthes, Besser & Mauke, 1843); Abraham Geiger, "Bruno Bauer und die Juden. Mit Bezug auf dessen Aufsatz: Die Judenfrage," *Wissenschaftliche Zeitschrift für jüdische Theologie* 5 (1844), issue 2, 199-234 and 325-371.

[38] Mendel Hess, "Der Frankfurter Reformverein," *Der Israelit des neunzehnten Jahrhunderts* 4 (1843), no. 46, 183-185 (quotations 183); no. 47, 187-188; no. 48, 191-192.

[39] Ludwig Philippson, "Wohin?," *AZJ* 7 (1843), no. 34, 502-503, here 502. For a conservative viewpoint, see Michael Sachs, "Gutachten über den Reformverein," *Zeitschrift für die religiösen Interessen des Judentums* 1 (1844), issue 2, 49-60 as well as the "Nachbemerkung" by Zacharias Frankel, ibid., 60-73.

[40] On the background to the circumcision controversy originating from Frankfurt, see Robert Liberles, *Religious Conflict in Social Context: The Resurgence of Orthodox Judaism in Frankfurt am Main*, 1838-1877 (Westport, CT: Greenwood Press), 1985, 23-65; Andreas Gotzmann, *Jüdisches Recht im kulturellen Prozeß. Die Wahrnehmung der Halacha im Deutschland des 19. Jahrhunderts* (Tübingen: J.C.B. Mohr, 1997), 251-302.

Samuel Hirsch too, who at this time was the Chief Rabbi in Luxembourg,[41] and who had in 1842, during his tenure as the rabbi of Dessau, with his work *Die Religionsphilosophie der Juden*, sought to demonstrate, in debate with Hegelianism, that Judaism was the superior religion in the matter of universalism,[42] turned sharply and determinedly against the "mendacious reform" of the Frankfurt "Friends of Reform," whom he accused of "stripping [Judaism] of all that was characteristic," and thus of calling into question its right to exist.[43] At the same time, Hirsch defended Judaism's sympathy with modern times, against Bruno Bauer's accusation of it being antiquated, particularistic and incapable of modernization, and asserted that it was "intimately acquainted" with the modern world view.[44] According to him, Judaism, neither a faith nor a nationality, fulfilled the role of a "born witness to history"[45] with the messianic task of realizing "here on Earth the kingdom of truth, of reason, of the truly rational lawfulness created from the spirit," but that required "removing everything from our life that makes it difficult or impossible for us to fulfil this task."[46] Like the "Friends of Reform," Hirsch too contested the authority of the Talmud: having arisen in a time of decline and doubt, it stood (he said) for the traditions of the past, and rabbinical Judaism had overlooked the fact that even Moses and the prophets had not viewed the ceremonies as immutable laws, but as the symbolic representation of the "inner religious concept."[47] Nevertheless, Hirsch regarded the central religious laws and ceremonies of Judaism, understood correctly and in harmony with progressive moral insight, as necessary means for envisioning its own messianic role, as symbols to make the abstract ideas and ideals capable of being

---

[41] On Hirsch, see *inter alia* Heinz Monz, "Samuel Hirsch (1815-1889). Ein jüdischer Reformator aus dem Hunsrück," *Jahrbuch für westdeutsche Landesgeschichte* 17 (1991), 159-180; Gershon Greenberg, "The Historical Origins of God and Man. Samuel Hirsch's Luxemburg Writings," *LBIYB* 20 (1975), 129-148.

[42] Samuel Hirsch, *Die Religionsphilosophie der Juden oder das Prinzip der jüdischen Religionsanschauung und sein Verhältnis zum Heidentum, Christentum und zur absoluten Philosophie* (1842) (Hildesheim: Olms, 1986).

[43] Idem, *Die Reform im Judenthum und dessen Beruf in der gegenwärtigen Welt* (Leipzig: H. Hunger, 1844), 39-55, here 50. On Hirsch's clash with Bauer, see idem, *Das Judenthum, der christliche Staat und die moderne Kritik. Briefe zur Beleuchtung der Judenfrage von Bruno Bauer* (Leipzig: H. Hunger, 1843).

[44] Idem, *Die Reform im Judenthum*, 38.

[45] Ibid., 60.

[46] Ibid., 39.

[47] Ibid., 17.

experienced through the senses. The Jews must therefore retain in their religion a "specifically Jewish symbolism," "which is suitable for always illustrating clearly, to them and to the world, this witness role for the holiness of history."[48] So as much as one must agree with the "Friends of Reform" that one must rid the ceremonial of all "that hinders us from participating, with all our intellectual and material powers, in preserving and furthering civil society,"[49] nonetheless central biblical symbols such as the Sabbath and circumcision must be preserved. Adopting a two-fronted position against the "Friends of Reform," who in his view did not offer an acceptable principle of reform because they did not assume an immutable essence of Judaism beyond the mutable forms, and contrary to Bauer's verdict concerning the alleged insurmountable Jewish particularism, Hirsch characterized Judaism—when compared to Christianity in its dogmatism—as the superior embodiment of the Universal and of human freedom. Since however the Jews were a people with a universal mission, they must remain recognizable as Jews and have rituals and ceremonies that reminded them of their sublime vocation.

David Einhorn was evidently fundamentally in agreement with Hirsch, even if—as is yet to be shown—there was soon to be disagreement about the concrete assessment of circumcision and the dietary laws. In a letter published in the *Allgemeine Zeitung des Judentums*, to a Christian friend who had shown himself to be impressed by the program of the Frankfurt radicals, he warned the association of the "Friends of Reform" that their program would lead only to subversion and to the "uprooting of Judaism, which it feigns to reform."[50] This would however cause a "disastrous schism" that would damage most deeply the struggle for emancipation and against the "fierce zeal for proselytizing." Einhorn did in fact share their conviction of Judaism's capacity for development, which was demonstrated by its entire history: the Talmud itself, he said, was an element of this development, "however much it had, on the other hand, undoubtedly contributed to the ossification of Jewish life." Reform based on the unshakable principles of "Mosaism"—monotheism and the belief

---

[48] Ibid., 64.
[49] Ibid., 67.
[50] David Einhorn, "Gutachtliche Äußerung eines jüdischen Theologen über den Reformverein an einen sich dafür interessierenden Christen," *AZJ* 8 (1844), no. 7, 87-89, here 87.

in revelation—was therefore wholly legitimate; one must "unleash the rigidified forms [....] through the breath of the living spirit," examine them historically, and "reduce their enormous number, under which Judaism sighs and gasps." However, reform seemed to him to cease to be legitimate where the divine nature of "Mosaism" was disputed, the progressive role that the Talmud had once played in Jewish history was not recognized, and thus a state of complete "lawlessness" was sanctioned.

> In its various stages, Judaism has in fact shown the possibility of progressive development in respect of the form and also the spirit of the Israelite teachings, to the extent to which it is deemed capable of entering ever more clearly and purely into human consciousness, and no Israelite who knows his religion will wish to deny it a perfectibility, according to which its essence, interconnecting everything, was destined from the start to triumph over the excluding form, but this could not and must not be discarded as a protective shell and—as it were —as Israel's priestly robes until it has penetrated humanity to its very core and to its full extent, and Mosaism has fulfilled its priestly mission with the arrival of the kingdom of the Messiah. On the contrary, every Israelite must protest most solemnly against an absolute development intended for the spirit of Mosaism, in that the divine, as something complete in itself, cannot permit such a movement, whose lines, on top of everything, run in a diametrically opposed direction, and thus such an assertion involves the non-divinity of Mosaism.[51]

This passage contains, in a nutshell, the foundations of Einhorn's thinking, which he systematized in his other work in various contexts, developed pugnaciously against Orthodoxy as well as moderate Reform, and which he continued to illustrate in ever new images in countless sermons. Recurring themes such as the distinction between "form" and "spirit" or "essence" of the teachings of Israel, the further development of the human consciousness and its increasing insight into the doctrine, the idea of the priestly mission of the Jewish people and the particular forms as Israel's "priestly robes"—all this here serves the purpose of attempting on the one hand to legitimize a reform that is consistent and clearly founded, and on the other hand to guard against a step too far, toward the dissolution of the traditional foundations of Judaism and an unhistorical rejection of rabbinical tradition, which threatened all to easily to extend to the

[51] Ibid., 88.

Mosaic Torah itself. In spite of the vehemence with which he himself would soon uncompromisingly contest the authority of the Talmud, as we shall show, Einhorn held fast all his life to a relative acknowledgement of its historical function in the course of advancing awareness of the revelation of God as well as of Israel's messianic role in history, and reacted sensitively to attacks on the Talmud, which in his view followed false motives and "could not possibly [intend] a reformation, but rather merely a complete destruction of Mosaism."[52]

This also seems to be the background to the fierce controversy between him and Holdheim immediately after the first rabbinical conference in Brunswick in 1844, in which Einhorn had not taken part. Holdheim, who in the course of his search for an acceptable religious authority had questioned the rabbinical literature ever more radically, until he reached the conclusion that the Talmud had harmfully preserved in the Diaspora the system of laws that bore the hallmarks of ancient Israel, and that the dispersion of Israel must count as the revelation which swept away once and for all the law revealed at Sinai, in order to make way for universalism,[53] reported in 1844, in the journal *Der Israelit des neunzehnten Jahrhunderts*, under the title "Was lehrt das rabbinische Judenthum über den Eid?" [What does rabbinical Judaism teach us about the oath?], on the unanimous recommendation of the Brunswick rabbinical conference of 1844 to get rid of the *more judaico* oath and the *Kol Nidre*.[54] In this context, he turned against an apologetic defense of this prayer, which was frequently cited by anti-Semites as proof of the unreliability of Jewish promises, and furthermore called for critical destruction of the theory of rabbinical Judaism—incontestable in his view—according to which oaths and vows can be dissolved which affect the mutual relations between human beings. "We who have the courage to give up the *Kol Nidre*," Holdheim emphasized, "must also have the courage

---

[52] Ibid., 89.

[53] Samuel Holdheim, *Ueber die Autonomie der Rabbinen und das Prinzip der jüdischen Ehe. Ein Beitrag zur Verständigung über einige das Judentum betreffende Zeitfragen* (Schwerin: C. Kürschner, 1844); idem, *Vorträge über die Mosaische Religion für die denkenden Israeliten* (Schwerin: C. Kürschner, 1844) (however, in the preface he explicitly rejected the ideas of the "Friends of Reform").

[54] On the rabbinical conferences of 1844-1847, see Meyer, *Response to Modernity*, 132-142. On the discussions about the *Kol Nidre*, see the *Protocolle der ersten Rabbiner-Versammlung, abgehalten zu Braunschweig vom 12ten bis zum 19ten Juni 1844* (Brunswick: F. Vieweg und Sohn, 1844), 33-42.

to rid ourselves of and decisively reject the theory of the dissolubil-
ity of oaths and vows, which is a foul stain in rabbinical Judaism"—
less from fear of disparagement or as a justification vis-à-vis
governments, but rather for the love of truth, which commands Jews
to "purify [their] own religion of blemishes."[55]

Holdheim's critics included David Einhorn, who accused him of
having misrepresented the position of the rabbinic sages with his
"condemnation of the *Kol Nidre*," and thus of having unjustly brought
discredit on the Talmud, which definitely did not justify the dissol-
ubility of oaths.[56] What appeared at first to be a factual dispute
between two experts about the appropriate interpretation of the rabbinical position, in which both mustered the arsenals of their profound knowledge of the Talmud, escalated—through a second,
extremely polemical article by Einhorn in the *Allgemeine Zeitung des
Judentums*—to become a heated debate, in which Holdheim was now
accused of hate for the Talmud and a radicalism that "hurls the
most dreadful of all accusations at rabbinical Judaism, and makes it
into a sewer of the most abominable vice and sin," "into a verita-
ble monster, the epitome of all depravity," just to demonstrate its
"non-divinity" and thus to be able to relinquish it.[57]

> Thus everything that Dr. Holdheim raises against me is empty sham
> knowledge and illusion, and if his current discussion has opened my
> eyes about anything, it is in relation to his endeavors, which until now
> I had respected. In this regard, I am happy to grant Dr. Holdheim
> that I have been sleeping. Now I have awoken, and with me truly all
> those who care about the truth and the honor of their co-religionists,

---

[55] Samuel Holdheim, "Was lehrt das rabbinische Judentum über den Eid?," *Der Israelit des neunzehnten Jahrhunderts* 5 (1844), no. 35, 277-280, here 279; see also idem, "Noch Einiges über die rabbinische Auflösbarkeit der Eide," *Der Israelit des neun-zehnten Jahrhunderts* 5 (1844), no. 41, 327-329.

[56] David Einhorn, "Die rabbinische Lehre von der Auflösbarkeit der Eide," *Der Israelit des neunzehnten Jahrhunderts* 5 (1844), no. 7, 375-378, here 378. Holdheim coun-tered that in his remarks, he had naturally assumed that even strict adherents to the rabbinical tradition had in practice gone beyond the Talmud in this point, but urged Einhorn to study the rabbinical sources more closely, in order to understand the character of the Talmudic view in this matter appropriately; see Samuel Holdheim, "Bemerkungen zu der Entgegnung des Herrn Dr. Einhorn auf meine zwei Aufsätze betreffend die rabbinische Lehre von der Auflösbarkeit der Eide," *Der Israelit des neunzehnten Jahrhunderts* 6 (1845), no. 2, 9-13; no. 3, 17-20.

[57] David Einhorn, "Antikritik. Dr. Holdheim's neuentdeckte Lehre des rabbinis-chen Judenthums in Bezug auf das Kol Nidre und die Auflösbarkeit assertorischer Eide," *AZJ* 9 (1845), no. 13, 194-196; no. 18, 274-275; no. 19, 289-292; no. 22, 333-335, here 195.

and who wish to see Judaism developed further in its present existence, purified of all that is harmful and useless, but not to see it slan-
dered and treacherously assassinated.[58]

However, unlike the case of the controversy between Holdheim and
Zacharias Frankel, against whose defense of the *Kol Nidre* the Schwerin
rabbi had actually directed his attack,[59] behind the vehemence of
the argumentation, which no doubt also reflects Einhorn's disputa-
tious temperament, there is no fundamental dissent about the assessment of rabbinical literature as well as of the practical reforms, even
if Holdheim's radical disavowal of the Talmud at this time evidently
did not fit in Einhorn's more cautious concept of a historical appreciation and critique of the rabbis. To him it was very important—
and in this he seems in 1845 to be closer to Abraham Geiger[60]—to
justify the reforms carefully, without fighting the law in which God's
will was manifested, undermining the authority of the Bible and
rejecting rabbinical literature in its historical importance as completely irrelevant. Holdheim, on the other hand, in his *Das
Ceremonialgesetz im Messiasreich* (1845), put forward the thesis that the
ceremonial laws had once—in the time of Mosaic theocracy—been
intended to separate Israel as a holy people from the rest of humanity, and in the messianic time of religious universalism that had now
begun they could therefore no longer claim any validity, and that
relinquishing them in favor of convictions, feelings and inner moral
obligations was a universalistic act. In this context he trenchantly
rebutted all attempts to show liberal reforms as being justified or
based in the Talmud as dishonest and useless:

> It is an unforgivable weakness that one should keep well away from,
> to press the flag of progress into the stiffened hands of the Talmud.
> It is high time that people felt strong enough in relation to the
> Talmud and confronted it with the awareness that has long since
> advanced beyond it, not to drag along behind them the heavy tomes
> with every step forwards, and without opening them, lying in wait

---

[58] Ibid., 335.

[59] See Samuel Holdheim, *Die erste Rabbinerversammlung und Herr Dr. Frankel* (Schwerin:
C. Kürschner, 1845), 10-11; idem, "Der Eid nach dem rabbinischen Judenthume,"
Literaturblatt des Orients 6 (1845), 164-69, 197-204, 215-20 and 229-34; Zacharias
Frankel, *Die Eidesleistung der Juden in theologischer und historischer Beziehung*, 2nd edition
(Dresden and Leipzig: Arnold, 1847).

[60] On Geiger's concern to preserve an emotional connection to the Jewish heritage, including the rabbinical literature, see Meyer, *Response to Modernity*, 89-99.

for an innocent remark, in order to justify the foundation of progress thereon.[61]

Instead of a lasting disagreement, at the rabbinical conferences in Frankfurt and Breslau in 1845/46, at which Einhorn definitely appeared amongst the radical reformers, his fundamental agreement with central convictions held by Holdheim became apparent for the first time. Against the resolute opposition of Zacharias Frankel, for whom Hebrew as a "holy language" was inseparably bound up with the essence of Judaism,[62] he spoke in favor of holding services in the vernacular, for the sake of the inwardness of thoughts, convictions and feelings during prayer, whilst Hebrew remained the language of "study of the law."[63] Language drew its holiness from the content that was conveyed, but had no religious quality itself. Einhorn furthermore rejected the doubts of Samuel Hirsch, who regarded it as unacceptable to consistently ban Hebrew from the services, as that would unnecessarily deepen the chasm between lay people and rabbis, who would then soon be the only ones to have mastered Hebrew,[64] and—like Holdheim—voted against retaining Hebrew for the majority of the liturgy: "We cannot strike against the rigid rock of dead language and let water flow from it in order to quench the people's thirst."[65] At the negotiations concerning the retention of the concept of the Messiah in prayer, Einhorn, like Holdheim and Hirsch, voted for the committee report, which envisaged doing without any political-national overtones, and spoke in favor of "the removal of all lusting for bloody sacrifices and political restoration," as well as for

---

[61] Samuel Holdheim, *Das Ceremonialgesetz im Messiasreich. Als Vorläufer einer größern Schrift über die Religiöse Reform des Judenthums* (Schwerin: C. Kürschner, 1845). On this, see the critical discussion by David Einhorn, "Dr. Holdheim's Schrift: Das Ceremonialgesetz im Messiasreich," *Literatur-Blatt zum Israeliten des 19. Jahrhunderts* 1 (1846), no. 37, 157-160; no. 38, 161-164; no. 39, 165-168.

[62] *Protokolle und Aktenstücke der zweiten Rabbiner-Versammlung, abgehalten in Frankfurt am Main, vom 15ten bis zum 28ten Juli 1845* (Frankfurt am Main: E. Ullmann, 1845), 22. On the discussion concerning Hebrew at the conference, see Gotzmann, *Eigenheit und Einheit*, 261-276.

[63] *Protokolle und Aktenstücke*, 27.

[64] Ibid., 30-31. On this, see the objection by Abraham Geiger, that one should not think of Judaism as "going around on the crutches of a language" and thus allow it to appear as a "national religion" (*ibid.*, 32-33).

[65] Ibid., 49. In later years, both Holdheim and Einhorn once again emphasized more heavily the relevance of Hebrew. On Holdheim in this regard, see the article by Katrien de Graef in this volume; in Einhorn's Reform prayer book *Olath Tamid* (Baltimore: C. W. Schneidereith, 1858) more than half the liturgy was Hebrew.

an interpretation of the messianic hope in the sense of Israel's contribution to the universal progress of humanity. It is interesting that in this connection, he explicitly saw the value of the concept of Israel's status as the chosen people as the "awareness of an undeniable advantage" also in the fact that it felt a "beneficial self-esteem in relation to the dominant church."[66]

As regards Einhorn's critical attitude to the rabbinical continuation of Mosaic law, there is a noteworthy report in which as the spokesman for the committee for the position of women, he worked out a masterly analysis of how the rabbis had additionally exacerbated the view of the social, legal and religious inferiority of women that was rooted in Mosaic law, and postulated for his day the complete religious equality of women with men.[67] Following on from Geiger's article of 1837,[68] and in clear agreement with Holdheim's position, who in his time was among the most firm critics of the treatment of women in the Jewish tradition,[69] Einhorn asked "whether a proportion of our co-religionists which is eminently receptive to religious impressions shall continue—as heretofore—to experience an insulting exclusion from sharing in several duties and rights, to the detriment of themselves and the whole religious community," and called for the rabbinical views that were characterized by antiquated thinking to be overcome:

> From their point of view, the rabbis were however fully entitled to systematically exclude the female sex from a significant portion of the religious obligations and rights, and the poor woman was not permitted to complain about the withholding of high, spiritual favors, since it was believed that God himself had uttered the condemnation of her; with so many insulting setbacks in civil life, she could not even complain that the house of God too was as good as locked against her, that she had to beg the rabbis for permission to make the daily expression of the Israelite creed like alms, she was not permitted to take part in religious instruction nor in certain holy parental duties, the performance of religious acts being sometimes waived, sometimes forbidden, and finally insulted most bitterly in the house of God by

---

[66] *Protokolle und Aktenstücke*, 74-75; see the votes of Holdheim (76-77) and Hirsch (78-79).

[67] *Protokolle der dritten Versammlung deutscher Rabbiner, abgehalten zu Breslau, vom 13. bis 24. Juli 1846* (Breslau: Leuckart, 1847), 253-265.

[68] Abraham Geiger, "Die Stellung des weiblichen Geschlechtes in dem Judenthume unserer Zeit," *Wissenschaftliche Zeitschrift für jüdische Theologie* 3 (1837), issue 1, 1-14.

[69] See Samuel Holdheim, *Die religiöse Stellung des weiblichen Geschlechts im talmudischen Judenthum* (Schwerin: C. Kürschner, 1846).

the daily benediction for the good fortune of not having been born a woman. [....] But for our religious awareness that all people are accorded an equal degree of natural holiness, and for which the distinctions in the holy Scripture in this case have only a relative and momentary validity, it is a sacred duty to express the complete religious equality of the female sex most emphatically. In this respect life, which is stronger than any theory, has certainly achieved something; but for complete equality there is much that is still lacking, and even the little that has already been done still lacks legal force. It is thus part of our vocation to express the equal religious obligation and entitlement of woman, as far as possible, as lawful [....].[70]

The extent to which Einhorn appeared as a critical ally of Holdheim is shown in the fact that he supported the latter's criticism of Abraham Geiger's report on the work of the Sabbath committee: this criticism emphasized the restoration of a "worthy Sabbath celebration," but left the question concerning the Sabbath's conflict with the working day of non-Jewish society open.[71] In his vote, Einhorn was in favor of a symbolic interpretation of the Sabbath, which placed the emphasis in the matter of the observance of the Sabbath primarily on the remembrance of the liberation from Egypt and the theological declaration of belief in God as the creator of the universe,[72] and in practice wanted to allow a flexible arrangement for the Sabbath rest, including commercial activity "by means of non-Jews."[73] In this, he

---

[70] *Protokolle der dritten Versammlung deutscher Rabbiner*, 264. The concrete demands of the committee were nevertheless formulated in relatively general terms (see ibid., 265). Only later, in America, was Einhorn to turn his ideas into practice in the congregation. Thus in 1858, in a sermon in Baltimore, he condemned the "gallery cage" of the women's galleries, and granted the women of his congregation the same religious rights and duties; see David Einhorn, "Predigt, vom Herausgeber dieser Blätter gehalten im Tempel der Har Sinai Gemeinde," *Sinai* 3 (1858/59), no. 1, 824; idem, "Über Familiensitze in den Synagogen," *Sinai* 6 (1861/62), no. 7, 205ff. Under his leadership, the Philadelphia Conference spoke in favor of a reform of the divorce law and of revising the liturgy of the wedding to express the equal rights of the partners; see Meyer, *Response to Modernity*, 256-257; and see *Protokolle der Rabbiner-Konferenz abgehalten zu Philadelphia, vom 3. bis zum 6. November 1869* (New York: S. Hecht, 1870), 19-39. On the reform of the position of women in American congregations in the nineteenth century, see Karla Goldman, *Beyond the Synagogue Gallery. Finding a Place for Women in American Judaism* (Cambridge, MA: Harvard University Press, 2000).

[71] *Protokolle der dritten Versammlung deutscher Rabbiner*, 20-21.

[72] Ibid., 26ff.

[73] Ibid., 57ff. In the event of a conflict with professional duties, for example in government employment, the basic principle applied that the Sabbath must, as a "symbolic duty, which does not claim eternal validity, give way to the purely religious [duty] of civil service" (ibid., 198.)

did not go so far as Holdheim, in whose view a worthy Sabbath celebration was ultimately only conceivable by being moved to the Sunday, since only in this way could the conflict with the demands of civil (non-Jewish) society be settled: "We wish to save the Sabbath for Judaism, and save it [Judaism] through the Sabbath, even if the symbolic shell is surrendered to transience."[74] In contrast to Holdheim and Hirsch, who were judging from the same radical perspective,[75] at no point was Einhorn willing to take the radical step of moving the Sabbath to the Sunday, not even in the far more assimilated American society in which he later lived.[76]

In another central question, that of the preservation or abandonment of the dietary laws, Einhorn was in agreement with Holdheim on the matter, but earned the latter's sharp criticism because he sought to justify getting rid of most of the *kashrut* rules on the basis of an interpretation of rabbinical literature. As a member of the committee of the rabbinical conference with competence for the question, in a series of articles in 1847 Einhorn lamented the alienation that arises from the conflict between the demands of everyday life and the dietary laws, since Jews who had broken the latter

---

[74] Ibid., 59-73, here 73.

[75] On Hirsch's opinion, see "Des Dr. Hirsch Votum über die Sabbathfrage," *Der Israelit des neunzehnten Jahrhunderts* 7 (1846), no. 34, 266ff. Hirsch pressed resolutely for a "complete balancing of teaching and life in relation to the Sabbath" (266), argued for it to be moved to Sunday, and rejected fears that this could be understood as a rapprochement toward Christianity (267). See idem, *Die Sabbathfrage vor der dritten Rabbinerversammlung. Ein Votum* (Berlin: Verlag des Verfassers, 1846).

[76] See David Einhorn, "Predigt gehalten am Schabuothfeste 5631 (1871) im Tempel der Adath-Jeschurun-Gemeinde zu New York," in idem, *Ausgewählte Predigten und Reden*, ed. Kaufmann Kohler (New York: E. Steiger, 1880), 306-313. There, Einhorn complained about his congregation's lack of attendance at services, but rejected the move to Sunday as not being very helpful: "It is just a shame that this radical cure would kill the patient off completely. I once heard at the Breslau rabbinical conference the apt remark [by Leopold Stein, see Meyer, *Response to Modernity*, 139]: One could certainly bury the Sabbath on the Friday evening, but one would wait in vain on Sunday for its resurrection. And that is how it is! For such a resuscitation would require a spirit of Elijah, who with his holy ardor was able to breathe life into the dead child, and no such ardor is to be found in this race, and least of all amongst those for whom the move is intended to take place, and such a dreadful chasm between the old and the new Israel is to come into being. Such an exchange with the wedding ring would be seen by numerous Jews who eagerly desire it as only as a renunciation of the God of Israel and marriage to Christianity, and thus the now unfaithful bride would now also extinguish the last embers of the old fire of love in the water" (312). As a compromise, he suggested the introduction of an additional Sunday service not of a Sabbatic nature, which would take place every four weeks (313).

saw in this a break, and soon gave up their commitment to Judaism altogether.[77] Consequently he was in favor of a concentration and reduction of the *kashrut* to essential practices which should commit specifically to the concept of "humanity to animals" (slaughter and the ban on cooking the flesh of an animal in its mother's milk, consuming blood), whilst all other rules, in particular those that brought about "social segregation" should be dropped.[78] In contrast to Holdheim, for whom the dietary laws were obsolete simply because of the invalidity of the ceremonial legislation in the modern era, he argued above all on the basis of cultural-historical considerations about the origins of the individual laws and with reflections on the question of their religious significance for the present.[79] But he also attempted to argue within the Halakhic system, and to prove by exegesis that even the rabbinical tradition had declared at least those biblical purity rules relating to sacrifices in the Temple to be invalid after its destruction. He argued, however, that the Talmud had misjudged the original connection of the dietary laws with these purity rules, and therefore continued to see them as autonomous law that continued to stand.[80] Holdheim agreed with Einhorn's concrete proposals, but rejected his argumentation, in particular his invocation of the Talmud, and accused him of having "torn away the cobwebs of the Talmudic view," but nevertheless still repeatedly "becoming entangled in them."[81] Instead of wanting to justify the removal of the dietary laws by exegesis from their original biblical meaning, what was important was to "hold on to the inner connection of the dietary laws with the rest of the Mosaic ceremonial law," and to provide proof of the non-binding nature of the overall system of the ceremonial laws.[82] The dietary laws were associated with the whole idea of symbolic purity and holiness within the Mosaic theocracy,

---

[77] David Einhorn, "Materialien für den Commissionsbericht über die Speisegesetze," *Der Israelit des neunzehnten Jahrhunderts* 8 (1847), no. 6, 41-43; no. 7, 49-51; no. 13, 97-100; no. 14, 105-108; no. 19, 147-150; no. 20, 153-156, particularly 41-42.

[78] Ibid., 156.

[79] Ibid., 98 and 106.

[80] Ibid., 42-43.

[81] Samuel Holdheim, "Materialien zu einem Commissionsbericht über die Speisegesetze," *Wissenschaftliche Zeitschrift für jüdische Theologie* 6 (1847), issue 2, 41-63, here 52. "Where it is question of doing away with biblical laws, may we invoke the Talmud, where in the same moment and in the same relation where it declares these laws to be eternally binding, we deny it?" (ibid., 51-52).

[82] Ibid., 41.

which from the point of view of Talmudic Judaism was interrupted only at times, ideally continuing to exist until its restoration. If one believed in the continuing binding nature of Mosaic law, then one must take the food and purity laws very seriously indeed. However, since Mosaic theocracy and the ceremonial law "had long been destroyed and overcome by progressive historical development," on the grounds of reason and contemporary understanding of moral holiness, one could declare ceremonial law to be invalid, in opposition to both the Bible and the Talmud: "We have stepped out of the whole sphere of thought of antiquity, and there is no power that can conjure us back into it."[83] The true religious idea behind the *kashrut* laws could no longer be found, and even if it could, one could "preserve [this idea] in our soul," without "symbolizing it like children" through observation of the dietary laws.[84] Here too, it is apparent that Holdheim—far more radically than Einhorn—dismissed the necessity of arguing on the basis of biblical and rabbinical tradition in order to demonstrate the legitimacy of the reforms. Abraham Geiger too then backed Einhorn up, and supported the idea that one should continue what the Talmud had expressed— even if not consistently enough due to the conflict with contemporary idolatry—, and argued for a more cautious approach: The dispute between two scholars "who stand at the pinnacle of scientific Jewish theology, such as Holdheim and Einhorn," shows that sufficient theological clarity has not yet been achieved, and the congregations who in many cases felt that the dietary laws were part of the essence of Judaism would have to be slowly and carefully convinced.[85]

---

[83] Ibid., 59.

[84] Ibid., 61-62. Samuel Hirsch too criticized Einhorn's argumentation in an open letter as inappropriate "begging from the Talmud," and an example of what happens if in the course of reform, one underestimates "the philosophical concept": "Reform is shaken loose from its soil, the actual religious life, and displaced into the gloomy schoolroom, where one argues with the Talmud about the exegesis of this or that syllable, and there it can truly no longer flourish"; see "Offener Brief von Dr. S. Hirsch," *Der Israelit des neunzehnten Jahrhunderts* 8 (1847), no. 30, 233-236, quotation 234. On his own symbolic interpretation of the—largely outdated—dietary laws (for example as a symbol for the priestly vocation of every Israelite or for the holiness of the laws of nature, see Samuel Hirsch, "Die Speisegesetze (Aus einem demnächst erscheinenden Handbuch für israelitische Religionslehrer)," *Der Israelit des neunzehnten Jahrhunderts* 7 (1846), no. 18, 137-140; no. 19, 145-148; no. 20, 154-159.

[85] Abraham Geiger, "Nachschrift," *Wissenschaftliche Zeitschrift für jüdische Theologie* 6 (1847), issue 2, 63-75, here 65.

In spite of their differences of opinion in the area of theoretical justification of the reforms, both reformers were evidently perceived as representing a common line in practice. When in 1847, Einhorn was appointed as the successor to Holdheim as chief rabbi in Schwerin, and was inducted into office by his friend, this evidently took place with the awareness of thereby ensuring the continuity of cautious but nonetheless consistent reform. In his inaugural sermon, he admitted that it was also a burden to have to be measured against a predecessor "who deserves to have lasting memorials erected in your midst, and to be recalled with blessings by your children's children."[86] He then expounded his understanding of the office of rabbi, which moved between the poles of "level-headedness and strength," swore to his duty to listen to the demands of the times, which consisted in "allowing the eternally living spirit of Judaism to emerge ever more from its mantle, to free itself ever more from the shell of the written letter and of ceremony, and thus to reveal itself in the true sense for the first time," and to "openly and without shyness" confront "unthinking lip service." In more drastic formulations, he called for people to overcome courageously the pain "which the heart feels when a corpse is laid to rest in which there once dwelt a soul that was precious to one, so that one's sphere of activity does not become a graveyard, upon which one stands as someone who calls up the dead, but becomes a pure beacon from which one kindles the light of purified religious insight."[87] However, according to Einhorn it would be a mistake to believe that Jewishness and humanity were already at the elevated level of complete knowledge of God which would allow appropriate "religious symbols" to be waived. The rabbi should aim to show the congregation "that Judaism has a soul which can continue to exist without a physical shell, and is indeed destined for such a disembodied life as the highest blossom of its strength." But level-headedness requires that to start with, only those ceremonies are done away with that have ceased to be "religious symbols" for the eternal truths and moral commandments of Judaism, and to guard against "wanting to divest Judaism immediately, making a mockery of all historical development, of each and every ceremony,

---

[86] David Einhorn, "Antrittspredigt gehalten am 4. September 1847 in der Synagoge zu Schwerin," in idem, *Ausgewählte Predigten und Reden*, 3-18, here 5.
[87] Ibid., 6-7.

including ceremonies that are full of vitality and content."[88]

Under the conditions of the times, above all in view of the decision by the Mecklenburg government to withdraw the civil rights that had only just been granted, to do away with religious autonomy and, supported by Orthodoxy, to reverse the reform process by force,[89] his confession that for all his love of peace, he would prefer "a sea whipped up by storms [....] to the peace of a stagnant swamp, which emits only pestilential vapors,"[90] became reality rather more swiftly than he would have liked. The conflict, which was smoldering right from the start, reached a peak when Einhorn was drawn into the public discussion about the anti-circumcision movement in Frankfurt, Hamburg and Berlin. When a liberal Jew from the town of Teterow in Mecklenburg refused to allow his son to be circumcised, but declared that he wished to bring him up as a loyal Jew, and pressed for him to be registered in the Jewish register of births and to be named in a religious service, the Schwerin Israelite High Council (*Oberrat*) was asked for an opinion on the case. The statement of 25 November 1847, signed by Einhorn, made clear his view that whilst circumcision was one of the most holy religious obligations for Jews, it did not cause one to belong to the Jewish community, so that any person born of Jewish parents was to be regarded as a Jew with all the rights and duties. Einhorn took the position that fundamentally, no Jew could "release himself from the covenant of Israel" by infringing ceremonial or religious commandments. He therefore called on the father to bring the child to the synagogue for naming:

> May God bless this child and furnish it with the virtues of an Israelite after his own heart, of an Israelite of circumcised heart, and may all those who see the continued existence of our divine religion, which our forefathers sealed as a covenant between God and Israel and the whole of humanity a thousand times with their precious blood, as being threatened by such events and are therefore troubled in the depths of their souls, be calmed by the thought that by its nature, the divine is immortal and that Judaism rests on the unshakable pillars of justice, truth and peace; pillars that never sway,

---

[88] Ibid., 16.

[89] On the policy of the Mecklenburg government, see Hans-Michael Bernhardt, *Bewegung und Beharrung. Studien zur Emanzipationsgeschichte der Juden im Großherzogtum Mecklenburg-Schwerin 1813-1869* (Hannover: Hahn, 1998).

[90] Ibid., 17.

> even if the Earth were to age like a garment and the sky were to dissolve like smoke.[91]

It is worth looking at the public debate that followed on from this event, above all because of Einhorn's vote, with that of the Rostock theologian Franz Delitzsch, who was committed to the Lutheran "Mission to the Jews." The expert on rabbinical literature who was recognized also by Jewish scholars and who was later to found the Leipzig *Institutum Judaicum*,[92] brought into the arena a conservative Christian voice, which with its opposition to the views of the Schwerin rabbi, in turn triggered a most interesting controversy between Holdheim and Einhorn about an appropriate justification of Jewish universalism as well as of reform. In his Rostock-based newspaper, Delitzsch disputed—on the basis of the Talmud—Einhorn's view that it was not circumcision that caused inclusion in the Jewish community, and accused him of painting an idealized picture, with his assertion that infringements of the commandments did not lead to separation from Judaism: after all, in theory the Talmud envisaged death for deliberate desecration of the Sabbath, and excommunication for lesser offenses. Einhorn, he said, spoke "of the Talmudic and rabbinical viewpoint as an alien one," and "what reasonable person, who is familiar with self-chosen religious services and unhealthy interpretations of scripture, would blame him in the light of our times?" Einhorn should, however, then have taken the Torah as the starting point, which (Genesis 17:14) clearly viewed non-circumcision as a breach of the covenant. According to him, instead of convincing the father of the meaning and obligatory nature of circumcision, the rabbi had backed him up through false grounds. He—Delitzsch—did not wish to attack the decision itself, but had gained the impression "that the path on which the true Israelite is freed from the binding nature of the Old Testament law and the penalty for infringement is a

---

[91] The document is cited in a series of articles that Einhorn later published in America; see David Einhorn, "Die Beschneidungsfrage," *Sinai* 2 (1857/58), no. 10, 699-708; no. 11, 731-740; no. 12, 763-772; *Sinai* 3 (1858/59), no. 1, 796-805; no. 2, 827-835; no. 3, 859-867; no. 5, 923-932; no. 6, 955-965 (declaration of the senior council 736-739, quotation 739).

[92] On Delitzsch's ambivalent relationship with Judaism, see Christian Wiese, *Challenging Colonial Discourse: Jewish Studies and Protestant Theology in Wilhelmine Germany* (Leiden: Brill Publishers, 2005), 122-136.

different one from that of unauthorized self-exemption, which thrusts between Judaism and Christianity a thing which is neither a shell with a core nor a core without a shell."[93]

Einhorn thereupon accused Delitzsch of spreading a false interpretation of the biblical and rabbinical sources, and defended the right of the Reform movement, in dealing critically with its own tradition, even where it contested the binding nature of ceremonial law, to rethink its religious practices in the present day. In particular, he complained of Delitzsch's missionarily inspired concluding remark, according to which Judaism could not overcome the ceremonial law in this way: "Prof. D[elitzsch] would like to think that the Jews are forced to undergo circumcision, so that they become capable of participation in the sacrificial lamb."[94] He furthermore accused the Christian theologian of a complete lack of knowledge of Talmudic law, and put forward the view that rabbinical literature had gone beyond the biblical idea that non-circumcision was a destruction of the covenant between God and Israel deserving of death; in that, and in the Talmudic insight that through birth, Jews were included into this covenant and bound to it, there was progress, even if the rabbinical view that the refusal of circumcision was a sin which entitled one to use compulsion against the father was an error which had to be overcome from the religious consciousness of the modern era. Thus in the case of reform one certainly did not need—as Delitzsch insinuated—to ignore rabbinical Judaism and get rid of tradition, but one could progress on its foundation, always being

---

[93] Einhorn, "Die Beschneidungsfrage," 763-767, here 766-767. At a later point Delitzsch described this "arbitrary self-exemption from Mosaic law" as a break away from Judaism "to that deism [....] that can no longer distinguish between the spirit of God and the spirit of Man, revelation and contemporary opinion, development and breaking away" (ibid., 831).

[94] Ibid., 768-772 and 796-801, quotation 801. In general, Einhorn lamented the predominance of a Protestant hatred of Jews, which was directed against all modern Jews "who walk upright, do not carry a sack on their shoulders, [....] or are even so bold as to dispute the eternal obligatory nature of the ceremonial law without belief in Jesus 'Christ'; for according to his [....] Christian rational ideas, by law the eternal Jew can and may exist only as a horrible caricature, and thus everything that comes forward against this dogma is necessarily a work of the devil. But what upsets him most is the Jewish efforts toward reform, which undermine the whole dogmatic foundations of Christianity, put an end to the eternal sanctimonious prating about the 'curse of the law' and 'Jewish separatism' and fill the Jew, the antichrist incarnate, with the proud consciousness of a world-encompassing mission" (idem, "Das katholische und protestantisch-pietistische Christenthum gegen die Juden," *Sinai* 3 (1858/59), no. 11, 1115-1127, here 1118).

aware that the Talmud itself announced the dissolution of the ceremonial law in the future.[95]

Delitzsch then moved the dispute to the question of the relation between "ethnic community" and "religious community" in Judaism. Einhorn, he claimed, was confusing the two concepts: according to Delitzsch, by the fact that it was born of Jewish parents, the child was a member of the Jewish people, but would become a member of the Jewish religious community based on belief and confession only on completion of circumcision, which was made obligatory by the revealed law: "Is it not clear as daylight that a Jew who ignores revelation and the Sabbath and the seal of the covenant, whilst not ceasing to be a member of the Jewish people, excludes himself from the confessional group of the Jewish religious and faith community?" By allowing Jews to spurn confession and order without having to fear any consequences with regard to their affiliation with the congregation, Delitzsch claims, Einhorn presents the view that a Jew belongs to the Jewish religious community simply through the fact that he is born into it and is "encompassed by it like a magic circle," without being able to escape it by his free decision.[96] It must however be stated, according to the Christian theologian, that only circumcision makes a Jew a full member of the Jewish congregation, whilst "arbitrarily exempting oneself from the law," as Einhorn extols, is a breaking away from Judaism to that "deism" "that [can] no longer distinguish [....] between spirit of God and the spirit of Man, revelation and contemporary opinions."[97] Einhorn thereupon countered this by stating that Delitzsch was mistaking the question as to the means by which a Jew is accepted into his faith community with the question of the means by which he leaves it again. The decree from the senior council addressed only the first question.[98] However, regardless of that, it was in fact the case that it was primarily the fact of being born into the community of the Jewish "line" that decides whether one belongs to Judaism, and this community "still does not refuse its motherly embrace, but rather continues to let its blessings flow" to someone who distances himself from it.[99] Finally,

---

[95] Einhorn, "Die Beschneidungsfrage," 796-798.
[96] Ibid., 827-831, here 828-829.
[97] Ibid., 831.
[98] Ibid., 859-861.
[99] Ibid., 926.

Einhorn referred to Israel's status as the chosen people as the cause for this position:

> Yes, Professor Delitzsch! If Judaism is the only positive religion under the sun that wishes to have its ceremonial decrees and prohibitions observed only by a single line, and regards it as its exclusive property to the extent that it even nurtures a distaste for proselytes, then it is and must also be the only positive religion under the sun to which one belongs by birth; then you shall have to give up your heretical and rationalistic resistance to confessional membership by means of fleshly origins; however, then the Israelite religious community has such wonderfully powerful arms that the Israelite cannot escape it through free self-determination, so that it does not let go even those who move over to another faith. You now call that an unbearable shackle, an outrageous tyranny. But Judaism answers you thus: the community of my confessors is the greatest good for all from the house of Jacob, and I hold them in a fast and loving embrace, even if they wish to leave this community [....]. And so I declare, from a holy conviction deep inside, that [....] whoever releases himself from a Mosaic cere- monial law because it no longer expresses any religious thought at all, and is thereby, according to his unshakable conviction, revoked by God, but by contrast holds fast with his innermost soul, with his whole life, to the eternal truths and purely religious laws of Judaism, has not only not fallen away from Judaism, but rather is to be regarded as an assiduous worker for the realization of the kingdom of the Messiah.[100]

Holdheim's reaction to the controversy between Einhorn and Delitzsch throws a revealing light on the differences between him and his suc- cessor in Schwerin as regards the interpretation of universalism in Judaism, and shows that he perceived him rather as a half-hearted reformer—at least in the matter of theoretical justification. As in all the controversies discussed so far, here too it was less a matter of the practical decision itself, which Holdheim agreed with, but rather of how it was legitimized theoretically. Holdheim had no sympathy at all for Delitzsch's motives, for he too saw in the inter- vention by the Christian theologian neither any expression of sym- pathy for Orthodoxy nor a disinterested scientific interest in the question of circumcision, but rather a presumptuous missionary encroachment, based on a complete lack of understanding for the motives of the Reform movement, and on the inappropriate con- viction that Jews who did not regard the Talmud as a canon of

---

[100] Ibid., 927-929.

equal standing to the Bible must "jump from the Bible with one
bound and land in the broad and torrential river of Christianity."
If Delitzsch, as an orthodox Christian, thought that only the belief
in the overcoming of the "law" through the miracle of the sacrificial death of Christ could free the core of the Old Testament from
its shell, then reformed Jews counted "such a belief in miracles as
part and parcel of the Old Testament shell," and instead regarded
"self-exemption" from outdated elements of the Jewish tradition as
legitimate and appropriate.[101] In this matter, Holdheim basically
agreed with Einhorn's opinion that, according to the Talmudic view,
circumcision does not constitute one's Jewishness, nor does omission of circumcision mean leaving the covenant. But as he had
already done with regard to the dietary laws, he opposed Einhorn's
argumentation with the aid of the Talmud, in particular the view
according to which rabbinical literature had advanced beyond the
drastic position of the Bible, but was still ensnared in the error that
had been overcome by the modern Reform movement, that non-
circumcision was a punishable sin.[102]

In contrast to the dispute concerning the justification for abolishing the dietary laws, this time it was not only a matter of overcoming ceremonial law as such, but a question that separated Holdheim
and Einhorn far more deeply from one another and which—as we
shall see—underlay the actual and lasting theoretical dissent between
them, and influenced important practical decisions: the question about
the relation between universalism and particularism, of Judaism's religious and ethnic dimension, its ethico-religious mission and Israel's
status as the chosen people. According to Holdheim, with his argumentation Einhorn was entangling himself in a "highly awkward
dilemma," for the Talmudic view, with which he was striving to
defend the lasting membership of Judaism even for the uncircumcised, implied that anyone who was born a Jew must—even against
his will—"eternally persist [in Judaism] and could not separate himself from it": But from the point of view of contemporary religious
consciousness—and here he tacitly conceded a point to Delitzsch—
that was in fact not progress, but a "sharply expressed contradiction

---

[101] Samuel Holdheim, "Literarische Fehhde zwischen Dr. Einhorn und Prof.
Delitzsch über die Beschneidungsfrage in Mecklenburg," *Der Israelit des neunzehnten
Jahrhunderts* 9 (1848), no. 5, 33-37; no. 6, 41-44, here 34.
[102] Ibid., 41-43.

to the principle of freedom of conscience."[103] If Einhorn wished to proceed consistently in the name of freedom of conscience against religious compulsion, then he could not invoke the principle of the Talmud, according to which one must remain a Jew even unwillingly. The idea of holding fast to the notion of chosenness, but disputing the binding nature of the laws that once applied by referring to the historical development of Judaism, would necessarily lead to internal contradiction. Rather, one must admit that the "contemporary reforming consciousness" did not oppose the binding nature of the ceremonial law "because it seeks to express the particular alliance with God with freer forms, but because this consciousness resists the assumption of such a particular alliance." For the abolition of circumcision therefore, there was no other way than the "short, but succinct admission":

> Since it is not the accident of birth, no longer the natural descent, but the morally free profession of belief in the truths of Judaism as well as their moral realization that exclusively determines participation in and renunciation of Judaism, then any outer testimony—since it essentially denotes nothing—has become empty, meaningless and superfluous.[104]

Einhorn protested vehemently against Holdheim's attack and defended his recourse to the Talmud with his attempt to convince traditional congregations which often still stood at the "stage of outward

---

[103] Ibid., 43. "What brutality lies in the thought: Because you were born a Jew, i.e. you sprang from such a seed, are you obliged your whole life long to remain in the same and to fulfil all the conditions of this bond or to reap the wrath of God and suffer punishment?" (ibid.).

[104] Ibid., 44. This is a quotation from idem, *Die Religionsprinzipien des reformirten Judenthums* (Berlin: B. Behr's Buchhandlung, 1847), 22; for a detailed treatment of Holdheim's justification for the abolition of circumcision, see also idem, *Ueber die Beschneidung zunächst in religiös-dogmatischer Beziehung* (Schwerin: C. Kürschner, 1844). A quite different argument from those of Holdheim and Einhorn was put forward by Samuel Hirsch, who took the view that circumcision belonged to those ceremonies of Judaism that most strongly symbolized the religious idea; a father who refuses to let his son be circumcised reveals a hostile attitude to Judaism. See Hirsch's expert opinion on circumcision in *Rabbinische Gutachten über die Beschneidung. Gesammelt und herausgegeben von...., Rabbiner, Als Manuskript gedruckt,* ed. Salomon Abraham Trier (Frankfurt am Main: Druck der I. F. Bach'schen Buch- und Steindruckerei, 1844), 48-57. On Hirsch's position in the circumcision controversy, see Judith Frishman, "True Mosaic Religion. Samuel Hirsch, Samuel Holdheim and the Reform of Judaism," in *Religious Identity and the Problem of Historical Foundation: The Foundational Character of Authoritative Sources in the History of Christianity and Judaism,* ed. Judith Frishman (Leiden: Brill Publishers, 2004), 195-222) particularly 204-208.

lawfulness" and would not have accepted an "uncircumcised intruder" into their community on the basis of Holdheim's free justification. It had therefore been indispensable "to demonstrate membership of the Jewish faith also for the uncircumcised of Jewish descent on a Talmudic basis." In order to gain recognition for the child as a member of the congregation of Israel, the members of the High Council had merely wished to establish a scientific fact from the Talmudic point of view, "albeit without thereby remotely declaring our own support for the Talmudic motive for this recognition"—so there was therefore no disagreement at all.[105] He also defended himself against the accusation that he did not understand that only religious conviction and not Jewish origin made a Jew a Jew, and that he adopted the view that it was not possible to leave Judaism: he would most certainly not grant that the descendants of baptized Jewish parents be bound to the Jewish congregation "right down to the thousandth generation."[106] In his view however, Holdheim mistook the difference between external compulsion and the inner moral obligation, originating from the covenant with God, from which even the principle of freedom of conscience could exempt no-one, just as it could not entitle anyone to refuse alms to the starving or to take one's own life. It was therefore not so much the principle of freedom of conscience as "the principle of equal holiness of all lines of Man" that—since it disputed the "particular holiness of the Jewish line" and the "Talmudic particularism"—pushed religious confession into the foreground instead of birth. So whilst Reform Judaism must hold fast to the notion of the chosen people, it must emphasize that with its interpretation in the sense of an ethico-religious mission amongst peoples, it specifically does not make the "holiness of lineage" and special privileges, religious duties, rights and capabilities into a criterion of belonging to the Jewish community, but rather the free declaration of belief in the "eternal truths" which it is Israel's providential task to spread amongst humanity.[107]

Holdheim, who held the view that in the messianic era that had

---

[105] David Einhorn, "Entgegnung," *Der Israelit des neunzehnten Jahrhunderts* 9 (1848), no. 14, 105-107; no. 15, 113-115, here 107. "Holdheim declares war on us, whilst unfortunately for his bellicosity, in this regard the sweetest and most beautiful peace reigns between us" (ibid.).

[106] Ibid., 113.

[107] Ibid., 115.

now dawned, together with the ceremonial law and the separation from heathen peoples, the notion of the chosen people as the expression of "theocratic holiness of the people" was obsolete,[108] could only contradict that. In his reply, he once again impressed upon him his thesis that according to the Reform view, which distinguished between those political elements that had been overcome by history and those religious elements that continued to remain valid, Judaism was no "ethnic community" [*Volksgenossenschaft*] or "tribal religion" [*Stammesreligion*] which limited its moral demands to a small circle bound by ethnic origin, but a "religion of humanity, and a world religion," a "religious community" [*Religionsgenossenschaft*] which thrived on the moral free conviction "of man's likeness to the divine and of the bond of love between God and himself."[109] Rather, one must understand that the "entire historical Judaism" rests on the idea of a particular covenant and of Israel being a special, chosen people, and one must replace this idea, which together with its "lack of freedom of conviction and of conscience is doomed to perish," with the idea of "the chosenness of humankind."[110] Countering Delitzsch's fictitious assumptions of a "religious community" that had separated off from the "ethnic community" in the rabbinical literature, Einhorn had aptly interpreted the view of historical Judaism:

> But we must wonder, and we cannot regret enough, that such a sharp mind as Einhorn's can penetrate only up to a certain limit, namely as far as a correct understanding of the historical facts, but cannot overcome them, and see how, through his sharp dialectics, he seems to think he can pull away the whole religious grounds from under his feet and walk happily over a gaping abyss. Professor Delitzsch has

---

[108] Holdheim, *Das Ceremonialgesetz im Messiasreich*, 40. Where even in Christian societies, the exclusive, particularistic understanding of truth is beginning to give way to the "notion of general love of man and general human rights," it is the duty of Judaism to lead all faiths with the idea of universalism. In an era where the world has "moved from statutory particularism to Messianic universalism," Judaism must give up all ideas of a chosen people, at least "if we wish to see in the downfall of our former folk tradition the beginnings of the Messianic kingdom, and in the destruction of statutory particularism the foundation stone for building up the universalism that is founded on pure humanity" (ibid., 72-73). Against this, see the emphasis on the relevance of the idea of the chosen in Einhorn, "Dr. Holdheim's Schrift: Das Ceremonialgesetz im Messiasreich," 165-167.

[109] Holdheim, "Volksgenossenschaft und Religionsgenossenschaft. Mit Rücksicht auf die literarische Fehde zwischen Dr. Einhorn und Prof. Delitzsch," *Der Israelit des neunzehnten Jahrhunderts* 9 (1848), no. 21, 161-163; no. 22, 169-172; no. 23, 177-180, here 162.

[110] Ibid., 169.

> painted for me, in faithful and lively brushstrokes, a picture of the
> historical Judaism that he regards as a fiction of Einhorn's, as a reli-
> gion of bondage. Einhorn demonstrated to him succinctly that this
> Judaism is no fiction, but truly historical. But the lack of freedom,
> the tyranny, that is inalienably attached to such a Judaism, and against
> which our better sense of morality, justice and freedom must rise up,
> these he seeks to sweeten for us with a few sweet, flattering words,
> which would at best garnish a sermon to an unscientific public, to
> transform the iron fetters into bonds of love, the chains of slavery
> into garlands of roses.[111]

Holdheim then goes on to say that with his emphasis on Israel's status as the chosen people, which holds the Jew in its loving embrace
even when he wishes to escape it, Einhorn does not even notice that
this is an "open declaration of war" on freedom of conscience.
Delitzsch, he notes ironically, has not recognized the true historical
Judaism, but has protested against it in the name of freedom, whereas
Einhorn recognizes it, but ignores the call of freedom that is raised
against it. His unforgivable basic error lies in the fact that he has
not understood that the truly historical Judaism has long been overcome by the idea of freedom of worship and freedom of conscience,
and that the exclusive "tribal religion" that is associated with the
notion of the chosen people has already suffered "a rift" through
the messianic ideas of the prophets; this rift, Holdheim claims, "is
increasingly widened by the reforming consciousness of the present
day, which in contrast to historical Judaism, rooted in a particular
covenant, links to prophetic universalism.[112]

It seems rather questionable whether Holdheim really did justice
to Einhorn's intention, in the dispute with Delitzsch, to defend the
freedom to withdraw from a symbol regarded as being devoid of
content without sanctions on the part of the congregation, by dis-
placing the discussion to the question of the right to distance oneself completely from Judaism. But what is decisive is that concealed
behind it is a fairly fundamental questioning of Einhorn's reform
philosophy, which Holdheim also expressed clearly at the end of his
response, when he accused him, with his insistence on the chosen
people and the recourse to rabbinical tradition, of not yet having
broken through to the freedom of a universal Judaism:

---

[111] Ibid., 179-180.
[112] Ibid., 180.

For our principles fight [....] in the name of free conviction against the tribal religion, against the innate and inalienable obligation; in a word, [they fight] most resolutely against the fetters and the tyranny of the old historical Judaism, about which we have as few illusions as Einhorn. We respect Einhorn as one of the most thorough authorities on Talmudic-historical Judaism amongst present-day rabbis and Jewish scholars; therefore, we do not doubt that he shall soon cross the boundary which he has placed before his knowledge like a bolt, and shall break through to full freedom. Only then will the whole Reform movement have won, in him, one of the most upright and honest pioneers, on which they can then rightly congratulate themselves.[113]

As in the earlier mutual critical references, this intellectual skirmish confirms Kaufmann Kohler's comparative characterization of Holdheim and Einhorn, according to which the former was above all the "bold herald, storming ahead, of messianic Judaism freed of the pressure of the Talmud," whilst the latter by contrast was the more cautious "harbinger and perfecter of the positive Jewish reform principle in doctrine and worship,"[114] who did not wish to distance himself from tradition in a comparably radical way, but wanted to include important elements of it in his interpretation of Judaism. However, for Einhorn's conservative opponents that attitude was nevertheless still radical enough to attack him as a destroyer of the traditional Jewish religion. Soon after the controversy surrounding circumcision, it became clear that his position in Schwerin had become untenable because of the Orthodox resistance to his theology and his liturgical reforms. He publicly defended his principles once more,[115] but in 1851 the incessant hostility and the petitions to the government from the Orthodox aiming at separation left him no choice but to take the position of rabbi to the reform congregation in Pest in Hungary. In his valedictory sermon, there were bitter notes—not just the "deep pain of separation, such as must fill a helmsman when he sees himself forced to leave his beloved ship, which he has guided safely around a number of dangerous rocks, under the most pressing dangers, without knowing who shall guide the rudder in his

---

[113] Ibid., 180.

[114] Kaufmann Kohler, *Grab- und Gedenkrede für Rabbiner Dr. David Einhorn, gehalten im Tempel Beth-El, New York* (Milwaukee: J. S. Moses, 1879), 8.

[115] *Den öffentlichen Cultus betreffende Differenzpunkte zwischen den verschiedenen religiösen Parteien in den israelitischen Gemeinden des Großherzogtums Mecklenburg-Schwerin, dargelegt vom israelitischen Oberrathe* (Schwerin: A. W. Sandmeyer, 1850).

place,"[116] but also the lamentation over a mixture of fanaticism and half-heartedness that he had encountered in the congregation, a lack of reason and religious enthusiasm. As a consequence, this had led to the disparagement of his endeavors and to the creation of the "delusion" "as if the religious concept of Judaism [....] was left cold and had to clothe itself in a cloud of countless ceremonies, in order to envelop our families and communities in a purifying and sanctifying manner."[117] What he found outrageous in particular was the resistance to his attempt to make visible the universalism of Judaism —a central theme of his theology—through liturgical reforms concerning the idea of the Messiah and Israel's status as the chosen people:

> Does your reason then not rebel against believing that in Israel, God had chosen for himself a noble blood line which he nonetheless, for the sake of its sins, has pushed around for almost two millennia as the slaves among the peoples, in order one day to lead them back to the promised land and then make all peoples their slaves? Can that which is not even human be called divine? Is it not far more appropriate to the first principle of the teachings of Moses: God is the father of all people—to accord Israel the high mission of ennobling, honoring and joining all the peoples of the Earth through his holy teachings, a mission of which we can truly be far more proud than of that noble blood line and which is already expressed unambiguously in that ancient promise to Abraham: all the families of the kingdom of Earth shall one day be blessed through you?[118]

Einhorn was aware that what awaited him in Pest was no simple task either, and so he left Schwerin anticipating that "in [his] new surroundings, much larger battles" awaited him there.[119] The "Pest Israelite Reform Association" had been established in the revolutionary year of 1848, against the background of the Hungarian national uprising against the Habsburg rule, and had been designed

---

[116] David Einhorn, *Abschiedspredigt gehalten am 13. December 1851 in der Synagoge zu Schwerin bei seinem Austritte aus dem Amte eines Großherzoglich Mecklenburg-Schwerinschen Landesrabbiners* (Schwerin: F. Hartig, 1852), 4. His successors (Baruch Isaak ben Israel Lipschütz, Salomon Cohn and Gabriel Fabian Feilchenfeld) were all strictly Orthodox. In *AZJ* 15 (1851), no. 46, 543, one voice from the community complained that Einhorn should not have been allowed to leave his congregation in this difficult time.

[117] Einhorn, *Abschiedspredigt*, 7.

[118] Ibid., 9-10.

[119] Ibid., 13-14.

according to the model of Holdheim's Berlin Reform congregation, including moving the Sabbath service to the Sunday and abolishing the dietary laws. The first rabbi for the congregation had been the young Hungarian radical reformer Ignaz Einhorn, who wished to liberate Judaism almost entirely from ceremonial forms, and defined it purely in terms of religious and moral principles.[120] When he had to leave Hungary following the failed uprising, the congregation appointed Holdheim's friend David Einhorn—in the hope that he would consolidate the situation. His inaugural sermon in January 1852 was anything but a revolutionary declaration of spiritual independence from the past; rather, it was a declaration of support for a Reform movement that must not limit itself to outward measures. It was not the opportunity to pray with an uncovered head, and not the organ that brought the congregation together, but the longing for a powerful religious life, from which one must however eliminate everything that contradicts modern moral sensitivities: "the presumptuous curses on heretics, the vengeful proclamations against enemies that no longer exist, the deep sighing over persecutions that are long gone and are presented as contemporary, the expression of warmest longing for the restoration of the Jewish kingdom and animal sacrifice [....]."[121] Against a rejection of the rabbinical tradition on principle, Einhorn—true to his reform principles—emphasized the function of Mosaic law as that of a divine educational law acting in history, which however in ethical respects sometimes bears "the unmistakable marks of its times."[122] He was, he said, not remotely minded "to accord the Talmud in general a divine spirit or even to call its moral standard, such as its concept of Mosaic law, our own," but one must preserve and develop the "divine treasure" concealed within it, instead of "breaking with olden times."[123] Regardless of

---

[120] On reform in Hungary and on Ignaz Einhorn, see Philipson, *History of the Reform Movement*, chapter 10; Meyer, *Response to Modernity*, 157-163; Michael Silber, "The Historical Experience of German Jewry and Its Impact on Haskalah and Reform in Hungary," in *Toward Modernity: The European Jewish Model*, ed. Jacob Katz (New Brunswick, NJ: Transaction Books, 1987), 117-157; see also the description by Ignaz Einhorn, *Die Revolution und die Juden in Ungarn. Nebst einem Rückblick auf die Geschichte der Letztern* (Leipzig: Carl Geibel, 1851) (on the Reform Association, 107-113).

[121] David Einhorn, "Antrittspredigt gehalten vor der Reformgenossenschaft zu Pesth im Januar 1852," in idem, *Ausgewählte Predigten und Reden*, 19-30, here 22.

[122] Ibid., 27.

[123] Ibid., 29-30.

this attempt at "traditionalization," with which Einhorn aimed simultaneously at legitimizing and curbing the eagerness for reform among
the Pest congregation, and regardless of his desire—as expressed in
the sermon—to bring about, as a constructive reformer, calm in a
chaotic situation in Pest, just two months after he took up office the
temple was closed by the Austrian government—not without the
influence of the moderate rabbi Löw Schwab.[124] In a time of restoration, the Hungarian Jews were supposed to return to their own traditions and all revolutionary movements, whether political or religious,
were supposed to be put in their place. Einhorn used the subsequent
years until his emigration to America to present the mature results
of his thinking in his main work, *Das Prinzip des Mosaismus und dessen
Verhältnis zum Heidenthum und rabbinischen Judentum* (1854), with which
he finally took his place alongside Holdheim and Hirsch as a representative of an autonomous reform philosophy.

2. "Particular Universalism": David Einhorn's Reform Philosophy in America

In 1855, Einhorn left behind him the Europe of anti-liberal responses
that had brought his ideas of reform such disappointment, and followed the call of the Har Sinai Reform congregation in Baltimore,
which had arisen out of an association of German Jewish lay people that was founded in 1842.[125] Like numerous other German Reform
rabbis of the time, including his colleagues from the days of the rabbinical conferences, Samuel Adler and Samuel Hirsch, as well as the
next generation of rabbis, amongst whom Bernhard Felsenthal and
Kaufmann Kohler stood out, Einhorn followed the call to the
"promised land of the Reform movement" with great hopes.[126] In
his last sermon in New York in 1879, the year of his death, he
described his emigration retrospectively in images from Exodus: From

---

[124] On Schwab's position in relation to the Reform congregation, see Samuel
Holdheim, *Das Gutachten des L. Schwab Rabbiners zu Pesth über die Reformgenossenschaft
daselbst* (Berlin: J. Sittenfeld, 1848).

[125] On the history of the Jews of Baltimore, see Isaac M. Fein, *The Making of an
American Jewish Community: The History of Baltimore Jewry from 1773 to 1920* (Philadelphia:
JPS, 1985).

[126] See Michael A. Meyer, "America: The Reform Movement's Land of Promise,"
in *The American Jewish Experience*, ed. Jonathan Sarna (New York: Holmes & Meier,
1986), 60-81.

the "house of bondage" of Germany and Hungary, where "the most noble endeavors [were] suppressed with iron force" and the "reactionary angel of vengeance and death" ruled, he had come to America with jubilation, to the "land of the future" that had been an ideal for him from his early youth, since there—encouraged by full freedom of worship and freedom of conscience, the Reform movement "could already beat its powerful wings."[127] Einhorn wanted to use this freedom in order now to finally implement his ideas for reform, unencumbered by conflicts and without governments taking decisions over one's head. The spiritual climate and the structural conditions—for example the freedom of each individual to join a Jewish congregation of his choice,[128] but also, in comparison with Europe, the lack of deep-rooted Orthodox congregations—were very favorable, although in America at this time, the Reform movement was only just beginning to develop gradually.[129] It is, therefore, no surprise that over the long term, Reform Judaism assumed far more radical forms there than in Germany where, following the failed revolution of 1848, the revolutionary ideological and practical initiatives of the 1840s became a moderate "liberal Judaism" that progressed only cautiously.

Einhorn was the first established rabbi to bring to America a fully developed theological vision of Judaism in the modern world. In his inaugural sermon, with which he introduced himself to his new congregation in Baltimore, he explained the distinction between the eternal law of Sinai embodied in the Decalogue, and the other divine rules that had to be understood as the material signs of the covenant, as recollections of religious-moral ideas and as protection from heathen influences, but, instead of being as such eternally valid, were rather to be developed further on the basis of the revealed word of God. According to him, the Reform movement endeavored to bring about an "unleashing of Judaism" in order to prevent "an unleashing from Judaism," and was aiming at a religious service and a way

---

[127] David Einhorn, "Abschiedspredigt gehalten am 12. Juli 1879 im Tempel der Beth-El-Gemeinde zu New York," in idem, *Ausgewählte Predigten und Reden*, 85-92, here 85-87.

[128] See Alan Silverstein, *Alternatives to Assimilation. The Response of Reform Judaism to American Culture, 1840-1930* (Hanover, NH: University Press of New England, 1994), 9-34.

[129] On the overall development of the Reform movement in nineteenth century America, see Meyer, *Response to Modernity*, 225-295.

of life that were deeply rooted in tradition, but which overcame antiquated religious views, customs and ceremonies, and showed the "Jewish
doctrine in its characteristic nature" to advantage. Just what exactly,
in Einhorn's view, constituted this "essence" of Judaism, that would
characterize the Jewish religion as a unique religious force even after
the "dwindling away of its entire ceremonial law," he formulated in
a passage that expresses the core of his theological convictions:

> The belief in one unique God, who reveals himself, eternal, invisible
> and without form, solely in his wonderful works and particularly in
> Man, and with his existence fulfils everything in the same way, Earth
> as Heaven, the transient as the eternal, the flesh as the spirit; the belief
> in the innate goodness and purity of all creation and in particular of
> the god-like beings blessed with reason, which no natural shackles can
> prevent from sanctifying themselves freely, and no other mediation
> than one's own free energy can lead to atonement and redemption;
> the belief in a humanity whose members, all from one and the same
> heavenly and earthly origin, have the same innate nobility, have a
> claim to the same justice, the same law and the same bliss, shall already
> be blessed here on Earth with such bliss when one day all nations
> merge to become a single people of God [....] that recognizes the
> Lord of the Universe alone as its king—and with the blood-soaked
> purple of mortal kingdoms shall lay to rest for ever the whole illusion
> of the glossed-over lie, egoism and persecution of one's brothers—these
> and similar teachings, whose first appearance had to be under the veil
> of the particular common touch in order not to blind human eyes
> with their majesty—even today they are Israel's own; to possess them
> is its sole pride, their recognition some day is its only hope. Every sin-
> gle one of these teachings encompasses treasures of world-redeeming
> thoughts, and it is our most sacred duty to lift these treasures up more
> and more from the deep well of our literature, to collect them, to
> show them in their full glory, to render them usable for life and to
> enrich heart and soul with them.[130]

In this credo, right at the beginning of his role in Baltimore Einhorn
summarized all the elements of his theology, anthropology and mes-
sianology which underlay his historico-theological understanding of
Judaism as a universal religion—discernible precisely in the divine
mission of the chosen people of Israel—and which were to influence decisively the theological debates of American Reform Judaism

---

[130] David Einhorn, "Antrittspredigt gehalten am 27. September 1855 im Tempel
des Har-Sinai-Vereins zu Baltimore," in idem, *Ausgewählte Predigten und Reden*, 21-44,
here 38-40.

in the subsequent decades. But in America too, immediately after his arrival there was conflict about the implications of his thinking for the way in which the Reform movement saw itself, and for the practice of reform. The dispute resulted from the peculiar coalition between the moderate reformers Max Lilienthal, Leo Merzbacher and Isaac M. Wise, the publisher of the *American Israelite* and future founder of the Hebrew Union College,[131] as well as the opponent of reform, Isaac Leeser, from Philadelphia,[132] who in 1855, at the Cleveland Conference, for the sake of the unity of American Judaism jointly lent their support to a resolution according to which all Israelites should bear witness to the divinity of the Bible and acknowledge the Talmud as a binding legal interpretation of it. In the first issue of his publication *Sinai*, Einhorn immediately published a sharp protest against this alliance to preserve the authority of the Talmud. To him, it seemed destined to fail since in his view, it glossed over the conflict between two systems of thought that were fundamentally opposed, one of which regarded "rabbinical particularism," and the other "prophetic universalism [to be] the soul of Judaism."[133] Einhorn's first essay in America reads like a standard raised against any compromise at all in this matter: radical as never before in his pronouncements in Germany, he emphasized what in his view were the drawbacks of the Talmud, which in the present day stood in the way of serious reform: unsuccessful hermeneutics, petty morality, idealization of the past and a particularistic vision of the future.[134] It sounds a little like an echo of Holdheim's criticism of his own earlier efforts to include rabbinical tradition in the justification of reforms, when he now expressed in drastic terms the view that with the Talmud in one's hand, one might at best "smuggle in" reforms through exegetic tricks, but, in doing so, one could not really justify them convincingly. Instead of, like Wise, "opening the door [to the Talmud] with much pomp, and then escaping from its force by

---

[131] On his biography and his work, see Sefton D. Temkin, *Creating American Reform Judaism: The Life and Times of Isaac Meyer Wise* (London: Littman Library of Jewish Civilization, 1998).

[132] See Lance Sussman, *Isaac Leeser and the Making of American Judaism* (Detroit: Wayne State University Press, 1995).

[133] David Einhorn, "Die Rabbiner-Conferenz zu Cleveland," *Sinai* 1 (1856/57), no. 1, 4-10, here 6.

[134] Idem, "Stellung des neuern Judenthums zum Talmud," *Sinai* 1 (1856/57), no. 1, 1-4; no. 2, 33-38; no. 3, 65-67.

a back door," he preferred—whilst acknowledging the wealth of
valuable educational material contained therein—"to declare its view
of biblical legitimacy as a stage of religious insight that has been
overcome."[135]

Having sharply distanced himself from rabbinical literature,
Einhorn entered into the midst of a controversy in which the voices
raised against him were not just traditional ones.[136] For less radical reformers such as Wise too, he went much too far and thus
risked splitting American Judaism. The dissent between the two
very different personalities has rightly been compared with that
between the radical reforming approach of Holdheim and the evolutionary concept of Abraham Geiger:[137] In his history of the Reform
movement, Michael Meyer has shown convincingly how in contrast to the latter dispute, this one led to a bitter conflict, which
was also accompanied by personal animosity, over the path of
reform in America and for ideological as well as practical
supremacy.[138] Whereas the original pugnacious thinker Einhorn
argued for uncompromising implementation of his reform ideas (he
once said that radical Reform wanted "a Judaism with the messianic royal cloak, whilst moderate reform [wanted] a Judaism with
Orthodox and reforming rags"[139]), Wise preferred a gradual pace
of progress, covered by tradition, which did not endanger his higher

---

[135] Idem, "Gegenerklärung," *Sinai* 1 (1856/57), no. 1, 27-29, here 28.

[136] See the dispute between Einhorn and his Orthodox colleague in Baltimore,
Rabbi Abraham Joseph Rice, who had likewise come from the Fürth *yeshiva*, in *The
Occident* 13 (1855/56), 448-453; 549-552 (Rice); The *Asmonean* 12 (1855), no. 9, 67-
68 (Einhorn). On Rice, see I. Harold Sharfman, *The First Rabbi: Origins of Conflict
between Orthodox and Reform. Jewish Polemical Warfare in pre-Civil War America: A Biographical
History* (New York: Simon, 1988). Einhorn also got involved in a strident battle with
Benjamin Szold, the conservative rabbi of the Oheb Schalom congregation in
Baltimore, who had been chosen on the recommendation of Zacharias Frankel;
Einhorn saw moderate reform as far more dangerous than traditional Judaism, since
it claimed to take account of the demands of the modern world; see David Einhorn,
"Das Schicksal der Oheb Schalom Gemeinde," *Sinai* 4 (1859/60), 321-339; idem,
"Abfertigung," *Sinai* 5 (1860/61), no. 1, 1-28; Benjamin Szold, *Der Enthüllte Einhorn*
(Baltimore: W. Polmyer, 1860). Later, the two combatants were reconciled; see
David Einhorn to Benjamin Szold, 5.9.1876 (unpublished papers of David Einhorn,
American Jewish Archives (AJA), MSS Coll 155/1).

[137] See Petuchowski, "Abraham Geiger and Samuel Holdheim," 151-159.

[138] Meyer, *Response to Modernity*, 235-263.

[139] David Einhorn, "Antrittspredigt gehalten am 31. August 1866 in der Adath-
Jeschurun-Gemeinde zu New York bei deren gleichzeitiger Tempelweihe," in idem,
Ausgewählte Predigten und Ansprachen, 60-72, see 70.

goal of promoting the unity of American Judaism. Einhorn, who despised half-hearted reform far more than he did strict Orthodoxy, since it seemed to him to be a "misshapen hybrid," therefore described Wise in his letters as a "lickspittle" and "Jewish pope,"[140] whilst Wise in turn suspected him of being a "deist, Unitarian, Sadducee and apostle of deistic rationalism," and called on him to openly give up Judaism.[141]

The opposing fronts were additionally aggravated by the fact that Wise, who had come to America in 1846 from Moravia, was in favor of consistent Americanization of the Jewish congregations,[142] whilst Einhorn, who in spite of his enthusiastic patriotism never felt at home in America, was convinced that the future and the success of reform depended on a lasting connection to its German intellectual origins, as well as to the German culture and language.[143] In contrast to Leeser and Wise who, against the background of mass immigration of German Jews to America, from the late 1840s onwards at the latest[144] raised the adoption of English as the language of everyday life and of worship to the status of the criterion for successful acculturation, Einhorn became the most prominent voice for the conviction held by many intellectuals among the immigrants

---

[140] David Einhorn to Bernhard Felsenthal, 25.5.1862 (AJA, MSS Col. 155).

[141] Isaac M. Wise, in: *The American Israelite* 2 (15.2.1856), 1-2. On the conflict between these two opposing figures in the American reform movement, see Martin B. Ryback, "The East-West Conflict in American Reform Judaism," *American Jewish Archives* 4 (1952), 3-25.

[142] See inter alia Leon Jick, *The Americanization of the Synagogue, 1820-1870* (Hanover, NH: University of New England Press, 1976); Naomi W. Cohen, *Encounter with Emancipation. The German Jews in the United States 1830-1914* (Philadelphia: JPS, 1984), 159-210; Jonathan Sarna, *JPS: The Americanization of Jewish Culture* (Philadelphia: JPS, 1989).

[143] On the discourse concerning the significance of the German language and culture for American Reform Judaism of the nineteenth century, see Michael A. Meyer, "German-Jewish Identity in Nineteenth Century America," in idem, Judaism within Modernity. Essays on Jewish History and Religion (Detroit: Wayne State University Press, 2001), 323-344; Abraham Barkai, *Branching Out: German-Jewish Immigration to the United States 1820-1914* (New York: Holmes & Meier, 1994), 152-190; Christian Wiese, "Inventing a New Language of Jewish Scholarship: The Transition from German Wissenschaft des Judentums to American-Jewish Scholarship in the Nineteenth and Twentieth Centuries," *Studia Rosenthaliana* 36 (2002/03), 273-304.

[144] On this, see Eric E. Hirshler, ed., *Jews from Germany in the United States* (New York: Farrar, Straus and Cudahy, 1955); Barkai, *Branching Out, passim;* Hasia Diner, *A Time for Gathering: The Second Migration, 1820-1880* (The Jewish People in America vol. 2), (Baltimore: Johns Hopkins University Press, 1992).

that the future of American-Jewish culture depended on its ability to transplant the values and achievements of modern German Judaism to America. Until the end of his days he refused to write and preach in English, as he felt that the German language was "the language of our spirit and our heart," "which called the idea of reform into being and has carried it up to now, as a guardian carries an infant, and at least for the time being must guard against passing its high office over to the English language and withdrawing the protective maternal arms from the child."[145] Einhorn's words express a sense of cultural superiority, which Wise for example—who regarded German as the language of the suppression of and disdain for Judaism, and believed that English on the other hand was the language of freedom, in which Jews could openly express their understanding of themselves for the first time in the history of the Diaspora—rejected.[146] As Gershon Greenberg has shown, Einhorn's position was far more ambiguous: America represented on the one hand the future of Judaism, a country in which after a thousand years of suppression, Judaism could blossom in freedom and realize its own messianic task —the "promised land," the "new Canaan," the "land of Zion."[147] But at the same time Einhorn felt a strong disdain for what to his taste was the all too superficial and anti-social American culture that was shaped by an idolization of the dollar, which he was apt to characterize as "humbug."[148] It seems as if Einhorn, disappointed by the political events in Europe, had a vision of a "messianic" America, but which to his sorrow lacked

[145] "Antrittspredigt gehalten am 31. August 1866 in der Adath-Jeschurun-Gemeinde zu New York bei deren gleichzeitiger Tempelweihe," in idem, *Ausgewählte Predigten und Ansprachen*, 65.

[146] See Isaac M. Wise, "German Culture," *American Israelite* 27 (1879), no. 24, 4.

[147] See for example David Einhorn, "Trauerrede, gehalten am 19. April 1865, als am Tage der Bestattung Abraham Lincolns, im Tempel der Keneseth-Israel-Gemeinde zu Philadelphia," in idem, *Ausgewählte Predigten und Reden*, 135-139.

[148] See Gershon Greenberg, "The Messianic Foundations of American Jewish Thought: David Einhorn and Samuel Hirsch," *Proceedings of the Sixth World Congress of Jewish Studies*, vol. 2, Jerusalem 1975, 215-226; idem, "The Significance of America in David Einhorn's Conception of History," in *American Jewish Historical Quarterly* 67 (1973), 160-184. This ambivalence runs like a recurrent theme through all Einhorn's sermons, to sermons on political or topical occasions; see *inter alia* David Einhorn, "Der Sieg der Ideen der Unabhängigkeitserklärung Amerikas. Predigt am 4. Juli 1861," in idem, *Ausgewählte Predigten und Reden*, 95-104; idem, "Predigt gehalten an dem zum Bitt- und Bußtage bestimmten 30. April 1863 im Tempel der Keneseth-Israel-Gemeinde zu Philadelphia," in ibid., 114-120.

what had once formed the basis of his hopes for Germany: a spirit of science, philosophy and religious depth. Just how much he ultimately remained in the conceptual world of his culture of origin, in spite of his rhetoric about the "new Zion," is shown by his farewell sermon in 1879, in which he described himself as "Ivri," as the "wanderer" who had come from his native Germany to the "blessed" republic of America:

> Proud as I am of this adoptive citizenship, and as much as my heart desires the well-being of this place of freedom, whose star-spangled banner guarantees protection for all those who are oppressed—I cannot and shall not forget that the old country, the land of thinkers, at present the foremost cultural country in the world and above all the country of Mendelssohn, the birthplace of the reform of Judaism which, nurtured and raised in a deeply scientific spirit, proudly developing as in an ever richer Jewish literature, gradually penetrated into other countries and was even carried over the ocean. If you now deprive it of the German spirit or—what amounts to the same thing, the German language—you will then have wrenched it from its topsoil and it must wilt, the beautiful flower! [....]. In a word: wherever the German language is banished—there, the reform of Judaism is nothing more than a glossy veneer, a decorative doll without a heart, without a soul, into which even the proudest temples and most majestic chorales cannot breathe any life![149]

One of the evils of America which Einhorn fought right from the start was slavery. He was convinced that in this question, the Reform movement had to prove itself in concrete moral terms if its ideas of a messianic "mission of Israel" were not to remain merely enthusiastic rhetoric. In connection with the social discussion about slavery in the southern states, and about the American Civil War, he stated clearly that keeping slaves was—apart from infringing the American principle of the freedom and equality of men—an unacceptable crime against God, who had created people in his image. When in 1861 he publicly and vehemently attacked the New York Orthodox rabbi Morris Raphall, who had theologically legitimized slavery with reference to

---

[149] David Einhorn, "Abschiedspredigt gehalten am 12. Juli 1879 im Tempel der Beth-El-Gemeinde zu New York," in idem, *Ausgewählte Predigten und Reden*, 90. He expressed his lasting connection to Germany most clearly in connection with the Franco-German war in 1870/71; see idem, "Predigt gehalten am 8. April 1871 zur Feier des deutschen Friedensfestes im Tempel der Adath-Jeschurun-Gemeinde zu New York," in ibid., 183-185.

Mosaic law,[150] his position in the state of Maryland became so pre-
carious that in the face of threats of violent attacks he had to leave
Baltimore with his family and move to Philadelphia. When his congregation asked him to come back, but to refrain from engaging in
politics from the pulpit in future, he indignantly rejected this request,
accepted the appointment as rabbi of the Keneseth Israel Temple
in Philadelphia, and denounced the hypocrisy with which parts of
the congregation of Har Sinai praised humanity and mercy as the
essence of Judaism:

> But whether a person has the right to buy and sell another human
> being like cattle—about that—God preserve us!—not a single word
> must be uttered, as it could cause a nervous breakdown in the audi-
> torium; at a stroke, the glowing pious enthusiasm turns pale—appar-
> ently shocked by the politics, but in fact because of politics![151]

Einhorn's inaugural sermon on 4th July 1861 in his new congregation in fact turned into a most impressive document of the passion
and clarity with which he underlined the political consequences of
the Jewish tradition, according to which all people are called to freedom and are born with inalienable human rights:

> Is it not the wording of the divine Sinai constitution: "I am the Lord
> your God, who brought you out of the land of Egypt, out of the
> house of bondage, in order to transform the burst iron chain into a
> golden engagement ring?" Can one think of any more specific procla-
> mation of the innate equality of all rational beings than the doctrine:
> "*bidmut elohim asah oto*"—"God created man in his image" and in
> this state, called him to rule over all living things, to the crown of
> creation?[152]

---

[150] See Morris J. Raphall, *The Bible View of Slavery* (New York: Rudd & Carleton,
1861); David Einhorn, "Dr. Raphael's Rede über das Verhältnis der Bibel zum
Sklaveninstitut," *Sinai* 6 (1861/62), no. 1, 2-22. As "a Jew, the offspring who praises
God every day for release from the bondage of Egypt and still today in most places
around the old world languishes under the yoke of slavery and cries to God" (3),
Raphall has wrongly cited the Bible as a justification of slavery, instead of looking
at Man's likeness (15-16) and proclaiming the humanity of Judaism; see also idem,
"Noch ein Wort über Dr. Raphael's Prosklaverei-Rede," *Sinai* 6 (1861/62), no. 2,
45-50; on the discussion of the American rabbinate about slavery during the Civil
War, see Bertram W. Korn, *American Jewry and the Civil War* (Philadelphia: JPS,
1957), 15-55.
[151] David Einhorn, "Die Politik auf der Kanzel," *Sinai* 6 (1861/62), no. 6, 169-
173, here 171.
[152] Idem, "Festpredigt gehalten am 4. Juli 1861 im Tempel der Keneseth-Israel-
Gemeinde zu Philadelphia," in idem, *Ausgewählte Predigten und Reden*, 95-113, here 99.

During his time of office in Philadelphia and then from 1866—when he took over as rabbi of the Adath Yeshurun congregation in New York, which merged in 1874 with the oldest congregation of German Jews in the city, Anshe Chesed, to become the Temple Beth El— Einhorn reached the pinnacle of his theological influence on the fate of Reform Judaism in America. In 1869, after having had to give up Sinai in 1862, he founded the weekly periodical *The Jewish Times. A Journal of Reform and Progress*, as the mouthpiece of radical reform. At the Philadelphia Conference, which took place in November 1869 at the house of Samuel Hirsch who—coming from Luxembourg— had become Einhorn's successor at the Knesset Israel congregation just a few years before (1866),[153] seven principles—naturally in the German language—were accepted as binding for American reform, which reflected both the spirit of Einhorn as well as the theology of Holdheim. Those involved were the most renowned Reform rabbis in America, including Isaac M. Wise, who wished to be counted amongst the "theological colleagues," who—as it was put in the call to the meeting—"revere decisive religious progress."[154] Although Hirsch, as the host, was elected president, the leadership clearly lay with Einhorn, whose textual proposals, which had been printed in advance, were the sole basis of the discussion.

The seven principles of Philadelphia can nevertheless be counted as a precise, condensed summary of the theological reform theory specific to him, which he had developed in Germany and since his emigration had consistently translated into the American cultural and political context. At the center stood the attempt to raise as the standard of Jewish identity, in clear antithetical sentences, the universal mission of a modern Judaism, which in its morality as well as in its hopes for the future was divested of all historically determined particular elements, to thus distance oneself programmatically from

---

[153] Evidently at Einhorn's suggestion, see Samuel Hirsch, *Rev. Dr. David Einhorn. Gedächtniss-Rede, gehalten vor seinem Sarge den 6ten November 1879*, Philadelphia 1879. On the development of Hirsch's philosophy of religion in America, see Gershon Greenberg, "Samuel Hirsch's American Judaism," *American Jewish Historical Quarterly* 64 (1973), 362-382.

[154] "Aufruf zu einer Rabbiner-Conferenz," *The Jewish Times* 1 (1869/70), no. 14, 8. Despite the later distancing from Isaac M. Wise, there was then a short phase of unity in the Reform movement—apparent in the *Union of American Hebrew Congregations* established in 1873, and the Hebrew Union College founded in 1875, in which Einhorn was involved.

traditional Orthodoxy and to confront anti-Jewish prejudices. Israel's
messianic aim was not the restoration of the Jewish state, the "repeated
separation from the peoples," but "the unification of all people as
God's children" in recognition of the uniqueness of God "to the unity
of all rational beings and their calling to moral observance"; the
destruction of the Second Temple and the exile, the *galut*, were not
to be understood as a "punishment for the sinfulness of Israel," but
as the expression of the divine intention "to send the members of
the Jewish line to all the corners of the Earth, to fulfil their high
priestly task of leading the nations to the true acknowledgement and
honoring of God"; "Israel's status as the people chosen for the religion" and as the carrier of the highest idea of humanity was to be
emphasized still, but only in the same breath as the universal mission of Judaism and the idea of the "equal love that God has for all
his children."[155]

In the Philadelphia principles, central topoi of the European
and American Reform movement of the nineteenth century are
voiced which had developed since the Enlightenment in the continual debate with the image of Judaism held by non-Jewish theologies and philosophies, and in the context of politico-social debates
about the integration into European society of a Judaism that was
allegedly determined by an indissoluble alien "special identity." At
the same time, they deal with a universalistic re-interpretation of
fundamental themes of Jewish tradition: about understanding Israel's
status as the chosen people, the interpretation of exile and suffering in *galut*, Jewish existence in the Diaspora existence, the vision
of the messianic future, the relationship between Judaism and
humanity and other religions, as well as the relevance of ceremonial law for the modern era. The internal Jewish discourse
about determining the relationship between universalism and particularism with a view to the Jewish religion, which became a central theme of the Reform movement, was indissolubly connected
there with the question—discussed from the philosophy of the
Enlightenment, Idealism and Romanticism—of the capacity of the
Jewish community for emancipation, and of the capability for

---

[155] *Protokolle der Rabbiner-Conferenz abgehalten zu Philadelphia, vom 3. bis zum 6. November 1869* (New York: S. Hecht, 1870), 86; on the practical resolutions in Philadelphia, see Meyer, *Response to Modernity*, 255-258.

modernization of Judaism as a religion—the latter at least was always consistently negated.[156]

In his *Jerusalem* (1783), Moses Mendelssohn, as a representative of the Haskalah, had attempted to demonstrate philosophically that Judaism could be unified with a universal rational religion, and interpreted the laws of the Torah, to which he held in the Orthodox sense, as a binding special revelation for the Jewish people alone, which—in contrast to the Christian dogmatism—had never been championed with missionary zeal and raised to the prerequisite of salvation.[157] In the face of the Kantian judgement that Judaism was a religion incapable of universalism, purely "statutory" in its observance in relation to the commands of the Torah, and which must be overcome, even the generation of Jewish champions of Enlightenment after Mendelssohn, many of whom deemed themselves Kantians, failed to reconcile rational religion and ceremonial law. The main aim of *meskilim* and early reformers such as Saul Ascher or Lazarus Bendavid lay in refuting Kant's verdict and modernizing Judaism theoretically as well as practically—and in fact through a consistent historical critique of the ceremonial laws and through reining in the rabbinical tradition in favor of the biblical-prophetic tradition.[158] A reformer such as Abraham Geiger likewise aimed at overcoming particularism, and initially even thought of himself as an adherent of a universal belief in God that was free of particular obligations and rituals, a "religion of humanity," before he reached the conviction that Judaism itself was an embodiment of a universal belief, provided it was carefully freed of the ballast of national elements through historical critique, without fundamentally

---

[156] See Michael A. Meyer, "Should and Can an 'Antiquated' Religion Become Modern? The Jewish Reform Movement in Germany as Seen by Jews and Christians," in idem, *Judaism within Modernity*, 209-222.

[157] Moses Mendelssohn, *Jerusalem oder Über religiöse Macht und Judentum* (Berlin: F. Maurer, 1783); idem, *Jerusalem, Or on Religious Power and Judaism*, trans. by Allan Arkush, with an introduction and commentary by Alexander Altmann (Hanover, NH: University of New England Press, 1983).

[158] On Mendelssohn and his students, see Michael A. Meyer, *The Origins of the Modern Jew* (Detroit: Wayne State University Press, 1967). On Kant's position, and on the Enlightenment, see inter alia Micha Brumlik, *Deutscher Geist und Judenhaß. Das Verhältnis des philosophischen Idealismus zum Judentum* (Munich: Luchterhand, 2000), 27-74; Adam Sutcliffe, *Judaism and Enlightenment* (Cambridge: Cambridge University Press, 2003); Francesco Tomasoni, *Modernity and the Final Aim of History: The Debate over Judaism from Kant to the Young Hegelians* (Dordrecht: Kluwer Academic Publishers, 2003).

discarding entirely the inner rabbinical tradition.[159] Compared with
that, Holdheim, as we have seen, drew far more radical conclusions,
and saw the relinquishment of the Talmud as the precondition for
the integration of the Jewish community into a modern Europe.

David Einhorn and Samuel Hirsch had transformed Holdheim's
approach into a more moderate historico-philosophical and -theo-
logical interpretation of Judaism, which in spite of different emphases,
was closely related. Challenged by Hegel's interpretation of the exclusive "spirit of Judaism" and of its "particular God," in his 1842 work
Religionsphilosophie der Juden[160] Hirsch outlined his view of matters as

---

[159] See Michael A. Meyer, "Universalism and Jewish Unity in the Thought of
Abraham Geiger," in *The Role of Religion in Modern Jewish History: Proceedings of Regional
Conferences of the Association for Jewish Studies. Held at the University of Pennsylvania & the
University of Toronto 1974*, ed. Jacob Katz (Cambridge, MA: The Association, 1975),
91-104; idem, "Abraham Geiger's Historical Judaism," in *New Perspectives on Abraham
Geiger. An HUC-JIR Symposium*, ed. Jacob J. Petuchowski (New York: Ktav Publishing
House, 1975), 3-16. Geiger regarded the results of the Philadelphia Conference with
a certain suspicion, and rightly understood them as a kind of declaration of independence by his friend Einhorn and the American Reform movement that overtook the
German one, which had just revealed relatively conservative leanings at the Leipzig
synod of 1869, in theoretical as well as practical radicalism; see Abraham Geiger, "Die
Versammlung zu Leipzig und die zu Philadelphia," *Jüdische Zeitschrift für Wissenschaft
und Leben* 7 (1869), 1-27, particularly his thorough critique of the Philadelphia Conference
(ibid., 7-24). Einhorn responded vehemently, and accused Geiger of entering into too
many compromises with conservative forces for the sake of the unity of congregations;
see David Einhorn, "Dr. Geiger und die Philadelphier Rabbiner-Conferenz," *The Jewish
Times* 2 (1870/71), no. 7, 107; no. 8, 123-124; no. 9, 139; no. 11, 171; no. 12, 187-
188. In private letters, Einhorn judged even more sharply, for example when he wrote
to Bernhard Felsenthal that Geiger's periodical was becoming "increasingly insipid and
weak" (Einhorn to Felsenthal, 29 November 1872) and complained that he slapped
"the true reformers in the face, now on one side, now on the other," and the conferences in Germany were full of "lack of character, and hypocrisy and superficiality"
(Einhorn to Felsenthal, 8 September 1873, both letters in the unpublished material of
David Einhorn, *AJA* MSS Coll 155). In his obituary for Geiger, Einhorn honored not
so much the reformer as the historian, "who with the magic wand of genius opened
up in our innermost sanctum, in the Bible, new worlds of truth, and with his powerful seer's eye penetrated into the most hidden and obscure parts of our history, in
order to extol Judaism [....]"; see David Einhorn, "Gedächtnisrede, gehalten am 21.
November 1874 zu Ehren Abraham Geigers im Tempel der Beth-El-Gemeinde zu
New York," in idem, *Ausgewählte Predigten und Reden*, 190-193, here 182-183.

[160] On Hegel's position in relation to Judaism, see *inter alia* Brumlik, *Deutscher Geist
und Judenhaß*, 196-249; Gudrun Hentges, "Das Janusgesicht der Aufklärung:
Antijudaismus und Antisemitismus in der Philosophie von Kant, Fichte und Hegel,"
in *Antisemitismus—Geschichte und Gegenwart*, ed. Samuel Salzborn (Giessen: Netzwerk
für Politische Bildung, Kultur und Kommunikation, 2004), 11-32; on the philosophical relation between Hirsch and Hegel, see Emil L. Fackenheim, "Samuel
Hirsch and Hegel," in idem, *Jewish Philosophers and Jewish Philosophy*, ed. Michael L.
Morgan (Bloomington, IN: Indiana University Press, 1996), 21-40.

a stage that had been overcome in the process of the self-development of the divine spirit. His particular emphasis was on the attempt to show that Judaism, based on its own religious sources including the Talmud, had the capacity to develop a systematic religious philosophy which took up the Hegelian body of thought, but which inverted it in respect of the criterion of universalism. He took particular pains here to assert the uniqueness and superiority of Judaism to Christianity. Whilst the latter developed into a missionary world religion, diluting its Jewish heritage by the incorporation of heathen elements that had been carried out by Paul, in particular the doctrine of original sin, Judaism preserved the prophetic inheritance of the philosophy of moral freedom to do good or evil. Like Mendelssohn before him, and later Abraham Geiger in his historical works, Hirsch thus acknowledged a world-historic "Christian mission" in the service of spreading Jewish ideas amongst the peoples of the world,[161] but ascribed to Judaism the equally universal mission, as the "light of the peoples," of exemplifying the belief in one God and a morality of freedom, and in this way contributing to the future rule of God in a world of freedom and justice.[162] In his book *Die Humanität als Religion* (1854), which is to be understood in connection with his defense of Jewish participation in the Freemason movement, he even went so far as to talk of a common universal Judeo-Christian religion, in which the two religions, Christianity and Judaism, remained separated from one another only by their different symbolic forms of expression for one and the same truth.[163]

David Einhorn too, to a greater extent than Holdheim, supported a philosophical interpretation of Judaism. In contrast to Hirsch, however, he concentrated not so much on the relationship to Christianity[164] as on the theoretical justification of the universalism of Judaism. In the center here stand those two elements which, from the point of

---

[161] Hirsch, *Die Religionsphilosophie der Juden*, 832-839.

[162] Ibid., 861-868.

[163] Idem, *Die Humanität als Religion in Vorträgen gehalten in der Loge zu Luxemburg* (Trier: C. Troschel, 1854); on this, see Jacob Katz, "Samuel Hirsch —Rabbi, Philosopher and Freemason," *Revue des Etudes Juives* 125 (1965), 113-126.

[164] But see David Einhorn, "Unterscheidungslehre zwischen Judenthum und Christenthum," *Sinai* 5 (1860/61), no. 7, 194-197; no. 8, 225-232; no. 11, 324-325; no. 12, 359; 6 (1861/62), no. 4, 101-105; no. 8., 239-243. See also idem, "Merkwürdige Rede eines neuorthodoxen jüdischen Predigers über das Verhältnis between Judenthum und Christenthum," *Sinai* 6 (1861/62), no. 5, 112-115.

view of non-Jewish philosophers and theologians of his time, represented the main obstacle for a modern, universal Judaism—ceremonial law and the doctrine of Israel being chosen. He therefore
attempts to re-interpret these afresh, and thus to invalidate non-
Jewish judgements. His book *Das Prinzip des Mosaismus und dessen
Verhältnis zum Heidenthum und Rabbinischen Judenthum*, which had been
published in Pest and planned to run to several volumes, but which
remained incomplete, and which we shall not interpret in detail here,
undertook to construct a positive theology of Judaism in contrast to
Orthodoxy and to Christianity, by way of a synthesis between modern philosophy and religious studies as well as traditional biblical
and medieval philosophical sources.[165] In contrast to other Reform
philosophies, this work is distinguished by a quite distinct theology,
which on the one hand explicitly makes a break with rabbinical literature, but on the other hand is strikingly characterized by traditional language and is rooted in traditional values. It is thus obviously
also a response to forces within the Reform movement who regarded
pre-modern Judaism as completely worthless.

In this work, in order to found Reform Judaism on true principles, Einhorn undertook the attempt to show, distinct from Moses
Mendelssohn's view of Judaism as "revealed law," that at the center of the Jewish religion there certainly were doctrines of faith, in
particular moral doctrines,[166] and to demonstrate that ceremonial
law, above all sacrificial worship—in contrast to the rabbinical view,
for which the entire law forms the heart of Judaism and is of a binding nature—, is characterized by its symbolic character, which must
be distinguished from its transitory shell.[167] The distinction between
the eternal nature of this moral law and the transitory form of the

---

[165] Idem, *Das Princip des Mosaismus und dessen Verhältnis zum Heidenthum und rabbinischen Judenthum* (Leipzig: C. L. Fritzsche, 1854). The book was originally planned
to have three volumes, but Einhorn was able to continue it only in a few essays
from the 1870s; see idem, "Das Prinzip des Mosaismus Teil 2," in *The Jewish Times*
4 (1872/73), no. 1, 17; no. 2, 37-38; no. 3, 57; no. 4, 77; no. 5, 97; no. 6, 117;
no. 7, 138; no. 8, 157; no. 9, 177; no. 11, 217. For an interpretation of the work,
see Philip Cohen, *Biblical Theology as Response and Reform*, Phil. Diss. (UMI), Ann
Arbor, Michigan 1993. Einhorn published an accessible version of his thoughts in
his work *Ner Tamid (Beständige Leuchte). Die Lehre des Judenthums, dargestellt für Schule und
Haus* (Philadelphia: Stein und Jones, 1866).
[166] Idem, *Das Princip des Mosaismus*, 4-13; Holdheim, *Das Ceremonialgesetz im Messiasreich*,
58-68 reached a similar judgement.
[167] Einhorn, *Das Princip des Mosaismus*, 66.

"symbols of remembrance and awakening" which served it as a medium allowed Einhorn a flexible hermeneutics, which permitted him to understand the Bible, which for him still had a revelatory quality, at the same time as a historical document that was not to be understood in absolute terms in its specific description of forms.[168] Half of the book is devoted to a detailed description of biblical sacrificial worship and to the attempt to develop a theory of sacrifice that shows that it was essentially a symbol for ethico-religious principles. The task was to reconstruct the latter, and to claim them for liberal Judaism. Here, Einhorn took up theories developed in contemporary Religious Studies—in particular those of Friedrich Creuzer and Karl Christian Wilhelm Felix Bähr, about the symbolic nature of ancient forms of religious service, but divested them of their Christo-centric traits and of the tendency for example to interpret the Mosaic religion as a symbolic preparation for the revelation of Christ, and instead used them in order to make a theoretical distinction between the eternal moral truths of Judaism and ceremonial law, likewise divine but subordinate to human reason.[169] It would be interesting to discover how Holdheim viewed the irony that a radical reformer such as Einhorn justified the universalism of Judaism

---

[168] Ibid., 1-3.

[169] Ibid., 66-148. He referred above all to Friedrich Creuzer, *Symbolik und Mythologie der alten Völker, besonders der Griechen*, 4 vols. (Leipzig: Heyer und Leske, 1819-1823), and to Karl Christian F. W. Bähr, *Symbolik des Mosaischen Cultus* (Heidelberg: Mohr, 1837) on Einhorn's examination of these two works, see Cohen, *Biblical Theology*, 271-320, and Gershon Greenberg, "Religionswissenschaft and Early Reform Jewish Thought: Samuel Hirsch and David Einhorn," in *Modern Judaism and Historical Consciousness. Identities—Encounters—Perspectives*, ed. Andreas Gotzmann and Christian Wiese (Leiden: Brill Publishers, 2007, forthcoming) 105-139. If Bähr, whose symbolic interpretation of central elements of biblical culture Einhorn fundamentally appreciated, had put forward the thesis that Mosaic Judaism had created a sacramental sacrifice system on the basis of its ideas of atonement, which justified a structural particularism, since it worked only for the Jewish group and necessarily excluded others, then Einhorn turned this interpretation on its head and emphasized the universalism of Judaism which was far more marked than in Christianity: Apart from the fact that the sacramental interpretation of the sacrificial worship was mistaken, since from a Jewish point of view, people who were free did not need a mediator, but themselves had the potential for atonement and reconciliation, Mosaism—in contrast to rabbinical Judaism—was universalistic and far more inclusive than Christianity, since anyone who lived in the land could take part in the sacrificial worship without needing to become an Israelite: "A stranger, yes even an idolater—participant in the sacrament! Bähr might just as well expect the Christian church to allow a non-Christian to partake of Holy Communion" (Einhorn, *Das Princip des Mosaismus*, 76).

with the aid of—of all things—a reconstruction of the notions of atonement and sacrifice of the ancient priestly legislation: His conviction that for the present day, any reference—including symbolic reference—to the ancient Jewish state and temple cult was obsolete allows us to surmise that he would not have had very much time for that.

In Einhorn's theologically instructive but nonetheless vivid sermons, the distinction between "essence" and "form" becomes the image of a divine revelation that casts the "light of doctrine" on the "lantern of the law, of the ceremony": Over the course of history, the lantern becomes dispensable to the extent to which it is possible to penetrate into the innermost core of Judaism, "where its eternal truths and moral commandments emit such a wealth of strength and light" that the outer ceremonial symbols lose their meaning.[170] Behind Einhorn's argumentation stands a concept of revelation that is peculiar to him, and which is based on Schelling's idea of an original, pre-biblical monotheism and a divine original revelation that develops into a growing "awareness of God" amongst humanity.[171] Interpreted in Jewish terms, through the distinction between an "original revelation" to Adam through the breath of creation and the revelation at Sinai, this idea opens up two decisive possibilities, which Einhorn explained systematically for the first time in his essay "Prinzipielle Differenzpunkte zwischen altem und neuem Judentum" [Principal points of difference between the old Judaism and the new].[172] First, it permitted—and that is an important idiosyncrasy that distinguishes Einhorn from Hirsch and Holdheim—a consistent universalistic interpretation of the earliest origins of Judaism. If Judaism —and its revelation—begins not with Abraham or with the special

---

[170] Einhorn, "Antrittspredigt gehalten am 4. September 1847 in der Synagoge zu Schwerin," in idem, *Ausgewählte Predigten und Reden*, 16.

[171] Friedrich W. J. Schelling, *Philosophie der Offenbarung (1841/42)* (Frankfurt am Main: Suhrkamp, 1977); also idem, *Philosophie der Mythologie. Nachschrift der letzten Münchner Vorlesungen 1841*, ed. Andreas Roser and Holger Schulten (Stuttgart-Bad Cannstatt: Fromman-Holzboog, 1996). On Einhorn's position on Schelling's metaphysical thinking, see Cohen, *Biblical Theology*, 79-98; on Schelling's position on Jews and Judaism, which was considerably more positive compared to that of thinkers such as Kant, Fichte and Hegel, see Brumlik, *Deutscher Geist und Judenhaß*, 250-279.

[172] David Einhorn, "Prinzipielle Differenzpunkte zwischen altem und neuem Judentum," *Sinai* 1 (1856/57), no. 6, 162-164; no. 7, 193-197; no. 10, 290-294; no. 11, 333-335; no. 12, 365-371; 2 (1857/58), no.1, 399-404; no. 5, 540-544; no. 6, 572-576; 7 (1862/63), no. 12, 320-327.

revelation at Sinai, but at the beginning of biblical prehistory, then it becomes the "essence of Man"—"its truths and obligations are by their nature implanted by God, axioms of the human spirit and thus innate in the actual sense of the word."[173] Secondly, in this way the reason that is given by God, part of Man's likeness to God, becomes the actual "organ" of revelation, which is imparted in the person's growing awareness.[174] The immutable moral law is part of this rational divine spirit in the person. The revelation of Sinai, which was limited to the people of Israel, and which in spite of the story of the epiphany is not an external but an internal process, brings the people of the covenant and the ceremonial law into play as an educational tool that is limited in time and space; the latter is at the same time divine and subject to change on account of advances in human reason. According to Einhorn, the "actual Shibboleth of reform Judaism" is as follows:

> In its essence, Judaism is even older than the Israelite line; as pure essence of Man, as the expression of the divine spirit that is innate in us, it is as old—as the human race. The origin and its course of development—it is rooted in Adam and reaches its pinnacle in messianically perfected humanity. It was not a religion, but a religious people that was newly created on Sinai, a priestly people that was first of all to show the ancient doctrine of God more deeply in itself, and then bring it to general rule.[175]

The "biblical particularism" that came into play at Sinai is thus "nothing other than a lever of unrestricted universalism."[176] The interpretation, characteristic of Einhorn since his beginnings, of the people of Israel being chosen in the sense of a universalistic principle, according to which, without distinguishing themselves from humanity in respect of innate dignity,[177] the people of Israel have fulfilled a specific providential role since the revelation at Sinai, finds its backing in the *Princip des Mosaismus*, in Einhorn's anthropology and doctrine of creation. On the basis of an exegesis of Genesis 1-2, he drafted as it were a philosophical *midrash*, for which he referred to the Bible, commentaries on the Bible, medieval Jewish philosophy

---

[173] Ibid., 293.
[174] Ibid., 401.
[175] Ibid., 539.
[176] Ibid., 293.
[177] See ibid., 325.

(above all, of Chasdai Crescas) and contemporary German philosophy. At the center stands the notion, also encountered in Schelling
and Franz Joseph Molitor, of "centralization," according to which
man, as a being called to freedom and "likeness to God," represents
the "reflection and central point of the divine forces of creation," or
the point of centralization between God's absolute transcendence and
his involvement in the existence of his creation.[178] History has a
divine/human center, and advances in the direction of a perfection
of religious morality. For Einhorn, however, Judaism assumes the
messianic role, which in this process, for Schelling, is reserved for
Christianity: Its purpose is to awaken the heathen world, which to
a certain extent also includes Christianity with its pagan elements,
to natural moral holiness, to focus the divine light in itself and not
to keep it to itself, but to send it out into the world. Reform Judaism,
according to Einhorn, rests "on the unshakable cornerstone of a revelation that encompasses all times and all races, and created on Sinai
only a central point in the people of the covenant, in which all its
rays should be focused, in order to provide light and love for the
one great organism of humanity."[179]

Einhorn's concept of an *am ha-cohanim* (a "priestly people") sum-
moned from history and of a Messiah "wandering"[180] in exile refers
to a further decisive aspect of his philosophy: his understanding of
the "mission of Israel" which he taught and preached with an intensity unmatched by any other reformer, as well as to his understanding
of the relationship between Israel and the peoples. For Einhorn—as
for Holdheim and Hirsch too—the motif of the messianic "mission
of Israel" is ever-present, but goes far beyond the motif that was
usual in the Reform movement—for example in the case of Abraham
Geiger and later of Leo Baeck—of Judaism as the chosen witness
for the pure "ethical monotheism" of the prophets. He developed
the motif, which had already dominated his early theological comments at the rabbinical conferences in Germany, most impressively
in his sermons, for example in 1859 at *tisha be-av* in his congregation in Baltimore, in an analysis of Isaiah 9:6: Certainly one should

---

[178] See Einhorn, *Princip des Mosaismus*, 13 and 22-32, quotation 27. On Molitor,
see Christoph Schulte, "Franz Joseph Molitors Philosophie des Judentums," *Menora.
Jahrbuch für deutsch-jüdische Geschichte* 6 (1995), 47-64.
[179] Einhorn, "Differenzpunkte," 544.
[180] Ibid., 327.

also remember the tears and blood of exile, of the Jewish people's tale of woe that is filled with horror, and the victims of hatred of the Jews. But contrary to any Orthodox theology of sin and *galut*, this day of remembrance was much more a day of rejoicing, the day on which, from the ruins of the Jewish state with its institutions, "the foundation stone and cornerstone was laid for the enormous edifice of the messianic kingdom": "We celebrate today nothing less than the birthday of the Messiah, in other words Israel at the beginning of its messianic, world-redeeming vocation"![181] One will hardly be mistaken if one understands this identification of Judaism as the Messiah of the peoples as an attempt at a Jewish reclaiming of the idea of the suffering servant of God and as a profound challenge to the universal messianic claim of Christianity.

In his sermon, Einhorn explicitly ascribed to the destruction of the second temple and the events at Sinai a revelatory quality of equal value, and thus justified that dialectic, characteristic for this thinking, of particularism and universalism which was to justify the autonomous continued existence of Judaism as a minority in Christian America: "From the flames of Sinai, God revealed himself to Israel through Moses, from the flames of the temple mount through Israel —to the whole of humanity!"[182] The liturgy for *tisha be-av* in Einhorn's reform prayer book *Olat Tamid* (1858), the 1896 English translation of which formed the basis for the *Union Prayer Book*,[183] reflects this radical re-interpretation of exile and at the same time that of the messianic: In the place of the people of Israel, who are punished for their sin, and who hope for the coming of the Messiah, the return to Zion and the restoration of the temple, there is a community that becomes the embodiment of the servant of God who suffers for the sake of the world, in other words itself has a messianic quality—as with Hirsch, Judaism becomes the epitome of the

---

[181] Idem, "Predigt gehalten am Erinnerungstag der Zerstörung Jerusalems 5619 (1859) im Tempel der Har-Sinai-Gemeinde zu Baltimore," in idem, *Ausgewählte Reden und Predigten*, 324-331, here 325.

[182] Ibid., 329.

[183] *Dr. David Einhorn's Book of Prayers for Jewish Congregations*, trans. by Emil G. Hirsch (Chicago: s.n., 1896); see Lou H. Silberman, "The Union Prayer Book: A Study in Liturgical Development," in *Retrospect and Prospect: Essays in Commemoration of the Seventy-Fifth Anniversary of the Founding of the Central Conference of American Rabbis 1889-1964*, ed. Bertram W. Korn (New York: Central Conference of American Rabbis, 1965), 46-61.

truth of the one God and of one human morality.[184] It is a consequence of this concept of the universal mission of a "priestly people" that Einhorn consciously describes himself in his farewell sermon
as a "Hebrew," as a "member of that line [....] that was chosen
to be the priest and Messiah for humanity,"[185] a special characteristic which, as is to be shown below, may vanish only after the mission has been fulfilled.

In connection with the motif of the messianic "mission of Israel,"
perhaps the most interesting disagreement between Einhorn and
Holdheim becomes apparent, since it is at this point that one can
establish a striking contrast in the weighting given to universalism
by the two thinkers. As the first aspect, we should mention the assessment of the practical-ritualistic effects of the ideal of universalism.
Let us recall Einhorn's discussion of Holdheim's work *Das Ceremonialgesetz
im Messiasreich* in 1846, in which he rejected the latter's radical dissolution of the particular traits of Judaism into a pure universalism,
emphasizing instead the lasting validity of the concept of Israel as
the chosen people, and asserting that the features of Jewish particularism—ceremonies and a certain separation from the non-Jewish
world—belonged to the "priestly vestments" of the Jews, which they
could not simply discard until the fulfillment of the messianic era.
This disagreement was echoed in a heated public controversy between
David Einhorn and Samuel Hirsch, in which the two of them quarreled, a few weeks after the Philadelphia Conference, about the consequences resulting from the universalism of Judaism for dealing with
mixed marriages and with conversion to the Jewish faith: This was,
as it were, a posthumous debate with Holdheim's legacy. In a series
of articles under the title "Darf ein Reformrabbiner Ehen zwischen
Juden und Nichtjuden einsegnen?" [May a reform rabbi consecrate
marriages between Jews and non-Jews?] Hirsch had interpreted the
rigorous rabbinical prohibition of mixed marriages in the tradition
of Ezra and Nehemiah as historically determined harshness, and
demanded that Reform Judaism should respect the state laws on

---

[184] David Einhorn, *Olath Tamid. Gebetbuch für Israelitische Reform-Gemeinden* (Baltimore:
C. W. Schneidereith, 1858); on the character of this prayer book, see Eric L.
Friedland, "Olath Tamid by David Einhorn," *HUCA* 45 (1974), 307-332; on the
relation of the prayer book to Einhorn's *Princip des Mosaismus*, see Cohen, *David
Einhorn: Biblical Theology as Response and Reform*, 338-410.
[185] Einhorn, "Abschiedspredigt," 91.

marriage and permit non-Jews to marry Jewish men or women, with-out requiring them to formally convert to Judaism and—in the case of a man—to undergo circumcision. Here, Hirsch was assuming that committed Christians would in any case not marry non-Jewish part-ners, because of the deep religious contradiction—so this must at most concern non-Jews who rejected the Christian dogmas, accepted the teachings of Judaism in principle, and would allow their chil-dren a Jewish upbringing, but "would not wish to take on the priestly vocation of Israel" and therefore were not obligated to its symbol, circumcision.[186] Hirsch argued consistently on the basis of the view held by Holdheim who, in 1850 in his book *Gemischte Ehen zwischen Juden und Christen*, had justified his practice of giving his rabbinical blessing to mixed marriages "in the name of the religion of the purest human love, in the name of Judaism," with the Reform movement's vision of emphasizing God as the father of all humankind, and with the will "to replace the holy people with the holy race of humankind, to replace the covenant between God and Israel with a covenant between God and humankind."[187] In the rabbinical literature, he argued, the prohibition of mixed marriages had nothing to do with the religious differences between the partners, but was influenced by the desire to preserve the purity of the ethnic character of the Jews as long as they represented a separate, autonomous people living in a theocracy, in accordance with the plan of history under God's sav-ing grace. But this time was long ago consigned to the past.

The dispute with Hirsch was ignited when Einhorn declared him-self strictly against the consecration of mixed marriages, and indeed not—as he never tired of emphasizing—for the reason of Talmudic "belief in the higher sanctity of the blood of the Jewish line," but because it was his firm conviction that this meant "hammering a nail into the coffin of the tiny Jewish race with its high calling."[188] The polemical sharpness with which Einhorn rejected a more liberal

---

[186] Samuel Hirsch, "Darf ein Reformrabbiner Ehen zwischen Juden und Nichtjuden einsegnen?," *The Jewish Times* 1 (1969/70), no. 27, 9-10; no. 28, 10-11; no. 30, 9-10; no. 31, 10; no. 32, 10; no. 33, 10; no. 34, 10; no. 35, 11; no. 36, 13, here no. 27, 10.

[187] Samuel Holdheim, *Gemischte Ehen zwischen Juden und Christen. Die Gutachten der Berliner Rabbinatsverwaltung und des Königsberger Konsistoriums beleuchtet* (Berlin: L. Lassar, 1850), 64-65.

[188] David Einhorn, "Die Beschlüsse der Rabbiner-versammlung," *The Jewish Times* 1 (1869/70), no. 45, 10-11, here 11.

practice was quite evidently connected with his concern about a potential dissolution of Jewish identity—in it, he did not see a sign of the
overcoming of particularism, but a threat to the universal mission of
Israel to spread and deepen the eternal truths and moral laws. In
Einhorn's estimation that if the barriers of separation in its history of
exile had been lifted, "the tiny Jewish line, a grain of sand amongst
the peoples,"[189] would long since have perished, one can certainly perceive an echo of the anti-Jewish calls—customary at that time above
all in Germany—for a gradual dissolution of the "special Jewish character" through assimilation and mixed marriages. Einhorn countered
that with the duty of Israel to hold fast to its special character, and
asked: "May [Judaism], through mixed marriages, lead its nationality,
the actual lever of its missionary activity, gradually towards destruction
or even just allow it to be weakened?"[190] Therefore although he tended
to be skeptical of conversions, from his point of view a precondition
for marriage between Jews and non-Jews was the formal conversion,
including ritual bath or circumcision.[191] Hirsch thereupon accused
Einhorn of thinking in the racist categories of Ernest Renan, and
accused him of proselytizing. "The hope [of Reform Judaism] is surely
not," he objected, "that one day all people shall become Jews, but that
without being Jews, they shall live in truth, morality and holiness."[192]

The fact that there was a misunderstanding here of Einhorn's position is shown by his reaction to the later writings of Samuel Holdheim,
in which the latter considered more closely the historical and "particular" aspects of Jewish tradition,[193] wrote in Hebrew,[194] and was

---

[189] Idem, "Noch ein Wort über gemischte Ehen," *The Jewish Times* 1 (1869/70),
no. 48, 10-13, here 11.

[190] Ibid., 11.

[191] Ibid., Einhorn adhered strictly to this principle in his congregational practice
too. In 1870, Einhorn reported to Kaufmann Kohler about a conflict with his New
York colleague, Rabbi James K. Gutheim, when the latter wished to marry a couple whom he [Einhorn] had refused to consecrate because the bride, the daughter
of a Jewish father and a non-Jewish mother, did not want to convert to Judaism;
see Einhorn to Kohler, 7.1.1870 (unpublished papers of Einhorn, *AJA* MSS Coll
155).

[192] Samuel Hirsch, "Der Nagel zum Sarge der winzigen jüdischen Race," *The
Jewish Times* 1 (1869/70), no. 47, 10-11, here 11; and see Einhorn, "Noch ein Wort
über gemischte Ehen," 10-13.

[193] See for example Samuel Holdheim, *Die Erhaltung des Judenthums im Kampfe mit
der Zeit: Ein Bild aus der Vergangenheit belehrend für die Gegenwart. Predigt gehalten im
Gotteshause der jüdischen Reformgemeinde zu Berlin* (am 11. Mai 1851) (Berlin: L. Lassar,
1851).

[194] Idem, *Ma'amar ha-'Ishut. 'Al Tekhunat ha-Rabbanim ve-ha-Kara'im—kolel Khakirot*

even able to speak of a lasting ethnic dimension of Judaism. Einhorn, who had remained in contact with Holdheim after his emigration to America, and often allowed him to speak through *Sinai*,[195] referred in 1857, in a review of his work *Ha-emuna veha-dea*,[196] to the latter's ever clearer loyalty to the Jewish tradition—which he found "a shining testimony to the deep sincerity with which the author carries not just Judaism, but Israel, under his heart."[197] But after this praise, he expressed this criticism: From the chapter "Von dem Ceremonial-oder Ritualgesetz" [On the ceremonial law or ritual law], he quoted a passage in which Holdheim relativized his original theses from *Das Ceremonialgesetz im Messiasreich*, and now emphasized that it was not a matter of extinguishing the characteristic features of the Jewish people, of divesting Judaism of its historical shell and "merging it as a monotheistic people with other peoples," on the contrary: "Israel would never cease"—as Holdheim's imperative now put it—"to be a historical people, [nor] Judaism to be a historical religion." Einhorn rightly saw Holdheim, with his demand for the recognition of a "characteristic spiritual life of historical Judaism" as taking a new direction.[198] On the one hand, he recognized in it a rapprochement between their positions, through which their earlier differences with regard to the relationship between universalism and particularism was overcome, not without emphasizing that Holdheim must then,

---

Shonot be-Makhalkot ha-Tsedokim ve-ha-Perushim ha-Kara'im ve-ha-Rabbanim 'al Zmanem ve-Sibbot Toldotem [Essay about marriage] (Berlin: s.n. 1861).

[195] See for example Samuel Holdheim, "Etwas über die Idee der talmudischen und der gegenwärtigen Reform des Judentums," *Sinai* 1 (1856/57), 446-452; 476-551; 676-579; idem, "Die historische Basis der Reform," *Sinai* 3 (1858/59), 365-369; 4 (1859/60), 10-14; 37-42; 70-75; 100-106; 133-135; 173-175; idem, "Die Wunder der Versöhnung. Predigt, am Morgengottesdienste des Versöhnungstages 5620 (8. Oktober 1859) gehalten im Gotteshause der jüdischen Reformgemeinde zu Berlin," *Sinai* 5 (1860/61), 268-276; "Holdheim's letzte, niedergeschriebene aber nicht gehaltene Predigt für das Neujahrsfest 5621," *Sinai* 7 (1862/63), 302-310.

[196] Idem, *Ha-emunah veha-deah: Jüdische Glaubens- und Sittenlehre. Leitfaden beim Religionsunterricht der jüdischen Jugend. Zunächst für die Religionsschule der jüdischen Reformgemeinde zu Berlin* (Berlin: Julius Springer, 1857). On this, see David Einhorn, "Stein's Thora umizwah und Holdheim's Haemuna wehadea," *Sinai* 1 (1856/57), no. 4, 507-511, here 507. Continuation under the title "Holdheim's Religionsbuch: Haemuna wehadea," *Sinai* 4 (1859/60), no. 2, 33-38; no. 3, 65-71; no. 4, 97-102; no. 5, 129-137.

[197] Ibid., 133.

[198] Cited after ibid., 134. Einhorn characterized this chapter as a "radiant cupola," that arches over the "splendid work of a genius burning with the eternal flame of youth" (ibid., 133).

to be consistent, also reject mixed marriages.[199] On the other hand, Holdheim's new emphasis on an "inextinguishable historical characteristic" seemed to him to go too far, at least insofar as he excluded a merging with other peoples for the messianic era too, and thus postulated an "eternal special characteristic of Israel." That was, he felt, a return to particularistic thinking, against which one must protest determinedly.[200] It was no coincidence that in this review of Holdheim, Einhorn allowed himself to be challenged more explicitly than in any other text to make a firm declaration of belief in the time-limitation of the messianic role of the "priestly people" of Israel, and outlined a picture of the future according to which one day all "natural special characteristics" would vanish:

> The messianic kingdom shall no longer require it, and equally dispensable will be the characteristic spiritual life of historical Judaism. Whatever there is in this spiritual life, in the history of Israel, even in the midst of a messianic humanity, that still has any power of sanctification, that shall and must penetrate in the totality of peoples and wed itself closely to their peculiarities, just as our spiritual life as well as our history has become at least in part the innermost property of countless non-Israelites; it is impossible for this to be claimed exclusively for the Israelite line without at the same time granting it eternal holiness. By contrast, whatever no longer possesses any power of sanctification at all or at least on the messianic plane in Jewish spiritual life, whilst that may well appeal to the Jewish nature as charming and delightful, and appear to the national egoism to be worthy of continued preservation, shall and must nonetheless perish along with the whole special nature of the line in the world-encompassing divine covenant. Judaism, as a historical religion, shall become the common property of the peoples, but then the priestly people shall exit the scene just as once the Aaronic priesthood did with the destruction of the temple, [....] then shall Israel merge entirely with the peoples amongst whom it lives, dispersed.[201]

This interpretation also differed clearly from Samuel Hirsch's vision of the future, for according to the latter's religious philosophy, the

---

[199] Ibid., 135.

[200] Ibid., 136.

[201] Ibid., 136-137. Einhorn thus implicitly accused Holdheim of a covert return to rabbinical thinking, for in his view the idea of a continuation of the "eternally separate hereditary nobility" even in the kingdom of the Messiah was a characteristic feature of the Talmud that separated him from Reform Judaism; see idem, "Prinzipielle Differenzpunkte zwischen altem und neuem Judenthum," 323-325.

"time of the Messiah" of the absolute religion, in which all peoples shall realize freedom on Earth and acknowledge God as the one and humans as free agents in his image, contains a lasting particular element: The peoples shall reconcile themselves with Israel, "become fond of" it, and bring it to Jerusalem—not so that it shall found a state there, but "in order to establish the religion of all religions, the Jewish national religion," which "shall be honored and loved by all people, and with which all people shall commune indirectly, but Israel shall commune directly."[202] According to Einhorn's historical theology, which differs from that of Holdheim and Hirsch by more than just a nuance in this respect, after the completion of its "mission," Judaism returns completely to the universalism of its Adamitic origins and loses any identity of its own. However, it remains Einhorn's secret when in history the time for this has come—and until then, Judaism is determined by a characteristic polarity of universalism and particularism, a "particular universalism"; indeed, as shown in the controversy surrounding mixed marriage and conversion, the emphasis is precisely on strict preservation of Israel's special nature.

We are thus faced with the paradox that Einhorn's radical historico-theological universalism, together with his theory of an Adamitic pre-existence of Judaism before Israel became a people, and of a future messianic self-dissolution of the chosen "priestly people," at one end of the special covenant relationship with God evidently required as a counterweight a strong particular element in the present, whilst Hirsch and Holdheim, who assumed a particular origin for Israel and adhered to a special identity of Judaism even in the messianic future, could call for a more liberal practice in relation to non-Jews in the present day. It is not at all easy to decide which position is actually the more universalistic one, and even the causes of the difference are complex: For one thing, Einhorn appears to have developed and intensified his historical theology—more strongly than other radical reformers—under influence of non-Jewish verdicts on the particular character of Judaism and the hopes for a future as a nation, but felt forced to limit the apparent practical implications of his extreme theoretical universalism: The means for this were provided by the trenchant recourse to the aspect of being chosen as the priesthood, which was associated with a particularly marked

---

[202] Hirsch, *Die Religionsphilosophie der Juden*, 882.

consciousness of the special nature of Judaism. The different his-
torico-political context too could—at least with regard to the difference from Holdheim—offer an explanation: Whilst Holdheim, in the
course of his disappointment about the restoration in Germany, lost
his enthusiasm for a boundless theoretical universalism, and reconsidered the historical dimension of Jewish tradition, Einhorn underwent a noticeable radicalization of his much more philosophically
influenced universalistic interpretation of the origins, present and
future of Judaism. A not inconsiderable role was evidently played
here by the American context, which on the one hand inspired
Einhorn to a sometimes practically enthusiastic belief in humanity
and progress,[203] but on the other hand he perceived in both the
American and American-Jewish communities' developments which
made him aware of the dangers that integration posed to the preservation of Jewish identity. These included not only an increasing tendency toward indifference to and neglect of religious life within the
Jewish community, but also the materialistic tendencies which Einhorn
felt to be a serious threat to spiritual progress.[204] As long as this danger was not banished, Israel's messianic mission seemed to be not
only unfinished, but more necessary than ever.

---

[203] In this regard, it is worth reading his New York sermon given in 1866 on
the occasion of the laying of the Atlantic telegraph line, with the title "Gott redet
durch Feuerfunken" [God speaks through sparks of fire]—an enthusiastic paean to
the continuing work of the spirit of God, which drives forward enlightenment and
brotherhood among humanity; see David Einhorn, "Predigt gehalten am 20. October
1866, aus Anlaß der Legung des atlantischen Telegraphen, im Tempel der Adath-
Jeschurun-Gemeinde zu New York," in idem, *Ausgewählte Predigten und Reden*, 176-
182. Einhorn saw in this event a sign that the world was on its way to "reaching
our proudest goal," "general enlightenment and unification, brotherhood among all
humankind in God, their father" (181).

[204] See for example the striking contrasting of the conflict between the achievements of civilization in America and the "hideous" materialism and indifferentism
in idem, "Predigt gehalten am Neujahrstage 5639 (1878) im Tempel der Beth-El-
Gemeinde zu New York," in ibid., 197-204, here 203; see also idem, *Predigt im
Tempel Beth-El dahier, am Sabbath Chanukkah* (New York: M. Thalmessinger & Co,
1874), particularly 7: "Our teaching still stands in bitterest enmity against on the
one hand the dark superstition that presages the most unreasoning dogmas, and on
the other hand a spreading scientific approach that takes pride in denying God, in
raw materialism, teaches the similarity of humans to apes instead of their likeness
to God, and has blind natural forces rather than the spirit of God hold sway over
the surging waves, sets a law without a legislator to rule the world. Light still has
to struggle violently with darkness [....]."

3. Conclusion: Theology of Transition

The strength of the historical and religious-philosophical reflections on a Jewish universalism in the European and American Reform movement lies in that which Shulamit Volkov has described as the "invention of a tradition," as a philosophico-ethical re-interpretation of important elements of Jewish tradition, which aimed at Judaism's claim to recognition as a legitimate religious and cultural force of the modern era. In this connection, it created an effective Jewish "counter-history" against the Christian-inspired philosophical and theological images of Judaism, which were mostly sustained by a harsh verdict on "Jewish particularism" and implied not only a cultural sense of superiority, but fatally reinforced anti-Semitic stereotypes of a "special identity" and "Jewish arrogance of being the chosen people," which stood in the way of integration. Against this, reformers such as Einhorn, Holdheim and Hirsch, but also Geiger, succeeded in producing a self-confident interpretation of Judaism as a religion of at least equal value, if not superior, with a messianic humanitarian mission which justified its claim to an equal place in a pluralistic culture. Overall, this strategy is characteristic of liberal Judaism in Germany, and enjoyed an impressive continuation in the achievements of Jewish Studies right into the twentieth century.[205] However, as Amos Funkenstein has shown in his thoughts on Jewish apologetics, the danger of a "counter-history" for one's own identity lies in the fact that one makes oneself too dependent on the opponent's premises.[206] To go on the offensive and champion the right of cultural particularity in a pluralistic society was, however, hardly possible in the nineteenth century, particularly in Germany, where

---

[205] See Susannah Heschel, "Jewish Studies as Counterhistory," in *Insider/Outsider: American Jews and Multiculturalism*, ed. David Biale, Michael Galchinsky, and Susannah Heschel (Berkeley: CA: University of California Press, 1998), 101-115; Christian Wiese, "Struggling for Normality. The Apologetics of Wissenschaft des Judentums in Wilhelmine Germany as an Anti-Colonial Intellectual Revolt against the Protestant Construction of Judaism," in *Towards Normality: Patterns of Assimilation and Acculturation in German Speaking Jewry*, ed. Rainer Liedtke and David Rechter (Tübingen: J.C.B. Mohr, 2003), 77-101.

[206] Amos Funkenstein, *Perceptions of Jewish History* (Los Angeles, CA: University of California Press, 1993), 48. See also Susannah Heschel, *Abraham Geiger and the Jewish Jesus*, 36-37; Heschel demonstrates this convincingly for Geiger's "counter-history" against the image of Judaism constructed by nineteenth century New Testament research.

Holdheim, Hirsch and Einhorn developed their systems of thought, in view of the mistrust of "special identities" and the extreme cultural reservations about the continued existence of Judaism in the modern era. The proposals presented by the radical reformers do in fact often display an internalization of the prevailing enemy picture of "particularism," and the consequent compulsion to emphasize the universalism of Judaism against non-Jewish prejudices so strongly that the unique nature of Jewish religiosity as it was lived, together with its identifiable forms, threatened to retreat into the background and arrive at a situation where Judaism—at least theoretically—dissolved into a universal ethical religion of humanity, losing its religious and ethnic identity.[207] On the other hand, it is noticeable particularly in the case of David Einhorn that trenchant adherence to the idea of the chosen as well as the polarity of Judaism's universal and particular elements concealed an effective potential for the preservation of identity which disputed such conclusions.

The historiography on the American Reform movement is in agreement on the fact that the "classical phase" of radical Reform that now followed, and characteristically had as its decisive figures in Einhorn's sons in law, Kaufmann Kohler and Emil G. Hirsch, can be seen as the posthumous victory of the ideas of the pugnacious reformer. In the English-language "Pittsburgh Platform" of 1885, determined by Kohler and more influential than the Philadelphia resolutions, on the one hand one can hear the echo of Einhorn's Reform philosophy. But it turned out to be more radical than would ever have been possible in Germany, and contained undertones—such as not recognizing the Bible as revelation—which pointed beyond Einhorn and are reminiscent of the early Holdheim.[208] However, this was a transitional phenomenon, just as Einhorn was a figure of transition from German to American Reform Judaism and a member of a very specific generation of immigrant intellectuals. On the basis of a detailed analysis of the further programs of the American Reform movement—from the *Columbus Platform* of 1939, with its emphasis on

---

[207] The most extreme consequence of this tendency can be seen in the *Society for Ethical Culture*, initiated by Felix Adler, the son of Samuel Adler; on this, see Benny Kraut, *From Reform Judaism to Ethical Culture. The Religious Evolution of Felix Adler* (Cincinnati: Hebrew Union College Press, 1979); on the reaction of the radical reformers, see Meyer, *Response to Modernity*, 264-266.

[208] See the text of the program in ibid., 387-388.

the importance of Hebrew and the rituals of Judaism, through the declaration *Reform Judaism: A Centenary Perspective,* formulated in 1976 in San Francisco, to the latest document, the *Statement of Principles for Reform Judaism* formulated in 1999 in Pittsburgh by the *Central Conference of American Rabbis*—it can be shown how much the questioning of optimism about historical progress brought about by the Shoah, the new awareness of the reality of a Jewish people that was triggered by Zionism, and the threat to Jewish identity through increased assimilation, have changed the religious and theological profile of liberal Judaism of the twentieth century towards a re-evaluation of its particular elements.[209] The age of the dominance of the Einhorn-Holdheim version of Reform thus soon belonged definitively to the past in America too.

---

[209] See Dana E. Kaplan, *American Reform Judaism: An Introduction* (New Brunswick, NJ: Rutgers University Press, 2003); idem, ed., *Contemporary Debates in American Reform Judaism: Conflicting Visions* (New York: Routledge, 2001); idem, ed., *Platforms and Prayer Books: Theological and Liturgical Perspectives on Reform Judaism* (Lanham, MD: Rowman & Littlefield, 2002).

BIBLIOGRAPHY

Primary Sources
Writings by Samuel Holdheim

Rede verfaßt und gehalten in Kempen (Berlin: Julius Sittenfeld, 1836).

Die Einsegnung des Neumondtages: Rede gehalten an den beiden Sabbathen vor dem Gedächtnißtage der Zerstörung Jerusalems des Jahres 5597 (5. August 1837) in der Synagoge zu Frankfurt an der Oder (Frankfurt an der Oder: F. W. Kosky, 1837).

Gebet und Belehrung vereinigt, sind die Bestandtheile des jüdischen Gottesdienstes. Rede gehalten am Sabath- und Neumondstage des Monats Schewat 5597 in der Synagoge und auf Verlangen herausgegeben (Frankfurt an der Oder: F. W. Koscky, 1837).

Religion, Gesetzmäßigkeit und Frieden in Israel wieder herrschend zu machen, ist der heilige Beruf des jüdischen Geistlichen. Rede (theilweise) gehalten am Sabath Paraschath Schekalim des Jahres 5597 (4. März 1837) in der Synagoge zu Frankfurt a.O. (Frankfurt an der Oder: F. J. Tempel, 1837).

Einiges zur Geschichte der Dogmatik der jüdischen Religionslehre: zur Promotion Leipzig vorgelegt (1838, Reprint Leipzig, 2001).

Es ist Pflicht jedes Israeliten für die Erhaltung der Religion seiner Väter zu sorgen: Rede gehalten am 1. Sabbath Chanukka des Jahres 5598 (23. December 1837) in der Synagoge zu Frankfurt an der Oder (Frankfurt an der Oder: F. J. Tempel, 1838).

Ob es Pflicht jedes Israeliten für die Erhaltung der Religion seiner Väter zu sorgen: Rede gehalten am I. Sabbath Chanukka ... 23. Dec. 1837 (Frankfurt an der Oder: F. W. Koscky, 1838).

Dibre Chaj. Worte Gottes oder Gottesdienstliche Vorträge gehalten in der Synagoge zu Frankfurt an der Oder (Frankfurt an der Oder and Leipzig: F. J. Tempel and E. L. Fritzsche, 1838-1840).

Antrittspredigt bei der feierlichen Introduction in sein Amt als Großherzogl. Mecklenburgischer Landesrabbiner in Schwerin (Schwerin: C. Kürschner, 1840).

Der religiöse Fortschritt im deutschen Judenthume. Ein friedliches Wort in einer aufgeregten Zeit (Leipzig: E. L. Fritzsche, 1840).

Gedächtnißrede zu der dem glorreichen Andenken Sr. Hochseligen Majestät des Königs Friedrich Wilhelm III. In der Synagoge zu Frankfurt a.O. am 23. Juni 1840 gehaltenen Todtenfeier (Leipzig: E. L. Fritzsche, 1840).

"Der neue Israelitische Tempel zu Hamburg," *Israelitische Annalen* 45 (1841), 353-355; 46 (1841), 362-365.

*Die sittliche Reinigung des Menschen. Predigt gehalten in der Synagoge zu Schwerin am Sabbath paraschat para (*13. März 1841) (Schwerin: C. Kürschner, 1841).

Jakob und Israel. Predigt für den Sabbath (paraschat wa-jischlach), gehalten zu Schwerin (12. December 1840 (Schwerin: C. Kürschner, 1841).

Ueber das Gebetbuch nach dem Gebrauche des neuen Israelitischen Tempelvereins zu Hamburg. Ein Votum von Dr. S. Holdheim (Hamburg: B. S. Berendsohn, 1841).

Zuruf an die israelitische Gemeinde in Frankfurt an der Oder: Des israelitischen Geistlichen Beruf und Stellung in unserer Zeit. Predigt, gehalten in der Synagoge zu Frankfurt an der Oder am Sabbath Nachmu 5600 (15. August 1840) (Schwerin: C. Kürschner, 1841).

Die drei Symbole des Ueberschreitungsfestes: Worte des Schmerzes und der Erhebung am Tage der feierlichen Beisetzung Sr. Königl. Hoheit des Allerdurchlauchtigsten Großherzogs und Herrn Paul Friedrich, 19. März 1842 (am Sabbath vor dem Ueberschreitungsfeste) im israelitischen Gotteshause zu Schwerin gesprochen (Schwerin: C. Kürschner, 1842).

Verketzerung und Gewissensfreiheit. Ein zweites Votum in dem Hamburger Tempelstreit mit besonderer Berücksichtigung der Erwiederung eines Ungenannten auf mein erstes Votum (Schwerin: C. Kürschner, 1842).

Was er uns war, und was er uns hätte werden können: Gedächtnißpredigt auf den Tod des hochseligen Großherzogs Paul Friedrich, am 17. April 1842, im israelitischen Gotteshause zu Schwerin (Schwerin: C. Kürschner, 1842).

"Gutachten des Landesrabbiners Herrn Dr. Holdheim in Schwerin," *Rabbinische Gutachten über die Verträglichkeit der freien Forschung mit dem Rabbineramte* (1842/43), vol. 1, 38-83.

Ueber die Autonomie der Rabbinen und das Princip der jüdischen Ehe: Ein Beitrag zur Verständigung über einige das Judenthum betreffende Zeitfragen (Schwerin: C. Kürschner, 1843; 2nd edition 1847).

Der glaubensvolle Muth des israelitischen Volkshirten dem Murren seiner Gemeinde gegenüber. Predigt, gehalten in der Synagoge zu Schwerin am Sabbath Chukkath (29. Juni 1844) (Schwerin: C. Kürschner, 1844).

"Noch Einiges über die rabbinische Auflösbarkeit der Eide," *Der Israelit des neunzehnten Jahrhunderts* 5 (1844), no. 41, 327-329.

Ueber die Beschneidung zunächst in religiös dogmatischer Beziehung (Schwerin: C. Kürschner, 1844).

Vorträge über die Mosaische Religion für denkende Israeliten (Schwerin: C. Kürschner, 1844).

"Was lehrt das rabbinische Judenthum über den Eid?," *Israelit des neunzehnten Jahrhunderts* 5 (1844), 277-280.

Zweite Mittheilung aus einem Briefwechsel über die neueste jüdische Literatur: Ein Fragment von Samson Raphael Hirsch, Landesrabbiner zu Emden. Beleuchtet von Dr. Samuel Holdheim (Schwerin: C. Kürschner, 1844).

"Bemerkungen zu der Entgegnung des Herrn Dr. Einhorn auf meine zwei Aufsätze betreffend die rabbinische Lehre von der Auflösbarkeit der Eide," *Der Israelit des neunzehnten Jahrhunderts* 6 (1845), no. 2, 9-13; no. 3, 17-20.

Das Ceremonialgesetz im Messiasreich: als Vorläufer einer grössern Schrift über die religiöse Reform im Judenthum (Schwerin: C. Kürschner, 1845).

Das Religiöse und Politische im Judenthum: Mit besonderer Beziehung auf gemischte Ehen. Eine Antwort auf Frankel's Kritik der Autonomie der Rabbinen und der Protocolle der ersten Rabbiner-Versammlung in Betreff der gemischten Ehen (Schwerin: C. Kürschner, 1845).

"Der Eid nach dem rabbinischen Judenthume," *Literaturblatt des Orients* 6 (1845), 164-69, 197-204, 215-20, 229-34.

Der Segen des Gotteshauses und der Gottesdienst in der Wahrheit: Zwei Predigten, gehalten in der israelitischen Gemeinde zu Goldberg 1845 bei der Einweihungsfeier der neuen Synagoge (11. Sept.) und dem darauf folgenden Sabbath (13. Sept. 1845), und auf Verlangen in Druck gegeben (Schwerin, C. Kürschner, 1845).

Die erste Rabbinerversammlung und Herr Dr. Frankel (Schwerin: C. Kürschner, 1845).

Predigt bei der am 2. April stattgefundenen Einweihung des Gotteshauses der Genossenschaft für Religion im Judenthum (Berlin: Behr's Buchhandlung, 1845).

Ueber Auflösbarkeit der Eide von S. L. Rappoport, beleuchtet von Samuel Holdheim (Hamburg: Hermann Cobert, 1845).

Vorschläge zu einer zeitgemäßen Reform der jüdischen Ehegesetze (Schwerin: C. Kürschner, 1845).

Die religiöse Stellung des weiblichen Geschlechts im talmudischen Judenthum. Mit besonderer Rücksicht auf eine diesen Gegenstand betreffende Abhandlung des Herrn Dr. S. Adler in den Protocollen der zweiten Rabbiner-Versammlung (Schwerin: C. Kürschner, 1846).

Sie hörten nicht auf Moses vor Kürze des Odems und vor schwerer Arbeit! Predigt am Sabbat Waera (24. Januar) in der Synagoge zu Schwerin (Schwerin: C. Kürschner, 1846).

Abschiedspredigt bei dem Scheiden aus seinem Amte als Landesrabbiner des Großherzogtums Mecklenburg-Schwerin am 28. August 1847 (Schwerin: C. Kürschner, 1847).

Antrittspredigt des Dr. Samuel Holdheim bei dessen Einführung in sein Amt als Rabbiner und Prediger der Genossenschaft für Reform im Judenthum zu Berlin (Berlin: B. Behr's Buchhandlung, 1847).

Die religiöse Aufgabe im neuen Vaterlande. Predigt, bei Gelegenheit der Befreiung der Israeliten Mecklenburg-Schwerins von der Abgabe des Schutzgeldes gehalten am Sabbath Chaije Sarah (14. November 1846) (Schwerin: C. Kürschner, 1847).

Die Religionsprincipien des reformirten Judenthums entworfen und den Reformgenossenschaften zur Prüfung und Annahme empfohlen (Berlin: B. Behr's Buchhandlung, 1847).

"Materialien zu einem Commissionsbericht über die Speisegesetze," *Wissenschaftliche Zeitschrift für jüdische Theologie* 6 (1847), issue 2, 41-63.

Über die Autonomie der Rabbinen und das Princip der jüdischen Ehe 2nd edition (Schwerin: C. Kürschner, 1847).

Das Gutachten des Herrn L. Schwab, Rabbiners zu Pesth, über die Reformgenossenschaft daselbst (Berlin: J. Sittenfeld, 1848).

Der Kampf bis zum Anbruch der Morgenröthe: Eine Predigt gehalten am 2. April, dem Stiftungstage der Genossenschaft für Reform im Judenthume zu Berlin, und auf Verlangen dem Druck übergeben (Berlin: L. Lassar, 1848).

"Literarische Fehhde zwischen Dr. Einhorn und Prof. Delitzsch über die Beschneidungsfrage in Mecklenburg," *Der Israelit des neunzehnten Jahrhunderts* 9 (1848), no. 5, 33-37; no. 6, 41-44.

"Volksgenossenschaft und Religionsgenossenschaft. Mit Rücksicht auf die literarische Fehde zwischen Dr. Einhorn und Prof. Delitzsch," *Der Israelit des neunzehnten Jahrhunderts* 9 (1848), no. 21, 161-163; no. 22, 169-172; no. 23, 177-180.

Die Würdigung der Arbeit. Eine Predigt gehalten im Tempel der Genossenschaft für Reform im Judenthum zu Berlin, am 29. October 1848 (Berlin: L. Lassar, 1848).

Einsegnung einer gemischten Ehe (Berlin: J. A. Stargardt, 1849).

Die geprüfte Vaterlandsliebe. Predigt gehalten am Tage vor Eröffnung der Preußischen Kammern (25. Februar 1849) im Tempel der Genossenschaft für Reform im Judenthum (Berlin: L. Lassar, 1849).

(anonymous), *Denkschrift der Genossenschaft für Reform im Judenthum zu Berlin, wegen Abänderung des von den jüdischen Staatsbürgern zu leistenden Eides* (Berlin: J. Draeger, 1850).

Gemischte Ehen zwischen Juden und Christen. Die Gutachten der Berliner Rabbinatsverwaltung und des Königsberger Konsistoriums beleuchtet (Berlin: L. Lassar, 1850).

Die rechte Buße. Predigt gehalten am Versöhnungsfeste 5611 (16. September 1850) im Gotteshause der jüdischen Reformgemeinde zu Berlin (Berlin: L. Lassar, 1850).

Die wesentlichen Erfordernisse eines ächt jüdischen Gottesdienstes. Predigt gehalten am zweiten Tage des Neujahrsfestes 5611 (8. September 1850) im Gotteshause der jüdischen Reformgemeinde zu Berlin (Berlin: L. Lassar, 1850).

Die Erhaltung des Judenthums im Kampfe mit der Zeit. Ein Bild aus der Vergangenheit belehrend für die Gegenwart. Predigt gehalten im Gotteshause der jüdischen Reformgemeinde zu Berlin (am 11. Mai 1851) (Berlin: L. Lassar, 1851).

Gebetbuch für jüdische Reformgemeinden (Berlin: 1851).

Neue Sammlung jüdischer Predigten worunter über alle Feste des Jahres gehalten im Gotteshause der jüdischen Reformgemeinde in Berlin, 4 vols. (Berlin: Carl David, 1852-1869).

Predigten über die jüdische Religion. Ein Buch der religiösen Belehrung und Erbauung für's jüdische Haus, gehalten im Gotteshause der jüdischen Reform-Gemeinde zu Berlin (Berlin: Carl David's Buchhandlung, 1853).

Welches Zeugniss gibt der Bau eines neuen Gotteshauses für unsere Gemeinde, und welche Hoffnungen knüpfen sich an dessen Vollendung? Predigt gehalten bei Gelegenheit des Richtfestes des neuen Gotteshauses der jüdischen Reform-Gemeinde zu Berlin (am 4. Dezember 1853) (Berlin: Carl David, 1853).

Predigten über die jüdische Religion: gehalten im Gotteshause der jüdischen Reform-Gemeinde zu Berlin, 4 vols (Berlin: Julius Springer, 1853-1869).

Stahl's christliche Toleranz beleuchtet (Berlin: Julius Abelsdorff, 1856).

"Etwas über die Idee der talmudischen und der gegenwärtigen Reform des Judentums," *Sinai* 1 (1856/57), 446-452; 476-551; 676-579.

Die jüdische Zeitrechnung: Eine Predigt am zweiten Tage des Neujahrsfestes 5617 (1. Oct. 1856), gehalten in der Synagoge der jüdischen Reformgemeinde zu Berlin (Berlin: Julius Springer, 1856).

Geschichte der Entstehung und Entwickelung der jüdischen Reformgemeinde in Berlin: im Zusammenhang mit den jüdisch-reformatorischen Gesammtbestrebungen der Neuzeit (Berlin: J. Springer, 1857).

Ha-emuna ve-ha-deah: Jüdische Glaubens- und Sittenlehre: Leitfaden beim Religionsunterricht der jüdischen Jugend. Zunächst für die Religionsschule der jüdischen Reformgemeinde zu Berlin (Berlin: Julius Springer, 1857).

"Der verbesserte Religionsunterricht," *Programm zur öffentlichen Prüfung der Zöglinge der Religionsschule am 2. April 1858* (Berlin: Friedländer, 1858).

Gebete und Gesänge für das Neujahrs- und Versöhnungsfest zum Gebrauche für die öffentliche und häusliche Andacht jüdischer Reformgemeinden (Berlin, J. E. Huber's Verlag, 1859).

"Die historische Basis der Reform," *Sinai* 3 (1858/59), 365-369; 4 (1859/60), 10-14; 37-42; 70-75; 100-106; 133-135; 173-175.

Jehova hu ha'elohim: Jehova ist der wahre Gott! Eine Neïlapredigt, gehalten am Abend des Versöhnungstages 5620 (8. October 1859) im Gotteshause der jüdischen Reformgemeinde zu Berlin und auf Verlangen dem Druck übergeben (Berlin: W. J. Peiser, 1859).

Licht im Lichte! oder das Judenthum und die Freiheit. Eine Festpredigt, gehalten am Wochenfeste Schabuoth 5519 (8. Juni 1859) im Gotteshause der jüdischen Reformgemeinde zu Berlin (Berlin: W. J. Peiser, 1859).

Moses Mendelssohn und die Denk- und Glaubensfreiheit im Judenthume (Berlin: J. C. Huber, 1859).

Der Sambation. Eine Sabbathpredigt gehalten im Gotteshause der jüdischen Reform-Gemeinde zu Berlin (20. Februar 1859) und auf Verlangen dem Druck übergeben (Berlin: W. J. Peiser, 1859).

Die Wunder der Versöhnung. Eine Predigt am Morgengottesdienste des Versöhnungstages 5620 (8. Ocober. 1859) gehalten im Gotteshause der jüdischn Reformgemeinde zu Berlin und auf Verlangen dem Druck übergeben (Berlin: W. J. Peiser, 1859).

Etwas über das gegenseitige Verhältniss zwischen der religiösen und der allgemeinen wissenschaftlichen Erziehung und Bildung (Berlin: H. S. Herrmann, 1860).

"Die Wunder der Versöhnung. Predigt, am Morgengottesdienste des Versöhnungstages 5620 (8. Oktober 1859) gehalten im Gotteshause der jüdischen Reformgemeinde zu Berlin," *Sinai* 5 (1860/61), 268-276.

Gott siehet! Predigt für den Neujahrstag des Jahres 5621 (1860) als Entwurf aus den hinterlassenen Papieren des kurz vor dem Neujahrsfeste verstorbenen Dr. Samuel Holdheim, Rabbiner und Prediger der jüdischen Reform-Gemeinde zu Berlin. Nebst einem Vorworte von Dr. Abraham Geiger, Rabbiner in Breslau (Berlin: Im Selbstverlage der Wittwe des sel. Verfassers, 1861).

Ma'amar ha-'Ishut. 'Al Tekhunat ha-Rabbanim ve-ha-Kara'im—kolel Khakirot Shonot be-Makhalkot ha-Tsedokim ve-ha-Perushim ha-Kara'im ve-ha-Rabbanim 'al Zmanem ve-Sibbot Toldotem (Berlin: s.n., 1861).

Vier Predigten für Neujahr und Versöhnungstag (Berlin: Im Selbstverlag der Wittwe des sel. Verfassers, 1862).

"Holdheim's letzte, niedergeschriebene aber nicht gehaltene Predigt für das Neujahrsfest 5621," *Sinai* 7 (1862/63), 302-310.

Sechs Predigten (Berlin: Im Selbstverlage der Wittwe des sel. Verfassers, 1863).

Other Primary Sources

Alexandersohn, Jonathan, *Ehrenrettung und auf Dokumente gestützte Widerlegung aller gegen mich vorgebrachten Beschuldigungen und Verunglimpfungen. Meine durch öffentliche Blätter einigermaßen schon bekannte Verfolgungsgeschichte. Ein merkwürdiges Aktenstück in den Annalen des Judenthums*, 2nd ed. (Frankfurt am Main: J. F. Bach, 1847).

Anonymous, *Entgegnung auf den Bericht des Ober-Vorsteher-Collegiums der hiesigen Israeliten-Gemeinde über die Rabbinats-Angelegenheit an die Mitglieder* (anonymous) (Breslau: H. Richter, 1842).

Anonymous, *Jude und Nicht-Jude, eine Erwiederung auf die Schriften der Triple-Allianz der Herren Doctoren Holdheim, Salomon und Frankfurter, von einem Ungenannten* (Amsterdam: s.n., 1842).

Anonymous, "Personalzeichnungen aus der Braunschweiger Rabbinen-Versammlung," *Der Israelit des neunzehnten Jahrhunderts* 5 (1844), 297-300.

Anonymous, "Holdheim und die rabbinische Lehre vom Eide," *Der Israelit des neunzehnten Jahrhunderts* 6 (1845), 118-119.

Anonymous, "Eingesandte Erklärung, hervorgerufen durch die 'Erklärung' des Dr. David Einhorn in Hoppsteten, in der allgemeinen Zeitung des Judenthums No. 18," *Der Treue Zionswächter* 2 (1846), no. 24, 203-205.

Anonymous, "Rabbi Wolf Hamburger und sein Schweif," *Der Israelit des neunzehnten Jahrhunderts* 7 (1846), no. 27, 212-213.

Anonymous, "Verhältnisse der Israeliten im Fürstentume Birkenfeld," *Der Israelit des neunzehnten Jahrhunderts* 8 (1847), no. 42, 335-336; no. 43, 342-344.

Anonymous, "Das Wesen des Judenthums," *Der Treue Zionswächter* 5 (1849), 366-367, 371-373.

Anonymous, "Der Staat in seinem Verhältnisse zur Kirche," *Der Treue Zionswächter* 5 (1849), 225-227, 233-234, 243.

Anonymous, "Schulnachrichten," *Programm zur öffentlichen Prüfung der Zöglinge der Religionsschule am 2. April 1858* (Berlin: Friedländer, 1858).

Anonymous, "Die letzten Vorgänge in Berlin," *AZJ* 24 (1860), 573-575.

Aub, Josef, "Die Rabbinerversammlung und ihre Gegner," *Sinai* 1 (1846), 357-62.

"Aufruf zu einer Rabbiner-Conferenz," *The Jewish Times* 1 (1869/70), no. 14, 8.

Bähr, Karl Christian F. W., *Symbolik des Mosaischen Cultus* (Heidelberg: Mohr, 1837).

Balz, Theodor Friedrich, *Die schädlichen Folgen der Beschneidung: Ein Sendschreiben an die hocherwürdige Versammlung der Herren Rabbiner in Frankfurt A.M* (Berlin: Als Manuscript gedruckt und privatim vertheilt, 1845).

Bamberger, Fritz, ed., *Das Buch Zunz: künftigen ehrlichen Leuten gewidmet* (Berlin: Soncino-Gesellschaft, 1931).

Bauer, Bruno, "Die Juden-Frage," *Deutsche Jahrbücher für Wissenschaft und Kunst* 5 (1842), 1093-1126.

— *Die Judenfrage* (Brunswick: Otto, 1843).

— *The Jewish Problem*, trans. Helen Lederer (Cincinnati, OH: Hebrew Union College Press, 1958).

Beer, Peter, *Geschichte, Lehren und Meinungen aller bestandenen und noch bestehenden religiösen Sekten der Juden und der Geheimlehre der Cabbalah*, 2. vols., (Brünn: Trassler, 1822-1823).

Bericht des Ober-Vorsteher-Collegiums an die Mitglieder der hiesigen Israeliten-Gemeinde über die gegenwärtig vorliegende Rabbinatsangelegenheit, 2 vols. (Breslau: H. Richter, 1842).

Bergson, Joseph, *Die Beschneidung vom historischen, kritischen und medicinischen Standpunkt mit Bezug auf die neuesten Debatten und Reformvorschläge* (Berlin: Verlag von Th. Scherk, 1844).

Berliner, Abraham, *Zur Lehr' und zur Wehr. Über und gegen die kirchliche Orgel im jüdischen Gottesdienste* (Berlin: Nathansen & Lamm, 1904).

Bernfeld, Simon, "Zacharias Frankel in Berlin," *AZJ* 62 (1898), No. 29-31, 343-346, 356-358, 368-370, 389-391, 404, 437-439, 461-463, 486-488, 536-538, 569f., 582f., 595-597, 606-608.

— *Mika'el Zaqs. Me'ora'ot hajjav u-fe'ulato ha-sifrutit* (Berlin: s.n., 1900).

— *Toledot ha-reformatsyon ha-datit be-yisrael* (Cracow: Achiasaf, 1900; 2nd edition Warsaw: Tushiyah, 1923).

Brecher, Gideon, *Die Beschneidung der Israeliten, von der historischen, praktisch-operativen und ritualen Seite zunächst für den Selbstunterricht. Mit einem*

Approbationsschreiben von Herrn Rabbiner H. B. Fassel (Wien: Selbstverlag, 1845).

— "Die Beschneidung vor dem ärztlichen Forum," *AZJ* 52 (1857), 709-710.

Brück, Moses, *Das mosaische Judenthum, In einer Andachtsstunde als Predigt vorgetragen am Wochenfeste 5597 und durch Anmerkungen erläutert* (Frankfurt am Main: J. C. Herrmann, 1837).

— *Rabbinische Ceremonialgebräuche in ihrer Entstehung und geschichtlichen Entwicklung* (Breslau: Schulz, 1837).

— *Pharisäische Volkssitten und Ritualien in ihrer Entstehung und geschichtlichen Entwicklung* (Frankfurt am Main: J. C. Hermann, 1840).

— *Der mosaische Gesetzescodex* (Ofen: s.n., 1847).

— *Reform des Judenthums, in 100 Thesen dargestellt* (Nagy-Becskerek: Bettelheim, 1848).

Cassel, David, *Die Cultusfrage in der jüdischen Gemeinde von Berlin* (Berlin: Adolf, 1856).

Chorin, Aron, Iggeret Elassaph, *Oder Sendschreiben eines afrikanischen Rabbinen an seinen Collegen in Europa, hg. mit einem deutschen Vorworte, Nachworte und Noch-Etwas von A. Chorin* (Prag: Landau, 1826).

— *Der treue Bothe an seine Religionsgenossen gesendet* (Prag: Selbstverlag, 1831).

Creizenach, Michael, *32 Thesen über den Talmud* (Frankfurt am Main: Jäger, 1831).

— *Schulchan Aruch oder encyclopädische Darstellung des Mosaischen Gesetzes wie es durch die rabbinischen Satzungen sich ausgebildet hat, mit Hinweisung auf die Reformen, welche durch die Zeit nützlich und möglich geworden sind*, 4 vols. [with changing titles] (Frankfurt am Main: Andreäische Buchhandlung, 1833-1840).

Creuzer, Friedrich, *Symbolik und Mythologie der alten Völker, besonders der Griechen*, 4 vols. (Leipzig: Heyer und Leske, 1819-1823.

Den öffentlichen Cultus betreffende Differenzpunkte zwischen den verschiedenen religiösen Parteien in den israelitischen Gemeinden des Großherzogtums Mecklenburg-Schwerin, dargelegt vom israelitischen Oberrathe (Schwerin: A. W. Sandmeyer, 1850).

Die Deutsche Synagoge oder Ordnung des Gottesdienstes für die Sabbath- und Festtage des ganzen Jahres zum Gebrauche der Gemeinde, die sich der deutschen Gebete bedienen, Part I (Berlin: In der Mauerschen Buchhandlung, 1817).

Dinaburg (Dinur), Ben Zion, "Iggrot Shir'," *Kiryat Sefer* 3 (1926/27), 222-35, 306-19.

Dreifuß, Moses, "Eine ganz neue Erklärung über das Gebot der Beschneidung," *Der Orient* 6 (1845), no. 39 (supplement), 611-15.

Ehrlich, Abraham, "Ele toledot rabbenu Jehiel Mikha'el Zaqs," *Ha-Maggid 40-46 (1866)*, 317-318, 341-342, 349-350, 357-358, 365.

Einhorn, David, "Gutachten des Herrn Rabbiners Dr. David Einhorn im Fürstenthume Birkenfeld," in *Rabbinische Gutachten über die Verträglichkeit der freien Forschung mit dem Rabbineramte* (1842/43) vol. 1, 125-139.

— "Gutachtliche Äußerung eines jüdischen Theologen über den Reformverein an einen sich dafür interessierenden Christen," *AZJ* 8 (1844), no. 7, 87-89.

— *Gedächtniss-Predigt bei dem Trauer-Gottesdienste wegen des Hinscheidens der Großherzogin Cäcilie von Oldenburg, gehalten in der Synagoge zu Hoppstaetten am 11. Februar 1844* (Birkenfeld: C. F. Kittsteiner, 1844).

— "Die rabbinische Lehre von der Auflösbarkeit der Eide," *Der Israelit des neunzehnten Jahrhunderts* 5 (1844), no. 7, 375-378.

— "Antikritik. Dr. Holdheim's neuentdeckte Lehre des rabbinischen Judenthums in Bezug auf das Kol Nidre und die Auflösbarkeit assertorischer Eide," *AZJ* 9 (1845), no. 13, 194-196; no. 18, 274-275; no. 19, 289-292; no. 22, 333-335.

— "Erklärung," *AZJ* 10 (1846), no. 18, 266.

— Dr. Holdheim's Schrift: Das Ceremonialgesetz im Messiasreich," *Literatur-Blatt zum Israeliten des 19. Jahrhunderts* 1 (1846), no. 37, 157-160; no. 38, 161-164; no. 39, 165-168.

— Materialien für den Commissionsbericht über die Speisegesetze," *Der Israelit des neunzehnten Jahrhunderts* 8 (1847), no. 6, 41-43; no. 7, 49-51; no. 13, 97-100; no. 14, 105-108; no. 19, 147-150; no. 20, 153-156.

— "Entgegnung," *Der Israelit des neunzehnten Jahrhunderts* 9 (1848), no. 14, 105-107; no. 15, 113-115.

— *Abschiedspredigt gehalten am 13. December 1851 in der Synagoge zu Schwerin bei seinem Austritte aus dem Amte eines Großherzoglich Mecklenburg-Schwerinschen Landesrabbiners* (Schwerin: F. Hartig, 1852).

— *Das Princip des Mosaismus und dessen Verhältnis zum Heidenthum und rabbinischen Judenthum* (Leipzig: C. L. Fritzsche, 1854).

— "Die Rabbiner-Conferenz zu Cleveland," *Sinai* 1 (1856/57), no. 1, 4-10.

— "Gegenerklärung," *Sinai* 1 (1856/57), no. 1, 27-29.

— "Stellung des neuern Judenthums zum Talmud," *Sinai* 1 (1856/57), no. 1, 1-4; no. 2, 33-38; no. 3, 65-67.

— "Prinzipielle Differenzpunkte zwischen altem und neuem Judentum," *Sinai* 1 (1856/57), no. 6, 162-164; no. 7, 193-197; no. 10, 290-294;

no. 11, 333-335; no. 12, 365-371; 2 (1857/58), no.1, 399-404; no. 5, 540-544; no. 6, 572-576; 7 (1862/63), no. 12, 320-327.

— "Stein's Thora umizwah und Holdheim's Haemuna wehadea," *Sinai* 1 (1856/57), no. 4, 507-511.

— "Holdheim's Religionsbuch: Haemuna wehadea," *Sinai* 4 (1859/60), no. 2, 33-38; no. 3, 65-71; no. 4, 97-102; no. 5, 129-137.

— "Die Beschneidungsfrage," *Sinai* 2 (1857/58), no. 10, 699-708; no. 11, 731-740; no. 12, 763-772; *Sinai* 3 (1858/59), no. 1, 796-805; no. 2, 827-835; no. 3, 859-867; no. 5, 923-932; no. 6, 955-965.

— *Olath Tamid. Gebetbuch für Israelitische Reform-Gemeinden* (Baltimore: C. W. Schneidereith, 1858).

— "Das katholische und protestantisch-pietistische Christenthum gegen die Juden," *Sinai* 3 (1858/59), no. 11, 1115-1127.

— "Predigt, vom Herausgeber dieser Blätter gehalten im Tempel der Har Sinai Gemeinde," *Sinai* 3 (1858/59), no. 1, 824.

— "Das Schicksal der Oheb Schalom Gemeinde," *Sinai* 4 (1859/60), 321-339.

— "Samuel Holdheim," *Sinai* 5 (1860/61), no. 10, 289-297.

— "Abfertigung," *Sinai* 5 (1860/61), no. 1, 1-28.

— "Unterscheidungslehre zwischen Judenthum und Christenthum," *Sinai* 5 (1860/61), no. 7, 194-197; no. 8, 225-232; no. 11, 324-325; no. 12, 359; 6 (1861/62), no. 4, 101-105; no. 8., 239-243.

— "Merkwürdige Rede eines neuorthodoxen jüdischen Predigers über das Verhältnis between Judenthum und Christenthum," *Sinai* 6 (1861/62), no. 5, 112-115.

— "Über Familiensitze in den Synagogen," *Sinai* 6 (1861/62), no. 7, 205-207.

— "Dr. Raphael's Rede über das Verhältnis der Bibel zum Sklaveninstitut," *Sinai* 6 (1861/62), no. 1, 2-22.

— "Noch ein Wort über Dr. Raphael's Prosklaverei-Rede," *Sinai* 6 (1861/62), no. 2, 45-50.

— "Die Politik auf der Kanzel," *Sinai* 6 (1861/62), no. 6, 169-173.

— *Ner Tamid (Beständige Leuchte). Die Lehre des Judenthums, dargestellt für Schule und Haus* (Philadelphia: Stein und Jones, 1866).

— "Noch ein Wort über gemischte Ehen," *The Jewish Times* 1 (1869/70), no. 48, 10-13.

— "Dr. Geiger und die Philadelphier Rabbiner-Conferenz," *The Jewish Times* 2 (1870/71), no. 7, 107; no. 8, 123-124; no. 9, 139; no. 11, 171; no. 12, 187-188.

— "Das Prinzip des Mosaismus Teil 2," in *The Jewish Times* 4 (1872/73), no. 1, 17; no. 2, 37-38; no. 3, 57; no. 4, 77; no. 5, 97; no. 6, 117; no. 7, 138; no. 8, 157; no. 9, 177; no. 11, 217.

— "Predigt im Tempel Beth-El dahier, am Sabbath Chanukkah" (New York: M. Thalmessinger & Co, 1874).

— *Ausgewählte Predigten und Reden*, ed. Kaufmann Kohler (New York: E. Steiger, 1880).

— *Dr. David Einhorn's Book of Prayers for Jewish Congregations*, trans. Emil G. Hirsch (Chicago: s.n., 1896).

Einhorn, Ignaz, *Die Revolution und die Juden in Ungarn. Nebst einem Rückblick auf die Geschichte der Letztern* (Leipzig: Carl Geibel, 1851) (on the Reform Association, 107-113).

Ele Divre Ha-Berith [...] Beit Din Zedek de K"K (Hamburg-Altona, s.n., 1819).

Frankel, Zacharias, *Historisch-kritische Studien zu der Septuaginta. Nebst Beiträgen zu den Targumim. Erster Band. Erste Abtheilung: Vorstudien zu der Septuaginta* (Leipzig: Vogel, 1841).

— "Schreiben des Oberrabbiners Dr. Frankel an die Direction des Tempelvereins zu Hamburg," *Orient* 3 (1842), 53-56, 61-64, 71-72.

— "Erwiderung auf das von Herrn Dr. Salomon, Prediger am neuen israelitischen Tempel zu Hamburg, an mich gerichtete Sendschreiben," *Literaturblatt des Orients* 3 (1842), 353-68, 377-84.

— *Anzeige und Prospectus einer Zeitschrift für die religiösen Interessen des Judenthums* (Dresden: Simion, 1843).

— "Nachbemerkung des Herausgebers," *Zeitschrift für die religiösen Interessen des Judenthums* 1 (1844), 60-73.

— "Review of Ueber die Autonomie der Rabbinen und das Princip der jüdischen Ehe by Samuel Holdheim," *Zeitschrift für die religiösen Interessen des Judenthums* 1 (1844), 204-208, 244-248, 273-288, 321-328.

— "Über Reformen im Judenthume," *Zeitschrift für die religiösen Interessen des Judenthums* 1 (1844), 3-27.

— "Über manche durch den Fortschritt der Medicin im Judenthum bedingte Reformen," *Zeitschrift für die religiösen Interessen des Judenthums* 2 (1845), 265-269, 289-301, 342-349, 369-380.

— "Review of Teshuvot be-anshe aven by Pinchas Menachem Heilprin," *Zeitschrift für die religiösen Interessen des Judenthums* 2 (1845), 159-160; 241-248; 278-284; 363-368.

— "Die Symptome der Zeit," *Zeitschrift für die religiösen Interessen des Judenthums* 2 (1845), 3-21.

— *Der gerichtliche Beweis nach mosaisch-talmudischem Rechte. Ein Beitrag zur Kenntniss des mosaisch-talmudischen Criminal- und Civilrechts. Nebst einer Untersuchung über die Preussische Gesetzgebung hinsichtlich des Zeugnisses der Juden* (Berlin: Veit, 1846).

— *Die Eidesleistung der Juden in theologischer und historischer Beziehung*, 2nd edition (Dresden and Leipzig: Arnold, 1847).

— "Grundlinien des mosaisch-talmudischen Eherechts," *Jahresbericht des jüdisch-theologischen Seminar* (Breslau, January 27, 1860), i-xlviii.

— "Der Rückblick," *MGWJ* 10 (1861), 1-19.

— "Schlaglichter," in *MGWJ* 11 (1862), 3-20.

Fränkel, Jacob A., "Zur Geschichte der Homiletik," *Literaturblatt des Orients* 37 (1840), 590-592.

Gebetbuch für die öffentliche und häusliche Andacht, nach dem Gebrauch des Neuen Israelitischen Tempels in Hamburg (Hamburg: B. S. Berendsohn, 1841).

Gebetbuch der Genossenschaft für Reform im Judenthum. Erster Theil: Allwöchentliche Gebete und häusliche Andacht (Berlin: Im Selbst-Verlag der Genossenschaft, 1848).

Gebete und Gesänge zu dem von der Genossenschaft für Reform im Judenthum eingerichteten Gottesdienst in Berlin, für das Neujahrsfest des Weltjahres 5606 (als Manuscript gedruckt) (Berlin: Im Selbst-Verlage der Genossenschaft, 1845).

Geiger, Abraham, "Heuchelei, die erste Anforderung an den jungen Rabbiner unserer Zeit," *Wissenschaftliche Zeitschrift für jüdische Theologie* 1 (1835), 285-306.

— "Die Gründung einer jüdisch-theologischen Fakultät – ein dringendes Bedürfnis unserer Zeit," *Wissenschaftliche Zeitschrift für jüdische Theologie* 2 (1836), 1-21.

— "Die Stellung des weiblichen Geschlechtes in dem Judenthume unserer Zeit," *Wissenschaftliche Zeitschrift für jüdische Theologie* 3 (1837), 1-14.

— *Über die Errichtung einer jüdisch-theologischen Facultät* (Wiesbaden: L. Riedel, 1838).

— "Die zwei verschiedenen Betrachtungsweisen. Der Schriftsteller und der Rabbiner," *Wissenschaftliche Zeitschrift für jüdische Theologie* 4 (1839), 321-333.

— *Der Hamburger Tempelstreit, eine Zeitfrage* (Breslau: F. E. C. Leuckart, 1842); reprinted in idem, *Nachgelassene Schriften*, vol. 1 (Berlin: Gerschel, 1875), 113-196.

— "Brief an Leopold Zunz" (1845), in idem, *Nachgelassene Schriften*, ed. Ludwig Geiger, vol. 5 (Berlin: Gerschel, 1875).

— "Review of Holdheim's Ueber die Autonomie der Rabbinen," in *Zur Judenfrage in Deutschland. Vom Standpunkte des Rechts und der Gewissensfreiheit, im Vereine mit mehreren Gelehrten herausgegeben von Wilhelm Freund* (Berlin: Veit, 1843), 164-74.

— "Bruno Bauer und die Juden. Mit Bezug auf dessen Aufsatz: Die Judenfrage," *Wissenschaftliche Zeitschrift für jüdische Theologie* 5 (1844), issue 2, 199-234 and 325-371.

— *Gutachten über die Beschneidung* (Frankfurt am Main: Druck der J.J. Bach'schen Buch- und Steindruckerei, 1844).

— "Nachschrift," *Wissenschaftliche Zeitschrift für jüdische Theologie* 6 (1847), issue 2, 63-75.

— "Die religiösen Thaten der Gegenwart im Judenthume," *Wissenschaftliche Zeitschrift für jüdische Theologie* 6 (1847), 1-16.

— *Israelitisches Gebetbuch für den öffentlichen Gottesdienst im ganzen Jahre: mit Einschluß der Sabbathe und sämmtlicher Feier- und Festtage, geordnet und mit einer neuen deutschen Bearb[eitung] ver[sehen] von Abraham Geiger* (Breslau: Heinauer, 1854).

— "Review of Samuel Holdheim, Sein Leben und seine Werke, by Immanuel Ritter," *Jüdische Zeitschrift für Wissenschaft und Leben* 3 (1864/65), 216-218.

— "Die Versammlung zu Leipzig und die zu Philadelphia," *Jüdische Zeitschrift für Wissenschaft und Leben* 7 (1869), 1-27.

— *Israelitisches Gebetbuch für den öffentlichen Gottesdienst im ganzen Jahre: mit Einschluß der Sabbathe und sämmtlicher Feier- und Festtage, geordnet und mit einer neuen deutschen Bearb[eitung] ver[sehen] von Abraham Geiger* (Berlin: Gerschel, 1870).

— *Nachgelassene Schriften*, ed. Ludwig Geiger, 5 vols. (Hildesheim: Olms, 1999; reprint of the edition of Berlin 1875).

Glassberg, Abraham et al., eds., *Die Beschneidung in ihrer geschichtlichen, ethnographischen, religiösen und medicinischen Bedeutung: Zum ersten Male umfassend dargestellt* (Berlin: Boas, 1896).

Gottesdienst-Ordnung für die Synagogen des Königreichs Würtemberg. Unter höchster Genehmigung festgesetzt von der Königl. israelitischen Oberkirchen-Behörde (Stuttgart: Hallberger, 1838).

Graetz, Heinrich, *Geschichte der Juden von den ältesten Zeiten bis auf die Gegenwart*, 2nd edition, vol. 11 (Leipzig: Leiner, 1869; edition Berlin: Arani, 1998).

— *Volkstümliche Geschichte der Juden*, vol. 3 (Leipzig: O. Leiner, 1888).

— *Geschichte der Juden von den ältesten Zeiten bis auf die Gegenwart*, 2nd edition, vol. 2 (Leipzig: O. Leiner, 1900).

— *History of the Jews*, vol. 5: *From the Chmielnicki Persecution (1648 CE) to the Period of Emancipation in Central Europe (c. 1870 CE)* (Philadelphia: JPS, 1895).

— *Tagebuch und Briefe*, ed. Reuven Michael (Tübingen: J.C.B. Mohr, 1977).

Großherzoglich Mecklenburg-Schwerinischer Staats-Kalender, Schwerin (1841), 177; (1842), 177; (1843), 174; (1844), 173; (1845), 171; (1846), 170; (1847), 170; (1848), 170.

Grün[e]baum, Elias, "Gutachten des Bezirksrabbiners… zu Landau in der Pfalz in der Frankfurter Reform-Angelegenheit, Abgegeben an Sr. Hochwürden, den Herrn Rabbinen Salomon Trier in Frankfurt a.M.," *Israelit des neunzehnten Jahrhunderts* 5 (1855), no. 16, 121-125; no.17, 129-132.

Güdemann, Moritz, "Zacharias Frankel: Von ihm und über ihn," *MGWJ* 45 (1901), 243-253.

GutsMuths, Johann Christoph Friedrich, *Gymnastik für die Jugend: Enthaltend eine praktische Anweisung zu Leibesübungen. Ein Beytrag zur nöthigsten Verbesserung der körperlichen Erziehung* (Schnepfenthal: Buchhandlung der Erziehungs-Anstalt, 1793).

— *Spiele zur Uebung und Erholung des Körpers und Geistes, für die Jugend und alle Freunde unschuldiger Jugendfreunden* (Schnepfenthal: Buchhandlung der Erziehungs-Anstalt, 1796).

Heilprin, Pinchas Menachem, *Teshuvot be-anshe aven: Holdheim ve-reav be mikhtavim sheloshah asar* (Frankfurt am Main: s.n., 1845).

Heinemann, Jeremias, *Sammlung der die religiöse und bürgerliche Verfassung der Juden in den Königlichen Preussischen Staaten betreffenden Gesetze, Verordnungen, Gutachten, Berichte und Erkenntnisse: Mit einem Anhang, welcher Gesetze fremder Staaten enthält*, 2nd enlarged edition (Glogau: Heymann, 1831; reprint Hildesheim: Olms, 1976).

Herzfeld, Levi, *Handelsgeschichte der Juden des Alterthums. Aus den Quellen erforscht und zusammengestellt* (Braunschweig: Johann Heinrich Meyer, 1879; 2nd ed., 1894).

Hess, Mendel, "Der Frankfurter Reformverein," *Der Israelit des neunzehnten Jahrhunderts* 4 (1843), no. 46, 183-185; no. 47, 187-188; no. 48, 191-192.

— "Review of Ueber die Autonomie der Rabbinen," in *Israelit des Neunzehnten Jahrhunderts* 5 (1844), 1-4; 9-12; 17-21; 25-28.

Hirsch, Samson Raphael, *Die Reform im Judenthum und dessen Beruf in der gegenwärtigen Welt* (Leipzig: Hunger, 1844).

—— *Zweite Mittheilungen aus einem Briefwechsel über die neueste jüdische Literatur. Ein Fragment* (Altona: J. F. Hammerich, 1844).

Hirsch, Samuel, *Die Religionsphilosophie der Juden oder das Prinzip der jüdischen Religionsanschauung und sein Verhältnis zum Heidenthum, Christenthum und zur absoluten Philosophie* (Leipzig: Hunger, 1842; reprint Hildesheim: Olms, 1986).

—— *Das Judenthum, der christliche Staat und die moderne Kritik. Briefe zur Beleuchtung der Judenfrage von Bruno Bauer* (Leipzig: H. Hunger, 1843).

—— *Die Reform im Judenthum und dessen Beruf in der gegenwärtigen Welt* (Leipzig: H. Hunger, 1844).

—— "Review of Holdheim's Ueber die Autonomie der Rabbinen," *Literaturnblatt des Orients* 44 (1843), 696-699.

—— "Des Dr. Hirsch Votum über die Sabbathfrage," *Der Israelit des neunzehnten Jahrhunderts* 7 (1846), no. 34, 266-268.

—— *Die Sabbathfrage vor der dritten Rabbinerversammlung. Ein Votum* (Berlin: Verlag des Verfassers, 1846).

—— "Die Speisegesetze (Aus einem demnächst erscheinenden Handbuch für israelitische Religionslehrer)," *Der Israelit des neunzehnten Jahrhunderts* 7 (1846), no. 18, 137-140; no. 19, 145-148; no. 20, 154-159.

—— "Offener Brief von Dr. S. Hirsch," *Der Israelit des neunzehnten Jahrhunderts* 8 (1847), no. 30, 233-236.

—— *Die Humanität als Religion in Vorträgen gehalten in der Loge zu Luxemburg* (Trier: C. Troschel, 1854).

—— "Darf ein Reformrabbiner Ehen zwischen Juden und Nichtjuden einsegnen?," *The Jewish Times* 1 (1969/70), no. 27, 9-10; no. 28, 10-11; no. 30, 9-10; no. 31, 10; no. 32, 10; no. 33, 10; no. 34, 10; no. 35, 11; no. 36, 13.

—— "Der Nagel zum Sarge der winzigen jüdischen Race," *The Jewish Times* 1 (1869/70), no. 47, 10-11.

—— Rev. Dr. David Einhorn. *Gedächtniss-Rede, gehalten vor seinem Sarge den 6ten November 1879*, Philadelphia 1879.

Jahn, Friedrich Ludwig and Eiselen, Ernst, *Die Deutsche Turnkunst zur Einrichtung der Turnplätze* (Berlin: Selbstverlag, 1816).

"Jahresbericht des Culturvereins. Berlin 1842," *Orient* 18 (1842), 139-141.

Johlson, Josef, *Ueber Die Beschneidung in historischer und dogmatischer Hinsicht: Ein Wort zu seiner Zeit. Den Denkenden in Israel zur Prüfung vorgelegt von Bar Amithai* (Frankfurt am Main: J. E. Hermann'sche Buchhandlung, 1843).

Jost, Isaak Markus, *Geschichte der Israeliten seit der Zeit der Makkabäer bis auf unsere Tage* (Berlin: Schlesinger, 1820-1828).

Kalisch, Moritz, *Berlins jüdische Reformatoren nach der Thronbesteigung Friedrich Wilhelms III. und IV. Eine religionsgeschichtliche Betrachtung* (Berlin: C. Feister, 1845).

Kalischer, Zvi H., "Einiges zur Widerlegung der Ansichten des Herrn Dr. Samuel Holdheim in seinem Werkchen: 'Ueber Die Beschneidung' enthaltend," *Der Orient* 6 (1845), no. 1 (supplement), 1-4.

Kayserling, Meyer, *Gedenkblätter: Hervorragende jüdische Persönlichkeiten des 19. Jahrhunderts* [Leipzig: Grieben, 1892].

Kayserling, Moritz, *Die jüdische Litteratur von Moses Mendelssohn bis auf die Gegenwart, in Die jüdische Litteratur seit Abschluß des Kanons. Dritter Band: Die Poetische, Kabbalistische, Historische und neuzeitliche Litteratur*, ed. Jakob Winter und August Wünsche (Berlin: Poppelauer, 1897).

Klein, "Die rituelle Circumcision: eine sanitätspolizeiliche Frage," *Allgemeine Medicinische Central Zeitung* (11 June 1853), 365-366.

Kohler, Kaufmann, *Grab- und Gedenkrede für Rabbiner Dr. David Einhorn, gehalten im Tempel Beth-El, New York* (Milwaukee: J. S. Moses, 1879).

— "David Einhorn. The Uncompromising Champion of Reform Judaism. A Biographical Essay," in *David Einhorn Memorial Volume. Selected Sermons and Addresses*, ed. Kaufmann Kohler (New York: Bloch, 1911), 403-455.

— "Samuel Hirsch," in idem, *Hebrew Union College and Other Addresses* (Cincinnati: Ark Publications, 1916), 75-81.

Lavater, Johann Caspar, *Physiognomische Fragmente zur Beförderung der Menschenkenntnis und Menschenliebe*, 4 vols. (Leipzig/Winterthur: Weidmann und Reich, 1775-1778).

Levit, Eugen, *Die Circumcision der Israeliten. Beleuchtet vom ärztlichen und humanen Standpunkte von einem alten Arzt* (Wien: Druck und Commissions-Verlag von Carl Gerold's Sohn, 1874).

Liepmann, Marcus, *Kurze Uebersicht der Verhältnisse der Einwohner mosaischen Glaubens in den Großherzogl. Meckl. Schwerinschen Landen* (Güstrow: J. M. Oeberg, 1833).

Löwenstein, Ludwig, *Die Beschneidung im Lichte der heutigen medicinischen Wissenschaft, mit Berücksichtigung ihrer geschichtlichen und unter Würdigung ihrer religiösen Bedeutung* (Trier: Commissionsverlag von Heinrich Stephanus, 1897).

Maier, Joseph von, *Israelitisches Gebet- und Andachtsbuch, zum Gebrauche bei der häuslichen und öffentlichen Gottesverehrung* (Stuttgart: Zu Guttenberg, 1848).

Maybaum, Sigmund, "Aus dem Leben Leopold Zunz'," *Zwölfter Bericht der Lehranstalt für die Wissenschaft des Judentums* (Berlin: s.n., 1894), 1-63.

Mendelssohn, Moses, *Jerusalem oder Über religiöse Macht und Judentum* (Berlin: F. Maurer, 1783).

— *Jerusalem, Or on Religious Power and Judaism*, trans. Allan Arkush, with an introduction and commentary by Alexander Altmann (Hanover, NH: University of New England Press, 1983).

Ordnung der öffentlichen Andacht für die Sabbath- und Festtage des ganzen Jahres. Nach dem Gebrauch des Neuen-Tempel-Vereins in Hamburg, ed. Seckel Isaak Fränkel and M. J. Bresslau (Hamburg: Fränkel und Bresslau, 1819).

Philippson, Gustav, *Die Judenfrage von Bruno Bauer näher beleuchtet* (Dessau: Fritsche und Sohn, 1843).

Philippson, Ludwig, "Wohin?," *AZJ* 7 (1843), no. 34, 502-503.

Pinner, Mose, *Denkschrift für die Juden Preußens besonders für die Juden Berlins, Oder Gründliche Darstellung der den jüdischen Vorständen zustehenden Rechte in religiöser, politischer und gesetzlicher Hinsicht* (Berlin: Selbstverlag, 1856).

— *Geschichte der neuesten Reformen der jüdischen Gemeinde Berlin's und deren Bekämpfung. Ein Beitrag zur Cultusgeschichte der Juden* (Berlin: Selbstverlag, 1857).

— *Kol Kore. Aufruf an die orthodoxen Rabbiner Europa's und die Nothwendigkeit einer streng orthodoxen allgemeinen Rabbiner-Versammlung* (Berlin: Selbstverlag, 1858).

Protocolle der ersten Rabbiner-Versammlung abgehalten zu Braunschweig vom 12ten bis zum 19ten Juni 1844 (Brunswick: Vieweg, 1844).

Protokolle und Aktenstücke der zweiten Rabbinerversammlung abgehalten in Frankfurt am Main vom 15ten bis zum 28ten Juli 1845 (Frankfurt am Main: Ullmann, 1845).

Protokolle der dritten Versammlung deutscher Rabbiner, abgehalten zu Breslau vom 13. bis 24. Juli 1846 (Breslau: Leuckart, 1847).

Protokolle der Rabbiner-Konferenz abgehalten zu Philadelphia, vom 3. bis zum 6. November 1869 (New York: S. Hecht, 1870).

Rabbinische Gutachten über die Verträglichkeit der freien Forschung mit dem Rabbineramte, 2 vols. (Breslau: L. Freund, 1842/43).

Rabinowicz, Saul Pinchas, *R. Zecharjah Frankel* (Hebrew) (Warsaw: s.n., 1898-1901), 78-81, 307-314.

Raphall, Morris J., *The Bible View of Slavery* (New York: Rudd & Carleton, 1861).

Rapoport, Salomon J., "Gutachten des Oberrabbiners Dr. Z. Frankel, Directors des jüdisch-theologischen Seminars in Breslau," *Mittheilungen vom DIGB* 2 (1875), 26.

Ritter, Immanuel Heinrich, *Geschichte der jüdischen Reformation, vol. 3: Samuel Holdheim. Sein Leben und seine Werke, Ein Beitrag zu den neuesten Reformbestrebungen im Judenthum* (Berlin: W. J. Peiser, 1865).
— "Samuel Holdheim, The Jewish Reformer," in: *JQR* 1 (1889), 202-15.
— *Die jüdische Reformgemeinde zu Berlin und die Verwirklichung der jüdischen Reformideen innerhalb derselben* (Berlin: W. J. Peiser, 1902).
Sachs, Michael, *Festgebete der Israeliten* (Berlin: Veit & Co, 1855/56).
— "Gutachten über den Reformverein," *Zeitschrift für die religiösen Interessen des Judentums* 1 (1844), issue 2, 49-60.
— *Festpredigten und Sabbatpredigten zum ersten und zweiten Buch Mose* (Berlin: Louis Gerschel, 1866/67).
Salomon, Gotthold, *Bruno Bauer und seine gehaltlose Kritik über die Judenfrage* (Hamburg: Perthes, Besser & Mauke, 1843).
Salomon, Moritz Gustav, *Die Beschneidung. Historisch und medizinisch beleuchtet* (Braunschweig: Friedrich Vieweg und Sohn, 1844).
Schelling, Friedrich W. J., -, *Philosophie der Mythologie. Nachschrift der letzten Münchner Vorlesungen 1841*, ed. Andreas Roser and Holger Schulten (Stuttgart-Bad Cannstatt: Fromman-Holzboog, 1996).
— *Philosophie der Offenbarung (1841/42)* (Frankfurt am Main: Suhrkamp, 1977).
Steinschneider, Moritz, *Die Beschneidung der Araber und Muhammedaner, mit Rücksicht auf die neueste Beschneidungsliteratur. Sendschreiben an Herrn Gideon Brecher* (Wien: Gedruckt bei Franz Edlen von Schmid und J. J. Busch, 1845).
Stern, Sigismund, *Die Aufgabe des Judenthums und des Juden in der Gegenwart* (Berlin: W. Adolf & Co, 1853).
— *Die Religion des Judenthums* (Berlin: W. Adolf & Co, 1853).
— *Geschichte des Judenthums von Mendelssohn bis auf die Gegenwart* (Frankfurt am Main: Literarische Anstalt, 1857).
Synagogen-Ordnung für die Synagogen des Großherzogthums Mecklenburg-Schwerin unter allerhöchster Genehmigung festgesetzt von dem großherzoglichen israelitischen Oberrath in Schwerin (Schwerin: Kürschner, 1843).
Szold, Benjamin, *Der Enthüllte Einhorn* (Baltimore: W. Polmyer, 1860).
Tictin [sic!], Salomon Abraham, *Darstellung des Sachverhältnisses in seiner hiesigen Rabbinats-Angelegenheit* (Breslau: H. Richter, 1842).
Trier, Salomon Abraham, ed., *Rabbinische Gutachten über die Beschneidung, gesammelt und herausgegeben* (Frankfurt: Bach, 1844).
Wise, Isaac M., "German Culture," *American Israelite* 27 (1879), no. 24, 4.
Wolff, Abraham, *Agende for det mosaiske Troessamfunds Synagoge i København, til Brug ved Gudstjenesten og andre høitidelige Leiligheder* (Copenhagen: sn., 1833).

Zunz, Leopold, *Etwas über die rabbinische Literatur nebst Nachrichten über ein altes bis jetzt ungedrucktes hebräisches Werk* (Berlin: Maurersche Buchhandlung, 1818).

Zunz, Leopold, "Thefillin," *Jahrbuch für Israeliten* 2 (1843-44), 133-138; printed in idem, *Gesammelte Schriften*, vol. 2, 172-176.

— *Kurze Antworten auf Kultus-Fragen* (Berlin: J. Springer, 1844).

— "Beurtheilung von 'Die mosaische Religion. Catechismus für den israelitischen Religionsunterricht in Schule und Haus', von Julius Löwenheim, Lehrer an der Stadtschule in Lengsfeld, Eisenach, 1864," *Rheinische Blätter* 16 (1865), 73-77; printed in idem, *Gesammelte Schriften*, vol. 2, (Berlin: Gerschel, 1875-76), 236-240.

— *Gutachten über die Beschneidung* (Frankfurt am Main: J. F. Bach, 1844), printed in idem, *Gesammelte Schriften*, vol. 2 (Berlin: Gerschel, 1875-76), 191-203.

Zunz, Leopold, "4 Mai 1845 Letter to Geiger," in *Abraham Geiger, Nachgelassene Schriften*, vol. 5 (Berlin: Gerschel, 1875), 184-185.

— *Der Ritus des synagogalen Gottesdienstes, geschichtlich entwickelt* (Berlin: J. Springer, 1858).

— *Gesammelte Schriften*, 5 vols. (Berlin: Gerschel, 1875-76).

— *Die gottesdienstlichen Vorträge der Juden, historisch entwickelt. Ein Beitrag zur Alterthumskunde und biblischen Kritik, zur Literatur- und Religionsgeschichte*, 2nd ed. (Frankfurt am Main: Kauffmann, 1892).

Secondary Sources

Agnon, S. Y., "Sipurim shel ashkenaz ve-agapehah," in *In zwei Welten: Siegfried Moses zum fünfundsiebzigsten Geburtstag*, ed. Hans Tramer (Tel Aviv: Verlag Bitaon, 1962).

Alexander, Gabriel E., "Die jüdische Bevölkerung Berlins in den ersten Jahrzehnten des 20. Jahrhunderts: Demographische und wirtschaftliche Entwicklungen," in *Jüdische Geschichte in Berlin. Essays und Studien*, ed. Reinhard Rürup (Berlin: Edition Hentrich, 1995), 117-48.

Altmann, Alexander, "Zur Frühgeschichte der jüdischen Predigt in Deutschland. Leopold Zunz als Prediger," *LBIYB* 6 (1961), 3-58.

— *Moses Mendelssohn. A Biographical Study* (Alabama: University of Alabama Press, 1973).

— *The New Style of Preaching in Nineteenth-Century German Jewry*, in idem, *Essays in Jewish Intellectual History* (Hanover, NH: University Press of New England, 1981), 190-245.

Amir-Moezzi, Mohammad Ali, *Le guide divin dans le shî'isme original: aux sources de l'ésotéricisme en Islam* (Lagrasse : Verdier, 1992).

Baader, Benjamin, *Gender, Judaism, and Bourgeois Culture in Germany, 1800-1870* (Bloomington. IN: Indiana University Press, 2006).

Barkai, Abraham, *Branching Out: German-Jewish Immigration to the United States 1820-1914* (New York: Holmes & Meier, 1994).

Baron, Salo W., "Aspects of the Jewish Communal Crisis in 1984," *JSS* 14 (1952), 99-144.

Bechtholdt, Joachim, *Die jüdische Bibelkritik im 19. Jahrhundert* (Stuttgart: Kohlhammer, 1995).

Bernhardt, Hans-Michael, *Bewegung und Beharrung. Studien zur Emanzipationsgeschichte der Juden im Großherzogtum Mecklenburg-Schwerin 1813-1869* (Hannover: Hahn, 1998).

Biberfeld, Philipp, "Dina DeMalkhuta Dina," in *Schriftenreihe des Bundes Jüdischer Akademiker*, vol. 2 (Berlin: Menorah, [1925]), 31-37.

Biemann, Erwin, Schmierer, Wolfgang, and Taddey, Gerhard, *Israelitische Oberkirchenbehörde im Königreich Württemberg: Inventar* (Stuttgart: Kohlhammer, 1996).

Biographisches Handbuch der Rabbiner, ed. Michael Brocke and Julius Carlebach, vol. 1: *Die Rabbiner der Emanzipationszeit in den deutschen, böhmischen und großpolnischen Ländern, 1781-1871*, ed. Carsten Wilke (München: K.G. Saur, 2004).

Bisschops, Ralph. "Metapher, Wert und Rang," *Revue Belge de Philologie et d'Histoire* LXVIII (1990), 636-645.

— "Metaphor as the Internalisation of a Ritual: With a Case Study on Samuel Holdheim (1806-1860)," in *Metaphor, Canon and Community: Jewish, Christian and Islamic Approaches*, ed. Ralph Bisschops and James Francis (New York and Bern: Peter Lang, 1999), 284-307.

Brämer, Andreas, *Rabbiner und Vorstand: Zur Geschichte der jüdischen Gemeinde in Deutschland und Österreich 1808-1871* (Wien: Böhlau, 1999).

— *Rabbiner Zacharias Frankel. Wissenschaft des Judentums und konservative Reform im 19. Jahrhundert* (Hildesheim: Olms, 2000).

— *Judentum und religiöse Reform: Der Hamburger Israelitische Tempel 1817-1938* (Hamburg: Dölling & Galitz, 2000).

Breuer, Mordechai, *Jüdische Orthodoxie im Deutschen Reich 1871-1918* (Frankfurt: Jüdischer Verlag bei Athenäum, 1986).

Brumlik, Micha, *Deutscher Geist und Judenhass. Das Verhältnis des philosophischen Idealismus zum Judentum* (Munich: Luchterhand, 2000).

Carlebach, Julius, "Deutsche Juden und der Säkularisierungsprozeß in der Erziehung. Kritische Bemerkungen zu einem Problembereich der jüdischen Emanzipation," in Liebeschütz and Paucker, eds., *Das Judentum in der Deutschen Umwelt 1800-1850*, 55-93.

— "The Foundations of German Jewish Orthodoxy - An Interpretation," *LBIYB* 33 (1988), 67-91.

Carlebach, Julius, ed., *Das aschkenasische Rabbinat. Studien über Glaube und Schicksal* (Berlin: Metropol, 1995).

Carter, Stephen, *The Culture of Disbelief: How American Law and Politics Trivialize Religious Devotion* (New York: Basic Books, 1993).

Chittick, William C., *A Shi'ite Anthology* (London: Muhammadi Trust, 1980).

Cohen, Naomi W., *Encounter with Emancipation. The German Jews in the United States 1830-1914* (Philadelphia: JPS, 1984).

Cohen, Philip, *Biblical Theology as Response and Reform*, Phil. Diss. (UMI), Ann Arbor, Michigan 1993.

Davidsohn, Magnus, "Die Umgestaltung des Gottesdienstes in der Alten Synagoge," *Israelitisches Familienblatt* 38 (1926), 11-13.

Diekmann, Irene, ed., *Wegweiser durch das jüdische Mecklenburg-Vorpommern* (Potsdam: Verlag für Berlin-Brandenburg, 1998).

Diner, Hasia, *A Time for Gathering: The Second Migration, 1820-1880* (The Jewish People in America, vol. 2), (Baltimore: Johns Hopkins University Press, 1992).

Donath, Leopold, *Geschichte der Juden in Mecklenburg von den ältesten Zeiten (1266) bis auf die Gegenwart (1874), Auch ein Beitrag zur Kulturgeschichte Mecklenburgs* (Leipzig: Leiner, 1874, reprint Walluf: Sändig, 1974).

Dorff, Elliot N. and Rosett, Arthur, *A Living Tree: The Roots and Growth of Jewish Law* (Albany, N.Y.: SUNY Press, 1988).

Dubnow, Simon, *Weltgeschichte des jüdischen Volkes*, vol. 9 (Berlin: Jüdischer Verlag, 1929).

Efron, John M., *Medicine and the German Jews: A History* (New Haven: Yale University Press, 2001).

Ehrenreich, E., "Der erste Synagogenchor in Berlin," *Gemeindeblatt der Jüdischen Gemeinde zu Berlin* 19 (1929), 66-68, 107-111.

Elbogen, Ismar, "Leopold Zunz zum Gedächtnis," *Fünfzigster Bericht der Lehranstalt für die Wissenschaft des Judentums* (Berlin: s.n., 1936), 14-32.

— "Zum Andenken an Leopold Zunz 2," *JJGL* 30 (1937), 140-172.

Ellenson, David, *Tradition in Transition: Orthodoxy, Halakhah and the Boundaries of Modern Jewish Identity* (New York: University Press of America 1989).

— "Traditional Reactions to Modern Jewish Reform: The Paradigm of German Orthodoxy," in Frank and Leamon, eds., *History of German Philosophy*, 732-758.

— "Samuel Holdheim on the Legal Character of Jewish Marriage: A Contemporary Comment on His Position," in *Marriage and its Obstacles in Jewish Law: Essays and Responses*, ed. Walter Jacob and Moshe Zemer (Tel Aviv: Freehof Institute of Progressive Halakhah, 1999), 1-26.

— *After Emancipation: Jewish Religious Responses to Modernity* (Cincinnati: HUC Press, 2004).

Ellenson, David and Jacobs, Richard, "Scholarship and Faith, David Hoffmann and his Relationship to Wissenschaft des Judentums," *Modern Judaism* 8 (1988), 27-40.

Erder, Yoram, "Early Karaite Conceptions about Commandments given before the Torah," *Proceedings of the American Academy for Jewish Research* 60 (1994), 101-140.

Fackenheim, Emil L., "Samuel Hirsch and Hegel," in idem, *Jewish Philosophers and Jewish Philosophy*, ed. Michael L. Morgan (Bloomington, IN: Indiana University Press, 1996), 21-40.

Fein, Isaac M., *The Making of an American Jewish Community: The History of Baltimore Jewry from 1773 to 1920* (Philadelphia: JPS, 1985).

Frank, Daniel and Leaman, Oliver, eds., *History of Jewish Philosophy* (London: Routledge, 1997).

Frevert, Ute, *Krankheit als politisches Problem (1770-1880)* (Göttingen: Vandenhoeck & Ruprecht, 1984).

Friedland, Eric L., "Olath Tamid by David Einhorn," *HUCA* 45 (1974), 307-332.

Frishman, Judith, "True Mosaic Religion. Samuel Hirsch, Samuel Holdheim and the Reform of Judaism," in *Religious Identity and the Problem of Historical Foundation: The Foundational Character of Authoritative Sources in the History of Christianity and Judaism*, ed. Judith Frishman (Leiden: Brill Publishers, 2004), 195-222.

Funkenstein, Amos, *Perceptions of Jewish History* (Berkeley, CA: University of California Press, 1993).

Galliner, Arthur, *Sigismund Stern, der Reformator und der Pädagoge* (Frankfurt am Main: Englert und Schlosser, 1930).

Geiger, Ludwig, *Geschichte der Juden in Berlin*, 2 vols. (Berlin: Guttentag, 1871-1890; reprint Berlin: arani, 1988).

— Michael Sachs und Moritz Veit. *Briefwechsel* (Frankfurt am Main: Kauffmann, 1897).

— "Geist der Rabbiner, Ein geplantes Werk von Leopold Zunz," *AZJ* 35 (1916), 413-414.

— "Zunz' Synagogenordnung für Prag (1836)," *AZJ* 41 (1916), 485-487.

— "Zunz' Gutachten über die Beschneidung (1844)," *AZJ* 80 (1916), 449-452.

Gilman, Sander L., *The Jew's Body* (New York: Routledge, 1991).

— "The Indelibility of Circumcision," *Koroth* 9 (1991), 806-817.

— *The Case of Sigmund Freud: Medicine and Identity at the Fin de Siécle* (Baltimore: The Johns Hopkins University Press, 1993).

— *Freud, Race and Gender* (Princeton, NJ: Princeton University Press, 1993).

Ginzberg, Louis, "Israel Salanter", in *Understanding Rabbinic Judaism. From Talmudic to Modern Times*, ed. Jacob Neusner (New York: Ktav Publishing House, 1974).

Glatzer, Nahum N., "Some of Zunz's Letters to the Ehrenbergs," *Proceedings of the American Academy of Jewish Research* 25 (1956), 63-90.

Glatz, Nahum N., ed., *Leopold Zunz. Jude, Deutscher, Europäer. Ein jüdisches Gelehrtenschicksal des 19. Jahrhunderts in Briefen an Freunde* (Tübingen: J.C.B. Mohr, 1964).

Goldman, Karla, *Beyond the Synagogue Gallery. Finding a Place for Women in American Judaism* (Cambridge, MA: Harvard University Press, 2000).

Gotzmann, Andreas, *Jüdisches Recht im kulturellen Prozeß. Die Wahrnehmung der Halacha im Deutschland des 19. Jahrhunderts* (Tübingen: J.C.B. Mohr, 1997).

— "Koscher und Trefe; die Veränderung der religiösen Praxis im Deutschland des 19. Jahrhunderts," *LBI Informationen* 7 (1997), 85-109.

— "The Dissociation of Law and Religion in Nineteenth-Century German-Jewish Education," *LBIYB* 43 (1998), 103-126.

— "Geschichte als Abkehr von der Vergangenheit. Zur Problematik historischer Identität im deutschen Judentum der Emanzipationszeit," *Aschkenas*, 9 (1999), 327-352.

— "Symbolische Rettungen. Jüdische Theologie und Staat in der Emanzipationszeit," in D. Langewiesche/H. G. Haupt (eds.), *Nation und Religion in der deutschen Geschichte*, ed. Dieter Langewiesche and Heinz-Gerhart Haupt (Frankfurt am Main: Campus, 2001), 516-547.

— "Zwischen Nation und Religion: Die deutschen Juden auf der Suche nach einer bürgerlichen Konfessionalität," in *Juden, Bürger, Deutsche. Zur Geschichte von Vielfalt und Differenz 1800-1933*, ed. Andreas Gotzmann, Rainer Liedice and Till van Rhaden (Tübingen: J.C.B. Mohr, 2001), 241-261.

— *Eigenheit und Einheit. Modernisierungsdiskurse des deutschen Judentums der Emanzipationszeit* (Leiden: Brill Publishers, 2002).

— "Der Geiger-Tiktin-Streit — Trennungskrise und Publizität," in *In Breslau zu Hause? Juden in einer mitteleuropäischen Metropole der Neuzeit*, ed. Manfred Hettling, Andreas Reinke, and Norbert Conrads (Hamburg: Dölling & Galitz, 2003), 81-98.

— "Jüdische Theologie im Taumel der Geschichte. Religion und historisches Denken in der ersten Hälfte des 19. Jahrhunderts," in *Judentum und Historismus. Zur Entstehung der jüdischen Geschichtswissenschaft in Europa*, ed. Ulrich Wyrwa (Frankfurt am Main: Campus, 2003), 173-202.

Graff, Gil, *Separation of Church and State. Dina de-Malkhuta Dina in Jewish Law, 1750-1848* (Alabama: The University of Alabama Press, 1985).

Graupe, Heinz Moshe, *Die Entstehung des modernen Judentums. Geistesgeschichte der deutschen Juden 1650-1942*, 2nd edition (Hamburg: Leibniz Verlag, 1977).

Green, Warren P., "The Karaite Community in Interwar Poland," *Nationalities Papers* 14 (1986), 101-109.

Greenberg, Gershon, "Samuel Hirsch's American Judaism," *American Jewish Historical Quarterly* 64 (1973), 362-382.

— "The Significance of America in David Einhorn's Conception of History," *American Jewish Historical Quarterly* 67 (1973), 160-184.

— "The Messianic Foundations of American Jewish Thought: David Einhorn and Samuel Hirsch," *Proceedings of the Sixth World Congress of Jewish Studies*, vol. 2 (Jerusalem: s.n., 1975), 215-226.

— "The Historical Origins of God and Man. Samuel Hirsch's Luxemburg Writings," *LBIYB* 20 (1975), 129-148.

— "Religionswissenschaft and Early Reform Jewish Thought: Samuel Hirsch and David Einhorn," in *Modern Judaism and Historical Consciousness. Identities – Encounters – Perspectives*, ed. Andreas Gotzmann and Christian Wiese (Leiden: Brill Publishers, 2007), 106-139.

Harris, Jay, *How do we know this?: Midrash and the Fragmentation of Modern Judaism* (Albany, N.Y.: SUNY Press, 1995).

Hayoun, Maurice H., "Samuel Holdheim (1806-1860), un rabbin adversaire du Talmud," *Revue des Études Juives* 105 (1992), 283-288.

Heinemann, Isaak, *Ta'ame ha-Mitsvot be-Sifrut Jisrael*, vol. 2 (Jerusalem: s.n., 1956).

Hentges, Gudrun, "Das Janusgesicht der Aufklärung: Antijudaismus und Antisemitismus in der Philosophie von Kant, Fichte und Hegel," in *Antisemitismus — Geschichte und Gegenwart*, ed. Samuel Salzborn (Giessen: Netzwerk für Politische Bildung, Kultur und Kommunikation, 2004), 11-32.

Heschel, Susannah, *Abraham Geiger and the Jewish Jesus* (Chicago: Chicago University Press, 1998).

— "Jewish Studies as Counterhistory," in *Insider/Outsider: American Jews and Multiculturalism*, ed. David Biale, Michael Galchinsky, and Susannah Heschel (Berkeley: CA: University of California Press, 1998), 101-115.

Hess, Jonathan, *Germans, Jews and the Claims of Modernity* (New Haven, Yale University Press, 2002).

Heymann, Aron Hirsch, *Lebenserinnerungen*, ed. Heinrich Loewe (Berlin: Poppelauer, 1909).

Hirsch, Heinz, *Spuren jüdischen Lebens in Mecklenburg*, 2nd ed. (Schwerin: Friedrich Ebert Stiftung, 1997).

— "Aspekte jüdischen Lebens in Mecklenburg im 19. und 20. Jahrhundert," in *Antijudaismus Antisemitismus Fremdenfeindlichkeit. Aspekte der Geschichte der Juden in Deutschland und Mecklenburg*, publ. by the Verein für Jüdische Geschichte und Kultur in Mecklenburg und Vorpommern (Schwerin: s.n., 1998), 113-135.

Hirshler, Eric E., ed., *Jews from Germany in the United States* (New York: Farrar, Straus and Cudahy, 1955).

Homa, Bernard, *Metzitzah* (London: [s.n.] 1960).

Homann, Ursula, "Juden in Mecklenburg-Vorpommern, Geschichte und Gegenwart," *Tribüne* 151 (1999), 186-196.

Horowitz, Elliot, "Ve-nahafokh hu': Yehudim mul sonehem be-hagigot ha-purim," *Tsiyon* 59 (1994), 129-168.

Horwitz, Rivka, "Zacharias Frankel's 1842 Idea of Jewish Independence in the Land of Israel" (hebr.), *Kivvunim* 6 (1980), 5-24.

— *Hashpa'at ha-Romantiqa 'al Chochmat Jisrael* (Jerusalem: Merkaz Zalman Shazar, 1984).

Itzhaki, Masha, *Juda Halévi. D'Espagne à Jérusalem 1075-1141* (Paris: Michel, 1997).

Jersch-Wenzel, Stefi and Rürup, Reinhard, eds., *Quellen zur Geschichte der Juden in den Archiven der neuen Bundesländer*, vol. 4: *Staatliche Archive der Länder Mecklenburg-Vorpommern, Sachsen und Thüringen* (Munich: K. G. Saur, 1999).

Jick, Leon, *The Americanization of the Synagogue, 1820-1870* (Hanover, NH: University of New England Press, 1976).

Judd, Robin E., *German Jewish Rituals, Bodies and Citizenship*, Ph.D. thesis University of Michigan 2000.

— "Circumcision and the Modern German-Jewish Experience" in *My Covenant in Your Flesh: Circumcision, Gender, and Culture across Jewish History*, ed. Elizabeth Mark (Hanover, NH: University Press of New England, 2003), 142-155.

— *Cutting Identities: Jewish Rituals and German Politics, 1843-1933* (Ithaca, NY: Cornell University Press, forthcoming 2007).

Kaplan, Dana E., ed., *Contemporary Debates in American Reform Judaism: Conflicting Visions* (New York: Routledge, 2001).

— *American Reform Judaism: An Introduction* (New Brunswick, NJ: Rutgers University Press, 2003).

— Kaplan, Dana, ed., *Platforms and Prayer Books: Theological and Liturgical Perspectives on Reform Judaism* (Lanham, MD: Rowman & Littlefield, 2002).

Kaplan, Marion, *The Making of the Jewish Middle Class* (New York: Oxford University Press, 1991).

Katz, Jacob, *Exclusiveness and Tolerance: Studies in Jewish-Gentile Relations in Medieval and Modern Times* (London: Oxford University Press, 1961).

— "Samuel Hirsch — Rabbi, Philosopher and Freemason," *Revue des Études Juives* 125 (1965), 113-126.

— *Out of the Ghetto: The Social Background of Jewish Emancipation, 1770-1870* (New York: Schocken Books, 1978).

— "A State within a State, The History of an Anti-Semitic Slogan," in idem, *Zur Assimilation und Emanzipation der Juden. Ausgewählte Schriften* (Darmstadt: Wissenschaftliche Buchgesellschaft, 1982), 124-54.

— "Die Halacha unter dem Druck der modernen Verhältnisse," in *Judentum im deutschen Sprachraum*, ed. Karl E. Grözinger (Frankfurt am Main: Suhrkamp, 1991), 309-324.

— *Ha-Halakha be-Mezar. Makhsholim al Derekh Ha-Orthodoxia Be-Hitavuta* (Jerusalem: Magnes Press, 1992).

— "The Controversy over brit milah during the first half of the Nineteenth Century" (Hebrew), in *Jewish Law in Conflict* (Hebrew), ed. Jacob Katz (Jerusalem: Magnes Press, 1992), 123-149.

— *Tradition and Crisis: Jewish Society at the End of the Middle Ages* (New York: New York University Press, 1993).

— "The Orthodox Defense of the Second Day of the Festivals," in idem, *Divine Law in Human Hands: Case Studies in Halakhic Flexibility* (Jerusalem: Magnes, 1998), 255-319.

Katz, Jacob, ed., *Toward Modernity: The European Jewish Model* (New Brunswick, NJ: Transaction Books, 1987).

Kleinberger, Aron, "Peraqim be-Toldot ha-Chevrah ha-yehudit bi-Yme ha-Beynayim u-va-'Et ha-chadashah," in *Tesisah le'umit be-Jahadut Germanyah ba-Machatsit ha-rishonah shel ha Me'ah ha-19*, ed. Emanuel Etkes and Yosef Salmon (Jerusalem: Magnes, 1980), 225-247.

Kober, Adolf, "Jewish Preaching and Preachers. A Contribution to the History of the Jewish Sermon in Germany and America," *Historia Judaica* 7 (1945), 103-134.

Koltun-Fromm, *Abraham Geiger's Liberal Judaism: Personal Meaning and Religious Authority* (Bloomington, IN: Indiana University Press, 2006).

Korn, Bertram W., *American Jewry and the Civil War* (Philadelphia: JPS, 1957).

Kraut, Benny, *From Reform Judaism to Ethical Culture. The Religious Evolution of Felix Adler* (Cincinnati: Hebrew Union College Press, 1979).

Landman, Leo, *Jewish Law in the Diaspora: Confrontation and Accomodation. A Study of the Development, Composition and Function of the Concept of Dina D'Malkhuta Dina—The Law of the Kingdom—the State—is the Law* (Philadelphia: Dropsie College for Hebrew and Cognate Learning, 1968).

Lieber, David L., ed., *Etz Hayim Torah and Commentary* (New York: JPS, 2001).

Liebeschütz, Hans, *Das Judentum im deutschen Geschichtsbild von Hegel bis Max Weber* (Tübingen: J.C.B. Mohr, 1967).

Liebeschütz, Hans and Paucker, Arnold, eds., *Das Judentum in der deutschen Umwelt 1800-1850. Studien zur Frühgeschichte der Emanzipation* (Tübingen: J.C.B. Mohr, 1977).

Liberles, Robert, *Religious Conflict in Social Context: The Resurgence of Orthodox Judaism in Frankfurt am Main, 1838-1877* (Westport, CT: Greenwood Press, 1985).

Lorenz, Ina, "Zehn Jahre Kampf um das Hamburger System, 1864-1873," in *Die Hamburger Juden in der Emanzipationsphase, 1780-1870*, ed. Peter Freimark and Arno Herzig (Hamburg: Christians-Verlag, 1989), 41-82.

Lowenstein, Steven M., "The 1840s and the Creation of the German-Jewish Religious Reform Movement," in *Revolution and Evolution, 1848 in German-Jewish History*, ed. Werner E. Mosse, Arnold Paucker, and Reinhard Rürup (Tübingen: J.C.B. Mohr, 1981), 255-297.

— *The Berlin Jewish Community: Enlightenment, Family, and Crisis (1770-1830)* (New York: Oxford University Press, 1994).

Lucas, Franz D. and Frank, Heike, *Michael Sachs — Der konservative Mittelweg, Leben und Wirken des Berliner Rabbiners zur Zeit der Emanzipation* (Tübingen: J.C.B. Mohr, 1992).

Mahler, Raphael, *Divre yeme yisrael: Dorot aharonim*, vol. 2 (Merhavjah: Sifriyat Po'alim, 1980).

Marcus, Jacob Rader, *Israel Jacobson—The Founder of the Reform Movement in Judaism* (Cincinnati: Hebrew Union College Press, 1972).

Marx, Karl, *On the Jewish Question*, trans. Helen Lederer (Cincinnati: HUC Press, 1958).

Maybaum, Sigmund, *Jüdische Homiletik nebst einer Auswahl von Texten und Themen* (Berlin: Dümmler, 1890).

Meyer, Michael A., *The Origins of the Modern Jew* (Detroit: Wayne State University Press, 1967).

— "Abraham Geiger's Historical Judaism," in *New Perspectives on Abraham Geiger. An HUC-JIR Symposium*, ed. Jacob J. Petuchowski (New York: Ktav Publishing House, 1975), 3-16.

— "Universalism and Jewish Unity in the Thought of Abraham Geiger," in *The Role of Religion in Modern Jewish History: Proceedings of Regional Conferences of the Association for Jewish Studies. Held at the University of Pennsylvania & the University of Toronto 1974*, ed. Jacob Katz (Cambridge, MA: The Association, 1975), 91-104.

— "The Religious Reform Controversy in the Berlin Jewish Community, 1814-1823," *LBIYB* 24 (1979), 139-155.

— "Alienated Intellectuals in the Camp of Religious Reform: The Frankfurt Reformfreunde, 1842-1845," *Association of Jewish Studies Review* 6 (1981), 61-86.

— *German Political Pressure and Jewish Religious Response in the 19th Century* (LBI Memorial Lectures 25) (New York: Leo Baeck Institute, 1981).

— "Ob Schrift? Ob Geist? — Die Offenbarungsfrage im deutschen Judentum des neunzehnten Jahrhunderts," in *Offenbarung im jüdischen und christlichen Glaubensverständnis*, ed. Jakob J. Petuchowski and Walter Strolz (Freiburg: Herder, 1981), 162-179.

— "Christian Influence on Early German Reform Judaism," *Judaica* 38 (1982), 164-177.
— "Methodological Prolegomena to a History of the Reform Movement in Modern Jewry," *HUCA* 43 (1982), 309-316.
— "America: The Reform Movement's Land of Promise," in *The American Jewish Experience*, ed. Jonathan Sarna (New York: Holmes & Meier, 1986), 60-81.
— "Modernity as a Crisis for Jews," *Modern Judaism* 9 (1989), 151-164.
— "Recent Historiography on the Jewish Religion," in *LBIYB* 35 (1990), 3-16.
— *Response to Modernity: A History of the Reform Movement in Judaism* (New York: Oxford University Press, 1988).
— "Recent Historiography on the Jewish Religion," *LBIYB* 35 (1990), 3-16.
— "'Ganz nach dem alten Herkommen'? The Spiritual Life of Berlin Jewry Following the Edict of 1823," in *Bild und Selbstbild der Juden Berlins zwischen Aufklärung und Romantik*, ed. Marianne Awerbuch (Berlin: Colloquium-Verlag, 1992), 229-243.
— "'How Awesome is this Place!', The Reconceptualization of the Synagogue in Nineteenth-Century Germany," *LBIYB* 41 (1996), 51-63.
— "German-Jewish Identity in Nineteenth Century America," in idem, *Judaism within Modernity*, 323-344.
— "Should and Can an 'Antiquated' Religion Become Modern? The Jewish Reform Movement in Germany as Seen by Jews and Christians," in idem, *Judaism within Modernity*, 209-222.
— Judaism within Modernity. Essays on Jewish History and Religion (Detroit: Wayne State University Press, 2001).
— "'Most of My Brethren Find Me Unacceptable': The Controversial Career of Rabbi Samuel Holdheim," in: *JSS* 9 (2003), no. 3, 1-19.
Meyer, Michael A. and Brenner, Michael, eds., *German Jewish History in Modern Times*, vol 2: *Emancipation and Acculturation, 1780-1871* (New York: Columbia University Press, 1997).
Miller, Philip E., "Evidence of a Previously Undocumented Karaite Presence in Galicia," *Studies in Bibliography and Booklore* 17 (1989), 36-42.
— *Karaite Separatism in Nineteenth-Century Russia: Joseph Solomon Lutski's Epistle of Israel's Deliverance* (Cincinnati: Hebrew Union College Press, 1993).

— "A Speculation on External Factors in the Formation of the Crimean Karaite (National) Identity," in *Judaism and Islam: Boundaries, Communication and Interaction. Essays in Honor of William M. Brinner*, ed. Benjamin H. Hary, John L. Hayes, and Fred Astern (Leiden: Brill Publishers, 2000), 335-342.

Monz, Heinz, "Samuel Hirsch (1815-1889). Ein jüdischer Reformator aus dem Hunsrück," *Jahrbuch für westdeutsche Landesgeschichte* 17 (1991), 159-180.

Morgenstern, Matthias, *Von Frankfurt nach Jerusalem. Isaac Breuer und die Bedeutung des Austrittsstreits für die deutsch-jüdische Orthodoxie* (Tübingen: J.C.B. Mohr, 1995).

Mosse, George L., *Toward the Final Solution: A History of European Racism* (London: Fertig, 1978).

Myers, David N., "The Ideology of Wissenschaft des Judentums," in Frank and Leaman, eds., *History of Jewish Philosophy*, 706-720.

— *Resisting History. Historicism and its Discontent in German-Jewish Thought* (Princeton, NJ: Princeton University Press, 2003).

Neusner, Jacob, *Rabbinic Judaism, Structure and System* (Minneapolis: Fortress Press, 1995).

Pasto, James, "Islam's 'Strange Secret Sharer': Orientalism, Judaism and the Jewish Question," *Comparative Studies in Society and History* 30 (1998) 437-474.

Pelli, Moshe, "Ha-reforma ha-datit shel Ha-rav 'haredi' Shaul Berlin," *HUCA* 42 (1971), 1-23 (Hebrew section).

Petuchowski, Jakob J., *Prayerbook Reform in Europe: The Liturgy of European Liberal and Reform Judaism* (New York: World Union for Progressive Judaism, 1968).

— "Abraham Geiger and Samuel Holdheim: Their Differences in Germany and Repercussions in America," *LBIYB* 22 (1977), 139-59.

Philippson, Martin, *Neueste Geschichte des jüdischen Volkes*, 2 vols. (Leipzig: Fock, 1907 and 1910).

Philipson, David, "The Reform Movement in Judaism," *JQR* 15 (1905), 508-521; 16 (1904), 485-503.

— "Samuel Holdheim, Jewish Reformer," *Central Conference of American Rabbis Year Book* 16 (1906), 305-329.

— *The Reform Movement in Judaism*, revised ed. (New York: Ktav Publishing House, 1967).

— "Some Unpublished Letters of Theological Importance," *HUCA* 2 (1925), 418-33; reprint 1968, 427-30.

Plaut, W. Gunther, *The Rise of Reform Judaism* (New York: World Union of Progressive Judaism, 1963).

Proudfoot, Wayne, *Religious Experience* (Berkeley, CA: University of California Press, 1985).

Rabbi, Ben, *Die Lehre von der Beschneidung der Israeliten, in ihrer mosaischen Reinheit dargestellt und entwickelt* (Stuttgart: Hallberger'sche Verlagshandlung, 1844).

Rahden, Till van, "Weder Milieu noch Konfession. Die situative Ethnizität der deutschen Juden im Kaiserreich in vergleichender Perspektive," in *Religion im Kaiserreich. Milieus — Mentalitäten — Krisen*, ed. Olaf Blaschke and Frank-Michael Kuhlemann (Gütersloh: Gütersloher Verlagshaus, 1996), 409-34.

Rahe, Thomas, "Leopold Zunz und die Wissenschaft des Judentums. Zum Hundersten Todestag von Leopold Zunz," *Judaica* 42 (1986), 188-199.

— "Religionsreform und jüdisches Selbstbewußtsein im deutschen Judentum des 19. Jahrhunderts," *Menora* 1 (1990), 89-121.

Romney Wegner, Judith, *Chattel or Person? The Status of Women in the Mishnah* (New York: Oxford University Press, 1988).

Rosenbloom, Noah H., *Tradition in an Age of Reform. The Religious Philosophy of Samson Raphael Hirsch* (Philadelphia: JPS, 1976).

Rosenfeld, Mosche N., "Talmudschule und jüdische Erziehung in Fürth," in *Kleeblatt und Davidstern. Aus 400 Jahren jüdischer Vergangenheit in Fürth*, ed. Werner J. Heymann (Emskirchen: Mümmler, 1990), 88-91.

Rotenstreich, Nathan, "For and against Emancipation: The Bruno Bauer Controversy," *LBIYB* 4 (1959), 3-36.

— *Tradition and Reality. The Impact of History on Modern Jewish Thought* (New York: Random House, 1972).

— *Jews and German Philosophy. The Polemics of Emancipation* (New York: Schocken Books, 1984).

Rudavsky, David, "The Historical School of Zacharias Frankel," *JSS* 5 (1963), 224-244.

Ryback, Martin B., "The East-West Conflict in American Reform Judaism," *American Jewish Archives* 4 (1952), 3-25.

Said, Edward, *Orientalism. Western Conceptions of the Orient* (London: Routledge & Kegan, 1978).

Salzberger, Georg, "Samuel Holdheim. Ein Vorkämpfer der Reform im Judentum," *Emuna* 7 (1972), 254-259.

Sarna, Jonathan, *JPS: The Americanization of Jewish Culture* (Philadelphia: JPS, 1989).

Schad, Margit, *Judentum als Lebensanschauung und Literatur. Michael Sachs (1808-1864) — Rabbiner, Prediger und Übersetzer* (Hildesheim: Georg Olms Verlag, 2006).

Schoeps, Hans-Joachim, "Friedrich Julius Stahl und das Judentum," in *Vergangene Tage: Jüdische Kultur in München*, ed. Hans Lamm (Munich: Langen Müller, 1982).

Scholem, Gershom, *Über einige Grundbegriffe des Judentums* (Frankfurt am Main: Suhrkamp, 1970).

Schorsch, Ismar "Zacharias Frankel and the European Origins of Conservative Judaism," *Judaism* 30 (1981), 344-54.

Schorsch, Ismar, "Moritz Steinschneider on Liturgical Reform," *HUCA* 53 (1982), 241-264.

— "Breakthrough into the Past: The Verein für Cultur und Wissenschaft des Judentums," *LBIYB* 33 (1988), 3-28.

— "The Ethos of Modern Jewish Scholarship," *LBIYB* 35 (1990), 55-71.

— "Scholarship in the Service of Reform," *LBIYB* 35 (1990), 73-101.

— *From Text to Context: The Turn to History in Modern Judaism* (Hanover, NH: Brandeis University Press, 1994).

— "Emancipation and the Crisis of Religious Authority: The Emergence of Modern Rabbinate," in idem, *From Text to Context*, 9-50.

Schulte, Christoph, "Franz Joseph Molitors Philosophie des Judentums," *Menora. Jahrbuch für deutsch-jüdische Geschichte* 6 (1995), 47-64.

Schur, Nathan, *History of the Karaites* (Frankfurt am Main: Lang, 1992).

— *The Karaite Encyclopedia* (= Beiträge zur Erforschung des Alten Testaments und des Antiken Judentums 38) (Frankfurt am Main: Lang, 1995).

Seeliger, Herbert, "Origin and Growth of the Berlin Jewish Community," *LBIYB* 3 (1958), 159-168.

Seligmann, Caesar, *Geschichte der jüdischen Reformbewegung von Mendelssohn bis zur Gegenwart* (Frankfurt am Main: Kauffmann, 1922).

Seraphim, Peter Heinz, *Das Judentum im osteuropäischen Raum* (Essen: Essener Verlagsanstalt, 1938).

Sharfman, Harold, *The First Rabbi: Origins of Conflict between Orthodox and Reform. Jewish Polemical Warfare in pre-Civil War America: A Biographical History* (New York: Simon, 1988).

Shochat, Esriel, *Al Khilufe Tekufot. Reshit HaHaskalah be-Yahadut Germaniya* (Jerusalem: Mossad Bialik, 1960).

Silber, Michael, "The Historical Experience of German Jewry and Its Impact on Haskalah and Reform in Hungary," in *Toward Modernity: The European Jewish Model*, ed. Jacob Katz (New Brunswick, NJ: Transaction Books, 1987), 117-157.

Silberman, Lou H., "The Union Prayer Book: A Study in Liturgical Development," in *Retrospect and Prospect: Essays in Commemoration of the Seventy-Fifth Anniversary of the Founding of the Central Conference of American Rabbis 1889-1964*, ed. Bertram W. Korn (New York: Central Conference of American Rabbis, 1965), 46-61.

Silverstein, Alan, *Alternatives to Assimilation. The Response of Reform Judaism to American Culture, 1840-1930* (Hanover, NH: University Press of New England, 1994).

Sinasohn, Max M., *Die Berliner Privatsynagogen und ihre Rabbiner* (Jerusalem: Sinasohn, 1971).

Sorkin, David, *The Transformation of German Jewry 1780-1840* (Detroit: Wayne State University Press, 1999).

Sussman, Lance, *Isaac Leeser and the Making of American Judaism* (Detroit: Wayne State University Press, 1995).

Sutcliffe, Adam, *Judaism and Enlightenment* (Cambridge: Cambridge University Press, 2003).

Synagogen in Berlin. Zur Geschichte einer zerstörten Architektur, 2 vols. (Berlin: Arenhövel, 1983).

Tänzer, Aron, "Samuel Holdheim als Rabbinatskandidat," *AZJ* 62 (1898), 19-20.

— *Die Geschichte der Juden in Hohenems und im übrigen Vorarlberg* (Meran: Elmenreich, 1905; reprinted Bregenz: Lingenhöle, 1982).

Temkin, Sefton D., *Creating American Reform Judaism: The Life and Times of Isaac Meyer Wise* (London: Littman Library of Jewish Civilization, 1998).

Thiemann, Ronald, *Religion in Public Life: A Dilemma for Democracy* (Washington, D.C.: Georgetown University Press, 1996).

Tomasoni, Francesco, *Modernity and the Final Aim of History: The Debate over Judaism from Kant to the Young Hegelians* (Dordrecht: Kluwer Academic Publishers, 2003).

Toury, Jacob, "Die Revolution von 1848 als innerjüdischer Wendepunkt," in Liebeschütz and Paucker, eds., *Das Judentum in der deutschen Umwelt*, 539-576.

— *Soziale und politische Geschichte der Juden* (Düsseldorf: Droste, 1977).

— "The Revolution that Did Not Happen (A Reappraisal of Reform-Judaism)," *ZRGG* 36 (1984), 193-203.

Trautmann-Waller, Céline, *Philologie allemande et tradition juive. Le parcours intellectuel de Leopold Zunz* (Paris: Cerf, 1998).

Trevisan-Semi, Emanuela, "A Brief Survey of Present-day Karaite Communities in Europe," *Journal of Jewish Sociology* 33 (1991), 97-106.

Türk, Moriz, "Das erste Gemeindestatut und die Genossenschaft für Reform im Judentum," in *Festschrift zum 70. Geburtstage von Moritz Schaefer* (Berlin: Philo-Verlag, 1927), 241-257.

Volkov, Shulamit, "Die Erfindung einer Tradition. Zur Entstehung des modernen Judentums in Deutschland," *Historische Zeitschrift* 253 (1991), 603-628.

Wexler, Paul, "Is Karaite a Jewish Language?," *Mediterranean Language Review* 1 (1983), 27-54.

Wiener, Max, *Jüdische Religion im Zeitalter der Emanzipation* (Berlin: Philo Verlag, 1933).

Wiese, Christian, "Inventing a New Language of Jewish Scholarship: The Transition from German Wissenschaft des Judentums to American-Jewish Scholarship in the Nineteenth and Twentieth Centuries," *Studia Rosenthaliana* 36 (2002/03), 273-304.

— "Struggling for Normality. The Apologetics of Wissenschaft des Judentums in Wilhelmine Germany as an Anti-Colonial Intellectual Revolt against the Protestant Construction of Judaism," in *Towards Normality: Patterns of Assimilation and Acculturation in German Speaking Jewry*, ed. Rainer Liedtke and David Rechter (Tübingen: J.C.B. Mohr, 2003), 77-101.

— "Ein 'aufrichtiger Freund des Judentums'? 'Judenmission', christliche Judaistik, und Wissenschaft des Judentums im deutschen Kaiserreich am Beispiel Hermann L. Stracks," in *Gottes Sprache in der philologischen Werkstatt. Hebraistik vom 15. bis zum 19. Jahrhundert*, eds. Gerald Necker and Giuseppe Veltri (Leiden: Brill Publishers, 2004), 277-316.

— *Challenging Colonial Discourse: Jewish Studies and Protestant Theology in Wilhelmine Germany* (Leiden: Brill Publishers, 2005).

— "Von Dessau nach Philadelphia: Samuel Hirsch's Philosophie im Kontext deutscher und amerikanischer Reformdebatten im neunzehnten Jahrhundert," in *Jüdische Bildung und Kultur auf dem Gebiet des heutigen Sachsen-Anhalt*, ed. Giuseppe Veltri and Christian Wiese (Berlin: Metropol, forthcoming 2007).

Wigoder, Geoffrey, *Encyclopedia of Judaism* (New York et al.: Macmillan, 1989).

Wilke, Carsten, "Bayerische Bildungspolitiker gegen den Talmud. Das Ende der 'sogenannten jüdischen Hochschule zu Fürth' (1819-1830)," in *Neuer Anbruch. Zur deutsch-jüdischen Geschichte und Kultur,* ed. Michael Brocke, Aubrey Pomerance, and Andrea Schatz (Berlin: Metropol, 2001), 113-126.

— "Der Talmud und den Kant": *Rabbinerausbildung an der Schwelle zur Moderne* (Hildesheim: Olms, 2003).

Wolbe, Eugen, *Geschichte der Juden in Berlin und in der Mark Brandenburg* (Berlin: Verlag Kedem, 1937).

Wolff, Eberhard, "Medizinische Kompetenz und talmudische Autorität: jüdische Ärzte und Rabbiner als ungleiche Partner in der Debatte um die Beschneidungsreform zwischen 1830 und 1850," in *Judentum und Aufklärung; jüdisches Selbstverständnis in der bürgerlichen Öffentlichkeit* ed. Arno Herzig, Hans-Otto Horch, and Robert Jütte (Göttingen: Vandenhoeck & Ruprecht, 2002), 119-149.

Ydit, Meir, "Karaite and Reform Liturgy," *CCAR Journal* 18 (1971), 53-61.

Yuval, Israel, "Ha-nakam veha-kelalah, ha-dam veha-alilah (me-alilot kedoshim le-alilot dam)," *Tsiyon* 58 (1993), 33-90.

Zajaczkowsky, Ananiasz, *Karaism in Poland* (Warsaw: Panstwowe Wydawn, 1961).

Zeugnisse jüdischer Kultur: Erinnerungsstätten in Mecklenburg-Vorpommern, Brandenburg, Berlin, Sachsen-Anhalt, Sachsen und Thüringen (Berlin: Wichern-Verlag, 1992).

INDEX